ADOLESCENCE: A CONTEMPORARY VIEW

THIRD EDITION

LINDA NIELSEN

WAKE FOREST UNIVERSITY

HARCOURT BRACE COLLEGE PUBLISHERS

FORT WORTH PHILADELPHIA SAN DIEGO NEW YORK ORLANDO AUSTIN SAN ANTONIO

TORONTO MONTREAL LONDON SYDNEY TOKYO

Vice President, Publisher	Ted Buchholz
Editor in Chief	Christopher P. Klein
Senior Acquisitions Editor	Jo-Anne Weaver
Senior Project Editor	Charles J. Dierker
Senior Production Manager	Kenneth A. Dunaway
Art Director	Sue Hart

Cover image: *The Night the Horse Got Loose* by Bill Rane. Oil on canvas, 39″ × 29¼″. From the collection of Dr. and Mrs. Troy Scott, Dallas, Texas.

ISBN: 0-15-500995-8

Library of Congress Catalog Card Number: 95-75132

Address for Editorial Correspondence: Harcourt Brace College Publishers, 301 Commerce Street, Suite 3700, Fort Worth, TX 76102.

Address for Orders: Harcourt Brace & Company, 6277 Sea Harbor Drive, Orlando, FL 32887-6777. 1-800-782-4479, or 1-800-433-0001 (in Florida).

Additional credits and copyright information appear on page 620 and constitute a continuation of the copyright page.

Printed in the United States of America

5 6 7 8 9 0 1 2 3 4   039   9 8 7 6 5 4 3 2 1

For my husband Steve—
playmate and
most intimate, romantic friend

TO THE INSTRUCTOR

Given all the other textbooks you might choose for a course on adolescence, why choose mine? In this third edition, I have tried to create for you and your students the kind of book I enjoy teaching from—a book that motivates and engages students. *Adolescence: A Contemporary View* not only requires them to analyze the data, but also encourages them to question the conclusions. They begin to recognize practical applications of what they are reading and to appreciate the vast differences in the lives of adolescents in our society.

EXTENSIVE AND CURRENT RESEARCH

Although we shouldn't judge any book solely on the basis of the sheer number of references, we do have an obligation to give our students as much up-to-date information as possible. Toward that end, the foundation of this book is an extensive research base featuring an unusually high percentage of recent studies and statistics—the number of sources approaches 1,600, more than 80% of which have been published since 1990. A few quick examples: The chapter on gender roles is based on almost 170 references, as is the chapter on adolescents in blended and single-parent families. Rather than devoting the tables, figures, or text to only a single study or to data from the 1980s, I have focused on information from the 1990s. I also emphasize longitudinal research and try to draw students' attention to the better designed studies with the most representative samples.

ENGAGING WRITING STYLE

No matter how extensive and current the research that underlies it, a book doesn't serve you well unless it's read and understood. In this third edition, therefore, I have adopted a more informal writing style than I used in the preceding two. My goal is to engage your students in material that they otherwise might consider "too dry and boring." My writing style, photographs, cartoons, graphics, self-quizzes, and boxed inserts are designed to entice your students to examine their own adolescence, their own families, and the lives of adolescents with whom they have very little in common. I want your students to feel carried along by the momentum of the prose and to feel more as though they are reading a letter from a friend than plodding through a dreary textbook. I have avoided jargon and provided an extensive glossary to help your students master the more difficult concepts and terminology. This book demands rigorous thinking from your students, yet also entertains and engages them.

CHALLENGING STUDENTS' IDEAS AND ASSUMPTIONS

Although I want your students to be entertained as they read, I also want to encourage them to question many of their own beliefs and assumptions. I want students to leave your classes saying, "I never thought about that before" and "After reading this, I'm not sure what I think about that now." In the same vein, I want your students to recognize the shortcomings of the research on which we base many of our beliefs about adolescents. In order to challenge students to reexamine or to question their own views, I have used several approaches. First, at the end of each chapter I have placed "Questions for Discussion and Debate," which are designed to provoke lively classroom discussions and to encourage your students to share their personal experiences and their differences. Some instructors also use these questions as assignments for papers or as the basis for out-of-class surveys or projects. Second, at the beginning of each chapter I point out the shortcomings of the research. In this way, your students can gain a better appreciation for "what we don't know," as well as an awareness of the difficulties involved in conducting research. I want students to understand that even the most well-designed studies might not necessarily yield "the truth." In other words, I want to draw your students into the process of critically evaluating the research, the theories, the experts' opinions, and the statistics. Third, I have presented a variety of viewpoints on controversial issues as well as research that supports contradictory viewpoints. Although students sometimes complain that "your chapter didn't tell us which view was right," I am complimented by their recognition of the complexity of certain questions and their appreciation for why even the most carefully conducted studies might yield contradictory findings.

PRACTICAL APPLICATIONS AND EXAMPLES FROM LIFE

Although I want them to understand that one "right" answer or one "best" solution isn't always possible, I also want students to see the many practical applications and real life examples of the theories and research. With this in mind, I have provided your students with many examples, case studies, successful programs, counseling strategies, and excerpts from adolescents' writing about their own lives. Given the emphasis I have put on practical applications, this book is ideally suited for students who are planning careers as teachers, counselors, health care workers, juvenile justice workers, and mental health professionals.

THOROUGH COVERAGE OF SINGLE-PARENT AND BLENDED FAMILIES

One of the major additions to this third edition is Chapter 9, "Adolescents in Single-Parent and Blended Families." Because millions of adolescents—the majority of adolescents in our country—no longer live with both of their biological parents, I have devoted an entire chapter to them and their families. Sadly, I have found that most college students have received very little up-to-date information about single-parent and blended families. As a consequence, many hold false assumptions and gross misconceptions about these families. Written specifically to redress this gap, Chapter 9, based on more than 200 recent references, dispels many of the myths about adolescents from single-parent and blended families. Varying from the approach of previous coverage of this topic, this chapter (1) focuses on teenagers rather than on young children, (2) separates the data on stepfathers and stepmothers, (3) presents the strengths of blended families, (4) examines the influence of the family's income and the teenager's gender, and (5) discusses the marital and family dynamics that underlie adolescents' reactions to their parents' divorce or remarriage. Students with divorced parents, stepparents, and unmarried parents repeatedly tell me how helpful this chapter is in helping them understand their own experiences and feelings.

COMPREHENSIVE COVERAGE OF RACE, GENDER, AND ECONOMIC ISSUES

Another reality I continue to emphasize is that the effects of race, family income, and gender are powerful forces that shape adolescents' lives. Not only do I devote a separate chapter to race and gender, but also I incorporate these two dimensions of adolescents' lives into all other chapters. For example, each of the following receives a separate discussion: ego and social development, school performance, SAT scores, vocational choices, religious preferences, drug use, pregnancy, suicide, and eating disorders—and each discussion emphasizes the influence of race, gender, and family income. With regard to race, I have expanded the information about Native American adolescents, recent immigrant families, and the differences among Hispanic American teenagers from various countries of origin. With respect to gender, I have expanded or added sections on each of these: sexual harassment in the schools; date rape; incest; and gender differences in social relationships, ego development, vocational choices, and interactions with family members.

Because the majority of college students come from families whose financial resources are much higher than average, I believe it is especially important to help them appreciate the profound impact that family income and the nation's economy have on adolescents. That's why I provide such in-depth coverage of these economic situations and financial issues: poverty, mothers' employment, the financial plight of teenage and unmarried parents, cutbacks in welfare and student aid, the homeless, rising college costs, lack of funds for public schools, and young workers' lack of academic and vocational skills. After reading these new sections of the book, students tell me they have come to understand the ways in which their own family's economic situation shaped their adolescence—whether good, bad, or somewhere in between. Perhaps more important for me, however, is that so many students say these sections of the chapters enabled them for the first time to understand how far removed their lives and their friends' lives were from the "average" adolescent in our country in terms of economic resources—and in terms of the far-reaching consequences of those resources.

THE FATHER'S ROLE IN ADOLESCENT DEVELOPMENT

With regard to gender biases, I have included far more information than other textbooks on the role that fathers play in adolescents' lives and development. Not only have I emphasized the research on adolescents and their fathers in the two chapters on families, but also I weave the research on fathers into other chapters, under such topics as these: society's definitions of fathering, the mother's role in a father's relationships with their children, adolescents who live with unmarried fathers, the father–daughter relationship, the father's influence on the teenage son, fathers and teenage aggression, early childhood attachment to fathers, fathers' parenting styles, fathers' feelings after divorce, fathers and custody, and the relationship between teenagers and their stepfathers. I do not follow the popular approach of simply presenting the research about "parents" as if these two people were a single entity—an entity that relates to children in the same way and that, therefore, has a similar effect on each child. By devoting equal attention to the research on fathers or by separating it from that on mothers, I offer a less biased, less restrictive, less sexist view of adolescents and each of their parents. After reading the research on fathers in this third edition, many students have said they are able to view their fathers, their parents' marriage, and interactions in their families with more insight and more compassion.

DIVERSE THEORETICAL PERSPECTIVES

As in former editions, the third edition embraces many different theoretical approaches. Rather than trying to sell students on any one view or theory, I offer as much diversity as possible and encourage them to probe the strengths and weaknesses of each. In this spirit, I offer extended discussions of biological theories, family systems' theories, and the links between adolescence and early childhood. With regard to early childhood, I focus more extensively on the connections between an adolescent's behavior and attitudes and his or her temperament, family experiences, family dynamics, and peer relationships as a young child. Thus, this new edition is much more developmental and more expansive than the previous two editions in its emphasis on early childhood and on the family.

NEW TOPICS

Topics from previous editions continue to receive special attention, including: date rape, incest, gay and lesbian youth, obesity, physical fitness, adolescent athletes, steroids, religion, teenagers with chronic or fatal illnesses, death and dying, shy teenagers, interracial dating, abortion, sexually transmitted diseases, and eating disorders. Besides the new chapter, "Adolescents in Single-Parent and Blended Families," these topics are also new:

- self-deception and errors in human reasoning
- schizophrenic, schizoid, and borderline personality disorders
- triangulation and enmeshment in families

- the influence of happily married parents and stepparents
- the effects of temperament
- chronic illness and ego development
- attention deficit disorders
- sexual harassment in schools
- parents' mental health and adolescent development
- extroverted versus introverted adolescents
- the importance of explanatory styles
- hostile attributions
- troubled peer relationships
- poverty
- mothers and teenage sons
- fathers and teenage daughters

I hope this new edition brings you and your students a great deal of pleasure.

TO THE STUDENT

To begin, I'd like you to read the first few pages of this preface addressed to your instructor. I want you to know what I believe is special about this new edition of my book, why I emphasize certain topics, and what I hope to accomplish by the way I present the material. I hope that reading and discussing my book will be a relevant, thought provoking, entertaining journey for you. I also hope you will feel emotionally and mentally stretched—challenged to re-examine some of your beliefs, willing to accept some new viewpoints, surprised and, yes, even a little upset by some of what you read.

How to Make an "A"

Now that I've got your attention, I have to admit that I can't guarantee that you'll make an "A" by reading this section. On the other hand, I can tell you how to use certain features of the book to increase the odds of your making a good grade.

First, the test questions that accompany this book come from three sources:

1. the bold-faced terms in every chapter
2. the "Review/Test Questions" at the end of every chapter
3. the figures and tables in each chapter

So you should do well on the tests if you can (1) provide definitions and specific examples of the bold-faced terms, (2) answer the review questions with specific statistics and specific findings from various research studies, and (3) summarize the data from the figures and graphs. In other words, don't ignore the graphs and figures, don't think you can do well on the tests merely by having a "pretty good idea" what the bold-faced terms mean, and don't assume that general answers to the review questions will be sufficient to pick the correct answers on multiple-choice questions. Although you don't need to memorize each exact statistic, you do need to be able to cite specific findings and statistics to support your answers to such questions as: "How well-off is the average adolescent financially after his or her parents divorce?" or "How good are the academic skills of adolescents today, compared to those of adolescents in the 1970s and 80s?"

Second, before you begin reading each chapter, take time to look at each of these:

1. the "Review/Test Questions" and the "Questions for Discussion and Debate" at the end of the chapter
2. the "Key Questions Addressed in this Chapter" listed at the front of each chapter
3. the headings and subheadings in the chapter outline
4. the glossary terms at the end of the chapter

These four steps will give you a very clear sense of what you need to memorize, attend to, and make notes on as you read.

GIVE ME SOME FEEDBACK

In closing, believe me when I say I would like to hear from you after or during your course. Please write. Let me know what you liked, what you disliked, and what you believe should be changed for the next edition. I am especially interested in your answers to these questions: Which sections of the book most affected you? What did you find especially helpful? Which sections were the most difficult to understand? What would you have liked more information about? And please don't feel limited to a couple of sentences or one-word responses—I'd like to know the "how and why" of your thoughts and reactions, too. (By the way, the responses of previous students helped shape the book you're reading. So, thanks in advance—my address follows the next section.)

ACKNOWLEDGMENTS

I haven't always enjoyed reading my reviewers' comments, but I always appreciate their efforts and insight. I would like to thank each of them for their candid comments and useful suggestions: Joan Corell, Westfield State College; Mary Lynn Crow, University of Texas at Arlington; Virginia Dansby, Middle Tennessee University; Daniel Houlihan, Mankato State University; Christine Readdick, Florida State University; Robert Schell, SUNY–Oswego; Ellen Slicker Middle

Tennessee University; Samuel Snyder; North Carolina State University; and Michelle Tomarelli, Texas A&M University.

Also I appreciate Acquisition Editors Tina Oldham, Eve Howard, and Jo-Anne Weaver for the attention they gave my project, as well as to all of those who have helped to design this third edition.

Above all, I am indebted to Steve, my husband, and to Nesha, my stepdaughter, for their patience and good humor during the two years I have so often disappeared from our family to work on this book. Hearing Nesha playing the piano as I worked, witnessing her transformation from a child to a young woman, and knowing how lovingly she has forgiven my mistakes and shortcomings, I am renewed and rejuvenated. I feel especially blessed to witness the wise, loving, nurturing ways in which my husband Steve is raising his daughter, to have his continual reassurance that I should trust my own voice and instincts as an author, and to bask in the daily pleasures and unfolding mysteries of living with him. Finally, I am grateful to Mattie, our short-legged, floppy eared, spoiled dog, who brings forth the child and the fool in me no matter what else is going on in our lives.

Linda Nielsen
Box 7266
Wake Forest University
Winston–Salem, NC 27109

TABLE OF CONTENTS

ABOUT THE AUTHOR

Linda Nielsen has worked with and written extensively about adolescents for more than 25 years. Published in such journals as the Harvard Educational Review and Educational Psychology Review, she is the author of *How to Motivate Adolescents* (Prentice Hall, 1981) and co-author of *Understanding Gender Roles and Moving Beyond* (U.S. Department of Education). A high-school teacher and counselor before becoming a psychologist, Dr. Nielsen has conducted workshops for teachers, parents, and counselors. Her research work includes federal projects for delinquent, learning-disabled, and emotionally troubled adolescents. She received the most outstanding author's award from the U.S. Center for Women Scholars in 1980 and was also the recipient of a postdoctoral fellowship from the American Association of University Women. Dr. Nielsen is a professor at Wake Forest University where she teaches classes in Adolescent Psychology and Fathers and Daughters, as well as courses in statistics, research, and women's studies.

TABLES, FIGURES, AND INSERTS

TABLES

FIGURES

INSERTS

ADOLESCENCE

ADOLESCENCE: THEORIES AND RESEARCH

Chapter Outline

Key Questions Addressed In This Chapter

1. How has the concept of adolescence developed and changed?
2. What are the basic differences among the various theories of adolescence?
3. What are the differences between the various ways of conducting research and gathering data about adolescents?
4. What are the shortcomings of the research on adolescents?
5. In what ways do we commonly misinterpret social science research?

"Leave me the hell alone, you old lop-eared heifer!" With these words from one of my ninth-grade students, I encountered a side to adolescence that was foreign to what I had known as a teenager. In those first few months as a high-school teacher, and later as a school counselor, I learned that *far* was what caused things to burn, "Jews are people who don't believe in God," and "rinsing with Coca-Cola after sex will stop you from getting pregnant." Naively I believed that if I just cared and empathized enough with my teenage students and clients, I could help them change many of the attitudes and behaviors that were causing them so much difficulty and pain. Yet over the years, my experiences as a teacher and therapist left me increasingly perplexed and frustrated. Why was I able to influence some of my teenage students and clients in ways that seemed to transform their lives but unable to make any impression whatsoever on others? Why did some of my students from low-income and physically abusive families succeed in school when others from wealthier, loving families failed? Why did some change their self-destructive behavior while others kept repeating their mistakes, continually shooting themselves in the foot?

My experiences as a teacher and counselor inevitably led me to become an adolescent psychologist. In my quest to answer the many unresolved questions that haunted me, I also examined many aspects of my own adolescence—the different nature of my relationship with each of my parents, the similarities and differences between my brother and me, the impact of adolescent experiences on my adult life. Having devoted 26 years of my life to studying adolescents, I have written this book as my way of sharing with you what the research and my own experiences have to offer. Before we embark, you might want to ask yourself: Why am I studying adolescence? What is it that I hope to achieve by examining the research, theories, and statistics? How do I think that having a better understanding of adolescence will benefit me?

As a way of preparing you for what is to come in future chapters, this first chapter focuses on two areas. First, we briefly examine the four different theoretical approaches to studying adolescence: biological theories, behavior and social learning theories, psychoanalytic theories, and cognitive stage theories. Then we examine the methods commonly used to gather data or conduct research on adolescents: survey, field, correlational, experimental, and longitudinal. Let's start by asking a basic question: How did the concept of adolescence come into being?

THE HISTORY OF ADOLESCENCE

The word *adolescence* comes from the Latin verb *adolescere*, which means to grow to maturity. Although the verb itself is old, the concept of adolescence, as we presently know it in our country, is relatively new. The idea of adolescence as a period of life that is somehow distinct from both childhood and adulthood did not exist before the 19th century. In fact, researchers paid relatively little attention to the teenage years until recent decades. For example, in the 1950s and

1960s, less than 2% of the articles published in professional journals about human behavior included teenagers (L'Abate, 1971). So how have we gotten to the point where adolescence is considered such an important topic? And why does the 10% of our population between the ages of 13 and 19 attract as much attention as they do in our society at large? The answers are related to three major changes in our society: industrialization, compulsory education, and the postwar baby boom (Anderson, 1992; Elder, 1980; Kett, 1977).

People in early modern England and America had clear ideas about the stage of life they termed "youth." Like us, they believed that the teenage years and the early 20s were a transitional time involving significant changes in our sexual, social, and vocational lives. Also like us, premodern Western societies were concerned about the problems of youth. But not until the 19th century did we refer to this age group as adolescents and begin paving the way for the scientific study of adolescence.

Within our country there were differences between the ways that youth were viewed in colonial New England and in the South. In the South the legal system mainly sought to protect youth from being financially exploited or physically abused. Issues related to a young person's age took a back seat to problems related to race and class. But in colonial New England churches and families were focused on indoctrinating youth with their traditional Puritan values. Indeed, there was a steady barrage of sermons and literature preoccupied with youths' sins and transgressions—above all, a preoccupation with teenage sexuality. Crimes related to sex were much more commonly prosecuted by the courts in New England than by courts in the South. In fact, the majority of prosecutions in colonial New England were for committing adultery and having children out-of-wedlock (Moran & Vinovskis, 1994).

During the early part of the 19th century, however, economic changes began taking place that laid the groundwork for the views we have today of adolescence. Until the turn of the century, we had been an agrarian society with very few jobs that required formal schooling. Our laws didn't require school attendance, and very few children were in school, especially beyond the age of 10 or 11. As our nation became more industrialized, however, fewer young people were needed as farm laborers and more were needed for jobs that required reading, writing, and mathematics. As a result, by 1918 all states required children to attend school and nearly one third of our 14- to 17-year-olds were students. During the Great Depression even more teenagers became full-time students because jobs were scarce. We also passed child-labor laws limiting the age, the types of jobs, and the hours that young people could work. As the numbers of teenagers in school steadily grew, adolescence increasingly came to be viewed as a distinct period of life. Rather than working side-by-side with adults—and rather than being educated in one-room schools with younger children—teenagers began spending most of their time exclusively with other teenagers in their schools. Moreover, larger numbers of adolescents were congregated together. From 1930 to 1960, the average size of a high school more than doubled from only 700 to an average of 1,600 students. Mainly through school then, an ever-more distinct adolescent subculture was forming—a culture with its own ways of speaking, dressing, socializing, dancing, and eating.

The connection between our notions about adolescence and our country's economic needs is also illustrated during periods of depression and wartime. When our economy is suffering from an economic depression, we need fewer workers because unemployment is high. When the economy is poor and jobs are scarce, it's usually in the country's best interests for adolescents not to be in the labor force where they might take jobs away from adult workers. Our nation's economic needs, therefore, affect our views about adolescence. For example, during economic depressions, the articles published on adolescence generally portrayed teenagers as too immature and too unskilled to enter the work force. In contrast, when our country has been at war, we need older teenagers to assume adult responsibilities as soldiers and by working in war-related industries. Indeed, during wartime, journal articles have tended to portray adolescents as mature enough to assume these adult roles (Enright & others, 1987). The point is that the way we view adolescence is at least partly connected to our country's economic and political concerns.

Adolescents also began attracting more attention after the 1950s because their numbers grew so rapidly. From 1960 to 1970 the number of Americans between the ages of 14 and 24 skyrocketed to an all-time high of 52% of the total population—a generation referred to as the "baby boom." Eager to cash in on the booming teenage market, businesses and the entertainment industry further contributed to our perceiving adolescence as a distinct group—a group that would be convinced through advertising that it "needed" such items as special clothing, cosmetics, hair products, movies, music, and television programs. By designing products and tailoring experiences specifically for teenage consumers, businesses and advertisers furthered our perceptions of adolescence as a period having little in common with children or adults—a stereotype that is not necessarily founded in reality, as you will see in future chapters.

In all of these ways then, our ideas about adolescence have been shaped and reshaped. Today, in a country of slightly more than 252 million people, roughly 24 million are teenagers. Nearly 30% of them are members of racial minorities, 18% are living in poverty, and only 40% are living with both of their biological parents (U.S. Department of Commerce, 1992 & 1993). How do researchers and theorists come to their conclusions about these 24 million young people? How do we go about trying to explain the behavior, the attitudes, and the differences among them?

THEORIES OF ADOLESCENCE

In studying adolescents, researchers and theorists approach the topic from several viewpoints. These approaches can be separated into four basic categories: biological theories, behavioral and social learning theories, psychoanalytic theories, and cognitive stage theories. In each chapter of this book, we examine the

Figure 1–1

America's adolescents

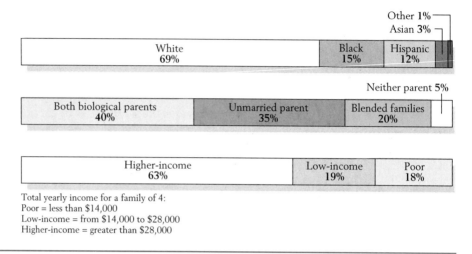

Source: U.S. Department of Commerce (1992). *Current population reports.* Washington, DC: Bureau of the Census.

Figure 1–2

The American population

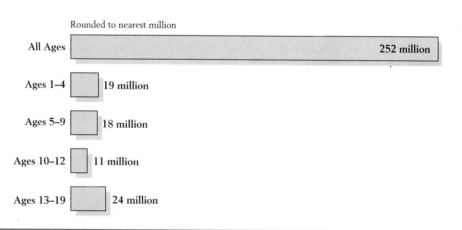

Source: U.S. Department of Commerce (1993). *Population estimates by age, sex, race & Hispanic origin.* Washington, DC: Bureau of the Census.

research from each of these viewpoints, noting their strengths and weaknesses. In order to appreciate the major differences between these theories at this point, let's consider their views on a few crucial questions: How much of an impact do biological and environmental influences have on adolescent behavior? How distinct and how important is adolescence compared to other periods of our lives?

BIOLOGICAL THEORIES

According to those who study adolescence from the biological viewpoint, certain aspects of human behavior are related to physiological factors such as hormone levels, inherited traits, or neurological disorders. Biological views dominated our beliefs and our research on adolescence during the early 1900s. One of the most important scholars of adolescent development, G. Stanley Hall, pioneered and popularized biological views of adolescence at the turn of the century. According to Hall, adolescence is a distinct and tumultuous time of life when our behavior is primarily determined by the way our species is genetically programmed. Hall believed that adolescents are genetically destined to be especially prone to rapid, rebellious, and sometimes life-threatening changes in behavior. Therefore Hall promoted the biological viewpoint that adolescence is universally a difficult, troublesome period of life (Hall, 1904).

From the biological viewpoint, many of the changes in a person's behavior during adolescence are related to the physiological changes that occur during the teenage years. Likewise, many of the differences we notice between teenagers are related to differences in their physiological makeup. As explained in future chapters, researchers have found associations between certain aspects of teenage behavior and physiological factors such as disorders in the neurological system, hormone imbalances, and inherited disturbances. For example, male delinquents who continue to engage in criminal activities beyond adolescence have lower levels of adrenal secretions than male delinquents who don't become criminals as adults (Magnusson & Bergman, 1994). Likewise, other aspects of our personalities remain basically unchanged from the time we are born. As shown in Chapter 5, our genes do play a part in how we behave and who we become in adolescence and beyond (Caspi, Elder, & Herbener, 1990; Chess & Thomas, 1993; Kagan, 1989; Robins & Rutter, 1990).

Much research supports the theory that certain aspects of an adolescent's behavior and mental health are influenced by biological factors. Most researchers who study adolescence from a biological viewpoint today, however, consider themselves advocates of **biosocial theories.** That is, biological and environmental factors work together to account for our behavior during adolescence. So when we are trying to understand an adolescent, we need to consider his or her genetic predispositions and other biological factors as well as aspects of the family and the immediate environment that might be influencing the person's behavior. In this sense then, biosocial theorists agree with behavioral and social learning theorists—to whom we now turn our attention (Galvin, 1992; Plomin, DeFries, & McClearn, 1990; Rowe, 1994; Udry, 1994).

BEHAVIORAL AND SOCIAL LEARNING THEORIES

Unlike strictly biological theories, behavioral and social learning theories are based on the premise that most of how we behave and who we become during and after adolescence is determined by environmental influences. Although behavioral and social learning theorists do not deny that biological factors influence our behavior, they emphasize the impact that our experiences have on our development. Among the most important environmental factors are the kinds of behavior and ways of thinking that are reinforced or punished at home, at school, by our peers, and by our society.

The idea that environmental factors play a large role in determining how people behave during adolescence initially gained wider recognition through the research of anthropologists Ruth Benedict and Margaret Mead. Both women pointed out that adolescents in other societies behave differently than American teenagers because each group is socialized differently. In opposition to Hall's still

Margaret Mead 1901–1978

popular views, Mead and Benedict were showing that adolescence is not a particularly stressful or rebellious period in every society. How children are socialized has an impact on how they think and behave when they become adolescents (Benedict, 1934; Mead, 1935).

Research emerging from sociology at the time also backed up these anthropological findings. Sociologists were finding that teenagers behaved in different ways according to the kind of families they came from—above all, how rich or how poor their families were. For example, teenagers from poor families were found to drop out of school, break the law, and get pregnant more often than teenagers from wealthier families (Havighurst, 1952; Hollingshead, 1949). Again, in contrast to views that were widespread at the time, adolescence was not a universal experience that affected all adolescents in the same ways. And much of what historically had been blamed on "being an adolescent" or "raging hormones" was related to environmental factors such as poverty.

In conjunction with these early sociological and anthropological studies, support was growing among psychologists for a theory being developed by B. F. Skinner known as **behavioral** or **Skinnerian** psychology. According to Skinner and other behavioral psychologists, most of an individual's behavior and attitudes are a result of the ways he or she has been reinforced or punished since birth. Thus adolescence is not seen as a stage of life per se that is distinct from childhood or adulthood. If adolescence is unique, it is mainly because teenage people are reinforced or have been socialized beforehand to behave in particular ways during this period of their lives (Skinner, 1953).

Modifying and expanding upon behavioral theories, **social learning theorists** believe that modeling affects our behavior and attitudes. That is, we imitate those people that we see receiving the kinds of rewards we ourselves would like to receive. For example, teenage boys who are very aggressive and antisocial often come from homes in which one or both parents acquiesced to the boys' whiny, aggressive behavior from the time they were very young children. When these parents are taught how to change their behavior, their teenage son's behavior often improves in turn (Andrews & Dishion, 1994). A contemporary of B. F. Skinner was Albert Bandura, one of the most renown social learning theorists, who points out that the beliefs and styles of thinking we have developed by the time we reach adolescence have a profound influence on how reinforcement and punishment affect us. Each adolescent has his or her own lens, so to speak, through which all experiences are given a personal interpretation and personal meaning. As a consequence of our particular style of reasoning and our personal beliefs of how the world works, reinforcement and punishment do not always affect all of us in exactly the same ways (Bandura, 1977;1989).

As you will see in future chapters, the behavioral and social learning theorists are correct in terms of the one fundamental belief they share in common—how we have been reinforced and punished as we're growing up *do* have an impact on many aspects of our teenage behavior and development. For example, teenagers who have grown up in poor families are the most likely to quit school, break the law, and have children out-of-wedlock—in large part because they have received too little reinforcement and too few role models for being studious, obeying the law, and postponing parenthood (Huston, 1993). Likewise, the kinds of behavior that parents reinforce and punish at home are closely linked with a teenager's mental health, peer relationships, and styles of thinking (Asher & Coie, 1990; Hinde & Stevenson, 1995; Robins & Rutter, 1990).

Psychoanalytic Theories

Like the behavioral and social learning theorists, **psychoanalytic theorists** believe that our teenage behavior and development are influenced by environmental factors—mainly by the kinds of experiences we have during the first few years of our lives in our families. Unlike other theorists, however, psychoanalytic theorists put the most emphasis on our early childhood experiences. Above all, how our mothers relate to us in the first few years of our lives supposedly shapes our ways of thinking and relating to people from there on. For example, teenagers who continually have trouble getting along or becoming intimate with people and becoming self-reliant have often had unloving, ambivalent, or overly-involved relationships with their mothers during early childhood. These teenagers have apparently developed maladaptive ways of reasoning and behaving around people based on problems in their relationships with their mothers as infants and preschoolers (Karen, 1994; Main, 1993).

Psychoanalytic theorists also see our development progressing in distinct stages during which certain psychological and sexual issues need to be resolved if we are to become well-adjusted adolescents and adults. Thus our teenage behavior is mainly determined by our early childhood experiences with our mothers and by how well we master the skills associated with each psycho-social stage. In order to understand why a particular teenager is behaving in certain ways, therefore, we should examine the dynamics within his or her family, especially the relationship between mother and child in the first few years of the child's life. Because the founder of psychoanalytic theories was Sigmund Freud, they are commonly referred to as **Freudian theories** (Freud, 1931;1949).

Contemporary psychoanalytic theorists such as Peter Blos and Erik Erikson have modified Freud's original theories. According to these more recent theories, the experiences we have after early childhood continue to influence our development. In particular, adolescence is viewed as an important period for shaping and reshaping certain aspects of ourselves. Indeed, adolescence is a crucial time for separating or "individuating" enough from our families to build close relationships with our peers and to function in the adult world. Like Freud, however, newer psychoanalytic theorists still consider our early childhood experiences with our parents and the dynamics within our families to have a significant impact on how we think and behave as teenagers (Blos, 1979; 1989; Erikson, 1968).

Cognitive Stage Theories

Like the Freudians, **cognitive stage theorists** believe that adolescent behavior is related to stages of development. Unlike the Freudians, however, the cognitive

Sigmund Freud, 1856–1939

stage theorists see the stages of human development as mental, not as psychological or sexual. Throughout childhood we supposedly move into more advanced
mental stages that enable us to reason, to solve problems, and to interact with
people in more mature ways. The process of maturing that we observe in most
adolescents, therefore, is seen as evidence of their having finally arrived at the
higher cognitive level—a stage referred to as "formal operational thinking." On

the other hand, those adolescents who think and behave in extremely immature ways are seen as being stuck, so to speak, in the childhood stage of reasoning referred to as "concrete operational thinking." Thus, adolescence is considered a distinct, unique phase of life because young people are advancing to a new cognitive stage that enables them to behave more maturely. These adolescent changes, however, are not considered to result mainly from environmental influences, family dynamics, or early childhood experiences. Because Jean Piaget is considered the founder of cognitive stage theories, they are often referred to as **Piagetian theories** (Piaget, 1954; 1965).

Jean Piaget, 1896–1980

If you're expecting that reading this textbook will show you which of these theories is correct and which are false, you're going to be disappointed. If this is your goal, you're going to get aggravated with researchers (and with me) for not giving you definitive, clear-cut answers to such questions as: "What causes some adolescents to abuse drugs?" "Why do so many teenagers get pregnant every year?" "Why was my adolescence so much easier than my brother's?" No one theory provides the answers to such questions. And there is no theory that consistently explains or establishes the causes of all types of teenage behavior. Instead, what you will discover in reading this book is that some theories do a better job than others explaining a particular type of teenage behavior. For example, manic depression and schizophrenia seem to be closely linked to genetic factors, whereas teenage pregnancy and delinquency seem to be much more closely linked to poverty than to any biological or genetic factor (Huston, 1993; Weiner, 1992).

The best way of approaching the research on adolescence then is to consider the analogy of the blindfolded people and the elephant. Without knowing what an elephant looks like, each blindfolded person has a hold of a different part of the elephant. When each person is asked to describe what the animal looks like on the basis of the data they have, they describe an entirely different animal. If you have hold of the trunk, and I have hold of the tail, we each have only a very small part of the total picture. Even though each person is very intelligent, logical, and honest, they arrive at different truths and different realities about elephants. In the same vein, researchers gathering data and hypothesizing about adolescence or particular adolescent behaviors have only part of the whole picture from their different theoretical perspectives. This shouldn't discourage you, however, or cause you to disdain the whole process of doing research and creating theories.

Unfortunately, very little research has been conducted from several different theoretical viewpoints simultaneously. Moreover, we social scientists have tended to underestimate or to ignore altogether the impact of genetic and other biological factors in our research and theories on adolescence (Ketterlinus & Lamb, 1994; Pattishall, 1994). So rather than feel you have to choose one theory over the others, try to approach your study of adolescents by taking a broader view— the view that each theory has something to contribute and that biological and environmental influences are continually dancing and interacting with one another as we develop during childhood and adolescence. Like the researchers, the more you do this, the more likely you are to get a clearer picture of your elephant or your adolescent.

CONDUCTING RESEARCH

Just as there are different theoretical approaches to studying adolescents, there are different ways of gathering information and conducting research. The most popular research methods are: surveys, field studies, correlational studies, experimental research, and longitudinal studies.

SURVEY AND FIELD RESEARCH

One of the simplest ways of gathering information about adolescents is through surveys. These surveys can be conducted by written responses, or by personal or telephone interviews. After administering the survey, the researcher tabulates the responses and tries to make generalizations based on the findings. The major shortcoming of survey research is that people sometimes lie or exaggerate in ways that give us a distorted view of what is actually going on. For example, in surveys teenagers report attending religious services more often than they actually do (Gallup, 1992; Kosmin & Lachman, 1993).

Rather than trusting what people say on surveys, therefore, some researchers go into the field to observe and record how people behave in their natural habitat. These **field researchers** go into schools, homes, shopping malls, and other places where teenagers are naturally found and record what they see. One disadvantage of field research is that when we know we are being observed and recorded, we tend to change our natural behavior. Another disadvantage is that the situations in which the field researcher chooses to observe people might not be representative of most of their behavior. For example, recording teenage behavior in a shopping mall might yield a very different picture than observing them in math class or on their school's athletic teams. The best field researchers, therefore, are those who manage to win the confidence of the people they are observing and who gather their data in the least obtrusive ways possible. For example, the sociologist Elijah Anderson has recorded the behavior of alienated young blacks by spending years of his life "hanging out" and working in their ghetto neighborhoods. In so doing, Anderson has earned a reputation as one of the few prominent "street sociologists" in our country (Anderson, 1992).

CORRELATIONAL RESEARCH

Correlational research is used to measure the strength of the relationship between two or more variables. For example, we might want to know how close a relationship there is between adolescents' grades and their family's income, or between how many hours of television adolescents watch each week and their age. The statistical formulas that are used to assess these relationships yield a number called a **correlation coefficient.** The coefficient is a number that ranges anywhere from .01 to 1.00 that is preceded by either a positive (+) or a negative (−) sign. The further the number is from .01 (the closer it is to 1.00), the stronger the relationship between the variables. So if the correlation between living with an unmarried parent and grades is .98, and the correlation between watching television and grades is .34, which of the two factors is more closely related to grades? Which of the two relationships or correlations is stronger? The answer is the parent's marital status because .98 is further from .01 than .34 is.

We need more information than this, however, about these relationships. We need to know the direction of the relationship. A negative sign ($-$) in front of the correlation coefficient means that as one factor increases, the other factor decreases. This is referred to as a **negative** or **inverse correlation.** A positive sign ($+$) means that as one factor increases or decreases so does the other—a **positive correlation.** For example, there might be a .98 relationship between the number of hours students watch television each week and their grades and a .98 relationship between hours spent watching television and how much junk food they eat. But even though the two correlation coefficients are exactly the same numerically, the two relationships aren't the same. In fact, there is a negative correlation between excessive television watching and teenagers' grades—as television watching increases, grades decrease. And there is a positive correlation between watching television and eating junk food—the more television we watch, the more junk food we tend to eat. Although the strength of the relationship is indicated by the correlation coefficient, we need the plus or the minus sign to tell us the direction of the relationship. This doesn't mean that if the relationship is negative, the results are "bad" or that if the relationship is positive, the results are "good." For example, there is a strong, positive relationship between heavy drinking and car accidents; but the results certainly aren't "positive" in any sense of the word.

The main drawback to correlational research is that too many people misuse or misinterpret the results to try to prove that one factor has caused the other to increase or to decrease. But correlations *neither prove nor disprove causality.* Correlational studies tell us merely how strong the relationship is that exists between the variables. Let's go back to our television viewing example. Although there is a negative correlation between excessive television watching and making high grades, we shouldn't misinterpret this to mean that watching television causes teenagers' grades to fall. In fact, children who watch the most television generally have the least well-educated parents who place less emphasis on reading for pleasure and on studying than the parents of children who watch less television. So watching television cannot be said to cause these students' poor grades (Barton & Coley, 1992; Bence, 1991). Likewise, as explained in Chapter 9, there is a positive correlation between living with an unmarried mother and dropping out of high school. But most unmarried mothers have extremely low incomes and live in school districts where children receive the poorest educations. It is just as likely, therefore, that poverty and poor schools are closer to being the causes of dropping out of high school than the mother's not being married. And, in fact, when family incomes are equal, a mother's marital status is not highly correlated with her children's dropping out of school (Hetherington, 1991; McLanahan, Astone, & Marks, 1993). Once again, it is a gross abuse of correlational studies to use them to try to prove or disprove causality.

EXPERIMENTAL RESEARCH

The only type of research that is designed to demonstrate cause and effect is **experimental research.** If the study is carefully designed, experimental research can help us determine the causes of various kinds of adolescent behavior and attitudes. Experimental studies, however, are supposed to meet a number of conditions before we trust their results. First, the study has to be arranged in such a way that the people being studied, called the **experimental group,** receive a specific treatment or are exposed to a specific condition without being influenced by other variables that might influence whatever is being measured. The variables that are being measured are referred to as the **dependent variables.** Any variable that the researcher believes might influence the dependent variables are referred to as **independent variables.** For example, suppose you want to know if a special series of announcements on television about the dangers of drunk driving will cause a decrease in the number of teenage traffic deaths. Your dependent variable would be the number of teenage traffic fatalities recorded by the police. You would use statistical formulas to compare the fatalities during the 6 months prior to the ads with the number of fatalities during a 6-month period at some point after the ads had been in effect. Your independent variable is the television campaign.

Second, there should be a **control group** of people who are as similar to the subjects as possible, but who have not been exposed to the treatment or to the specific situations under study. For example, if you are using only 9th-grade students from wealthy, midwestern families in your experimental group, then you need a group of ninth graders from similar backgrounds for your control group. Third, in the best experimental studies, researchers consider other variables that might interfere with or confound the results of the treatment. These are referred to as **confounding variables** or **extraneous variables.** In your drinking and driving study, for instance, a teenager's age, gender, race, and family income might influence how effective the television announcements are in changing their driving and drinking habits. Although researchers can't eliminate extraneous factors, they can try to measure their impact by including them in the study as additional independent variables. For example, you would use statistical formulas that compare the traffic fatalities before and after the television announcements by age, gender, race, and family income.

When experimental studies are carefully designed and when the statistical formulas are correctly applied and interpreted, they offer us the most reliable information about causality. Experimental studies, therefore, have the advantage of being able to assess which approaches to particular teenage problems are the most effective. For example, is the best way to reduce traffic fatalities through television announcements or by taking teenagers to the scenes of fatal accidents? One of the major disadvantages of experimental research, however, is the time, training, and money involved in conducting well-designed studies. Another drawback is that poorly designed experimental studies can be misinterpreted or misused in ways that lead us to the wrong conclusions about cause and effect.

LONGITUDINAL RESEARCH

Often, however, researchers are not interested in trying to prove causality. Instead, they want to find out how the passage of time affects people's behavior or attitudes. In order to do this, researchers use two methods. In a **cross-sectional study,** researchers gather data on the dependent variable or variables from several groups of people of different ages. For example, you might ask a group of 13-year-olds and a group of 19-year-olds how often they use particular types of drugs. After feeding your data into the correct statistical formulas, you would then make generalizations about how the passage of time seems to have affected teenagers' drug use. The obvious disadvantage of cross-sectional research is that extraneous variables other than the passage of time might account for any differences that are found. For example, unlike the 13-year-olds, the 19-year-olds might have grown up during a time when antidrug campaigns on television and in schools were widespread and when several nationally renowned athletes died from drug overdoses. So, if you found that the older teenagers used far fewer drugs than the younger teenagers, you would be wrong to conclude that growing older causes teenagers to become wiser in regard to using drugs.

The better approach would be to use a **longitudinal study** in which data are gathered from the same group of people across a period of time. This group should be **cohorts,** meaning that they should share many of the same characteristics in common mainly because they are the same age. So let's go back to your drug study. If you designed a longitudinal study, you would ask a group of 13-year-olds about their drug use and then ask them again when they are 19. Better yet, you could ask them about their use of drugs every year from the time they are 13 until they are 19. After putting your data into the correct statistical formulas, you could then make some generalizations about how teenagers' drug use changes as they age. The advantage of longitudinal research is that there are fewer confounding variables to confuse the results than there are in cross-sectional studies. The disadvantage is that longitudinal studies are difficult to conduct because they involve keeping track of the same group of people over a period of time. As a result, longitudinal studies are relatively scarce. For this reason, I have made a special point throughout this book to highlight the longitudinal research for you. Given the advantages of longitudinal data, you should pay particular attention to these findings.

SHORTCOMINGS AND MISINTERPRETATIONS OF RESEARCH

As researchers, editors, and authors, we do the best we can to present people with accurate information. Nevertheless, none of us is immune from making mistakes when it comes to conducting, interpreting, or disseminating our research and statistics. You need to be aware, therefore, of a few of the most common shortcomings in the published research: (1) inappropriate generalizations, (2) race and gender bias, (3) confusion over medians and means, and (4) the fallibility of human reason.

Regardless of whether the research is based on surveys, field studies, correlations, experiments, or longitudinal studies, the results should be generalized only to people who are similar to those who participated in the study. For this reason, most researchers try to have a **representative** or **random sample** of subjects who represent a wide range of different characteristics. In many cases, however, this isn't possible. For example, if you're conducting research on high-school students, you might have access to only white, college-bound 10th graders in a predominantly upper-middle-class school. In this case, your sample isn't representative of all high-school students in this country, and your results should be generalized to only white, college-bound 10th graders in upper-middle-class schools. If the subjects aren't representative of all adolescents across the country, this doesn't discredit or undermine the importance of the study. Indeed, the data might be very valuable for understanding problems or potential of a certain kind of group. Nevertheless, we should apply the results or the statistical data only to people who are similar to those in the study. Unfortunately, we often fail to notice the particular characteristics of the adolescents in a study, thus making the mistake of generalizing to teenagers who have little, if anything, in common with the researchers' subjects.

In this vein, a second shortcoming in much of our research is that we have focused too exclusively on white, male, middle-class teenagers. Most researchers have not seen to it that half of the subjects in their studies are female, that nearly 30% are members of racial minorities, or that 18% are living in poverty before generalizing their results to "American teenagers." This isn't to say that conducting research or gathering statistics only about white teenage boys or only about middle-class teenagers is unethical or wrong. It isn't. But what is wrong is to create theories and generalizations about adolescent development or adolescent behavior primarily or exclusively on the basis of studies with restricted or nonrepresentative samples. Whatever theories or data emerge from any study should be restricted only to teenagers of that gender, race, or economic background. The problem is that many of our theories and generalizations about teenagers have typically been derived only from studies of white, male, middle-class adolescents. As a consequence, these theories, generalizations, beliefs, and recommendations often have not been relevant for teenage girls, minority youth, or teenagers from low-income families. Because our literature on adolescents is heavily biased with research on males, we might say that "adolescent" psychology is, more accurately, the psychology of white, male teenagers (Adelson 1980; Fausto-Sterling, 1991; Pattishall, 1994; Schiebinger, 1993).

Moreover, much of the data we have collected on female and minority adolescents has been gathered and interpreted in ways that give us distorted, inaccurate, or very limited ideas about these teenagers. For reasons we discuss in Chapters 6 and 7, researchers have traditionally focused on the differences rather than the similarities between white, male teenagers and other groups of adolescents. Also, much of our research and theory has been based on the premise that female and minority teenagers are inferior to white, male teenagers (Fisher, 1991; Fausto-Sterling, 1991; Harding, 1993; Tuana, 1993). Although researchers are increasingly aware of these racial and gender biases, you still need to keep these potential sources of bias in mind as you read what has been published.

A third source of confusion in adolescent research or statistics about adolescents involves the concepts of means and medians. When statisticians and researchers use the word **mean,** they are referring to the arithmetical average. To compute the mean, you add all of the numbers in the distribution and then divide by the total number of entries. Say you're a high-school teacher with four students in your math class. What is the mean family income of your students if their families' incomes are $20,000, $10,000, $320,000, and $10,000? The mean income is $90,000 because $360,000 divided by four equals $90,000. Now assume that you haven't been allowed to see the actual incomes for each of your student's families. Instead, you are simply given a statement at the top of your class roster: "The mean family income for your math class is $90,000." If you don't understand what the mean represents, you might make a gross error, namely, assuming that you are going to be teaching a fairly wealthy group of teenagers.

Because the mean can give us such a distorted picture of a group, researchers and statisticians should present their information in terms of means and medians. The **median** is the number or balancing point above and below which half of the values in the group fall after they have been ranked from lowest to highest. Using the example of your hypothetical math class, the median family income would be $25,000 because 50% of the incomes ($10,000 & $20,000) fall below $25,000 and 50% of the incomes ($30,000 & $320,000) fall above $25,000. Knowing the mean and the median incomes, you would realize that the majority of your students come from fairly low-income homes, but that somebody's family has a whoppingly big income. Unfortunately, too many students and other readers of statistics wrongly think *mean* and *median* are synonymous. As a consequence, they make gross misjudgments and incorrect generalizations. When you're reading statistics, it's important not to confuse the medians and the means because the two concepts convey very different kinds of information.

ERRORS IN HUMAN REASONING

Last, but not least, we are all prone to making certain kinds of cognitive errors—errors that arise from drawing on our personal experiences, from our personal biases, and from the shortcomings in human reasoning. As researchers and as consumers of the data, we are all occasional victims of our own flawed reasoning. Before you begin your study of adolescents, therefore, you need to recognize some of our common cognitive errors (Gilovich, 1991).

First, our minds want to find meaningful, predictable patterns where maybe none exist. Our tendency to impose order and meaning to the data encourages us to see as "fact" what is sometimes only a possibility, hypothesis, or well-educated guess. For example, look at Figure 1–3. Pretend that each dot represents an attack on someone by teenage hoodlums. Are you in any more danger of being attacked in one part of town than in another? Given our tendency to want to impose order,

Figure 1–3

Misinterpreting research data

Imagine that each dot represents at attack on innocent people by a band of teenage hoodlums. Are you any more likely to be attacked in one part of town than in another?

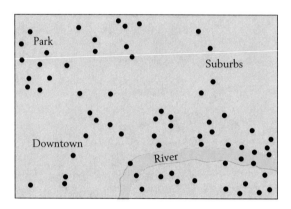

many of us think we're in the most danger down by the river. In reality, however, the dots are randomly scattered, not clustered. You can see the randomness better if you bisect the figure with a diagonal line instead of seeing it as quadrants.

Second, we tend to pay the most attention to the research and statistics that confirm our own beliefs and feelings. For example, if you believe that teenagers should be allowed to buy alcoholic beverages when they're 18, you will pay most attention and remember best those statistics that support your belief. We tend to ask questions and seek information in ways that support our own hunches or views. So no matter how much data is put in front of us, we often refuse to accept it when it doesn't fit with our preconceived expectations or personal experiences. "I'll see it when I believe it" often seems to be a more accurate description of us than "I'll believe it when I see it." Confronted with information or theories that threaten to turn our views upside down, each of us occasionally reasons like Galileo's critics, who refused to consider the possibility that the earth was not the center of the solar system and who put Galileo under house arrest for the last 8 years of his life.

Third, we do more than simply ignore information that fails to support our views. We also subject these statistics and studies to the most critical scrutiny. We usually seek out additional information or criticize the researchers' methods only when the outcomes are not what we expect or not what we want to hear. Ironically, when we are exposed to a mixed body of evidence, most of us become even more convinced of the soundness of our original beliefs.

Fourth, most of us are more prone to believe those findings and statistics that flatter the groups to which we belong than those that are embarrassing or critical.

Our self-serving biases also influence what we consider to be "enough" evidence, or a "sound" study, or an "expert" on the topic. We generally dig deepest and search for the most data when we don't like the initial conclusions. Likewise, most researchers are more likely to run additional experiments if the results of their initial study do not support their favored hypothesis than if the initial results confirm their hypotheses.

Fifth, we tend to exaggerate the amount of statistical support that exists for those beliefs in which are the most emotionally invested. For example, we're more likely to exaggerate the research that supports our personal views on topics such as abortion and interracial dating than on topics such as teenage obesity and teenager's poor math skills. We are also likely to exaggerate the extent to which the experts confirm our particular views.

Sixth, most of us rely too much on our own experiences and not enough on research findings and statistics. When data confirm our experiences, we generally accept them with very little doubt or difficulty. When the data don't reflect our experiences, however, we tend to trust experience and to question or reject the research. Considering the fact that there are roughly 24 million teenagers in our country—almost a third being members of racial minorities, a fifth living in poverty, less than half living with both biological parents, and only a fifth eventually graduating from college—most college students are on especially shaky ground when they try to generalize about adolescence on the basis of their own lives.

Finally, for most of us our beliefs are like personal possessions. Just as we acquire and keep those belongings that make us feel good, we acquire and cling to those beliefs that make us feel good. Even when the research and statistics fail to support us, we cling fervently to those beliefs and theories that make us feel best about ourselves and about those for whom we care. So when a writer or researcher challenges our views, we often feel as if that person is trying to steal our possessions—trying to take something precious away from us (Abelson, 1986).

Keeping each of these kinds of errors in mind, you can approach the theories, the research, and the statistics on adolescents with a more open mind. Although you cannot always prevent your reasoning from being faulty, you can learn to ask yourself such questions as: "How would someone who doesn't believe the way I do explain these results?" "Which of my beliefs are being challenged by these statistics?" "Why am I so upset by, or so reluctant to accept, these findings?"

Review/Test Questions

1. How has the concept of adolescence developed historically, and how have our nation's economic or political needs affected our views?

2. How many teenagers are there in our country and how do they differ by race, family income, and type of family?

3. What are the fundamental differences and similarities among the various theoretical approaches to studying adolescence?

4. In what ways have our views of adolescence changed since the time of Stanley Hall and Sigmund Freud?

5. What are the advantages and disadvantages of each of the ways of conducting research or gathering information about adolescents?

6. Define and give an example of independent, dependent, and confounding variables.

7. How do the mean and median differ? Why is this important?

8. Define and give two examples of correlation coefficients and negative, positive, and inverse correlations.

9. Give an example of how each of the following might cause someone to misinterpret research findings or statistics: random samples, faulty generalizations, cross-sectional studies, sexist and racist biases, and confounding variables.

10. What are some of the shortcomings in our research on adolescence?

11. What are some of the errors you are most likely to make in reading or interpreting research and statistics about adolescents?

Questions for Discussion and Debate

1. What are your reasons for studying adolescent psychology? How are the experiences in your own life related to your interest in adolescence?

2. What are the advantages and disadvantages of our society's having defined adolescence as such a distinct and unique period of life?

3. To which of the theories of adolescence are you most drawn? Why?

4. If you were a researcher with unlimited funds, what three questions about adolescents or adolescence would you try to answer? What type of research would you be employing to answer your questions? What would be your independent, dependent and confounding variables?

5. Find a correlational study and an experimental study in a recent journal of adolescence and discuss the strengths and weaknesses of each.

6. Considering your own experiences and your personal biases, what mistakes do you think you might be most likely to make in interpreting or judging the research and statistics on adolescents?

Glossary

behavioral psychology, p. 9
biosocial theories, p. 7
cognitive stage theories, p. 10
cohort group, p. 17
confounding variable, p. 16
control group, p. 16
correlation coefficient, p. 14
correlational research, p. 14

cross-sectional research, p. 17
dependent variable, p. 16
experimental group, p. 16
experimental research, p. 15
extraneous variable, p. 16
field research, p. 14
Freudian theories, p. 10
independent variable, p. 16

inverse correlation, p. 15
longitudinal research, p. 17
mean, p. 19
median, p. 19
negative correlation, p. 15
Piagetian theories, p. 12
positive correlation, p. 15
psychoanalytic theories, p. 10

References

Abelson, R. (1986). Beliefs are like possessions. *Journal for the Theory of Social Behavior, 16,* 222–250.

Adelson, J. (1980). *Handbook of adolescent psychology.* New York: Wiley.

Anderson, E. (1992). *Streetwise.* Chicago: University of Chicago.

Andrews, D., & Dishion, T. (1994). Microsocial underpinnings of adolescent problem behavior. In R. Ketterlinus & M. Lamb (Eds.), *Adolescent problem behavior* (pp. 187–209). Hillsdale, NJ: Erlbaum.

Asher, S., & Coie, J. (1990). *Peer rejection in childhood.* New York: Cambridge University Press.

Bandura, A. (1977). *Social learning theory.* Englewood Cliffs, NJ: Prentice Hall.

Bandura, A. (1989). Human agency and social cognitive theory. *American Psychologist, 44,* 1175–1184.

Barton, P., & Coley, R. (1992). *American's smallest school: The family.* Princeton, NJ: Educational Testing Services.

Bence, P. (1991). Television and adolescents. In R. Lerner, A. Petersen & J. Brooks-Gunn (Eds.), *Encyclopedia of adolescence* (pp. 1123–1126). New York: Garland.

Benedict, R. (1934). *Patterns of culture.* Boston: Houghton Mifflin.

Blos, P. (1979). *On adolescence.* New York: Free Press.

Blos, P. (1989). *Father and son.* New York: Free Press.

Caspi, A., Elder, G., & Herbener, E. (1990). Childhood personality and the prediction of life course patterns. In L. Robins & M. Rutter (Eds.), *Straight and devious pathways from childhood to adulthood* (pp. 13–36). New York: Cambridge University.

Chess, S., & Thomas, A. (1993). Continuities and discontinuities in temperament. In R. Robins & M. Rutter (Eds.), *Straight and devious pathways* (pp. 205–220). New York: Cambridge University.

Elder, G. (1980). Adolescence in historical perspective. In J. Adelson (Ed.), *Handbook of adolescent psychology* (pp. 3–46). New York: Wiley.

Enright, R., Levy, V., Harris, D., & Lapsley, D. (1987). Do economic conditions influence how theorists view adolescents? *Journal of Youth and Adolescence, 16,* 541–559.

Erikson, E. (1968). *Identity: Youth in crisis.* New York: Norton.

Fausto-Sterling, A. (1991). *Myths of gender: Biological theories about women and men.* New York: Basic Books.

Fisher, C. (1991). *Ethics in applied developmental psychology.* New York: Abelex.

Freud, S. (1931). *The standard edition of the complete psychological works of Sigmund Freud.* London: Hogarth Press.

Freud, S. (1949). *An outline of psycho-analysis.* New York: Norton.

Gallup, (1992). *The religious life of young Americans.* Princeton, NJ: Gallup International Institute.

Galvin, R. (1992). The nature of shyness. *Harvard Magazine, 94,* 40–45.

Gilovich, T. (1991). How we know what isn't so: The fallibility of human reason in everyday life. New York: MacMillan.

Hall, S. (1904). *Adolescence.* Englewood Cliffs, NJ: Prentice Hall.

Harding, S. (1993). *The racial economy of science.* Bloomington, IN: Indiana University Press.

Havighurst, R. (1952). *Developmental tasks and education.* New York: McKay.

Hetherington, M. (1991). Families, lies and videotapes. *Journal of Research on Adolescence, 1,* 323-348.

Hinde, R., & Stevenson, J. (1995). *Relation between relationships within families.* Cambridge: Oxford University Press.

Hollingshead, A. (1949). *Elmstown's youth.* New York: Wiley.

Huston, A. (1993). *Children in poverty.* New York: Cambridge University.

Kagan, J. (1989). *Unstable ideas: Temperament, cognition and self.* Cambridge, MA: Harvard University.

Karen, R. (1994). *Becoming attached.* New York: Time Warner.

Kett, J. (1977). *Rites of passage: Adolescence in America.* New York: Basic Books.

Ketterlinus, R., & Lamb, M. (1994). *Adolescent problem behaviors.* New York: Erlbaum.

Kosmin, R., & Lachman, S. (1993). *One nation under God.* New York: Harmony.

L'Abate, L. (1971). The status of adolescent psychology. *Developmental Psychology, 4,* 201-205.

Magnusson, D., & Bergman, L. (1994). Juvenile and persistent offenders. In R. Ketterlinus & M. Lamb (Eds.), *Adolescent problem behaviors* (pp. 81–93). Hillsdale, NJ: Erlbaum.

Main, M. (1993). *A typology of human attachment organization.* New York: Cambridge University.

McLanahan, S., Astone, N., & Marks, N. (1993). The role of mother only families in the reproduction of poverty. In A. Huston (Ed.), *Children in poverty.* New York: Cambridge University.

Mead, M. (1935). *Sex and temperament in three primitive societies.* New York: American Library.

Moran, G., & Vinovskis, M. (1994). Children at risk in early modern England, colonial America & 19th century America. In R. Ketterlinus & M. Lamb (Eds.), *Adolescent problem behaviors* (pp. 1–17). Hillsdale, NJ: Erlbaum.

Pattishall, E. (1994). Research agenda for adolescent problems. In R. Ketterlinus & M. Lamb (Eds.), *Adolescent problem behavior* (pp. 209–217). Hillsdale, NJ: Erlbaum.

Piaget, J. (1954). *The construction of intelligence in children.* New York: Basic Books.

Piaget, J. (1965). *The moral judgment of the child.* New York: Free Press.

Plomin, R., DeFries, J., & McClearn, G. (1990). *Behavioral genetics.* New York: Freeman.

Robins, L., & Rutter, M. (1990). *Straight and devious pathways from childhood to adulthood.* New York: Cambridge University.

Rowe, D. (1994). Genetic and cultural explanation of adolescent risk taking. In R. Ketterlinus & M. Lamb (Eds.), *Adolescent problem behavior* (pp. 109–127). Hillsdale, NJ: Erlbaum.

Schiebinger, L. (1993). *Nature's body: Gender in the making of modern science.* Boston: Beacon Press.

Skinner, B. (1953). *Science and human behavior.* New York: Free Press.

Tuana, N. (1993). *The less noble sex.* Bloomington, IN: Indiana University.

Udry, R. (1994). Integrating biological and sociological models of adolescent problem behaviors. In R. Ketterlinus & M. Lamb (Eds.), *Adolescent problem behaviors* (pp. 93–109). Hillsdale, NJ: Erlbaum.

U.S. Department of Commerce (1992). *General population characteristics.* Washington, DC: Bureau of the Census.

U.S. Department of Commerce (1993). *Population estimates by age, sex, race & Hispanic origin.* Washington, DC: Bureau of the Census.

Weiner, I. (1992). *Psychological disturbance in adolescence.* New York: Wiley.

PHYSICAL DEVELOPMENT

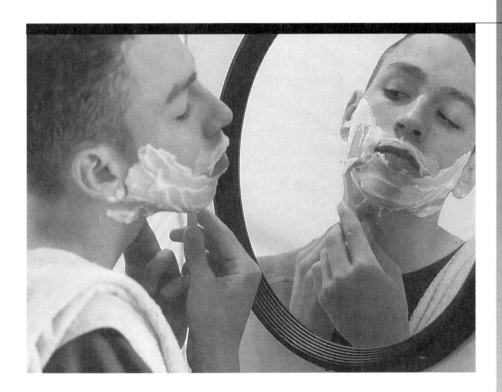

Chapter Outline

Key Questions Addressed In This Chapter

1. What physical changes occur during adolescence and in what sequence?
2. How is the physical development of males and females alike and different?
3. How do physical changes affect adolescents' personalities?
4. How do hormonal changes during adolescence affect their behavior?
5. How physically fit and healthy are most adolescents today?
6. How does an adolescent's physical appearance affect his or her development?
7. How do hormones affect adolescents' moods and personalities?
8. How do adolescents' habits affect physical problems later in their lives?
9. In what ways do exercise and sports benefit adolescents?
10. What are the disadvantages and advantages of being an adolescent athlete?

PUBERTY: WHAT, WHEN, AND WHY?

Before the age of 16, it happens to all of us—puberty begins. The word puberty comes from the Latin verb *pubescere*, which means "to grow hairy or mossy." Today in our society puberty signifies the period of life during which our bodies become physically capable of reproducing. For girls, the first menstrual period is seen as the clearest sign that puberty is well underway. For boys, however, the passage into puberty is not as evident to outside observers or as clearly marked by a single event like menstruation.

Technically, puberty has begun long before our body actually starts showing outwardly that we're entering adolescence (Higham, 1980; Katchadourian, 1970). First the structure in our limbic system known as the **hypothalamus** signals our pituitary gland to release the hormones known as **gonadotropins.** A year or so before our body shows any outward signs of puberty, while we are asleep our pituitary gland begins to release these gonadotropins into our body. These gonadotropins cause the ovaries and the testes, known as the **gonads,** to speed up their production of **estrogen** in girls and **testosterone** in boys. Although both males and females have estrogen and testosterone in their bodies from birth to death, when puberty begins the ovaries increase the amount of estrogen in a girl's body by six times its childhood level. Likewise in boys, although they always have some estrogen in their bodies, the testes produce 20 times the amount of testosterone when puberty begins.

In other words, what matters at puberty is how much estrogen or testosterone the individual's body produces, not whether these hormones are present in the body. Indeed, by adding estrogen or testosterone through medications, we can alter our appearance as males or females. For example, teenage girls who have a genetic abnormality that prevents their bodies from producing enough estrogen at puberty would retain their child-like body without estrogen supplements. At puberty these girls are given estrogen pills that enable them to develop a more normal female appearance. Likewise, if a male wants to have a sex-change operation, he takes estrogen shots or pills, which cause his body to develop fuller breasts and hips, to lose some of his body hair and muscle mass, and to pitch his voice higher. On the other hand, when male or female athletes take **steroids,** synthetically produced hormones similar to the natural **androgen** hormones that cause masculine characteristics, they develop a more masculine appearance— more muscle mass, more body hair, and deeper voices. Female athletes who use steroids also stop menstruating in response to the additional male hormones.

What is it, though, that determines when we'll enter puberty? Why are some of us such late bloomers, while others of us are way ahead of our peers physically? Although we're not altogether sure about the answer, some researchers believe that puberty begins when the percentage of fat relative to our body's overall weight reaches the right proportions (Frisch, 1991). That is, until we achieve a certain weight and have enough body fat, the hypothalamus refuses to give the gonadatropins the go-ahead. This hypothesis might help explain why teenagers from richer families who have good diets and tend to have heavier body weights and more fat usually mature before children who are malnourished. It's also true that as our society's diet and health have improved during the past 100 years, children have started maturing earlier. Mainly due to better nutrition and better health care, most adolescent boys now enter puberty around the age of 12 and finish growing by age 19. Most girls enter puberty around 11 and stop growing at about age 17. Likewise, teenage girls who lose too much of their body fat, as is the case with many Olympic gymnasts and with all anorexics, stop having their periods until they gain back enough fat.

But weight and fat tissue aren't the only factors that seem to affect how fast we mature physically. For example, it's not clear why teenagers living in higher altitudes and those from small families enter puberty sooner than children living in lower altitudes and those from large families. Even the seasons might have some bearing on how fast we mature—fewer girls start to menstruate in the spring than in any other season (Beau, Baker, & Haas, 1977; Malina, 1979; Peterson & Taylor, 1980).

The fact remains, however, that the best way to predict when a child is physically going to become an adolescent is to look at his or her parent's physical development. Although this method isn't 100% foolproof, most of us mature at about the same age our parents did. So if your mother started menstruating when she was 11 and your father had a beard by the time he was 14, odds are that you're going to develop at about the same rate they did.

CHANGES IN THE HEAD AND FACE

Did you notice in your own adolescence that some of your childhood problems, such as trouble with your tonsils or adenoids, seemed to improve? During puberty our lymphatic tissues begin to shrink, causing us to grow out of some of the allergic reactions, colds, and sore throats that plagued us as younger children. Unfortunately, this gain is offset by another loss: our vision. Rapid changes in the eyes from the ages of 11 to 14 often produce shortsightedness, the inability to see things far away. After the fifth grade, then, many of us become aware that we need glasses. Changes in our vocal cords also make us aware that our voices are changing. A teenage girl's voice does become somewhat lower. But the most noticeable changes are for boys because their vocal cords double in length, causing their voices to drop nearly an octave.

At the same time the vocal chords are enlarging, so is the nose—much to the disappointment of many adolescents who become fixated on having a big nose. In early adolescence, the hairline recedes and the facial bones grow in such a way that the nose and chin are proportionately larger than the rest of the face. As the face continues to grow and assumes its final contours, however, the nose and chin assume a size more proportionate to the face. But until that time, many adolescents complain about the size of their nose. Although we can't alter this pattern, we can reassure teenagers who are obsessing on the size of their nose by explaining that everyone's nose, not just theirs, grows to its full size before the rest of the face catches up.

CHANGES IN HEIGHT

Adolescents fortunate enough to be satisfied with the size of their nose might not be satisfied with their height. As Insert 2–1 illustrates, as a society we are fixated on the idea of boys' being tall—at the very least, taller than girls (Gillis, 1982). Once again, the best way for a teenager to predict how tall he or she will be is to look at their same-sex parent. It's genetically possible, of course, for two very short parents to have a very tall child. But generally, when it comes to our final size and shape, "the acorn doesn't fall far from the tree." That is, most of us end up with a body shaped very similar to our same-sex parent's body.

In terms of how fast our various parts grow, the body plays a mean trick on us as adolescents. Our parts grow at different rates, leaving us feeling awkward and out of proportion. Our legs finish growing before our arms do, and our hands and feet reach their full size before the arms and legs reach theirs. Moreover, teenagers usually gain most of their height in the spring, yet don't gain weight until the fall. The result is that teenagers have a legitimate reason to feel awkward and out of proportion until their body completely finishes growing. They are justified in

---

Insert 2–1

Should Short Adolescents Take Hormone Shots?

Should perfectly healthy teenagers be given a synthetic drug to make them grow taller? The growth hormone, first manufactured in 1985 for children whose bodies are incapable of producing it, is now being used experimentally with children whose hormones are normal but who want to be taller for social reasons in a society like ours in which being tall is valued—especially if you're male. Citing evidence that short people tend to fall behind others in terms of their school grades, income, and popularity, advocates of the drug insist that being short can be a social handicap. With the experiment only recently underway, it is not yet clear whether the drug will actually increase an individual's height, or merely prod the body to reach more quickly the natural height it would have achieved eventually anyway. But if the drug works, the question is: Do we want to use drugs just to improve the appearance of perfectly normal, healthy children?

Source: G. Cowley & M. Hager (1992, July 13). A drug to grow on. *Newsweek*, p. 59.

feeling self-conscious about being "too skinny and gangly," or "all feet," or "all legs" at certain periods of their growth. What we might do, then, is to explain to them well ahead of time how these changes are going to occur so they might at least feel "normal" in their newly forming body.

In terms of our final height, most of us grow about 10 inches taller from the ages of 11 to 18. During our fastest year of growth, we grow about 3 to 5 inches. By the end of adolescence, then, most boys are about 5'10" and most girls are about 5'5". In contrast to the 1890s when only about 5% of all males grew taller than 6 feet, today nearly 25% of teenage boys are at least 6 feet tall.

MUSCLE DEVELOPMENT AND PHYSICAL ABILITIES

Although our height usually increases by about 20% during our adolescence, our weight might actually double. By the time adolescence ends, boys generally weigh about 25 pounds more than girls. This extra weight is primarily due to the fact that males are taller and have a higher proportion of muscle to fat tissue than females. A boy's muscle tissue usually doubles during adolescence, while a girl's increases by only 50%. Only about 12% of a man's total body weight is due to his fat tissue, in contrast to about 20% to 25% of a woman's total weight.

These differences in muscle and fat tissue have naturally led us to wonder: How do teenage boys and girls stack up against each other in terms of their athletic and physical abilities? First, keep in mind that we are discussing only averages when we say that boys are usually 5 inches taller and 25 pounds heavier than girls when they finish growing. In other words, many girls are taller and heavier than many boys. Consequently, these girls can often outperform many boys in physical activities because of their size. Likewise, adolescent girls who exercise regularly or who are athletes have more muscle and less fat than teenage boys who are not physically fit. Athletic girls also have higher oxygen intake, more stamina, and more muscle strength than unathletic boys (Peterson & Taylor, 1980).

In regard to specific physical abilities, a female's higher proportion of body fat and lighter bones give her an advantage over males in activities requiring stamina, such as long distance running or swimming. Females also are usually more loose-jointed, which enables them to outperform males in such tasks as touching the floor with the palms of the hands. On the other hand, most tasks requiring upper body strength, such as lifting heavy weights or doing chin-ups, are easier for males because of their additional muscle tissue. Until adolescence, most boys and girls are well-matched physically in terms of their weight, height, and muscle tissue. But once testosterone causes teenage boys' muscles to develop, and they grow taller and heavier, they can generally outperform girls in sports such as basketball or soccer unless the girl has been exercising or has the size and height to compete. In short, if a teenage boy and girl are about the same weight and height and exercise about the same, the boy will have the advantage in most physical activities requiring upper body strength; and the girl will have the advantage in activities requiring long distance stamina or muscle flexibility (Thomas & French, 1985).

Insert 2–2

Myths about Females and Physical Exercise

Should programs for female students' athletic development receive the same amount of money as those for male students?

Which are True?

1. If girls lift weights, they will develop muscles as large as boys'.

2. Jogging causes the breast tissues to sag.

3. Some exercises can increase the tissue in the breasts.

4. Vigorous exercise, such as playing on the school's basketball team, makes menstrual cramps worse.

5. Teenage girls cannot perform as well athletically during their menstrual period.

6. Being hit hard on the chest during sports causes permanent damage to a girl's breast tissue.

7. A girl's reproductive organs are more vulnerable to injury playing sports than a boy's reproductive organs.

8. Males generally have more flexible muscles than females.

9. Females have less physical stamina relative to their body size than males.

10. Adolescent girls have too much body fat to compete as well as males in sports such as swimming.

All of the above are false.

FAT TISSUE AND BODY SHAPE

BODY FAT

One of the changes during adolescence that disturbs many girls is the increase in **adipose tissue,** or fat, as most of us so fondly call it. If a male or female's estrogen reaches high enough levels, fat tissue increases. But at puberty, a boy's estrogen level remains basically unchanged from childhood, while his testosterone level increases dramatically. The result is a net decrease in the percentage of fat tissue in his body. He loses his baby fat and begins to look more angular and more muscular. His fat tissue, composing only 12% to 15% of his total body weight, is distributed mainly around his abdomen. When a male is overweight, then, he gets a pot belly, rather than first putting on inches around his hips or thighs as females do. The teenage boy's shape also changes in that his shoulders and chest become larger in proportion to his lower body. Because he has less fat covering his muscle tissue, his muscles also will be more apparent than a teenage girl's, particularly in his upper body.

For the teenage girl, although her testosterone level remains basically unchanged from childhood, her estrogen level skyrockets. This causes her body to add more fat tissue and to distribute it around her hips, stomach, thighs, upper arms, and breasts. During puberty her body reaches a level of 20% to 25% fat, even if she is not at all overweight and even if she exercises regularly. No matter how much she exercises or how much weight she loses, a teenage girl's fat still will be distributed mainly in these areas of her body, preventing her from achieving the straight, hip-less shape she had before puberty.

BREAST DEVELOPMENT

Given our particular society's definitions of beauty, most teenage girls don't mind the fat tissue which their additional estrogen adds to their breasts. In some areas of Puerto Rico and Italy, both boys and girls have developed larger breasts as a consequence of eating poultry that had been treated with high doses of estrogen (Bongiovani, 1983). When it comes to breasts, in our own society before boys start producing large enough amounts of testosterone to develop their muscles, some of them worry about their breasts being too fleshy or too flabby.

In girls, breast development is one of the first signs that puberty has begun. The increases in estrogen in the girl's body cause her breasts to develop in stages many months before she starts to menstruate. First the **areola,** the area around the nipple, becomes thicker and darker. Depending on the amount of pigment in the skin, the areola can range from light pink to very dark brown. Because the nipples grow before the breast tissue, many girls feel embarrassed. Moreover, the fat tissue in each breast does not necessarily grow at the same rate, which leaves some girls feeling abnormal even though this is, in fact, quite normal. The breasts also get larger because the **mammary glands,** which produce milk during pregnancy, are developing. Most of the breast, however, is fat tissue, not muscle or glands. For this reason, no amount of exercise can increase the size of the breast itself. What exercise can do, however, as you can see from looking at professional female body builders, is increase the size of the pectoral muscles that underlie the fat tissue in each breast. Enlarging this muscle through exercise gives males and females the appearance of having a larger chest. False advertising about special breast creams aside, only two factors determine the size of a woman's breasts: what she inherits from her mother and how much fat tissue she has throughout her body. That is, if a teenage girl or woman loses 30 pounds, her breasts get smaller because they are mostly fat tissue.

Because all fat tissue retains water, a teenage girl's breasts usually become somewhat fuller around the time she is having her period each month. Due to the monthly fluctuations in her body's hormones, all of her fat tissues will retain more water at this time of month. Consequently, most girls notice that their breasts are more tender and swollen during these days, and they should be reassured that this discomfort passes as their estrogen levels rise again after the period ends. Unfortunately, many girls are dissatisfied with the size or shape of their breasts. In a society obsessed with the size of the female breast, teenage girls are quick to pick up on the message that only breasts of a certain size and shape are desirable. Like adolescent boys who worry about their penis being too small, many teenage girls make themselves unhappy by believing their breasts are not pretty because they are either too small, too large, or unshapely.

WEIGHT CONTROL AND NUTRITION

LOSING AND GAINING WEIGHT

In an effort to look skinnier, many teenagers—especially girls—are dieting or exercising in ways that make little sense in terms of how the body actually works and that can be extremely dangerous as well. If we could somehow do a better job educating adolescents about how their bodies actually lose and gain weight, perhaps we could at least reduce some of their dangerous dieting. How is it then that the body loses or gains weight and what is the best way for a teenager to get his or her body to look skinnier or to look heavier (Harris, 1991; McGlynn, 1990; Wolfe, 1991)?

First, in teenagers' attempts to lose or to gain weight, it's important that they understand that the scales are not the best way to measure how much "fat" they're really losing or gaining. The number of pounds that appears on the scales is the weight of more than merely fat. Those pounds also reflect two other components of the body that fluctuate in weight—muscle tissue and water. In fact, how much water we have in our bodies changes almost daily, depending on such factors as how much we've exercised, how much salty food we've eaten, and how hot or cold the weather is. For example, a teenage boy who jogs 4 miles on a hot day can lose as much as 5 pounds of water. But once he replenishes his liquids, his weight will go back up. Likewise, a girl who has eaten a lot of salty food or is close to the time she's going to start her period is retaining more water in her body tissues than usual. So if she's been dieting, she might be shocked to discover that her weight has increased, and she might wrongly assume that she's as "fat" as ever. But if she cuts down her salty foods and waits a few days until her period ends, she'll magically lose weight again. The weight of the water in the body is the reason why so many of the weight loss products that teenagers buy seem to work. These products are **diuretics,** meaning that they cause the body's tissues to empty themselves of water, giving the false impression that you're not as fat because the number of pounds on the scales goes down. In reality, though, diuretics do nothing to alter the amount of fat in the body. They just dehydrate you.

The weight on the scales also can confuse teenagers because fat tissue weighs less than muscle tissue. In other words, if you had one cup full of your fat tissue and one cup full of your muscle tissue, the cup of muscle would weigh almost two and a half times more than the fat. So if you are exercising a lot, two things are happening: You are burning up your fat tissue and you are adding more muscle tissue. On your scales, though, you can actually gain a few pounds even though you are literally losing fat and gaining muscle. In fact, your clothes might start to fit looser and you might see more muscles developing, even though your weight does not go down. Not understanding this physiological fact, teenagers can get discouraged when they are trying to lose fat through exercising because they keep relying on the numbers on the scales to measure their success.

Finally, most adolescents make foolish choices when it comes to trying to lose or gain weight because they don't understand the basic facts about calories and fat tissue. First, a body has to burn up 3,500 calories worth of energy in order to lose one pound of fat tissue. So, for example, if a boy eats an 800-calorie sandwich and goes out to play two hours of basketball, which burns up about 700 calories, he still has 100 calories to spare and has not burned any of his body's fat. In other words, if a teenager wants to lose one pound of fat in a week, he or she would have to burn up 500 more calories each day than he or she eats. This is why losing fat is a gradual, slow process that involves exercising as well as cutting back what we eat. Second, what adolescents choose to eat influences how quickly they feel hungry again. The adolescent who eats complex carbohydrates, like bread, cereals, and pasta, will have longer-lasting energy and won't feel hungry as quickly as the one who eats foods high in sugar.

In order to decide how much to eat in a day in order to lose fat tissue, adolescents first have to determine about how many calories they burn up in the course of their typical day. Those who don't do any exercise other than what's required to move themselves from place to place during the day should decide what weight they would like to be, then multiply that number by 12 to determine the number of calories they should eat each day to reach that weight. But teenagers who get a lot of exercise, like athletes, could multiply by 18 or 20, depending on how much of a workout they're getting every day. So, for instance, if a 160-pound boy wants to lose 20 pounds, he should be eating only 1,680 calories a day, unless he's going to do some exercise (Bailey, 1978).

Third, adolescents also need help understanding the importance of their **basal metabolic rate,** which is the speed at which the body converts calories into energy. People with a low basal metabolism burn calories at a slow rate and, therefore, cannot eat as much food without gaining weight. People with high metabolic rates, though, can eat more food and burn up the extra calories before they are converted into fat. From the ages of 11 to 20, everyone's metabolic rate is slowing down somewhat. Teenagers need to understand, then, that they can get away with eating more and not exercising without gaining weight at the age of 14 than they can at 20. Moreover, young people need to be educated to understand that exercising not only burns up calories during the activity itself but also raises the body's basal metabolic rate after the exercise is over. Given this, older adolescents need to build regular exercise into their lives and cut back on what they're eating if they want to avoid what is known in college as "the freshmen fifteen" (pounds) or, at 40, as "middle age spread" (Brownwell & Stein, 1988).

OBESE ADOLESCENTS

In short, the best way to lose weight is not to cut back on the amount you're eating but to increase the amount you exercise. This is the reason why the main difference between adolescents who are obese and those who aren't is how much they exercise, not how much they eat. Obese teenagers also skip more meals, snack more between meals, eat more quickly, and eat less nutritious food than other adolescents. This is why programs that succeed in helping obese teenagers lose weight require that they exercise every day, as well as cut back their calories. Although 90% of obese adolescents have at least one parent who is also overweight, even a genetic tendency to gain weight can almost always be controlled by exercise and diet (Morrill, 1991; Wishon, 1991).

A very important contributor to adolescent overeating is stress. Not only do some obese teenagers have tense relationships with their parents, but some of their parents also tend to be overly protective and to discourage their child's independence in ways that seem to be contributing to the child's overeating. Given our society's emphasis on being thin, most obese teenagers have less self-confidence than other people of normal weight. Realizing this, a number of weight loss programs for teenagers focus on building self-confidence while teaching about food and exercise (Kimm, 1991; Morrill, 1991). Unfortunately, 80% of those adolescents who are extremely overweight don't adopt better eating and exercising habits. So they remain overweight throughout their lives, posing serious problems to their physical health (Sigman & Flanery, 1992).

WEIGHT AND GENDER

When it comes to which teenagers actually do need to lose weight, girls overestimate and boys underestimate how fat they really are (Koff & Rierdan, 1991; Page, 1991; Wadden, 1991; White, Schiecker, & Dayan, 1991). Most teenage girls who are dieting or who say they're too fat are actually the right weight for their height and age. Sadder still, most girls start worrying about being too fat before they even become adolescents. In contrast, many teenage boys who actually do need to lose weight don't see themselves as overweight. Instead, most boys complain about not being tall enough or muscular enough (Bell, 1988; Gillis, 1982; Martel & Biller, 1987). Even female athletes put themselves on dangerous diets in order to meet our society's ideal of "thin enough" (Carruth & Goldberg, 1990).

The 70% of all teenage girls who have been on a diet need to know that dramatic up and down swings of weight can increase their risk of later heart disease. Recognizing the dangers of continual dieting, the federal government has changed the standard tables for what the ideal weight is for males and females according to height and age. Fortunately, the number of dieters in our society has dropped from 65 million in 1986 to 48 million in 1991, reflecting our growing concern for our health rather than for unnaturally thin bodies. But too many teenage girls still are abusing their bodies by dieting when their weight is perfectly normal (Kramer, 1991). For example, in a survey of nearly 37,000

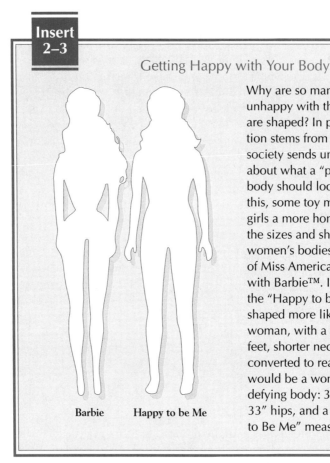

Insert 2–3

Getting Happy with Your Body

Why are so many adolescent girls unhappy with the way their bodies are shaped? In part, their dissatisfaction stems from the fact that our society sends unrealistic images about what a "pretty" adult female body should look like. Realizing this, some toy makers are sending girls a more honest message about the sizes and shapes of real women's bodies by creating a line of Miss America dolls to compete with Barbie™. In contrast to Barbie, the "Happy to be Me" doll is shaped more like an average woman, with a wider waist, larger feet, shorter neck and shorter legs. If converted to real life, a Barbie doll would be a woman with a gravity-defying body: 36" bust, 18" waist, 33" hips, and a size-5 shoe. "Happy to Be Me" measures 36–27–38.

Barbie   Happy to be Me

adolescents, three times as many females as males who weren't overweight said they were overweight; and 16% of the senior high girls were on a diet compared to 2% of the males. Worse yet, 40% of the senior high girls disliked their bodies in contrast to only 15% of their male counterparts (Harris, Blum, & Resnick, 1991).

Most teenage girls' obsession with thinness is directly tied to two overriding messages that they receive from our adult society. First, males of all ages can be more overweight than females and still be considered sexy, attractive, and socially desirable. Second, physical appearance is more important if you're female than if you're male. Put more bluntly, you'll do a lot better socially as a physically unattractive male than as a physically unattractive female—especially if your culture values extreme thinness in females (Adams, 1991; Bordo, 1993; Friedman, 1989; Wolf, 1992). The closest message to the one that girls receive about their weight is the one boys receive about their height—a male needs to be "tall enough" which means, at the very least, taller than the female he's with (Gillis, 1982; Martel & Biller, 1987). Well before we reach adolescence, most of us have

Insert 2–4

Fat, Food, and Exercise: Facts and Fictions

Which are True?

1. The best way to lose weight is to cut back on what you eat.

2. Exercise raises your basal metabolic rate.

3. Eating grapefruit helps the body burn calories faster.

4. Two vigorous 6-minute exercises burn up more fat than one slow, continuous 12-minute exercise.

5. Exercising can make you look skinnier without your actually losing any pounds.

6. By increasing your exercise, you instead might increase your weight.

7. If you eat before you go to bed, you will gain more weight than if you eat earlier in the evening.

8. A good way to lose weight is to eat a big breakfast, medium lunch, and small dinner.

9. You can eat as much as you want of certain kinds of food and never gain weight.

10. It's possible to get headaches from the caffeine in certain chocolate candies.

Numbers 2, 5, 6, 8, and 10 are true.

---

adopted these two standards: a male really can't be "too" tall and a female can seldom be "too" skinny. It's also important to point out that most African American adolescents haven't been socialized to adopt such exaggerated, unhealthy ideas about female thinness (Wade, 1991).

Carried to the extreme, our society's obsession with female slenderness contributes to the rise in two eating disorders among teenage and young adult females, psychological disorders discussed in Chapter 14. Although some males also have these disorders, they are almost exclusively female illnesses. The first, **anorexia nervosa,** is a disorder in which the person literally starves himself or herself to death unless someone intervenes. The second, **bulimia,** also known as "binging and purging," is a disorder in which one overeats and then forces oneself to throw up, or takes laxatives to force the food out of the body before the calories have time to be absorbed. Most females with these two eating disorders are teenagers or young adults who are obsessed with our society's ideals of thinness and who suffer from very negative feelings about their own appearance (Fisher & Brone, 1991).

Realizing the damage that our exaggerated notions about female thinness have done to many girls in terms of their physical health and their self-esteem, some efforts are being made to send girls a healthier and more anatomically accurate message about their bodies. For example, the older image of the beautiful female body is personified by the Barbie™ doll—a doll with proportions that in real life would nearly topple over a woman, given Barbie's shoe size and other body measurements. On a more positive note, the recent "Happy to Be Me" doll represents a more biologically correct version of what a healthy woman's body looks like and gives girls a more reasonable image to compare themselves to ("Barbie backlash," 1992). But, as shown in Chapter 6, most adolescent boys are much more satisfied with how they look and much less obsessed with their weight and appearance than girls their age.

Nutrition and Health

In addition to girls' dangerous dieting habits, most teenagers are unknowingly harming themselves as a consequences of their poor eating habits (Carruth & Goldberg, 1990; Freedland & Dwyer, 1991; McGlynn, 1990). In terms of their overall health, adolescents with poor eating habits are retarding their body's growth or damaging their muscle and bone tissue. Because of the rapid growth in our bodies during adolescence, we need large amounts of calories to build healthy bones and tissues. During their peak growing years a teenage boy needs 2,500 to 3,000 calories a day and a teenage girl needs 2,000 to 2,500. Although it's usually girls who do the most damage to themselves by eating too little, many teenage boys also undereat or eat too little of the kinds of foods that build bones and tissue.

Too many adolescents also are damaging their bodies by eating foods that contain too much fat. As most people know by now, high cholesterol from fatty foods contributes to heart disease. But most adolescents don't seem to realize that the condition of their cardiovascular system at age 40 or 50 will depend on what kinds of food they've been eating all their lives. Especially for those teenagers who smoke, are overweight, have high blood pressure, or have a family history of heart disease, the food they eat is closely connected to how healthy they will be as adults. For example, obesity has increased more than 50% among African American adolescents during the past 15 to 20 years, contributing to high rates of hypertension and diabetes as adults (Robinson & Ward, 1991). In order to help adolescents recognize this connection between the present and the future, some schools are testing students' cholesterol levels and alerting those who are at high risk for developing later disease (Flax, 1991). But on the whole, our teenagers still aren't doing a very good job cutting back on their fat intake or on the high amounts of sugar they consume (Carruth & Goldberg, 1990; Freedland & Dwyer, 1991).

Given the power of advertising and the fact that the average teenager spends 15,000 hours in front of the television before the age of 18, one of our most effective ways of changing young people's eating habits could be through television (Story, 1990). For example, 15-year-old girls' eating habits and feelings about their own weight are related to the kinds of messages they get from magazines and television (Newell, 1990). Another approach is to do a better job educating adolescents about nutrition at school. For example, the Heart Healthy Cook-off program in Pawtucket, New York, is teaching teenagers new eating habits by having them analyze recipes, make healthy substitutions in each recipe, and then cook the healthier food. The students are then judged for the food's presentation, taste, and nutritional value (Carleton, 1991). If more such programs existed, adolescents would no doubt be healthier.

Many adolescents also don't realize that what they eat can be having an influence on their grades, their aches and pains, and their moods. For example, teenagers who complain of frequent headaches, constipation, or stomach pains often are creating these problems themselves by what and when they eat. Skipping meals—especially breakfast or lunch—or eating too little food lowers the body's blood sugar levels and can create headaches and drowsiness. Not eating enough fiber also can cause stomach pains and constipation. A poor diet can contribute to drowsiness and inattentiveness in class, which in turn can influence a student's grades. In fact, drowsiness from not eating enough can literally be fatal—not only to teenagers but to others. A number of car accidents are caused by teenagers who have dozed off at the wheel traveling to and from school, killing or injuring themselves, their passengers, and other motorists. Too many teenagers also die or seriously injure themselves at work in accidents caused by drowsiness or lack of energy from poor eating habits. Because most parents don't monitor how much sleep their teenage children are getting or what they are eating during the day, many adolescents are creating problems for themselves that could be remedied in large part by getting more sleep and changing their eating habits (Carskadon, 1990).

PHYSICAL FITNESS

FITNESS TRENDS

When it comes to physical fitness, how do today's adolescents stack up? In general, not very well. Given their bad eating habits and their lack of exercise, teenagers are now more overweight and more out of shape than teenagers in the 1970s and '80s. For example, the average 13-year-old boy can do only 3 chin-ups and takes more than 10 minutes to run one mile. Nearly 65% of children from ages 6 to 17 fail to meet the standards set by the President's Council on Physical Fitness. Obesity has increased 54% in the past 20 years among children ages 6 to 11 and 40% among those ages 12 to 17. The average 13-year-old boy, for example, needs to lose 9 pounds. About 25% of all teenagers are overweight and only one fifth of them will get their weight down to normal during their adult lives. Almost 35% already have factors that put them at risk for later heart disease and 42% have high cholesterol. All in all, today's children and adolescents are the most overweight and least exercised generation in the history of our country—less physically fit than children in 20 other countries (American Athletic Union, 1989; Harris, 1991). But as Table 2–1 illustrates, getting regular exercise in activities such as swimming, running or biking can keep teenagers in good shape.

Table 2–1

Scorecard on 14 Sports for Adolescents

Below is a summary of how seven experts rated 14 sports. A score of 21 indicates maximum benefit. Ratings were based on exercising four times a week for 30 min to 1 hr.

	Stamina	Muscular Endurance	Muscular Strength	Flexibility	Balance	Weight Control	Muscle Definitions	Digestion	Sleep	Total Score
Jogging	21	20	17	9	17	21	14	13	16	148
Bicycling	19	18	16	9	18	20	15	12	15	142
Swimming	21	20	14	15	12	15	14	13	16	140
Skating	18	17	15	13	20	17	14	11	15	140
Handball Squash	19	18	15	16	17	19	11	13	13	140
Skiing	19	19	15	14	16	17	12	12	15	139
Basketball	19	17	15	13	16	19	13	10	12	134
Tennis	16	16	14	14	16	16	13	12	11	128
Calisthenics	10	13	16	19	15	12	18	11	12	126
Walking	13	14	11	7	8	13	11	11	14	102
Golf	8	8	9	8	8	6	6	7	6	66*
Softball	6	8	7	9	7	7	5	8	7	64
Bowling	5	5	5	7	6	5	5	7	6	51

*Ratings for golf are based on the fact that most people use a golf cart or caddy. If waliking, the fitness value increases.

Source: U.S. Department of Health and Human Services (1980). *Children and youth in action: Physical activities and sports.* (p.29). Washington, DC: Author.

PSYCHOLOGICAL BENEFITS OF EXERCISE

Not only could getting more exercise help adolescents lose weight, lower their cholesterol levels, and be more energetic, it also could give their self-esteem a boost. Regular exercise seems to reduce depression and lift our spirits, no matter what our age. Some researchers believe we feel better after exercising because our body increases its production of endorphins (Carr, 1981). **Endorphins** are chemicals automatically released by the brain whenever the body is seriously injured, as a natural anesthetic to dull intense physical pain. Some evidence suggests that our bodies also release these endorphins, which act like antidepressant drugs, when we exercise. This could explain why, for example, teenagers in a drug abuse program who were required to exercise every day became less depressed, improved their self-esteem scores, and used fewer drugs afterward than those teenagers in the program who did no physical exercise (Collingwood, 1991). Although not all researchers agree that endorphins are responsible for our good feelings after exercising, it's still clear that regular exercise usually helps adolescents feel more self-confident, improves their moods, and helps them cope more effectively with the stressful situations in their lives (Harris, 1991; Risser, 1989; Tucker, 1990; Tuckman & Hinkle, 1988).

ADOLESCENTS' HEALTH-RELATED BEHAVIORS

Given the sorry shape most adolescents are in when it comes to their overall physical fitness, why aren't they doing a better job taking care of their bodies? Because physical fitness not only affects how they look but also how they feel, why are so many teenagers refusing to exercise, continuing to overeat, and neglecting to eat nutritiously? Unfortunately, it seems most adolescents refuse to change their health habits even after we give them the information about how their choices are harming them (Irwin & Orr, 1991; Millstein & Litt, 1990). For example, even adolescents with life-threatening diseases such as chronic asthma often cause their own death or severe attacks because they refuse to follow their doctor's directions for taking their medicine (Stelzer, 1991).

Why? Part of the reason might be the adolescent attitude that "it can't happen to me." As explained in Chapter 3, some Piagetian psychologists believe that young adolescents, unlike older teenagers, aren't capable of recognizing that they're as mortal and vulnerable to illness and injury as the rest of us. But regardless of whether Piaget's explanation is correct, it's nonetheless true that older adolescents are usually better at taking care of their health and safety than young teenagers (Millstein & Litt, 1990). Another factor that seems to influence teenagers' attitudes toward their health is gender. In living out our society's male gender role, most boys put themselves at greater physical risk than girls in trying to prove their masculinity. As a consequence, teenage boys have higher death and injury rates than girls and more illnesses related to not following their doctors' orders (Miller & Wood, 1991; Stelzer, 1991). For example, in a survey of nearly 38,000 adolescents, almost half of the girls but only a third of the boys said they wear a seatbelt regularly, and nearly twice as many senior high boys as girls drink heavily on a weekly basis (Harris, Blum, & Resnick, 1991). Whether we're talking about wearing seatbelts, drinking heavily, driving fast, following their doctors' orders for taking asthma medicines, or taking dares other males might present them with, boys do a much poorer job than girls in taking care of their physical selves (Penley & Willis, 1992; Stelzer, 1991).

Careless, lax attitudes about their own health and safety seem to be contributing to many adolescents' needless deaths and injuries. In fact, adolescents are the only age group in our country whose death rate has increased during the past 30 years. Advances in modern medicine have reduced death rates from disease in every age group, including adolescents. But death and injuries from motor vehicle accidents, shootings, stabbings, drug use, alcohol abuse, and suicide have kept the teenage death rate on the increase. Every 7 minutes a child in the United States is arrested for a drug offense. Every 20 minutes an adolescent dies from a motor vehicle accident. Every 80 minutes one is a homicide victim, and every 90 minutes one commits suicide (Millstein & Litt, 1990; Robinson, 1991).

MALE REPRODUCTIVE SYSTEM

Basic Components

Although most adolescents are not as physically fit as teenagers were in the past, they are becoming physically mature at an earlier age. As a result of better medical treatment and better foods, teenagers today are entering puberty at around the age of 12 or 13. The first sign that puberty is beginning for boys is the growth of the penis and testicles. The two parts of the penis are the **glans,** or rounded head, which is the most sensitive area, and the **shaft,** which becomes engorged with blood during an erection (see Figure 2–1). Most boys in our society have a **circumcised** penis, meaning that the skin covering the glans, called the **foreskin,** was surgically cut and folded back shortly after birth. Circumcision historically has been performed as a religious rite and as a measure for preventing infections that might develop from bacteria trapped underneath the foreskin. Circumcision is the most common surgical procedure in our country. By the 1970s, however, the American Academy of Pediatrics concluded that, given our standards of cleanliness today, no medical reason remains for subjecting baby boys to this unnecessary cosmetic surgery. Most baby boys nowadays are circumcised because their parents want their son's penis to look a certain way, not because health risks are involved in not being circumcised. It appears, however, that more and more parents are choosing not to have this elective surgery performed on their sons. For example, in 1985 only 60% of the male newborns were circumcised—a decrease of 10% from 1979 (Smith, 1987). The result, obviously, is a higher percentage of boys entering puberty in this decade who are uncircumcised. If the trend continues, circumcised teenagers might eventually feel somewhat uncomfortable socially because they won't "look right" in comparison to the majority of their peers.

Circumcised or not, a boy's reproductive glands, the **testicles,** grow larger during adolescence, causing the skin sack that houses them, the **scrotum,** to enlarge as well. Although both testicles are the same size, the left one generally hangs slightly lower than the right—a fact boys need to know so they won't feel embarrassed or abnormal. The primary functions of the scrotum are to maintain the right temperature for sperm production and to protect the testicles from injury. In situations of physical danger or in cold weather, the scrotum contracts, pulling the testicles nearer to the body for protection and for extra warmth so sperm can survive. Likewise, in warm weather or after hot showers, the scrotum relaxes, causing the testicles to descend further from the body as a way of keeping the body cool enough for sperm to be produced.

Inside the testicles the **vas deferens** tubes carry sperm from the testicles to the **seminal vesicles** where they are stored. If the vas deferens tubes were unwound, they would stretch the length of several football fields. The seminal vesicles and the **prostate gland** produce **semen,** the fluid ejaculated during an orgasm. The semen, also called **seminal fluid,** is mainly composed of protective fluids that help the sperm survive in the acidic environment of the vagina. Semen is ejaculated

Figure 2–1

Male pelvic organs

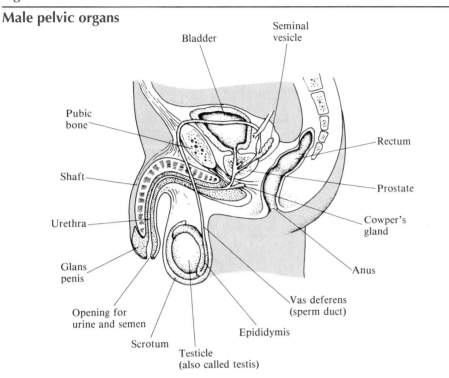

Bladder

Seminal
vesicle

Pubic
bone

Rectum

Shaft

Prostate

Urethra

Cowper's
gland

Glans
penis

Anus

Opening for
urine and semen

Vas deferens
(sperm duct)

Scrotum

Epididymis

Testicle
(also called testis)

through the **urethra,** the same tube that carries urine out of the body from the bladder. A single ejaculation contains about 400 million sperm, which propel themselves by moving their tails in a swimming motion. Although adolescent boys usually have fewer sperm and their sperm swim slower than a man's, they are very capable of impregnating an egg—as far too many young teenagers have discovered. Moreover, live sperm are present in the few drops of liquid that the penis releases when a boy is sexually excited, which can result in a girl's getting pregnant even though her boyfriend doesn't have an orgasm—a fact we need to share with more young people before they discover this reality through an unwanted pregnancy.

EMOTIONAL REACTIONS

Most teenage boys are nervous or confused at some point as their body is developing. Not only is it embarrassing to have an erection at inopportune times at school or at work, but it creates real tension knowing that you can't control what your own body is doing at times like these. In fact, an erection can be caused by the friction of clothes or by the need to urinate, not only by something sexually arousing. Then there is also the embarrassment of having **wet dreams** or **nocturnal emissions,** orgasms that occur while a boy is asleep.

Just as most girls worry about the size and shape of their breasts, teenage boys often worry about the size and appearance of their penis. Despite the fact that almost every male's penis is about 5 or 6 inches long when aroused, the size of penises vary considerably when they are relaxed. This means that teenage boys see a variety of sizes and shapes in other boys' genitals, which can cause them to worry about their own adequacy. Most teenage boys also are too naive to understand that female sexual pleasure has less to do with the size of their partner's penis and more to do with their partner's willingness to please.

Boys also worry, of course, about aspects of their appearance other than their genitals: "Do I have too much hair on my body?" "Do I have too little hair on my chest?" "Why can't I grow a mustache?" "Why aren't my shoulders broader?" "My upper arms are too skinny." "I don't have the muscles most other guys have." "My calves look like bird legs." "My chest caves in" (Bell, 1988). Nevertheless, most teenage boys are more satisfied with how they look than are most teenage girls, for reasons discussed at length in Chapter 6 (Adams, 1991; Koff, Rierdan, & Stubbs, 1990).

FEMALE REPRODUCTIVE SYSTEM

BASIC COMPONENTS

The girl's primary sexual organ, the **clitoris,** has a glans and a shaft similar to the penis. The glans is covered by a protective hood of skin, the **prepuce,** and the shaft is buried underneath the skin, rather than exposed above the surface like the shaft of the penis. Also like a male, the female's clitoris becomes enlarged by the additional flow of blood when she is sexually aroused. Under the right circumstances when the clitoris is sufficiently stimulated, an orgasm occurs. Given this anatomical fact, teenagers start to discover that it's not the movement of the penis inside the vagina that causes a female's orgasm, but the stimulation of nerves near the clitoris. In the event a girl is very aroused but does not have an orgasm, she can experience the same physical discomfort as a boy whose testicles ache from the extra blood in his aroused tissues—a condition referred to as "blue balls."

Next to the clitoris is the urethra, the tube that carries urine outside the body from the bladder. The small urethral opening is almost invisible because it is surrounded by the **labia,** the folds of skin that protect the genital area. The more noticeable opening is the vaginal entrance. The **vagina** is the passageway through which a baby passes from the uterus to the outside of the body. It is also the area that accommodates the penis during intercourse. Unlike what many adolescents initially believe, the vagina is not a hollow space or an open cavity. The walls of

Figure 2–2

Female pelvic organs

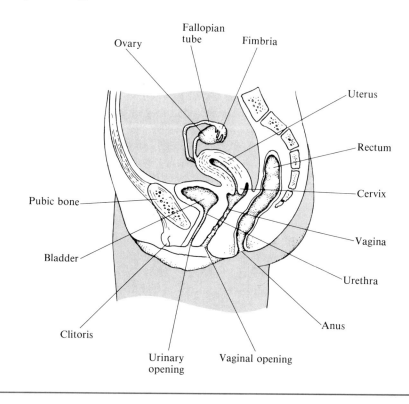

the vagina are touching one another unless something like a penis or a tampon separates them.

At the entrance to the vagina is the **hymen,** a thin membrane that partially blocks the vaginal opening. Although many adolescents are confused on this point, the hymen, also called the cherry or the maidenhead, doesn't have to be "broken" when a girl loses her virginity. Obviously the hymen can't completely block the vaginal opening because menstrual fluids and other natural secretions need an opening to pass through. Moreover, the hymen is often stretched without notice during a girl's childhood when she is playing or when she inserts tampons. But unless there is some physical abnormality, this stretching of the hymen is seldom accompanied by intense pain or excessive bleeding, despite the exaggerated depictions of being "deflowered" that adolescents encounter in some movies or books.

At the opposite end of the vagina is the bottom portion of the uterus, the **cervix.** The **os** is the tiny opening between the vagina and the uterus. During childbirth, the os dilates and expands to a width that allows the baby to pass through. Otherwise the os is so small that it does not feel like an opening to the touch. If girls understood their own anatomy, they would not worry, as some do, that a tampon can somehow get lost or pushed into some other part of the body by mistake. The os is far too small for this.

The **uterus,** or **womb,** lies on the opposite side of the os from the vagina. About the size of a small, upside-down pear and located low in the abdominal area, the uterus is composed of thick muscles. During pregnancy the fertilized egg implants itself in the walls of the uterus, grows for nine months, and then, through contractions of the uterine muscles, the baby is pushed out into the world. When a girl is having menstrual cramps, she is feeling the muscles of her uterus contract. At the top of the uterus are the **Fallopian tubes** through which the unfertilized egg passes each month from the ovaries to the uterus. Unlike males who continually produce new sperm, the egg that is released each month has been stored in the female's ovaries since the moment of her birth.

Menstruation

Before the age of 16, almost all girls have started to menstruate. Unless the egg is fertilized by sperm, the uterus sheds its lining. This monthly shedding of the uterine lining is called **menstruation** and marks the beginning of **menarche**—the girl's official passage from childhood to puberty. If the egg is fertilized, the uterine lining is kept for housing and nourishing the developing fetus, so no menstrual period occurs until after the baby is born. Because a teenage girl can skip periods for reasons other than pregnancy, such as stress or extreme weight loss, a blood or urine test is needed to determine whether she's pregnant. Although we refer to the menstrual fluid as blood, it's actually a mixture of the tissue, mucus, and blood that had lined the uterus. Not understanding this, some teenage girls believe they are losing blood from their body's circulatory system and fear they will become weak or anemic when they're menstruating. But unless a disorder or disease is causing heavy, irregular bleeding, menstruating doesn't cause anemia.

Most teenage girls have irregular periods in the first year or two after they start menstruating—a situation which understandably frightens those teenage couples who are having sex without using contraceptives. Skipping a period every now and then, however, is perfectly normal for teenage girls. Once their periods become regular, most girls menstruate every 25 to 35 days, for 3 to 5 days. Like teenage boys, adolescent girls also are somewhat less fertile than adults, in this case because their bodies don't necessarily release an egg each month. Nevertheless, teenage girls are clearly fertile enough that one million of them get pregnant every year—mostly by accident.

Although most girls have some discomfort while they're menstruating, such as mild cramping, tender breasts, or lower back pain, only a small percent have pain severe enough to interfere with their normal daily activities. Most teenage girls don't have an intensely negative reaction to having their periods. Even though they are inconvenienced and sometimes embarrassed, if a period starts unexpectedly in some public situation, most girls don't feel that their periods are an earth-shattering experience. This doesn't mean that girls never feel depressed or physically debilitated during their periods. Some do. But how well a girl feels during her period is determined both by her attitude and by physical factors beyond her control. Some girls have enough discomfort that they take medicines to ease the pain. Others have pain and depression caused by their extremely low levels of calcium, progesterone, or prolactin. So menstrual pain isn't "only in their heads" (Boston Women's Health Collective, 1991; Hood, 1991b; McGrory, 1990).

Though only a minority, some girls suffer from more dramatic mood shifts immediately before or during their periods—a condition referred to as **premenstrual syndrome,** or **PMS.** Although a number of strategies, including changes in diet and exercise, help alleviate some of these symptoms, the debate continues as to the actual causes of PMS (Hood, 1991b). Despite the ongoing debate, the fact remains that those girls who are taught to believe that having a period is going to be painful and depressing usually do feel worse than those girls who are taught to believe that having their period "isn't going to be that big a deal" (Hood, 1991a). For example, in a study involving hundreds of women from 10 different countries, although the physical symptoms that accompanied menstruation were the same, the extreme mood shifts associated with PMS were basically a phenomenon only in the western countries (Erickson, 1987).

In discussing girls' menstrual cycles and moods, it's important to note several major findings from our most recent research. First, a woman's moods have less to do with the time of the month than with the time of the week. Both men and women are usually in a better mood on the weekends than during the week. Second, males also have changes in their hormone levels and in their moods throughout a month—which we call "normal ups and downs" rather than a "syndrome." For example, when their plasma testosterone levels increase, males' good humor and hand-steadiness often decrease. Third, among males and among females, some of us shift our moods more often or more quickly than others. Fourth, there are large differences among people of the same gender in terms of how closely their hormone levels are associated with their moods or behavior. That is, high levels of a particular hormone in one person might be associated with a behavior such as aggression; but a high level of that same hormone in another person has no association with that same behavior. In short, after almost 50 years of research, the menstrual cycle has not been shown to have any consistent effect on females' cognitive performance, work performance, or academic performance. In contrast, male hormones have been found to be related to certain kinds of behavior. For example, in a study of almost 4,500 men, unusually high testosterone was associated with delinquency, drug use, sexual promiscuity, violence, conduct disorders, and abusiveness (Dabbs & Morris, 1990). Still, even these findings are correlational, not causal. So the bottom line is that although males and females have monthly cycles or regular fluctuations in their hormone levels, these hormonal changes haven't been established as a cause for any particular behavior or mood (Tavris, 1992).

Rather than focusing on the debate over how many of a girl's menstrual symptoms are influenced by her negative expectations, we should work instead to create more positive images of menstruation so young girls won't create negative prophecies that might contribute to whatever physical or emotional discomfort some of them inevitably do experience. But unfortunately many male and female teenagers still have extremely negative images associated with menstruation (Bell, 1988; Hood, 1991b; Stubbs, Rierdan, & Koff, 1989). Think back to your own adolescence and ask yourself: How did I first find out about menstruation? Which images came into my mind when I thought about menstruation? What slang words and jokes did I hear about menstrual periods? Many adolescents still get the message that menstruation is something dirty or shameful (Buckley & Gottlieb, 1988; Delaney, Lupton, & Toth, 1988). Too many teenage girls still feel ashamed buying tampons or sanitary napkins, especially if a male is around. Moreover, the words we use and the items we sell tell teenagers what our society thinks of this natural bodily process: "sanitary" napkins, feminine "hygiene" products, "that time" of the month, and the many slang expressions and jokes that demean and insult menstruating women. Even the advertisements in teenage magazines send the message that menstruation is unclean—a hygienic crisis of some sort that needs to be hidden by devising fail-safe security systems for peace of mind (Havens & Swenson, 1988).

Furthermore, certain health risks are associated with teaching girls that menstruation is dirty. Believing that they have to make themselves clean after having a period, too many girls use douches that contribute to vaginal infections and skin irritations. Not only is douching unnecessary after a menstrual period, it can flush minor vaginal infections into the uterus where more serious infections are likely to develop (Boston Women's Health Collective, 1991). In short, as a society we would serve girls better by sending them more positive messages about menstruation.

Pregnancy

During a normal monthly cycle, teenage girls are most likely to get pregnant about 2 weeks after their period ends. At this midpoint in the 28-day cycle, one or more eggs are released from the ovaries, a process known as **ovulation.** If this egg is penetrated by one of the 400 million sperm present in one ejaculation, the egg is fertilized and fetal development begins. When the egg isn't fertilized, it disintegrates inside the uterus and approximately 2 weeks later the girls starts her period. Because the egg survives only 24 to 48 hours after it is released from the ovary, the girl is only fertile for about 2 days a month.

With odds like these, it might seem surprising that so many teenage girls accidentally get pregnant every year. Yet one reason why these accidental pregnancies occur is that sperm, unlike the egg, live much longer than 2 days after they have been released inside a female's body. Sperm can live 5 to 6 days inside the Fallopian tubes. Therefore, a girl who has unprotected intercourse 6 days before she is actually fertile can still get pregnant. This is one of the main reasons why the "rhythm method" of birth control, in which a couple tries to avoid pregnancy by not having intercourse on the 2 days the female is fertile, is so unsuccessful. The second reason is that there is no reliable way to predict exactly which 2 days each month a girl or woman will be fertile. If we did a better job helping adolescents understand these facts, more young couples might be spared the pain of their unwanted teenage pregnancies.

ABNORMAL DEVELOPMENT

Due to genetic abnormalities, some children's reproductive systems do not mature normally during adolescence. Boys with **Klinefelter's syndrome** are born with an extra *X* chromosome. Although these boys have a penis and testicles, they do not develop normally during adolescence. Their muscles, body hair, and voices fail to develop normally due to their low testosterone levels. The opposite condition, being born with an extra *Y* chromosome, makes boys mature sooner, grow taller, and suffer from more severe acne than genetically normal males due to their excessively high testosterone levels. A similar condition among females, **Turner's syndrome,** causes the child to be born with female genitals, but without ovaries. As a result, she is unable to produce enough estrogen as a teenager to develop her secondary sex characteristics. By receiving supplements of estrogen or testosterone, these teenagers can be helped to develop a more normal appearance (McCauley, 1987). It was once believed that these youngsters would be mentally retarded or would have high rates of mental illness. More recent research, however, shows that although these youths do have certain academic and social problems, they are not retarded or mentally ill. As teenagers, many of these children have problems making friends and fitting in with their peer group. Girls with Turner's syndrome also tend to be more hyperactive and inattentive than other girls. Likewise, boys with Klinefelter's syndrome have more problems with language and reading skills and are more unassertive, inactive, and withdrawn than other teenage boys. These boys are not, however, as once suspected, more aggressive or more involved in delinquent or criminal behavior. Moreover, those whose families work with them diligently to overcome their difficulties are often able to develop relatively normal lives, both mentally and socially (Mandoki, 1991).

HORMONES, MOODS, AND BEHAVIOR

Genetic abnormalities such as Klinefelter's and Turner's syndromes clearly show us that the levels of estrogen and testosterone in our bodies during puberty do affect our secondary sex characteristics. But in genetically normal adolescents, how much do these hormones affect behavior and personality? How much are an adolescent's shifting moods due to his or her hormones? How responsible are hormones for the differences we notice between male and female sexual behavior? Do our adolescent hormones somehow cause us to develop a different personality from what we had as younger children?

LIMITATIONS OF THE RESEARCH

Before examining whether hormones influence adolescents' moods and behavior, it's important to keep several shortcomings of the research in mind. First, hormones might have more impact on younger adolescents than on older teenagers. Second, other factors in the adolescent's life that have an impact on behavior, such as whether they are living with one parent or with two parents, need to be considered before making conclusive statements about the impact of hormones. Third, we don't yet know how long it takes for a rise or fall in hormones to influence behavior, yet most studies compare adolescents' behavior and their hormone levels only over very short periods of time. Fourth, hormone levels change throughout the day, yet researchers seldom measure adolescents' hormones at night when they are at their peak. Likewise, most researchers have measured adolescents' hormones through blood tests, yet samples from saliva and urine might be more accurate. Then, too, hormone levels are affected by factors such as how much sleep, food, or sexual activity the adolescent has recently had (Buchanan, Eccles, & Becker, 1992).

Finally, we know that it is possible for our moods and our behavior to raise or lower our hormone levels. For example, in males and females testosterone levels often increase after we've been in a fight. In other words, just because a researcher might find higher than average levels of a hormone following certain behaviors, such as fighting or yelling, it doesn't prove that an increase in the hormone caused that behavior to occur (Carlson, 1986). For all these reasons, our conclusions about how hormones affect adolescents' behavior need to be viewed cautiously.

HORMONES AND SEXUAL BEHAVIOR

One of the first questions that comes to mind, of course, is: Do the dramatic changes in our hormones during adolescence affect sexual behavior? The answer is maybe. On the one hand, boys and girls with higher androgen levels are more likely than those with less androgen to masturbate, think about sex, and make plans to have intercourse within the next year. On the other hand, when it comes to when adolescents actually have sex, it seems that factors other than hormones have the most influence. For example, regardless of their hormones levels, boys who are popular with girls are the most likely to be having sex. Likewise, regardless of her hormone levels, a girl who plays sports and whose father lives with her is less sexually active than other girls. In other words, although hormone levels do increase adolescents' interest in sex, they don't seem as strong as other forces in determining when an adolescent becomes sexually active (Udry, 1988).

HORMONES AND MOODS

There also seems to be some relationship between levels of some hormones and teenagers' moods under certain conditions. For example, teenage boys who are easily frustrated, irritable, and impatient tend to have higher levels of testosterone than calmer boys. Likewise, teenage girls with more testosterone tend to be more uninhibited, resourceful, and enterprising than other girls. In regard to estrogen, when young teenage girls' estrogen levels are at their highest, they tend to feel more irritable and depressed. Ironically, however, older teenage girls and women usually feel more energetic and are in their best moods when their estrogen levels are high. This finding serves as a reminder that our hormones probably affect us differently depending on our age. Young adolescents and those who mature early do seem to change their moods more quickly, feel their moods more intensely, and experience a wider variety of moods than older teenagers. This might be due to the fact that their hormones are fluctuating more dramatically than in later adolescence. Even so, most teenagers are very much like they were when they were younger children when it comes to their day-to-day moods (Buchanan, Eccles, & Becker, 1992).

On the other hand, it's important not to accept the stereotype that adolescents are moodier than adults and younger children. Although it is true that adolescents tend to feel negative emotions more often than younger or older people, they also feel positive emotions more often. Most adolescents feel happy and content, not moody and dissatisfied, most of the time. Another bit of good news is that adolescents' bad moods generally don't last as long as those of adults. Although adolescents' moods tend to change more often than adults' during a day, this is partly related to the fact that adolescents switch back and forth between more different types of activities each day than adults do—which, in turn, causes their moods to change more frequently. All in all, then, adolescents shouldn't be described as moodier than other age groups (Larson, 1991).

EARLY AND LATE MATURATION

Hormones also have an indirect influence on certain aspects of teenage behavior because they help to determine how early or how late children start looking grown up. As we know from our own experiences, how mature we look often affects how we feel about ourselves and how other people treat us. In general, boys who mature early feel better about themselves and have more social advantages than later-maturing boys. In contrast, girls who mature early tend to feel worse about themselves than girls who mature later. Not only can our self-concept be affected by how early or how late we mature physically, so can the way other people treat us. What does the research show us about early and late maturing teenagers (Buchanan, Eccles, & Becker, 1992; Brooks-Gunn, 1991; Ellis, 1991)?

First, given our society's emphasis on being athletic and looking masculine, maturing early usually gives boys an advantage in terms of their popularity and their freedom from adult supervision. Because they are more physically developed than other boys, they have the edge in sports and they attract more attention from girls. As a result, boys who mature early are usually more self-confident and more socially mature, which often leads to dating more often than less physically mature boys their age. One disadvantage of maturing early, though, is that adults tend to expect more from these young males than they may be able to

**Insert
2–5**

Adolescents' Feelings About Their Bodies

"Where I go to school, I'd say 80% of the boys work out with weights. It's pointless, because what happens is the standards just go up."

"I had to shave a lot earlier than most of my friends. I was already shaving every day by the time I was 15, and even though I felt macho, it really was a pain in the neck."

Females

"Sometimes when I'm alone, I stand in front of the mirror and stare at myself. I stare at all the things I can't stand, like I absolutely can't stand my legs. They're so short and my thighs are huge."

"There were some days in high school when I'd shave under my arms and then cover my armpits with adhesive tape. It wasn't much good for my skin, but on those days I knew for sure I wouldn't perspire on my blouse!"

"There's a difference between what you want and what you think other people want. I don't think hairy legs are that bad. It doesn't bother me on me, and it doesn't bother me on other girls."

"I'm glad I haven't gotten my period yet. I'm still a kid. No way do I want to worry about that every month."

Males

"All of a sudden I realized my voice was low. On the telephone people started thinking I was my father, not my mother!"

Source: R. Bell (1988). *Changing bodies, changing lives.* New York: Random House.

handle intellectually or emotionally. For example, a 6-foot-tall, 14-year-old boy who already needs to shave every morning is often given more responsibility and less adult supervision than a 17-year-old boy who is 5'3" and looks 13. But merely because one boy looks much older than another is no reason to think his intellectual skills or life experiences have prepared him to be treated as if he were older.

In cases like these, adolescents who look much older than they are may be more likely to get into trouble because they are being given more independence than they are actually prepared for.

Second, girls who mature extremely early are not advantaged in the same way that most early maturing boys are. Although girls don't want to be the last ones in their peer group to develop a womanly body, they usually don't like being the first either. Developing a womanly body and starting to menstruate years before other girls is stressful for most girls. Having mature bodies doesn't mean that these young girls are ready to be treated in a sexual way. Yet, not knowing her actual age, many males seem to relate to the well developed young girl as if she were a much older adolescent. For example, a 5th-grade girl with a womanly figure is often exposed to the same kinds of sexual stares, comments, and come-ons that a 10th grade girl has to cope with. The problem, of course, is that 5th-grade girls with 10th-grade bodies are still only 10 or 11 years old when it comes to their social and intellectual skills. Whether or not they are ready emotionally, however, most of these girls start dating earlier and have sex sooner than other girls their age.

Third, early maturing girls also tend to be more dissatisfied with their appearance than those who develop later. That is, early maturing girls are the most likely to complain that they are too fat. In part this happens because girls who inherit a shorter, stockier body type from their mothers usually do mature earlier than girls with taller, leaner bodies. So, in fact, they are somewhat heavier than other girls their age. Then, too, girls who mature early have more fat tissue around their hips, breasts, and thighs as a response to their higher estrogen levels than girls who are further behind them physically. Although early maturing girls often like being among the first to start their periods and to wear a bra, by 9th or 10th grade they are more dissatisfied with their bodies than girls who matured later.

Fourth, early maturing girls and boys often are given more freedom and responsibility than they can really manage. These girls and boys tend to hang out with older teenagers, get involved in more delinquent behavior, and get into more trouble at school than peers whose bodies mature later. They also have more conflict with their parents than teenagers who mature later. It also seems that early maturing boys and girls are less motivated academically than those who mature on time. Of course this might be related to the fact that they start dating sooner than their peers and are, therefore, less interested in their school work than in their social lives.

Finally, by the time we reach late adolescence most of the differences between early and late maturation seem to have diminished. It also seems that how mature our bodies are has less impact than what grade we're in at school when it comes to such things as when we start dating, smoking, or drinking. So if most of the teenagers in your school start dating in the eighth grade, that's probably when you'll start dating, too, no matter how physically mature or immature your body is. Likewise, how we feel about maturing early or late often depends on our particular goals and on what our friends think. For example, female dancers and gymnasts want to mature late because being extremely thin is an advantage in their profession and among their friends. Consequently, teenage gymnasts who develop last are happier than those who develop early (Iversen, 1990). On the other hand, if you're a sixth-grade boy whose goal is to become a star football player, then developing early is a blessing, not a curse.

ADOLESCENT ATHLETES

MALE ATHLETES

When it comes to sports, maturing early almost always benefits boys because it gives them the muscle mass, weight, and height they need for a competitive edge. Overall 3.4 million boys participate in school sponsored athletics. Football is still most boys' first choice, with 947,757 boys playing football and 517,217 playing basketball. Football, however, is losing popularity faster than other sports. In fact, 4,000 fewer teenage boys played football in 1990 than in 1989, and participation has declined 16% since 1975. One of the reasons for football's decline is that more boys are choosing sports such as soccer, which pose less risk of serious injury. In 1975 only 115,811 boys were playing soccer; but by 1990 this number had grown to 220,777. More teenage boys also are getting jobs after school rather than playing football, and stricter rules about having a certain grade-point-average keep many boys from going out for a team. Whatever the reason for the decline, some high schools have dropped football altogether and are using soccer as their centerpiece for homecoming and other former football traditions (National Athletic Trainers Association [N.A.T.A.], 1988; National Federation of State High Schools Association [N.F.S.H.S.A.], 1991).

The advantages of being a male athlete are apparent to most of us when we recall the popularity that the jocks enjoyed in high school. Aside from adding to a boy's popularity, participating in sports is supposed to help young men build character by teaching them good sportsmanship, self-discipline, self-sacrifice, teamwork, cooperation, and concentration. Sports also are supposed to teach teenage boys ways of overcoming obstacles they will face in other areas of their lives. For still others, especially those from poor families, being a star athlete is a way many boys hope to gain fame and fortune in the future—or, at the very least, a way to win an athletic scholarship to college. But how true are these claims? Is this what most teenage boys get from their experiences on athletic teams?

Whatever valuable lessons a boy might be learning as an athlete, they do not seem to translate into helping him as a student. In the most extensive study of high-school athletes involving nearly 13,000 students over a 6-year period, being an athlete didn't improve students' grades or make them any more likely to finish high school (Women's Sports Foundation, 1989). This suggests that whatever character-building lessons these athletes learned were not carrying over into their schoolwork or their future jobs. Being an athlete does not improve a male's high-school or college grades, and often seems to hurt him academically. Realizing this, in the 1980s the National Collegiate Athletic Association passed Proposition 48.

Table 2–2

Ten Most Popular Boys' and Girls' Sports, 1989–90

Boys' Sports	Participants
Football	947,757
Basketball	517,271
Baseball	413,581
Track & Field (Outdoor)	405,684
Wrestling	233,856
Soccer	220,777
Cross Country	155,806
Tennis	136,939
Golf	122,998
Swimming & Diving	85,112

Girls' Sports	Participants
Basketball	389,688
Track & Field (Outdoor)	308,810
Volleyball	293,688
Softball (Fast Pitch)	205,040
Tennis	128,076
Soccer	111,711
Cross Country	104,876
Swimming & Diving	84,760
Filed Hockey	50,237
Golf	40,418

Source: National Federation of State High School Association (1990). *National Federation Handbook.* Kansas City, MO: Author.

Under this legislation, all high-school athletes applying to college have to score at least 700 out of a possible 1600 on the Scholastic Aptitude Test, or 15 out of 36 on the American College Test, and have at least a "C" average in 11 required high-school courses. As a result, most high schools now have "no pass, no play" rules that require athletes to maintain a "C" average in order to play. Although this sounds like a clever way to encourage athletes to balance their schoolwork with sports, some teachers lower their standards or make special exceptions so that the best athletes can squeeze by with the required "C"s (Mathis, 1989).

But if an athlete can win a scholarship to college or can land a contract to play professionally, why does it matter if his grades in high school or college suffer? Although this argument is compelling, the fact remains that only a handful of high-school athletes are good enough to earn college scholarships, and only one in 10,000 high-school athletes gets a contract for professional sports. Even then, among those

How do you feel about high-school sports?

who make it to the pros, many are left without the educational skills to support themselves or their families when their athletic careers end (N.F.S.H.S.A., 1991).

Male high-school sports also raise another question: Is it fair to use taxpayers' money to give such a large share of the school's budget to programs that serve such a small percentage of students? What about spending more of the school's athletic money on activities that more students could enjoy? Even among athletes, is it fair to give males so much more money and attention than females, or to give the basketball and football players so much more money than the soccer or tennis players? There is also the question of placing so much attention on high-school athletes while ignoring students who excel in other activities. Where are the cheerleaders, pep rallies, and awards banquets honoring the stars on the debate team, the French club, or volunteer service clubs? These uncomfortable ethical questions remain unanswered.

Another troubling question is whether sports are worth the physical injuries to teenage athletes. Many children suffer permanent physical damage from sports before the age of 18, most of whom are young teenagers. These injuries include permanent damage to bones and joints, as well as damage to immature hearts, kidneys, and muscles. In 1988 alone, 503,706 teenage boys were injured playing football—14,000 of whom needed surgery, usually for knee injuries. More disturbing still, these injuries increased from 1987 to 1988. Doctors also are seeing more injuries in children, such as tendinitis and stress fractures in bones, that were once seen only in adults (N.A.T.A., 1988).

Finally, there is the question of whether most sports actually do build character (Danish, Petipas, & Hale, 1990). Are most teenage athletes learning to be good sports and not to get angry when they lose? Are they learning to be competitive or merely aggressive? Are they learning to limit their physical aggression to the game? Although many teenage athletes do learn these lessons, many others do not. Evidence suggests, for instance, that high-school athletes become less sensitive to other people's needs, behave more aggressively off the courts and fields, and become more sexist than boys who don't play sports (N.A.T.A., 1988). There is also the question of whether sports are any better than many other less expensive and less dangerous activities for teaching these character-building lessons. Why not teach these same lessons through less physically aggressive activities that more students can enjoy?

Given the physical and academic risks associated with being a high-school athlete, more counselors are trying to work with boys and their parents on issues related to identity development and future careers. Indeed, many parents need to be more involved in this kind of counseling because many high-school athletes tell us they feel pressured by their parents (Goldberg, A., 1991; Hellstedt, 1990).

FEMALE ATHLETES

And what about female athletes? Nearly 1.9 million girls are playing a sport at their school. Their first choice continues to be basketball, still growing in popularity with more than 10,000 additional girls playing in 1990 than in 1989. Golf also has gained nearly 10,000 new female players, replacing softball as the 10th most popular girls' sport. Nearly 112,000 girls are playing soccer (N.A.T.A., 1988). But how much do these adolescents benefit from their involvement in sports? Are the gains worth the losses? Should we adults place more restrictions on female athletes to protect them against certain physical or emotional harm?

Girls who choose to participate in sports are usually in a much different situation than male athletes. To begin with, almost twice as many boys as girls play sports so, of course, in most schools female athletes are not nearly as much the norm as male athletes. Sadly, many female athletes tell us that their male and female classmates disapprove of their participating in sports other than tennis, skating, or gymnastics, which are considered feminine enough. Although most male athletes are more popular and self-confident than other boys as a consequence of playing sports, the opposite is too often the case for female athletes. Indeed, teenage girls who play contact sports are ridiculed in some schools for being too masculine, or are believed to be lesbians (Cohen, 1993; Desertrain & Weiss, 1988; Hargreaves, 1993; Kane, 1988).

Most school policies also are less supportive of female than of male athletes. Girls' teams usually are given less money, poorer facilities, fewer coaches, and a less desirable schedule. They are seldom given the same support as male athletes in regard to pep rallies, publicity in school and local papers, scholarships, or academic tutoring. In order to redress some of these inequities, the federal government passed a law in 1975 called **Title IX,** which states that "no person in the United States shall, on the basis of sex, be excluded from participation in, be denied the benefits of, or be subjected to discrimination under any education program or activity receiving federal financial assistance" (Title IX, 1978). Despite this federal law, female athletes in high school and college continue to receive less support than males (Cohen, 1993; Hargreaves, 1993).

ATHLETES AND STEROIDS

Most of us are aware that many college and professional athletes use steroids to improve their performance. Steroids are synthetic drugs that mimic testosterone in their masculinizing effects on the body. By increasing their muscle mass, steroids give male and female athletes an advantage over their competitors. So much for the good news. The bad news is that steroids increase their chances of developing cancer and liver problems, becoming infertile or impotent, and dying from a heart attack. Some of the other side effects include: puffy face and neck, stunted growth, outbursts of uncontrollably aggressive behavior, unexpected moods swings, and depression (Fuller & LaFountain, 1988).

What is shocking is not that so many adult athletes use these drugs, but that more and more teenage athletes are using them. Although steroids are illegal except when prescribed by doctors for treating certain diseases, such as severe asthma, even adolescent athletes can get their hands on these drugs without much trouble. The federal Food and Drug Administration estimates that illegal sales of steroids total about $100 million a year in our country. Roughly 2% of all teenagers have at some time used steroids. Almost all of these youngsters are male, and most—but not all—are high-school athletes (Johnston, O'Malley, & Bachman, 1993).

Why do teenage boys use steroids? Roughly one third are trying to improve their appearance by making themselves more muscular. The rest use them mainly to improve their athletic performance. Nearly half of these boys say they will continue using steroids even if it is absolutely proven to increase their chances of being sterile, developing cancer, or dying from a heart attack. Even though they know the drug is illegal, most boys say they have a right to take the drug because their behavior isn't hurting anybody except themselves. If they can look more muscular or improve their athletic skills, most of these boys are willing to take the chance. Worse yet, many of these boys' high-school coaches say the scientific evidence is not convincing enough yet for them to tell their players not to use steroids. Not surprisingly, then, more than two thirds of the boys who have used or are using steroids say their coaches approve; and nearly half say their parents know but have said nothing to them (Fuller & LaFountain, 1988; Goldberg, 1990; Schmidt, 1989; Yesalis, 1991).

CONCLUSION

Although our physical maturation doesn't change us into entirely new personalities, our body's growth does influence the way we see ourselves and the way others see us. As we have seen, adolescents' rates of maturation affect certain aspects of their behavior as well as how others behave toward them. Moreover, having a body that is able to reproduce life is a profound change for a young person that doesn't escape anyone's attention. Although most adolescents aren't obsessed in negative ways with the physical changes occurring in their bodies, they certainly are adjusting to their new bodies in ways that can be simultaneously annoying and amusing—both to themselves and to others. As future chapters explain, adolescents' appearance and physical maturity is also an influential factor in their relationships with parents and peers, as well as in their self-confidence.

Review/Test Questions

1. When and why does puberty begin?
2. How do the head and face change during adolescence? What problems can this create for some adolescents?
3. In what ways do the physical changes in adolescent males and females differ and in what ways are they the same?
4. How do height and weight change during adolescence? How can these changes affect adolescents positively and negatively?
5. What mistakes do many teenagers make when attempting to lose weight? What do they need to know about the body in order to lose weight more successfully and less dangerously?
6. How do the physical abilities of teenage males and females differ? Why?
7. How physically fit are today's adolescents? Cite specific statistics to support your answer.
8. How do our society's definitions of male and female beauty negatively affect some adolescents? How does the importance of physical appearance differ for males and females?
9. How can adolescents' eating, exercising and sleeping habits affect them at school and in other aspects of their moods or behavior?
10. How do obese adolescents' habits differ from other teenagers'? What are the most

effective ways of helping overweight teenagers lose weight?
11. How could we improve adolescents' health habits?
12. Using Figures 2–1 and 2–2 as your guide, explain the function of each part of the male and female reproductive system.
13. How do Turner's and Klinefelter's syndromes affect adolescents?
14. How do adolescent males and females feel about menstruation? Where do these feelings come from? How do most teenage girls react to having their periods?
15. In what ways do hormones influence adolescents' behavior, personalities, or moods?
16. How does early and late maturation affect male and female adolescents?
17. What types of sports are adolescent athletes engaged in, and how has their popularity changed in recent years? Why?
18. What are the advantages and disadvantages of being an adolescent athlete? How do these differ for males and females? Why?
19. What are steroids and how prevalent are they among teenagers? Why?
20. In what ways can adolescents' physical appearance affect their personalities, their success at school, and their popularity among their peers?

Questions for Discussion and Debate

1. How would you go about helping more adolescents get into better physical condition and develop healthier eating habits?

2. How would you help adolescent girls feel less obsessed about being overweight and feel more satisfied with their appearance?

3. In what positive and negative ways did your physical appearance affect your development or your personality as an adolescent?

4. What aspects of your physical self did you want to change when you were a teenager and why? How do you feel about yourself physically now? Why?

5. What are your happiest and your unhappiest memories associated with your physical development or your appearance as an adolescent?

6. What misinformation about your own sexuality and your own physical development did you have when you were an adolescent?

7. What appealed to you as an adolescent in terms of male and female attractiveness? How have your attitudes changed or remained the same? Why?

8. As an adolescent, how did you feel about female athletes and male athletes? And now? Why?

9. What were the wisest and the most foolish habits you developed as an adolescent in terms of your own fitness and health?

10. How could high-school sports and physical fitness programs be improved?

Glossary

adipose tissue, p. 31
androgen, p. 27
anorexia nervosa, p. 37
areola, p. 32
basal metabolic rate, p. 34
bulimia, p. 37
cervix, p. 45
circumcised, p. 42
clitoris, p. 44
diuretics, p. 33
endorphins, p. 40
estrogen, p. 27
fallopian tubes, p. 46
foreskin, p. 42
glans, p. 42
gonadotropins, p. 27

gonads, p. 27
hymen, p. 45
hypothalamus, p. 27
Klinefelter's syndrome, p. 49
labia, p. 44
mammary glands, p. 32
menarche, p. 46
menstruation, p. 46
nocturnal emissions, p. 44
os, p. 45
ovulation, p. 48
Premenstrual syndrome
    (PMS), p. 47
prepuce, p. 44
prostate gland, p. 42
scrotum, p. 42

semen, p. 42
seminal fluid, p. 42
seminal vesicles, p. 42
shaft, p. 42
steroids, p. 27
testicles, p. 42
testosterone, p. 27
Title IX, p. 57
Turner's syndrome, p. 49
urethra, p. 43
uterus, p. 46
vagina, p. 44
vas deferens, p. 42
wet dreams, p. 44
womb, p. 46

References

Adams, G. (1991). Physical attractiveness and adolescent development. In R. Lerner, A. Petersen & J. Brooks-Gunn (Eds.), *Encyclopedia of adolescence* (pp. 785–789). New York: Garland.

American Athletic Union. (1989). *Physical fitness trends in American youth*. Washington, DC: Author.

Bailey, C. (1978). *Fit or fat*. New York: Houghton Mifflin.

Barbie backlash. (1992, October 26). *Winston Salem Journal*, pp. 1, 15.

Beau, C., Baker, P., & Haas, J. (1977). Effects of high altitude on adolescent growth. *Human Biology, 49*, 109–124.

Bell, R. (1988). *Changing bodies, changing lives*. New York: Random House.

Bongiovani, A. (1983). Epidemic of premature telarche in Puerto Rico. *Journal of Pediatrics, 103*, 245–246.

Bordo, S. (1993). *Unbearable weight: Feminism, Western culture and the body*. New York: Norton.

Boston Women's Health Collective, (1991). *Our bodies, ourselves*. New York: Random House.

Brooks-Gunn, J. (1991). How stressful is the transition to adolescence for girls? In M. Colten & S. Gore (Eds.), *Adolescent Stress* (pp. 131–156). New York: Aldine De Gruyter.

Brownwell, K., & Stein, J. (1988). Metabolic and behavior effects of weight loss and regain. In S. Stunkard & A. Baum (Eds.), *Perspectives on behavioral medicine* (pp. 233–245). Hillsdale, NJ: Erlbaum.

Buchanan, C., Eccles, J., & Becker, J. (1992). Are adolescents victims of raging hormones? *Psychological Bulletin, 111*, 62–107.

Buckley, T., & Gottlieb, A. (1988). *Blood magic: The anthropology of menstruation*. Berkley, CA: University of California.

Carleton, R. (1991). Pawtucket heart health program. *Annals of the New York Academy of Sciences, 623*, 322–326.

Carlson, N. (1986). *Physiology of behavior*. Boston: Allyn & Bacon.

Carr, D. (1981). Physical conditioning facilitates secretion of beta endorphin. *New England Journal of Medicine, 305*, 560–563.

Carruth, B., & Goldberg, D. (1990). Nutritional issues of adolescents. *Journal of Early Adolescence, 10*, 122–140.

Carskadon, M. (1990). Patterns of sleep and sleepiness in adolescents. *Pediatrician, 17*, 5–12.

Cohen, G. (1993). *Women in sport*. New York: Sage.

Collingwood, T. (1991). Physical fitness effects on substance abuse risk factors. *Journal of Drug Education, 21*, 73–84.

Dabbs, J., & Morris, R. (1990). Testosterone, social class, and antisocial behavior. *Psychological Science, 1*, 209–211.

Danish, S., Petipas, A., & Hale, B. (1990). Sport as a context for developing competence. In T. Gullotta, G. Adams & R. Montemayor (Eds.), *Developing social competency in adolescence* (pp. 169–195). Newbury Park, CA: Sage.

Delaney, J., Lupton, M., & Toth, E. (1988). *The curse: A cultural history of menstruation*. Urbana, IL: University of Illinois.

Desertrain, G., & Weiss, M. (1988). Being female and athletic. *Sex Roles, 18*, 567–583.

Ellis, N. (1991). An extension of the Steinberg accelerating hypothesis. *Journal of Early Adolescence, 11*, 221–235.

Erickson, K. (1987). Menstrual symptoms and menstrual beliefs: National and cross-national patterns. In B. Ginsburg & B. Carter (Eds.), *Premenstrual Syndrome*. New York: Plenum.

Fisher, C., & Brone, R. (1991). Eating disorders in adolescence. In R. Lerner, A. Peterson & J. Brooks-Gunn (Eds.), *Encyclopedia of adolescence* (pp. 156–172). New York: Garland.

Flax, E. (1991, November 12). Schools test children for cholesterol. *Education Week*, p. 6.

Freedland, J., & Dwyer, J. (1991). Nutrition in adolescent girls. In R. Lerner, A. Petersen & J. Brooks-Gunn (Eds.), *Encyclopedia of adolescence* (pp. 714–724). New York: Garland.

Friedman, R. (1989). *Body love: Learning to like our looks.* New York: Harper & Row.

Frisch, R. (1991). Puberty and body fat. In R. Lerner, A. Petersen & J. Brooks-Gunn (Eds.), *Encyclopedia of adolescence* (pp. 884–892). New York: Garland.

Fuller, J., & LaFountain, M. (1988). Performance enhancing drugs in sport. *Adolescence, 22*, 969–976.

Gillis, J. (1982). *Too tall, too small.* Champaign, IL: Institute for Personality and Ability Testing.

Goldberg, A. (1991). Counseling the high school athlete. *School Counselor, 38*, 332–340.

Goldberg, L. (1990). Effect of a steroid education program on high school football players. *Adolescent Health Care, 11*, 210–214.

Hargreaves, J. (1993). *Sporting females: History and sociology of women's sports.* New York: Routledge.

Harris, D. (1991). Exercise and fitness during adolescence. In R. Lerner, A. Petersen & J. Brooks-Gunn (Eds.), *Encyclopedia of adolescence* (pp. 324–327). New York: Garland.

Harris, L., Blum, R., & Resnick, M. (1991). Teen females in Minnesota. *Women and Therapy, 11*, 119–135.

Havens, G., & Swenson, I. (1988). Imagery associated with menstruation in advertising targeted to adolescent women. *Adolescence, 23*, 89–97.

Hellstedt, J. (1990). Early adolescent perceptions of parental pressure in the sport environment. *Journal of Sport Behavior, 13*, 135–144.

Higham, E. (1980). Variations in adolescent development. In J. Adelson (Ed.), *Handbook of adolescent psychology* (pp. 472–495). New York: Wiley.

Hood, K. (1991a). Premenstrual syndrome. In R. Lerner, A. Petersen & J. Brooks-Gunn (Eds.), *Encyclopedia of adolescence* (pp. 830–831). New York: Garland.

Hood, K. (1991b). Menstrual cycle. In R. Lerner, A. Petersen & J. Brooks-Gunn (Eds.), *Encyclopedia of adolescence* (pp. 642–646). New York: Garland.

Irwin, C., & Orr, D. (1991). Health research in adolescence. In A. Lerner, A. Peterson & J. Brooks-Gunn (Eds.), *Encyclopedia of Adolescence* (pp. 284–298). New York: Garland.

Iversen, G. (1990). Psychosocial aspects of delayed puberty in the competitive female gymnast. *Sport Psychologist, 4*, 155–167.

Johnston, L., O'Malley, P., & Bachman, J. (1993). *National survey results on drug use: 1975–1992.* Rockville, MD: National Institute on Drug Abuse.

Kane, M. (1988). Female athletic role as a status determinant of high school adolescents. *Adolescence, 23*, 253–264.

Katchadourian, H. (1970). *The biology of adolescence.* San Francisco: Freeman.

Kimm, S. (1991). Self-concept measures and childhood obesity. *Journal of Developmental & Behavioral Pediatrics, 12*, 19–24.

Koff, E., & Rierdan, J. (1991). Perceptions of weight & attitudes toward eating in early adolescent girls. *Journal of Adolescent Health, 12*, 417.

Kramer, S. (1991, July 8). Forget about losing those last 10 pounds. *Time*, pp. 50–51.

Larson, R. (1991). Adolescent moodiness. In R. Lerner, A. Petersen & J. Brooks-Gunn (Eds.), *Encyclopedia of adolescence* (pp. 658–662). New York: Garland.

Malina, R. (1979). Secular changes in size and maturity. *Society for Research in Child Development Monographs, 179*, pp. 610–615.

Mandoki, M. (1991). A review of Klinefelter's syndrome in children and adolescents. *Journal of the American Academy of Child & Adolescent*

Psychiatry, 30, 167–172.

Martel, L., & Biller, J. (1987). *Stature and stigma: Biopsychosocial development of short males.* Lexington, MA: Lexington Books.

Mathis, N. (1989, May 17). No pass, no play. *Education Week,* p. 12.

McCauley, E. (1987). The Turner syndrome. *Child Development, 58,* 464–473.

McGlynn, G. (1990). *Dynamics of fitness.* Dubuque, IA: W. C. Brown.

McGrory, A. (1990). Menarche: Responses of early adolescent females. *Adolescence, 25,* 265–270.

Miller, B., & Wood, B. (1991). Childhood asthma. *Journal of Asthma, 28,* 405–414.

Millstein, S., & Litt, I. (1990). Adolescent health. In S. Feldman & I. Litt (Eds.), *At the threshold* (pp. 431–455). Cambridge, MA: Harvard University Press.

Morrill, C. (1991). Adolescent obesity. *School Counselor, 38,* 347–351.

National Athletic Trainers Association. (1988). *High school football injuries.* Oak Park, IL: Author.

National Federation of State High Schools Association. (1991). *National Federation Handbook.* Kansas City, MO: Author.

Newell, G. (1990). Self-concept as a factor in the quality of diets of adolescent girls. *Adolescence, 25,* 117–130.

Page, R. (1991). Indicators of psychosocial distress among adolescent females who perceive themselves as fat. *Child Study Journal, 21,* 203–212.

Penley, C., & Willis, S. (1992). *Male trouble.* Minneapolis: University of Minnesota.

Peterson, A., & Taylor, B. (1980). The biological approach to adolescence. In J. Adelson (Ed.), *Handbook of adolescent psychology* (pp. 117–158). New York: Wiley.

Risser, W. (1989). Exercise for children. *Pediatrics in Review, 10,* 131–140.

Robinson, C. (1991). Working with adolescent girls: Strategies to address health status. In C. Gilligan, A. Rogers & D. Tolman (Eds.), *Women, girls, and psychotherapy* (pp. 241–253). New York: Haworth.

Robinson, T., & Ward, J. (1991). Cultivating resistance among African American female adolescents. In C. Gilligan, A. Rogers & D. Tolman (Eds.), *Women, girls, and psychotherapy* (pp. 87–104). New York: Haworth.

Schmidt, P. (1989, May 17). Officials are aware of steroid use. *Education Week,* p. 8.

Sigman, G., & Flanery, R. (1992). Eating disorders. In E. Greydanus & M. Wolraich (Eds.), *Behavioral pediatrics* (pp. 181–201). New York: Springer-Verlag.

Smith, R. (1987, September 12). Doubts about circumcision. *Newsweek,* p. 42.

Stelzer, J. (1991). Medical noncompliance. *Family Systems Medicine, 9,* 121–125.

Story, M. (1990). Study group report on the impact of television on adolescent nutritional status. *Journal of Adolescent Health Care, 25,* 117–130.

Stubbs, M., Rierdan, J., & Koff, E. (1989). Developmental differences in menstrual attitudes. *Journal of Early Adolescence, 9,* 480–498.

Tavris, C. (1992). *Mismeasure of woman.* New York: Simon & Schuster.

Thomas, J., & French, K. (1985). Gender differences across age in motor performance. *Psychological Bulletin, 98,* 260–282.

Title IX. (1978). Washington, DC: Office of Civil Rights.

Tucker, L. (1990). Physical fitness and psychological distress. *International Journal of Sport Psychology, 21,* 185–201.

Tuckman, B., & Hinkle, J. (1988). An experimental study of the physical and psychological effects of aerobic exercise on schoolchildren. In B. Melamed (Ed.), *Child Health Psychology* (pp. 221–232). Hillsdale, NJ: Erlbaum.

Udry, J. (1988). Biological predispositions & social control in adolescent sexual behavior. *American Sociological Review, 53,* 709–722.

Wadden, T. (1991). Salience of weight related worries in adolescent males and females. *International Journal of Eating Disorders, 10,* 407–414.

Wade, J. (1991). Race and sex differences in adolescent self perceptions of attractiveness and self-esteem. *Personality and Individual Differences, 27,* 552–565.

White, D., Schiecker, E., & Dayan, J. (1991). Gender differences in categorizing adolescents weight status. *Psychological Reports, 148,* 831–843.

Wishon, P. (1991). Adolescent obesity. *International Journal of Adolescence & Youth, 2,* 43–51.

Wolf, N. (1992). *The beauty myth: How images of beauty are used against women.* New York: Doubleday.

Wolfe, S. (1991). *Women's health alert.* Reading, MA: Addison Wesley.

Women's Sports Foundation (1989). *Minorities in sports.* New York: Author.

Yesalis, C. (1991). Anabolic steroids, nonmedical use by adolescents. In R. Lerner, A. Petersen & J. Brooks-Gunn (Eds.), *Encyclopedia of adolescence* (pp. 44–49). New York: Garland.

COGNITIVE DEVELOPMENT

CHAPTER OUTLINE

KEY QUESTIONS ADDRESSED IN THIS CHAPTER

1. How should intelligence be measured and defined?
2. What are the advantages and disadvantages of traditional IQ tests?
3. How do cognitive stage theories explain adolescents' mental development?
4. How do adolescents and younger children compare in terms of their memory, decision making skills, and problem solving strategies?
5. What are the shortcomings of cognitive stage theories?
6. How does cognitive socialization explain adolescent cognition?
7. What factors contribute to an adolescent's intellectual abilities?
8. How do creative and highly intelligent teenagers differ from their peers?
9. How can we increase creativity and intelligence among the young?
10. What are the causes of mental retardation, and in what ways can we better serve the needs of these adolescents?

Why do some 14-year-olds solve problems more maturely and make decisions more carefully than some 17-year-olds? What kinds of thinking skills do most of us develop during our adolescence that we lacked as younger children? What is intelligence, and how can we best measure it? What exactly do our adolescent IQ scores determine about us? Why do some of us, as children and as adolescents, have better memories than others? Can we improve adolescents' decision making and problem solving skills? Do those of us who are especially creative or who have high IQ scores have a more difficult adolescence than our peers? Is something special going on in the homes of gifted and creative adolescents that has helped them develop their special talents?

Questions such as these are answered, for the most part, by those psychologists and researchers studying cognitive development and by **psychometricians,** people who are trying to define and to measure intelligence. The psychometric approach focuses on defining and measuring intelligence, creativity, mental retardation, and giftedness. In measuring our mental abilities, of course, these researchers are simultaneously raising the controversial issue of how much our intellectual abilities and creativity are influenced by our genes rather than by our environment. Understandably, then, this research raises quite a ruckus because it involves race and gender comparisons.

The two main approaches to the study of cognitive development are the Piagetian and the information processing approach. **Piagetian psychologists** endorse the theories of the famous Swiss developmental psychologist, Jean Piaget. Their primary interest is to describe the stages we might pass through in developing more mature ways of solving problems and relating to other people. The second group of researchers is much more specific in terms of studying the exact ways in which children and adolescents process information. Referred to as using the **information processing approach,** these researchers are examining the specific ways in which we memorize, analyze, reason, and make decisions as we age. This approach to understanding intelligence is a detailed, step-by-step analysis of our cognitive processes at different ages in our lives. While the Piagetian psychologists are trying to describe the kinds of skills we develop at different stages in childhood and adolescence, the information processing researchers are trying to explain how the brain actually works in processing information. Psychometricians, on the other hand, are trying to measure what we know, not how we think. To begin, then, let's look at what the psychometric approach has to say about defining and measuring adolescents' intelligence.

DEFINING AND MEASURING INTELLIGENCE

What do we mean when we say one person is more intelligent than another? Who, for example, is more intelligent—the 14-year-old with the vocabulary of a college senior who makes straight "A"s in English or the 14-year-old who has uncanny insights into other people's behavior and can navigate by the stars without a compass, but makes "C"s in school? To most people in our society, including most researchers, the word *intelligent* encompasses three aspects of behavior. The first is the ability to solve practical problems by being logical, seeing many sides of a problem or issue, and being open-minded. The second is having good verbal and reading skills—the size of your vocabulary, your ease and comprehension in reading, and your skills in carrying on a conversation. The third is having social skills appropriate to our age—being sensitive to social cues from other people, being able to admit our mistakes, and showing an interest in the people around us. When judging how intelligent we or other people are, in our country we're especially likely to be judging one another's verbal skills—the size of our vocabulary in writing or speaking and the speed and ease with which we use these words (Snyderman & Rothman, 1987).

But do these definitions accurately identity those of us who are extremely intelligent from those of us who are of average or below average intelligence? Is it possible, for example, that a person can be extremely intelligent in some areas, such as music or math, but extremely "dumb" in others; and that, as a consequence, it's unfair to use a single IQ score from a written test to categorize this person's overall intelligence? Is it also possible that our definitions of intelligence might differ, depending on which culture we are being raised in or what race or gender we are?

As you've probably already expected, researchers are divided in their opinions on these issues. The traditional viewpoint is that a person's overall intelligence can be defined and measured by a written test and that this test score is a relatively accurate measure of intelligence, regardless of the person's culture, race, economic background, or gender. Given this perspective, the two most popular ways of defining and measuring adolescents' intelligence are still the Stanford-Binet IQ test and the Wechsler Adult Intelligence Scale.

Traditional IQ Tests

The French psychologist, Alfred Binet, originally designed his test for the purpose of deciding which French children had too little intelligence to benefit from being educated in regular public schools. As understanding of intelligence and testing grew, Lewis Terman at Stanford University revised Binet's test in 1916. Since then the **Stanford-Binet** has been updated several times, most recently in 1985 (Thorndike, Hagan, & Sattler, 1985). This test determines IQ mainly by scoring our verbal skills—defining words, interpreting proverbs, explaining abstract terms, and describing the similarities between two seemingly different words. Some nonverbal skills also are assessed, such as abilities to trace a path through a maze and compute certain math problems.

Believing that the Stanford-Binet placed too much emphasis on verbal skills, David Wechsler developed his IQ test in 1939. Like the Stanford-Binet, the Wechsler Adult Intelligence Scale, or **WAIS,** and the Wechsler Intelligence Scale for Children, or **WISC,** have been revised several times since their inception. The WISC-IIIR (third revision) measures intelligence by deriving separate scores from six verbal and five nonverbal subtests. As Insert 3–1 illustrates, these subtests

Insert 3–1

Sample IQ Test Questions

Verbal subtests

General information
The individual is asked a number of general-information questions about experiences that are considered normal for individuals in our society.
For example, "How many wings does a bird have?"

Similarities
The individual must think logically and abstractly to answer a number of questions about how things are similar.
For example, "In what way are boats and trains the same?"

Arithmetic reasoning
Problems measure the individual's ability to do arithmetic mentally and include addition, subtraction, multiplication, and division.
For example, "If two buttons cost 14¢, what will be the cost of a dozen buttons?"

Vocabulary
To evaluate word knowledge, the individual is asked to define a number of words. This subtest measures a number of cognitive functions, including concept formation, memory, and language.
For example, "What does the word *biography* mean?"

Comprehension
This subtest is designed to measure the individual's judgment and common sense.
For example, "What is the advantage of keeping money in the bank?"

Digit span
This subtest primarily measures attention and short-term memory. The individual is required to repeat numbers forward and backward.
For example, "I am going to say some numbers and I want you to repeat them backward: 4 7 5 2 8."

Performance subtests

Picture completion
A number of drawings are shown, each with a significant part missing. Within a period of several seconds, the individual must differentiate essential from nonessential parts of the picture and identify which part is missing. This subtest evaluates visual alertness and the ability to organize information visually.
For example, "I am going to show you a picture with an important part missing. Tell me what is missing."

Picture arrangement
A series of pictures out of sequence are shown to the individual, who is asked to place them in their proper order to tell an appropriate story. This subtest evaluates how individuals integrate information to make it logical and meaningful.
For exmaple, "The pictures below need to be placed in an appropriate order to tell a meaningful story."

Insert 3–1

Sample IQ Test Questions

Object assembly

The individual is asked to assemble pieces into something. This subtest measures visual-motor coordination and perceptual organization.

For example, "When these pieces are put together correctly, they make something. Put them together as quickly as you can."

Block design

The individual must assemble a set of multicolored blocks to match designs that the examiner shows. Visual-motor coordination, perceptual organization, and the ability to visualize spatially are measured.

For example, "Use the four blocks on the left to make the pattern on the right."

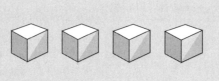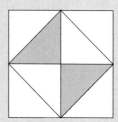

Coding

This subtest evaluates how quickly and accurately an individual can link code symbols and digits. The subtest assesses visual-motor coordination and speed of thought.

For example, "As quickly as you can, transfer the appropriate code symbols to the blank spaces."

Code

●	□	★	△	⫽
1	2	3	4	5

Test

★	⫽	□	△	●	□	△	★	⫽	□	●	△	★	⫽

Table 3–1

IQ Ranges and Classifications

IQ Scores	Classification	Percent in General Population
Above 130	Very superior	2%
120–129	Superior	6–7%
110–119	Bright	16%
90-110	Average	50%
80-89	Dull-normal	16%
70-79	Borderline	6-7%
Below 70	Mental defective	2%

Source: Wechsler, D. (1981a & 1981b) *Wechsler Intelligence Scales for Children and Adults.* New York: Psychological Corporation.

measure abilities to define words, solve math problems, arrange pictures in a logical sequence so that they tell a story, reproduce designs with colored blocks, assemble puzzles, trace a path through a picture of a maze, identify missing parts of pictures, and answer an assortment of questions on general topics (Wechsler, 1981a).

Both the Stanford-Binet and the WISC-IIIR compute the final IQ score by comparing individuals' performance to that of other people their same age. If your performance is about average for people your age, your IQ score will turn out to be roughly 100. But if your performance is considerably above or below that of people your age, your score reflects this. For example, if you're only 16 years old, but your performance on the test is the same as the average 20-year-old's, your IQ score will be about 125. On the other hand, if you're 16, but your IQ score is only 75, you have the mental age of the average 12-year-old. As you can see from Table 3–1, IQ scores are converted into different categories—from very superior to mental defective—which are then used in situations such as assigning adolescents to various types of educational or rehabilitation programs.

ALTERNATIVE DEFINITIONS OF INTELLIGENCE

Although the Stanford-Binet and the Wechsler tests are still the most popular ways of defining and measuring intelligence, not all researchers agree that these are the best. Robert Sternberg, for example, has proposed his triarchic theory of intelligence (Sternberg, 1985). According to Sternberg, human intelligence is comprised of three components: how well we analyze problems and use abstract thinking, the ways in which we put our former experiences to use in solving unfamiliar problems, and our practical knowledge. Analytical and abstract thinking are the types of skills measured on traditional IQ tests. But experiential intelligence

Insert
3–2

Under the Eye of the Clock: The True Story of Christopher Nolan

"Can any sane, able-bodied person sense how it feels to have evil-intentioned limbs constantly making a mockery of you?" Christopher Nolan

As an adolescent, Christopher Nolan began writing his prize-winning autobiographical novel, *Under the Eye of the Clock,* which was published in 1990 when he was 22 years old. What is remarkable about this author, however, is not the relatively young age at which he started his novel. It is the fact that Christopher Nolan cannot talk, cannot smile, cannot chew his own food, cannot walk, and cannot control his arms. In fact, Christopher Nolan was 11 years old before he was able to communicate anything to those around him other than by rolling his eyes upward. But with a new drug that enabled him to move his neck, a unicorn stick strapped to his forehand, years of special education, and a mother who held his chin from behind while he "wrote," Nolan was able to tap out his thoughts on a typewriter. During the first 11 years of his life, the Nolan family read and sang to Christopher, taught him the alphabet by stringing letters from the kitchen ceiling, and learned how to respond to his grunts and few gestures. Refusing to believe that their son was mentally retarded, the Nolans eventually sold their farm to move to Dublin where they could enroll Christopher in a special school. There therapists spent years trying to teach him to type. All the while, Christopher was composing poems inside his mind and reciting them to himself again and again. Since his adolescence, the typing stick has allowed him to express himself and to continue composing and writing poetry, essays and novels. As an adolescent, his book of poetry, *Dam-Burst of Dreams,* heralded the beginning of his literary career. Critics are now comparing his work to other famous Irish writers like Joyce and Becket—the brilliant work, not of "a physically disabled writer," but of "a writer who is also physically disabled."

is our ability to solve familiar problems in a quick and automatic enough way that we reserve energy to solve unfamiliar problems more effectively. Being intelligent also entails having the practical knowledge to get ourselves out of trouble in real-life situations, to get along with other people, and to apply what we know in ways that make sense in a particular situation. The first type of intelligence can be seen as book learning, the second as learning from experience, and the third as common sense. But according to Sternberg, our intelligence can't be accurately measured without seeing how well we can adapt to a particular type of situation. In other words, what's intelligent in one situation might turn out to be downright stupid in another.

Howard Gardner also believes that intelligence goes far beyond what is measured on tests such as the Wechsler and Stanford-Binet. Gardner believes that we have seven different types of intelligence or seven "frames of mind" that contribute to our overall intelligence: linguistic, logical-mathematical, bodily-kinesthetic,

Insert 3–3

Encouraging Adolescents' Seven Intelligences

How can we encourage adolescents to develop their skills in the seven kinds of intelligence proposed by Howard Gardner? One approach is to develop new criteria for grading students, as teachers working with Gardner have done in their art, music, and writing classes:

Production

A. Craft: Being in control of the basic techniques & principles

B. Pursuit: Developing your work over time by revising, pursuing the problem in depth, and returning to a problem or theme from a variety of angles

C. Invention: Experiment, take risks, solve problems creatively, set your own problems to work on

D. Expression: Express ideas or feelings in your work

Reflection

A. Ability to assess your own work

B. Ability to evaluate others' work

C. Ability to use criticisms and suggestions

D. Ability to learn from other works

E. Ability to articulate your goals

Perception

A. Capacity to make fine discriminations about works

B. Awareness of sensuous aspects of experience: Example—responding to visual patterns made by shadows

C. Awareness of physical properties and qualities of materials: Example—textures of paper, sounds of words

Approach to Work

A. Engagement: Works hard, meets deadlines, shows care and attention to detail

B. Ability to work independently

C. Ability to work collaboratively with others

D. Ability to use cultural resource: Know where to go for help

Source: Gardner, H. (1993) *Multiple Intelligences.* New York: Basic Books, p. 150.

spatial, musical, interpersonal, and intrapersonal. In other words, Gardner is among those who believe that our intelligence should be defined and measured more on the basis of how we behave in everyday situations than on how we score on written tests (Gardner, 1993).

Traditional IQ tests, college entrance exams, and experiments such as Piaget's measure linguistic and logical-mathematical intelligences. In contrast, spatial intelligence is the ability to create mental models of the physical world and to maneuver by using those models. For example, sailors, sculptors, and engineers need this kind of intelligence. Musical intelligence, of course, is best exemplified by the Amadeus Mozarts and Leonard Bernsteins of the world. Bodily or **kinesthetic intelligence** is the ability to solve problems or create something by using your whole body. Dancers, surgeons, and athletes exhibit this form of intelligence.

Gardner also proposes two kinds of personal intelligence—interpersonal and intrapersonal. Interpersonal, or social intelligence, is the ability to understand other people and to know how to get along well with them. Successful teachers, salespeople, and political or religious leaders rely on this kind of intelligence. Finally there is intrapersonal intelligence—the ability to see ourselves accurately and to use what we know about ourselves to create a happy life for ourselves. This form of intelligence is closest to what we might commonly think of as wisdom, or insight, or introspection.

Gardner also believes that each of the seven kinds of intelligence develop at somewhat different rates. For example, our kinesthetic intelligence develops earlier than our linguistic intelligence; therefore, adolescents with athletic intelligence can be identified sooner than those who have intellectual gifts in areas such as poetry or music. Likewise, any one of our seven forms of intelligence can be destroyed by physical damage to the brain while leaving the others intact. Moreover, any one of the seven can emerge in an extreme form in genius and even in people otherwise considered retarded or mentally disabled. For example, as Dustin Hoffman portrayed in the film *Rainman*, some people with the mental disability known as autism possess superior abilities in one particular area, such as drawing, music, or math. As Insert 3–2 illustrates with the true story of Christopher Nolan, Gardner is correct in that there are cases of people who are diagnosed as retarded or autistic and later emerge as true geniuses (Nolan, 1990).

Although our society has considered linguistic and logical-mathematical skills to be the most important in deciding how intelligent a person is, Gardner considers all seven kinds of intelligence as equally valuable. As a consequence, he believes our schools should alter their curriculum and teaching methods in ways that would do a better job encouraging all seven kinds of intelligence. Insert 3–3 illustrates one way Gardner and the teachers he works with have devised for encouraging students to develop their seven intelligences.

CULTURAL BIAS IN DEFINING INTELLIGENCE

Another consideration in trying to decide how to define and measure intelligence is race or cultural background (Anastasi, 1988; Herstein & Murray, 1994; Lonner, 1990). To begin with, cultures sometimes differ in regard to what kind of thinking or what kind of behavior is considered wise or intelligent. For example, in white, middle-class society in our country, being outspoken and answering questions quickly is generally considered a sign of intelligence. But in other societies, the intelligent person is the one who speaks very little and who answers questions slowly after moments of silent thinking. Within our own country white and nonwhite adolescents are often raised with different values and different definitions of intelligence when it comes to such things as how to go about solving the kinds of problems that appear on IQ tests.

Robert Williams and Daryl Wing Sue are among the experts who question the validity of IQ tests for assessing the intelligence of Americans who aren't from the white middle-class (Sue, 1991; Williams, 1975). For example, what if this question were asked of three children from different U.S. subcultures: "If five blackbirds are sitting on a wire and one flies away, how many would be left?" Unlike many whites or blacks, many Native Americans would answer "zero" because they know from their cultural heritage or from experience that when one blackbird flies away, they all do. The point is that if adolescents from different racial and cultural backgrounds are going to have a fair test of their intelligence, we need to ask them questions that are more culturally appropriate than many that are asked on traditional IQ tests. For example, when Williams was 15, his school counselor suggested that he become a bricklayer because he was good with his hands and had scored only 82 on his IQ test. Ignoring this advice, Williams earned a doctorate in psychology, became one of the founders of the American Association of Black Psychologists, and established an eminent reputation as an author and college professor.

Given these concerns about cultural fairness, psychologist Janet Mercer developed an alternative to traditional IQ tests—the System of Multicultural Pluralistic Assessment test, referred to as the **SOMPA** (Mercer & Lewis, 1978). This IQ test was designed for assessing nonwhite children younger than 12 while taking into consideration their families' economic backgrounds, any neurological problems the children might have, and assessments of the children's behavior at home and at school. The final score, called the Estimated Learning Potential, adjusts the child's IQ score from the Wechsler on the basis of information from the SOMPA. According to one of our leading experts on psychological testing, Anne Anastasi, the SOMPA is a powerful tool for preventing IQ test scores from being misused to misdiagnose children from impoverished homes or from nonwhite cultures (Anastasi, 1988).

VALIDITY AND RELIABILITY OF IQ TESTS

Related to the issue of race and cultural background, IQ tests also have been criticized for not being valid or reliable (Anastasi, 1988; Locurto, 1991). **Validity** refers to whether any test is actually measuring what it claims to be measuring. For example, if I ask you to stand on my bathroom scales and let me weigh you while explaining that I am testing to determine how athletically skilled you are, you could claim that my test is not a valid measure. I am accurately measuring something, but not your athletic skills. Likewise, as we have seen, opponents of traditional IQ tests agree that they are testing something, but the *something* isn't intelligence—or is only a narrow or shallow manifestation of intelligence. According to the tests' critics, what we have been measuring with IQ tests is a variety of different skills, words, and attitudes that people have learned from their families, schools, and neighborhoods. From this standpoint, IQ tests are not valid measures of anyone's intelligence, although the test might be measuring what we have learned about white, middle-class culture. Those who support the use of these IQ tests, of course, argue that the tests are valid measures of intelligence, regardless of a person's race, sex, economic class, or life experiences.

Reliability means how constant or how consistent a person's score on any test is over time. In other words, if you took an IQ test or an SAT test or a jogging test

12 months ago, would you score about the same if you took those tests this afternoon? If your scores are similar across time, then the test is considered reliable. But if your scores change dramatically over time, then the test is not valued as a reliable measuring instrument. Those who support IQ tests point out that most of our IQ scores do remain remarkably constant throughout our lives. The tests' opponents, however, point out that, even though they might be in the minority, some children's scores do change dramatically when they are retested—changes of as much as 50 points in some cases.

These changes in a person's scores might occur for a number of reasons, given the conditions under which IQ testing takes place (Anastasi, 1988). First, unlike tests administered by classroom teachers, IQ tests are administered by one psychologist who—alone in a room with the child—asks the questions out loud, explains the directions, uses a stopwatch to time certain answers, and interprets the answers before arriving at the final IQ score. Some evidence suggests that the race, gender, and personality of the psychologist can influence a person's performance on the test. In other words, if you feel intimidated or nervous around the particular psychologist who happens to be giving you the test, you might not do as well as you would with a psychologist who made you feel more at ease. Likewise, because portions of the test are timed and because performance is based on doing a good job following verbal directions, some young people get very nervous, which could, of course, affect their scores. Even if the psychologist does a good job putting the youngster at ease, factors other than intelligence, such as not feeling well physically or being preoccupied with something going on at home or at school, can lower a person's score on any particular day.

The Pros and Cons of IQ Testing

Given that IQ tests are surrounded by so much controversy, why do we keep using them? Are there any advantages to these tests? If, as the critics argue, IQ tests aren't measuring intelligence, then are they useful for measuring anything? Let's examine the evidence (Locurto, 1991).

Overall, IQ scores generally do a pretty good job of predicting how well children and adolescents will do in school. That is, there is anywhere from about a +.40 to +.60 correlation between IQ scores and educational success. But, and this is a very important "but," this connection is mainly for people whose IQ score is either extremely high or extremely low. For the vast majority of us whose IQ scores fall within the average range, IQ is only moderately accurate as a predictor of how successful we are at school or in the world beyond school. Motivation, maturity, self-discipline, and dedication seem to play equally as important a role as intelligence for most of us. Moreover, IQ scores predict our achievements in elementary school better than our achievements in high school or college.

One of the most famous illustrations is a study that Lewis Terman began in the 1920s in which he followed the lives of 1528 California schoolchildren with average IQs of 150 over a period of 50 years (Terman, 1959). These children, who became known as "Terman's Termites," did turn out to be above average in school achievement, physical health, athletics, emotional maturity, and character. For instance, 70% of them graduated from college compared to only 8% of other Americans their age. Their incomes, job status, and overall happiness also were well above average. Even those who only earned a high-school degree earned about as much money as college graduates in the general population. So doesn't this prove that IQ scores predict life success? No. Why? First, most of these people had well-educated, financially secure parents. Second, high IQ produced a wide variety of different outcomes. For example, nearly 40% of the women who had graduate degrees became housewives. And the men who achieved the most financially and professionally had parents who were more likely to encourage initiative, independence, and academic success than men with similar IQs who achieved less. So clearly, IQ wasn't the only factor influencing their success.

Nevertheless, IQ scores remain our most valuable tool for identifying which children have the very poorest and the very highest intellectual skills. These IQ scores, in turn, can enable us to give those students who need the most help and those who are truly gifted the special attention they need at school. Beyond school, IQ scores also are more closely associated with occupational and social success than any other test currently available. So if you are trying to gauge which 5-year-old will grow up to be the most socially and academically successful adolescent, an IQ score still would be your best bet. But, as "Terman's Termites" show us, factors other than intelligence—such as self-discipline and motivation—can be as important as intellectual abilities in determining how successful any of us will be in school, at work, or in our personal lives. Without belaboring the point further, remember: there is not a direct path from any child's IQ score to his or her achievements, income, or personal happiness in the real world.

Unfortunately, IQ tests historically have been misused as the only criterion used to assign students to the special education track for "slow learners" or the "educable mentally retarded." A number of tragic outcomes have resulted from this misuse of the tests. First, although most of our IQ scores stay relatively constant across time, some children are misdiagnosed on the basis of one testing and truly don't have mental handicaps that justify their being segregated into the "special ed" curriculum. Second, students who are labeled as "special ed kids" are socially and academically stigmatized by this kind of labeling—a label that follows them throughout their years in school. Third, too many students relegated to the special education track don't receive the kind of education that could help them overcome many of their deficits. As shown in Chapter 10, special education too often becomes a dumping ground for those children that most teachers don't want to work with and that most other students don't want to associate with. Fourth, most slow learners don't benefit intellectually or socially from being kept apart from brighter students (Jones, 1992).

Given these concerns, most states have modified the way they use IQ tests (Elliott, 1987). Some states have abandoned them altogether for assigning children to special education classes. Others use the scores, but only in combination with teachers' opinions, parents' reports, students' grades, and achievement tests. Slowly, then, the use of IQ tests is declining. In trying to find a happy medium between the two warring sides of the debate, perhaps it's best to consider IQ tests as useful to an extent as one way of identifying young children who need special help in order to succeed in school. As long as the IQ score is backed up by other evidence, such as feedback from parents and teachers, both the brightest and the slowest students might benefit from their use.

Intelligence: Inherited or Acquired?

Aside from the debate about the advantages and disadvantages of IQ testing, another issue has intrigued researchers for decades: How much of our intelligence is inherited, and how much is acquired through the kinds of experiences we have as we're growing up? Given the thousands of studies addressing this question, what have we learned?

First, IQ is partly dependent on what happens to us while we're growing up and can, therefore, be improved through certain kinds of experiences (Locurto, 1991). For example, older adolescents who have received special kinds of training to improve their cognitive skills have improved their IQ scores (Anastasi, 1988; Feurerstein, 1979; Spitz, 1986). The IQ scores of poor children who are adopted at an early age by wealthier families also tend to improve. Unfortunately, adolescents who were malnourished in the first few years of their lives often have lower IQ scores even when they received good diets later in childhood (Drotar, 1985; Salt, Galler, & Ramsey, 1988). Some children's low IQ scores also seem to be related to the high levels of lead in their blood—lead in their drinking water from old plumbing, from objects painted with lead based paint, or from heavy traffic fumes in inner cities. Poor children are the most likely to contract lead poisoning which, in turn, has been associated with lower IQ scores, more learning disabilities, and inattentiveness at school (Viadero, 1986). It's now estimated that about half of the differences between people's intelligence is due to environmental factors (Plomin, DeFries, & McClearn, 1990).

On the other hand, intelligence doesn't seem to be as malleable as many researchers previously thought—and it's still not altogether clear which environmental factors are the most important in shaping intelligence (Locurto, 1991; Plomin, DeFries, & McClearn, 1990). For example, although preschool programs have generally failed to raise most poor children's IQ scores or to have long-lasting effects on their later school achievements, most adopted children do make intellectual gains. On the other hand, adopted children's improvements aren't as closely tied to the family's income as researchers had expected. This means that money probably isn't as influential as other factors within the home unless the family is extremely poor or extremely wealthy. What our present research is telling us is that we still haven't identified any single way to improve all children's IQs. But what is clear is that our intelligence is determined both by genetic and by environmental factors.

Insert 3–4

Characteristics of Piaget's Concrete and Formal Thinking

Concrete Thinking

Concept of equivalence

The ability to understand that if A=B and B=C, then A=C:

You notice that your sister's feet are smaller than yours. Later that day, you notice that your cousin's feet are bigger than yours. Without having to look at your sister's and your cousin's feet side by side, you know that your cousin wouldn't be able to wear your sister's shoes.

Concept of Reversibility

The ability to work backward and forward, to rotate objects in your mind, and to imagine something as it had looked before it was completed:

You notice that a brick in the wall looks like a flat rectangle; but, having noticed the thickness of the wall, you can imagine how the brick would look if it were removed from the wall and stood on its narrow end.

The Concept of Class Inclusion

The ability to reason simultaneously about each part of a whole as well as about the whole itself:

You understand that when you have 10 candy bars and 8 of them are chocolate, you have more "candy" than you have "chocolate candy."

Associativity

The idea that the sum is independent of the order in which things are added:

You understand that 4 + 2 + 3 will add up to the same as 2 + 4 + 3.

Formal Operational Thinking

Abstract Reasoning

The ability to solve problems and understand situations without having to see the actual objects or people involved:

You are able to understand and to discuss concepts such as justice and love.

Combinational Analysis

The ability to formulate several different possibilities in trying to find the solution to a problem:

After reading a recipe, you bake a cake. When you take it out of the oven, it's as flat as a pancake. You're able to figure out that either (1) you put too much of something in or (2) you left something out or (3) your had the temperature set wrong or (4) somebody didn't write the recipe down correctly or (5) a combination of any of the above.

Propositional Thinking

The ability to generalize what you learned in one situation or in one type of problem solving to another similar situation or problem:

A few weeks after your cake mishap, you're trying to bake bread. You remember each of the four things that might have gone wrong in baking your cake and you try to avoid repeating these mistakes with the bread.

Perspective Taking

The ability to consider problems or approach situations from viewpoints other than your own:

In arguing with your parents about your curfew, you can understand why they worry about you when you're out past midnight.

PIAGET'S APPROACH TO COGNITIVE DEVELOPMENT

In contrast to the psychometric approach, Piagetian psychologists are not interested in measuring "what" children and adolescents know, but in describing "how" they go about knowing it. That is, Piagetians are interested in finding out how children and adolescents solve problems and how they reason about social or moral situations or issues. Piaget's theories dominated the study of cognitive development for nearly four decades. Like other stage theorists, Piagetians believe that we act and think more maturely or more intelligently as we age primarily because we are advancing from one cognitive stage to a more sophisticated stage. In other words, Piagetians assume that the way young children and adolescents actually "think" is essentially different and that their different thinking skills aren't primarily due to the experiences they have as they age. Although Piaget's theories have come under heavy fire in recent years, they still contribute much to our understanding of childrens' and adolescents' problem solving skills (Inhelder & Piaget, 1958; Overton & Montangero, 1991; Piaget, 1972).

Cognitive Stages Between Birth and Adolescence

According to Piaget, we advance through three cognitive stages before beginning adolescence: sensorimotor, preoperational, and concrete operations. From the time we are born until we are about 18 months old, we are in our **sensorimotor stage.** During this stage, we can respond only in simple, generalized ways to the objects and people around us. Our biggest advance during this stage comes when we acquire the concept of **object permanence**—the ability to realize that people and objects still exist even when we can't actually see them. In other words, we're able to understand that our father still exists even when he leaves the room after putting us to bed at night. Until we acquire this new mental skill, we are easily entertained by games such as hide-and-seek or a Jack-in-the-box because we are astounded when something that we thought had literally disappeared suddenly reappears. As your own parents can remind you, a less amusing side of not having this skill is that infants and toddlers become very upset when a parent or a toy disappears from sight, because they believe the person or object no longer exists. Once we have acquired this important skill of keeping objects and people alive in our heads by being able to create a mental symbol for them, we have left our sensorimotor stage behind and advanced to the preoperational stage.

Up until about the age of 7, while we are in our **preoperational stage,** our mental skills advance rapidly as we learn to speak and to think in terms of symbols. Not only can we start attaching various meanings to our mental symbols, but also we can start imagining objects as merely representations of the real thing. For example, we can play with our baby dolls and our toy trucks and pretend they are real babies and real trucks like the ones we see around us in real life. We become capable of engaging in more mature kinds of play and to enjoy more experiences that involve distinguishing between what is real and what is only a representation of reality.

Although our language and our imagination are developing, however, we see the world around us from a very egocentric point of view. In Piaget's terminology, egocentrism is not synonymous with the word "egotistical," meaning self-confident and proud. **Egocentrism** is the child's inability to interpret or to consider experiences from any perspective other than his or her own. Without the ability to consider any other person's point of view, we often seem to be extremely selfish during this period of our lives. For example, we can't understand that refusing to share our favorite toy with our friend is hurting the other person's feelings. But egocentrism also means that we don't have the ability to solve certain kinds of intellectual problems because we aren't able to manipulate the variables in our mind in such a way that we can come up with the right answer. For example, if you arrange the pieces of a jigsaw puzzle upside down on a table in front of a 5-year-old, she might not be able to assemble it even though she has put that same puzzle together dozens of times before when the pieces were arranged right side up. Because she is egocentric, she isn't able to take the perspective of what the puzzle looks like from the other side of the table. Not being able to work the upside-down puzzle doesn't mean this child is selfish, self-centered, or egotistical. But, in Piaget's terms, her behavior is egocentric because she is able to approach the problem only from her own immediate visual viewpoint. She literally can't stand back and see how to solve the problem by assuming the perspective of someone sitting on the other side of the table.

As we age, however, we move into the stage of **concrete operations** in which we are improving our skills in solving problems that require us to consider things from more than one perspective. Between the ages of 7 and 12, we also come to understand the **rule of equivalence:** If A is equal to B in some way, such as its weight or length, and if B is equal to C, then A and C also are equal. In acquiring the principle of **associativity,** we also realize that the order in which numbers are arranged does not affect how they are added together. For example, 4+2 and 2+4 both equal 6. We also come to realize that an object or a person can belong to several different categories at the same time. For example, an 8-year-old boy can finally understand that his puppy is part of the categories of dog and pet, and that dog is part of an even larger category called animals. Then, too, we grasp the principle of **reversibility:** If you take four cards out of a stack of six, separate these four into two stacks, then put them all back into one stack, you still have the same six cards. We also master the principle of **class inclusion:** If you have eight white buttons and two red, you have more things in the category of buttons than you have in the category of red or white. Children who have not mastered this concept, however, will get confused when we ask them questions or give them problems to solve that require separating and combining things that belong to several different categories.

Two other principles acquired during our concrete operational stage are conservation and serialization. **Conservation** is the principle that helps us understand that we can change the shape of liquids and solids without changing their weight or their amount. In other words, not until we're about 7 years old can we understand that if we put one scoop of ice cream into one huge cone, and then put the same size scoop into five smaller cones, we still have the same amount of ice cream. Similarly, not until we master **serialization** can we arrange objects in correct order in terms of some abstract dimension such as their length or weight. For example, the 5-year-old won't be able to arrange different sized leaves in the proper order from biggest to smallest, but a 10-year-old will.

COGNITIVE STAGES DURING ADOLESCENCE

According to the Piagetians, many of the changes we undergo as adolescents in terms of how we solve problems and how we relate to other people are a consequence of our entering the stage of **formal operations.** During our teenage years, Piagetians believe we are evolving from our concrete operational thinking to our stage of formal reasoning. In other words, at no single age or one exact moment do we develop formal reasoning. Consequently, Piagetians are not surprised by the differences in the ways adolescents of exactly the same age are thinking and behaving. So a 17-year-old boy might be reasoning, thinking, and behaving in ways that are far more immature than his 14-year-old sister if he is still in the stage of concrete reasoning while she has already entered the more advanced stage of formal reasoning.

If we advance beyond the stage of concrete thinking, our reasoning supposedly becomes more logical, more abstract, and less egocentric. We develop the skills referred to as **critical thinking**—grasping the deeper meaning of problems, seeing different perspective and approaches, remaining open-minded when evidence doesn't fit our preexisting beliefs or expectations. Because we can think more abstractly and less egocentrically, we become more interested in discussing hypothetical issues and in considering solutions to hypothetical problems. The "what ifs" that were beyond our comprehension or that bored us as young children now become more interesting to us. On the other hand, if we are still in the concrete stage of thinking, we too readily accept a hypothesis as true without first questioning its underlying premises. We also are more limited in terms of coming up with only one or two possible solutions to a problem until we enter our formal reasoning stage. As a consequence, older teenagers are supposedly better at questioning hypotheses, generating explanations on their own for why certain things might be happening, and solving problems that require taking account of several different perspectives at the same time.

To get a feeling for the kinds of experiments that Piaget's theories are based on, look at Insert 3–5. What's the right answer? Which principles are being tested in this experiment? According to Piaget, at your age you should easily see that either block will make the water level go up to exactly the same amount because size, not weight, is the only variable that matters. According to Piagetians, as our formal thinking develops, we also should become more willing to abandon our illogical thinking and admit when we're on the wrong track. We should become less pig-headed and less defensive as we outgrow our concrete operational thinking. Yet even after getting the wrong answer and then watching the experimenter demonstrate the right answer, some teenage students still reach the conclusion of one who said, "Oh, I see. The water went up the same in both containers even

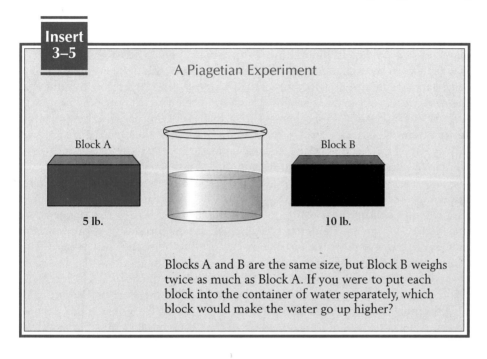

Insert 3–5

A Piagetian Experiment

Block A

5 lb.

Block B

10 lb.

Blocks A and B are the same size, but Block B weighs twice as much as Block A. If you were to put each block into the container of water separately, which block would make the water go up higher?

though one of those cubes weighs more than the other. Hmmm. You must have *magic* water!" (Burbules & Linn, 1988).

Another consequence of formal operational reasoning is being able to appreciate and to use satire, irony, parodies, and metaphors. So our sense of humor becomes more sophisticated because we can understand the satire and metaphors in what we hear, read, and see around us. For example, a 12-year-old might find a particular movie boring because she truly doesn't understand its humor. But her 15-year-old brother might think the movie is hilarious because he grasps the double meanings in the words and understands how satire and parody are being used to make certain scenes funny. In this case, according to Piagetians, the sister isn't any less intelligent than her brother. She simply hasn't yet entered the stage of formal reasoning.

ADVANCING TO HIGHER COGNITIVE STAGES

Given the skills that the Piagetians tell us we acquire when we advance to our formal reasoning stage, it's natural enough for us to wonder: How can we help adolescents get there faster? In fact, how do we make the shifts from one stage to the next higher one during our childhood and adolescence? What can parents and teachers do to help children, at whatever age, advance more quickly to a more mature stage of thinking?

According to Piaget's theories, we organize the information that comes into our mind by putting the data into our **schema** or **schemata.** Each separate schema allows us to keep data from our former experiences stored and organized in such a way that when we encounter new data, we aren't overcome by continually having to categorize and interpret it from scratch. When we encounter new information, then, we rely on our existing schema to interpret the new data or show us how to react in a new situation. Our schemata are actively selecting and interpreting information from the outside world in order to make sense of them on the basis of our former experiences and knowledge. **Assimilation** is Piaget's term for this process of storing and interpreting new data in ways that conveniently fit into our existing schemata, or mental compartments. At the same time, however, our schemata have to be reworked or redone on those occasions when new data and new experiences simply won't fit into our existing mental compartments. When this happens, we experience the uneasy, unpleasant feelings of **disequilibrium** or **cognitive dissonance.** We feel mentally out of balance because the new data "just won't fit" or "doesn't compute" with our existing schemata. In order to get rid of this feeling of disequilibrium, we change our existing schemata so that the new data fit more logically. Piaget used the term **accommodation** to describe this process of adjusting or updating our schema to make sense of our new experiences or new information.

Piaget believed that, as a consequence of the different kinds of experiences we have as children and adolescents, we encounter different amounts of cognitive dissonance that, in turn, cause our schema to advance at different rates. For example, young children who usually play with much older children are more likely to encounter experiences and information that don't fit with their existing schema. These children, then, would be more likely to experience the disequilibrium that encourages them to accommodate the new data by changing their existing schema. Likewise, an adolescent whose stepmother spends a lot of time with her discussing things in ways that require formal operational thinking is more likely to experience disequilibrium and to change her schema than the adolescent who spends most of her time babysitting her younger sister. On the other hand, Piagetians do not believe we can design our schools or homes in such a way that we can push children from one stage to another at our will. A certain amount of biological maturation is necessary before these kinds of experiences can have any real impact on helping us advance to a higher cognitive stage.

Obviously, though, we often encounter new information that doesn't make sense in terms of our existing schemata, but we don't change our schemata one iota—hence the cliché, "you can lead the horse to water, but you can't make it drink." Why not? We often react like the student who chose to believe that the experimenter was using magic water rather than accommodate the new evidence by changing our existing schema. Of course Piagetians are aware that we all sometimes refuse to change our existing schema in order to accommodate new and contradictory information—a fact that accounts, in large part, for why some children and adolescents are still functioning at a lower stage of cognitive development than others. As the next chapter shows, Freudian psychologists also recognize this mental refusal to change our schema even in the light of information that doesn't fit. But the Freudians use different terminology from Piaget, telling us that the subconscious mind plays a number of mental tricks on us in the form of our defense mechanisms, in order to sublimate, discredit, or somehow destroy whatever new data don't fit into our existing system of beliefs—especially when the new information or new experience contradicts those beliefs stored in our schema about how wonderful, how bright, and how perfect we ourselves are.

APPLYING PIAGET'S THEORIES TO SCHOOL SETTINGS

Teachers, of course, have been especially interested in applying Piaget's theories in the schools. A few examples illustrate how his theories about concrete and formal operational thinking can be translated into practical suggestions for educators (Linn & Songer, 1991). According to Piaget, students who are still using concrete operational thinking will have a hard time solving science or math problems that require them to generate several different hypotheses at once or to question the assumptions underlying a hypothesis. As an English or history teacher, you might also notice these students having a harder time analyzing or interpreting ideas than students who have advanced to the stage of formal operational thinking. Likewise, as a physics teacher, you might have trouble explaining the logic of certain physics problems to students who are still using concrete thinking. In all of these cases, the teachers should use more concrete or less abstract ways of teaching the material.

Another way of applying Piaget's ideas is to try teaching students more advanced ways of thinking—teaching them how to think more critically. Classroom activities and homework assignments are designed in ways that supposedly will teach students' the kinds of skills that Piaget associates with formal operational thinking. Attempts to teach critical thinking, of course, wouldn't meet with Piaget's wholehearted approval because he believed our cognitive stages are mainly the consequence of aging, not experience. Nevertheless, a number of these classroom programs have succeeded in teaching adolescents to use more of the skills that Piaget referred to as formal operational thinking (Perkins, Segal, & Voss, 1992; Resnick, 1986).

SHORTCOMINGS OF PIAGET'S THEORIES

Although Piaget's theories have been an important catalyst in studying adolescents' cognitive development, and although they still form the basis of some of the most current theories in the field, they have come under fire as research continues to contradict many of Piaget's predictions. Among the many shortcomings in Piaget's work, one of the most noteworthy is that he reached his conclusions mainly by observing his own children. In any event, Piaget's theories no longer dominate the field of cognitive development as they did prior to the 1980s. Recent research has pointed out a number of contradictions and inconsistencies in Piaget's predictions and conclusions (Keating, 1990; Overton & Montangero, 1991; Rybash, Roodin, & Santrock, 1991).

First, contrary to Piaget's predictions, we adults often rely on concrete operational thinking and young children sometimes use formal operational reasoning. In other words, children and adults might not use completely different types of thinking to solve problems as Piaget assumed. So if older children appear to think better than younger children, or if adolescents don't solve problems as well as adults, it might be because we have more experiences and more information at our disposal as we age, not because we have moved into a more advanced cognitive stage.

Second, the kind of reasoning we use at whatever age we are does seem to depend on the kinds of experiences we've had in our lives. For example, adolescents who go through special training to learn more abstract ways of thinking do use more formal operational thinking. Likewise, college graduates seem to use more advanced reasoning skills than those who never attend college, suggesting that college experiences do have an impact on our reasoning skills. Likewise, in those nonindustrialized countries where formal operational thinking isn't as highly valued or as necessary, adults use concrete reasoning more often than do adults in industrialized countries. Findings such as these contradict Piaget's belief that our experiences or our society's values don't have much impact on the kinds of reasoning skills we develop.

Third, we seem to move back and forth between formal and concrete reasoning depending on what type of problem we're trying to solve and on how familiar we are with a particular situation or type of problem. Most of us use formal reasoning in situations or with problems we're most familiar with and in those areas in which we already have the most background knowledge. So our most advanced or most logical thinking generally takes place only after we already have learned a great deal about a particular subject or already had a number of experiences of the same general type. Contradicting Piaget's theory, apparently we don't arrive at the stage of formal reasoning and leave our concrete reasoning skills behind us like an outgrown pair of shoes.

Fourth, our intuitions and visual illusions seem to interfere with our logical thinking. For example, look at Insert 3–6. What's the right answer? If you can think abstractly about the laws of motion and avoid being led astray by visual illusion, you should be able to come up with the right answer—"B." Because the ball continues moving forward and then slightly downward as gravity exerts pressure, it hits the ground slightly in front of where it was dropped, following a parabolic arc. But if you're like half of the college students at Johns Hopkins University who were asked this question, you got the wrong answer (McCloskey, 1983). It seems that solving physics problems often involves what we're choosing to concentrate on as the backdrop. Because the ball does fall straight down relative to the moving person who dropped it, we might wrongly reason that it fell straight down relative to the floor. In any case, Piaget's theories overlook the fact that our scientific thinking skills are often based more on our intuitions and our visual misperceptions than on logical reasoning (Kuhn, 1991; McCloskey, 1983).

Fifth is the issue of how old we're supposed to be when we advance from one cognitive stage to the next. In another contradiction of Piaget, many of us don't

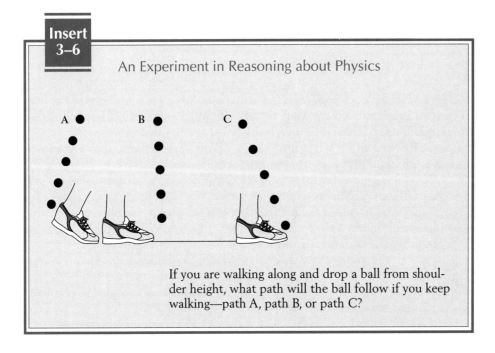

An Experiment in Reasoning about Physics

If you are walking along and drop a ball from shoulder height, what path will the ball follow if you keep walking—path A, path B, or path C?

acquire certain formal reasoning skills until we become adults. For example, many of us don't give up our simplistic ways of seeing and interpreting the world around us as adolescents. It seems that we need adult experiences to teach us how to think in more relative terms—for example, to see that a particular personal problem can't be solved by looking for a single correct solution. Only as adults do many of us start seeing that "truth" or "reality" often depends on whose values or from which perspective we're looking at a situation. For example, a very bright 19-year-old might not be able to understand until's she's older that her stepfather isn't "an evil, dishonest person" simply because he didn't tell the truth in one particular situation. Likewise, even as young adults, many of us aren't able to do the kind of introspective, insightful thinking that Piaget assumed would accompany formal operational thinking. In fact, it seems that certain kinds of wise thinking develop only very late in life. In short, much of what Piaget predicts should happen in terms of advanced reasoning during adolescence or early adulthood happens much later, if at all (Baltes & Baltes, 1993; Rybash, Roodin, & Santrock, 1991).

Finally, our inborn disposition and our gender seem to be closely related to certain aspects of thinking and behavior that Piaget claimed were due to cognitive stages. For instance, those of us who were open-minded, considerate of other people's feelings and perspectives, and insightful about the deeper meaning of things when we were adolescents, might have been that way since birth (Keating, 1990). For now, suffice it to say that, when it comes to aspects of reasoning such as perspective taking, there might be more than a grain of truth to the old aphorism: "You can't make a silk purse out of a sow's ear."

SUPPORT FOR PIAGET'S THEORIES

Despite the shortcomings of Piaget's theories, however, a number of his predictions and observations are well documented in other research (Keating, 1990; Overton & Byrnes, 1991). From early adolescence on, most of us do think more abstractly, become more self-reflective, are better at considering more than one issue at a time, and interpret situations and resolve problems from a more open-minded perspective and in more relative terms. When it comes to logical and mathematical topics, moral reasoning, understanding their interactions with other people, and social or political issues, adolescents' responses to problems are usually more sophisticated than those of younger children. When it comes to scientific reasoning, it's also true that older adolescents usually are better than younger adolescents at generating, testing, and evaluating hypotheses about cause-and-effect relationships. Likewise, older adolescents do a better job comparing the evidence to a theory and changing their minds when the evidence doesn't fit their predictions or contradicts their hypotheses. Before adolescence, however, we generally ignore or modify any evidence that doesn't support our own theories.

Interestingly, too, young adolescents have a harder time than younger children or older adolescents deciding what the right answer is even *after* seeing the evidence. Young adolescents often say, "I can't tell what the right answer is," when younger children can recognize the correct answer quickly. What seems to be happening here is that during early adolescence we start becoming aware, as Piaget predicted, that not all situations and problems have simple or absolute right and wrong solutions. Although we are smarter and more mature in being able to understand that not everything has an answer and that things aren't always black and white, we appear dumber because we're so hesitant and so skeptical that we refuse to see the answer in situations that do have a clear-cut answer. We overgeneralize about uncertainty to the point of fooling ourselves into believing that no evidence or no reasoning is really reliable. Even though our mental skills have in fact advanced, as young adolescents we literally outsmart ourselves in ways that make others see us as having lost ground intellectually.

INFORMATION PROCESSING

Although Piagetians have contributed much to our understanding of cognition, they have not shown us what kinds of cognitive activities adolescents and children engage in when they are solving various kinds of problems or performing certain tasks. This is the goal of researchers who study information processing and who are exploring such questions as: Why do adolescents have better memories than younger children? How and why do the attention spans of children and adolescents differ? How do adolescents and children solve problems differently? How do we develop our critical thinking skills? What strategies do adolescents use in solving different types of problems and can we help them learn more efficient strategies?

MEMORY

The information processing research shows us a number of interesting differences between adolescents and younger children (Keating, 1990; Overton & Byrnes, 1991). First, we do have better memories and can hold more thoughts in mind at the same time when we're adolescents than when we were young children. In part, this is because we use more devices and clues to help us store and retrieve new information. But no matter how old we are, what we remember and how long we remember it also has much to do with our emotions and our moods at the time an event happens or at the time we're trying to memorize something. For instance, an 8-year-old girl might remember more than her 17-year-old brother about a particular event if she was more emotionally involved than he was at the time. So our moods and emotions do influence how much we remember and under what conditions we most easily recall that information (Bower, 1982; Brown & Kulik, 1977).

PROCESSING SPEED

We also process information faster as we move through adolescence. For example, on tasks that involve matching letters and mentally rotating objects in order to imagine them from several different angles, 10-year-olds take almost twice as long as young adults, yet 12-year-olds take only one and a half times as long (Hale, 1990). Then, too, as Inserts 3–4 and 3–5 illustrate, adolescents are better than children at solving science or math problems that require an understanding of the relationships between variables such as weight and volume.

COGNITIVE MONITORING

During adolescence we also get better at cognitive monitoring—observing, criticizing, and modifying our own thinking skills. In other words, we get better at watching and analyzing how our own minds are working. You're able, for example, to realize that you have a pretty poor memory compared to your classmates and that you need to develop special strategies to help you remember more. So you go out and buy yourself an organizer calendar and a new kind of notebook that helps you get your class notes better organized. Another aspect of cognitive monitoring is realizing that everybody makes mistakes in their thinking from time to time and that our first answers aren't always right. So, for example, as an adolescent you're more likely than you were as a child to go back and check your answers on tests a second time before handing them in to your teachers.

COGNITIVE SOCIALIZATION

Unlike the information processing approach, the cognitive socialization approach has not yet made many direct contributions to the research on adolescent cognition (Keating, 1990). Nevertheless, these theories are worth noting because they do offer a viable explanation for the many differences among adolescents concerning analyzing and interpreting data and experiences. According to the **cognitive socialization approach,** the kinds of social interactions we have during our childhood and adolescence—above all, our conversations with other people—have a profound impact on shaping our cognitive structures and thinking skills (Vygotsky, 1978).

So far most of this research has focused on how the particular culture and social class in which we are raised influences our cognitive development (Cole & Means, 1981). Consequently, the cognitive socialization approach is criticized for being more like sociology than psychology. Nevertheless, some psychological studies are showing that adolescents who participate in high-school courses in which they are regularly required to participate in small group discussions develop higher order thinking skills (Perkins, Segal, & Voss, 1992). Such research suggests that the types of conversations and interactions adolescents have with other students, their parents, and their teachers do have a significant impact on shaping which kinds of cognitive skills they will eventually develop.

Furthermore, the logic underlying the cognitive socialization approach makes sense. Why wouldn't the types of experiences we have as children and adolescents have an impact on the kinds of thinking skills we eventually develop? For example, most teenagers in the United States watch more than 15,000 hours of television before the age of 18 and see 20,000 TV ads each year. Yet the messages in these ads and the ways in which these messages are presented encourage lower-level reasoning skills—the kind of thinking that is the very opposite of what most schools are trying to encourage and what researchers, like Piaget, consider part of formal reasoning (Keating, 1990). Despite the fact that relatively little hard evidence has been collected in the area of cognitive socialization, it's important for us to keep abreast of the research that emerges from this approach to studying adolescents' cognitive development.

MENTAL RETARDATION

No matter which approach we take in trying to understand adolescents' cognitive growth, it is clear that some adolescents can never develop the skills associated with concrete or formal operational thinking due to genetic defects that retard their mental development. Being **mentally retarded** is technically defined as having scored below 70 on traditional IQ tests and having difficulty adapting to the demands of everyday life. Using this definition, about 5 million people in our society are mentally retarded.

Among adolescents and adults who have been classified as mentally retarded, however, there are vast differences in the skills that they are capable of learning (Matson & Mullick, 1990). People who score between 50 and 70 on their IQ tests can usually be taught to read and write and can learn vocational skills in special education classes that allow them to become financially self-supporting. Children scoring between 35 and 55 on IQ tests, however, must usually live with their parents or in a shelter for the retarded throughout their adult lives. Although these adolescents can be trained to take care of their own hygiene and can perform tasks that are useful in the family or in a sheltered environment, they will not be able to live on their own without the daily supervision of other adults. Adolescents whose IQ scores fall between 20 and 40 usually have speech and motor impairments and need help performing many of their day-to-day hygiene tasks. Although some of these adolescents can learn some simple occupational tasks, they are not able to support themselves financially because they must be under the constant supervision of adults. Children whose IQ scores fall below 20 require fairly constant custodial care throughout their lives and cannot benefit from special educational training, given the severity of their retardation.

Mental retardation can be caused by both genetic and environmental factors (Matson & Mullick, 1990). **Down's syndrome,** for example, is a genetic abnormality that often causes mental retardation and is associated with certain physical characteristics such as slanted eyes, a short neck, and a very rounded face. Because the incidence of Down's syndrome increases dramatically for babies whose mothers or fathers are past the age of 40, this particular form of retardation can be reduced by older men and women choosing not to have children or by terminating pregnancies in which tests have shown that the fetus has this defect. Other mentally retarded children, however, have no family history of retardation and have no evidence of brain damage or a genetic abnormality. In these cases, a severely impoverished environment at home might cause the retardation, especially in families in where the child was malnourished as an infant and toddler (Drotar, 1985; Lozoff, 1989). Deciding whether a child's retardation is caused by genetic factors or by the family's environment, however, is a question researchers remain unable to answer. Parents with very low IQs can, of course, pass retardation along to their children through their genes. But even if their children are born with perfectly normal intelligence, these parents also might pass the retardation along because of being unable to provide their children with an enriching, stimulating environment.

In either case, we are slowly coming to understand in our society that very few mentally retarded adolescents are in any way dangerous to other people and that many more of these young people than we had ever before imagined can be helped to lead productive lives.

CREATIVITY AND GIFTEDNESS

In contrast to mentally retarded adolescents, those who are highly intelligent or highly creative are seldom feared or seldom pitied in our society. But there are a

How creative are you? How have teachers or family members
affected your creativity?

number of stereotypes and myths surrounding exceptionally creative and intellectually gifted youth. To begin with, many people assume that creativity and intellectual giftedness are one in the same. But, in reality, adolescents who are extremely
creative in art, music, or dance don't necessary have extremely high IQ scores and
those who have exceptionally high intelligence aren't necessarily creative. In general, creative adolescents do have above-average or high IQ scores; but this doesn't
mean that creativity and high intelligence go hand-in-hand (Seisberg, 1993).

DEFINING CREATIVITY

One way to distinguish creative adolescents from those who are intellectually
gifted is to consider the differences in their convergent and divergent thinking
abilities. **Convergent thinking** is characterized by the kinds of questions asked on
IQ tests—questions that require a single correct answer and that rely heavily on
direct, logical, predictable ways of thinking. But the kind of thinking involved in
creativity is **divergent thinking**—generating many different answers to a problem
and coming up with solutions or answers to questions or situations that actually
might not have any correct answer. The more divergent our thinking is, the more
creative we are considered to be. Highly creative adolescents can approach problems or create solutions that are especially novel and unusual compared with
most people their age. Three of the most popular tests for measuring adolescents'
creativity are Guilford's Creativity Tests for Children, Torrance's Tests for Creative
Thinking, and the Khatena-Torrance Creative Perceptions Inventory (Guilford,
1967; Khatena & Torrance, 1976; Torrance, 1966).

Roots of Creativity and Giftedness

Although disagreement continues about how to disginguish "creative" from "intellectually gifted" students, it's generally agreed that anyone whose IQ score is higher than 120 and who also demonstrates a special talent or skill can rightly be referred to as "gifted." But whether we're studying highly creative or highly intelligent teenagers, it's clear that their intelligence or talent isn't the only thing that sets them apart from other people their age. Indeed, a child's intellectual skills or special talent doesn't seem to be the most important factor determining whether he or she will someday be recognized as a genius or an exceptionally creative person. Although it's tempting for those of us who don't have any exceptional skill, talent, or intellectual prowess to believe that people are simply born that way, this isn't what the research shows (Davis & Rimm, 1993; Harring, McCormick, & Harring, 1994; Seisberg, 1993; Tomlinson-Keasey & Little, 1990). Often, for instance, highly gifted or creative teenagers are religiously commited to practicing and perfecting their talent. These young people have the self-discipline, will power, and dedication to perfect their special talent to a level of true brilliance and genius. If there's one thing that keeps resurfacing in the research it's this: From childhood on, the geniuses or extremely intelligent and creative people have an amazing amount of will power and self-discipline. It is this drive and dedication that enable them to stay motivated enough to perfect their talent through rigorous training, tedious practice, and repeated failure. Moreover, their self-motivation and need to excel or express themselves creatively seems to come from within themselves, not solely from trying to win the approval of other people, or making high grades, or winning. In short, as Thomas Edison is credited for saying about himself, "Genius is one percent inspiration and ninety-nine percent perspiration."

Also, although many of us seem to want to believe that highly creative or extremely intelligent people have some sort of special immunity from the criticism and negative feedback the rest of us endure, this isn't true. In fact, these adolescents have to learn to be exceptionally objective and brutally honest with themselves about their own shortcomings in order to perfect their skills or art. This is especially the case with creative youngsters who are willing to take risks and to fail, as well as to be criticized and corrected.

Not only do those teenagers who ultimately reach the pinnacle of creativity and intelligence have to be able to accept criticism, they also must have enough strength of character to tolerate rejection, public humiliation, and failure—at least on occasion. The fortitude to keep working despite rejection and criticism is a trademark of most people who eventually achieve eminence in their field. Van Gogh, for example, sold only one painting in his lifetime. Gertrude Stein submitted her poetry to editors for 20 years before a poem was finally accepted, and Rodin's sculptures were repeatedly rejected. Stravinsky was run out of Paris by an angry audience and critics when he first presented his musical masterpiece, the "Rite of Spring." The world-famous Frank Lloyd Wright was one of the most widely rejected architects of his time. More than a dozen publishers rejected the poetry of e.e. cummings—a fact that his mother noted in her dedication when she finally financed the publishing of his work: "With no thanks to . . ." followed by the long list of the publishers who had rejected her son's work (White, 1982). The point is that self-motivation, dedication, and the ability to accept criticism and rejection are part of the make-up of those gifted or intelligent children who eventually become recognized as the most creative or most intelligent in their area of expertise.

Finally, most teenagers who already have been recognized, or who will some-day be recognized, as exceptionally creative or intelligent people haven't devel-oped their abilities without the help of their families and teachers. Whether children are talented in music, art, dance, sports, or an academic area such as math, they seldom realize their full potential unless their parents are willing to dedicate much of their own lives to helping them get special training and unless the family is willing, in many ways, to revolve around their needs. One of the biggest sacrifices, of course, is often financial because special tutors, coaches, and programs cost money. Obviously these sacrifices and the family's intense focus on the child's exceptionality often create stress for the parents and any other siblings, as well as the child with the exceptional talent or skills.

One of the most famous studies illustrating this point is Blooms' research on famous concert pianists, sculptors, mathematicians, neurologists, and Olympic ath-letes. These famous people had parents who emphasized the importance of hard work and self-discipline by modeling it in their own behavior. Regardless of how much schooling or what kind of jobs they had, these parents made sure that their child received formal instruction from a special coach, mentor, or teacher. These adults who achieved excellence in art, music, or athletics had spent 25 to 30 hours a week as adolescents perfecting their special talent under the direction of their expert teacher or coach. Interestingly, what was exceptional about these children's teachers or coaches wasn't as much their own skill as their ability to make the ini-tial learning, which is often tedious and boring, into something pleasurable and to offer continual support for the child's early efforts. These teachers set high stan-dards, but offered far more praise and encouragement than humiliation and criti-cism. Still, most of the children weren't recognized as talented or gifted until after the age of 11 or 12. It had taken years of practicing and perfecting their talent before these young teenagers could stand out as exceptional (Bloom, 1985).

Social and Psychological Well-Being

But is it worth it? Don't young people with these exceptional talents, creativ-ity, or brilliance pay a price when it comes to their social and psychological well-being? Doesn't being so intelligent or so talented create a host of emotional problems for them that other people their age don't have to put up with? No, not generally. Although it's tempting to conjure up images of psychologically dis-turbed geniuses like Vincent Van Gogh who cut off his ear in a fit of depression and despair, geniuses or highly creative people aren't significantly more prone to madness, suicide, depression, or to the sorts of social or personal miseries that the rest of us encounter. For example, some parents and teachers worry that putting mathematically precocious students into classes with much older students or into special accelerated programs will interfere with their social development. But this hasn't seemed to be the case (Richardson & Benbow, 1990). Considering mental health, friendship, and social skills, exceptionally gifted and creative adolescents get along as well as, or better than, most people their age (Colangelo & Kerr, 1990; Cornell, 1990; Harring, McCormick, & Harring, 1994; Tomlinson-Keasey & Little, 1990).

On the other hand, this same research shows that being extremely intelligent or extremely creative doesn't prevent these adolescents from having many of the same social or psychological problems as other people their age. So we shouldn't make the mistake of assuming that they don't need as much help as other teenagers when they're showing signs of stress or maladjustment. For example, being creative or intelligent doesn't prevent adolescents from being depressed or trying to kill themselves (Delisle, 1990; Hayes & Sloat, 1990). Like other adolescents, many gifted students also feel more anxious, more depressed, and lonelier during junior high school than during high school (Kline & Short, 1991a, 1991b). Life for gifted girls, though, is usually more stressful than for gifted boys, especially during their teenage years. Most highly intelligent girls feel more social rejection and receive less attention from their teachers and counselors than gifted boys—a topic we'll discuss at length in Chapters 6 and 10 (Hollinger, 1991; Kline & Short, 1991b; Sadker & Sadker, 1993).

EDUCATING CREATIVE AND GIFTED STUDENTS

As far as our public schools are concerned, many educators and parents believe we're not doing enough for our most talented students (Davis & Rimm, 1993). At present, nearly 5% of all students are enrolled in classes for the gifted and talented or academically gifted students, commonly referred to as **"GT"** or **"AT"** classes. But most of the adolescents who are chosen for these classes are selected on the basis of their former grades and their IQ scores, which excludes many students who are extremely creative in areas such as art or music (Davis & Rimm, 1993).

Other questions also arise: How should we educate the gifted? How much money should we devote to their education relative to other students? Because girls, minorities, and low-income students have been so underrepresented in gifted programs, how should we decide which students to accept? Moreover, because federal support for gifted education plummeted during the Reagan years and forced many schools to abandon these programs, how are we going to pay for those programs that already exist, let alone fund new programs? For example, should we, as some schools already are doing, use Howard Gardner's theories of multiple intelligence to identify gifted students? Or, as critics contend, will this result in too many students being allowed into these specially funded programs for the gifted? As we will see in Chapter 10, our society is confronted with the awesome challenge of trying to figure out how to provide the best education for

How have your special talents and intelligence
affected your development?

gifted, average, and mentally handicapped students at a time when our national
achievement scores are falling and the cost of education is rising.

CONCLUSION

As we have seen, Piagetian research and the research on information processing have contributed greatly to our understanding of the differences between
children's and adolescents' reasoning. Likewise, the psychometricians have
refined traditional IQ tests and have offered us new ways of defining and measuring human intelligence. As our research continues to become more sophisticated and more expansive, many of our stereotypes about the gifted and the
retarded also are falling by the wayside, providing many of these young people
with an easier adolescence. As discussed in the next chapter, the research on cognitive development also is providing many insights into adolescents' reasoning
and behavior in moral and social situations.

Review/Test Questions

1. How do the psychometric, stage theories, and information processing approaches to adolescents' cognitive development differ?

2. Describe each of Piaget's stages of cognitive development by providing specific examples of behavior that demonstrate the major advances within each stage.

3. How do Sternberg's and Gardner's definitions of intelligence differ from those tested by traditional IQ tests?

4. What are the strengths and weaknesses in Piaget's theories?

5. What are the advantages and disadvantages of traditional IQ tests?

6. How are adolescents affected by our prevailing definitions of intelligence and creativity?

7. How do IQ scores seem to be related to environmental and to genetic factors?

8. What are some of the myths surrounding gifted, creative, and mentally handicapped adolesccents and what statistics or research refute these myths?

9. In what ways are highly creative and gifted adolescents different from other people their age?

10. What issues are we having to confront in regard to educating creative, gifted, and mentally handicapped students?

11. What causes mental retardation?

12. What myths about mentally retarded people has our research helped dispel?

13. Using a situation that adolescents typically encounter, provide a specific example of: cognitive dissonance, egocentrism, formal and concrete reasoning.

14. Provide a specific example of valid, invalid, reliable, and unreliable ways of measuring and testing.

15. Describe five specific types of problems that adolescents usually are able to solve but that typically confuse younger children.

Questions for Discussion and Self-Exploration

1. What's your IQ and how do you feel about it? If you had a child with a relatively low IQ score, would you tell him or her what the score was? Why?

2. How would you devise an IQ test that was fair to people regardless of race, gender, or cultural background?

3. How should teachers and counselors use students' IQ scores?

4. How do you feel about segregating children into special classes for slow, fast, or gifted students on the basis of their IQ scores? Why?

5. How do you feel when you're around a mentally retarded person? Why? How have your feelings changed as you've aged?

6. What do you believe we should be doing differently in our schools for mentally retarded and for gifted adolescents?

7. What experiences in your family or at school encouraged your creativity or your special skill? Which discouraged your creativity or your talent?

8. In what ways do you believe your family and your teachers have helped your cognitive development? In what ways have they hindered you?

9. When you read the story about Christopher Nolan, how do you feel? Who or what do you believe is responsible for his success?

10. How well do you believe Piaget's theories explain your cognitive development?

Glossary

accommodation, p. 84
assimilation, p. 84
associativity, p. 81
A.T. or A.G., p. 95
cognitive dissonance, p. 84
cognitive socialization
    approach, p. 90
class inclusion, p. 81
concrete operations, p. 81
conservation, p. 81
convergent thinking, p. 92
critical thinking, p. 82
culture fair test, p. 75

disequilibrium, p. 84
divergent thinking, p. 92
Down's syndrome, p. 91
egocentrism, p. 81
formal operations, p. 82
G.T., p. 95
information processing theo-
    ries, p. 67
kinesthetic intelligence, p. 73
mentally retarded, p. 90
object permanence, p. 80
Piagetian psychologists, p. 67
preoperational stage, p. 80

psychometrics, p. 67
reliability, p. 75
reversibility, p. 81
rule of equivalence, p. 81
schema, p. 84
sensorimotor stage, p. 80
serialization, p. 82
Stanford-Binet, p. 68
SOMPA, p. 75
validity, p. 75
WAIS-R, p. 68
WISC-III R, p. 68

References

Anastasi, A. (1988). *Psychological testing.* New York: MacMillan.

Baltes, P., & Baltes, M. (1993). *Successful aging.* New York: Cambridge University Press.

Bloom, B. (1985). *Developing talent in young people.* New York: Ballantine.

Bower, G. (1982). Mood and memory. *American Psychologist, 36,* 129–148.

Brown, R., & Kulik, J. (1977). Flashbulb memories. *Cognition, 5,* 73–99.

Burbules, N., & Linn, M. (1988). Response to contradiction: Scientific reasoning during adolescence. *Journal of Educational Psychology, 80,* 67–75.

Colangelo, N., & Kerr, B. (1990). Extreme academic talent. *Journal of Educational Psychology, 82,* 404–409.

Cole, M., & Means, B. (1981). *Comparative studies of how people think.* Cambridge, MA: Harvard University Press.

Cornell, D. (1990). Self-concept and peer status among gifted program youth. *Educational Psychology, 82,* 456–463.

Davis, G., & Rimm, S. (1993). *Education of the gifted and talented.* New York: Allyn & Bacon.

Delisle, J. (1990). The gifted adolescent at risk. *Journal for the Education of the Gifted, 13,* 212–228.

Drotar, D. (1985). *New directions in failure to thrive.* New York: Plenum.

Elliott, R. (1987). *Litigating intelligence: IQ tests, special education and social science in the courtroom.* Westport, CT: Auburn.

Feurerstein, R. (1979). *The dynamic assessment of retarded performers.* Baltimore, MD: University Park Press.

Gardner, H. (1993). *Multiple intelligences.* New York: Basic Books.

Guilford, J. (1967). *The nature of human intelligence.* New York: McGraw Hill.

Hale, S. (1990). A global developmental trend in cognitive processing speed. *Child Development, 61,* 653–663.

Harring, N., McCormick, L., & Harring, T. (1994). *Exceptional children and youth.* New York: MacMillan.

Hayes, M., & Sloat, R. (1990). Suicide and the gifted adolescent. *Journal for the Education of the Gifted, 13,* 229–244.

Herstein, R., & Murray, C. (1994). *The bell curve.*

New York: Free Press.

Hollinger, C. (1991). Facilitating the career development of gifted young women. *Roeper Review, 13*, 135–139.

Inhelder, B., & Piaget, J. (1958). *The growth of logical thinking from childhood through adolescence.* New York: Basic Books.

Jones, C. (1992). *Enhancing self-concepts and achievement of mildly handicapped students.* New York: Charles Thomas.

Keating, D. (1990). Adolescent thinking. In S. Feldman & G. Elliot (Eds.). *At the threshold.* Cambridge, MA: Harvard University Press.

Khatena, J., & Torrance, P. (1976). *Khatena Torrance creative perceptions inventory.* Chicago, IL: Stoelting.

Kline, B., & Short, E. (1991a). Changes in the emotional resilience of gifted adolescent boys and girls. *Roeper Review, 68*, 184–187.

Kline, B., & Short, E. (1991b). Changes in emotional resilience of gifted adolescent females. *Roeper Review, 13*, 118–121.

Kuhn, D. (1991). Higher order reasoning in adolescence. In R. Lerner, A. Petersen & J. Brooks-Gunn (Eds.), *Encyclopedia of adolescence* (pp. 917–920). New York: Garland.

Linn, M., & Songer, N. (1991). Cognitive and conceptual change in adolescence. *American Journal of Education, 99*, 379–417.

Locurto, C. (1991). *Sense and nonsense about IQ.* Westport, CT: Greenwood Press.

Lonner, W. (1990). An overview of cross-cultural testing and assessment. In R. Brislin (Ed.), *Applied cross-cultural psychology.* Newbury Park, CA: Sage.

Lozoff, B. (1989). Nutrition and behavior. *American Psychologist, 44*, 231–236.

Matson, J., & Mullick, J. (1990). *Handbook of mental retardation.* Elmsford, NY: Pergamon.

McCloskey, M. (1983). Intuitive physics. *Scientific American, 248*, 122–130.

Mercer, J., & Lewis, J. (1978). *System of multicultural pluralistic assessment.* New York: Psychological Corporation.

Nolan, C. (1990). *Under the eye of the clock.* New York: St. Martin's.

Overton, W., & Byrnes, J. (1991). Cognitive development. In R. Lerner, A. Petersen & J. Brooks-Gunn (Eds.), *Encyclopedia of adolescence.* New York: Garland.

Overton, W., & Montangero, J. (1991). Jean Piaget. In R. Lerner, A. Petersen & J. Brooks-Gunn (Eds.), *Encyclopedia of adolescence.* New York: Garland.

Perkins, D., Segal, J. & Voss, J. (1992). *Informal reasoning and education.* Hillsdale, NJ: Erlbaum.

Piaget, J. (1972). Intellectual evolution from adolescence to adulthood. *Human Development, 15*, 1–12.

Plomin, R., DeFries, J., & McClearn, G. (1990). *Behavioral genetics.* New York: Freeman.

Resnick, L. (1986). *Education and learning to think.* Washington, DC: National Research Council.

Richardson, T., & Benbow, C. (1990). Long-term effects of acceleration on the emotional adjustment of mathematically precocious youths. *Journal of Educational Psychology, 82*, 464–470.

Rybash, J., Roodin, P., & Santrock, J. (1991). *Adult development and aging.* Dubuque, IA: W. C. Brown.

Sadker, D., & Sadker, M. (1993). *Failing at fairness: How America's schools cheat girls.* New York: MacMillan.

Salt, P., Galler, J., & Ramsey, F. (1988). The influence of early malnutrition on behavioral development. *Development and Behavioral Pediatrics, 9*, 1–5.

Seisberg, R. (1993). *Creativity: Beyond the myth of genius.* New York: Freeman.

Snyderman, M., & Rothman, C. (1987). Survey of expert opinion on intelligence and aptitude testing. *American Psychologist, 42*, 137–144.

Spitz, H. (1986). *The raising of intelligence.* Hillsdale, NJ: Erlbaum.

Sternberg, R. (1985). *Triarchic theory of intelligence.* Cambridge, England: Cambridge University Press.

Sue, D.W. (1991). *Counseling the culturally differ-ent.* New York: Wiley.

Terman, L. (1959). *The gifted group at mid-life.* Stanford, CA: Stanford University Press.

Thorndike, R., Hagan, E., & Sattler, J. (1985). *Stanford-Binet intelligence scale.* Chicago, IL: Riverside.

Tomlinson-Keasey, C., & Little, T. (1990). Predicting educational attainment, occupational achievement, intellectual skill, and personal adjustment among gifted men and women. *Journal of Educational Psychology, 82,* 442–455.

Torrance, P. (1966). *Torrance tests for creative thinking.* Princeton, NJ: Personnel Press.

Viadero, D. (1986). Lead in water poses major health risk to schoolchildren. *Education Week, 6,* 12.

Vygotsky, L. (1978). *Mind in society.* Cambridge, MA: Harvard University Press.

Wechsler, D. (1981a). *Wechsler adult intelligence scale—Revised.* New York: Psychological Corporation.

Wechsler, D. (1981b). *Wechsler intelligence scale for children—Revised.* New York: Psychological Corporation.

White, J. (1982). *Rejection.* Reading, MA: Addison Wesley.

Williams, R. (1975). The bitch 100: A culture specific test. *Journal of Afro American Issues, 3,* 103–116.

SOCIAL, MORAL, AND EGO DEVELOPMENT

CHAPTER OUTLINE

KEY QUESTIONS ADDRESSED IN THIS CHAPTER

1. According to Piaget and Kohlberg, in what ways do our moral and social reasoning skills change from childhood through adolescence?

2. How do enmeshment, triangulation, and generational boundaries within the family affect social and ego development during adolescence?

3. What kinds of relationships with parents interfere with healthy ego development and mature social reasoning?

4. What are the shortcomings of Piaget's and Kohlberg's theories?

5. According to social learning theorists, what factors influence our moral and social development as adolescents?

6. How do parenting styles relate to adolescent ego development?

7. How does early childhood relate to adolescent social development?

8. How do fathers affect adolescents' ego development?

9. What are Erikson's and Freud's stages of ego development and what issues need to be resolved at each of these stages?

10. Why are some adolescents much less mature than others in terms of their ego development and social and moral reasoning?

DEFINITIONS OF MATURITY AND IMMATURITY

Why is it that some adolescents are much more close-minded, stubborn, judgmental, critical, and intolerant than others? Why is a 14-year-old sometimes more mature than a 19-year-old when it comes to listening to other people's opinions, accepting other people's mistakes, and recognizing the motives underlying another person's behavior? Why are some adolescents so self-righteous and unwilling to admit their own mistakes? Are these characteristics that adolescents can outgrow or can be trained to change, or are they relatively permanent aspects of their personalities that have been with them since early childhood? In short, why do some teenagers think and behave so immaturely when others their age are so much more mature? To researchers and psychologists these forms of maturity or immaturity are matters of social and moral reasoning and ego development.

SOCIAL REASONING

Social cognition or **social reasoning** is the way we apply our cognitive skills to our interactions with other people (Bornstein & Bruner, 1993; Kurtines & Gewirtz, 1992; Lapsley, 1990). Our social reasoning forms the basis for how we act toward other people, how we judge them, and how we interpret their behavior. Social cognition includes the skills and attitudes that are at the very root of being able to establish satisfying, loving relationships: empathizing with other people, being tolerant of others' opinions, interpreting people's behavior from several viewpoints, listening to other people's opinions, being willing to change our minds about someone in the face of new data or new experiences, and forgiving others when they make mistakes or fail to live up to our expectations.

An important aspect of mature social cognition is becoming less naive and more perceptive in terms of being able to recognize the motives underlying other people's behavior. For example, if you discover that your father has lied to you about the reason why he and your mother got divorced, you can see that his motives might have been good if he was trying to protect you from knowing something that could hurt you, even though you still know that his lying was bad. In this case, if your social reasoning skills are mature, you are more willing to forgive your parent because you can understand his or her motives for lying to you.

Mature social reasoning also involves learning how to evaluate what you hear, what you read, or what you're told in terms of how trustworthy or how biased the information might be. Adolescents with immature reasoning skills can be more easily fooled or brainwashed into believing things that aren't true because they're not as sophisticated in terms of considering the motives that underlie what people say and do. They're also not as sophisticated in terms of being able to see a situation from several different points of view at the same time. For example, an immature 16-year-old might not realize that his mother can be loving, but also can lie and deceive when it comes to certain topics. His immature social reasoning makes him view his mother in overly simplistic ways as either all good and saintly or all evil and wicked. When his reasoning matures, however, he'll be able to integrate his mother's good side and her bad side in a way that allows him to perceive her more realistically.

As our social reasoning matures, we also learn to base our opinions of people on their general, overall patterns of behavior rather than judging them on the basis of how they behave in one particular situation or how they behave around one particular person. For example, a teenager with immature social reasoning might dump her best friend because "she always ignores me when we get around boys, which proves she doesn't value me at all." Rather than recognizing that her friend's overall pattern of behavior is kind and loving, she converts the situation into an "either-or" choice. This tendency to interpret and react to situations and to categorize people in overly simplistic extremes is called **dualistic** or **absolutist thinking.** Everything and everyone is either one extreme or the other, as if there are only one or two absolute choices or interpretations for any given situation. For example, if her stepfather does something that makes her father mad, the immature teenager might decide once and for all that her stepfather is "a rotten person who never treats anyone well," rather than concluding, as a more mature teenager would, "my stepfather and father don't get along, but basically they're both nice guys." Obviously teenagers with immature reasoning have more trouble getting along with people because they interpret the world in such simplistic, absolute, dualistic ways: right or wrong, good or bad, love or hate, honest or dishonest, brilliant or stupid.

This dualistic reasoning also contributes to prejudice and stereotyping. In this regard, it's important to realize that one of the crucial changes in maturing adolescents is the ability to recognize their own parents' shortcomings and to abandon their child-like stereotypes of "mommy" and "daddy." In fact, adolescents who are still seeing their own parents as their heroes or as saints often are having trouble getting along with other teenagers as a consequence of their childish visions of the world. In this sense, then, the teenager who angrily accuses his or her parent of being a "fallen hero" is showing some progress toward maturity. Likewise, parents who are overwrought when their teenage child no longer sees them as "perfect" are trying to imprison the family in a fantasy land where parents are to be adored and revered, rather than loved for the flawed human beings we all are.

Obviously one of the most important abilities that adolescents must acquire in order to get along maturely with other human beings is the ability to empathize—the ability to recognize another person's feelings and points of view, then the ability to put our own feelings and opinions aside from time to time for the sake of a relationship. With empathy comes the understanding that many situations are too complex for a simple right or wrong judgment or a simple solution. With empathy comes greater forgiveness, greater tolerance, greater compassion. With empathy comes more self-restraint in terms of trying not to say or do things that would hurt other people.

Finally, a greater understanding of our own behavior and our own motives comes with mature social reasoning (Damon & Hart, 1988). As we become more empathic and less critical of other people, we see more of our own imperfections, prejudices, and mistakes. We are more willing to admit our mistakes, to apologize, and to recognize our own hypocrisy in judging others by standards we don't always live up to either. We are also better at recognizing the motives underlying our behavior. For example, if your father goes away on an exciting vacation without you, you realize that your anger at him when he comes home is motivated by your own jealousy, not by any wrong your father has done to you. Then, too,

---

Insert 4–1

Immature Social and Moral Reasoning

The following characteristics describe adolescents whose general ways of reasoning and behaving are egocentric. These traits represent **preconventional reasoning** and **arrested ego development**. How would you describe yourself at the age of 16? And now? How would you rate each of your parents?

1 = almost never, infrequently   10 = almost always, usually

Me/Parents

____ ____ **Absolutist/Dualistic**
Reasons in terms of "either-or," absolutes and extremes

____ ____ **Close-minded**
Rejects data that contradict his/her beliefs

____ ____ **Defensive**
Rationalizes and gets defensive rather than admit mistakes or apologize

____ ____ **Egocentric/Self-centered**
Inconsiderate of other people's feelings

____ ____ **Impulsive/Impetuous/Unreflective: Uncontrolled ego**
Fails to consider consequences of his/her behavior

____ ____ **Indecisive**
Easily confused or unable to make decisions

____ ____ **Inflexible/Brittle ego**
Adapts poorly to change or the unfamiliar

____ ____ **Intolerant/Critical**
Sets high standards for others and quick to reject, punish, and criticize

____ ____ **Irresponsible/Helpless/Self-pitying**
Whatever happens, it's never his/her fault

____ ____ **Judgmental/Punitive**
Harshly judgmental without considering other's motives or circumstances

____ ____ **Naive/Gullible**
Unable to recognize the motives underlying other people's behavior

____ ____ **Self-righteous/ Hypocritical**
Unwilling to judge self by high standards applied to others

____ ____ **Self-conscious/The imaginary audience**
Assumes everyone is always watching and talking about him/her

____ ____ **Stereotyped reasoning**
Stereotypes others and exaggerates their behaviors

____ ____ **Unempathic/Insensitive**
Unable to consider others' feelings and perspectives

____ ____ **Unforgiving**
Judges harshly and forgives reluctantly

mature social reasoning means learning more self-control. That is, we consider the consequences of what we say and do before blurting things out or acting impetuously—not only the consequence for ourselves, but the consequences for other people as well. In short, if your social reasoning is advancing during adolescence, you are becoming less self-deceptive, less egocentric, less close-minded, less self-righteous, less judgmental, and less pig-headed. Obviously these changes make you easier to get along with and help you establish close friendships and satisfying romantic relationships. As you can see from Insert 4–1, the ways of thinking and behaving that characterize adolescents with immature social reasoning, which are referred to as **egocentric thinking,** aren't appealing at any age.

MORAL REASONING

Another aspect of our thinking and behavior that usually improves during adolescence is our moral reasoning. Many of the skills involved in social and moral reasoning are the same. Moral reasoning refers to the ways we think about right and wrong and our subsequent behavior, especially in ethically difficult situations. Moral reasoning, therefore, includes such questions as: On what grounds do we judge the rightness or wrongness of particular acts in ourselves and in others? What punishment is fair for a particular mistake or crime? What extenuating circumstances should we consider before judging or punishing people? How closely should we abide by the rules or orders handed down by parents or authorities? When should we trust our own judgments, especially if they go against what we've been told by those in authority? When should we put someone else's needs or feelings or welfare ahead of our own or ahead of our family's?

Not only are researchers trying to find out how children and adolescents might differ in the ways they go about answering such decisions, they also are trying to determine why some of us never seem to develop very mature ways of reasoning about ethical or moral issues. Why are some people so judgmental and unforgiving while others are tolerant and kind-spirited? Why do some of us so sheepishly follow the codes or rules laid down by those in authority, even when it leads to cruel or inhumane treatment of other people? Why are some of us so rigid and self-righteous when it comes to our own particular beliefs?

ADOLESCENT VERSUS ADULT REASONING

As you study the descriptions in Insert 4–1, you're probably saying to yourself, "But a lot of adults I know behave like this!" And you're probably right (though you've probably also decided that those descriptions don't fit you, of course). To begin with, then, you need to know that the research isn't telling us that all of us will achieve advanced levels of thinking and behaving by the time we leave adolescence. As the preceding chapter showed, many adolescents and adults don't reach Piaget's higher levels of cognitive thinking. Likewise, the social and moral reasoning of some adults remains remarkably immature. Also keep in mind that our overall level of social or moral reasoning doesn't predict how we'll behave in every single situation. At times even the most immature, egocentric teenager or adult will behave with empathy and unselfishness; and under some circumstances even the most mature thinker will behave in self-centered, childish ways. The descriptions of our levels of social and moral reasoning, therefore, aren't meant to predict how teenagers or adults will interpret or behave in every conceivable situation. These levels of reasoning represent the predominant or characteristic ways that an individual thinks and behaves in most situations, most of the time.

During adolescence, however, most of us do become less egocentric (Bornstein & Bruner, 1993; Damon, 1988; Eisenberg, 1991; Keating, 1990). For example, older adolescents usually are more forgiving and less punitive than younger adolescents when it comes to how they view other people's mistakes, crimes, and "sins." As older adolescents, most of us also tend to be more tolerant of other people's political and religious views (Adelson, 1991; Avery, 1989; Benson, Donahue, & Erickson, 1989; Kurtines & Gewirtz, 1992). Most parents also tell us that adolescents are easier to get along with when they're older because they're less egocentric and more empathic (Steinberg, 1990).

It isn't possible, of course, to pinpoint an exact age when we make our greatest advances in social and moral reasoning. Some experts believe we mature the most from 11 to 14, mainly reaching our adult level of reasoning by the time we're 16 (Keating, 1990). Other experts, however, believe that certain aspects of our reasoning, such as empathy, might not reach their full maturity until late adolescence or our early 20s (Lapsley, 1990). Then again, as we'll see later in this chapter, when we mature might have more to do with certain dynamics within our families than with our actual age.

EXPLANATIONS FOR ADOLESCENTS' SOCIAL MATURITY AND IMMATURITY

Basically there are four different explanations for why some adolescents think and behave more maturely or more immaturely than others: (1) cognitive stage theories, (2) psychoanalytic theories, (3) social learning theories, and (4) biological theories. In this chapter we examine the cognitive stage, psychoanalytic, and social learning theories regarding parenting styles. In the next chapter we examine the biological views.

According to cognitive stage theorists, our social and moral maturity is primarily determined by the level of mental development we have achieved—a level that is determined both by our chronological age and by the types of experiences we've had throughout childhood. Arguing against this, social learning theorists believe that our teenage maturity is primarily determined by the behaviors our parents or other adult caretakers have taught us since birth. Our adult caretakers also influence our maturity because we model ourselves after certain aspects of how they think and behave. In comparison to cognitive stage theorists, then, social learning theorists give more credit—or, in some cases, blame—to our parents and other caretakers for how we think and behave as adolescents. On the other hand, the psychoanalytic researchers tell us that our social and moral

How socially mature were you as an adolescent?

reasoning as teenagers is part of our overall ego development—a process that has been occurring since birth and that has been occurring in distinct stages. The psychoanalytic and social learning theorists agree on one very important point: How maturely or immaturely we think and behave as adolescents is closely related to how our parents have related to us from birth. So let's start by examining the cognitive stage theorists' explanations for our social and moral reasoning as adolescents.

COGNITIVE STAGE THEORIES OF SOCIAL AND MORAL REASONING

PIAGET'S THEORIES

According to Piaget and his followers, our social and moral reasoning develops in stages, as discussed in Chapter 3 (Piaget, 1965). In testing these theories,

Piagetians give children and adolescents hypothetical situations involving moral dilemmas and ask them what they would do and why. For example, Piagetians ask young children: Which boy is "naughtier"—the boy who breaks two cups while he is trying to sneak jam out of the closet or the boy who breaks 12 cups by accident?

According to Piaget, between the ages of 4 and 7 our reasoning is based on very simplistic rules because we are in the stage of **moral realism.** In this stage we determine what is right and wrong according to a few overly simplistic, rigid rules handed down to us by our elders. When anyone, including ourselves, misbehaves, we judge the behavior on the basis of a series of fairly simplistic questions: Forgetting the person's motives or intentions, what was the consequence of the act, and how much damage was actually done? How likely is it the person will be caught? Had someone in a position of authority explained that this behavior was wrong?

According to the ways a child reasons, our motives and intentions matter neither in terms of deciding our guilt or innocence nor in deciding how we should be punished. So the young child decides that the boy who broke 12 cups is definitely naughtier and should be punished more than the boy who broke two cups, even though the two-cup culprit had the intentions and motives of a thief. Our egocentric reasoning relies almost exclusively on the rules and ethics handed down by those in positions of authority—namely, our parents. These rules and moral codes are not to be questioned, no matter what the extenuating circumstances. Once again, then, the poor clumsy child who broke the 12 cups is judged guilty and deserves to be punished because he did more damage.

How has your moral reasoning changed since adolescence?

As we approach adolescence, Piaget believes we enter the stage of **autonomous morality** in which our reasons for obeying or disobeying rules have more to do with our own values and less to do with being afraid of getting caught and punished. So, for example, teenagers who are still stuck in a child-like stage of reasoning might say they don't do drugs only because they're afraid of getting caught, while those who are developing more mature reasoning will say they don't do drugs because they've decided for themselves that drugs might harm their bodies. If we're adopting more mature reasoning, we become more concerned with considering the motives underlying a person's mistakes or "sins" and more concerned with the extenuating circumstances before passing judgments on ourselves or on others. In the case of Piaget's hypothetical story about the boys and the cups, we'd ask ourselves: Was the boy who was trying to snitch the jam hungry? Had he been unfairly deprived of food by his parents? Was he simply being a little glutton or in fact trying to pester his mother? If we are becoming more autonomous in our thinking, we start to question the rules, ethical codes, and punishments passed on to us by parents, political and religious leaders, and other authorities. Given our advanced thinking abilities, we start to see the contradictions in people's behavior and we recognize the hypocrisy in the world around us.

If our moral reasoning matures, we also begin to see more than one side to a story—in fact, we see more than two sides, or three sides, or a dozen sides. We begin to understand that some rules and punishments need to be modified because there isn't a simple answer or simple solution to what is right and wrong in a particular situation. It's not as easy for us as it was when we were reasoning childishly to separate the "bad guys" from the "good guys." We look beyond the mistakes people make and consider the motives and circumstances that existed at the time. For instance, we see that a person might steal or lie or cheat for a "good" reason and so shouldn't be punished so harshly. We also recognize that a person's mistakes in one situation don't necessarily represent their overall, general behavior. For example, an adolescent with mature reasoning can understand that a person who is poor might cheat on an income tax return in order to get enough money to help a sick spouse, but this doesn't necessarily mean he or she is "an untrustworthy person."

In the stage of autonomous morality, situations that once seemed so clear-cut and simple to us as young children now seem complicated, unclear, ambiguous, and unsolvable. We are taking off the rose-colored glasses of our childhood, which made us see situations and people in terms of "black or white," "good or bad." With more autonomous thinking comes more empathy, more perspective taking, more tolerance, more forgiveness—less critical, less judgmental, less self-righteous attitudes toward others and toward ourselves. Unfortunately, adolescents who remain at more child-like levels of reasoning also remain more unforgiving, intolerant, critical, judgmental, and harsh. The famous adolescent psychologist Joseph Adelson compares adolescents with these more immature levels of reasoning to Atilla the Hun when it comes to the swift and harsh ways they judge and punish other people (Adelson, 1982).

Insert 4–2

Kohlberg's Stages of Moral Development

Childhood: Preconventional Reasoning

Stage 1: Heteronomous Morality

Obeys rules mainly out of fear of punishment

Respects and obeys those in authority

Reasons egocentrically: Does not consider others' needs or perspectives

Stage 2: Individualism

Obeys rules in order to get rewards

Develops the concept of fairness and equal exchange in relationships

Places emphasis on keeping agreements and promises in deciding what's moral

Begins to recognize that other people have needs and feelings of their own

Early Adolescence: Conventional Reasoning

Stage 3: Interpersonal Expectations and Conformity: Good Boy-Nice Girl

Values mutual agreements and society's expectations more than individual's needs or circumstances

Tries to live up to other people's expectations

Makes decisions on the basis of what others think and approve

Believes in Golden Rule: Do to others as you would have them do to you

Stage 4: Social Systems and Conscience: Law and Order

Fulfills duties and abides by laws to maintain a fixed order

Upholds the status quo

Judges goodness on basis of contributions to a society or group

Tries to avoid any changes in the established order of things

Considers an individual's needs secondary to those of society

Late Adolescence/Early Adulthood: Postconventional Reasoning

Stage 5: Social Contact

Realizes that each society's rules and values differ

Believes that certain values, such as freedom, should be applied to all people

Emphasizes equality and mutual obligation within a democratic system

Reasons from a rational, not an emotional, perspective

Recognizes that certain moral dilemmas are too complicated to resolve

Finds it difficult to integrate moral, legal, and societal viewpoints

Stage 6: Universal Principles

Believes that principles should take precedence over society's or authorities' rules and codes

Will violate laws when necessary to act in accord with a principle

Transcends any one society's or any one religion's view of morality

KOHLBERG'S THEORIES

Perhaps the most well-known of Piaget's followers was the late Lawrence Kohlberg, whose research on moral development has dominated the field (Kohlberg, 1984). As Insert 4–2 shows, Kohlberg categorized our moral reasoning into stages. Like Piaget, Kohlberg tested his theories by giving children and adolescents hypothetical situations like the one described in Insert 4–3 and then asking them to explain how and why they came up with their answers. Like Piaget, Kohlberg found that most children are in the **preconventional stage** in which we reason very **egocentrically**—judging people and interpreting situations from only our own self-centered point of view. As we move into adolescence, however, Kohlberg believes that most of us start becoming less egocentric, progressing toward a much less self-centered, less judgmental position.

Kohlberg sees us slowly and erratically advancing from **conventional reasoning** to **postconventional reasoning** during adolescence. Those of us with conventional reasoning are still pretty conforming in terms of following the rules and believing in the ethics passed down from those in authority. For the most part, we judge ourselves and other people in terms of society's conventional expectations and our own parents' particular set of rules and beliefs. As a consequence, as adolescents

---

Insert 4–3

Kohlberg's Tests of Moral Reasoning

In trying to determine children's and adolescents' stages of moral reasoning, Kohlberg and his followers asked them to respond to a series of questions about certain hypothetical dilemmas. How would you respond to Kohlberg's questions about Heinz's moral dilemma: Is what Heinz did wrong? Is it a husband's moral duty to steal for his wife in a situation like this? Did the druggist have the right to charge so much for the medicine? What should a good husband do in a situation like this? Why?

The Story of Heinz

In Europe a woman was near death from a special kind of cancer. There was one drug that the doctors thought might save her. It was a form of radium that a druggist in the same town had recently discovered. The drug was expensive to make, but the druggist was charging 10 times what it cost him to make the drug. The sick woman's husband, Heinz, went to everyone he knew to borrow the money, but he could get only half of what the drug cost. He told the druggist that his wife was dying and asked him to sell the drug cheaper or let him pay later. But the druggist said, "No. I discovered the drug so I deserve to make money from it." So the desperate husband broke into the druggist's store and stole the drug for his wife.

we aren't especially tolerant of religious, political, or personal views that differ from our own. As we move toward more postconventional reasoning, we become increasingly open-minded, flexible, tolerant, and universal in our values and thinking. We realize that rules and moral codes are relative and flexible, often determined by one particular religion's or one society's values. Consequently, we begin to act in accord with our own internalized principles, even if this entails breaking laws or defying authorities or religious teachings that we once yielded to when we were younger.

So how many of us get to these more advanced levels of reasoning? According to Kohlberg's model for measuring moral development, only about 10% of us reach the most advanced levels of reasoning in our early 20s. Likewise, very few of us reach the stage of "social systems and conscience" before the age of 10, but nearly 50% of us reach this stage as adults. On the other hand, how advanced we become on Kohlberg's scale is also related to how much formal education we receive after high school and how much interaction we have with people who think more maturely than we do. For example, college graduates usually become more mature in terms of their moral and social reasoning than they were when they entered college, as do high-school students who regularly participate in class discussions with students who are reasoning at more mature levels (Kohlberg, 1984; Kurtines & Gewirtz, 1991; Rest, 1986).

THE IMAGINARY AUDIENCE AND PERSONAL FABLE

Another explanation for why young adolescents generally are not as good as older adolescents at empathizing with other people is that they are being held captive by two beliefs: the imaginary audience and the personal fable. Agreeing with Piaget, the psychologist David Elkind argues that young adolescents are still in a cognitive stage that holds them back from developing empathy and from considering others' perspectives. Elkind tells us that young adolescents are extremely self-focused and self-conscious because they're preoccupied with the idea that they're continually being watched, monitored, and judged by other people, even by people who don't even know them and who'll never see them again. Although in reality there is no audience out there continually observing or judging them, the belief in this **imaginary audience** makes young adolescents too self-focused to consider what's going on in other people's lives or what feelings and perspectives other people are having (Elkind, 1978; Elkind & Bowen, 1979). Although not all psychologists agree with Elkind that young adolescents believe in an imaginary audience any more than a number of adults do, it is nonetheless true that most of us do tend to be less self-conscious and less self-absorbed at the end of adolescence than we were at the beginning (Hudson & Gray, 1986).

Elkind's second explanation for why young adolescents usually are more self-absorbed and inconsiderate than older adolescents is their belief in the personal fable. The **personal fable** is the belief that we are somehow magically invincible or immune from the natural laws and consequences that apply to other people. We believe that no harm can come to us, as it does to other people, if we do things like use drugs, get drunk and drive, or have sex without using a contraceptive. Our personal fable is a form of arrogance and self-centeredness that gives us a false sense of security. We can take risks and say and do foolish or unkind things without having to pay any penalty. In terms of our social and moral reasoning, the result is that we often don't consider other people's feelings or opinions because we act as though we are somehow beyond the laws that apply to human relationships. Elkind believes we move into a more advanced stage of cognitive development by middle adolescence, leaving our personal fables and our imaginary audience behind.

Shortcomings of Cognitive Stage Theories

How well do the cognitive stage theories hold up? How accurately do they predict the differences between younger and older adolescents? Are children and adolescents as different as Piaget and Kohlberg maintain? In their favor, these theories are fairly accurate in that our thinking does advance in the sequence proposed by Piaget and Kohlberg. For example, we do begin questioning those in authority before we develop our own personal code of ethics. Other parts of cognitive stage theories, however, don't hold up as well (Eisenberg, 1991; Keating, 1990; Kurtines & Gewirtz, 1992; Lapsley, 1990).

First, the cognitive stages seem to occur much later than predicted. Moreover, some very young children think and behave in ways that are supposed to occur only much later in life. Because the power of a stage theory rests primarily on how accurately it predicts the ages at which we will develop certain skills, this is a major shortcoming in Piaget's and Kohlberg's models. There is also the question of how well our real life behavior actually matches our answers to the kinds of hypothetical situations posed by these experimenters. For example, high-school and college students whose scores on Piaget's tests showed them to be in the stage of formal operational reasoning behaved no less egocentrically than students whose scores showed them to be in the more childish level of the concrete operational stage (O'Connor & Nikolic, 1990).

Perhaps more important, social learning and psychoanalytic theorists show that our moral and social maturity as teenagers is closely tied to the ways we've been reinforced while growing up. Perhaps it's not so much which stage we're in as what ways of thinking our parents have taught us. For example, adolescent and college students' political reasoning is remarkably similar to their parents' (Liebes, Katz, & Ribak, 1991). As you'll see in the remainder of this chapter, our social reasoning and behavior is closely linked to the kind of relationship we had with each parent during our early childhood and to certain dynamics within our families. Such findings indicate that how we reason might be much less affected by a stage than by our childhood experiences—above all, by how our parents interact with us and with each other while we're growing up.

In addition, the ways that moral development has traditionally been measured have been criticized. Among others, James Rest points out that the hypothetical stories used to assess children and adolescents aren't very representative of real-life situations (Rest, 1986). Critics also point out that scoring Kohlberg's tests is complicated and subject to the experimenter's personal interpretations. To compensate for these shortcomings, Rest has developed his own test for measuring Kohlberg's stages of moral reasoning, the Defining Issues Test. One of Rest's stories, for example, asks adolescents a series of questions about whether the editor of the school's newspaper should defy the principal's orders to shut down the paper because some of the stories have caused students to start protesting against school policies that they consider unfair. Among the questions asked are: Does the principal have the right to tell the students what to do when the welfare of the school is at stake? Is the editor of the newspaper in any way violating other people's rights by publishing his or her own opinions?

Another criticism of Kohlberg's work is that it is culturally biased (Miller & Bersoff, 1992). According to Kohlberg, those of us who make our moral decisions on the basis of our individual rights are more advanced than those of us who put the community's needs first. In some cultures, however, considering the good of the group or community or valuing the sacredness of all forms of life is considered more ethical than valuing the individual's well-being and individual efforts. People living in cultures with these values, therefore, score lower on Kohlberg's tests and are considered to be less morally advanced than those of us raised in a society in which individuality is so heavily emphasized. The ways we're socialized to think and behave as males and females also influences our moral and social development. Indeed Kohlberg's theories have been criticized heavily for inadequately explaining female moral development because most of his research was conducted only with males—topics we delve into in the next chapter.

Perhaps the most important shortcoming of cognitive stage theories is this: Longitudinal studies show that many aspects of our moral and social reasoning and behavior are remarkably consistent from early childhood through adolescence. That is, some aspects of our personalities seem to be largely determined by our genetic inheritance, which, in turn, influences how we reason and behave socially and morally. Tolerance and empathy, for example, seem to be influenced by the interplay of our genetic temperament and our early childhood experiences with our mothers, as explained in the following sections. Moreover, many of us seem to reason and behave very much as we did when we were preschoolers when it comes to many aspects of our moral and social reasoning. Remember, though, that despite their shortcomings, cognitive stage theories are correct in predicting that most of us become at least somewhat more mature in our social and moral reasoning skills during our adolescence.

PSYCHOANALYTIC THEORIES OF DEVELOPMENT

DEFINING EGO DEVELOPMENT

Another way of looking at how our reasoning develops as we age is from the psychoanalytic perspective. Psychoanalytic theorists present their ideas in terms of the development of a person's ego. Although the word *ego* conjures up the negative images associated with the word *egotistical,* psychologists use the term in a positive sense. A person's **ego** is the basic structure around which his or her personality is organized (Hauser, Powers, & Noam, 1991; Lapsley, 1988; Marcia, 1991).

Ego development is the progress we make toward achieving two goals. The first step is to develop the kinds of thinking and behavior that enable us to get along well with people and eventually to form intimate, fulfilling, committed relationships. Obviously this involves learning how to think and behave in less self-centered ways. The other goal in ego development is to become self-reliant and separate enough from each of our parents to fashion an identity of our own. This process, referred to as **individuation,** begins in the first few years of our lives, reaching its highest pitch during adolescence. Individuation means learning to have thoughts, feelings, decisions, identities, and values that don't necessarily agree with those of our parents. Without becoming individuated, we are unable to become self-reliant or self-confident enough to form an identity that is truly our own.

Another way of looking at ego development is that from the time we're born, we're moving along two crisscrossing paths—the path to achieving intimacy with other human beings and the path to discovering "who am I?" apart from anyone

How have your race and gender affected your social maturity?

else. To succeed on either path, we have to accomplish the same two goals: to become less egocentric and to become individuated from our families. These paths are crisscrossing and intersecting because in order to have an intimate, fulfilling relationship with another person, we have to become self-reliant and individuated enough to have a self to offer.

Two aspects of ego development are especially worth noting: ego control and ego resilience. **Ego control** is basically synonymous with self-control—the ability to restrain our impulses by considering the impact our behavior has on other people. Rather than blurting out whatever we think or acting out whatever we feel, those of us who develop ego control usually stop to consider the consequences before we speak or act—the consequences for ourselves and for other people. Obviously this aspect of ego development makes it easier for us to get along well with other people, as well as to succeed in the world of work and school.

Another positive aspect of ego development is **ego resilience.** Those of us with a resilient ego adapt fairly well to change, the unpredictable, and the unfamiliar. We're generally able to modify our behavior in ways that suit the situations in which we find ourselves. For example, if we're at a party where we don't know many of the people, we can size up the situation and make pretty good decisions about how we ought to behave in that particular setting. In contrast, those of us with a **brittle ego** are fairly inflexible or rigid in terms of adapting to the unpredictable and the unfamiliar. We come across as uptight, nervous, uncomfortable, aggravated, or downright hostile and angry whenever we're in unfamiliar or unpredictable situations. For example, a teenager with a brittle ego has a much harder time adapting to a new stepparent or to college than does the teenager with a more resilient ego. As will be discussed in the next chapter, teenagers with extremely brittle egos can also be said to have a neurotic disposition.

Saying that an adolescent has a strong or healthy ego, therefore, doesn't imply anything negative in terms of selfishness or egotism. To the contrary, an adolescent with a well-developed ego behaves more unselfishly, more empathically, and more maturely than someone with a weak ego. When a teenager's ego has not matured very much beyond child-like, egocentric thinking and behavior, he or she is said to have **arrested** ("stopped") **ego development.** Compared to people their age, teenagers with arrested development get along more poorly with others, are not as self-reliant, have more psychological problems, and are less successful at creating an identity of their own (Block, 1971; Harter, 1990; Hauser, Powers, & Noam, 1991; Marcia, 1991).

The most well-known person to study ego development was Sigmund Freud. According to Freudian theories, the way your ego develops is primarily determined by early childhood experiences—above all, by the relationship you had with your mother. Thus, the basic structure of your personality (the ego) is shaped by the time your are 5 or 6 years old. More contemporary psychoanalytic theorists like Erik Erikson believe that Freudians place too much emphasis on our early childhood experiences and not enough on our experiences during adolescence and adulthood.

FREUD'S THEORIES

According to Freud, our maturity or immaturity and the ways we relate to people are primarily determined by our early childhood relationships with each parent. Early childhood is the crucial period for developing our expectations and lifelong patterns of thinking and behaving. Because our mother is almost always our primary caretaker, Freudians believe that the way she relates to us has the most profound impact on our ego development. From our mothers, we learn our fundamental attitudes about ourselves, about relating to other people, about what to expect from life, and about how to get what we want (S. Freud, 1931, 1949; A. Freud, 1958, 1977).

The Freudians also believe that we go through a sequence of stages during which we learn—or fail to learn—specific skills and attitudes that lead to the development of a mature ego. During each childhood stage, we either achieve more mature ways of thinking and behaving or we remain stuck in a child-like pattern from there on. In other words, those teenagers who are extremely immature and who get along poorly with people failed to acquire more mature ways of thinking and behaving at various stages as they grew up. By examining each of Freud's stages, we can see which behaviors and attitudes a troubled or immature teenager has failed to learn as a child.

Birth–age 2: Oral stage   Freud referred to this first period of life as the **oral stage.** If we feel securely loved by our parents, we acquire a sense of basic trust—the belief that our basic needs will be met by those who love us. Above all, Freudians believe that our lifelong sense of trust or distrust comes from our mothers. As infants, the question "Can I trust?" is answered by how well she meets our physical needs. This kind of trust is not to be confused with foolishly trusting every strange person we meet or with trusting everything that people tell us. The trust that psychologists are referring to is the attitude that we can depend on those who love us. If we feel this, we then feel secure and confident enough to interact with people outside our families and with the world around us. The more trust we develop at this age, the more self-confidence we carry with us throughout our lives. If we don't acquire this feeling of trust from other mothers, however, we interact fearfully and reluctantly from then on. For example, from the Freudian view, teenagers who seldom interact with their peers, who are extremely afraid or anxious in new situations, and who interact passively with the world can be seen as not having achieved this basic trust in the first few years of their lives.

Ages 2–4: Anal stage   If we've acquired trusting attitudes, then between the ages of 2 and 4 we attempt to become much more self-reliant—Freud's **anal stage.** This is the time for us to start seeing ourselves as people who are separate from each of our parents—the time to start the process of individuation that should proceed throughout childhood and adolescence. In this anal stage, both parents, especially the primary caretaker, have to encourage or sometimes even force us to become increasingly self-reliant and willing to assume the initiative for interacting with other children. At this time our parents are also supposed to teach us our lifelong attitudes about self-control. Primarily through toilet training, we learn our first lessons about the importance of self-control. So those children who do not succeed in becoming toilet trained, or feeding themselves, or learning other kinds of self-control like most children their age, will likely have problems related to poor self-control and impulsiveness throughout their lives. Likewise, those children who are overly disciplined or overly concerned about such issues as toilet training will likely have problems related to being too self-controlled and not relaxed enough—the condition Freudians refer to as "anal retentive."

Another extremely important lesson that needs to be learned in the anal stage is the understanding that we aren't the only people in the world who have needs and feelings. Our caretakers must teach us something about mutuality—the idea that we need to give, not only take, in a relationship. Learning about mutuality also lays the foundations for us to be empathic toward other people throughout our lives. Our primary caretaker must teach us that we can't continually do all the taking and act as though other people have no feelings and are here only to meet our needs. Indeed this is the time in our lives when our primary caretaker lays the foundation for us eventually to be able to empathize, cooperate, and compromise—to give of ourselves to other people. At this very young age, we either adopt a style of relating to people that is basically self-centered, narcissistic, self-indulgent, demanding, and unempathic, or we adopt a style that is basically reciprocal, unselfish, tolerant, cooperative, and empathic.

So what is it exactly that the caretakers of empathic, cooperative, mature teenagers seem to have done differently than the caretakers of egocentric, self-indulgent, demanding teenagers? First, empathic teenagers usually have mothers who ignored or punished their extremely egocentric behavior as toddlers, even though they simultaneously made their child feel loved. Second, their mothers didn't give in to their every whim or frequently acquiesce to their whining or to their tantrums. Third, their mothers taught them as toddlers that they couldn't selfishly and dependently expect all their needs and demands to be met by another person—especially not without giving something in return. Empathic, giving, cooperative teenagers learned early in their lives that we all sometimes have to give, to compromise, to be tolerant, to delay gratification, and to empathize with other people's feelings if we want to be in a relationship.

What happens if we don't develop this sense of mutuality and autonomy as toddlers? First, even as teenagers, we will tend to be childishly dependent and very possessive toward other people. Second, we will selfishly expect other people to continually meet our needs and acquiesce to our demands without believing that we need to compromise or to give anything back in return. Third, having failed to learn about mutuality and empathy, we don't do a very good job recognizing or responding to other people's feelings or viewpoints. Fourth, we will have very little self-control, behaving however we please without regard to the impact on other people. In short, if we haven't learned what we were supposed to learn in this anal stage, we act like selfish, demanding, out-of-control toddlers. For example, teenagers who are always flying into rages whenever they don't get their way probably were infantilized or indulged by one or both parents during this early childhood period when they were supposed to be learning about self-reliance, self-restraint, empathy, and reciprocity.

Ages 4–5: Phallic stage   By time we reach the age of 4 or 5, the Freudians believe we have acquired our lifelong styles of relating to people. So as 4- and 5-year-olds, we are faced with other turning points in our ego development. This is the period Freudians refer to as our **phallic stage.**

In order to relate well to people later in our lives, in the phallic stage we have to resolve our **Oedipal issues.** We do this by identifying with our same-sex parent and giving up an infantile dependence on our opposite-sex parent. **Identification** is the process of becoming bonded enough to our same-sex parent that we model our behavior after him or her from then on. From the psychoanalytic viewpoint, if we're going to become socially and sexually well-adjusted and develop a healthy ego later in life, we have to identify with our same-sex parent at this point. For instance, a 19-year-old boy who has never had a date, is not close to his father, and is extremely dependent on his mother could be seen as having failed to resolve his Oedipal issues as a preschooler. For teenagers in similar situations, psychoanalytic theorists might have us ask: Why didn't this teenager become identified with his or her same-sex parent as a 5-year-old? What was going on in the family that prevented this teenager from resolving these Oedipal issues as a preschooler?

In other words, during the phallic stage we have our chance to avoid the fate of the tragic Greek character, Oedipus—a man who kills his father and unknowingly marries his mother. Obviously, Freudians aren't saying that teenagers with unresolved Oedipal issues literally kill or literally marry their parents. Metaphorically speaking, however, these teenagers do "kill" their relationship with their same sex-parent and ruin their chances of becoming intimate with someone their own age if they "marry" themselves emotionally to their opposite-sex parent. And like Oedipus, who eventually turns against his own mother and mourns his lost relationship with his father, some teenagers become extremely angry at the parent to whom they have been emotionally wedded since their early childhood (Bowen, 1978; Hauser, Powers, & Noam, 1991; Karen, 1994; Main, 1993).

According to Freudians, the phallic stage is also when we are most prone to acquire a lifelong sense of guilt. If either parent used guilt or pity to try to bond us to them, then we might never outgrow the feeling of being responsible for that parent's happiness. This guilt, in turn, interferes with our ego development, making it difficult for us to become intimate with people outside our family. As one male psychiatrist explains it, "My mother worshipped me and I adored her. But she did not want me to grow up and leave her. I felt a special responsibility for her. I was nearly 40 before I could protect myself from her" (Pittman, 1993, p. 148). As the writer Erma Bombeck more whimsically puts it, "Guilt: the gift that keeps on giving."

What do the Freudians say will happen if a teena[ge] Oedipal issues by becoming identified with their same-se[x] hood? First, they will have trouble becoming intimate with comfortable about their own sexuality. Second, even as adults, be overly dependent on their opposite-sex parent. Third, these te[enagers] a distant, competitive, jealous, and combative relationship with the[ir par]ent (Biller, 1993; Blos, 1989). Indeed, many societies throughout th[e world] traditionally celebrated the son's bonding to his father and the daughter[']s to her mother in ritualized initiation ceremonies welcoming them into th[e world] of manhood or womanhood (Bly, 1990; Corneau, 1991; Osherson, 1993).

Not all Freudian theorists, however, believe that daughters have to res[olve] these Oedipal issues as sons do. Unlike the son, the daughter doesn't have to p[ull] away from her primary caretaker in order to identify with the adult who is supposed to be her primary role model. In this sense, the son's development might be more complicated than the daughter's because he needs to shift his primary allegiance away from his mother toward his father (Chodorow, 1978). You might be among those who disagree with these Freudian views. Nevertheless, teenage boys who are socially mature, not overly dependent on their mothers, fairly self-reliant, and relatively comfortable around girls have usually had close relationships with their fathers since early childhood (Biller, 1993; Phares & Compas, 1992; Snarey, 1993).

Ages 5–12: Latency stage   By the time we start elementary school, Freudians say we are entering the **latency period.** During the next 6 or 7 years, we need to acquire the belief that we can complete projects and achieve goals to levels that make us proud of ourselves. We acquire the self-confidence that we can set a goal, work hard to achieve it, and measure up to standards we set for ourselves. If we don't acquire these industrious habits and attitudes about ourselves, as adolescents we feel inferior or incompetent at most of what we do. We never believe that we quite measure up to our own standards or to the standards of others. Between the ages of 6 and 12, it's especially important for our parents to help us see ourselves as industrious, productive, capable people—to see ourselves as people who can achieve goals that we've set on our own without the constant supervision, encouragement, or involvement of either parent.

Adolescence: Genital stage   The fifth and final Freudian stage is the **genital stage**—the time for establishing intimate, sexual relationships with peers. Whatever conflicts with our parents that have not been resolved from earlier stages will reappear during our teenage years. Moreover, as teenagers it is normal for us occasionally to backslide or "regress" into behaving like we did as younger children. For example, teenagers who are usually self-reliant and self-motivated might regress to being very passive and dependent on their parents. These lapses into infantile behavior aren't cause for alarm as long as they are relatively short-lived. If the regressive behavior continues for long or is extreme, however, there might be cause for concern. An adolescent who seems to be regressing to a

have more serious psychological prob-
t or schizoid personality disorders, or
ated lightly. As discussed at the end of
y that therapists can help these ado-
ure ego development (Blos, 1979).

)RIES

ik Erikson placed more emphasis
early childhood shape our ego
veloping in specific stages. And,
re certain new ways of thinking
evelop a healthy, mature ego

age of "trust versus mistrust."
and emotional needs, the
oing to be a good, safe, and
iet, the stage is set for fearing to people and approach-

Psychoanalytic Theories of Development

er doesn't resolve these
parent in early child-
their peers or feeling
these children will
enagers will have
same-sex par-
world have
's bonding
e world
olve

, Erikson believes we are in the stage of "autonomy
e acquired a basic sense of trust, we become much more
-reliant, and adventuresome—a period many parents have jokingly
erred to as "the terrible twos" because we children become so feisty and independent. If, however, we have a parent who is either overly protective and indulgent or who punishes us too harshly, we are apt to develop feelings of self-doubt
and shame that follow us from there on.

As 4- and 5-year-olds, Erikson sees us in the stage of "initiative versus guilt." If
our ego is developing along a healthy path, we are rapidly broadening our contact
with other children and eagerly exploring the world beyond the family. Although
we still feel shy or afraid from time to time, our fears don't stop us from venturing
forth and initiating contact with other children on our own. If we're developing a
sense of initiative, we're striving to achieve certain goals on our own rather than
turning to either parent to meet our every need or solve our every problem.
During this time it's especially important that our parents not be overly critical
and not use guilt as their main method for trying to control our behavior. It's also
especially important that neither parent allow us to cling to them in infantile ways.

If we don't acquire this sense of initiative, how does this affect us as adolescents? First, we move through childhood doubting our own worth and withdrawing from the world around us. So by time we reach adolescence, we aren't
nearly as self-motivated or as self-reliant as most other people our age. We're passive. We don't venture out or explore life unless we're pushed or prodded. We
depend on one or both parents in childish ways. If we have overly moralistic,
extremely inflexible ways of reasoning, we can also be said to have acquired too
great a sense of guilt in early childhood.

Erikson's fourth stage is "industry versus inferiority," which roughly spans the period from ages 6 to 12. If we acquired a sense of initiative as preschoolers, we are enthusiastically interacting with other children and excited about learning. During these years, the risk is that we will develop feelings of inferiority that will undermine our sense of adventure and self-reliance.

As adolescents, we are in Erikson's fifth stage, "identity versus identity confusion." If all has gone well in the previous stages, we use our teenage years to explore many different roles and options—social, personal, and vocational. If the adults in our families have helped us acquire a sense of trust, autonomy, initiative, and industry, then we are equipped to interact and to reason in ways that enable us to develop our identities. If, however, we have failed to acquire these attitudes as we've been growing up, then we will not be as self-reliant and socially mature as other people our age. Again, this process of individuating or becoming separate from our families is one that should have begun when we were preschoolers. Although individuation doesn't require rejecting the adults who love us, it does entail becoming separate and self-reliant enough to have opinions, feelings, and identities that may differ from theirs.

Our early adult years are seen by Erikson as the time for establishing truly intimate relationships—the stage of "intimacy versus isolation." If young people have not developed an identity of their own, they are not likely to be able to achieve intimacy with someone else. Thus, these adults remain emotionally isolated from other people, even though they may marry and have children of their own.

In the middle of our lives, Erikson says we enter the stage of "generativity versus stagnation." Here we are either focused on helping younger people develop themselves or we recognize that we have done nothing to help the next generation. Then, in the final stage of life, we become even more introspective about what we have done with our lives. In evaluating our lives, we feel either a sense of satisfaction and pride or of sadness and gloom—the stage of "integrity versus despair."

ATTACHMENTS TO PARENTS

Another way of appreciating the impact that our parents have on our ego development is to consider the research on **attachment theory**. This research underscores the link between our early childhood relationships with each parent and the ways we reason and relate to people throughout our lives. According to attachment theorists, roughly 70% of us are securely attached to our primary caretaker in early childhood. This means we felt loved by our mothers without being overly dependent, overly protected, or overly involved with her. As a consequence, we are self-confident and self-reliant enough to learn the skills we need in order to get along well and to become intimate with people (Belsky & Cassidy, 1994; Bowlby, 1988; Greenberg, Cicchetti, & Cummings, 1990; Karen, 1994; Main, 1993; Parkes, Stevenson-Hinde, & Marris, 1991).

Unfortunately, the other 30% of us are not securely attached to our mothers during early childhood. If we had an overly protective mother who allowed us to depend on her in extremely infantile, self-centered ways, we learned to relate to people in anxious/avoidant ways. Even as teenagers and adults, we are extremely possessive, jealous, demanding, and self-centered. When we don't get what we want, we pout, get angry, and throw temper tantrums like we did as little children. We tend to drive people away because we suffocate them with our infantile, dependent, clingy, jealous ways. Because we expect and demand so much from others, we continually feel angry, dissatisfied, and disappointed in them. We also tend to be extremely shy, socially withdrawn, and overly dependent on our families (Belsky & Cassidy, 1994; Karen, 1994; Main, 1993; Parkes, Stevenson-Hinde, & Marris, 1991).

At the other extreme are those of us who had a mother who was distant, unaffectionate, rejecting, or physically abusive. We tend to relate to people in anxious/resistant ways. As toddlers, teenagers, and adults, we usually are relatively outgoing and independent. Despite our self-reliance, however, we have trouble becoming emotionally intimate with anyone because our own mothers were not intimate with us. As teenagers and as young adults, we tend to be somewhat aggressive, emotionally distant, suspicious, exploitative, and impulsive (Belsky & Cassidy, 1994; Karen, 1994; Main, 1993; Parkes, Stevenson-Hinde, & Marris, 1991).

FATHERS AND EGO DEVELOPMENT

One of the shortcomings of attachment theories, Freud's theories, and Erikson's theories is their underemphasis on the father's impact on a child's ego development. In fact, some critics have pointed out that psychoanalytic theorists are either blaming or praising mothers for everything and letting the fathers off the hook completely (Caplan, 1989). Because we explore the father's importance in detail in Chapter 8, for now we'll highlight only a few major points.

When fathers are as actively involved as mothers in parenting their infants and toddlers, children's ego development generally benefits in several ways. First, these children tend to be more outgoing, to cry less, to be less overly dependent on their mothers, and to explore things around them more eagerly. Second, these children are more at ease around unfamiliar people, more socially mature, more self-controlled, and more empathic. Third, these benefits generally seem to carry over into adolescence. Fourth, the benefits of early bonding between father and child seem to be greater for boys than for girls. In fact, being intimately bonded to his father in early childhood seems to be more closely related to a teenage boy's ego maturity than being close to his father during the teenage years. In short, when a teenager's ego development is arrested, it is probably as much a consequence of too little fathering as of too much or inadequate mothering (Biller, 1993; Elicker & others, 1992; Koestner, Franz, & Weinberger, 1990; Phares & Compas, 1992; Snarey, 1993).

CHRONIC ILLNESS, PHYSICAL HANDICAPS, AND EGO DEVELOPMENT

Another important aspect is the considerable impact that a child's physical health can have on his or her ego development. Some teenagers who are physically handicapped or who have a chronic illness, such as asthma, epilepsy, or diabetes, have more arrested ego development than physically healthier teenagers. Some unhealthy children have trouble relating well to people, becoming self-reliant, and developing their own identities. On the other hand, a number of handicapped and chronically ill teenagers have very mature egos (Cohen, 1990; Minuchin & Nichols, 1994; Orr & Pless, 1991). So what is it that distinguishes one group from the other? There seem to be two answers—overprotectiveness and enmeshment.

When a young child is chronically ill, some parents get into the habit of infantilizing and indulging the child in areas of his or her life that have nothing to do with the illness itself. The overly protective parent continually makes excuses for the growing child's immature, demanding, self-centered behavior. It's perfectly understandable, of course, why parents need to be extremely attentive to a sick child, especially when the child is too young to take care of himself or herself. Unfortunately, some parents carry their attentiveness and protectiveness too far. For example, parents might still be using their child's chronic illness as an excuse for the fact that their 17-year-old daughter is too self-centered, infantile, and demanding to make friends. Although loving and well-intended, these parents undermine their child's self-control, social skills, self-reliance, self-confidence, and initiative. Having had so little expected of them at home, these children don't learn how to empathize, compromise, or assume responsibility for the consequences of their behavior (Apter, 1991; Bowen, 1978; Miller & Wood, 1991; Minuchin & Nichols, 1994).

Second, a parent and a child with a chronic illness or physical impairment are apt to become overly involved in one another's lives in ways that interfere with the child's ego development—a situation known as enmeshment. These children and parents are overly focused and overly entangled in one another's lives. For example, working with a housewife and her asthmatic son with arrested ego development, a therapist noticed that the mother had very low self-esteem, was depressed, and was unhappily married. Whenever she was mad at her husband or dissatisfied with her life, she obsessed on her son's asthma. She had also become excessively involved in other areas of her son's life. In these ways, she made herself feel needed and important. Without an identity of her own, the mother had to convince herself and her son that her "important job" was to take care of him— which, in turn, resulted in his never learning to take care of himself (Tavris, 1992). In any event, a parent's overinvolvement is one reason why some physically unhealthy teenagers have failed to develop an ego or social reasoning as mature as that of most other people their age (Garrison & McQuiston, 1990; Rosen, 1991; Sholevar & Perkel, 1990).

FAMILY SYSTEMS THEORIES

The way in which our ego develops is also partly influenced by certain dynamics and roles within our families. Each family member comes to assume certain

Parents Who Contribute to Arrested Ego Development

Adolescents who have problems making friends or establishing intimate relationships are frequently in an enmeshed or triangulated relationship with a parent or have a parent who often acts depressed, dependent, or helpless. The following checklist characterizes these parents. Which represent your relationship with each of your parents or stepparents?

1 = almost never, seldom   10 = almost always, very frequently

The Parent's Personality

Mother/Father

____ ___Seems depressed and helpless

____ ___Tries to appear fragile and victimized

____ ___Seems generally unhappy with her/his life

____ ___Acts and talks in ways that make people pity her/him

____ ___Presents herself/himself as a helpless, innocent victim

____ ___Blames other people for the bad situations in her/his life

____ ___Makes people feel guilty or disloyal for disagreeing with her/him

____ ___Makes people believe that things "just never turn out right" for her/him

____ ___Acts as if she/he is usually being unfairly mistreated by others

Parent's Style of Relating to Children

____ ___Makes children feel responsible for protecting the family

____ ___Reminds children how much she/he has sacrificed and suffered for them

____ ___Tries to make children feel disloyal for disagreeing with her/his opinions or feelings

____ ___Encourages child to be overly dependent on her/him

____ ___Makes children believe her/his life would be meaningless without them

____ ___Continually solves children's problems for them

____ ___Tries to make children feel guilty or sorry for her/him

____ ___Refuses to punish infantile or demanding behavior

____ ___Excuses child's aggressive, dependent, or childish behavior

____ ___Grants children an equal voice with adults in almost all family matters

____ ___Gets angry at any other adult who points out their children's problems

____ ___Wants everybody in the family involved in everybody else's business

Parent's Relationship with Spouse or Partner

____ ___Puts children's desires ahead of the adult couple's well-being

____ ___Discusses marital, divorce, or dating problems with the children

____ ___Criticizes the spouse or partner in front of the children

____ ___Aligns with child against the other parent or partner

____ ___Keeps secrets with children from the other parent or partner

____ ___Mocks or criticizes the other parent or partner behind his/her back

____ ___Grants children the right to decide what the adult couple will do

roles that enable the group to function as a whole, even though the roles are sometimes very destructive for a child's ego development. The research that examines how our roles and relationships within the family affect our development is referred to as **family systems theories.** With regard to adolescents' ego development, four aspects of family systems' theories are especially relevant: (1) enmeshment, (2) generational boundaries, (3) triangulation, and (4) marital happiness (Hinde & Stevenson, 1995; Minuchin & Nichols, 1994).

ENMESHMENT

A relationship in which two people are overly involved in each other's lives is referred to as **enmeshment.** When a parent and child are enmeshed, they behave as though they share the same feelings, same perspectives, same thoughts, and same needs. For reasons examined more closely in Chapter 8, mothers are far more likely than fathers to be enmeshed with one of their children. Indeed, one expert on enmeshment, Salvador Minuchin, uses the words *mochild* or *chother* to describe relationships where the mother and child are thinking and behaving almost as if they were one entity (Minuchin & Nichols, 1994). Enmeshed children focus too little on their own ego development and too much on their parent. As a result, by time they reach adolescence, these enmeshed children have not developed the social maturity, self-reliance, close friendships, and self-confidence of most people their age (Bowen, 1978; Harter, 1990; Hauser, Powers, & Noam, 1991; Parker, 1983).

Enmeshment can also be defined as a collapse of ego boundaries between the child and the parent. A **boundary** is an unwritten, yet clearly understood set of expectations that protects each person's identity, feelings, and opinions from being overly entangled with another person's. For example, a mother is violating her son's ego boundary when she convinces him to despise someone who has treated him very well for years, but whom she hates for reasons of her own. The son is also violating his mother's boundary when he involves himself in her problems with her husband, ex-husband, or boyfriend. No matter what the situation, the enmeshed parent and child are continually into each other's business and confused about whose problems, feelings, opinions, illnesses, decisions, friends, and lives are whose. These children come to believe that love and friendship require people to merge together so that whatever is happening to one of them should literally reverberate through the other. In some cases, enmeshed teenagers cannot even distinguish what they think and feel from what the enmeshed parent thinks and feels. On the other hand, when teenage and adult children begin to realize the negative impact of their enmeshment, they can become extremely angry and hostile toward the parent they have been so entangled with since early childhood (Bowlby, 1988; Karen, 1994; Main, 1993; Minuchin & Nichols, 1994).

GENERATIONAL BOUNDARIES

Another family dynamic that interferes with a child's developing a mature ego is the collapse of generational boundaries. **Generational boundaries** are the unwritten rules and expectations that grant adults more privileges and more power than children. For example, a teenage girl is defying a generational boundary when she tries to tell her father how he ought to spend his money, or when she tries to tell her divorced mother who she can and cannot date or marry. Generational boundaries not only protect the intimacy and sanctity of a marriage, but they also give children the security of knowing that the adults' relationship is the secure, exclusive, intimate core around which children's lives will revolve. In some families, these generational boundaries collapse to the point that the child and adult actually exchange roles. That is, either the child becomes the center around which the family revolves or the child acts as a peer, a counselor, or a parent to one of the adults—a damaging situation known as **role reversal.** For example, a parent is violating generational boundaries by using a child as a confidante or counselor on financial or sexual matters. Rather than focusing enough on their own ego development and concerns, these children assume the emotional burden of acting as their parent's best friend. For example, a teenage daughter might take on the burden of helping her divorced mother solve her financial problems rather than leaving the financial concerns up to her mother and her mother's boyfriend.

How have each of your parents affected your ego development?

Generational boundaries help children develop several important aspects of a mature ego. First, boundaries help children develop self-control (ego control) and flexibility (ego resilience) by teaching them to respect authority and respect other people's relationships. Indeed, when parents or stepparents fail to protect the privacy, the intimacy, and the centrality of their marriage, a child is apt to be drawn into an enmeshed relationship and become burdened by the parent's needs for emotional intimacy. Teenagers with immature social and ego development have often sensed or been explicitly told by one of their parents, "You children are always more important than our adult relationship, so you can always count on your wishes being put ahead of ours." In contrast, as one well-adjusted son from a family with strong generational boundaries said, "My parents made it very clear without actually saying it that they came first to each other and the rest of us kids as a group came second" (Snarey, 1993, p.337). In these ways, an intimate marriage and strong generational boundaries help teenagers develop mature egos and satisfying relationships with their peers (Harter, 1990; Hauser, Powers, & Noam, 1991; Hinde & Stevenson, 1995).

TRIANGULATION

A third situation that can interfere with a child's ego and social development is **triangulation,** which occurs when any two family members align themselves with one another against a third person in the family as a way of avoiding their own personal problems. A triangle that commonly interferes with a child's ego development is one in which the child and the mother are aligned together as a couple against the father. In discouraging intimacy between the father and child, some mothers literally tell the child, "Your father doesn't understand you as well or love you as much as I do." In some families, the mother and child mock and criticize the father. Yet without the father to ally themselves against, many of these mothers and children have little else to bind them together. As these children age, they become increasingly disengaged from their father and less involved in focusing on important aspects of their own ego development (Bowen, 1978; Hauser, Powers, & Noam, 1991; Hinde & Stevenson, 1995; Minuchin & Nichols, 1994).

If the parents divorce, enmeshed or triangulated children often disengage altogether from their fathers, which can undermine their ego development even further. Even before the divorce, however, these fathers are frequently relegated to the role of the outsider, the scapegoat, or the "bad" parent. In Chapter 9 we examine the extremely damaging consequences these family triangles can have for teenagers (Guttman, 1993; Hetherington, 1991; Kalter, 1990; Wallerstein, 1991; Warshak, 1992).

Why is it that one child in the family falls prey to triangulated or enmeshed relationships but others don't? Why do some mothers become enmeshed or triangulated with a child but the vast majority don't? Among the most important factors are the mother's family background, her mental health, and the child's inborn or genetic disposition. A child born with an extremely dependent, introverted, or fearful disposition is more likely to end up enmeshed with a parent than is a child with an outgoing, independent disposition. If the mother is unhappily married, depressed, or generally dissatisfied with her life, she is more apt to become enmeshed with one of her children than if she is happily married and relatively satisfied with her life (Blechman, 1990; Radke-Yarrow, 1991; Rubin, Lemare, & Lollis, 1990; Waxler & others, 1992). For example, a mother who isn't happily married generally tries to keep her young adult children living at home and clings to them longer than the happily married mother (White & Edwards, 1990). Likewise, a mother who was raised by emotionally distant or rejecting parents is more apt to become enmeshed and triangulated with one of her children than is the mother who came from a loving, secure family (Ainsworth & Eichberg, 1991; Bowen, 1978; Main, 1993; Minuchin & Nichols, 1994). For example, the mother who is enmeshed with her son often has unhappily married or divorced parents, a father who exploited or abused her, and a mother who is unloving and self-centered. The mother turns to her son, rather than to her husband, for emotional intimacy and self-esteem, inadvertently interfering with her son's ego and social development in the process (Pianta, Egeland, & Stroufe, 1990).

When we look at families hampered by triangulation, weak boundaries, or enmeshment, we commonly find a child with arrested or troubled ego development. A number of these extremely shy, socially isolated adolescents suffer from dependent personality, schizophrenic, and anxiety disorders (Goldstein, 1990; Minuchin & Nichols, 1994; Zimbardo & Radl, 1981). Those who are enmeshed with a parent also tend to have a number of stress-related illnesses such as migraine headaches and frequent allergy attacks (Bowen, 1978; Miller & Wood, 1991; Minuchin & Nichols, 1994; Parmelee, 1989; Rodin, 1990). When these conditions exist in their families, teenagers are more apt to have trouble relating to people their age, creating an identity of their own, and becoming self-reliant (Baumrind, 1991; Cooper & Cooper, 1992; Eisenberg, 1991; Harter, 1990; Hauser, Powers, & Noam, 1991; Marcia, 1991; Putallaz & Heflin, 1993).

Marital Happiness

Teenagers whose social and ego development have been adversely affected by triangulation, enmeshment, or collapsed generational boundaries generally have one thing in common—their parents are divorced or unhappily married. In contrast, teenagers who are the most well-adjusted socially and who have mature egos usually come from homes where happily married adults are meeting each other's needs for intimacy (Blechman, 1990; Cowan & Cowan, 1992; Hinde & Stevenson, 1995; Parke & Ladd, 1992). For example, adolescents living with happily married adults generally get along better with their peers and have more flexible, individuated egos than those living with unhappily married adults (Liddle, 1994; McDonough & Cooper, 1994).

As mentioned, the father plays an important role in a child's ego development. For this reason, it's worth noting that unhappily married fathers tend to have poorer relationships with their children than do unhappily married mothers. An unhappily married man seems to pull back further or to be pushed back further from his children than does the unhappily married woman. This might be related to the fact that enmeshment and triangulation are more common between mothers and children. It also might be that unhappily married men are not as close to their children to begin with as happily married men. Mothers might also have an easier time than fathers separating marital problems from their roles as parents. For whatever reason, children's relationships with their fathers tend to suffer more than their relationship with their mothers when the marriage is unhappy (Belsky & others, 1991; Cowan & Cowan, 1992; Snarey, 1993).

In closing, we need to mention briefly that a mother having a job outside the home is also associated with her children's social and ego development. In general, teenagers whose mothers have always worked outside the home have more mature egos and are more self-reliant than children whose mothers are full-time homemakers (Cowan & Cowan, 1992; Lerner & Galambos, 1991; Minuchin & Nichols, 1994; Richards & Duckett, 1991). This might be due partly to the fact that fathers tend to be closer to their children when the mother has a job than when she is a full-time housewife (Biller, 1993; Gilbert, 1993; Paulson, Koman, & Hill, 1990; Richards & Duckett, 1991; Snarey, 1993; Warshak, 1992).

What experiences helped you become individuated from your parents?

SOCIAL LEARNING THEORIES: PARENTING STYLES

Like family systems and psychoanalytic theorists, social learning theorists believe that our teenage behavior is largely determined by our earlier experiences. Social learning and psychoanalytic theorists also agree that experiences with our parents usually have the most profound impact. The ways in which parents influence us are discussed in detail in Chapter 8. So for now let's focus on the impact of parenting styles.

One illustration of how parenting styles, marital happiness, and enmeshment sometimes work together to affect a child's ego development is the longitudinal research of Jack Block—a study that followed the development of 171 people from junior high school into early adulthood. Block found that, as teenagers and as adults, the children with the most mature egos, the most satisfying relationships, and the fewest psychological problems, generally had parents who were happily married and loving yet consistently firm in disciplining their children—a style referred to as democratic parenting. These parents weren't afraid to punish their children and didn't allow children to become aligned with one parent against the other. In contrast, the children who grew up having the most immature or troubled ego development usually had parents who weren't happily married. These children also tended to be enmeshed with their opposite sex parent—an adult who was tense, gloomy, unhappy with life, sexually inhibited, and overly protective and indulgent toward the child. The mothers often played the role of self-sacrificing martyrs and tried to make their sons feel sorry for them (Block, 1971).

As adolescents and as adults, the children with arrested ego development were easily discouraged, socially immature, childishly dependent on their parents, and extremely critical of other people. They also were distrustful, fearful, brooding, inflexible, defensive, self-pitying, lacking in self-confidence, and quite irritable, explosive, and hostile. They seldom dated, had few if any friends, and weren't emotionally intimate with anyone. As they aged, these adolescents usually got worse, not better. By their mid-20s most of them felt cheated, victimized, and soured on life, often suffering from an assortment of psychological problems. Many felt detached even from their own parents, spouses, and children. Whatever tactics they had relied on to avoid dealing with their arrested ego development finally wore out, leaving these adults with the same types of problems they had throughout their teenage years (Block, 1971).

In short, the adults we live with do have an impact on our ego development and on our social and moral reasoning. Naturally then researchers have asked: What exactly do our parents and stepparents do that facilitates or impedes these aspects of our development? In attempting to answer this, researchers typically classify parenting styles into four basic categories: dictatorial, permissive, indifferent, or democratic. As you'll see, how well adolescents get along with other people and how maturely they reason are closely related to the parenting style they have grown up with (Baumrind, 1991; Cooper & Cooper, 1992; Eisenberg, 1991; Hauser, Powers, & Noam, 1991).

DICTATORIAL PARENTING

Adults using a dictatorial style are overly strict, punitive, critical, and controlling of children's behavior. In these families there's plenty of adult supervision and control but not enough affection. There is not enough give and take between adults and children. Dictatorial adults generally act as though "children should be seen but not heard." They expect the children to yield to their authority without question. They don't feel any need to explain the reasons for their rules or to make compromises that take their children's ideas or feelings into account. Instead, they are quick to punish, slow to reward, and often abide by the philosophy "spare the rod and spoil the child."

Adolescents growing up in these families typically respond in one of two ways. Either they become extremely submissive or they become aggressive and defiant. In terms of their social reasoning, most of these adolescents aren't very mature because they haven't had many chances at home to develop skills such as perspective-taking and empathy. Even those who are well-behaved and obedient, however, often feel misunderstood and unloved. Unfortunately, this harsh, dictatorial style of parenting, especially toward male children, seems to be passed down from one generation to another. That is, adolescents whose grandparents used harsh, aggressive methods to discipline their children tend to have extremely strict parents (Simons & others, 1991).

Families that are run in a dictatorial manner usually have the most conflict when their children reach adolescence and want to be granted more freedom and more say. As their reasoning becomes more sophisticated, teenagers are able to recognize more of the shortcomings in a parent's logic and more of the hypocrisy in adults' behavior. This can start a vicious cycle: These teenagers are likely to question their parent's authority and to challenge those rules and regulations that they believe are unreasonable or hypocritical—obviously, this doesn't go over well in a household run by adults with dictatorial ways of parenting. Although these teenagers usually succeed at school, because they are so well monitored at home, they are usually less self-confident, less socially mature, and less relaxed than teenagers from less dictatorial families. Boys from these homes tend to be more hostile and girls more submissive than teenagers from less restrictive families. These adolescents are also likely to choose jobs and make decisions that they believe will please their parents.

PERMISSIVE PARENTING

At the other extreme are adults who are too permissive and too indulgent with their children. These indulgent, overly protective parents clearly make their children feel loved by being very involved, affectionate, and attentive. Unfortunately, these loving parents handicap their children by refusing to set standards for mature behavior or to punish immature, aggressive, or egocentric behavior. Under the guise of "not wanting to hurt my son's self-esteem" or "wanting my daughter to know that I love her no matter how she behaves," the indulgent parent undermines teenage maturity and ego development by rewarding, permitting, or excusing infantile, self-centered, or antisocial behavior. One expert on permissive parenting explains that when a three-foot tyrant is taller than all other family members, that child is standing on the shoulders of one of the parents (Minuchin & Nichols, 1994).

Some permissive parents use a style referred to as **coercive parenting.** In a coercive relationship, the parent who is generally too permissive occasionally tries to gain control over the child by threatening, nagging, scolding, pleading, or crying. Instead of enforcing firm, consistent discipline, the coercive parent might threaten to withdraw love or try to make the child feel guilty: "How can you do this to me if you love me?" "If you really loved me, you'd do what I'm asking." A coercive mother might also shift her responsibilities as a disciplinarian onto the father: "Just wait until your father gets home!" When coercive tactics fail, as they usually do, the parent loses control and starts behaving in infantile or aggressive ways toward the child—screaming, slamming doors, throwing things, hitting, or verbally abusing the child (Patterson, Reid, & Dishion, 1992).

In general, the mother in these families is more permissive than the father, especially with her son—and especially when she isn't married (Block & Gjerde, 1988; Hetherington, 1991; Patterson, Reid, & Dishion, 1992; Rubin, Lemare, & Lollis, 1990). Although some fathers are too permissive as parents, they tend to be this way with their daughters more than with their sons (Snarey, 1993). As discussed, permissive parenting is also relatively common when a child has a physical handicap or a chronic illness.

Although adolescents with a permissive parent usually get their way at home, they don't get their way in the world beyond the family where their immature, manipulative, or aggressive behavior offends and hurts the people around them. Having been successful with these various strategies with their permissive parent(s), these teenagers generally rely on the same behaviors with people outside the family. In short, these teenagers lack the maturity of most people their age and behave much like egocentric preschoolers: flying off the handle, throwing tantrums, sulking, running away—refusing to work toward solving problems with people. Permissive parenting has thus succeeded in teaching children a self-defeating attitude that contributes to arrested ego development: "I don't have to assume responsibility for how I act because I've never had to pay much of a price for my self-centered, manipulative, immature, or aggressive behavior at home." Such children often become adolescents who are too self-centered, childish, demanding, aggressive, or socially inept to get along well with people, let alone to be self-reliant enough to create identities of their own (Hauser, Powers, & Noam, 1991; Patterson, Reid, & Dishion, 1992; Rubin, Lemare, & Lollis, 1990). Children who have not received enough discipline at home are also more apt to end up with problems such as low self-esteem, schizoid personality disorders, depression, eating disorders, anxiety disorders, and personality disorders (Goldstein, 1990; Parker, 1983; Putallaz & Heflin, 1993; Rodin, 1990).

INDIFFERENT PARENTING

Another type of permissive parent is the one who is too indifferent, emotionally detached, or rejecting to offer much guidance or discipline. These parents provide neither enough love nor enough discipline and supervision. Although they don't indulge their children in overly protective ways, these parents are permissive in that they fail to provide clear-cut guidelines for mature behavior or to punish and discipline children in ways that teach more mature social and moral reasoning. These indifferent parents teach their children egocentric, self-defeating ways of thinking and behaving. Basically these teenagers have learned: "I don't have to control my feelings or my behavior. I don't have to empathize with other people's feelings or respect their opinions. I'm entitled to have people do what I want, when I want—especially those people who supposedly love me."

DEMOCRATIC PARENTING

The best of all parenting styles is referred to as the democratic approach. If you're lucky, you were raised by adults who used a democratic style of parenting. These adults are loving and affectionate, yet firm and consistent when it comes to disciplining children. As a result, their children generally have the most mature egos, the most independent identities, and the most satisfying peer relationships (Baumrind, 1991; Cooper & Cooper, 1992; Harter, 1990; Hauser, Powers, & Noam, 1991; Montemayor & Flannery, 1991; Steinberg & others, 1991).

So what is it that these democratic adults are doing right? First, they're not afraid to establish and enforce clearly defined rules and expectations. These adults don't tolerate egocentric, immature, coercive, or aggressive behavior—at least not for long. On the other hand, democratic adults are self-confident and wise enough to allow their children to question and to disagree with them, especially during adolescence. These adults are teaching their children how to empathize, how to assume other people's perspectives, how to be flexible, and how to express their feelings and opinions in relatively considerate ways. Unlike permissive parents, democratic parents don't let their children rule the roost or trespass across the generational boundaries. They don't rule with an iron hand; but they don't give children the upper hand either. These adults also foster ego development by refusing to rescue children repeatedly from the negative consequences of their own actions. For example, if a teenager spends the entire weekend watching television, but begs her parent to let her stay home from school on Monday because she isn't prepared to take her test, the democratic parent refuses while the permissive parent goes along with the scheme. While permissive parents too often rescue their children, democratic parents allow children to experience enough frustration, failure, embarrassment, and punishment to learn to assume responsibility for their own behavior.

Democratic parenting also helps children develop mature egos and more satisfying peer relationships by enabling them to maintain a close relationship with both parents as teenagers. Historically most psychologists believed that adolescents had to reject and rebel against their parents in order to mature and create identities of their own. Most research now shows, however, that feeling close to our parents helps us become self-reliant, self-confident, socially well-adjusted adults. In fact, adolescents who are extremely distant and detached from their

---

Insert 4–5

An Adolescent With Arrested Ego Development

Find a specific example of each of the following in this hypothetical family: enmeshment, triangulation, egocentrism, dualistic reasoning, modeling, temperament, brittle ego, Oedipal issues, arrested ego development, boundaries, and individuation.

Although he is attractive and bright with financially well-off, well-educated parents, at age 19 Joe has no friends and has never been on a date. He has no hobbies and spends most of his time alone watching old movies on television. He complains continually that "there isn't anybody at my high school I'd want to be friends with or date. Besides, things never work out my way like they do for everybody else." The few times that classmates have invited him to join them, Joe finds something that doesn't suit him. For one reason or another, the people never meet his expectations. Most days he's in a very grumpy mood, complaining continually how boring and miserable life is.

As a young child, Joe was often hospitalized for chronic ear infections. His mother still talks about how much she sacrificed to take care of him as a young child. As an infant, Joe was easily frustrated, often fussy, and adapted poorly to any change in routines. He seldom initiated any contact with other children, depending instead on his mother to play with him or to find playmates for him. When Joe's mother feared he was getting "too attached" to his baby-sitter, she quit her part-time job and stayed at home full-time until he was a teenager.

For the past 19 years, Joe's father has tried to convince his wife to "let the boy tough things out a little on his own so he can grow up." Still, the mother refuses to discipline her son and excuses his infantile, angry, demanding behavior by saying that "He's just shy and lacks self-confidence." Despite the problems in their marriage and her chronic depression, the wife says they need to focus more on Joe's problems and less on marital issues. "After all, the kids come before anything else." When her husband finally convinced her to leave the children for a week for a second honeymoon, she phoned home twice to see how Joe and his older sister were getting along.

The older Joe gets, the more his mother confides in him about her problems. Joe has reassured his mother that if she ever gets divorced, he'll live with her because "you need me." Joe has also grown increasingly hostile toward his father, describing him as "always criticizing me and trying to push me into doing things." When the father suggested that Joe might want to see a counselor to learn how to make friends and examine his anger and immaturity, Joe and his mother angrily accused the father of "trying to punish" Joe. In high school, Joe fantasized a lot about going to college because he believed "once I leave this town, my whole life is going to be better." After Joe gets to college, however, his mother allows him—against his father's wishes—to come home almost every weekend because he hasn't made any friends. Now Joe is considering transferring to another college next year.

families are often immature and troubled in regard to their own ego development (Baumrind, 1991; Cooper & Cooper, 1992; Harter, 1990; Hauser, Powers, & Noam, 1991).

In concluding our discussion of parenting styles, keep two other findings in mind. First, children's inborn temperaments influence how their parents relate to them. That is, some of us are born with a disposition that makes it easier for our parents to relate to us in more democratic ways. Second, most parents believe that their parenting style is the best, despite any evidence to the contrary. Even the most dictatorial adults usually see themselves as more laid back and more fair-minded than they actually are; and even the most permissive parents see themselves as being simply understanding and nurturing. Because most of us relate to our children very much as our own parents related to us, our parenting styles feel normal and right—in part because we're accustomed to this kind of parenting from our childhood (Patterson, Reid, & Dishion, 1992). When it comes to judging ourselves as parents and stepparents, nature didn't make us perfect. It did the next best thing: Nature made us blind to our own faults.

CONCLUSION

Going back to the question at the beginning of this chapter: Why do some adolescents behave and reason less maturely than others their age? As we've seen, a number of different theories account for these differences. Although psychologists disagree about whether these differences are the consequences of cognitive stages, the types of relationships we have with our parents, or experiences beyond our families, several conclusions remain undisputed. First, some adolescents are clearly much more mature than others their age in terms of their social, moral, and ego development. Second, differences in our social and moral reasoning do account for how well or how poorly we get along with people and how maturely we make decisions as adolescents. Third, most adolescents do become more mature with regard to their social and moral reasoning, although not everyone winds up with the same level of maturity as adults. Fourth, adolescents with more advanced ego development and more mature social and moral reasoning are easier to live with, to teach, to befriend, to date, and to counsel than are those with arrested ego development and childish levels of reasoning.

In the next chapter we expand our exploration of social and moral reasoning and ego development by considering the biological viewpoints. We also extend further into social learning theorists' explanations by examining the differences in male and female social development and by looking at other experiences in our families that affect social relationships with our peers. The next chapter also leads to the question that inevitably lies at the end of the path: How do we help adolescents develop more mature egos and more adaptive ways of reasoning and behaving?

Review/Test Questions

1. Describe 10 ways in which the reasoning and behavior of adolescents with arrested ego development differ from that of other adolescents their age.

2. According to Kohlberg and Piaget, what are the stages we move through as children and adolescents? How do our ways of thinking and behaving change if we make the appropriate advances at each stage?

3. Give an example of each of the following: egocentrism, dualistic thinking, moral realism, postconventional reasoning, brittle ego, and regression.

4. What are the shortcomings or criticisms of Kohlberg's and Piaget's theories?

5. How do the imaginary audience and the personal fable relate to an adolescent's social or moral reasoning?

6. What is ego development? What exactly do we mean when we say some adolescents have mature or immature egos?

7. What changes in our thinking and behavior should occur at each of Freud's and Erikson's stages of development? How do adolescents who haven't mastered the skills or overcome the crises associated with each of these earlier childhood stages think and behave?

8. What is an Oedipal complex? What problems develop for adolescents who haven't resolved their Oedipal issues? What increases the odds of an adolescent's having unresolved Oedipal issues?

9. What is individuation and how can adults help or hinder it?

10. In what ways does each parenting style affect an adolescent's social reasoning and ego development?

11. What are five specific ways in which families affect adolescents' moral and social reasoning?

12. Why is it important for adolescents that their fathers be actively involved in their early lives?

13. How can each of the following affect an adolescent's moral, social, and ego development: chronic illness, enmeshment, triangulation, and role reversals?

14. How does the parents' marriage affect adolescents' maturity or skills in terms of ego development or social reasoning?

Questions for Discussion and Debate

1. Based on your answers to the checklists in this chapter's inserts, in what ways have each of your parents affected your moral, social, and ego development?

2. What experiences do you believe have helped you mature most in terms of moral and social reasoning?

3. How would you compare your levels of social and moral reasoning with your siblings'? What do you think accounts for your similarities and your differences?

4. Think of someone you know who seems to have arrested ego development. What factors do you think have interfered with their ego development and social reasoning?

5. How did the imaginary audience and the personal fable affect you or your friends as adolescents?

6. How much of your ego development and social reasoning was influenced by a cognitive stage? by reinforcement and punishment? by dynamics in your family?

7. How would you go about helping the boy described in the hypothetical Insert 4–5 story? What do you see as contributing to his arrested ego development?

8. Considering Kohlberg's and Piaget's stages of social and moral reasoning, how much do you agree or disagree with their definitions of maturity and ethical reasoning?

9. Why do you think men's and women's styles of relating to their children are often so different? How or what do you think each of your parents or stepparents has contributed to your ego development?

10. Thinking back to how each of your parents, stepparents or other adults raised you, what mistakes do you think they made in terms of helping you develop mature social reasoning?

Glossary

absolutist thinking, p. 104
anal stage, p. 118
arrested ego development, p. 117
attachment theory, p. 123
autonomous morality, p. 110
boundary, p. 127
brittle ego, p. 117
coercive parenting, p. 134
conventional reasoning, p. 112
dualistic thinking, p. 104
ego, p. 116

ego resilience, p. 117
egocentric thinking, p. 106
egocentrism, p. 112
enmeshment, p. 127
family systems theories, p. 127
generational boundary, p. 127
genital stage, p. 121
identification, p. 120
imaginary audience, p. 113
individuation, p. 116
latency stage, p. 121

moral realism, p. 109
Oedipal issues, p. 120
oral stage, p. 118
personal fable, p. 113
phallic stage, p. 120
postconventional reasoning, p. 112
preconventional stage, p. 112
role reversal, p. 128
social cognition, p. 103
triangulation, p. 129

References

Adelson, J. (1982). How children learn the principles of community. *American Educator, 15,* 60–67.

Adelson, J. (1991). Political development. In R. Lerner, A. Petersen & J. Brooks-Gunn (Eds.), *Encyclopedia of adolescence* (pp. 792–794). New York: Garland.

Ainsworth, M., & Eichberg, C. (1991). Effects of mother's unresolved loss of an attachment figure. In C. Parkes, J. Hinde & P. Marris (Eds.), *Attachment across the life cycle* (pp. 160–183). New York: Routledge.

Apter, A. (1991). Behavioral profile and social competence in temporal lobe epilepsy. *American Academy of Child and Adolescent Psychiatry, 30,* 887–892.

Avery, P. (1989). Adolescent political tolerance. *High School Journal, 72,* 168–174.

Baumrind, D. (1991). Parenting styles and adolescent development. In R. Lerner, A. Petersen & J. Brooks-Gunn (Eds.), *Encyclopedia of adolescence* (pp. 746–758). New York: Garland.

Belsky, J., & Cassidy, J. (1994). Attachment: Theory and evidence. In M. Rutter, D. Hays & S. Baron (Eds.), *Developmental principles and clinical issues in psychology and psychiatry.* Blackwell, England: Oxford.

Belsky, J., Youngblade, L., Rovine, M., & Volling, B. (1991). Patterns of marital change and parent child interaction. *Journal of Marriage and the Family, 53,* 487–498.

Benson, P., Donahue, M., & Erickson, J. (1989). Adolescence and religion: Review of the literature from 1970–1986. *Research in the Social Scientific Study of Religion, 1,* 153–181.

Biller, H. (1993). *Fathers and families: Paternal factors in child development.* Westport, CT: Auburn House.

Blechman, E. (1990). *Emotions and the family.* Hillsdale, NJ: Erlbaum.

Block, J. (1971). *Lives through time.* Berkeley, CA: Bancroft Books.

Block, J., & Gjerde, P. (1988). Parental functioning and the home environment in families of divorce. *Journal of the American Academy of Child and Adolescent, 27,* 207–213.

Blos, P. (1979). *On adolescence.* New York: Free Press.

Blos, P. (1989). *Father and son.* New York: Free Press.

Bly, R. (1990). *Iron John: A book about men.* Reading, MA: Addison Wesley.

Bornstein, M., & Bruner, J. (1993). *Interaction in cognitive development.* Hillsdale, NJ: Erlbaum.

Bowen, M. (1978). *Family therapy in clinical practice.* New York: Aronson.

Bowlby, J. (1988). *A secure base.* New York: Basic Books.

Caplan, P. (1989). *Don't blame mother.* New York: Harper & Row.

Chodorow, N. (1978). *The reproduction of mothering.* Berkeley: University of California.

Cohen, P. (1990). Common and uncommon pathways to adolescent psychopathology and problem behavior. In L. Robins & M. Rutter (Eds.), *Straight and devious pathways* (pp. 242–259). New York: Cambridge University.

Cooper, C., & Cooper, R. (1992). Links between adolescents' relationships with parents and peers. In R. Parke & G. Ladd (Eds.), *Family peer relationships* (pp. 135–157). Hillsdale, NJ: Erlbaum.

Corneau, G. (1991). *Absent fathers, lost sons.* Boston: Shambhala.

Cowan, C., & Cowan, P. (1992). *When partners become parents.* New York: Basic Books.

Damon, W. (1988). *The moral child.* New York: Free Press.

Damon, W., & Hart, D. (1988). *Self-understanding in childhood and adolescence.* New York: Cambridge University Press.

Eisenberg, N. (1991). Prosocial development in adolescence. In R. Lerner, A. Petersen & J. Brooks-Gunn (Eds.), *Encyclopedia of adolescence.* New York: Garland.

Elicker, J., Englund, M., & Stroufe, L. (1992). Predicting peer competence and peer relationships from early parent–child relationships. In R. Parke & G. Ladd (Eds.), *Family peer relationships: Modes of linkages.* Hillsdale, NJ: Erlbaum.

Elkind, D. (1978). *The child's reality.* Hillsdale, NJ: Erlbaum.

Elkind, D., & Bowen, R. (1979). Imaginary audience behavior in children and adolescents. *Developmental Psychology, 15,* 38–44.

Erikson, E. (1968). *Identity: Youth in crisis.* New York: Norton.

Freud, A. (1958). *The ego and the mechanisms of defense.* New York: International University Press.

Freud, A. (1977). *Normality and pathology in childhood.* New York: International Universities Press.

Freud, S. (1931). *The standard edition of the complete psychological works of Sigmund Freud.* London: Hogarth Press.

Freud, S. (1949). *An outline of psycho-analysis.* New York: Norton.

Garrison, W., & McQuiston, S. (1990). *Chronic illness during childhood and adolescence.* Thousand Oaks, CA: Sage.

Gilbert, L. (1993). *Two careers, one family.* Berkeley, CA: Sage.

Goldstein, M. (1990). Family relations as risk factors for schizophrenia. In J. Rolf (Ed.), *Risk and protective factors in the development of psychopathology* (pp. 408–424). New York: Cambridge University.

Greenberg, M., Cicchetti, D., & Cummings, E. (1990). *Attachment in the preschool years.* Chicago: University of Chicago.

Guttman, J. (1993). *Divorce in psychosocial perspective.* Hillsdale, NJ: Erlbaum.

Harter, S. (1990). Self and identity development. In S. Feldman & G. Elliot (Eds.), *At the threshold* (pp. 352–388). Cambridge, MA: Harvard University.

Hauser, S., Powers, S., & Noam, G. (1991). *Adolescents and their families: Paths of ego development.* New York: Free Press.

Hetherington, M. (1991). Families, lies and videotapes. *Journal of Research on Adolescence, 1,* 323–348.

Hinde, R., & Stevenson, J. (1995). *Relation between relationships within families.* Cambridge, England: Oxford University Press.

Hudson, L., & Gray, W. (1986). Formal operations, the imaginary audience, and the personal fable. *Adolescence, 21,* 751–765.

Kalter, N. (1990). *Growing up with divorce.* New York: Ballantine.

Karen, R. (1994). *Becoming attached.* New York: Time Warner.

Keating, D. (1990). Adolescent thinking. In S. Feldman & G. Elliot (Eds.), *At the threshold.* Cambridge, MA: Harvard University.

Koestner, R., Franz, C., & Weinberger, J. (1990). The family origins of empathic concerns. *Journal of Personality and Social Psychology, 58,* 709–717.

Kohlberg, L. (1984). *The psychology of moral development.* New York: Harper & Row.

Kurtines, W., & Gewirtz, J. (1991). *Moral behavior and development.* Hillsdale, NJ: Erlbaum.

Kurtines, W., & Gewirtz, J. (1992). *The moral development of forgiveness.* Hillsdale, NJ: Erlbaum.

Lapsley, D. (1988). *Self, ego, and identity.* New York: Springer.

Lapsley, D. (1990). Continuity and discontinuity in adolescent social cognitive development. In R. Montemayor, G. Adams & T. Gulotta (Eds.), *From childhood to adolescence.* Newbury Park, CA: Sage.

Lerner, J., & Galambos, N. (1991). *Employed mothers and their children.* New York: Garland Publishing.

Liddle, H. (1994). The anatomy of emotions in family therapy with adolescents. *Journal of Adolescent Research, 9,* 120–157.

Liebes, T., Katz, E., & Ribak, R. (1991). Ideological reproduction. *Political Behavior, 13,* 237–252.

Main, M. (1993). *A typology of human attachment organization.* New York: Cambridge University Press.

Marcia, J. (1991). Identity and self-development. In R. Lerner, A. Petersen & J. Brooks-Gunn (Eds.), *Encyclopedia of adolescence* (pp. 529–534). New York: Garland.

McDonough, M. & Cooper, C. (1994). Marital relationships and the regulation of affect in families of early adolescents. *Journal of Adolescent Research, 9,* 67–87.

Miller, B., & Wood, B. (1991). Childhood asthma. *Journal of Asthma, 28,* 405–414.

Miller, J., & Bersoff, D. (1992). Culture and moral judgment. *Journal of Personality and Social Psychology, 56,* 157–273.

Minuchin, S., & Nichols, M. (1994). *Family healing.* New York: Simon & Schuster.

Montemayor, R., & Flannery, D. (1991). Parent adolescent relations in middle and late adolescence. In R. Lerner, A. Petersen & J.

Brooks-Gunn (Eds.), *Encyclopedia of adolescence* (pp. 729–734). New York: Garland.

O'Connor, B., & Nikolic, J. (1990). Identity development and formal operations as sources of adolescent egocentrism. *Journal of Youth and Adolescence, 19,* 149–158.

Orr, D., & Pless, B. (1991). Chronic illness. In R. Lerner, A. Petersen & J. Brooks-Gunn (Eds.), *Encyclopedia of adolescence* (pp. 541–544). New York: Garland.

Osherson, S. (1993). *Finding our fathers: The unfinished business of manhood.* New York: Fawcett.

Parke, R., & Ladd, G. (1992). *Family–peer relationships: Modes of linkage.* Hillsdale, NJ: Erlbaum.

Parker, G. (1983). *Parental overprotection: A risk factor in psychosocial development.* New York: Grune & Stratton.

Parkes, C., Stevenson-Hinde, J., & Marris, P. (1991). *Attachment across the life cycle.* New York: Tavistock/Routledge.

Patterson, G., Reid, J., & Dishion, T. (1992). *A social learning approach: Antisocial boys.* Eugene, OR: Castalia.

Paulson, S., Koman, J., & Hill, J. (1990). Maternal employment and parent–child relations. *Journal of Early Adolescence, 10,* 279–295.

Phares, V., & Compas, B. (1992). The role of fathers in child and adolescent psychopathology. *Psychological Bulletin, 111,* 387–412.

Piaget, J. (1965). *The moral judgment of the child.* New York: Free Press.

Pianta, B., Egeland, B., & Stroufe, A. (1990). Maternal stress and children's development. In J. Rolf, A. Masten, K. Nuechterlain & .W. Weintraub (Eds.), *Risk and protective factors in the development of psychopathology* (pp. 215–236). New York: Cambridge University.

Putallaz, M., & Heflin, A. (1993). Parent–child relations and peer rejection. In S. Asher & J. Coie (Eds.), *Peer rejection in childhood* (pp. 189–217). New York: Cambridge University.

Radke-Yarrow, M. (1991). Attachment patterns in children of depressed mothers. In C. Parkes (Ed.), *Attachment across the life cycle.* New York: Routledge.

Rest, J. (1986). *Moral development.* New York: Praeger.

Richards, M., & Duckett, E. (1991). Maternal employment and adolescents. In J. Lerner & E. Duckett (Eds.), *Employed mothers and their children* (pp. 85–123). New York: Garland.

Rodin, J. (1990). Risk and protective factors for bulimia nervosa. In J. Rolf (Ed.), *Risk and protective factors in the development of psychopathology* (pp. 361–383). New York: Cambridge University.

Rosen, D. (1991). Growth and sexual maturation for adolescents with chronic illness or disability. *Pediatrician, 18,* 105–120.

Rubin, K., Lemare, L., & Lollis, S. (1990). Social withdrawal in childhood. In S. Asher & J. Coie (Eds.), *Peer rejection in childhood* (pp. 51–72). Hillsdale, NJ: Erlbaum.

Sameroff, A., & Emde, R. (1989). *Relationship disturbances in early childhood.* New York: Basic Books.

Sholevar, G., & Perkel, R. (1990). Family systems intervention and physical illness. *General Hospital Psychiatry, 12,* 363–372.

Snarey, J. (1993). *How fathers care for the next generation.* Cambridge, MA: Harvard University.

Steinberg, L. (1990). Autonomy, conflict and harmony in the family relationship. In S. Feldman & G. Elliot (Eds.), *At the threshold* (pp. 255–569). Cambridge, MA: Harvard University Press.

Steinberg, L., Mounts, N., Lamborn, S., & Dornbusch, S. (1991). Authoritative parenting and adolescent adjustment across varied ecological niches. *Journal of Research on Adolescence, 1,* 19–36.

Tavris, C. (1992). *Mismeasure of woman.* New York: Simon & Schuster.

Wallerstein, J. (1991). The long term effects

of divorce on children: A review. *Journal of American Academy of Child Psychiatry, 30,* 349–360.

Warshak, R. (1992). *The custody revolution: The fatherhood factor and the motherhood mystique.* New York: Poseidon.

Waxler, C., Denham, S., Iannotti, R., & Cummings, M. (1992). Peer relations in children with a depressed caregiver. In R. Parke & G. Ladd (Eds.), *Family-peer relationships* (pp. 317–344). Hillsdale, NJ: Erlbaum.

White, L., & Edwards, J. (1990). Emptying the nest and parental well-being. *American Sociological Review, 55,* 235–242.

Zimbardo, P., & Radl, S. (1981). *The shy child.* New York: McGraw Hill.

5

SOCIAL DEVELOPMENT AND PERSONALITY

CHAPTER OUTLINE

KEY QUESTIONS ADDRESSED IN THIS CHAPTER

1. How do adolescent friendships differ from those of younger children?
2. How does physical appearance affect adolescent friendship?
3. In what ways do friends contribute to one another's social reasoning and ego development?
4. How does temperament affect teenage friendships and social reasoning?
5. Which psychological disorders are associated with not getting along well with peers? Which are associated with immature social reasoning as adolescents?
6. How do explanatory styles affect adolescents' peer relationships?
7. Which environmental factors influence a person's temperament?
8. How are counselors, parents, and teachers helping adolescents with troubled peer relationships or poor social and moral reasoning?
9. What are the consequences of not having close friends during adolescence?
10. How do parents contribute to or detract from an adolescent's social development?

As most of us remember from our own teenage years, our peers assumed a more primary role as our families faded further into the background of our day-to-day lives. Although most of us were still close to our parents and stepparents as teenagers, we spent increasingly more time with people our own age and less time with our families or by ourselves. An essential part of healthy adolescent development is being able to make friends, to become emotionally intimate with a peer, and to learn better ways for getting along with people. In fact, those adolescents who aren't able to establish satisfying relationships with their peers often suffer from a host of problems, ranging from low self-esteem and acute loneliness to delinquency and suicide. Commonly, peers become so important that they cause more stress and unhappiness for most adolescents than do family members (Compas & Wagner, 1991; Dornbusch & others, 1991; Eisenberg, 1991).

Given the importance of having friends and developing mature social reasoning, researchers have devoted considerable attention to adolescents' social development. In this chapter we address these questions: In what ways are our adolescent friendships different from those we had as younger children? Why are most of us able to make close friends as adolescents, but some of us aren't? What benefits do we derive from having friends? And what happens to those of us who spend most of our teenage years alone and virtually friendless? How do male and female adolescents relate differently to people? Why are most teenage boys less advanced in their social development than most teenage girls? How can family members, teachers, or therapists help adolescents whose poor social development prevents them from getting along well with people?

CHARACTERISTICS OF ADOLESCENT FRIENDSHIPS

Before looking at why some adolescents are so much more successful than others in making friends and getting along with people, let's look at the changes in friendship and social reasoning that typically occur during our teenage years (Eisenberg, 1991; Hartup & Overhauser, 1991; Savin-Williams & Berndt, 1990).

ADOLESCENT DEFINITIONS OF FRIENDSHIP

As we move into adolescence, our expectations and definitions of friendship usually change. Before adolescence we choose our friends mainly on the basis of who can share activities with us. For example, in sixth grade if you and your next door neighbor both enjoy playing soccer, you'll probably get to be friends. But if you like playing soccer and your neighbor likes playing only computer games, you probably won't be friends. As one sixth grade boy put it, "Friends are easy to make. All you have to do is go up to a guy, say hello, and ask him if he wants to play ball; then he's a friend. If he don't want to play ball, then he's not a friend unless you decide to play something else" (Smollar & Youniss, 1982, p. 281).

By the time we reach adolescence, however, most of us expect to give and to get more from a friendship than merely playing together. Above all we're looking for loyalty and intimacy before we're willing to consider someone a real friend. We expect such friends to discuss problems and share feelings with us, and we want to feel comfortable enough to share ours with them. We're searching for peers who can offer us emotional support, pump us up when we feel down, and accept us for who we are, even when we make mistakes or fall short of their expectations.

During adolescence we begin realizing that becoming intimate and getting along well with people involves being less selfish and more considerate of other people's feelings. We're discovering that it's not enough anymore merely to watch television or play computer games with someone. If we want intimacy and under-standing, we also must be more willing to disclose our own personal thoughts and feelings. In the terms used by developmental psychologists such as Piaget and Kohlberg, as adolescents we have to develop less "egocentric" ways of thinking and behaving if we're going to have close friends.

Most teenagers also gain a better understanding of the concept of reciprocity. They start comprehending that one person can't do most of the taking and the

How have your ideas about friendship changed since adolescence?

other most of the giving if a relationship is going to last, or if two people are going to become intimate. Not only do we become more sensitive to the inequalities in our relationships, most of us also start trying harder to balance the give and take in our relationships with our peers and our families. Although it's clear that not all adolescents grasp these ideas about reciprocity, most at least move in the direction of being more giving and more empathic. Yet, although we become less ego-centric, we become more selective about potential friends than we were as younger children. We begin to look for more sophisticated traits such as selfless-ness and the ability to empathize. And even though we still enjoy a certain amount of time with some people simply because we happen to like the same activities, we realize that these playmates aren't the same as real friends.

As our social reasoning matures, we also start realizing that we don't have to interact with people in terms of putting them into overly simplistic, either-or categories. Unlike young children, we understand that we can relate to people at levels other than "friend" or "not a friend." This more mature reasoning enables us to interact with our peers at a variety of different levels—some can be friends; only a few can be best friends; but many can be acquaintances that we enjoy on a more limited, more casual basis. Learning this allows a sort of liberation: We don't have to throw relationships away or refuse to get to know people simply because we can't fit them into some overly simplistic category. As a consequence of our more expansive ways of perceiving relationships, we're able to interact with a larger number of people in a variety of ways. For example, most adoles-cents are able to understand that a stepparent can still be family and friend with-out having to be related to as parent. Thus, about 80% of all high-school students say they have five or six "good" friends, but only one or two "best" friends (Savin-Williams & Berndt, 1990).

TIME WITH FRIENDS

Typically, teenagers begin to spend less and less time at home. With going to school, working part-time jobs, studying, dating, and hanging out with friends, most teenagers spend only about 20 minutes a day interacting with their families. For adults who complain about children spending too much time in front of the TV set, the good news is that adolescents watch less and less television. Although girls spend more time than boys talking to their friends on the phone, both males and females spend about 20 hours a week with friends. Most adolescent friend-ships are also fairly stable and long-lasting. For example, the majority of 14-year-olds have a close friendship that has lasted anywhere from 1 to 5 years. Indeed, fewer than 10% of all adolescents have no contact with their classmates outside of school (Savin-Williams & Berndt, 1990).

SIMILARITY AMONG FRIENDS

Although many adults worry that other teenagers who have nothing in com-mon with their children will lead them astray, most adolescents who become friends are about the same age and share similar values, goals, family backgrounds, race, and religion. Consequently, friends tend to think and behave in similar ways when it comes to drinking, smoking, attending church, dating, graduating from high school or college, and using drugs. In fact, the longer two adolescents are friends, the more similar they become. All in all then, adults don't need to worry much about their teenage children being transformed into totally different people by other teenagers who have nothing in common with them to begin with (Savin-Williams & Berndt, 1990; Tolson & Urberg, 1993).

Although interracial friendships are still rare, friendships between males and females are even more uncommon. In fact, only about 5% of teenagers are friends with someone of the other sex compared to 15% who are friends with someone of another race (Hallinan & Williams, 1989; Hartup & Overhauser, 1991). It seems that both male and female adolescents get more self-confirmation and feel freer to explore the "who-am-I" issues with friends of their own sex (Lempers & Lempers, 1993).

As mentioned, most adolescents' "birds-of-a-feather" tendencies also extend to the ages of their friends. It's unusual for adolescents to be friends with people who are considerably older or younger. So should parents worry if their teenage children do start making friends with teenagers who are several years older? Maybe. In some cases young teenagers who hang out with older teenagers are more sexually active and more involved in delinquent behavior. On the other hand, this doesn't prove that older teenagers are a bad influence. The research doesn't demonstrate whether the younger adolescents were more prone to delinquency or more sexually active than other people their age *before* they started associating with older teenagers. Children whose bodies mature at a young age also tend to hang out with older teenagers because they're more alike in terms of their physical maturity. Because physically mature youths tend to be more interested in sex than others their age, their higher rate of sexual activity might have much more to do with their physical maturity than with the age of the people they're associating with (Savin-Williams & Berndt, 1990).

PHYSICAL APPEARANCE AND FRIENDSHIP

What about physical appearance? How important are looks to adolescents in terms of dates and friendships? As is true with adults, the most attractive adolescents are usually perceived by their peers and by adults as possessing more positive personality traits than unattractive youths. In other words, most of us tend to assume that good-looking teenagers are going to be more intelligent, more sociable, more sexual, more poised, more self-confident, more kind, more flexible, more self-disciplined and more enjoyable to be around than unattractive teenagers. Believing this, we unknowingly interact with attractive adolescents in ways that build their self-confidence; and we give them the benefit of the doubt when they show us the more undesirable sides of their personalities. So we inadvertently help attractive teenagers live up to our positive preconceptions of the appealing people we thought they would be before we got to know them. Not only their peers, but also teachers and other adults tend to hold these beliefs about attractive adolescents (Adams, 1991).

Although these findings are pretty discouraging when we think about what they seem to imply for unattractive adolescents, the situation isn't really that glum. First, the initial benefits that go along with being physically appealing tend to wear off as people spend more time around these adolescents. With enough contact and enough time, adults and adolescents eventually recognize the attractive teenager's shortcomings and the unattractive teenager's assets. It is true that attractive teenagers initially get more attention and that a girl's looks affect her popularity more than a boy's. However, in the long-run—regardless of gender—physical appearance doesn't determine how well-liked most adolescents are or whether they have friends and dates. Appearance usually has a significant impact on teenagers' friendships and social lives only for the very small minority who are extraordinarily beautiful or handsome or who are terribly ugly or disfigured (Coie, 1993).

THE IMPORTANCE OF FRIENDS

No matter what our age, we value friends. During our teenage years, though, our friends are especially important to our development. Perhaps more than at any other time of life, having or not having friends as teenagers affects our ego development, our identity, our self-esteem, and our mental health. This is why it's extremely important for adults to intervene on behalf of children who are still

How did your friends help and hinder your adolescent development?

having persistent problems making friends or getting close to their peers by the time they reach adolescence.

EGO DEVELOPMENT

One of the greatest benefits of having close friends and interacting with other teenagers in a variety of situations is the chance to develop a more mature ego and more mature social reasoning. As discussed, two aspects of ego development are crucially important during adolescence. The first is learning how to get along better with people by adopting less egocentric ways of reasoning and behaving. This involves not only becoming better at recognizing and empathizing with the motives that underlie another person's actions, but also analyzing our own behavior and motives more honestly and more objectively. Surprisingly, perhaps, our peers often help us achieve this maturity better than do our families. Other teenagers generally give us greater opportunities to become more empathic, more objective, more tolerant, more forgiving, and more flexible (Bornstein & Bruner, 1993; Gullotta, Adams, & Montemayor, 1990; Harter, 1990; Kandel, Raveis, & Davies, 1991; Marcia, 1991).

The other important aspect of teenage ego development is individuation—learning to see ourselves as separate from the adults we love, becoming more self-reliant, and assuming more responsibility for our own behavior and decisions. Without becoming more individuated, we aren't able to create truly intimate, satisfying relationships with people outside the family—either as adolescents or as adults. Our teenage peers help us realize that our own opinions, feelings, decisions, and identities don't have to replicate those of the adults we love. Although individuation doesn't require rejecting or emotionally detaching from the adults we love, it does entail not feeling guilty or disloyal when we have feelings, make decisions, or reach conclusions that are different from theirs.

Remember, too, that some parents don't support or encourage their teenager's individuation or self-reliance. At one extreme are those parents and children who are enmeshed in one another's lives—a situation that might prevent individuation from occurring even when the "child" is 40 years old. At the other extreme are those parents or stepparents who push their teenagers to grow up or to leave home too soon. Less extreme are the majority of parents who occasionally feel confused, uncomfortable, or maybe even a little sad as they watch their teenagers pulling away from them in the ways that are a necessary part of individuation. Regardless of how families respond, teenagers seldom can become individuated without having friends and interacting with people their age on a regular basis.

Although interacting with our peers helps our egos mature throughout childhood, our peer relationships are especially important during adolescence when most of us are on the brink of leaving home and living apart from our families. Without having had years of experience interacting with other teenagers, we aren't likely to develop the thinking and behavior that enable us to lead satisfying lives away from our families. In short, our friends can help us avoid becoming an adolescent or a young adult with arrested ego development like the person described in Insert 5–1.

Insert 5–1

Characteristics of Adolescents with Troubled Peer Relationships

Adolescents who have the most problems making friends and relating well to other people usually have arrested ego development, egocentric ways of thinking, external locus of control attitudes, or a difficult temperament. The following characteristics represent immature, child-like levels of social reasoning and ego development. How would you rate yourself now and as you were as an adolescent?

1 = very seldom, almost never   10 = frequently, almost always

**Arrested Ego Development:
Immature Social and Moral Reasoning**

Now   Then

____ ____ Interprets situations from an absolutist, either-or position

____ ____ Rejects contradictory information or opinions

____ ____ Uses many defense mechanisms to avoid admitting mistakes

____ ____ Doesn't consider other people's perspectives or feelings

____ ____ Fails to consider the impact of words and actions before reacting

____ ____ Sets high standards for others but doesn't apply them to self

____ ____ Rejects, punishes, and criticizes others quickly

____ ____ Judges others without considering their motives or their past behavior

____ ____ Fails to see the motives underlying people's behavior

____ ____ Stereotypes other people

____ ____ Forgives other people for their mistakes slowly or begrudgingly

____ ____ Categorizes or judges people on the basis of a few isolated incidents

____ ____ Shows little empathy or compassion for others

____ ____ Unable to see more than one or two solutions to interpersonal problems

____ ____ Unable to consider the circumstances that influence people's behavior

**Negative Explanatory Style and
External Locus of Control Attitudes**

____ ____ Refuses to accept responsibility for poor relationships with other people

SELF-AWARENESS AND SELF-ESTEEM

We also need other teenagers to help us mature in another important way—to gain more insight into our own behavior and motives (Damon & Hart, 1988; Eisenberg, 1991). Our teenage friends give us opportunities to gain a better understanding of other people's motives and behavior, as well as our own. Our friends and the people we date usually provide us with feedback about our own

____ ____ Blames bad moods, bad situations, or personal failures on other people

____ ____ Refuses to assume responsibility for improving unpleasant situations

____ ____ Blames problems on bad luck or circumstances beyond control

____ ____ Unwilling to change behavior in ways that could foster greater happiness

____ ____ Manifests a "poor me" attitude of sadness, passivity, and helplessness

____ ____ Rejects advice on how to improve unhappy situations

Difficult Temperament

____ ____ Exhibits introverted temperament

____ ____ Displays intense, unpredictable, easily aroused emotions

____ ____ Prefers self-pitying to self-satisfied

____ ____ Remains physically passive, inactive

____ ____ Shows reserve rather than affection

____ ____ Seems insecure and anxious rather than secure and calm

____ ____ Relies on disorganization and carelessness rather than organization and carefulness

____ ____ Prefers routines to variety

____ ____ Seems anxious and insecure rather than calm and secure

Infancy and Early Childhood

____ ____ Showed problems related to eating, sleeping, or toilet training

____ ____ Was difficult to soothe when crying

____ ____ Preferred physical inactivity or physical hyperactivity

____ ____ Clung to mother excessively in comparison to other children the same age

____ ____ Displayed short attention span, was easily distracted

____ ____ Cried profusely for long periods of time when separated from mother

____ ____ Suffered from allergies, bed-wetting, or other physical signs of stress

shortcomings, our own hypocrisy, and our own errors in social and moral reasoning. They serve as mirrors that allow us to see ourselves differently than we do in our families—both our good and our bad points, our lighter side and our darker side, our beauty and our beast.

Our teenage friends and the people we date also help build our self-esteem and self-confidence in ways that even the most supportive, loving family members simply can't. Think back and remember the countless times your own parents or stepparents complimented you for something, then compare the impact of their efforts with one terrific compliment from someone your own age. Not only do those of us with close friends have more self-esteem as teenagers, we also make better grades and enjoy school more than those of us who are lonely and virtually friendless (Savin-Williams & Berndt, 1990).

DRUGS, DELINQUENCY, AND SCHOOL FAILURE

Adolescents who have close friends and get along fairly well with people are also less likely to abuse drugs and alcohol, to break the law, or to quit school than those who are socially rejected or ignored (Asher & Coie, 1990; Coie, 1993; Compas & Wagner, 1991; Page & Cole, 1991). Why? First, adolescents who have very few or no friends almost always have very low self-esteem and immature social and moral reasoning skills. Given their immaturity and their low self-esteem, it's not especially surprising that they would abuse drugs and alcohol, break the law, or be disinterested in school. Second, most adolescents who have trouble making friends also make bad choices when it comes to people they associate with. They generally try to become friends with other immature, troubled teenagers rather than with more socially mature, well-adjusted teenagers. Remember, teenagers tend to choose friends who are like themselves. As a result, lonely or troubled teenagers wind up hanging around with the very people who are least likely to teach them, or expect from them, more mature behavior.

MENTAL HEALTH

Finally, whether adolescents have close friends is important for two other reasons. First, having a close friend seems to help most adolescents cope better with their problems. For example, when your parents are going through a divorce or when your boyfriend or girlfriend has jilted you, having a close friend can help get you through the tough times. Second, noticing which adolescents don't have close friends can help adults identify those adolescents who have, or might develop, serious psychological disorders. One of the most common symptoms of many mental disorders is being unable to get along well with, or become close to, peers. Among both adolescents and adults, people who spend most of their free time alone have more emotional and psychological problems than people who spend most of their leisure time with another person. Especially for teenage boys, continually having troubled relationships with peers or not having friends is frequently a symptom of psychological disturbance. This isn't to say that not having friends *causes* a person to develop a psychological disorder. It's simply that adolescents with psychological problems usually have been thinking and behaving in ways that don't attract peers throughout their childhood. Having a close friend seems to act as a buffer against serious mental disorders (Asher & Coie, 1990; Bornstein & Bruner, 1993; Clarizio, 1994; Harrington, 1994; Hartup & Overhauser, 1991; Larson, 1990).

As Insert 5–2 illustrates, being extremely shy, socially isolated, and unable to maintain a close relationship as an adolescent often indicates a psychological disorder. For example, adolescents who are so shy or so withdrawn that they rarely relate to people outside their immediate family might be suffering from an

Insert 5–2

Psychological Disorders Associated with Poor Peer Relationships

Schizophrenic Disorders

Few or no close friends

No intimate relationships

Grossly immature social reasoning and behavior

Extremely angry, irritable and negative

Emotionally cold, distant, or apathetic

Little or no interest in sex or dating

Avoidant Personality Disorder

Few or no social activities

Restrained in intimate relationships

Shy and inhibited in new social situations

Self-concept as socially inept, unappealing, or inferior

Clinical Depression

Loss of interest in people

Poor peer relationships

Separation Anxiety Disorder

Worries of loss of, or harm coming to, parents

Worries and stress due to separations from family

Reluctance or refusal to go to school

Fears being alone at home without family

Dependent Personality Disorder

Needs others to assume responsibility for him/her

Excessive needs to be nurtured

Uncomfortable or feelings of helplessness when alone

Desperate in seeking relationships

Antisocial Personality Disorder

Aggressive or violent with peers

Impulsive, irresponsible, deceitful

Reckless disregard for other people

Little or no remorse, empathy, or guilt

Conduct Disorder

Bullying, threatening, and intimidating to others

Violent fights, use of weapons

Physically cruel to people or animals

Frequent lying and breaking of promises

Theft and destruction of property

Oppositional Defiant Disorder

Argumentative, hot-tempered, defiant

Deliberately annoys people

Frequently blames others for his/her mistakes

Touchy, angry, spiteful

Source: Adapted from: *Diagnostic and Statistical Manual of Mental Disorders.* (1994). Washington, DC: American Psychiatric Association.

avoidant personality disorder or a social anxiety disorder. Being unable to make friends and not dating also might indicate that an adolescent is too dependent on the family or too afraid of self-reliance—symptoms of **dependent personality disorders** or **separation anxiety disorders.** It's also worth noting that a number of shy, withdrawn, isolated adolescents are clinically depressed. Some of the earliest and most recognizable symptoms of teenage depression are not having close friends, not dating, and not being intimate with anyone outside the family (American Psychiatric Association, 1994; Rubin, Lemare, & Lollis, 1990).

Even more disturbing, the same combination might be symptomatic of **schizophrenia,** one of the most serious of all psychotic disorders. Schizophrenia and the related **schizoid personality disorder** almost always surface during adolescence when these teenagers' social isolation and emotional detachment stands out so clearly. Schizophrenic adolescents are unable to become emotionally attached to anyone or to maintain an ongoing friendship. By early adulthood, the schizophrenic's thinking and behavior usually become so distorted and so removed from reality that he or she is incapable of functioning without medication or hospitalization. We discuss this disorder in Chapter 15. So for now the important thing to remember is that adolescents who are extremely shy, socially withdrawn, virtually friendless, and emotionally detached even from members of their own family might be manifesting the first symptoms of schizophrenia.

Other adolescents, however, don't have friends because of being too aggressive, defiant, abusive, or violent. Many of these teenagers are suffering from psychological problems categorized as **conduct disorder, antisocial personality disorder,** or **oppositional defiant disorders**—all of which stem from the adolescent's basic disregard for society's rules and for other people's feelings or well-being. About half of those teenagers who are rejected by most of their peers are shunned for being too aggressive or too violent (Peplar & Rubin, 1994). Because these disorders are associated with delinquency and violence, we discuss them in Chapter 15 in connection with teenage crime and violence. By comparing the characteristics of the various mental disorders described in Insert 5–2, you will recognize a common thread: being unable to create a satisfying, emotionally attached, intimate, or ongoing relationship with a peer.

In sum, our teenage friends give us the chance to advance our social and moral reasoning skills, build our self-esteem, fashion an identity separate from our parents, and buffer ourselves against serious psychological problems. Without a close friend and without frequent contact with people our age, no matter how intelligent we are or how loving our families, it's unlikely that we'll develop the skills or attitudes to have truly intimate or satisfying relationships. Failing to develop more mature ways of thinking and behaving during our teenage years also puts us at greater risk for psychological and social problems in our adult lives (Michalos, 1991; Myers, 1992).

WELL-ADJUSTED VERSUS TROUBLED ADOLESCENTS

Now that we've seen the importance of friends to adolescent development, we're led to the question: Why are some adolescents much better at getting along with people and more mature in their social reasoning than others? Before exploring this question, you need to keep two things in mind. First, how well or how poorly teenagers get along with people is usually obvious very early in their lives. By the time we're five or six years old, clear differences have already

How popular were you as an adolescent? Why?

emerged in terms of how well we empathize, compromise, cooperate, tolerate frustration, listen, consider others' feelings and opinions, and assume the initiative for interacting with people. Even at this early age, some of us are much more self-disclosing, more compassionate, more tolerant, and more sociable than others. To put it more bluntly: Teenagers who are hard to get along with and who don't have close friends have usually had these problems since they were very young children (Dunn, 1993).

Second, there's a difference between the social problems that well-adjusted adolescents have and those that indicate psychological disorders or arrested ego development. For example, simply because an adolescent might go for a few months without a close friend or without dating doesn't mean that he or she has arrested ego development or a psychological disorder. It's normal for most teenagers to endure a few weeks or even a few months of feeling lonely or being dissatisfied with their friendships and their social lives. There are any number of perfectly understandable reasons why teenagers might temporarily find themselves without a friend or with nobody to date—being new in a school, being preoccupied with a family problem, or making the transition from junior high to high school, for example. Furthermore, our junior-high years seem to be tougher than those of senior high when it comes to making friends and enjoying our social lives (Asher & Coie, 1990).

So when we're discussing troubled adolescents who don't get along well with people because of their difficult temperaments, or arrested ego development, or a psychological disorder, we're not referring to the vast majority of teenagers who are sometimes lonely and unhappy about not having friends or dates. "Troubled," or "maladjusted," or "arrested development" refers to adolescents who have chronic problems making friends or getting along with people month after month or, in extreme cases, year after year. These are the young people who drag their social and emotional problems with them into their adult lives unless someone intervenes to help them get the professional help they need. Because serious problems are almost always apparent in early childhood, millions of children would benefit from more intensive help from their families, their teachers, and professional therapists. If we were more focused on helping young children whose social and ego development clearly lags behind their peers, by the time they reached adolescence more of them would have satisfying friendships that can bring much joy and maturity (Asher & Coie, 1990).

It's important to remember that an adolescent's social development involves more than how he or she actually behaves around people. Social development also includes how adolescents reason about social matters: What are their overall styles of interpreting the world around them—hostile? pessimistic? optimistic? egocentric? accusatory? It's important to explore these cognitive patterns because they are closely related to how we interact with other people (Gullotta, Adams, & Montemayor, 1990; Myers, 1992).

To determine why some adolescents develop positive, productive ways of interpreting their experiences but others develop destructive and self-defeating patterns, the next section addresses the research on temperament and the research on explanatory styles. The third factor that affects adolescents' social relationships is gender—a topic explored in the Chapter 6.

TEMPERAMENT AND SOCIAL RELATIONSHIPS

DEFINING TEMPERAMENT

In trying to figure out why some adolescents do better than others at getting along with people, the most obvious place to start is at the beginning—birth. **Temperament** or **disposition** consists of those ways of behaving and interpreting experiences that appear very early in our lives and that seem to remain relatively unchanged as we age. Those researchers who study temperament or personality traits are referred to as **trait theorists.** As shown in Figure 5–1, temperament or disposition is primarily defined by two groups of traits—extroversion or introversion, and emotional stability or instability. Where one's personality fits on a scale of extroversion–introversion can be referred to as a measure of that person's sociability, whereas emotional instability can be referred to as neuroticism or as being emotionally labile. Some researchers have added a third trait, activity level, which indicates how energetic or how self-motivated the person is (Capaldi & Rothbart, 1992; Eysenck & Eysenck, 1963; Plomin, DeFries, & McClearn, 1990).

Sociability, that is, one's degree of introversion versus extroversion, is a trait that involves more than merely how outgoing or how relaxed an adolescent is around other people. **Introverts** are not only shy, withdrawn, and uncomfortable around people, but they also tend to avoid or withdraw from new experiences

Figure 5–1

Personality traits: Aspects of temperament

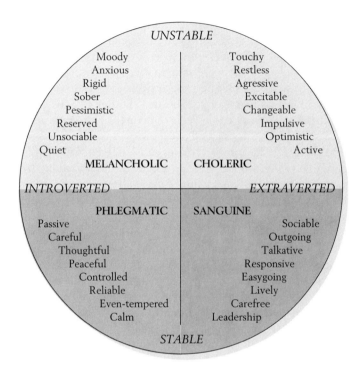

and challenging tasks. Introverted teenagers tend to be more somber, lethargic, reserved, unaffectionate, and unenthusiastic. In contrast, **extroverts** are more curious, outgoing, risk-taking, fun-loving, energetic, and responsive when interacting with the unfamiliar or attempting challenging things.

The second major aspect of temperament is emotionality, meaning how often, how easily, how unpredictably, and how intensely a person's emotions are aroused. Emotionally stable adolescents are better at regulating their emotions and behavior than emotionally "unstable" adolescents, whose dispositions are referred to as **labile** or **neurotic.** Emotionally stable teenagers are relatively self-regulated, calm, even-tempered, flexible, and easy-going. They're able to calm down soon after getting upset. Adolescents with more neurotic, labile dispositions are impulsive, reactive, touchy, excitable, moody, intense, and unpredictable. They are too quickly and too easily angered, hurt, and offended—and very slow to calm down or cool off. The emotionally labile adolescent is often described by peers as moody, high strung, hot-tempered, volatile, easily stressed, and hypersensitive.

These adolescents have too little self-control and overreact to other people's remarks or behavior.

According to some researchers, another important aspect of emotionality is the degree to which one seeks pleasure. Regardless of whether a person is an extrovert or an introvert, he or she can possess either a joyful disposition that finds pleasure in the world or a joyless disposition that can't seem to find pleasure in anything. Extroverted pleasure seekers find enjoyment primarily through interacting with other people and through participating in exciting or somewhat risky physical activities. Introverted pleasure seekers find joy in more private, less risky activities such as hiking, painting, or gardening. Whether an extrovert or an introvert, having a disposition that enables you to create joyful experiences for yourself is a definite plus for your social and psychological well-being as an adolescent (Capaldi & Rothbart, 1992; Plomin, DeFries, & McClearn, 1990).

As shown in Figure 5–1, we can view an adolescent as belonging to one of four temperamental categories or personality types: extroverted, introverted, dysthymic, or hysteric. Each personality type carries with it certain social and psychological benefits or risks (Chess & Thomas, 1993; Eysenck & Eysenck, 1963; Harrington, 1994; Myers, 1992; Seligman, 1991; Strack & Argyle, 1990).

The most fortunate group of adolescents are those with a relatively extroverted, emotionally stable disposition. Fairly sociable and even-tempered, these teenagers generally get along well with people and have the fewest psychological problems. The next most fortunate are the introverted teenagers with fairly calm, stable, self-controlled personalities. Although they have more trouble getting to know people than extroverts, their calm, reasonable dispositions can still work in their favor socially. These emotionally stable introverts aren't especially prone to psychological disorders, although extreme shyness is often related to anxiety disorders or dependent personality disorders.

In contrast to these two types of emotionally stable teenagers are the two kinds of emotionally unstable adolescents—those with neurotic dispositions and those with melancholic or **dysthymic** dispositions. Introverted, emotionally unstable teenagers have the highest risk for developing psychological problems such as depression, paranoia, and schizoid or schizophrenic personalities. Although these shy, socially isolated teenagers aren't physically aggressive or violent, their emotional instability makes them very difficult to get along with. Shy and passive around their peers, these adolescents are often very demanding, aggressive, moody, uncontrollable, inflexible, and overreactive around their families. The second group of emotionally unstable teenagers are extroverts who are aggressive, combative, and sometimes violent around their families and peers. Most delinquents and teenagers with mental disorders related to violent, defiant, or criminal behavior are in this category.

The Impact of Heredity

The question that inevitably comes to mind next is: How much of a teenager's disposition is determined by genetic make-up and how much is shaped by environmental factors? To answer this question, many researchers start by study-ing the behavior of a group of infants and then follow their dispositions as toddlers, children, and adolescents. To assess dispositions of infants, researchers measure such things as how long it takes someone to soothe them when they're crying, how often they cry or fret, how they behave around unfamiliar objects and new people, and how long they continue crying when separated from their mothers. These early infant studies and other research have led to the generally accepted conclu-sion that certain aspects of our temperaments are indeed influenced by genetic factors. In other words, how well or how poorly we get along with other people as adolescents is partly determined by the disposition we are born with (Block & Gjerde, 1991; Chess & Thomas, 1993; Kagan, 1989; Robins & Rutter, 1990).

The importance of heredity in shaping temperament is perhaps best demon-strated by the research of one of the world's leading experts on child and adoles-cent development, Jerome Kagan. After a lifetime of studying shy children and adolescents, Kagan concludes: "Now when I look at a shy two-year-old, I envision an excitable amygdala [part of the central nervous system]; twenty years ago I saw a child who had been punished for particular social behaviors or had experi-enced discomfort in peer or adult interactions. This change in perspective has altered my attitude toward the small number of adults I know who have a very short fuse. I used to invent a history of life events that created their temper; and I privately blamed them for not using their will to prevent their past history from influencing them. Currently, I am more forgiving; after all, it is not their fault that they were born with a reactive limbic circuit" (Kagan, 1989, p. 6). As explained further on in the section on adolescents with introverted temperaments, Kagan has found that extremely shy teenagers and adults start life with neurological and chemical differences that predispose them to be shy (Galvin, 1992).

The link between certain aspects of our personalities and our genetic inheri-tance is also demonstrated in the field of **psychopharmacology**—the study of drugs and chemicals that are part of the genetic makeup of our bodies or that affect our dispositions and behavior. As discussed in Chapter 15, certain drugs change teenagers' moods and behaviors. More astounding still, a new antidepres-sant drug called Prozac seems to be changing some people's temperaments by altering the chemical make-up of their brains' neurotransmitters. For a number of depressed people, Prozac not only has alleviated their depression but also made their dispositions more extroverted, more calm, and less melancholic. This research in biopsychology has been establishing connections between the chemi-cals in our brains and certain behaviors or ways of thinking that have traditionally been viewed as unchangeable parts of our temperament such as aggressiveness, hyperactivity, and depression (Kramer, 1993).

The Impact of Environment

So is the research telling us that the way we relate to people as adolescents is basically determined by the disposition we were born with? When it comes to those adolescents who don't get along well with people, should we shrug our shoulders and tell ourselves there's nothing anyone could have done to change the outcome? Doesn't temperament have anything to do with the experiences we have while we're growing up?

First, when trait theorists say there's a genetic influence on our temperaments, they don't mean that we will definitely inherit the exact disposition of one of our parents. For example, if both of your parents are extremely shy, you might still have been born with a very outgoing, extroverted disposition. Furthermore, the current thinking is that only about 40% of a person's temperament can be accounted for by genetic factors. This leaves 60% to be determined by environmental factors. Second, some aspects of temperament seem to be less affected by our genes than others. The two traits most influenced by our genes are how extroverted we are and how stable or controlled our emotions are. Aspects of our temperament such as the motivation to achieve, risk taking, rebelliousness, empathy, tolerance for ambiguity, or the need to be intimate with other people seem to be most closely connected to the experiences we have as we're growing up (Plomin, DeFries, & McClearn, 1990).

Third, traits theorists recognize that the situation a person is in affects how he or she will behave at that particular point in time. That is, simply knowing a person's basic disposition doesn't give us some superhuman power to predict exactly how he or she is going to act in every conceivable situation (Gullotta, Adams, & Montemayor, 1990). A person's basic temperament determines the way he or she behaves and reasons *most* of the time in situations that are *similar* to ones they've been in before. Because most of us choose the same situations to be in day after day, we generally display the same dispositions day after day. Yet, a 16-year-old who is basically introverted can be very quiet in school but fairly talkative at home. So you can't jump to the conclusion that your brother's or sister's terrible disposition comes entirely from "bad" genes (of course, you inherited the good genes from your favorite relatives' side of the family, right?).

Fourth, we know that a child's basic disposition can be affected for better or for worse by the experiences he or she has, especially by experiences with the parents during the first few years of life. For example, children born with extremely introverted or extremely aggressive temperaments do become more sociable when both parents consistently relate to them in ways that develop more mature, more sociable behavior (Grauerholz & Koralweski, 1991). Which aspects of an adolescent's disposition will recede and which will flourish also depends on how much stress is in the family and on each parent's mental health (Plomin, DeFries, & McClearn, 1990; Robins & Rutter, 1990). Poverty, conflict between parents, and child abuse also increase the odds that the most negative aspects of a child's disposition will grow by time he or she reaches adolescence (Myers, 1992; Robins & Rutter, 1990; Strack & Argyle, 1990).

On the other hand, your basic disposition can't somehow be exchanged or swapped for a better one merely by controlling the experiences you have. In fact, the way infants and toddlers respond to an experience is largely determined by their basic disposition. As the familiar metaphor illustrates, a child with a melancholic temperament sees a "half empty" glass of water. But the more optimistic child sees the same glass of water as "half full." Children and adolescents who have sullen, volatile, fearful, inflexible, withdrawn, or aggressive temperaments react more negatively to unpleasant events and stress than do those with more upbeat, stable, outgoing, and flexible dispositions. We can't simply add up the good and bad things that happen in a child's life to explain why some adolescents have more agreeable dispositions than others. In fact, a number of socially well-adjusted teenagers and adults with very pleasant dispositions have encountered more stressful, negative events than socially maladjusted people their age who have very disagreeable dispositions (Argyle, 1990; Michalos, 1991; Myers, 1992). So the bottom line is that an adolescent's temperament is determined both by genetic factors and by the experiences he or she has.

PARENTS' INFLUENCES ON TEMPERAMENT

Given that our temperaments are shaped in part by the experiences we have at home, researchers have naturally wondered: Which parent has the greater influence over a child's temperament, or which parent's temperament is the child's more likely to resemble?

Some evidence suggests that the opposite-sex parent has the most impact on certain aspects of our dispositions. For example, one of the most careful and thorough longitudinal studies that followed young adolescents into their 40s found that those with the most maladaptive dispositions were most like the opposite-sex parent. The sons with the most difficult dispositions, most debilitating psychological problems, and most troubled social relationships were most like their mothers; and the troubled daughters were most like their fathers. As a consequence, Block concludes: "A good father married to a neurotically ineffective woman cannot produce a good son; and a good mother married to a neurotically ineffectual man cannot produce a good daughter" (Block, 1971, p. 260). Block also reported that the most troubled adolescents didn't admire (they did not "want to grow up to be like") their opposite-sex parent—the parent they were most like temperamentally and the parent who seemed to have had the greater influence over their development. This suggests that the parent we most admire isn't necessarily the parent we'll be most like when it comes to our dispositions. For reasons discussed in Chapter 8, mothers and fathers seem to have different impacts on their sons' and on their daughters' development.

Other evidence, however, suggests that each parent's own disposition determines which child he or she will influence most. That is, within any family, each child's temperament simply seems to "fit better" with one parent's than with the other's, regardless of gender (Dunn, 1993). Likewise, it seems that whichever parent is the least psychologically well-adjusted has the most influence over the child who has the most social, psychological, or developmental problems. For example, a depressed parent usually has more impact on the overly dependent, fearful child than on the more outgoing, self-reliant child. This connection between the most troubled parent and the most vulnerable child is especially sad because children with difficult dispositions also react more negatively to stress and problems within the family (Hetherington, 1991; Patterson, Reid, & Dishion, 1992; Rubin, Lemare, & Lollis, 1990).

CONTINUITY OF TEMPERAMENT

Because our experiences in our families do affect our development, researchers have also pursued the answer to these questions: How much do our temperaments change as we age? As adolescents, do most of us have the same dispositions we had as young children? And, as adults, do most of us have the same basic personalities we had as adolescents?

On the whole, the research shows that the two most important aspects of our dispositions—how extroverted we are and how stable or self-regulated our emotions are—remain fairly constant from very early childhood on. Because these two aspects of temperament have such a powerful influence on how well we get along with other people, most of us as adolescents relate to people very much as we did as young children. In other words, most teenagers with chronic problems in making friends, dating, or becoming intimate with others have had similar problems since they were preschoolers. So the good news is that if you have friends because of your relatively pleasant disposition as a 5-year-old, you're probably still going to have friends and a pleasant disposition as a teenager. The bad news is that if your disposition made it hard for you to relate well to people as a 5-year-old, you're probably going to be in the same predicament as a teenager. Unless someone intervenes to redirect our early childhood dispositions, there is an underlying continuity to our basic social and emotional style. Although the troubled adolescent often turns out to be better as an adult than we would have guessed, on the whole the child with a difficult disposition becomes the teenager and the adult with a difficult disposition (Block & Gjerde, 1991; Halverson, Kohnstamn & Martin, 1994; McCrae & Costa, 1986).

Among many others, two longitudinal studies illustrate how unvarying our temperaments tend to be. In a 30-year study of 75 upper middle-class white children, those who were timid, fearful, shy, tense, and overly dependent on their mothers as preschoolers had trouble making friends and getting along with people throughout childhood and adolescence as a consequence of their difficult temperaments. As adults, these individuals were still basically as gloomy, socially withdrawn, dissatisfied, emotionally detached, and unenthusiastic about most of what was going on around them as they had been as very young children (Chess & Thomas, 1993). In another study, ill-tempered, irritable, impulsive, and explosive 40-year-old men who had frequent temper tantrums as children and adolescents were more likely to have lower paying jobs and to be divorced than men with more pleasant childhood dispositions. Likewise, extremely shy 40-year-old men who had brittle egos as young boys and teenagers were still socially withdrawn, reluctant to make decisions, lacking insight into their own motives and behavior, and less committed to a stable career or marriage than more outgoing men with similar educations, physical appearance, and incomes (Caspi, Elder, & Herbener, 1990).

However, the way your temperament shows itself does change as you age. For example, if you're a physically aggressive, hyperactive 4-year-old who tears the arms off your teddy bear during daily temper tantrums, you might express your disposition as a teenager by smashing car windows or hitting people when you're upset. Or if you're a sullen, fearful, extremely shy 4-year-old who gets your parents to cave in to your demands by crying uncontrollably for hours, you might express yourself as a teenager by sulking and refusing to talk to your parents for days whenever you don't get your way.

Growing older, though, usually doesn't bring dramatic changes in those aspects of our disposition that affect how *well* we relate to other people. On the other hand, how we behave during our first 2 years of life is a less reliable predictor than how we behave as adolescents. That is, as we age, our present disposition becomes a better predictor of how we'll behave in the future. This is why it's extremely important for families and schools not to ignore or excuse those adolescents whose early childhood problems are still with them. The longer that

How did your physical health and your physical skills affect your personality as a teenager?

problems such as aggression or social immaturity continue, the more likely it is that these problems will follow us throughout our lives. Likewise, the earlier we intervene in a child's life, the better. This includes efforts to reshape problematic aspects of temperament, such as frequent temper tantrums, excessive crying or pouting, physical aggressiveness, hyperactivity and chronic inattentiveness, over-reliance on either parent, or extreme shyness. So let's now examine how an adolescent's temperament affects peer relationships and psychological development. Then let's look at those aspects of our families that seem to have the most impact on our temperaments as we're growing up.

INTROVERTED ADOLESCENTS

Is being shy a great disadvantage for teenagers? No, having an introverted disposition does not doom a teenager to unhappy relationships with his or her peers. In fact, somewhat shy teenagers who are relatively calm, self-controlled, good humored, and sweet tempered get along much better with their peers than the emotionally volatile and reactive extroverted teenagers who are basically out of control. In terms of a teenager's social and mental well-being, what generally matters most is how emotionally calm, good-natured, and stable he or she is, not how shy or how outgoing. As explained later, shy teenagers can be helped to become more sociable without drugs or therapy through assertiveness or social skills training.

Serious social and psychological problems, however, do plague those shy adolescents whose dispositions are very melancholic, overly reactive, volatile, and lacking in self-control. These are the teens with neurotic dispositions. Not only are these shy people extremely difficult to get along with as teenagers, they were also irritable, fretful, easily stressed, generally unhappy, and difficult to please as infants and toddlers. These introverted, emotionally volatile, somewhat angry adolescents also tend to have "insecure-attached" relationships with their mothers. Thus, they usually relate to people in "attached-avoidant" ways—extremely demanding, egocentric, distant, and hard to please, yet also extremely jealous, possessive, overly dependent, and clingy with the people they like or love (Belsky & Cassidy, 1994; Elicker, Englund, & Stroufe, 1992; Greenberg, Cicchetti, & Cummings, 1990; Karen, 1994).

It's this group of extremely introverted, high-strung, and moody teenagers that researchers such as Jerome Kagan believe are genetically predisposed to develop their withdrawn, emotionally overreactive dispositions. Kagan's view is that about 10% to 15% of all children are born with a predisposition to shyness, but that only 2% are still extremely inhibited by time they reach adulthood. Fortunately, most shy children receive the kind of parenting and peer experiences that help them overcome their extreme shyness by the time they reach adolescence. The other 2% continue to have serious social and psychological problems associated with their severe shyness and emotional reactivity (Galvin, 1992; Kagan, 1989; Kagan & Snidman, 1991).

As infants and as teenagers, when these children are around people other than their families or are faced with a new or challenging task or situation, they react physically with allergy attacks, bed wetting, constipation, stomach aches, headaches, or other physical symptoms of stress. During adolescence these extreme physical reactions can be part of disorders such as **social phobia** or acute **anxiety disorders.** According to Kagan, some children are born with what amounts to a hair-trigger brain circuit that contributes to their overreactivity and with chemical or neurological differences that contribute to their shyness. For a child born with this relatively rare condition, very little is required to overstimulate the amygdala, a small structure deep in the brain that helps control heart rate and perspiration. Even mild stress might cause these teenagers' hearts to pound and their palms to sweat, or bring on a migraine headache, an asthma attack, or a stomach ache. These teenagers, referred to a **temperamentally inhibited,** might also have excessive levels of a neurotransmitter called norepinephrine—a chemical similar to adrenaline, the fight-or-flight chemical that pumps us up when we're afraid or nervous. As detailed in Chapter 15, these shy teenagers often seem to profit from a combination of drug therapy, intensive counseling, and social skills training.

On the other hand, a genetic predisposition toward shyness doesn't entirely explain the behavior of these extremely introverted, rather angry teenagers. These teenagers also tend to share similar kinds of relationships with their parents. As young children, many of these teenagers were overly protected by and overly involved with their mother—often to the point of being emotionally estranged or even alienated from their father. Often their parents are unhappily married and their mothers are depressed and chronically dissatisfied with their own lives. Moreover, a number of their mothers lived with an emotionally cold, divorced mother, were rejected by their own fathers, and find it difficult to be emotionally intimate with adult males. Such family situations often lead the mother and shy child to become excessively dependent on each other and to interact in ways that make the child's shyness, social immaturity, and depressive ways of thinking and behaving even worse. Although shy and mild-mannered away from home, many of these teenagers are extremely self-centered, demanding, hostile, insensitive, and infantile at home—behavior that one or both parents have reinforced since early childhood. For reasons that are not altogether clear, sons are more likely than daughters to end up in this group of troubled and troublesome introverted teenagers. And, as we will see in Chapter 15, some of these shy yet hostile teenagers have schizoid personality disorders that require intensive therapy if they are to improve (Belsky & Cassidy, 1994; Elicker, Englund & Stroufe, 1992; Kagan, 1989; Karen, 1994; Putallaz & Heflin, 1993; Radke-Yarrow, 1991; Rubin, Lemare & Lollis, 1990; Waxler & others, 1992).

Regardless of how much of a teenager's shyness is related to these genetic or biological factors, extreme shyness becomes more of a social handicap as a child ages. Although extremely shy teenagers are no more likely to become delinquent or to drop out of school, they are more likely to abuse drugs and alcohol and to have psychological problems such as depression, schizoid personalities, anxiety disorders, paranoia, or dependent personality disorders (Larson & Richards, 1991; Page, 1990; Page & Cole, 1991; Rubin, Lemare, & Lollis, 1990).

Extremely shy adolescents who also have pessimistic, passive styles of interpreting their world are especially prone to clinical depression or suicide. These introverted, melancholic adolescents tend to have troubled relationships with people throughout their lives unless they receive professional help (Argyle, 1990; Caspi, Elder, & Herbener, 1990; Kupersmidt, Coie, & Dodge, 1993; Larson, 1990; Myers, 1992). Unfortunately, many parents refuse to seek help for their socially isolated, shy teenager—choosing instead to make excuses or ignore the teenager's social and emotional problems as they have since their child's first few years of life.

AGGRESSIVE ADOLESCENTS

About 50% of those adolescents who are rejected by their peers are disliked for being too aggressive, hostile, or, in some cases, physically violent (Asher & Coie, 1990). Only a small minority of teenagers condone physically aggressive or violent behavior. The vast majority of teenagers don't want to be around peers who are physically aggressive, violent, hostile, or physically threatening (Asher & Coie, 1990; Dunn, 1993; Peplar & Rubin, 1994).

Teenage violence and delinquency is discussed in Chapter 15, but let's take a brief look at the topic as it relates to trait theories. Some researchers report that aggressive or violent teenagers are born with extroverted, emotionally unstable dispositions. Even as young children, these teenagers were too easily excited, too impulsive, too touchy, too volatile, too reactive, and too unrestrained. Because aggressive and violent teenagers are usually much more defiant and aggressive than other children even as preschoolers, the current view is that aggression is caused by the combination of inborn temperament, inadequate parenting, family stress, and poverty. Indeed, aggressive teenagers have often been physically or sexually abused or raised in poverty (Cicchetti, 1992; Parke & Ladd, 1992; Peplar & Rubin, 1994). Other evidence suggests that teenage aggression might also be related to abnormal hormone levels. Both teenage males and females who are extremely impulsive, irritable, aggressive, destructive, and delinquent have been found to have unusually high levels of certain hormones that might be contributing to their aggressive, emotionally labile dispositions (Brooks-Gunn, 1991; Buchanan, Eccles, & Becker, 1992).

Some evidence also suggests that the neurological disorder referred to as **attention deficit hyperactivity disorder (ADHD)** can contribute to aggressive, defiant behavior. Once referred to as "minimal brain damage" or "hyperactivity," attention deficit disorders are closely linked with teenage delinquency, violence and aggression, and adult criminality. ADHD is addressed in Chapter 15, but it's important to mention that this neurological disorder might make some teenagers somewhat more aggressive, impulsive, and defiant. The symptoms are usually severe enough that 90% of these children are identified before the age 6 (American Psychiatric Association, 1994; Farrington, Loeber, & VanKammen, 1990).

EXPLANATORY STYLES AND SOCIAL RELATIONSHIPS

PERCEPTION AND PERSONALITY

As we've seen, our dispositions affect our relationships with people in large part by influencing how we interpret or perceive our experiences and other people's actions. Before examining how our patterns of thinking affect our teenage

---

Insert 5–3

Locus of Control Inventory

1. Do you believe most problems will solve themselves?

2. Are you often blamed for things that just aren't your fault?

3. Do you believe it doesn't pay to try hard because things seldom turn out?

4. Do you believe most parents listen to what their children say?

5. When you get punished, does it usually seem that it's for no good reason?

6. Do you usually find it hard to change a friend's opinions?

7. Do you believe that it is nearly impossible to change your parents' minds?

8. Do you believe that when you do something wrong there is very little you can do to make it right?

9. Do you believe that most students are just born good at sports?

10. Do you believe that a good way to handle problems is not to think about them?

11. Do you believe that if someone hits you, there isn't much you can do to stop it?

12. Have you felt that when people were mean to you it's for no reason?

13. Do you usually believe you can change what might happen by what you do?

14. Do you believe that when bad things are going to happen they are just going to happen no matter what you do?

15. Do you usually find it useless to try to get your way at home?

16. Do you believe that when somebody your age wants to be your enemy there is little you can do?

17. Do you usually believe that you have little to say about you get to eat?

18. Do you believe that when someone doesn't like you there is little you can do?

19. Do you usually believe it's useless to try in school because other students are just smarter than you?

20. Do you believe that planning ahead makes things turn out better?

21. Do you believe you usually have little to say about what your family does?

Scoring: Give yourself 1 point for answering "no" to questions 4, 13, and 20 and for answering "yes" to the others. The higher your score, the more pessimistic or "external" your locus of control attitudes are, or the more "learned helplessness" you have. The lower your score, the more optimistic or "internal" your locus of control attitudes are.

Source: S. Nowicki & B. Strickland (1973). A locus of control scale for children. *Journal of Consulting and Clinical Psychology, 40,* 148–154.

relationships though, we need to understand several fundamental findings about the connection between our perceptions and our behavior (Gilovich, 1991; Gullotta, Adams, & Montemayor, 1990).

First, as we go about perceiving and interpreting our experiences, all of us routinely exclude certain information about ourselves and other people from our thinking. For example, most of us ignore, forget, or "don't see" behavior in another person that contradicts our preconceived expectations or beliefs. For instance, if you believe that athletes aren't good students or that stepparents aren't very loving people, then you won't be as likely to see, hear, or remember information that contradicts your beliefs. Likewise, if you believe a particular person can do no wrong, then almost no matter what he or she does, you won't be very likely to "see" it. Most adolescents, like the rest of us, behave in accord with the principle: "I'll see it when I believe it," not "I'll believe it when I see it."

Second, how we explain our experiences to ourselves depends on our overall style of analyzing the world around us—our habitual ways of interpreting whatever bits of information we have allowed into our thinking. This is where our dispositions seem to come into play. Those of us with aggressive temperaments tend to interpret our world in hostile, defensive ways. Those of us with easygoing, stable dispositions usually give a more optimistic interpretation to other people's actions and to our experiences. Those with melancholic temperaments interpret events in gloomy, pessimistic ways. For example, if someone you're interested in dating doesn't give you a very enthusiastic response when you finally get up your nerve to say "hello," your disposition will partially influence how you react. As a melancholic, introverted person, you might say to yourself: "I made a fool of myself. Nobody has any interest in getting to know me. It's not worth trying to talk to anyone else in this school." As a more extroverted, calm person, you might tell yourself: "Well, maybe I picked a bad time. I'll try again tomorrow. Nothing ventured, nothing gained."

Third, when we're interacting with other people or deciding how to respond to a particular situation, we're seldom aware that we've excluded certain information. We're also generally unaware that our overall temperament or mood at any particular moment is coloring our interpretations of "reality" in ways that might be self-defeating. For example, if you have a splitting headache, you're probably going to give a more negative interpretation to your best friend's ignoring you than if you're feeling great after acing a final exam. In any event, the point is that teenagers' temperaments seem to be fairly consistently related to their overall style of interpreting other people's actions, as well as interpreting their own behavior and the situations in which they find themselves.

These different styles of interpreting or explaining the world to ourselves are referred to as our **explanatory styles,** or our **locus of control attitudes,** or our **attributional styles.** Most of us interpret our world in a style that is relatively stable day in and day out—stable enough to be considered a part of our temperament by the time we reach adolescence. Your individual explanatory style includes: how you explain to yourself why things are the way they are in your life, why other people behave the way they do, and why you and other people are succeeding or failing at this or that. The study of explanatory styles falls into an area of psychology known as **attribution theory**—the study of how or to what we attribute the things that happen to us in our lives and to what we attribute other people's behavior.

One of the most important and most well-researched aspects of explanatory styles is our **locus of control attitudes**—how much control we believe we have over what is happening or what will happen to us. People with **internal locus of control** attitudes generally feel and believe that their own behavior and their own decisions do influence how other people react to them and the situations in which they find themselves. In contrast, adolescents with **external locus of control** attitudes seldom see the connection between their own behavior and their circumstances. Instead, they behave as though they are virtually powerless when it comes to changing the unpleasant situations in their lives. Looking at Nowicki and Strickland's Locus of Control inventory in Insert 5–3, you can see the differences between the thought patterns of adolescents with external and internal explanatory styles (Nowicki & Strickland, 1973).

Another important aspect of explanatory style is how accurately we recognize the motives that underlie another person's behavior. On the one hand, it's not wise to have a style of thinking that is so naive or so optimistic that we can't ever recognize negative motives such as greed, jealousy, or hate. On the other hand, it's equally harmful to our relationships to continually attribute negative, hostile motives to other people's actions. By the time we reach adolescence, most of us aren't seriously handicapped by attributing motives that are "too good" to other people—at least, not in most situations. Yet, a number of adolescents *are* seriously handicapped by continually attributing other people's behavior to extremely negative, hostile motives. These adolescents are said to have a hostile attribution bias, which makes it very difficult for them to get along well with other people (Asher & Coie, 1990; Elicker, Englund, & Stroufe, 1992; MacKinnon & others, 1992; Parke, 1992; Waxler & others, 1992).

Our explanatory styles are related to how we behave around other people and to our mental health. Given the importance of our explanatory styles, psychologists are trying to answer questions such as these: Why is it that some adolescents interpret other people's behavior in ways that bring friendship, love, and intimacy into their lives? Why is it that some teenagers have pessimistic or hostile styles of explaining other people's behavior? Why do some adolescents interpret other people's behavior optimistically, and others interpret the world through such a dark, gloomy lens? Why do the latter continually impede their relationships and own development by using such immature ways of interpreting other people's behavior?

Adolescents with Optimistic Explanatory Styles

When it comes to explaining the causes of the good and bad events in their lives, adolescents with internal locus of control attitudes are willing to assume a considerable share of the responsibility for their situations and for their own feelings and

Insert 5–4

Adolescents with Extroverted Temperaments and Optimistic Explanatory Styles

The following list characterizes adolescents who have relatively extroverted temperaments and optimistic explanatory styles. How well do each of these describe you during adolescence? How well do these traits describe someone you know who has trouble making friends, getting along with people, and being emotionally intimate.

    1 = seldom, very infrequently   10 = almost always, very often

Me	*Other*	
____	____	1. **Loves and respects self**
____	____	2. **Focuses on more of the good in people than the bad**
____	____	3. **Perseveres in the face of obstacles and failure**
____	____	4. **Feels happy about life in general**
____	____	5. **Feels satisfied with most friendships**
____	____	6. **Sets own goals and usually achieves them**
____	____	7. **Focuses on how to solve problems rather than ruminating**
____	____	8. **Avoids obsessing on personal shortcomings and past failures**
____	____	9. **Envisions success and happiness for the future**
____	____	10. **Feels well physically**
____	____	11. **Tolerates frustration and criticism pretty well**
____	____	12. **Focuses on more positive than negative things from the past**
____	____	13. **Prefers upbeat people, stories, movies, and music**
____	____	14. **Chooses long-term rewards instead of immediate pleasures**
____	____	15. **Feels more satisfied than dissatisfied with life**
____	____	16. **Recalls childhood as a pretty happy one**
____	____	17. **Thinks parents did a pretty good job of child-rearing**
____	____	18. **Avoids comparisons to people who have or achieve more**
____	____	19. **Feels grateful for good things in life**
____	____	20. **Copes with stress relatively well**

moods. On the whole, these young people recognize the connections between their own behavior, how other people respond to them, and how things turn out for them—whether it's grades at school, a relationship with a friend, or success at a sport. These adolescents tend to take a self-motivated, active, energetic approach to solving problems with other people, to making their own lives better, and to changing their own bad moods. As Insert 5–4 illustrates, adolescents with these optimistic explanatory styles generally reason and behave in ways that attract, rather than repel, other people (Buchanan & Seligman, 1994; Seligman, 1991).

In terms of the quality of their relationships, these adolescents have an advantage over teenagers with helpless, external control attitudes. Instead of continually blaming other people or factors beyond their control for what's going on in a relationship, they assume a large part of the blame or credit for how others respond to them. For example, when things aren't going well with a friend, a teenager with internal control is likely to ask herself: "What am I saying or doing that's contributing to this problem? What could I change about my approach that might make things better?" Because these adolescents aren't usually accusing and blaming everybody else when they're frustrated or unhappy, they're more enjoyable to be around—even when problems in a relationship do arise. They understand that "the harder I work at something, the more 'luck' I have."

Being introspective and honest enough with themselves to admit to some of their own shortcomings, they assume their fair share of responsibility in making relationships work and in getting along with people. As you'd expect, adolescents with optimistic, self-motivated explanatory styles usually have more intimate, satisfying friendships and happier social lives than teenagers with pessimistic, helpless patterns of reasoning (Asher & Coie, 1990; Bandura, 1991; Buchanan & Seligman, 1994; Page, 1991; Strack & Argyle, 1990; VanBuskirk & Duke, 1991). Extremely pessimistic, hostile, or helpless explanatory styles are also closely correlated with various mental illnesses—a topic discussed at length in Chapter 15.

Adolescents with Pessimistic, Helpless Explanatory Styles

This same body of research also shows that adolescents who don't have intimate, satisfying friendships and who don't get along very well with most people often have external locus of control attitudes, also referred to as **learned helplessness** or **learned pessimism.** These adolescents often don't recognize the connection between their own behavior and how people react to them. Nor do they assume responsibility for how their behavior affects the happy or unhappy circumstances in their lives. Whether they've failed a test, been cut from a team, had an argument with a parent, or been unable to make friends, it's usually always somebody else's fault—seldom, if ever, their own. Rather than assuming some of the responsibility, these young people continually blame other people or blame factors beyond their control for most of what's wrong in their lives. If not blaming another person, these adolescents blame external factors like "bad luck." Or they blame their problems on a trait that they believe can't be altered in any way—"my hot-tempered nature" or "my shyness" are responsible, "but I can't do anything about it since that's just who I am." These pessimistic, passive ways of interpreting their experiences are common among teenagers who are rigid, sober, unsociable, moody, withdrawn, self-pitying, and anxious.

Given their pessimistic, passive explanatory styles, these teenagers tend to be unmotivated and self-pitying, often venting much of their hostility and frustration on those around them. Rather than doing something constructive to improve a particular situation or to pull themselves out of a bad mood, they remain passive and lethargic, or disgruntled and grumpy, or hostile and defensive. Rather than looking toward the future as an opportunity for making changes in their own lives, these adolescents stay gloomily or angrily focused on the negative aspects of their lives. They also tend to dwell obsessively on their past failures and disappointments. Being too focused on the negative parts of the past, they feel hopeless about the future. Not surprisingly, these adolescents don't have much success making friends or maintaining relationships, given their accusatory, passive ways of thinking. For example, if they don't have friends, it's "because everybody at my school is such a loser," or if they make a bad grade it's "because the teacher was boring and didn't like me." Needless to say, even though these adolescents want friends, most people don't enjoy being around them. Misery loves company, but company doesn't love misery.

At the other extreme, some adolescents interpret their experiences in ways that are far too self-blaming. They not only assume too much of the responsibility for how a relationship is going, they also hold themselves responsible for things that truly are beyond their control. Wrongly assuming that every problem is their fault, these adolescents aren't very comfortable to be around because they are too self-effacing and apologetic. Anytime anything goes wrong, these adolescents hold themselves totally responsible. If an adolescent continually assumes too much responsibility for too many of the things that don't turn out right, their social relationships suffer because other teenagers see them as "too down on themselves."

All in all, adolescents who are the most satisfied with their social relationships have locus of control attitudes that aren't excessively external or excessively internal. They think in ways that enable them to assume responsibility for much of what they're feeling and experiencing, yet still acknowledge the reality that certain aspects of our lives *are* beyond our control. Sometimes nobody in class does well on a test because the teacher was in a grumpy mood during the grading; sometimes an accident or an argument really isn't your fault; and sometimes your parents argue and make everyone in the family miserable no matter how you behave. As the theologian Reinhold Niebuhr said in his Serenity Prayer: "God, give us grace to accept with serenity the things that cannot be changed, courage to change the things which should be changed, and the wisdom to distinguish the one from the other."

ADOLESCENTS WITH HOSTILE EXPLANATORY STYLES

Another aspect of explanatory style that interferes with an adolescent's social development is **hostile attribution bias.** Adolescents with a hostile attribution style continually ascribe negative, hostile, or malicious motives to other people when, really, their motives were benign or their behavior was simply careless or accidental. Interpreting the world from this hostile stance, these adolescents are easily angered, hurt, and offended. They overreact to what other people say or do, rather than give others the benefit of the doubt or a chance to explain themselves. This unwillingness to communicate also enables these teenagers to perpetuate and exaggerate their distorted beliefs about reality. Whether a classmate accidentally bumps into them or a teacher jokes with them lightheartedly, these teenagers tend to react either by lashing out verbally or physically or by withdrawing into a hostile silence (Asher & Coie, 1990; Elicker, Englund, & Stroufe, 1992; Parke, 1992; Waxler & others, 1992).

Most adolescents with this biased, hostile way of interpreting the world are physically or verbally aggressive and can best be categorized as having an extroverted, emotionally unstable disposition. Many delinquent and violent teenagers have a hostile attribution bias (American Psychiatric Association, 1994). A hostile explanatory style is associated with a number of psychological disorders, such as paranoia and schizoid personality disorders, that render the adolescent's reasoning extremely distorted and maladapted. Some adolescents with hostile explanatory styles are extremely shy and passive, isolated in their own private world while interpreting life through a very hostile, negative lens. Unlike shy teenagers with emotionally stable dispositions, shy adolescents with these hostile styles get along very poorly with people as a consequence of their overly reactive, unstable, neurotic dispositions. Whether socially withdrawn and silently hostile or extroverted and outwardly aggressive, these adolescents create a reality for themselves that makes it difficult, if not impossible, for them to relate well to people or to be psychologically well-adjusted.

Adolescents with Depressive Explanatory Styles

Because we discuss depression in Chapter 15, it's worth mentioning now only that many adolescents who have hostile attribution biases or external locus of control attitudes are clinically depressed. Many teenagers who have had problems getting along well with their peers throughout childhood seem to have acquired hostile or external explanatory styles very early in their lives (American Psychiatric Association, 1994; Harrington, 1994; Kupersmidt, Coie, & Dodge, 1993).

In terms of adolescents' social development and psychological well-being, one of the worst situations is having external locus of control attitudes and a ruminating style of thinking. Rumination is the habit of obsessing on the people or events that make us sad or angry. Of course looking back at the past isn't always a bad thing. In fact, one sign of a teenager's social maturity is the ability to look back at the past, examine what went wrong, and try to figure out ways of behaving in the future that will prevent those mistakes from recurring. However, looking back at the past does much more harm than good if the adolescent has a hostile attribution bias or extremely external locus of control attitudes. These teenagers look back and obsess on what went wrong without taking any positive action to improve their situations in the future. They stew in their own juices, making themselves angrier or more depressed. For example, if someone has supposedly wronged them, rather than talking it over or trying to figure out constructive ways to deal with the situation, ruminating teenagers with helpless, pessimistic, or hostile explanatory styles throw more fuel on their own emotional fires. Brooding or ruminating about the past are common symptoms of clinical depression (American Psychiatric Association, 1994; Cohen, 1990; Seligman, 1991).

In terms of their peer relationships, these brooding teenagers can't see any way out of the hole they have dug themselves into socially. For example, in a survey of nearly 1,300 high-school students, not having friends was the strongest predictor of feeling hopeless and helpless (Page, 1991). Many friendless adolescents adopt a brooding, depressing, passive explanatory style referred to as "sad passivity" (VanBuskirk & Duke, 1991). These teenagers passively or angrily wrap their ruminating, hopeless, hostile, pessimistic explanatory style around themselves like an old, familiar blanket—a blanket that offers temporary comfort—but ultimate suffocation.

PARENTS' IMPACT ON EXPLANATORY STYLES

Given the impact that explanatory styles have on teenagers' social development and mental health, researchers naturally ask: Where do our explanatory styles come from? Why do some adolescents have such hostile or such helpless, pessimistic styles? The answer generally seems to lie in the parents' explanatory styles—above all, the mother's. This isn't to say that our fathers don't influence our explanatory styles. Those fathers who are actively involved in their children's day-to-day lives, especially during the preschool years, do have an impact on explanatory styles (Biller, 1993). Nevertheless, most children spend far more time around their mothers, especially in the first few years of life, when explanatory styles seem to become established. As a consequence, most of us are more similar to our mothers than to our fathers in regard to our attribution styles. So if you're a teenager who has relatively optimistic ways of interpreting the world and if you assume responsibility for most of what is happening in your own life, then your parents probably modeled and reinforced these ways of thinking and behaving while you were growing up—especially your mother. In regard to your teenage friendships or your social maturity, the best parents are those who continually show you through their own behavior that you're not powerless or helpless when it comes to influencing how other people relate to you or how you choose to relate to them (Seligman, 1991; Sigel, McGillicuddy & Goodnow, 1992).

Unfortunately not all parents help their children develop positive explanatory styles. For reasons having to do with their own poor mental health and their own maladaptive ways of interpreting the world, some parents encourage depressive, or helpless, or hostile explanatory styles in their children. Clinically depressed teenagers typically have very helpless, pessimistic explanatory styles as do many of their mothers. Indeed, a mother's psychological problems, especially depression, are closely associated with teenage disorders such as depression, dependent personality disorders, anxiety, and social phobia (Blechman, 1990; Hopo & Biglan, 1990; Karen, 1994; Pianta, Egeland & Stroufe, 1990; Radke-Yarrow, 1991; Waxler & others, 1992). Likewise, a father's psychological problems are most closely associated with teenage disorders that involve aggressive, violent, or delinquent behavior in teenage boys (Phares & Compas, 1992). Even though the father's mental health is most closely related to the son's aggressive behavior, teenage boys with hostile attribution styles often have a mother with these same negative, reactive ways of interpreting other people's behavior. Perhaps the mother has the most influence over the son's style of thinking, but the father has the most influence over whether the son learns to control his aggressive, impulsive behavior (Asher & Coie, 1990; Elicker, Englund, & Stroufe, 1992; MacKinnon & others, 1992; Parke, 1992; Peplar & Rubin, 1994; Putallaz & Heflin, 1993).

It's important to remember, though, that a parent doesn't have the same influence over each child in the family. As discussed earlier, each parent might have the greatest influence over the opposite-sex child (Block, 1971). It also seems that each parent has the greatest impact over a particular type of behavior. For instance, mothers do generally have the most influence over whether their sons develop depressed explanatory styles, but fathers generally have the most influence over whether sons develop enough self-control not to act aggressively and impulsively (Phares & Compas, 1992; Snarey, 1993; Warshak, 1992).

On the other hand, each person's temperament might be more important than gender in determining who is going to have more influence over a child's explanatory styles. On the whole, whichever child in a family has the most dependent, most introverted, or most emotionally unstable temperament is the most easily influenced by a parent. Unfortunately, whichever parent is the most emotionally unstable or psychologically troubled generally has the greatest impact on that susceptible child. This association between the least well-adapted parent and child might explain why those adolescents with extremely introverted or extremely aggressive dispositions often have pessimistic or negative explanatory styles like their mothers (Elicker, Englund, & Stroufe, 1992; MacKinnon & others, 1992; Peplar & Rubin, 1994; Waxler & others, 1992).

Obviously our parents don't sit down with us, describe their attributional styles, and tell us to adopt them. In large part we seem to acquire a parent's attributional style simply by observing how he or she deals with day-to-day events. As children, our antennae are constantly tuned in to the way our parents talk about the causes of their feelings and the causes of what's going on in their lives. In regard to hostile attribution bias, does each parent show us through his or her own life that there are a number of reasons other than intentional malice why people say or do things that make us sad or angry? For example, a parent who is hurt or angry at someone might usually respond in a forgiving, optimistic, self-motivated way that conveys something along these lines: "I'm mad at her for what she did, but I really don't know what her motives were because I don't even know her that well. Besides, I guess I've really got to be honest and admit that I did a few things that provoked her." Or the parent might react with a hostile interpretation: "I don't even want to hear her side of it. She's evil and intentionally set out to ruin my life without my ever doing anything to hurt her."

Our parents also influence our attributional styles by the way they respond to us when we're having problems with our peers. For example, assume you're 14 and complaining about your latest social failure: "I wasn't invited to this weekend's party which just goes to prove that everybody at school thinks I'm a loser." Your parent can respond with a pessimistic, external style: "You poor thing! I know just how you feel. People really are so insensitive, aren't they? Remember, sweetie, there's not much you can do until you graduate and get away from here." Or your parent could respond with a more self-directed, optimistic explanatory style: "I'm really sorry. Hey, why not throw a party of your own so you won't feel so bad?"

Finally, and probably most important, we might acquire our explanatory styles not so much by watching what our parents literally say or do but by observing *how* they say or do it—their tone of voice, the expressions on their faces. For example, in reply to your question about why they're so unhappy with their jobs, parents might say, "It's basically my own fault that I don't have a better job by this point in my life because I didn't work very hard during my 20s and 30s." The tone of voice might send you the opposite message: "Nothing ever turns out right for me no matter what I do." In comparing your own explanatory style to those of your parents, think back to your childhood and ask yourself: How did each parent typically react when things went wrong or when someone made them sad or angry? When I think back on the tone of voice and the expressions on their faces, do I see either of my parents as a downtrodden, helpless, victimized person? Were either of them usually blaming other people for their bad moods or for the unhappy circumstances in their lives?

HELPING ADOLESCENTS WHO HAVE TROUBLED PEER RELATIONSHIPS

Can we help those adolescents who don't get along well with people as a consequence of their immature or maladjusted social reasoning and arrested ego development? In trying to answer this question, let's examine five different strategies being used to help these adolescents. The first approach is integrating activities into the school curriculum that are designed to advance adolescents' social reasoning skills. The second approach is teaching adolescents more mature social skills through programs run by school counselors or private therapists. The third approach uses family therapy aimed at helping parents and teenagers relate to each other in ways that will advance the adolescent's social reasoning and social skills. Fourth is a form of individual therapy known as "cognitive restructuring," which is designed to teach adolescents less pessimistic, less hostile, less self-defeating ways of interpreting the world. Finally, in the most extreme cases, therapists use drugs, such as antidepressants, in conjunction with individual therapy to help teenagers acquire more adaptive ways of relating to people.

IDENTIFYING TROUBLED ADOLESCENTS

Among those adolescents who don't get along well with their peers, about half are too aggressive and overreactive, and the other half are too withdrawn and passive (Coie, 1993). Aggressive adolescents aren't hard to identify in terms of knowing who needs counseling because their aggressive, defiant, or violent behavior doesn't escape the notice of teachers or family members—at least not for long. Withdrawn, socially isolated adolescents are less likely to get the professional help they need because their behavior usually isn't causing anyone enough trouble to warrant seeing them as "troubled" or as psychologically maladapted. One question that needs to be asked is: How can family members and teachers recognize which introverted adolescents do need professional help? Five questions can help us identify these adolescents (Harrington, 1994; Hartup & Overhauser, 1991; Myers, 1992).

First, exactly how much time is the adolescent spending alone or with someone in the family instead of with a peer? Most adolescents spend about 20 hours a week with their friends, so this can serve as a general yardstick. Second, it's even more important to ask: How is the adolescent spending his or her time alone, and what kind of mood is he or she usually in? Moping around the house, aimlessly wandering around complaining about being bored or unhappy, sleeping too much, or watching hour after hour of television are common symptoms of depression and disorders such as social phobia and dependent personality disorders. A school counselor or therapist should be consulted when a shy, lonely adolescent often seems listless and sullen, or hostile and ill-tempered, or downtrodden, unenthusiastic, and emotionally detached. Physical signs of stress, such as headaches or digestive ailments, are also common among these troubled youth.

Third, has the adolescent recently been able to maintain at least one close friendship over a period of time? If so, then there's not as much cause for alarm as if he or she hasn't been able to be intimate with anyone on an ongoing basis. Most teenagers have at least three or four people they pal around with, plus at least one close friend. The socially isolated, shy teenager who associates with only

What were your greatest problems with your friends as a teenager?

one person or who hasn't been close to anyone for a long period of time might be developing very serious disorders such as schizoid personality disorders or severe clinical depression. Fourth, how old is the adolescent? Having no close friends, not dating, and spending most of their time alone is more closely linked to psychological disorders for 18-year-olds than for 13-year-olds (Compas & Williams, 1990; Dornbusch & others, 1991; Larson & Asmussen, 1991).

Fifth, is the adolescent extremely introverted and passive around his or her peers but outspoken, demanding, hostile, aggressive, impulsive, or downright uncontrollable at home? If so, this usually indicates problems within the family itself that are contributing to the adolescent's social withdrawal and anger. Adolescents who are extremely isolated and withdrawn around their teachers and peers, but very outspoken, demanding, and hostile at home, often come from families in which they are overly enmeshed with a depressed or chronically unhappy mother and overly distanced from their father (Waxler & others, 1992).

School Activities for Moral and Social Reasoning

Both Piaget and Kohlberg believed that our moral and social reasoning becomes more mature by interacting with people whose reasoning skills are superior to ours. Piaget and Kohlberg also believed we become more mature by finding ourselves in situations in which we have to re-examine our decisions and our ways of reasoning. This is why interacting with peers who are psychologically well-adjusted and whose social reasoning is fairly mature is so crucial during childhood and adolescence. In this spirit, a number of teaching techniques and school programs have been designed to help adolescents toward more mature, less egocentric reasoning. As Insert 5–5 illustrates, one of these classroom approaches, referred to as **values clarification,** was introduced in some schools during the 1960s. In these values clarification activities, adolescents are asked to examine their ways of reasoning about social and moral issues. The teacher, however, doesn't express any of his or her own values or religious ideas. The point of values clarification techniques is not to help students develop a particular set of values, but to help them develop more logical, less egocentric ways of reasoning (Raths, Harmin, & Simon, 1978).

A somewhat different approach is to use class discussions and class activities to teach specific aspects of social reasoning and ego development such as empathy, perspective taking, and compromise. These activities are intended to teach adolescents that some ways of reasoning are definitely more ethical or definitely more mature than others. For example, in these discussions the teacher does point out to students when their responses are egocentric, self-righteous, or lacking empathy by asking such questions as: "How would you feel if someone did that to you? What motives did the person have for doing that? How would you feel if the situation were reversed? What do you think the people in this situation are thinking or feeling?" In other words, the adult voices opinions and challenges those of

Insert 5–5

Should Schools Teach Moral Reasoning?

Some researchers and educators believe we should use certain structured exercises to help adolescents develop more mature ways of reasoning and behaving in situations involving moral matters. Following is a description of a classroom activity in which a high-school teacher is using one of these approaches to moral education known as **values clarification.** What do you think about this approach to moral education?

Teacher: So some of you think it's best to be honest on tests, is that right? And some of you think dishonesty is all right? And I guess some of you are not certain? Well, are there any other choices, or is it just a matter of honesty and dishonesty?

Sam: You could be honest some of the time and dishonest some of the time.

Teacher: Does that sound like a possible choice, class? Are there any other alternatives to choose from?

Tracy: You could be honest in some situations and not in others. For example, I'm not honest when a friend asks me about an ugly dress.

Teacher: Are there any other choices?

Sam: It seems to me you have to be all one way or all the other.

Teacher: Just a minute, Sam. As usual we are first looking for all of the alternatives that there are in the issue. Later on you can discuss this and see if you are able to make a choice and if you want to make your choice part of your actual behavior.

Ginger: Does this mean we can decide for ourselves whether we should be honest on tests in here?

Teacher: No. It means you can decide on the value. I personally value honesty, and although you may choose to be dishonest, I will insist that we be honest on tests here. In other areas of your life you may have more freedom to be dishonest. But one can't do anything any time, and in this class I expect honesty.

Ginger: But how can we decide for ourselves? Are you telling us what to value?

Teacher: Not exactly. I don't mean to tell you what to value. That's up to you. But I mean that in this class, not elsewhere necessarily, you have to be honest on tests or suffer the consequences. I merely mean that I can't give tests without the rule of honesty. All of you who choose dishonesty as your value may not practice it here, that's all I'm saying. Further questions anyone?

Source: L. Raths, M. Harmin, & S. Simon. (1978). *Values and teaching.* Columbus, OH: Merrill.

the students when their reasoning seems self-centered, intolerant, close-minded, insensitive, or hypocritical.

The good news is that many students who participate in these programs do seem to start reasoning more maturely. The bad news is that these programs don't seem to have much impact in terms of changing the way adolescents actually behave in moral or social situations. Also, the influence of the programs seems to be much stronger on younger adolescents than on older teenagers (Damon, 1988).

Social Skills Training

An approach that has been more successful in helping adolescents get along better with their peers is social skills training, in which adolescents meet in groups to learn exactly which aspects of their behavior are making it difficult for them to get along with other people, to make friends, or to date. These school programs also teach young people how to go about resolving different problems with their families and peers. Some also teach students new ways of interpreting their experiences—new explanatory styles (Coie, 1993; Gullotta, Adams, & Montemayor, 1990; Johnson, Jason, & Betts, 1990).

Using videotapes, peer tutoring, role playing, and discussions, adolescents in these training programs get the chance to practice more mature social skills and more advanced social reasoning. For example, adolescents are asked to record how often they behave in certain ways each day: How often today did you spontaneously say "hello" to someone? How often today did you smile or compliment someone? Given only one or two behaviors to record and to practice each week, the adolescent records how the other person responds after each encounter. The daily record keeping helps adolescents see the connection between their behavior and other people's responses.

In working with adolescents who are too aggressive and too reactive around their peers, social skills programs concentrate on teaching such skills as self-control, negotiation, empathy, and relaxation procedures. The emphasis is on helping these students learn to control their impulsive, angry behavior by developing less aggressive ways of resolving conflicts or expressing their feelings. Activities in moral and social reasoning are designed to increase the adolescent's sense of fairness, justice, and concern for others' feelings. The group leaders act out real-life situations with these aggressive teenagers, helping them figure out step-by-step what they could say and do differently. Sometimes these scenes are videotaped and played back to the group as a way of assessing their own strengths and weaknesses.

As you can see from Insert 5–6, social skills training programs also are designed for shy high school and college students who want to become more outgoing and less incapacitated by their shyness. These programs have succeeded in helping many adolescents and young adults relate better to their peers, their teachers, and their employers, as well as boosting self-esteem (Johnson, Jason, & Betts, 1990; Zimbardo & Radl, 1981).

Cognitive Restructuring: Changing Explanatory Styles

The self-recording assignments used in social skills training programs have also helped improve adolescents' explanatory styles. Adolescents with hostile attribution biases and those with pessimistic, passive styles have developed more optimistic, less hostile ways of interpreting the world through a form of therapy referred to as cognitive restructuring. In supportive yet persistent ways, the therapist challenges the adolescent's hostile, or pessimistic, or helpless pattern of

Insert 5–6

Overcoming Shyness

Some high schools and a number of colleges offer programs to help shy students become more sociable and more self-confident. Following are suggestions for overcoming shyness derived from one of the leading researchers in the field whose "shyness clinics" are among the best in the country.

Step One: The Decision to Change

Being shy provides you with a number of benefits. People feel sorry for you and offer to do things for you because you seem too afraid to do them yourself. People spend time with you because your sad shyness makes them feel guilty for leaving you alone. If this sort of prison is not for you, then take the first step and decide that you don't want shyness to continue to intrude on your life.

Step Two: Behavioral Assessment

List the situations in which you're shy rather than label yourself "a shy person." Then rank each situation from the most to the least frightening.

Step Three: Building Self-Esteem

1. Make a list of all your very best qualities.
2. Make a list of your most glaring flaws, labeling it "things to improve."
3. Focus on one of your strong points and develop it further.
4. When you're about to do something that you're afraid of failing at, be sure you do everything you can beforehand to be fully prepared.
5. Avoid doing things that make you feel guilty or ashamed of yourself.
6. Try to do one thing each day to make you feel good (exercise, reorganize your work area, write to a friend, paint, do a small chore, read).

Step Four: Your Personal Appearance

Make a list of all the things you can do to improve your physical appearance. Start with things like keeping your hair clean, getting a good hairstyle, making sure your clothes are neat and clean.

Step Five: Learn to be Your Own Best Friend

Shy people have more trouble than other people enjoying themselves when they're alone. So make a list of activities that people do alone that you could enjoy if you weren't so focused on being alone, and do more of these things. Then start "going public" alone by doing things like browsing in a bookstore, shopping, running errands, jogging, or biking.

Step Six: Practice Social Skills

1. Watch other people who are enjoying themselves. Look at what they do, listen to what they are saying, and follow their examples. Here are some of the things you'll observe them doing: smiling, making eye contact, leaning forward and nodding, laughing, asking questions, complimenting people, doing favors for people, showing an active interest in others.
2. If you're afraid to ask someone for a date, write out a script, and practice it before phoning the person.
3. Choose courses in which you can talk rather than hiding in large lectures.
4. Tell your teachers that you're shy about speaking in class but that you're going to try.

Source: P. Zimbardo and S. Radl (1981). *The Shy Child.* New York: McGraw Hill.

interpreting an event—leading the client toward less distorted, less self-defeating interpretations of reality (Nielsen, 1981; Seligman, 1991).

We discuss some of these techniques in Chapter 15; but let's look at one example now. Many adolescents who don't get along well with their peers, or who reason immaturely as a consequence of psychological problems, have a distorted way of interpreting their experiences referred to as **splitting** or **displacement.** The adolescent directs anger at someone who is not responsible. Very often the person who actually deserves the anger is one of the adolescent's parents—a parent who has been discovered doing something that he or she wishes the child didn't know about. If that particular parent happens to be the one the adolescent most needs to feel love for and loved by, he or she might play a mental trick on themselves. In order to keep loving the parent who has done the "bad" thing, the adolescent interprets reality in such a distorted way that the parent seems "all good." The anger they still feel for that parent has to go somewhere. So it gets directed at another person—the other parent, a stepparent, or a peer—whose behavior is misinterpreted in ways that enable the adolescent to see him or her as "all bad." Extremely self-critical adolescents with low self-esteem seem to direct a large part of the anger at themselves. These adolescents then end up developing very distorted styles of interpreting the world around them. As a consequence, they "rewrite" the past and react to the present in ways that have little to do with actual events. The therapist's job is to help these young people develop more adaptive explanatory styles by recalling the information that is being denied, examining that information more thoroughly and objectively, and understanding why they felt the need to deny those realities in the first place (Bowlby, 1988; Miller, 1990).

As explained in Chapter 15, changing adolescents' explanatory styles is at the heart of many techniques and programs being used to help delinquent, violent, and aggressive adolescents. Cognitive restructuring techniques are also among the most successful techniques for adolescents who are suffering from such disorders as anorexia, depression, schizoid behavior, anxiety, social phobia, and other personality disorders.

FAMILY THERAPY

Social skills training and classroom activities that encourage more mature social reasoning aren't enough for those young people whose problems stem from more serious psychological disorders such as depression and personality disorders. Although many therapists recommend social skills training programs for their teenage clients, adolescents with serious, longstanding social problems also need individual or family counseling in order to catch up socially and psychologically with their peers. Depending on the problem, the therapist might recommend either individual therapy, family therapy, or a combination of both. Along with counseling, the therapist also decides whether the adolescent needs medication for depression, hyperactivity, or other debilitating disorders—a topic also addressed in Chapter 15.

Family therapy can be best for some troubled teens. Indeed, some adolescents can't learn to get along better with their peers until they understand some of the dynamics in the family that are contributing to their social or emotional problems. For example, family therapy is often useful for adolescents whose peer problems are related to being enmeshed with a parent or to having been raised by an overly indulgent parent. A number of teenagers who are extremely shy, socially immature, and extremely dependent on one or both parents have an enmeshed or overly indulgent parent. Unhealthy dynamics within the family often are contributing to—and sometimes the primary cause of—these adolescents' problems. If you look ahead into the boxes in Chapter 15, you can see some specific examples of how therapists work with the entire family (Bowen, 1978; Hanson, Gottesman, & Heston, 1990; Parker, 1983; Perry, Frances, & Clarkin, 1990; Minuchin & Nichols, 1994).

Family therapy can also be helpful for extremely aggressive, antisocial teenagers, most of whom are boys (Patterson, Reid, & Dishion, 1992). In these families the therapist is trying to help parents learn more effective ways to change their teenager's behavior. Because many of these teenage boys have an overly indulgent mother and an uninvolved or overly dictatorial father, the therapist is often trying to teach each parent to adopt a style of parenting that is a little more like their spouse's. Therapists also have helped adolescents with hostile or pessimistic explanatory styles by teaching their parents less hostile, less helpless ways of thinking. In these programs parents who have hostile, or helpless, or depressed, or pessimistic explanatory styles are being taught to behave in more optimistic, self-directed ways around their children. The changes in the parent's behavior, in turn, seem to help their teenage children develop less self-defeating ways of interpreting the world around them (Seligman, 1991).

CONCLUSION

In summarizing our discussion of social development and friendship, several major points stand out. Above all, having friends during adolescence is essential if we're going to be psychologically well-adapted and if we're going to become more mature in our ways of thinking and behaving. Without teenage friends, we're not only lonely, we're also at risk for developing a host of very serious social and psychological problems that often follow us throughout out adult lives. We've also seen that how well or how poorly we get along with people as teenagers depends on a combination of factors: our cognitive stages, our temperaments, our explanatory styles, and our levels of ego development. To complicate matters further, each of these factors is influenced by still other circumstances such as chronic illness, neurological disorders, or psychological disorders of the child, plus the explanatory styles, mental health, and the styles of parenting of the adults who raised us. Looking more closely into our families, we've also seen that social and ego development are affected by enmeshment, triangulation, generational boundaries, and marital happiness.

Clearly, a number of explanations are possible in answer to the two basic questions we started out with: Why are some adolescents so much more mature than others when it comes to their social and moral reasoning? Why do some adolescents get along so much poorer or so much better with people compared with other people their age? In the next chapter we continue exploring these two questions by examining the impact of gender on adolescents' social and ego development.

Review/Test Questions

1. How do adolescent friendships differ from those of younger children?

2. How does physical appearance affect adolescent friendships?

3. How do teenage friends affect each other in regard to mental health, ego development, social reasoning, drug use, and delinquency?

4. How does temperament affect our teenage friendships and social reasoning?

5. How do labile adolescents think and behave differently from emotionally stable teenagers?

6. How are extroverted teenagers different from introverted teenagers other than being more outgoing?

7. What aspects of temperament are most advantageous and most disadvantageous when it comes to getting along well with people as a teenager?

8. What psychological disorders are associated with not getting along well with our peers and immature social reasoning as adolescents?

9. How do explanatory styles affect adolescents' peer relationships?

10. In what ways do teenagers with hostile attribution biases think and behave differently from other adolescents?

11. Why do some adolescents have such self-defeating explanatory styles?

12. What environmental factors influence the shape a child's temperament will take by the time he or she is an adolescent?

13. What are the three or four symptoms used to diagnose adolescents with the following psychological disorders: anxiety disorders, dependent personal disorders, schizoid personality disorders, depression, conduct disorders, separation anxiety disorders, and antisocial personality disorders?

14. How stable are our personalities? Cite the findings from specific studies to support your answer.

15. How do adolescents with external locus of control attitudes think and behave differently from those with internal locus of control attitudes?

16. How do counselors go about changing adolescents' explanatory styles?

17. How can we help adolescents develop more mature social reasoning?

18. What is cognitive restructuring therapy, and how is it supposed to improve adolescents' relationships with their peers?

19. What are the consequences of not having close friends during adolescence?

20. In what ways can family therapy be used to help adolescents become more mature in terms of their behavior and social reasoning?

Questions for Discussion and Debate

1. How did your friendships change from childhood to adolescence and from adolescence to college? According to this chapter, what accounted for these changes?

2. In what positive and negative ways do you think each of your parents has shaped or influenced your basic temperament? How did he or she do this?

3. How would you describe your temperament? In what regard has it stayed the same, and in what regard has it changed since your preschool years? Since adolescence? Why?

4. What aspects of your ego development and social reasoning did your teenage friends contribute to and detract from?

5. Considering the different psychological problems described in the boxes in this chapter, to which of these disorders do you think your behavior as an adolescent was most similar? How and why have these symptoms changed or not changed in the past few years?

6. What aspects of your family's dynamics do you think were most helpful and most harmful to your ego and social development?

7. How would you describe your explanatory styles and the styles of each of your parents? How have each of your parent's or your life's experiences affected how your explanatory styles developed and changed over the years?

8. Which aspects of your temperament and explanatory styles created the most problems for you with your peers as an adolescent? Which were the most beneficial? What would you like to change now about your temperament or your explanatory styles?

9. What programs or techniques would you design to help adolescents get along better with their peers? Consider shyness, aggression, pessimism, hostile attribution bias, and depression.

10. In what ways has family therapy, individual counseling, an experience, or a book you've read helped you to change some aspect of your temperament or explanatory style? On the basis of your experiences, how would you recommend that other college students or adolescents go about changing certain aspects of themselves if they choose?

Glossary

acute anxiety disorders, p. 167
antisocial personality disorder, p. 156
attention deficit hyperactivity disorder (ADHD), p. 168
attribution theory, p. 171
attributional styles, p. 170
avoidant personality disorder, p. 155
conduct disorders, p. 156

dependent personality disorder, p. 155
displacement, p. 184
disposition, p. 158
dysthymic, p. 160
explanatory styles, p. 170
external locus of control, p. 171
extrovert, p. 159
hostile attribution bias, p. 174
internal locus of control, p. 171

introvert, p. 158
labile, p. 159
learned helplessness, p. 173
learned pessimism, p. 173
locus of control attitudes, p. 170
neurotic/neuroticism, p. 159
oppositional defiant disorders, p. 156
psychopharmacology, p. 161

schizoid personality disorder,
    p. 156
schizophrenia, p. 156
separation anxiety disorder,
    p. 155

social phobia, p. 167
splitting, p. 184
temperament, p. 158
temperamentally inhibited,
    p. 167

trait theorists, p. 158
values clarification, p. 180

References

Adams, G. (1991). Physical attractiveness and adolescent development. In R. Lerner, A. Petersen & J. Brooks-Gunn (Eds.), *Encyclopedia of adolescence* (pp. 785–789). New York: Garland.

American Psychiatric Association. (1994). *Diagnostic and statistical manual of mental disorders IV.* Washington, DC: Author.

Argyle, M. (1990). The happiness of extroverts. *Personality and Individual Differences, 11,* 1011–1017.

Asher, S., & Coie, J. (1990). *Peer rejection in childhood.* New York: Cambridge University Press.

Bandura, A. (1991). Self-efficacy: impact of self-beliefs on adolescent life paths. In R. Lerner, A. Petersen & J. Brooks-Gunn (Eds.), *Encyclopedia of adolescence* (pp. 112–116). New York: Garland.

Belsky, J., & Cassidy, J. (1994). Attachment: Theory and evidence. In M. Rutter, D. Hays & S. Baron (Eds.), *Developmental principles and clinical issues in psychology and psychiatry* (pp. 120–135). Blackwell, England: Oxford University Press.

Biller, H. (1993). *Fathers and families: Paternal factors in child development.* Westport, CT: Auburn House.

Block, J. (1971). *Lives through time.* Berkeley, CA: Bancroft Books.

Blechman, E. (1990). *Emotions and the family.* Hillsdale, NJ: Erlbaum.

Block, J., & Gjerde, P. (1991). Preadolescent antecedents of depressive symptomatology at age 18. *Journal of Youth and Adolescence, 20,* 217–231.

Bornstein, M., & Bruner, J. (1993). *Interaction in cognitive development.* Hillsdale, NJ: Erlbaum.

Bowen, M. (1978). *Family therapy in clinical practice.* New York: Aronson.

Bowlby, J. (1988). *A secure base.* New York: Basic Books.

Brooks-Gunn, J. (1991). How stressful is the transition to adolescence for girls? In M. Colten & S. Gore (Eds.), *Adolescent stress* (pp. 131–156). New York: Aldine De Gruyter.

Buchanan, C., Eccles, J., & Becker, J. (1992). Are adolescents victims of raging hormones? *Psychological Bulletin, 111,* 62–107.

Buchanan, G., & Seligman, M. (Eds.). (1994) *Explanatory style.* Hillsdale, NJ: Erlbaum.

Capaldi, D., & Rothbart, M. (1992). Development and validation of an early adolescent temperament measure. *Journal of Early Adolescence, 2,* 153–173.

Caspi, A., Elder, G., & Herbener, E. (1990). Childhood personality and the prediction of life course patterns. In L. Robins & M. Rutter (Eds.), *Straight and devious pathways from childhood to adulthood* (pp. 13–36). New York: Cambridge University Press.

Chess, S., & Thomas, A. (1993). Continuities and discontinuities in temperament. In R. Robins & M. Rutter (Eds.), *Straight and devious pathways from childhood to adulthood* (pp. 205–220). New York: Cambridge University Press.

Cicchetti, D. (1992). Peer relations in maltreated children. In R. Parke & G. Ladd (Eds.), *Family peer relationships: Modes of linkage* (pp. 345–383). Hillsdale, NJ: Erlbaum.

Clarizio, H. (1994). *Assessment and treatment of depression in children and adolescents.* Brandon, VT: Clinical Psychology Publishing Co.

Cohen, P. (1990). Common and uncommon pathways to adolescent psychopathology and problem behavior. In L. Robins & M. Rutter (Eds.), *Straight and devious pathways from childhood to adulthood* (pp. 242–259). New York: Cambridge University Press.

Coie, J. (1993). Toward a theory of peer rejection. In S. Asher & J. Coie (Eds.), *Peer rejection in childhood* (pp. 365–413). New York: Cambridge University Press.

Compas, B., & Wagner, B. (1991). Psychosocial stress during adolescence. In M. Colten & S. Gore (Eds.), *Adolescent stress* (pp. 67–92). New York: Aldine De Gruyter.

Compas, B., & Williams, R. (1990). Stress, coping, and adjustment in mothers and young adolescents. *American Journal of Community Psychology, 18,* 525–545.

Damon, W. (1988). *The moral child.* New York: Free Press.

Damon, W., & Hart, D. (1988). *Self-understanding in childhood and adolescence.* New York: Cambridge University Press.

Dornbusch, S., Mont-Reynaud, R., Ritter, P., Zeng-yin, C., & Steinberg, L. (1991). Stressful events and their correlates among adolescents of diverse backgrounds. In M. Colten & S. Gore (Eds.), *Adolescent stress* (pp. 111–131). New York: Aldine De Gruyter.

Dunn, J. (1993). *Young children's close relationships.* Newbury Park, CA: Sage.

Eisenberg, N. (1991). Prosocial development in adolescence. In R. Lerner, A. Petersen & J. Brooks-Gunn (Eds.), *Encyclopedia of adolescence.* New York: Garland.

Elicker, J., Englund, M., & Stroufe, L. (1992). Predicting peer competence and peer relation-

ships from early parent–child relationships. In R. Parke & G. Ladd (Eds.), *Family peer relationships: Modes of linkages.* Hillsdale, NJ: Erlbaum.

Eysenck, S., & Eysenck, H. (1963). The validity of assessments of extraverion and neuroticism and their factorial stability. *British Journal of Psychology, 54,* 51–62.

Farrington, D., Loeber, R., & VanKammen, W. (1990). Long term criminal outcomes of hyperactivity-impulsivity-attention deficit and conduct problems in childhood. In L. Robins & M. Rutter (Eds.), *Straight and devious pathways from childhood to adulthood* (pp. 62–81). New York: Cambridge University Press.

Galvin, R. (1992). The nature of shyness. *Harvard Magazine, 94,* 40–45.

Gilovich, T. (1991). *How we know what isn't so: The fallibility of human reason in everyday life.* New York: MacMillan.

Grauerholz, E., & Koralweski, M. (1991). *Sexual coercion.* New York: Lexington Books.

Greenberg, M., Cicchetti, D., & Cummings, E. (1990). *Attachment in the preschool years.* Chicago: University of Chicago.

Gullotta, T., Adams, G., & Montemayor, R. (1990). *Developing social competencies in adolescence.* Newbury Park, CA: Sage.

Hallinan, M., & Williams, R. (1989). Interracial friendship choices in secondary schools. *American Sociological Review, 54,* 67–78.

Hanson, D., Gottesman, I., & Heston, L. (1990). Long range schizophrenia forecasting. In J. Rolf (Ed.), *Risk and protective factors in the development of psychopathology* (pp. 424–444). New York: Cambridge University Press.

Harrington, L. (1994). *Depressive disorder in childhood and adolescence.* New York: Wiley.

Harter, S. (1990). Self and identity development. In S. Feldman & G. Elliot (Eds.), *At the threshold* (pp. 352–388). Cambridge, MA: Harvard University Press.

Hartup, W., & Overhauser, S. (1991). Friendships. In R. Lerner, A. Petersen & J.

Brooks-Gunn (Eds.), *Encyclopedia of adolescence* (pp. 378–384). New York: Garland.

Hetherington, M. (1991). Families, lies, and videotapes. *Journal of Research on Adolescence, 1,* 323–348.

Hops, H., & Biglan, A. (1990). Maternal depression and children's behavior. In G. Patterson (Ed.), *Depression and aggression in family interaction* (pp. 115–125). Hillsdale, NJ: Erlbaum.

Johnson, J., Jason, L., & Betts, D. (1990). Promoting social competencies through educational efforts. In T. Gullotta, G. Adams & R. Montemayor (Eds.), *Developing social competency in adolescence* (pp. 139–167). Newbury Park, CA: Sage.

Kagan, J. (1989). *Unstable ideas: Temperament, cognition, and self.* Cambridge, MA: Harvard University Press.

Kagan, J., & Snidman, N. (1991). Temperament and allergic symptoms. *Psychosomatic Medicine, 53,* 332–340.

Kandel, D., Raveis, V., & Davies, M. (1991). Suicidal ideation in adolescence. *Journal of Youth and Adolescence, 20,* 289–309.

Karen, R. (1994). *Becoming attached.* New York: Time Warner.

Kramer, P. (1993). *Listening to Prozac.* New York: Viking.

Kupersmidt, J., Coie, J., & Dodge, K. (1993). The role of poor peer relationships in the development of disorder. In S. Asher & J. Coie (Eds.), *Peer rejection in childhood* (pp. 274–309). New York: Cambridge University Press.

Larson, R. (1990). The solitary life. *Developmental Review, 10,* 155–183.

Larson, R., & Asmussen, L. (1991). Anger, worry, and hurt in early adolescence. In M. Colten & S. Gore (Eds.), *Adolescent stress* (pp. 21–42). New York: Aldine De Gruyter.

Larson, R., & Richards, M. (1991). Daily companionship in childhood and adolescence. *Child Development, 42,* 156–164.

Lempers, J., & Lempers, D. (1993). Comparison of same-sex and opposite-sex friendships during adolescence. *Journal of Adolescent Research, 8,* 89–108.

MacKinnon, C., Lamb, M., Arbuckle, B., Baradaran, L., & Volling, B. (1992). The relationship between biased maternal and filial attributions and the aggressiveness of their interactions. *Development and Psychopatholgy, 4,* 403–415.

Marcia, J. (1991). Identity and self-development. In R. Lerner, A. Petersen & J. Brooks-Gunn (Eds.), *Encyclopedia of adolescence* (pp. 529–534). New York: Garland.

McCrae, R., & Costa, P. (1986). *Emerging lives, enduring dispositions.* Boston: Little Brown.

Michalos, A. (1991). *Life satisfaction and happiness: Global report on student well-being.* New York: Springer Verlag.

Miller, A. (1990). *Banished knowledge: Facing childhood injuries.* New York: Doubleday.

Minuchin, S., & Nichols, P. (1994). *Family healing.* New York: Simon & Schuster.

Myers, D. (1992). *The pursuit of happiness.* New York: Morrrow.

Nielsen, L. (1981). *Motivating adolescents.* Englewood Cliffs, NJ: Prentice Hall.

Nowicki, S., & Strickland, B. (1973). Locus of control scale for children. *Journal of Consulting & Clinical Psychology, 40,* 148–154.

Page, R. (1990). Shyness and sociability. *Adolescence, 25,* 803–806.

Page, R. (1991). Loneliness as a risk factor in adolescent hopelessness. *Research in Personality, 25,* 189–195.

Page, R., & Cole, G. (1991). Loneliness and alcoholism risk in late adolescence. *Adolescence, 26,* 925–930.

Parke, R. (1992). Familial contribution to peer competence among young children. In R. Parke & G. Ladd (Eds.), *Family peer relationships: Modes of linkage* (pp. 107–134). Hillsdale, NJ: Erlbaum .

Parke, R., & Ladd, G. (1992). *Family peer relationships: Modes of linkage.* Hillsdale, NJ: Erlbaum.

Parker, G. (1983). *Parental overprotection: A risk factor in psychosocial development.* New York: Grune and Stratton.

Patterson, G., Reid, J., & Dishion, T. (1992). *A social learning approach: Antisocial boys.* Eugene, OR: Castalia.

Peplar, D., & Rubin, K. (1994). *The development and treatment of childhood aggression.* Hillsdale, NJ: Erlbaum.

Perry, S., Frances, A., & Clarkin, J. (1990). *A DSM casebook of treatment selection.* New York: Bruner-Mazel.

Phares, V., & Compas, B. (1992). The role of fathers in child and adolescent psychopathology. *Psychological Bulletin, 111,* 387–412.

Pianta, B., Egeland, B., & Stroufe, A. (1990). Maternal stress and children's development. In R. Rolf (Ed.), *Risk and protective factors in the development of psychopathology* (pp. 215–236). New York: Cambridge University Press.

Plomin, R., DeFries, J., & McClearn, G. (1990). *Behavioral genetics.* New York: Freeman.

Putallaz, M., & Heflin, A. (1993). Parent–child relations and peer rejection. In S. Asher & J. Coie (Eds.), *Peer rejection in childhood* (pp. 189–217). New York: Cambridge University Press.

Radke-Yarrow, M. (1991). Attachment patterns in children of depressed mothers. In C. Parkes (Ed.), *Attachment across the life cycle* (pp. 115–127). New York: Routledge.

Raths, L., Harmin, M., & Simon, S. (1978). Values and teaching. New York: Merrill.

Robins, L., & Rutter, M. (1990). *Straight and devious pathways from childhood to adulthood.* New York: Cambridge University Press.

Rubin, K., Lemare, L., & Lollis, S. (1990). Social withdrawal in childhood. In S. Asher & J. Coie (Eds.), *Peer rejection in childhood* (pp. 51–72). Hillsdale, NJ: Erlbaum.

Savin-Williams, R., & Berndt, T. (1990). Friendship and peer relations. In S. Feldman & G. Elliot (Eds.), *At the threshold: The developing adolescent* (pp. 277–308). Cambridge, MA: Harvard University Press.

Seligman, M. (1991). *Learned optimism.* New York: Random House.

Sigel, I., McGillicuddy, A., & Goodnow, J. (1992). *Parental belief systems: Psychological consequences for children.* New York: Springer Verlag.

Smollar, J., & Youniss, J. (1982). *Adolescent relations with mothers, fathers & friends.* Chicago: University of Chicago Press.

Snarey, J. (1993). *How fathers care for the next generation.* Cambridge, MA: Harvard University Press.

Strack, F., & Argyle, M. (1990). *The social psychology of subjective well-being.* Oxford, England: Pergamon Press.

Tolson, J., & Urberg, K. (1993). Similarity between adolescent best friends. *Journal of Adolescent Research, 8,* 274–288.

VanBuskirk, A., & Duke, M. (1991). Coping style and loneliness in adolescents. *Genetic Psychology, 152,* 145–157.

Warshak, R. (1992). *The custody revolution: The fatherhood factor and the motherhood mystique.* New York: Poseidon.

Waxler, C., Denham, S., Iannotti, R., & Cummings, M. (1992). Peer relations in children with a depressed caregiver. In R. Parke & G. Ladd (Eds.), *Family peer relationships: Modes of linkage* (pp. 317–344). Hillsdale, NJ: Erlbaum.

Zimbardo, P., & Radl, S. (1981). *The shy child.* New York: McGraw Hill.

6

GENDER ROLES AND ADOLESCENT DEVELOPMENT

Chapter Outline

Key Questions Addressed In This Chapter

1. How do Freudians, cognitive psychologists, sociobiologists, and social learning theorists account for gender differences?
2. What are the shortcomings in the research on gender differences?
3. How do gender roles influence adolescent development?
4. How are adolescents socialized into their gender roles?
5. What are the positive and negative consequences associated with each gender role?
6. In what respects do adolescent males and females generally differ in regard to their academic skills, self-esteem, and vocational plans?
7. How could we help more adolescents overcome sexist attitudes and behaviors?
8. In what ways do gender roles affect adolescents' ego development, individuation, communication styles, and friendships?
9. How are gender roles related to adolescents' health and safety?
10. To what extent are adolescents androgynous?

GENDER ROLES AND ANDROGYNY

DEFINING THE TERMS

An adolescent's gender and race often profoundly affect his or her personal feelings and self-concept. Unfortunately, race and gender remain two of the most potent sources for the stereotypes, prejudice, and discrimination that affect millions of people—often with disturbingly acute effects on our young. In short, there's no way to escape the influence that race and gender have on our development or on the way others interact with us. In the next chapter we examine how race affects our adolescent development. In this chapter we explore the impact of gender.

To begin, we can ask: If our society has supposedly become less sexist in recent decades, then why are most teenage girls still choosing to enter the same kinds of lower paying jobs that women had in their mother's generation. And why are far more boys still choosing to become doctors, corporate executives, and scientists? Why are teenage boys still doing better than most of their female classmates in advanced math and science? Why do most female college graduates still average the salary of male high-school graduates? Why are adolescent girls usually more depressed and less self-confident than boys?

Questions such as these are at the heart of two larger questions: How much have our society's gender roles actually changed? What accounts for the gender differences that we still see in certain areas such as aggression and self-esteem? In exploring these questions, other hotly debated issues arise: How much do hormones influence male and female behavior? To what extent do our schools, our parents, and the media influence our masculinity or our femininity? How much of a gender gap is there between today's teenagers? How much less sexist are teenagers than their elders—if at all? Does male and female development during childhood and adolescence differ? In what ways? Do these differences pose threats to the individual's mental, physical, or emotional well-being?

Before exploring these questions, we need to define several crucial concepts. The term *gender* or *sex* refers to a person's being anatomically male or female. In contrast, **gender role** or **sex role** refers to those characteristics, interests, and activities that a society defines as appropriate for males and for females. In our society, for example, being the major breadwinner of the family and being physically aggressive traditionally have been considered major components of the male gender role. Likewise, raising the children and adorning the body with jewelry and make-up are part of our society's expectations for the female gender role. In other societies, however, these particular aspects of gender roles are reversed: Men take care of the children; women are more physically aggressive; and men spend more time than the women applying make-up and wearing jewelry. Having reported these kinds of gender role differences in her cross-cultural research in the 1930s, the famous anthropologist Margaret Mead caused quite a stir among those who had long believed that the way males and females behave is universal because gender differences are determined by our genes and hormones (Mead, 1935).

Although findings such as Margaret Mead's are no longer a surprise to most of us today, in earlier decades such research unearthed an upsetting reality: The ways we males and females behave are heavily influenced by the expectations and customs of our particular society and historical period. For example, a teenage boy in 1954 who wore an earring and a pastel-colored shirt would have been criticized for being too feminine. But behaving the same way in the 1980s and 90s, he would be accepted as masculine—or even macho—by teenagers in most parts of our country. In the same way, teenage girls and women who smoked publicly during the 50s were considered unladylike and too masculine. But by the 1980s, our society's gender roles had changed in such a way that smoking was being marketed to females as lady-like, sexy, and liberated.

Although each person's sex is genetically determined as either male or female, our gender roles are determined by our particular society's definitions of masculinity and femininity. Even though gender roles differ somewhat from culture to culture, most adolescents in industrialized nations are growing up with remarkably similar gender roles. Moreover, a 30-nation survey shows that our definitions of masculinity and femininity are still fairly similar to the roles assigned to males and females in much earlier decades (Williams & Best, 1989).

Nevertheless, one of the most dramatic changes in psychology in the past 20 years has been a shift in attitudes about gender roles (Doyle & Paludi, 1991; Huston & Alvarez, 1990). Until the late 1970s, most psychologists and educators believed that children and teenagers should be socialized to conform to our society's prescribed gender roles. As responsible adults, it was our duty to teach "boys to be boys" and "girls to be girls" and to disapprove of those who refused to be molded into their proper gender roles. But during the 1980s this attitude shifted, and the concept of androgyny increasingly gained support among psychologists. Derived from the Greek words for man, *andro*, and woman, *gyne*, **androgyny** means a combination of both masculine and feminine personality traits. During the 1970s most psychologists assumed that masculine and feminine traits were mutually exclusive. For instance, if you had the feminine traits of sensitivity and nurturance, you couldn't also have the masculine traits of assertiveness and independence. Nowadays, however, psychologists realize that a person can develop both masculine and feminine attitudes and behaviors, if their society encourages them to develop these characteristics.

In studying gender and androgyny, remember that gender roles and sexual orientation are two different concepts. **Sexual orientation** refers to whether a person is heterosexual, homosexual, or bisexual. But the term *gender roles* refers to our society's ways of defining masculine and feminine. For example, most homosexual males typify the male gender role in terms of their attitudes, appearance, and behavior; and most lesbians fit our society's definitions of femininity. Some heterosexual males and females, however, don't fit their gender roles in terms of the way they dress, the jobs they do, or how they behave. The 16-year-old, 6'3," 200-pound football hero and the beautiful, soft-spoken, 17-year-old homecoming queen, who both happen to be gay, still fit our culture's gender roles, although their sexual orientations are in the minority. Conversely, the effeminate male in a fashion design class, and the rough-and-tumble tomboy in shop class, who both are heterosexual, do not fit cultural gender roles. So don't confuse sexual orientations with gender roles.

Almost all psychologists nowadays agree that one of the main reasons males and females behave differently is that we have been socialized since birth to adopt certain attitudes and behaviors that fit our particular society's gender roles. Nevertheless, the debate still rages as to how much influence a society can have over our male and female differences. What about the influence of our male and female hormones? What about genetic differences that might cause males and females to behave differently? What about differences in our brains that might cause us to process information differently? It's also a question of which aspects of our society are the most influential in determining our behavior and attitudes. Questions like these intrigue researchers, especially regarding adolescence, when our hormones and our behavior as males and females are undergoing some of their most dramatic changes.

LIMITATIONS OF THE RESEARCH

Before examining the research, let's consider the shortcomings we have to work with when studying male and female behavior (Epstein, 1988; Fausto-Sterling, 1991; Hare-Mustin & Marecek, 1988; Schiebinger, 1993; Tuana, 1993).

RESEARCH NEGLECT AND PUBLICATION BIAS

First and foremost, most adolescent research, as well as research with older subjects, has been conducted with white males, not with female or nonwhite subjects. Therefore, much of what we know about adolescent development from our research doesn't apply to teenage girls or to teenagers from minority groups. In fact, the famous adolescent psychologist, Joseph Adelson, tells us that adolescent psychology as we know it is more accurately "the psychology of adolescent boys" (Adelson, 1980). Consequently, assessing the similarities and differences between adolescent males and females is restricted by having so few studies that have included teenage girls or minority youth.

Moreover, when researchers have included teenage girls in their work, studies that find differences between males and females are more likely to get accepted for publication than studies that don't find differences between the sexes. In other words, the information we get from professional journals, newscasts, newspapers, and magazines overemphasizes the differences between males and females and underemphasizes our similarities. This is also true, by the way, for studies that compare various racial groups, rich and poor, delinquent and non-delinquent, and so forth. That is, when we researchers find differences between blacks and whites or between males and females, our results generally make their way into the professional literature and into the news faster than when we find similarities between different groups of people. Although this shortcoming is being redressed in more professional journals and in the media, many of our assumptions about males and females are still based on research from the past that reported our differences rather than our similarities.

SAMPLING ERRORS AND EXPERIMENTER BIAS

As discussed in Chapter 1, researchers should generalize their conclusions only to people who are similar to the individuals who participate in the study. Unfortunately, when it comes to looking at gender differences, too many generalizations have been made on the basis of studying children and adults with genetic or hormonal defects. More disturbing still, some of our assumptions about what is normal or natural in human males and females are based on studies with animals and insects.

Because gender roles play such a major part in our lives, very few people who serve as subjects in our research studies, or those of us who analyze the data, are free from our sexist expectations and biases. When it comes to our observations of male and female behavior, we generally remember only the information that fits our gender stereotypes. In other words, it's difficult for researchers to be objective in collecting and interpreting data about male or female behavior because so much of what we see—and how we interpret it—is based on our own gender role expectations.

Remember, too, from our discussion of trait theories that the way an individual behaves in one situation might not represent how he or she will react in a different setting or situation. This is particularly important when it comes to gender differences because most male and female subjects are observed in very different types of situations when researchers are collecting data about their behavior. For example, in a study of 11 different cultures, both males and females started acting more nurturing when they were around infants (Whiting & Edwards, 1988). Yet most researchers do not collect data about how males behave in situations that tend to bring out their feminine traits, such as caring for young children. Likewise, data is often gathered about females in situations in which their masculine behavior is least likely to come forward. For example, if you were to count the number of teenage girls and boys crying during a sad movie, you might conclude that girls are more emotional and more sensitive than boys. But, if you counted the number of male players crying after losing their championship game, you might reach different conclusions about male sensitivity and emotionality. Consequently, when considering studies that compare male and female adolescents, you need to consider the types of situations in which these teenagers were observed.

CORRELATIONAL DATA AND DISSEMINATION BIAS

As explained in Chapter 1, we shouldn't make cause and effect statements based on correlational data. Unfortunately many of the supposed differences between males and females comes from correlational, not experimental, research. For example, it is true that many girls with high testosterone levels are more aggressive and athletic than other girls. But does this prove that testosterone causes aggression, and does this explain why boys are generally more aggressive than girls? No. Why? First, both girls and boys with higher than normal testosterone levels look more masculine and are, therefore, treated differently than teenagers with normal testosterone levels. It could be then that their appearance, not their testosterone levels, causes people to act more aggressively toward them and encourages more aggressive behavior in these children. In considering differences between males and females, therefore, it's important to remember that most studies relating hormones to behavior are merely correlational.

Finally, the ways in which we interpret and disseminate information about gender differences or about male and female behavior too often reflect the values or concerns of whichever group in that society has the most power and influence. Perhaps it's no surprise then that psychology and other social sciences have traditionally been **androcentric,** or male centered, in the types of questions researchers ask and the ways in which the data are interpreted. For example, research showing that males tend to be more aggressive than females has routinely been used as an argument for keeping women out of combat positions in the military—positions that also happen to pay more and have greater chances for advancement than noncombat positions (Mitchell, 1991; Muir, 1993; Pearsall, 1990; Wekesser, 1991). But the same data has not been used to argue that men are not as well-suited as women for high offices, such as the presidency or military policy makers, where males' aggressive behavior might contribute to more foolhardy decisions. The point here is not whether women should be in combat. The point is that the same research data can be used to support a male point of view or to maintain the status quo, when the same data could as easily have been used to argue for a female or a racial minority point of view. When reading about male and female adolescents, therefore, it's important to train yourself to interpret the data in ways that could serve the needs, goals, or values of either gender.

THEORIES OF GENDER DIFFERENCES

The longstanding debates about gender differences have usually centered around the question: Does nature or nurture have the greater influence in determining our behavior and attitudes as males and females? In attempting to answer this question, researchers and psychologists have grouped themselves into several camps according to which group of theories they believe best explains our behavior. As discussed, these four main groups are biological theories, Freudian theories, cognitive theories, and social learning theories.

Few psychologists nowadays would deny that our genes, hormones, and perhaps even certain evolutionary trends might have an impact on certain human behavior. Likewise, when it comes to gender differences, the debate among psychologists isn't so much *whether* biological factors play a part, but a debate over *how much* of an interplay exists between biological and environmental factors and which is dominant. In the realm of research on gender differences, biological researchers have focused primarily on three areas: evolutionary influences, brain lateralization, and hormones.

Evolution and Genetics   According to supporters of sociobiology, much of our behavior is determined by biological factors that have evolved for the survival and betterment of our species (Wilson, 1978). From this viewpoint, the ways in which males and females behave differently have been genetically programmed as universal traits into our species. So, for example, sociobiologists contend that teenage girls are generally more nurturing and less aggressive than boys, despite our more liberal gender roles, because these traits are passed along to us genetically as a way of ensuring that females will care for the young and males will protect their families. Likewise, sociobiologists contend that teenage boys are more sexually active and more promiscuous than girls as a result of their genetic programming to repopulate the species, not as a consequence of how our society has reinforced a double standard of sexual behavior. Some sociobiologists also explain our gender differences by generalizing from their observations of other mammals. For instance, the fact that many male animals have sex with more than one female of their species is used as evidence that men and boys are genetically predisposed to sexual behavior that our society labels promiscuous.

As you might expect, sociobiologists have their critics (Fausto-Sterling, 1991). For instance, archaeological and fossil records show that among our early ancestors, males and females shared the tasks of gathering food. The women didn't sit around camp taking care of the young while the men went out hunting aggressively for large game. In fact, the supposedly aggressive, domineering male "killer apes" were predominantly vegetarians, not carnivores that lived off large prey they had hunted and killed. Moreover, animals of different species assume a number of variations in the gender roles. For example, male owl monkeys and marmosets take care of the young, handing them over to the mothers only for nursing. Also, many female primates are far from "monogamous," copulating, even when pregnant, with any number of males. As for males' being genetically programmed to aggressively protect their families from harm, some of the biggest, strongest male baboons are the first guys clamoring up the trees to safety when enemies approach, leaving the females and the young behind to fend for themselves.

But what does this business about cave dwellers and monkeys have to do with our study of adolescents and gender roles? Quite a bit, in fact, because there are still people who believe that male and female behavior is primarily determined by our genes and that the behavior of monkeys and humans is closely linked. When we propose ways of helping adolescents become more liberated from their

Insert 6–1

Cognitive Difference between Males and Females

Problem-Solving Tasks Favoring Women

Women tend to perform better than men on tests of perceptual speed in which subjects must rapidly identify matching items—for example, pairing the house on the far left with its twin:

In addition, women remember whether an object, or a series of objects has been displaced:

On some tests of ideational fluency, for example, those in which subjects must list objects that are the same color, and on tests of verbal fluency, in which participants must list words that begin with the same letter, women also outperform men:

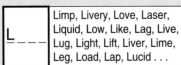

Women do better on precision manual tasks—that is, those involving fine-motor coordination–such as placing the pegs in holes on a board:

And women do better than men on mathematical calculation tests:

77	14 x 3 − 17 + 52
43	$2(15+3)+12-\dfrac{15}{3}$

Problem-Solving Tasks Favoring Men

Men tend to perform better than women on certain spatial tasks. They do well on tests that involve mentally rotating an object or manipulating it in some fashion, such as imagining turning this three-dimensional object

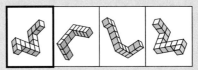

or determining where the holes punched in a folded piece of paper will fall when the paper is unfolded:

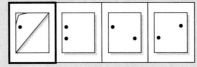

Men also were more accurate than women in target-directed motor skills, such as guiding or intercepting projectiles:

They do better on disembedding tests, in which they have to find a simple shape, such as the one on the left, once it is hidden within a more complex figure:

And men tend to do better than women on tests of mathematical reasoning:

1,100	If only 60 percent of seedlings will survive, how many must be planted to obtain 660 trees?

Source: D. Kimura (1992, September). Sex differences in the brain. *Scientific American,* pp. 119–125.

gender roles, therefore, we encounter opposition from those who believe we are "tampering with nature."

Brain lateralization, hemisphericity, or **bilateralization** refer to the fact that each side of the brain seems to control certain mental and physical functions. Apparently, the left hemisphere controls our verbal abilities and emotions while the right controls our mathematical abilities, visual spatial abilities, and artistic or musical talent. This seems to hold true for both genders. The search for proof of differences in the male and female brain has been conducted for quite some time. Earlier in this century, for example, researchers rationalized the positions of girls and women in our society by saying that female brains have less thinking capacity because females can't consume as much food as males and, therefore, have fewer nutrients available for their brains. Although today's research is more sophisticated, many questions remain in the search for proof of differences between male and female brain function (Fausto-Sterling, 1991; Kimura, 1992; Tavris, 1992).

Because they tend to have an advantage in tasks that require mental rotation of an object or navigation along an unknown route, could males be more right-brain dominant? Because they generally outperform males in computing math calculations, matching items, and recalling landmarks, could females be more left-brain dominant? Is it possible that the hemispheres in males and females are somehow connected differently since women's scores on vocabulary tests are affected when either hemisphere of their brain is damaged, but men's scores are affected only by injuries to the left hemisphere? Does this imply that female brains are more **bilateralized**—that they can process verbal information in either hemisphere but males can't? Given that left-handedness and verbal skills are both thought to be controlled by the right hemisphere, what are we to make of the finding that females and left-handed males rely more on verbal skills than on visual spatial skills when solving certain types of problems than do right-handed males? Consider that 3 to 4 times more males than females stutter, and 10 times more boys than girls have reading disabilities. So are males less adept than females in these verbal and reading skills because their brains process information differently? Some researchers think so.

Although intriguing to many people, the research on brain lateralization is still too meager and contradictory to draw any reliable conclusions. But perhaps more important, theories on brain lateralization don't explain why the sexes are becoming more similar in terms of their performance on these particular problem-solving tasks. Nor can biological theories explain why the kinds of experiences that teenagers of both sexes have in and out of school are related to how well they do on certain visual-spatial skills (Baenninger & Newcombe, 1990). The theories on brain lateralization also seem to have overstepped their bounds, given our limited understanding of how the human brain works. Roger Sperry, the Nobel Prize-winning neurobiologist whose experiments helped establish our theories on brain lateralization, has lamented that hypotheses and generalizations about brain hemisphericity have gotten out of hand. As Sperry himself points out, the brain operates as a closely integrate whole, not as two absolutely separate and distinct halves (Sperry, 1982). For example, when a child's brain is damaged on one side, the undamaged hemisphere takes over all the brain's functions—which is not the case, by the way, when an adult's brain is damaged. Most brain researchers today believe that the two lobes complement one another and can sometimes take over one another's functions (Tavris, 1992).

One further concern about theories of sex differences in the brain is that researchers keep changing their minds about which lobe of the brain accounts for the superiority of one sex over the other. Originally the left lobe was considered the seat of intellect and reason. The right lobe was considered the passionate, instinctive, irrational, and emotional side. Guess which sex was thought to have left-brain superiority? But in the 1960s and 1970s, the right lobe was suspected as the source of genius, inspiration, creativity, and mathematical talents. Guess which sex was thought to have right-brain dominance? The answer to both questions? Male (Tavris, 1992).

Despite the inconclusive evidence, many people persist in believing that certain gender differences in adolescents can be explained by these brain lateralization theories. Some people state, as if it were fact, that females are more intuitive and more emotional than males because of their "right-brain dominance" and that males are more rational and analytical because of their "left-brain preferences." Not only are such beliefs not yet supported by the research, they overlook a much more important reality: Males and females are far more similar than different in verbal, mathematical, musical, artistic, and visual-spatial abilities (Tavris, 1992).

Hormones   In searching for biological explanations for certain gender differences, researchers are also exploring any possible relationships between our hormones and our behavior. For example, boys with androgen deficiencies seem to perform more poorly on solving certain kinds of visual-spatial problems than boys with normal androgen levels. Likewise, some children who were accidentally exposed to masculinizing hormones while still in the womb are more aggressive than other children as teenagers. It has even been reported that males' performance on spatial ability tests drops in the springtime when their testosterone levels are lowest (Carlson, 1986).

On the other hand, the link between a person's hormones and his or her behavior or cognitive performance hasn't been established. The links between hormones and male or female behavior are generally contradictory, inconsistent, and weak. The strongest correlations so far have been between physical aggressiveness and unusually high levels of testosterone in some teenage boys and men. Even here though, the data is correlational and can't be used to prove that high testosterone levels cause aggressiveness. For example, behaving aggressively raises testosterone levels in males and females. So it might be that a male who behaves aggressively for reasons other than his hormone level actually elevates his testosterone level rather than the other way around. Likewise, decades of research on women's menstrual cycles have failed to find any consistent or demonstrable links between hormone levels and female performance at work, at school, or at cognitive tasks (Buchanan, Eccles, & Becker, 1992; Dabbs & Morris, 1990; Fausto-Sterling, 1991; Paikoff, Brooks-Gunn, & Warren, 1991; Tavris, 1992).

In contrast to these biological or genetic theories, psychoanalytic or Freudian theorists argue that how we behave as males and females is primarily determined by how we resolve the issues associated with our childhood stages of ego development. Indeed, the major childhood event determining how our "femininity" and "masculinity" will develop is whether we resolve our Oedipal or Electra Complex as young children (Erikson, 1968; Freud, 1977).

By way of brief review, Oedipus becomes king after murdering his father, then unknowingly marries his own mother. For a while, the incestuous couple rules their kingdom happily, having four children together—who are, of course, half siblings to Oedipus. When Oedipus learns his true identity, he blinds himself with his mother's brooch, whereupon the queen kills herself. The miserable, blind Oedipus then wanders the land, totally dependent on his daughter\half-sister, Antigone, as his guide. Not only is Antigone unable to marry anyone because she has to take care of her father\half-brother Oedipus; but she also ends up being put to death for an act of loyalty to one of her brothers.

Around the age of 4 or 5, we are supposedly jealous of the attention our same-sex parent is getting from our opposite-sex parent. In order to resolve this frustrating situation, we have to "fall out of love" with our opposite-sex parent and bond, or "identify" with, our same-sex parent. If we fail to bond in this way with the correct parent, then as teenagers and adults we will lack the self-confidence and social maturity to create intimate, heterosexual relationships. In other words, teenagers with unresolved Oedipal issues are the "mommies' boys" and "daddies' girls" who haven't broken free of their child-like dependence and reverence for their opposite-sex parent. As a consequence, these teenagers seek out very dependent relationships with someone who will "mother" or "father" them in very protective, possessive, child-like ways. Or, as a consequence of not having bonded to their same-sex parent as a young child, these teenagers develop homosexual orientations. Even as adults, these males and females fail to live up to our society's gender role expectations in that they are too dependent on their opposite-sex parent to meet their emotional needs. Moreover, they relate to their same-sex parent in extremely competitive, jealous ways.

Freudians also believe that we learn our gender roles from observing and imitating our same-sex parent. In other words, boys living with a single mother or girls living with a single father wouldn't learn appropriate gender role behavior. But this assumption is not supported by contemporary research on teenagers from single-parent families (Huston & Alvarez, 1990). It's also important to recognize that many contemporary theorists, as well as Freud himself, believe that Oedipal issues don't affect girls the same as boys. Indeed, Freud didn't believe in an Electra complex. More contemporary interpretations of Oedipal issues cast a different light on male and female development (Kaschak, 1992). According to Freud, in the first few years of our lives we have a fairly exclusive, self-centered, demanding, relationship with our mothers. But around 4 or 5, we're supposed to grow up a little in the sense that we should stop relying so heavily on our mothers to meet our every need. In the myth, Oedipus doesn't overcome his complex in that he turns to another woman, Antigone, to meet his needs after his mother dies. Even though Oedipus gets a second chance to stop using women as extensions of himself to "mother" him, he has his own daughter\half-sister sacrifice her life to his needs. In the same way, boys in our society can be said to have failed to resolve their Oedipal complex as long as they feel entitled to be taken care of and to have their needs met by self-sacrificing females—if not by mother herself, then by other females in their lives. By overcoming his child-like dependence and demanding self-centeredness with his own mother, a son is more apt to become less demanding, less engulfing, and less egocentric with other females as he ages.

Likewise, Antigone can be interpreted as representative of the traditional female gender role—the woman who continually sacrifices herself and puts her own needs aside for the men in her life. Girls who can overcome their "Antigone complex" would then stand a better chance of becoming women who realize that their central purpose is not to lead a life of self-denial and self-sacrifice in order to please men and boys. Exactly as a son needs to stop seeing his mother, and eventually other females, as people who are there primarily to meet his needs, the daughter must stop seeing herself as her father's possession whose primary function is to meet his needs and eventually the needs of other males (Kaschak, 1992).

COGNITIVE THEORIES

In contrast to the psychoanalytic view, cognitive psychologists believe that we acquire our gender roles in stages, much like the stages of cognitive development described in earlier chapters. Around the age of 3, we begin to identify ourselves as either male or female. During the next couple of years we learn to correctly identify other people's gender. For example, by the age of 5 we have learned that, even if a man dresses up in women's clothes, he is still male. The cognitive viewpoint assumes that we become aware of our gender and start behaving in ways that fit our gender role without needing to be reinforced to adapt to the role. In contrast, social learning theorists believe that we learn to behave in masculine or feminine ways through the rewards, approval, and punishment that we get from the people around us (Kohlberg, 1966).

Another variant of cognitive theory is **gender schema theory.** Because we are all exposed to more incoming information than we can process, we must screen out or ignore certain information. While processing new information, we are trying to make it fit with our existing beliefs and our previously stored data. These pre-existing beliefs and facts are organized by our internal cognitive structures, our schema. As shown in the discussion of Piaget in Chapter 3, a **schema** is a set of ideas or an organizational framework that helps us categorize, process, interpret, and remember new information (Levy & Carter, 1989).

When it comes to our behavior and attitudes as males and females, we remember incidents and store information that conform to our existing beliefs about males and females. We also ignore or discount experiences and information that contradict our existing beliefs about each gender. For example, if taught that women who choose not to have children are unhappy and maladjusted, a female teenager literally will not take into account the many childless women she knows who are happy and well-adjusted. According to gender schema theory, adolescents and adults who conform to traditional sex roles have schema that organize all incoming information into similar restricted categories. In contrast, adolescents who step beyond our culture's gender roles have schemata that allow them to organize incoming information on bases other than gender stereotypes. In other words, even though both groups of adolescents are exposed to the same information, they are processing the data differently according to their existing schema.

SOCIAL LEARNING THEORIES

As explained in the preceding chapter, social learning theorists believe that most of our behavior and attitudes are consequences of reinforcement and punishment since birth, as well as the models available to imitate. In regard to gender roles, these same principles apply. So girls who are reinforced for being aggressive and competitive will grow up being more androgynous than girls who are reinforced for being passive and subservient. Likewise, boys who are reinforced for showing their emotions openly and for being artistic will grow up being more androgynous than boys who are reinforced for concealing their feelings and for abandoning their interests in the arts. For example, boys who grow up in cultures that reinforce their taking care of younger children act more maturely and more sociably around their peers as teenagers than boys who are raised in societies like ours in which boys seldom care for younger children (Whiting & Edwards, 1988). In short, social learning theorists contend that how we are socialized determines how we behave as males and females (Huston & Alvarez, 1990; Lynch, 1991).

COMPARISONS OF GENETIC AND ENVIRONMENTAL INFLUENCES

Whether studying biological or social learning theories, the basic problem is that no ethical way exists to conduct research on humans that allows us to test the effects of various hormones, to alter various parts of the brain, or to tamper with genetic codes in ways that might answer many of our questions about gender differences. The closest we can come to this type of research is to observe adolescents who have been born with abnormalities involving their hormones and genes. As seen in Chapter 2, babies born with Turner's syndrome and Klinefelter's syndrome do not produce enough estrogen or testosterone as adolescents, respectively, to develop their secondary sex characteristics. Even when these teenagers are given synthetic hormones to help their bodies develop, the girls tend to be more aggressive and the boys more passive than other teenagers. This suggests that, at least in the case of passive and aggressive behavior, our genes might partly account for why most males are more aggressive than most females. On the other hand, this conclusion is complicated by the fact that these children look different from other children of their same sex while they are growing up. In comparison to other girls, these females have a more masculine body, which might, in turn, cause people to treat them differently than girls who look more feminine. This would then be proof that the environment, not their genes, is primarily responsible for their behaving more aggressively than other girls.

Studying children who are born as hermaphrodites, however, has given us a better understanding of the relative impact of the environment and genes on our male and female behavior. **Hermaphrodites** are children born with a mixture of male and female sexual glands and organs. That is, the child might have both a penis and a vagina, or might have what seems to be a penis but have ovaries rather than testicles. After a more complete physical examination, doctors might discover that a "he" is actually a "she" whose vaginal lips were fused together, resembling a scrotum, and whose clitoris was enlarged, resembling a penis. Because the correct gender of these children is sometimes not discovered until years after they are born, they are often raised as if they were one sex, when in fact they are chromosomally and hormonally the other sex. For example, not until the "boy" approaches puberty and no testicles descend, yet "his" breasts are enlarging, might it be discovered that "he" has ovaries and a uterus. He has been successfully socialized into a male gender role, but he is genetically female (Money & Ehrhardt, 1972).

Studies of hermaphroditic children show that their behavior and attitudes conform to the gender role into which they are socialized, despite their actual biological sex. In other words, it's not what these teenagers are genetically that determines their masculine or feminine behavior. It's how they are raised, how others treat them, and what they themselves believe they are from the time of their birth. For example, among rural villages in Santo Domingo "girls" sometimes discover at adolescence (when their voices deepen, the clitoris grows into a small penis, and the testicles descend) that genetically they are "boys"—in fact, it's common enough that such children have been tagged with a local term that means "penis at 12." Even though they were raised as girls, most of these teenagers switch gender roles, and adapt to their anatomy as males who marry and become fathers. The research on hermaphroditic children undermines theories that attempt to explain gender differences too exclusively in terms of genes and hormones and lends more credibility to social learning theories (Imperato-McGuinley, 1979).

SEX ROLE SOCIALIZATION

FAMILY

Much of our data about gender supports the social learning theorists' position: Most of how we behave as males and females depends on how we are socialized. Above all, our parents' and stepparents' attitudes and behaviors influence our ideas about masculinity and femininity. Despite all the discussion about women's liberation, the fact remains that most adults still treat their sons and daughters differently at home. Most encourage their sons to be more self-reliant, assertive, competitive, ambitious, outspoken, athletic, and sexually active than their daughters. Even during infancy, female children are generally talked to more, picked up more often when they cry, and prevented from roaming as far or playing as roughly as male infants. Most families also give sons more toys and games that require math, science, and visual-spatial skills. Even household chores are assigned in most families on the basis of traditional gender stereotypes. Like most of their fathers and stepfathers, most teenage boys are still expected to shovel the snow, take out the garbage, and cut the grass. And like most of their mothers or stepmothers, most teenage girls are still doing the cooking, cleaning, and childcare for younger siblings (Bartko & McHale, 1991; Eccles, Jacobs, & Harold, 1990; Thorne, 1993).

When it comes to their children's educational and vocational plans, most adults also continue to react along stereotyped gender lines. For example, when money is short, parents lower their plans for their daughter's education more than they lower their plans for their son (McLoyd, 1989). On the other hand, some families are less sexist than others. When both adults in their family are earning an income, adolescents tend to have less restrictive attitudes about gender roles than in families with a mother who is a full-time housewife. In these two-income families, the happier the father is with his wife's having a job and the less sexist he is in the way he treats her, the higher his daughter's academic and vocational goals tend to be. Teenage boys whose mothers earn incomes also seem to have less sexist attitudes than boys whose mothers are housewives (Barber & Eccles, 1992; Gilbert, 1993; Lerner & Galambos, 1991). The gender role attitudes that older members of a family pass down to the young are also related to the level of industrialization of their society. Adults and adolescents in industrialized countries tend to be less sexist and more androgynous than people in less developed countries (Williams & Best, 1989).

The adults' religious beliefs can also have an impact on their teenagers' gender-related beliefs and behavior. In extremely orthodox or conservative families, traditional gender roles are more strictly and rigidly enforced. For example, females might be restricted to less influential positions in religious ceremonies, prayers, and rituals. The parents' religious beliefs can either reinforce or reject the ideology that females should be submissive to males in family and religious matters (Brod, 1988; Heschel, 1990; Ho, 1990).

SCHOOLS

Beyond the family, adolescents' attitudes and behavior are shaped almost daily by what goes on in their schools. Students' views of what is appropriate for males and females in our society and their future expectations for their own lives are influenced by their school's curriculum, the ways their teachers interact with male and female students, school policies, and the teaching methods used in the classroom. Despite the fact that **Title IX** legislation was passed in the early 1970s in order to guarantee male and female students an equal education, most schools are still sexist and androcentric in their ways of educating students. Studies and

Insert 6–2

The Thin Gray Gender Line

Should schools that are supported by taxpayers' money have the right to enroll only students of one sex? According to a federal judge's 1991 ruling in Virginia, yes. Virginia Military Institute won the right to continue its policy of excluding female students on the grounds that female students would prevent the male cadets from "bonding" through their hazing rituals. This decision goes against the Supreme Court's 1982 ruling that forbids gender discrimination in schools receiving federal or state funding. In the 1982 case, the justices said that a tax-supported female nursing school in Mississippi had to admit male students. The ruling in favor of V.M.I., which receives $9 million each year from Virginia's state budget, also seemed strange in that only several months before in Operation Desert Storm, women in the military had died fighting for their country alongside their male comrades.

Source: E. Mitchell (1991, July 1). The thin gray gender line. *Time,* p. 66.

surveys conducted throughout the past 5 years continue to show that most schools' policies, the curriculum, teaching techniques, and teachers' interactions with students remain more advantageous for boys than for girls (American Association of University Women [AAUW] 1992; Henderson & Dweck, 1990; Mortenson, 1991; Sadker & Sadker, 1993).

Curriculum   Despite the fact that 51% of public school students are girls, the curriculum is typically more relevant and more well-suited to the lives and learning styles of boys. The content of textbooks, the photographs used to illustrate the texts, the questions asked on tests, and out-of-class assignments more often reflect interests and viewpoints that relate to male students. For example, the required reading lists for high-school students across the nation have changed very little since 1963 in that the authors are predominantly white males. Efforts to modernize and expand the required reading to include more works by female and minority authors have been virtually ineffective in most schools (Applebee, 1989). This is not to say that the curriculum should exclude works by white or male authors, but that adolescents could benefit from a more diversified curriculum that reflects the interests and experiences of female and minority students.

Likewise, most schools are not doing well in teaching girls to use computers—a skill that affects not only their present experiences, but also their future job prospects. At school, teenage boys generally have more exposure than girls to computers and are taught more about computer programming to prepare them for a greater variety of future careers. Most girls' experiences with computers in school are still limited to learning how to type on computers for secretarial jobs or for the lower-paying jobs as computer operators. Given their educational experiences, is it surprising that only 8% of the lower-paid computer operators are male in contrast to 76% of the higher-paid computer specialists?

Interactions with Teachers   As is true with the curriculum, most teachers also reinforce traditional gender roles in their ways of relating to students and in their teaching methods. From elementary school through college, male students generally receive more attention, more praise, more questions, and more feedback from their teachers than do their female classmates. Most teachers also give male students more remedial help. Boys tend not to be penalized for calling out answers and taking risks; but many girls who do the same are reprimanded for being "rude." Likewise, when teachers are asked to remember their favorite students, the ones they like best are assertive males and the ones they like least are assertive females. These patterns appear to hold true, by the way, whether the teachers are male or female, white or minority, urban or suburban. Also, despite the stereotype that females talk more than males, male students do most of the talking during class and interrupt the teacher and other students more than their female classmates.

Teaching Techniques   Most teachers also continue to use methods that appeal more to male than to female students. Because males are usually socialized outside of school to be more assertive and more competitive than females, they feel more comfortable than girls with teaching techniques and assignments that rely on competing against other classmates (Muir, 1993). In contrast, female students usually feel more comfortable helping and cooperating with their classmates, rather than competing in an individualistic, aggressive manner. As in most sports, the "I win, you lose" philosophy is the basis for most classroom activities and grading systems. Especially in math and science classes, female students are more afraid of making mistakes and taking risks and are less self-confident than their male classmates. In part this is happening because math and science teachers generally don't give girls the same encouragement or the same chances as boys to experiment on their own with the problems. Many math and science teachers also continue to send the same message as many other adults in our society: Boys are naturally better at math and science, and girls are better at English and the arts.

Further complicating the situation for female students, they are expected to feel comfortable competing against and outperforming boys in the classroom—a direct contradiction to how they are socialized to behave around the boys they are trying to impress socially. Boys, on the other hand, aren't in this same kind of bind socially and academically. They can develop one set of traits—assertiveness, outspokenness, independence, competitiveness—that serves them well in succeeding as students and succeeding socially with girls. By using more cooperative teaching methods and by arranging academic activities in which girls and boys are not necessarily competing against each other, teachers can help girls overcome some of the stress of their double bind.

These findings might make us wonder: Do teenage girls benefit from being in classes without boys where they feel more free to express themselves and where teachers might give them more attention? In general, yes. Reviews of the research show that girls who attend coeducational high schools and colleges usually have lower educational aspirations, more stereotyped attitudes about women's roles, and lower intellectual self-esteem than those who attend all-girls' schools. In all-girls' high schools and colleges, the students also tend to be more competitive, more verbally assertive in class, and more interested in academics than girls in coeducational schools. Moreover, these differences seem to persist years after they have graduated from their all-girls' high schools and colleges. In contrast, whether boys attend all-male or coeducational high schools and colleges seems to make relatively little impact on their achievements and attitudes. Because most coeducational schools are more oriented toward male than female students, this finding makes sense (Lee & Marks, 1990).

Because coeducational high schools and colleges are the norm, we need to find ways to incorporate these findings about the benefits of single-sex education for girls into coeducational classrooms. In other words, we need to identify what it is about all-girls' schools that we can provide for girls in coeducational environments. One possibility is to segregate certain classes by sex so that girls can receive the attention they need in traditionally male-oriented courses such as math and science. Another option is to establish a school committee to oversee ways of making the curriculum, teaching methods, and school policies more conducive to girls' interests and learning styles (Lee & Marks, 1990).

Sexual Harassment of Students   As Insert 6–3 demonstrates, another problem facing teenage girls that seldom affects boys is sexual harassment or sexual involvement with their teachers—a problem that exists at the high-school and college level. Not only do some male teachers flirt with their female students, make sexual comments to them, and hug or touch them, some also go so far as to have sex with their students. Male teachers in our high schools and colleges who become sexually involved with their female students are often violating federal laws against having sex with a minor, as well as violating professional ethics and school policies. Teenage boys, of course, are not immune from being sexually harassed or having sex with a teacher. But the problem is still far more common

Insert 6–3

High-School Teachers Harassing Female Students

"I'm 18 and a senior now. Last year I finally confronted one of my history teachers after class one day and asked if it was really too much to drop all the honey-cookie-pieface-lambchop stuff, adding that I considered it sexist and demeaning. His eyes nearly popped out of his head. When I pointed out that none of the guys in my class are "Hot Harold" or "Studmuffin Sam," he whined,"But I'm not interested in guys!" Another teacher drooled all over my friend, "I'll give you a 96 if you'll give me a 69." And another thought it was appropriate to say to a young woman wearing a skirt, "Why don't you lift that up for me?" Now I'd like to make absolutely clear that I don't think every teacher at this high school is a deranged psycho rapist. But too often I've felt like a second rate student, expected to cater to every grungy Mr. Wonderstud whose class I happened to be in."

Source: Miranda Van Gelder (October, 1991) High School Lowdown. *MS.*, p. 56.

among male teachers and female students at the high-school, college, and graduate school levels (AAUW, 1993; Deich & Weiner, 1990; Gittins, 1990; Stein, Marshall, & Tropp, 1993).

MEDIA, LITERATURE, AND LANGUAGE

Beyond the school walls, adolescents' attitudes about gender roles are influenced by television, magazines, and language in our culture at large. By the age of 4, most children have spent between 2,000 and 3,000 hours watching television—nearly 15,000 hours by time they turn 18 (Nielsen, 1988). What messages about the roles of males and females in our society are they getting during these thousands of hours of TV exposure? Unfortunately, with few exceptions, television still depicts males and females in stereotyped roles. Men and boys are generally portrayed as active, industrious, ambitious and financially self-sufficient, while most women and girls are still depicted in roles related to childcare, food preparation, housework, and marriage, or as helpmates and sexual partners. This is especially unfortunate because adolescents' attitudes have been shown to become less sexist after seeing males and females depicted in nontraditional roles on television (Faludi, 1991; Liebert & Sprafkin, 1988; Remafedi, 1990).

Turning our attention to what most teenagers are reading, we see similar patterns. Teenage magazines and romance novels also send the message to girls that their self-worth primarily depends on self-sacrifice, beauty, and popularity with boys (Peirce, 1990; Smith, 1990). As they're growing up, most adolescents are also receiving messages about gender from fairy tales and nursery rhymes. For example, what female roles, virtues, and attitudes are being presented in "Little Miss Muffet," "Cinderella," "Sleeping Beauty," and "Snow White"? Now contrast those messages with the male roles in "Jack and the Beanstalk" and "The Little Engine that Could." Indeed, did you have any trouble remembering the gender of the industrious, hardworking, determined, successful little engine? But aren't fairy tales merely a meaningless form of entertainment for children? Aren't we stretching things a little too far by trying to connect fairy tales to gender role socialization? No, at least not according to a number of psychologists, including the world famous Bruno Bettelheim who wrote in great detail about the ways in which fairy tales are used throughout the world to socialize children into accepting the values and roles sanctioned by their society (Bettelheim, 1976; Binchy, 1988; Crowley, 1989; Zipes, 1991).

Adolescents also receive messages about gender roles through the language they hear and the wording of what they read. For example, what gender first comes into your mind for the people described by the following underlined words? The medical student heard his professor lecture in his same raspy voice. The firemen, mailmen, and chairmen were talking about their forefathers. Now, using nonsexist language, what gender first comes to mind? The medical students heard their professor's raspy voice. The firefighters, postal workers, and department heads were talking about their ancestors. In the same way that derogatory words for various racial groups and for gay people convey negative messages, derogatory words describing girls and women reinforce negative images. For example, consider the judgments and messages we convey when we refer to an unmarried, older man as a "bachelor" and to his female counterpart as "an old maid" or a "spinster." The traditional words we choose to use or the new words we create do reflect the roles we have established, or want to establish, for males and females in our society. By using nonsexist language and by refusing to use pejorative words, therefore, we are helping to create less restrictive roles, more positive images, and more expansive expectations for children and adolescents (Lakoff, 1990; Mills, 1992).

Defining Masculinity and Femininity

So our schools, families, media, fairy tales, musical lyrics, religion, toys, and language all work together to send us the messages about how we're supposed to behave as males and females in our particular societies. But, as you can see even within your own lifetime, our society is continually readjusting its definitions of "masculinity" and "femininity"—as are other societies, and as societies have throughout history. Gender roles have always shifted and evolved in ways that bewilder the elders and confuse the young. Our present situation is no exception. For example, at times in our country, females were stereotyped as oversexed, and men were assigned responsibility for keeping custody of their children after a divorce (Rotundo, 1993).

**Insert
6–4**

Where Are the Male Dancers?

Dance companies are looking for more men but aren't having much luck. "Where's the prince?" asks an editorial in *Dance* magazine. The shortage of classically trained male dancers has reached such proportions that the ballet critic for *The New York Times* laments, "We are back to the same old story—forced to acknowledge that the United States is less receptive to the development of male classical dancing than it should be." Even in our supposedly more liberated society, boys are still reluctant to become professional dancers, fearing that they will be ridiculed or ostracized for doing something "sissy" or accused of being gay.

Source: L. Shapiro (1989, April). Where are all the men? *Newsweek*, p. 62.

Moreover, there seems to be more disagreement since the late 1980s over what males' roles should be than over females' roles (Shweder, 1994). Adolescent males today aren't being given any simple or straightforward prescription for what it takes to "be a man" in our society. To the contrary, male researchers and writers whose work has been rapidly emerging since the late 1980s as a "men's movement" or "masculinists" are not at all in agreement on what teenage boys or men need to be doing in terms of living up to their gender role expectations. A number of male writers believe that boys and men need to become more emotional, more empathic, more nurturing, less competitive, and more intimately connected to other people—in short, develop more of the "feminine" traits in themselves (Betcher & Pollack, 1993; Doty, 1993). Among these writers is the cofounder of Men Against Pornography, who believes that when a boy's definition of manhood includes domination, possessiveness, pornography, and competition for status, he ought to choose to be a "person of conscience" instead of a "man" (Stoltenberg, 1993). In this same vein, some men are urging other teenage and adult males to create more intimate relationships with their own fathers, as women have traditionally done with their mothers (Corneau, 1991; Keyes, 1992; Pittman, 1993).

On the other hand, other male authors believe there's not much that needs to be changed about our present definitions of manhood (Thomas, 1993). In this camp are those who argue that males have more right to complain about their gender role than females do because women's roles allow them more often to freeload off men. For example, teenage girls aren't drafted in wartime, and men are still expected to be the primary breadwinners for families (Farrell, 1993).

Male researchers and writers are also in disagreement over the longstanding question: How much of boys' and men's behavior is cultural and how much genetic? Some males still contend that masculinity and femininity are in the deepest parts of our being from birth onward. Our society isn't inventing gender roles and socializing us into them. We're merely discovering these ingrained aspects of ourselves as we're growing up (Hawley, 1993). Likewise, a psychotherapist at London Men's Center contends that it's a "universal fact of life" that men are controlling and destructive and that they basically dislike females (Jukes, 1993).

Finally there are those male writers who try to inspire other males to discover and define what is truly "masculine" for themselves by participating in initiation rituals and sharing experiences in their lives with other males. Through the study of myth, singing, and dancing, by initiated ritual and the bond of shared experiences, these males work at becoming open enough to bring forth new definitions of masculinity on their own (Bly, 1990; Meade, 1994). One male reviewer of the literature summarizes this approach to redefining male gender roles: "Some respected elders of the tribe are supposed to show up and let you in on some deep secret about what it means to really be a man. Unfortunately, in our post modern society we have no respected tribal elders or deep secrets, only a male identity crisis due in part to literature written largely by men in their 40s who are groping around in the dark looking for their "dignity" (Shweder, R., 1994, p. 3). So when it comes to helping adolescents understand what it means to "be a man" or to "be

How do you feel about girls playing basketball, football, or field hockey?

a woman," we adults aren't in agreement either. Keeping this in mind, let's now turn our attention to the question: Just how different are teenage males and females?

GENDER DIFFERENCES: HOW MUCH AND HOW MANY?

So we know that gender roles are still very much alive in our society. Still, we might wonder: What differences *do* exist between male and female adolescents? What measurable distinctions can be made? How much are teenagers being influenced by the messages they usually receive about male and female roles through their schools, our media, and our language? When compared to teenagers in their parents' generation, are adolescents much different today in regard to their gender roles? In an attempt to answer complex questions like these, let's examine the research in regard to these aspects of adolescent development: intellectual and academic self-confidence, vocational choices, physical and social self-esteem, math and verbal skills, identity formation, social reasoning, friendships, stress and depression, and aggression and risk taking. Also keep in mind that adolescents' attitudes, behavior, and choices do tend to get less sexist as they age. In other words, young adolescents are usually more rigid, more traditional, and more uptight about issues and attitudes related to gender and gender roles than are older adolescents (Galambos, Almeida, & Petersen, 1993; Lynch, 1991; Nelson & Keith, 1990).

INTELLECTUAL AND ACADEMIC SELF-CONFIDENCE

When it comes to how they feel about their intellectual abilities and academic skills, teenage girls are usually less confident than boys, even when their achievement scores and grades are equivalent. In general, from junior high school through college, female students lose more of their intellectual self-confidence than most male students (AAUW, 1992; Frederick & Nicholson, 1992; Henderson & Dweck, 1990; Holland & Eisenhart, 1991; Sadker & Sadker, 1993).

A few specific examples illustrate these gender differences. In a review of 70 research studies involving more than 63,000 students, high-school and college girls lost more of their confidence about doing math than did the male students (Hyde, 1993). Even among the brightest teenagers in our country who have won the prestigious national Westinghouse Talent Search Award, the female winners have less confidence about themselves intellectually than the boys (Campbell, 1991). Sadly, the brightest girls often seem to lose more of their intellectual self-confidence than less gifted girls as they move through high school and college. The brightest girls also feel increasingly stressed by trying to figure out how to remain attractive to boys without hiding their intellectual talents (Bakken, Hershey, & Miller, 1990; Cangelosi & Schaefer, 1991; Kline & Short, 1991; Kramer, 1991).

VOCATIONAL DEVELOPMENT

Because most girls feel less self-confident intellectually than boys, it's not surprising that most are still preparing for the same kind of work that the females in preceding generations have chosen—teaching, nursing, secretarial work, and other jobs that don't involve much math or science. And because most boys are still being socialized to believe that they have no choice except to be the major (or the sole) breadwinner for their future family, they, too, are restricting their vocational choices. This isn't to say that teenagers' vocational choices are as restrictive as they've been historically. For example, since 1960 the number of women's college degrees in agriculture have increased from 1% to nearly 30%, in architecture from 3% to 35%, and in pharmacy from 11% to 53%. More girls now graduate from high school than boys, and almost as many women as men graduate from college. Nevertheless, nearly one fourth of all female college graduates earn their degree in teaching, nursing, or home economics, in contrast to only 14% earning a degree in engineering. Like girls, the vast majority of boys are still restricting themselves to jobs traditionally filled by men. For example, most boys with artistic talents in areas like dance are still discouraged from pursuing their interests. Even among college graduates, most males still avoid the fields traditionally considered "women's work." For example, males still earn nearly 90% of the undergraduate degrees in engineering and 70% in architecture and agriculture (Lapan & Jingeleski, 1992; Mortenson, 1991).

How do you feel about a male being a seamstress, a nurse, a cosmetologist, or a kindergarten teacher?

Unfortunately, the jobs that most teenage girls are preparing for pay less and offer fewer chances for advancement than the jobs most teenage boys are preparing themselves for. Women who work full-time still earn 30% less than men who work full-time. Likewise, the average female college graduate still earns less, on average, than a male with only a high-school diploma. And female high-school graduates earn less, on average, than a male high-school dropout. Although high school and college girls from higher-income families and those whose mothers have careers tend to choose better paying, less traditional jobs, the vast majority are still choosing the lower-paying jobs traditionally held by women (Campbell, 1991; Faludi, 1991; Lapan & Jingeleski, 1992; Schulenberg, Goldstein, & Vondracek, 1991).

Given that nearly half of all women end up divorced and that 80% of all mothers are employed, most teenage girls still aren't making the best decisions for themselves in terms of their future incomes. By preparing themselves for jobs that don't require much math or science and jobs that will enable them to meet the demands of being a wife and mother, a female typically ends up with a much lower-paying job than a male. Likewise, most teenage and college males are still choosing jobs that will allow them very little time with their future families and that place them in the position of having to be a family's main breadwinner throughout all of their adult lives (Gustafson, 1991).

MATH AND VERBAL SKILLS

Given that teenage girls generally have less confidence in their intellectual abilities than boys, we might wonder whether there is any legitimate reason for their feelings. How do teenage girls and boys compare in terms of their math and verbal skills? Do girls have a justifiable reason for feeling less confident intellectually than boys?

Let's start with math skills. Boys do better in math than girls, right? Wrong. Both sexes perform about the same in math problems except at the most advanced levels of math. Until high school, girls generally surpass boys in doing math computations. But female high-school and college students do fall behind males in terms of the most advanced math skills—not a surprise because, starting in high school, girls quit enrolling in as many math courses as boys. Why? First, teenage girls usually gets the message at school and at home that females aren't good at math and that women don't need math in order to get good jobs. For example, in 1992 the National Council of Teachers of Mathematics wrote a letter to the Mattel toy company criticizing their newest "Teen Talk" Barbie, a speaking doll that includes in its prerecorded repertoire the statement: "Math class is tough." Given their exposure to such messages, it's not surprising that girls tend to take fewer math courses than boys in high school and college.

Yet when female students do take the same number of math courses as male students, their achievement scores are similar. Unfortunately, the choice to avoid math limits a girl's future job options and excludes her from many of the higher-paying jobs. Fortunately, however, since some girls are receiving more encouragement to keep enrolling in math courses, female students are catching up to males in their advanced math skills (Campbell, 1991; Fennema, 1990; Hyde, 1993).

But high school and college girls surpass boys in verbal skills, right? Wrong again. In vocabulary, writing, anagrams, and reading comprehension males and females are basically alike throughout their school careers (Fennema, 1990; Hyde, 1993; Linn & Hyde, 1991).

Appearance and Self-Esteem

When it comes to their physical appearance and self-confidence, girls generally feel more inferior than boys—and their negative feelings increase as they age. Especially when it comes to their weight, teenage girls dislike their bodies more than boys. In fact, even when boys are overweight, they are more satisfied with their bodies than girls who don't need to lose weight. Whereas teenage boys are most likely to feel bad when they're too short, most girls feel bad because they think they're not thin enough. Not only do girls feel much worse about their appearance, they also base more of their happiness and self-esteem on how they look than most boys do (Adams, 1991; Kaschak, 1992; Koff, Rierdan, & Stubbs, 1990; Phelps, 1993; Wadden, 1991; Wade, 1991; Wolf, 1992).

A few recent studies illustrate the severity of this problem. In a survey of 36,000 teenagers in Minnesota, females differed from males most dramatically in the areas of body image and concern about how they looked. Only 15% of the senior high-school boys, but 40% of the girls, disliked their appearance. Three times as many girls as boys believed they needed to lose weight (Harris, Blum, & Resnick, 1991). In a nationwide survey of almost 3,000 students in grades

4 through 10, girls disliked their appearance more than boys at every age level. By 10th grade, twice as many girls as boys disliked their looks (AAUW, 1992).

The large difference between how most males and females feel about their appearance has serious consequences for girls. First, our overall self-esteem is more closely connected to how we feel about our appearance than to any other aspect of ourselves during the teenage years, including our grades, athletic skills, or popularity with peers. So girls' feelings about their physical selves often lowers their self-esteem and can be a contributing factor to depression (Friedman, 1989; Wolf, 1992). Second, chronic dieting can create other problems for teenage girls: sleepiness and inability to concentrate at school, cessation of menstrual periods, irritability, hypertension, and retarded bone and muscle growth. Although just as many males are overweight, females do more dieting even though they are bio-logically programmed to store fat reserves in their thighs and hips. Even those girls who are thin are overly focused on losing weight. Girls who think they need to lose weight when their weight is actually normal are more stressed and depressed than girls who like their bodies. Their obsession with thinness is emo-tionally and psychologically damaging (Newell, 1990; Page, 1991). Even more distressing, the fact that so many teenage girls believe they need to lose weight is contributing to an increase in life-threatening eating disorders (Bordo, 1993; Fisher & Brone, 1991). All in all, we are doing a very poor job helping teenage girls feel satisfied with their bodies and their looks.

IDENTITY DEVELOPMENT

As noted in preceding chapters, several important developments have to take place during adolescence to enable us to fashion an identity of our own. First, we have to develop a more realistic image of ourselves by narrowing the gap between our actual skills and temperament and our overly idealistic, childhood fantasies of who we would like to be. As an adolescent, if I can't narrow this gap between who I am and who I want to be, I won't have much self-esteem, let alone be able to develop an identity of my own. Second, taking into consideration the feedback we get about who we are from other people, we have to develop independent cri-teria within ourselves on which we base our self-confidence so that we're not always relying on the judgments of others to feel good about ourselves or to form an identity. Third, we have to formulate a relatively consistent image of who we are as individuals, which involves integrating the contradictions that we see in our own behavior and attitudes. These steps to forming an identity also involve learn-ing to distinguish between your "true" and your "false" self—the person you really are and the person you pretend to be in order to win approval from people (Harter, 1990).

Unfortunately, more girls than boys leave adolescence without having achieved these steps toward identity formation. Why? First, most girls are socialized to keep their identities "flexible" in order to accommodate the needs of their future husbands and children. Second, girls are encouraged to focus more on achieving intimacy with other people than on fashioning an identity separate from these relationships. Third, girls are more likely than boys to stop or to "foreclose" their identities before they explore their options and experiment with different roles and paths. This happens largely because forming an identity requires a person to think and behave in ways that are considered "unfeminine": taking risks, questioning authorities, asserting opinions, and putting personal needs and interests ahead of others' expectations. Many of the teenage girls who try to form identities of their own, as boys do, encounter considerable disapproval (Brown & Gilligan, 1992; Gilligan, 1991; Hancock, 1989; Josselson, 1992; Kaschak, 1992; Richards, 1991).

One of the more important aspects of forming an identity, after having figured out what our interests and talents are, is preparing ourselves for our future jobs. Most girls, however, are still encouraged to prepare themselves for the kinds of jobs that don't "interfere too much" with being someone's wife and mother. Despite the fact that nearly half of all marriages end in divorce and that 80% of all mothers are employed, most teenage girls are still basing their identities on the expectation that a husband will be taking care of them financially. Likewise, most teenage boys are still being told to base their vocational plans on having to be the major breadwinner for their future family. Thus, forming an identity during adolescence, which is a large part of our ego development, takes different paths for males than for females. Illustrating this, a survey of 65 studies involving more than 9,000 people shows that these sex differences in personality and ego development are greater in junior and senior high school than at any other time in our adult lives (Cohn, 1991).

Another way of looking at gender differences in identity formation is to consider the importance of building connections to other people versus listening to your own "voice" about what you feel, what you need from others, and what you want from your own life. Most teenage boys have been socialized all their lives to fear or feel uncomfortable with "too much" emotional intimacy and connection to other people. Most teenage girls, however, have been raised to fear not being in a close, harmonious relationship with others. As a result, most teenage girls shape their identities around their fears of being abandoned by people for being too self-centered, too outspoken, too demanding, too self-reliant, or too assertive. And most boys shape their identities around their fears of losing their independence to someone they love, being suffocated or stifled by intimacy, and becoming "too feminine" in terms of showing their feelings or their dependence on others. Unlike the teenage boy, the teenage girl's concern for connectedness with other people shapes her identity around such questions as: "Do you love me? Is everything okay in our relationship? How can we get closer?"

For the adolescent girl, the down side of this path is often becoming overly reliant on other people's opinions and approval, failing to develop her intellectual skills and other talents, foreclosing her identity without exploring her options, and concealing her own feelings and needs in order to keep everyone else happy. For the adolescent boy, the down side of his path usually is failing to develop intimate relationships and friendships and becoming overly focused on his own personal achievements and development. Most boys are encouraged to express what they *think*—not *feel*—and what they want from others. But most girls are encouraged to muffle their own "voice" so as not to create problems in their relationships. At adolescence, girls tend to "lose their voices" by sacrificing or stifling who they truly are in order to please or create intimacy with other people. Unlike most teenage boys, most girls believe they must form an identity on the basis of what everyone will approve of—the "nice girl" who is not "too" outspoken, self-reliant, self-focused, intellectually challenging, ambitious, competitive, or demanding (Brown & Gilligan, 1992; Gilligan, 1991; Gilligan & Rogers, 1993).

SOCIAL AND MORAL REASONING

Given the importance of close, harmonious relationships to a girl's self-esteem and identity, it's not surprising that teenage girls usually have more mature social skills than most boys their age. In general, teenage boys are further behind girls in regard to those aspects of social reasoning that influence how well we get along with other people. In comparison to girls, teenage boys are usually not at good at recognizing the motives underlying other people's behavior or at expressing concern for others' feelings. Most teenage girls are also better at controlling their aggressive impulses, coming up with ways to resolve problems with people, and forgiving or accepting people's shortcomings and mistakes (Cohn, 1991; Dunn, 1993; Hauser & Bowlds, 1990; Kaschak, 1992; Maccoby, 1990).

According to Carol Gilligan, one of the most well-known and controversial researchers in the field comparing male and female moral reasoning, females generally reason from a less self-centered, more empathic viewpoint than males. Because most males are socialized to relate to people in less intimate, more self-focused ways, their reasoning about social and moral issues is also more focused on self-reliance and on their own welfare and feelings than is most girls'. Most males reason as though their primary responsibility is to themselves; whereas most females reason as though other people's needs and feelings come before their own. Thus males are more apt to reason and relate to people on the basis of principles like justice, fairness, and self-reliance; and girls more apt to reason on the basis of intimacy, harmony, and cooperation. From this viewpoint, teenage boys and men need to become more considerate of other people, more focused on creating intimacy, and less concerned with their own welfare. In contrast, teenage girls and women need to be more focused on self-reliance, less controlled by the needs and wishes of others, and more responsible for their own vocational and intellectual development (Brown & Gilligan, 1992; Gilligan, 1982; Gilligan, Lyons, & Hanmer, 1990; Gilligan, Rogers, & Tolman, 1991).

An example from Gilligan's research illustrates how she and her colleagues go about reaching their conclusions. In asking children what they should do in situations where they have to decide between meeting their own needs and meeting the needs of another person, one boy answered: "You go about one fourth for the other person and about three fourths for yourself. The most important thing in your decision should be yourself. Don't let yourself be guided totally by other people, but you have to take them in consideration." In contrast a girl answered,

"Well, it really depends on the situation. If it's just a responsibility to your job or to somebody that you barely know, then maybe you put yourself first. But if it's somebody you really love, and love as much or more than you love yourself, then you've got to decide what you love more—that person or yourself. You can't just decide, I'd rather do this or I'd rather do that" (Gilligan, 1982, p. 36). Another way of stating Gilligan's conclusions is that females are superior to males in the sense of being more empathic and less self-centered.

As you might expect, Gilligan's conclusions haven't gone without criticism. First, other researchers haven't found significant differences between male and female reasoning even using Gilligan's techniques (Tavris, 1992). That is, male and females usually reason more alike than differently. For example, a survey of the research on compassion, altruism, and caretaking—even at the expense of one's own interests—failed to find differences between males and females. Although females were more likely to *express* their sympathy and concern verbally, they weren't any more likely than males to *behave* empathically when it came to actually helping or sacrificing for others (Kohn, 1990). Moreover, a person's financial status, temperament, and cultural upbringing might have as much or more influence over his or her social reasoning. For example, in comparison to Anglo Americans, Israelis and African Americans of both sexes tend to place less emphasis on the individual's needs and more emphasis on the good of the community in their social and moral reasoning (Stack, 1986).

Aside from Gilligan's research, our assumptions that males and females differ in regard to empathy, self-sacrifice, and compassion are also influenced by the types of situations we have traditionally allowed each sex to participate in. Because females of all ages are more likely than males to be working at jobs or assigned tasks at home that involve nurturing, serving, and taking care of other people, we could jump to the conclusion that males wouldn't be equally as good at these particular tasks because they aren't as empathic or compassionate. Yet, as mentioned, our behavior is clearly influenced by societal conditioning. For example, historically women have been forbidden to join men in combat during war, except in roles as nurses. And men, even those who are extremely passive and nurturing, have been drafted involuntarily into combat. Yet you wouldn't be so naive as to assume that these soldiering and nursing assignments in the military prove that males are less empathic, more war-like, or less compassionate than females, would you? In fact, throughout history females have been as militant in wartime as males in whatever ways their society has allowed them to participate. And females voluntarily join aggressive, "white power" hate groups in our own country during peacetime (Elshtain, 1987; Muir, 1993; Pearsall, 1990; Wekesser, 1991).

All and all then, it might be safest to conclude that most females are more open than males in expressing their empathy and compassion for others with words, with tears, and with other nonverbal signs of concern. And it is true that the way we assign jobs at home and in the work force on the basis of gender does deprive most boys and men of an equal chance to develop or express those traits that Gilligan and others see as underdeveloped in most males. So by being less gender stereotyped in the work force, in our schools, and in our families, we can help teenage boys focus more on empathy, compassion, and selflessness and girls focus more on balancing their own welfare with the needs of others.

PEER RELATIONSHIPS

With their peers and other people, teenage boys usually aren't as intimate or as easy to communicate with as most girls. As Insert 6–5 illustrates, most males and females even use different linguistic styles to communicate their thoughts and feelings. On the whole, males interrupt more, listen less attentively, and focus more on themselves in a conversation. Most teenage girls use conversation as one way of maintaining and building closeness; but most teenage boys use conversations as ways to assert their opinions, demonstrate their expertise, or highlight their own accomplishments (Lakoff, 1990; Tannen, 1991).

Although girls are assertive with their friends, they usually express their needs in less aggressive, less confrontational ways. Female friends also tend to spend more time than male friends discussing personal issues, helping each other solve problems, and revealing intimate information about themselves. In contrast, when teenage boys get together, they are usually sharing an activity rather than talking to one another. Boys are also more likely than girls to criticize, threaten, and boss one another. Given these gender differences, it's not surprising that most teenage girls know their friends better, are more satisfied with their friendships, and feel less lonely than most teenage boys. Boys also tend to be less willing than girls to be influenced by another person's opinions, especially when boys think they're being watched by other people. Moreover, most of these differences in male and female friendships are apparent when we're only 5 or 6 years old and continue well into our adult years (Feiring & Lewis, 1991; Hartup & Overhauser, 1991; Lempers & Lempers, 1993; Savin-Williams & Berndt, 1990; Thorne, 1993).

Most boys lag behind girls in these areas as children; and the differences usually become larger during adolescence. Most male and female children who have trouble making friends, getting along with people, or being intimate with people outside the family don't catch up to their peers as adolescents—in fact, the differences get larger. But because most girls are further ahead than most boys in their childhood social development, in a sense boys look even worse than girls during adolescence. Indeed, compared to teenage girls, boys seem to have more social problems from their early childhood than from the transition to adolescence itself (Petersen, Kennedy, & Sullivan, 1991). This might partially help explain why older adolescent boys feel more stressed by their peer relationships than do girls their age (Larson & Asmussen, 1991).

FAMILY RELATIONSHIPS

Most teenage boys are also harder to get along with at home than most teenage girls. Parents and stepparents tell us that adolescent boys are harder to influence, harder to control, and harder to communicate with—especially for mothers and stepmothers (Camara & Resnick, 1989; Smetana, Yau, Restrepo, & Braeges, 1991;

Insert 6–5

Male and Female Conversational Styles

Females focus more on interdependence; males more on independence:

She: "How can you do this when you know it's hurting me?"

He: "How can you try to limit my freedom?"

She: "But it makes me feel awful."

He: "You're trying to control me."

Females focus more on acknowledging feelings; males more on giving advice:

She: "I felt awful when it happened, and I didn't know what to do."

He: "Well, I've got an idea what you could do. Why don't you. . ."

She: "I don't want you to fix it for me! I want you to see how I feel."

Females focus more on establishing a connection by sharing problems; males more on discussing the experience:

He: "I'm really upset about flunking that test."

She: "Yeah, I think I did badly on it, too."

He: "Why don't you care about what's going on in my life for a change?"

She: "But I do! I was just trying to show you that I understand how you feel."

Females focus more on asking questions and exploring the problem. Males tend to downplay or dismiss the problem:

David: "I'm going to feel ridiculous if Rachel ignores me again tomorrow."

Todd: "Well, it won't seem so bad after awhile, I guess."

David: "I really want to try to get back together with her."

Todd: "Yeah. It's tough. By the way, did you see that game Sunday?"

Rachel to Anne: "I don't know what I'm going to do if David doesn't speak to me tomorrow."

Anne: "I'll bet you're really worried. Exactly what did he say to you today?"

Rachel: "Nothing. Nada. Zip. Zero."

Anne: "How awful. What do you think you'll do tomorrow if he gives you the cold shoulder again?"

Females are more willing to ask for advice. Males interpret asking for information as a form of powerlessness:

She: "We're late and we're lost. Let's just stop and ask for directions at that gas station."

He: "No, I'll find it. It's around here somewhere."

Females are more likely to minimize differences in expertise. Males are more likely to want to demonstrate their expertise:

She: "You've done a great job so far sticking with me while I'm explaining this difficult topic. Just stop me whenever you don't understand."

He: "It's really not that difficult. Watch."

Females tend to give intimate details and reveal weaknesses. Males tend to see this as a breech of trust or invasion of privacy:

She: "Well, exactly what did she say to you when she got so mad?"

He: "Oh, I don't know. Just stuff."

She: "Then what did you say?"

He: "I don't remember exactly."

Females tend to misinterpret challenges as personal attacks. Males tend to perceive intellectual challenges less personally:

He: "I don't agree with you at all. Why do you believe that?"

She: "Why are you criticizing me? I really don't want to argue about this."

He: "I'm not being critical. I just want to know why you think that."

Females are more likely to make indirect requests. Males are more likely to make straightforward, decisive statements:

She: "We could try that new pizza place, if you want."

He: "I'd rather go back to Joe's Diner."

She: "Well, I guess."

He: "Don't beat around the bush. Just tell me where you want to eat."

Source: D. Tannen (1991). *You just don't understand: Women and men in conversation.* New York: Morrow.

Steinberg, 1990). For reasons discussed fully in Chapter 9, when parents divorce or remarry, sons usually adapt more poorly and react with more hostility than daughters. Most boys create more problems than do girls, not only for their divorced parents, but also for their stepfamilies (Cherlin & others, 1991; Colten, Gore, & Aseltine, 1991; Furstenberg & Cherlin, 1991; Pasley & Ihinger-Tallman, 1994; Wallerstein, 1991; Warshak, 1992).

But let's hold on before we put too much blame on teenage boys for being more difficult at home than most girls. Indeed, parents might be partially responsible for their sons' behavior. To begin with, adults fight and argue more in front of their sons than in front of their daughters. Parents also involve sons in more of their marital arguments, often forcing sons to choose sides between parents (Emery, 1989; Forehand, 1991; Hetherington, 1991; Maccoby, 1990; Wallerstein, 1991). After a divorce, a mother is also more likely to criticize her former husband to her son and to make more negative comments about men in general to her son than to her daughter (Greene & Leslie, 1989; Hetherington, 1991; Kalter, 1990; Pianta, Egeland, & Stroufe, 1990; Wallerstein, 1991; Warshak, 1992).

Is it really so surprising, then, that most teenage boys react more negatively than most teenage girls do? Not only are they exposed to more of their parents' stress, boys also react to this stress with more outward hostility and aggression than girls. In other words, even though teenage girls might feel stressed by problems between their parents, they don't usually react by being more hostile or aggressive toward their peers or family as boys do. As a consequence, girls' peer relationships don't generally suffer as much as boys' when things aren't going well between their parents. Even though many of us still act as though boys are tougher than girls, they are actually more vulnerable and weaker than girls in the sense that their psychological well-being and peer relationships are affected more negatively by their parents' problems (Asher & Coie, 1990; Cherlin et al., 1991; Colten, Gore, & Aseltine, 1991; Hetherington, 1991; Robins & Rutter, 1990).

In regard to family matters, teenage boys are also more negatively affected than girls in several respects by having too little contact with their fathers. Especially after divorce, most sons see very little of their fathers. But even when their parents are still married to one another, boys who aren't very involved with their fathers or whose fathers are emotionally distant grow up to have more psychological, social, and educational problems than boys who spent a lot of time with their fathers while growing up. Teenage boys whose fathers have been actively involved and emotionally close to them, especially during early childhood, are more self-disciplined, self-directed, self-reliant, empathic, socially mature, academically successful, and psychologically healthy than boys whose fathers were physically absent or emotionally uninvolved—a topic we discuss at length in Chapter 8 (Biller, 1993; Corneau, 1991; Lamb, 1989; Pittman, 1993; Snarey, 1993; Warshak, 1992).

Psychological Disorders

Male Disorders   Compared to teenage girls, teenage boys also have more psychological disorders that interfere with relating well to other people. From early childhood on, boys vastly outnumber girls in almost every mental disorder associated with being well-adjusted around other people, being intimate with people, and creating satisfying friendships. These disorders include: attention deficit disorders, delinquency, schizoid personality disorders, antisocial personality disorders, aggressive or violent behavior, and avoidant or socially phobic personality disorders. Boys also have more negative and more hostile attribution styles than girls—ways of interpreting the world that are associated with a host of psychological disorders and with violent, aggressive behavior. By late adolescence, only 3% to 5% of all teenagers are depressed enough to be diagnosed as "clinically depressed," with females outnumbering males two to one. But teenage boys outnumber girls two to one in personality and conduct disorders (Asher & Coie, 1990; Ebata, Petersen, & Conger, 1990; Peplar & Rubin, 1994; Robins & Rutter, 1990).

One of the reasons for this difference is that males in our society are socialized to express their sadness and depression by being hostile or aggressive toward other people. Girls, on the other hand, are socialized to keep their sad, depressed feelings privately inside themselves. As a consequence, girls are more likely to be diagnosed as clinically depressed in part because their symptoms have come to be associated with depression. But adults aren't as prepared to recognize boys' anger and hostility as symptoms of depression. Instead, depressed boys are more likely to be diagnosed as having such illnesses as antisocial or schizoid personality disorders. Put differently, boys' psychological disorders are more likely than girls' to show up in their social lives and their maladapted relationships with people. For example, suicidal boys date less and spend more time alone than other boys, which is not as often true for suicidal girls (Kandel, Raveis, & Davies, 1991). So when teenage boys aren't dating or don't get along well with other boys or with their families, we need to consider the possibility that their behavior is a symptom of a psychological disorder, not merely a symptom of social immaturity or a difficult disposition. Because depressed boys are nearly three times more likely than depressed girls to succeed in killing themselves, we need to pay special attention to this link between male anger, hostility, aggression, and depression (Harrington, 1994; Peplar & Rubin, 1994).

Let's consider a few specific examples that represent the overall conclusions from the research on the link between male anger and various forms of psychological maladjustment or stress. Among adolescents whose parents had divorced, the teenage girls scored higher than the boys on tests for depression, but the boys showed much more hostility, displayed more angry outbursts, and had higher external locus of control attitudes (Colten, Gore, & Aseltine, 1991). In one study that followed a group of people from the age of 14 to 41, the males who were extremely self-critical, inflexible, and maladjusted socially as teenagers were far angrier than they were self-critical as adolescents and as adults. In contrast, teenage girls who were extremely self-critical, inflexible, and maladjusted socially were as self-critical 36 years later, but didn't show much anger either as teenagers or as women. In other words, the males expressed their self-criticism, inflexibility, and maladjustment by being angry, but the females remained overly critical of themselves rather than expressing their bad feelings as anger toward others (Koestner, Zuroff, & Powers, 1991). Likewise, 18-year-old boys who are diagnosed as clinically depressed have usually been hostile, angry, and antisocial from the age of 3; whereas clinically depressed girls turned their depression inward (Gjerde, Block, & Block, 1991). Shy, socially isolated teenage and young adult males who are eventually diagnosed as having schizophrenia and schizoid personality disorders are also much more hostile, aggressive, and angrier as children and adolescents than schizophrenic females (Hanson, Gottesman, & Heston, 1990).

Female Disorders   Despite these differences in the ways that males and females express their depression, teenage girls are almost twice as likely as boys to be diagnosed as depressed. Some estimates show that about one third of all girls have symptoms of mild depression at some time during adolescence, compared to only 15% of the boys (Harrington, 1994; Millstein & Litt, 1990).

Aside from the preceding discussion about males' expressing depression through anger and aggression, what else might account for the higher rates of clinical depression among teenage girls? In part, the answer might lie in the fact that, unlike boys, girls' self-images usually become more negative during adolescence, especially in regard to how they feel about their appearance. As Chapter 2 explained, girls who mature early feel more stressed and more depressed than early maturing boys (Petersen, Kennedy, & Sullivan, 1991). Remember too that moods, behavior, and hormone levels haven't been linked in any strong or consistent way, meaning that we can't blame adolescent hormones for girls being more depressed than boys (Buchanan, Eccles, & Becker, 1992; Paikoff, Brooks-Gunn, & Warren, 1991). Recall, also, that girls exercise far less than boys and that exercise is one way adolescents and adults reduce stress and depression (Brown & Siegel, 1988). This implies that girls not only are more depressed, but also they aren't as likely to be reducing their stress and depression by exercising.

Aside from these physical sources of stress, we have also seen that teenage girls not only tend to be less assertive and more confused about balancing success against popularity with boys, but they receive less attention in school and have less self-esteem than boys. Understandably these circumstances can lead to feeling helpless, angry, stressed, and depressed. Moreover, because girls generally feel more responsible than boys for maintaining harmonious or intimate relationships with other people, they may tend to feel more stress than boys do in their relationships with other people. Because girls generally invest more of themselves in relationships and because their self-esteem is more closely tied to maintaining harmony and intimacy, they may be more deeply affected than most boys by the ups and downs in their personal lives. It's also worth noting that even when girls become adults their depression is often associated with trying to maintain close relationships with other people without losing their own identity (Jack, 1991). Another source of stress and depression for many teenage girls is found within their own families. Girls are far more likely than boys to be the victims of incest, rape, battering, and sexual harassment.

CHRONIC ILLNESS AND PHYSICAL DISORDERS

Part of the reason why teenage boys have more psychological and social problems associated with not getting along well with people is that certain factors are against them physically from the outset. When it comes to the kinds of childhood illnesses or neurological problems that interfere with social and psychological well-being, boys are the weaker sex. As discussed in preceding chapters, teenagers who are born with illnesses such as asthma, or with neurological problems such as attention deficit disorders, generally aren't as mature or as psychologically well-adjusted as other people their age. Boys, however, are born with more of these types of physical handicaps and disorders than girls. These types of physical impairments thus put young boys at greater risk of developing social and psychological problems as they pass through childhood and adolescence (Asher & Coie, 1990; Cohen, 1990; Ebata, Petersen, & Conger, 1990; Harrington, 1994; Robins & Rutter, 1990).

These physical disadvantages might also help explain why it's easier to predict a teenage boy's psychological and social problems from his behavior as a preschooler than it is to predict a teenage girl's. That is, a boy's behavior as a preschooler is a more reliable indicator than a girl's preschool behavior of social and psychological problems as teenagers. For example, a 4-year-old boy who is too aggressive or too shy to get along well with his peers is more likely than a 4-year-old girl with these same problems to be acting basically the same way as a teenager (Asher & Coie, 1990; Kagan, 1989; Kupersmidt, Coie, & Dodge, 1993). So if we want to help teenage boys have fewer social and psychological problems, we need to work harder at intervening during the first 4 or 5 years in the life of a boy who is behaving in ways that so often predict future problems. As discussed, these include excessive aggression, hyperactivity, shyness, social isolation, overdependence on either parent, hostility and anger, and physical symptoms of stress such as frequent allergy attacks or bed-wetting.

AGGRESSION, DEFIANCE, AND RISK TAKING

Physical disorders might also help account for the fact that teenage boys are usually more aggressive, more defiant, more uncontrollable, and more violent than girls. While a boy's aggression and misbehavior might be his way of expressing depression, it is also his way of living up to society's traditional definition of masculinity. From infancy through adulthood, we have historically reinforced and encouraged more physically and verbally aggressive behavior in males than in females (Huston & Alvarez, 1990; Pleck, Sonnenstein, & Ku, 1993). As addressed in Chapter 2, aggression and hormones in humans have not yet been clearly linked. So we can't simply blame hormones for males being more aggressive than females (Buchanan, Eccles, & Becker, 1992; Fausto-Sterling, 1991; Tavris, 1992). For example, teenage boys who have the most sexist beliefs about masculinity are the most likely to be having trouble in school, using drugs, drinking, and breaking the law (Pleck, Sonnenstein, & Ku, 1993).

Table 6–1

Males and female adolescents: Who's better off?

Similarities

Math and verbal reasoning
Memory
Vocabulary and reading comprehension
Verbal aggressiveness
Moods and moodiness
Shifts in hormones
Need for love and attachment
Nurturance
Need for achievement
Sexual capacity and desire
Feeling emotions
Undergraduate college degrees

Differences	Who's better off?
Advanced mathematics	males
Dieting & eating disorders	males
Career choices & incomes	males
Intellectual self-confidence	males
Body image & self-esteem	males
Clinically depressed	males
Graduate school degrees	males
Suicide	females
Aggressive personality disorders	females
Verbalizing empathy and concern	females
Verbally expressing feelings	females
Stuttering and dyslexia	females
Physical aggression & violence	females
Being murdered	females
Being killed in an accident	females
Drinking and drug abuse	females
Resolving arguments	females
Getting along with people	females
Creating close friendships	females
High-school degrees	females
Identity formation	?
Styles of speaking & communicating	?

The unfortunate outcome of living up to our society's traditional ideas regarding masculinity is that adolescent boys injure and kill themselves (and others) and expose themselves to diseases at a much higher rate than adolescent girls. Boys kill themselves more often than girls by speeding, drinking, and taking risks while driving. Boys create more illness and earlier deaths for themselves by adopting the "masculine" teenage habits of smoking, drinking, and using drugs. Having learned to act out their anger and frustration through physical aggression, boys also kill one another fighting far more often than girls. Even in terms of violence toward his own body, the teenage boy is more aggressive than the teenage girl. Although teenage boys don't attempt suicide as often as girls, they succeed far more often than girls because they use more violent methods, such as hanging and shooting, whereas suicidal girls are more apt to be rescued because they overdose on pills rather than using weapons. As a result, teenage boys die at twice the rate of teenage girls from suicide, traffic accidents, and murder. In fact, murder is the leading cause of death for black teenage males, accounting for nearly half of their deaths (Millstein & Litt, 1990; Waldron & Lye, 1990).

CONCLUSION

In summarizing the data on gender and teenage development, three points stand out. First, there are more similarities between the two sexes than there are differences, especially in the later years of adolescence. Second, there are more differences among members of the same sex than between the two sexes in almost all areas of development and skills. Third, many of the differences that once existed between teenage boys and girls are diminishing as a consequence of changes in how we are raising and educating children. At the same time, we can't ignore the reality that gender stereotypes still affect most adolescents' development. Although most teenagers today are less sexist in terms of their attitudes and choices than teenagers in the past, their lives are far from free of stereotypes and restrictions based on gender. As Table 6–1 illustrates, gender differences remain in areas that are clearly influenced by how we are choosing to educate and socialize young people in our society. Overall, the big questions remain: Why are many people so focused on finding differences rather than similarities between the sexes? What function does the quest for gender differences serve?

Review/Test Questions

1. How do cognitive, social learning, and Freudian theorists account for gender differences?

2. What are the limitations of the research on gender differences?

3. What are five of the different ways in which we socialize children into our society's gender roles?

4. What is androgyny, and how androgynous are today's adolescents? Cite specific studies

or statistics to support your answer.

5. In what ways are the traditional male and female gender roles advantageous? Disadvantageous?

6. To what extent do gender differences affect the following areas of adolescent development: self-esteem, vocations, math and verbal skills, aggression, mental health, communication styles, and peer and family relationships?

7. In what regard and to what extent are adolescent males and females different in terms of their social, athletic, and academic development?

8. How are stress, depression, and aggression related to gender roles?

9. What types of studies do biological theorists conduct in their attempts to study gender differences?

10. How are schools usually more advantageous for boys than for girls?

11. What does the research on hermaphrodites teach us about gender differences or gender roles?

12. What is Title IX?

13. What is brain hemisphericity and how is this research related to gender differences?

14. What is the difference between sexual orientation and sex roles?

15. In what ways are the media and public education androcentric?

Questions for Discussion and Debate

1. What were the advantages and disadvantages of being male or female when you were an adolescent? What did you, or do you still, envy most about the other gender?

2. How androgynous do you think you are? Why?

3. What impact did each of your parents have on your gender role attitudes? How exactly did they influence your attitudes and behavior? What do you wish they would have done differently?

4. What specific changes would you like to see brought about in public education that would help expand the educational, vocational, and personal options for both male and female adolescents?

5. Think about your three favorite fairy tales. How does each portray gender roles? (Remember that even inanimate objects and animals have gender roles in these tales.) Repeat this exercise with your three favorite television programs and your two favorite popular songs.

6. In your own lifetime, what changes have you noticed in gender roles? How do you think these changes have affected you, your friends, and family?

7. What experiences have you had at school, in sports, or in your family that illustrate any of the theories or research in this chapter?

8. Comparing the teenagers of today with your adolescence, what differences do you notice in regard to their gender roles and attitudes?

9. Assuming that a research study could be designed that would answer your question, what would you most like to know about gender and gender roles that hasn't yet been answered?

10. How do you feel about female adolescents being allowed to attend military institutions and to enter the military as a career? Why?

Glossary

References

Adams, G. (1991). Physical attractiveness and adolescent development. In R. Lerner, A. Petersen, & J. Brooks-Gunn (Eds.), *Encyclopedia of adolescence* (pp. 785–789). New York: Garland.

Adelson, J. (1980). *Handbook of adolescent psychology.* New York: Wiley.

American Association of University Women. (1992). *How schools shortchange girls.* Washington, DC: Author.

American Association of University Women. (1993). *Hostile hallways: Sexual harassment in America's schools.* Washington, DC: Author.

Applebee, A. (1989). *A study of book length works taught in high school English courses.* Albany: State University of New York.

Asher, S., & Coie, J. (1990). *Peer rejection in childhood.* New York: Cambridge University Press.

Baenninger, M., & Newcombe, N. (1990). The role of experience in spatial test performance. *Sex Roles, 17,* 80–93.

Bakken, L., Hershey, M., & Miller, P. (1990). Gifted adolescent females' attitudes toward gender equality. *Roeper Review, 12,* 261–264.

Barber, B., & Eccles, J. (1992). Long-term influence of divorce and single parenting on career goals. *Psychological Bulletin, 111,* 108–126.

Barbie backlash. (1992, October l). *Winston-Salem Journal,* p. 15.

Bartko, W., & McHale, M. (1991). Household labor of children from dual versus single earner families. In J. Lerner & N. Galambos (Eds.), *Employed mothers and their children* (pp. 159–177). New York: Garland .

Betcher, R., & Pollack, W. (1993). *In a time of fallen heroes.* New York: Atheneum.

Bettelheim, B. (1976). *The uses and abuses of enchantment.* New York: Knopf.

Biller, H. (1993). *Fathers and families: Paternal factors in child development.* Westport, CT: Auburn House.

Binchy, M. (1988). *Rapunzel's revenge.* Greenwood, SC: Attic Press.

Bly, R. (1990). Iron John: *A book about men.* Reading, MA: Addison Wesley.

Bordo, S. (1993). *Unbearable weight: Feminism, Western culture and the body.* New York: Norton.

Brod, H. (1988). *A mensch among men: Exploration of Jewish masculinity.* Freedom, CA: Crossing Press.

Brown, J., & Siegel, J. (1988). Exercise as a buffer of life stress. *Health Psychology, 7,* 341–353.

Brown, L., & Gilligan, C. (1992). *Meeting at the crossroads: Women's psychology and girls' development.* Cambridge, MA: Harvard University.

Buchanan, C., Eccles, J., & Becker, J. (1992). Are adolescents victims of raging hormones? *Psychological Bulletin, 111,* 62–107.

Camara, K., & Resnick, G. (1989). Styles of conflict resolution and cooperation. *American Journal of Orthopsychiatry, 56,* 560–579.

Campbell, J. (1991). The roots of gender inequity in technical areas. *Journal of Research in Science Teaching, 28,* 251–264.

Cangelosi, D., & Schaefer, C. (1991). A 25-year follow-up study of ten exceptionally creative adolescent girls. *Psychological Reports, 68,* 307–311.

Carlson, N. (1986). *Physiology of behavior.* Boston: Allyn & Bacon.

Cherlin, A., Furstenberg, F., Lansdale, P., Kiernan, K., Robins, P., Morrison, D., & Teitler, J. (1991). Longitudinal studies of effects of divorce on children in Britain and the U.S. *Science, 252,* 1386–1390.

Cohen, P. (1990). Common and uncommon pathways to adolescent psychopathology and problem behavior. In L. Robins & M. Rutter (Eds.), *Straight and devious pathways from childhood to adulthood* (pp. 242–259). New York: Cambridge University.

Cohn, L. (1991). Sex differences in the course of personality development. *Psychological Bulletin, 109,* 255–266.

Colten, M., Gore, S., & Aseltine, R. (1991). Patterning of distress & disorder in a sample of high school aged youth. In M. Colten & S. Gore (Eds.), *Adolescent stress* (pp. 157–180). New York: Aldine De Gruyter.

Corneau, G. (1991). *Absent fathers, lost sons.* Boston: Shambhala.

Crowley, E. (1989). *Sweeping beauties: Fairytales for feminists.* Greenwood, SC: Attic Press.

Dabbs, J., & Morris, R. (1990). Testosterone, social class, and antisocial behavior in a sample of 4,462 men. *Psychological Science, 1,* 209–211.

Deich, B., & Weiner, L. (1990). *The lecherous professor.* Urbana: University of Illinois Press.

Doty, W. (1993). *Myths of masculinity.* New York: Crossroads.

Doyle, J., & Paludi, M. (1991). *Sex and gender.* Dubuque, IA: W. C. Brown.

Dunn, J. (1993). *Young children's close relationships.* Newbury Park, CA: Sage.

Ebata, A., Petersen, A., & Conger, J. (1990). The development of psychopathology in adolescence. In J. Rolf, A. Masten, D. Cicchetti, K. Nuechterlein, & S. Weintraub (Eds.), *Risk and protective factors in the development of psychopathology* (pp. 308–334). New York: Cambridge University.

Eccles, J., Jacobs, J., & Harold, R. (1990). Gender role stereotypes and parents' socialization of gender differences. *Journal of Social Issues, 46,* 183–201.

Elshtain, J. (1987). *Women and war.* New York: Basic Books.

Emery, E. (1989). Family Violence. *American Sociological Review, 44,* 321–328.

Epstein, C. (1988). *Deceptive distinctions: Sex, gender and the social order.* New York: Sage Foundation.

Erikson, E. (1968). *Identity: Youth in crisis.* New York: Norton.

Faludi, S. (1991). *Backlash: The undeclared war against American women.* New York: Crown.

Farrell, W. (1993). *The myth of male power.* New York: Simon & Schuster.

Fausto-Sterling, A. (1991). *Myths of gender: Biological theories about women and men.* New York: Basic Books.

Feiring, C., & Lewis, M. (1991). Transition from middle childhood to early adolescence. *Sex Roles, 24,* 489–509.

Fennema, R. (1990). *Math and gender.* New York: Columbia Teachers College.

Fisher, C., & Brone, R. (1991). Eating disorders in adolescence. In R. Lerner, A. Peterson, & J. Brooks-Gunn (Eds.), *Encyclopedia of adolescence* (pp. 156–172). New York: Garland.

Forehand, R. (1991). A short-term longitudinal examination of young adolescents. *Journal of Abnormal Child Psychology, 19,* 97–111.

Frederick, J., & Nicholson, H. (1992). *The explorers' passage: Studies of girls and math, science and technology.* Indianapolis: Girls National Resource Center.

Freud, A. (1977). *Normality and pathology in childhood.* New York: International Universities Press.

Friedman, R. (1989). *Body love: Learning to like our looks.* New York: Harper & Row.

Furstenberg, F., & Cherlin, A. (1991). *Divided families.* Cambridge, MA: Harvard University Press.

Galambos, N., Almeida, D., & Petersen, A. (1993). Masculinity, femininity and sex role attitudes in early adolescence. *Child Development, 61,* 1905–1914.

Gilbert, L. (1993). *Two careers, one family.* Berkeley, CA: Sage.

Gilligan, C. (1982). *In a different voice.* Cambridge, MA: Harvard University Press.

Gilligan, C. (1991). Women's psychological development. In C. Gilligan, A. Rogers, & D. Tolman (Eds.), *Women, girls, and psychotherapy* (pp. 5–33). New York: Haworth.

Gilligan, C., Lyons, N., & Hanmer, T. (1990). *Making connections.* Cambridge, MA: Harvard University Press.

Gilligan, C., & Rogers, A. (1993). Reframing daughtering and mothering. In J. Mens-Verhulst, K. Schreurs, & L. Woertman (Eds.), *Daughtering and mothering* (pp. 125–135). New York: Routledge.

Gilligan, C., Rogers, A., & Tolman, D. (1991). *Women, girls and psychotherapy.* New York: Haworth Press.

Gittins, N. (1990). *Sexual harassment in schools.* Washington, DC: National School Boards.

Gjerde, P., Block, J., & Block, P. (1991). Preadolescent antecedents of depressive symptomatology at age 18. *Journal of Youth and Adolescence, 20,* 217–231.

Greene, R., & Leslie, L. (1989). Mothers' behavior and sons' adjustment following divorce. *Journal of Divorce, 12,* 235–251.

Gustafson, S. (1991). *Female life careers.* Hillsdale, NJ: Erlbaum.

Hancock, E. (1989). *The girl within.* New York: Fawcett.

Hanson, D., Gottesman, I., & Heston, L. (1990). Long range schizophrenia forecasting. In J. Rolf (Ed.), *Risk and protective factors in the development of psychopathology* (pp. 424–444). New York: Cambridge University Press.

Hare-Mustin, R., & Marecek, J. (1988). The meaning of difference. *American Psychologist, 43,* 455–464.

Harrington, L. (1994). *Depressive disorder in childhood and adolescence.* New York: Wiley.

Harris, L., Blum, R., & Resnick, M. (1991). Teen females in Minnesota. *Women and Therapy, 11,* 119–135.

Harter, S. (1990). Self and identity development. In S. Feldman & G. Elliot (Eds.), *At the threshold* (pp. 352–388). Cambridge, MA: Harvard University Press.

Hartup, W., & Overhauser, S. (1991). Friendships. In R. Lerner, A. Petersen, & J. Brooks-Gunn (Eds.), *Encyclopedia of adolescence* (pp. 378–384). New York: Garland.

Hauser, S., & Bowlds, M. (1990). Stress, coping and adaptation. In S. Feldman & G. Elliot (Eds.), *At the threshold* (pp. 414–431). Cambridge, MA: Harvard University Press.

Hawley, R. (1993). *Boys will be men.* New York: Eriksson.

Henderson, V., & Dweck, C. (1990). Motivation and achievement. In S. Feldman & G. Elliott (Eds.), *At the threshold: The developing adolescent* (pp. 308–329). Cambridge, MA: Harvard University Press.

Heschel, S. (1990). Jewish feminism and women's identity. *Women and Therapy, 10,* 31–39.

Hetherington, M. (1991). Families, lies and videotapes. *Journal of Research on Adolescence, 1,* 323–348.

Ho, C. (1990). Domestic violence in Asian American communities. *Women and Therapy, 9,* 129–150.

Holland, D., & Eisenhart, M. (1991). *Educated in romance: Women, achievement and college culture.* Chicago: University of Chicago Press.

Huston, A., & Alvarez, M. (1990). The socialization context of gender role development in early adolescence. In R. Montemayor, G. Adams, & T. Gulotta (Eds.), *From childhood to adolescence* (pp. 312–345). Newbury Park, CA: Sage.

Hyde, J. (1993). Meta-analysis and the psychology of women. In F. Denmark & M. Paludi (Eds.), *Handbook on the psychology of women.* Westport, CT: Greenwood Press.

Imperato-McGuinley, J. (1979). Androgens and the evolution of male gender identity among pseudo-hermaphrodites. *New England Journal of Medicine, 43,* 236–237.

Jack, D. (1991). *Silencing the self: Women and depression.* New York: HarperCollins.

Josselson, R. (1992). *The space between us.* San Francisco: Jossey-Bass.

Jukes, A. (1993). *Why men hate women.* New York: Columbia University Press.

Kagan, J. (1989). *Unstable ideas: Temperament, cognition and self.* Cambridge, MA: Harvard University Press.

Kalter, N. (1990). *Growing up with divorce.* New York: Ballantine.

Kandel, D., Raveis, V., & Davies, M. (1991). Suicidal ideation in adolescence. *Journal of Youth and Adolescence, 20,* 289–309.

Kaschak, E. (1992). *Engendered lives.* New York: Basic Books.

Keyes, R. (1992). Sons and fathers: *A book of men's writing.* New York: HarperCollins.

Kimura, D. (1992, September). Sex differences in the brain. *Scientific American,* pp. 119–125.

Kline, B., & Short, E. (1991). Changes in resilience: Gifted adolescent females. *Roeper Review, 13,* 118–121.

Koestner, R., Zuroff, D., & Powers, T. (1991). Family origins of adolescent self-criticism and its continuity into adulthood. *Journal of Abnormal Psychology,* 100, 191–197.

Koff, E., Rierdan, J., & Stubbs, M. (1990). Gender, body image & self concept in early adolescence. *Journal of Early Adolescence, 10,* 56–68.

Kohlberg, L. (1966). A cognitive development analysis of children's sex role concepts and attitudes. In E. Maccoby (Ed.), *The development of sex differences* (pp. 82–133). Stanford, CA: Stanford University.

Kohn, A. (1990). *The brighter side of human nature: Altruism and empathy.* New York: Basic Books.

Kramer, L. (1991). An ethnographic study of gifted adolescent girls. *Journal of Early Adolescence, 11,* 340–362.

Kupersmidt, J., Coie, J., & Dodge, K. (1993). The role of poor peer relationships in the development of disorder. In S. Asher & J. Coie (Eds.), *Peer rejection in childhood* (pp. 274–309). New York: Cambridge University Press.

Lakoff, R. (1990). *Talking power: The politics of language.* New York: Basic Books.

Lamb, M. (1989). *The father's role.* Hillsdale, NJ: Erlbaum.

Lapan, R., & Jingeleski, J. (1992). Circumscribing vocational aspirations in junior high school. *Journal of Counseling Psychology, 39,* 81–90.

Larson, R., & Asmussen, L. (1991). Anger, worry, and hurt in early adolescence. In M. Colten & S. Gore (Eds.), *Adolescent stress* (pp. 21–42). New York: Aldine De Gruyter.

Lee, V., & Marks, H. (1990). Sustained effects of single sex secondary school experience. *Journal of Educational Psychology, 82,* 578–592.

Lempers, J., & Lempers, D. (1993). Comparison of same sex and opposite sex friendships during adolescence. *Journal of Adolescent Research, 8,* 89–108.

Lerner, J., & Galambos, N. (1991). *Employed mothers and their children.* New York: Garland.

Levy, G., & Carter, D. (1989). Gender

schema, gender constancy, and gender role knowledge. *Developmental Psychology, 25,* 444–449.

Liebert, R., & Sprafkin, J. (1988). *The early window: Effects of television on children and youth.* New York: Pergamon.

Linn, M., & Hyde, J. (1991). Cognitive and psychosocial gender differences. In R. Lerner, A. Petersen, & J. Brooks-Gunn (Eds.), *Encyclopedia of adolescence* (pp. 139–150). New York: Garland.

Lynch, M. (1991). Gender intensification. In R. Lerner, A. Petersen, & J. Brooks-Gunn (Eds.), *Encyclopedia of adolescence.* New York: Garland.

Maccoby, E. (1990). Gender and relationships. *American Psychologist, 45,* 513–552.

McLoyd, V. (1989). Socialization and development in a changing economy. *American Psychologist, 44,* 293–302.

Mead, M. (1935). *Sex and temperament in three primitive societies.* New York: American Library.

Meade, M. (1994). *Men and the water of life.* San Francisco: Harper.

Mills, J. (1992). *Womanwords: Dictionary of words about women.* New York: Free Press.

Millstein, S., & Litt, I. (1990). Adolescent health. In S. Feldman & G. Elliot (Eds.), *At the threshold* (pp. 431–457). Cambridge, MA: Harvard University.

Mitchell, E. (1991, July 1). The thin gray gender line. *Newsweek,* p. 66.

Money, J., & Ehrhardt, A. (1972). *Man, woman, boy, girl.* Baltimore, MD: Johns Hopkins University Press.

Mortenson, T. (1991). *Equity of higher educational opportunity for women, Black, Hispanic and low income students.* Iowa City, IA: American College Testing.

Muir, K. (1993). *Arms and the woman.* London: Hodder & Stoughton.

Nelson, C., & Keith, J. (1990). Comparisons of female and male early adolescent sex role atti-

tude. *Adolescence, 97,* 183–204.

Newell, G. (1990). Self concept as a factor in the quality of diets of adolescent girls. *Adolescence, 25,* 117–130.

Nielsen, A. (1988). *Nielsen report on television.* Northbrook, IL: Nielsen Company.

Page, R. (1991). Indicators of psychosocial distress among adolescent females who perceive themselves as fat. *Child Study Journal, 21,* 203–212.

Paikoff, R., Brooks-Gunn, J., & Warren, M. (1991). Effects of girls' hormonal status on depression and aggressive symptoms. *Journal of Youth and Adolescence, 20,* 191–215.

Pasley, K., & Ihinger-Tallman, M. (1994). *Stepparenting: Issues in theory, research & practice.* New York: Greenwood Publishing.

Pearsall, P. (1990). *Women at war.* New York: Ashgate Publishing.

Peirce, K. (1990). A feminist perspective on the socialization of teenage girls through Seventeen magazine. *Sex Roles, 23,* 491–500.

Peplar, D., & Rubin, K. (1994). *The development and treatment of childhood aggression.* Hillsdale, NJ: Erlbaum.

Petersen, A., Kennedy, R., & Sullivan, P. (1991). Coping with adolescence. In M. Colten & S. Gore (Eds.), *Adolescent stress* (pp. 93–110). New York: Aldine De Gruyter.

Phelps, L. (1993). Figure preference and body dissatisfaction in adolescence. *Journal of Adolescent Research, 8,* 297–310.

Pianta, B., Egeland, B., & Stroufe, A. (1990). Maternal stress and children's development. In J. Rolf, A. Masten, K. Nuechterlain, & .W. Weintraub (Eds.), *Risk and protective factors in the development of psychopathology* (pp. 215–236). New York: Cambridge University.

Pittman, F. (1993). *Man enough: Fathers, sons and the search for masculinity.* New York: Putnam's Sons.

Pleck, J., Sonnenstein, G., & Ku, I. (1993). Problem behaviors and masculine ideology in adolescent males. In R. Ketterlinus & M. Lamb (Eds.), *Adolescent problem behaviors.* Hillsdale, NJ: Erlbaum.

Remafedi, G. (1990). Report on the impact of television portrayals of gender roles on youth. *Journal of Adolescent Health Care, 11,* 59–61.

Richards, M. (1991). Adolescent personality in girls and boys. *Psychology of Women Quarterly, 15,* 65–81.

Robins, L., & Rutter, M. (1990). *Straight and devious pathways from childhood to adulthood.* New York: Cambridge University.

Rotundo, E. (1993). *American manhood.* New York: Basic Books.

Sadker, D., & Sadker, M. (1993). *Failing at fairness: How America's schools cheat girls.* New York: Macmillan.

Savin-Williams, R., & Berndt, T. (1990). Friendship and peer relations. In S. Feldman & G. Elliot (Eds.), *At the threshold: The developing adolescent* (pp. 277–308). Cambridge, MA: Harvard University Press.

Schiebinger, L. (1993). *Nature's body: Gender in the making of modern science.* Boston: Beacon Press.

Schulenberg, J., Goldstein, A., & Vondracek, F. (1991). Gender differences in adolescents' career interests. *Journal of Research on Adolescence, 1,* 37–61.

Shweder, R. (1994, January 9). *New York Times Book Review,* p. 3.

Smetana, J., Yau, J., Restrepo, A., & Braeges, J. (1991). Conflict and adaptation in adolescence: Adolescent–parent conflict. In M. Bolten & S. Gore (Eds.), *Adolescent stress* (pp. 43–64). New York: Aldine De Gruyter.

Smith, L. (1990). *Becoming a woman through romance.* New York: Routledge.

Snarey, J. (1993). *How fathers care for the next generation.* Cambridge, MA: Harvard University.

Sperry, R. (1982). Some effects of disconnecting the cerebral hemispheres. *Science, 217,* 1223–1226.

Stack, C. (1986). The culture of gender: Women and men of color. *Signs, 11,* 321–324.

Stein, N., Marshall, N., & Tropp, L. (1993). *Secrets in public: Sexual harassment in our schools.* Wellesley, MA: Wellesley College.

Steinberg, L. (1990). Autonomy, conflict and harmony in the family relationship. In S. Feldman & G. Elliot (Eds.), *At the threshold* (pp. 255–569). Cambridge, MA: Harvard University Press.

Stoltenberg, J. (1993). *The end of manhood.* New York: Dutton.

Tannen, D. (1991). *You just don't understand: Women and men in conversation.* New York: Morrow.

Tavris, C. (1992). *Mismeasure of woman.* New York: Simon & Schuster.

Thomas, D. (1993). *Not guilty: The case in defense of men.* New York: Morrow.

Thorne, B. (1993). *Gender play: Girls and boys in school.* New Brunswick, NJ: Rutgers University Press.

Tuana, N. (1993). *The less noble sex.* Bloomington, IN: Indiana University.

Wadden, T. (1991). Salience of weight related worries in adolescent males and females. *International Journal of Eating Disorders, 10,* 407–414.

Wade, J. (1991). Race and sex differences in adolescent self perceptions of attractiveness and self-esteem. *Personality and Individual Differences, 27,* 552–565.

Waldron, I., & Lye, D. (1990). Relationships between teenage smoking & attitudes toward women's rights. *Women and Health, 16,* 23–46.

Wallerstein, J. (1991). The long term effects of divorce on children: A review. *Journal of American Academy of Child Psychiatry, 30,* 349–360.

Warshak, R. (1992). *The custody revolution: The fatherhood factor and the motherhood mystique.* New York: Poseidon.

Wekesser, C. (1991). *Women in the military.* New York: Greenhaven Press.

Whiting, B., & Edwards, C. (1988). *Children of different worlds.* Cambridge, MA: Harvard University Press.

Williams, J., & Best, D. (1989). *Sex and psyche: Self-concept viewed cross-culturally.* Newbury Park, CA: Sage.

Wilson, E. (1978). *Sociobiolgy.* Beverly Hills, CA: Sage.

Wolf, N. (1992). *The beauty myth: How images of beauty are used against women.* New York: Doubleday.

Zipes, J. (1991). *Don't bet on the prince.* New York: Routledge.

Zipes, J. (1994). *Fairy tales as myths.* Louisville, KY: University of Kentucky Press.

7

ADOLESCENTS FROM MINORITY CULTURES

CHAPTER OUTLINE

KEY QUESTIONS ADDRESSED IN THIS CHAPTER

1. How has our population changed in terms of race?
2. In what ways does racism affect many adolescents?
3. How do adolescents from various racial groups compare in terms of their education, family incomes, out-of-wedlock births, parents' marital status, and health?
4. In what ways are African, Native, and Hispanic American adolescents often unique?
5. What are the major problems confronting each racial minority in our society?
6. How much educational progress has each minority group made in our society?
7. In what ways are Asian American teenagers not the "model" minority?
8. How does being a recent immigrant affect adolescents and their families?
9. In what ways is our research biased or inadequate in regard to minority adolescents and their families?
10. What pitfalls do we need to avoid in studying minority youth?

OUR MULTICULTURAL SOCIETY

DEMOGRAPHIC TRENDS

Although Hispanic, African, Asian, and Native American adolescents are still referred to as "minorities," in some ways this is a misleading choice of words. By the year 2000, non-Hispanic whites will make up only about 60% of the population under the age of 18. Although minorities now constitute only 30% of our young people, within the next 5 years roughly 20% of all teenagers will be African Americans, 15% Hispanic Americans, 3% Asian Americans, and 1% Native Americans. In many of our public school systems, "minority" youth are already the majority. For example, only 7% of the public school students in San Antonio and less than 15% in Phoenix, Chicago, Birmingham, and San Francisco are white. As Figure 7–1 shows, only about half of the children in Texas, California, and New Mexico are white. What else do our national statistics tell us about these changes in our population (Roberts, 1994; U.S. Department of Commerce, 1993)?

Figure 7–1

Minority enrollment in public schools

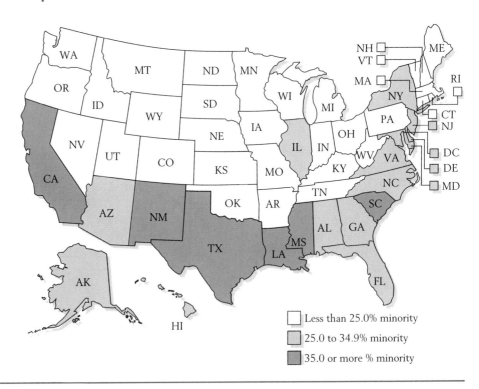

☐	Less than 25.0% minority
▫	25.0 to 34.9% minority
■	35.0 or more % minority

Source: National Center for Education Statistics (1993). *The condition of education.* Washington, DC.

Table 7–1

America's immigrants: Where do they go?

California: Population 40% immigrant

Mexico—70%
Philippines—4%
El Salvador—3%
China—2%
Others—19%

Texas: Population 12% immigrant

Mexico—80%
El Salvador—4%
Vietnam—2%
Others—14%

New York: Population 10% immigrant

Dominican Republic—12%
Former Soviet Union—10%
Jamaica—6%
China—5%
India—5%
Others—62%

Florida: Population 8% immigrant

Mexico—30%
Haiti—21%
Cuba—6%
Jamaica– 4%
Colombia—4%
Others—35%

Source: U.S. Department of Commerce (1993). *Population projections by states.* Washington, DC: Bureau of the Census.

To begin with, we might ask: What accounts for the growing numbers of minorities in our society? In large part the answer is the change in our immigrant population. Since 1970, about 10.5 million people legally immigrated to the United States, with another 3 million estimated to have entered illegally. About one third of 1% of our population are newly arriving immigrants, most of whom settle in California, Texas, New York, and Florida. At present we accept more immigrants than all other industrialized nations in the world combined. But the change is not so much in the actual numbers of immigrants, since we have had higher percentages at earlier periods in our history. The change is that most immigrants are now coming from Hispanic and Asian countries.

During the 1980s our Asian-American population increased by more than 100%, the fastest-growing minority in terms of percentage increases. Most of these families immigrated from China and the war-torn countries of Vietnam, Cambodia, and Laos. Most had enjoyed a relatively high standard of living before immigrating and were among the most well-educated people in their homeland. As a consequence, most Asians who arrived during the 1980s distinguished themselves through their educational and financial achievements in the United States as they assimilated. Most Asian American adolescents and their families live in three states: California, New York, and Hawaii. Nearly one fourth are of Chinese heritage, followed by people of Filipino and Japanese heritage.

Yet in terms of actual numbers, most of our immigrants since 1970 have come from Hispanic countries. Roughly 60% come from Mexico, 15% from Puerto Rico, 5% from Cuba, and 20% from other South American and Caribbean countries. Most Hispanic American youth live with their families in California, Texas, and New York. As you can see from Table 7–1, no state has been reshaped more dramatically by immigration than California. More than half of all immigrants in the United States settle there or in New York. In fact, Hispanic people now constitute a slim majority in Los Angeles, and more than one in eight Americans speaks a language other than English at home—mostly Spanish. Because the term *Hispanic* is favored in some parts of the country and *Latino* or *Chicano* is preferred in others, these terms are used interchangeably in this chapter. Likewise, although the term *American* can refer to people living on either the North American or South American continents, in this textbook the term is used to refer specifically to those living in the United States.

WHO'S WHITE?

As our society has become more multicultural, it has become increasingly difficult to answer the question: Who is white? More to the point, when it comes to how we treat one another socially, the question might be more aptly asked: Which adolescents can reach the point of being treated socially and financially as if they are white and which cannot?

Despite its significance, the question of who is white is not easy to answer. Why? First, in one decade alone—1970 to 1980—the number of racially mixed marriages in our country nearly doubled. As of the mid-1990s, about 2% of all U.S. marriages are interracial. As a result, there are now more than 1 million children who cannot be categorized either by appearance or genetic make-up as belonging to any one race. Likewise, many teenagers who might look white are the racially mixed descendants of white slave owners and the black women they often raped and exploited. Given their interracial background, light-skinned black Americans, sometimes referred to as "high yellows," are often able to "pass"

—that is, to be perceived and treated as white, although genetically they are not. However, no matter how light their skin, these racially mixed adolescents are not considered or treated as if they are white as long as their face or hair has African features (Roberts, 1994).

Trying to think of adolescents as members of a particular race is also complicated by immigration from Hispanic and Asian countries where skin color ranges from pinkish white to dark black within the same race. Commonly enough, one adolescent is treated as white and another as a minority, even though they are actually members of the same race. Our perceptions of some people as "more white" than others are also influenced by their financial and academic accomplishments. That is, we tend to treat minority teenagers more like white Americans when they come from upper-income, well-educated families. Jewish and Asian American teenagers serve as examples. In a related way, although the 8 million Californians with Hispanic ancestry consider themselves Latinos, only half identify themselves as being a member of a race. In other words, being treated as if you are white, black, Asian or Hispanic is becoming less a matter of skin tone than of physical features and other distinguishing characteristics such as your speech, your level of education, and your social customs. Again, the importance of race is less one of "Who is white?" than "Who can be treated as if they are white?" (Hacker, 1992).

Amidst the confusion over how to categorize people along racial lines, one fact remains: Our teenage population has become increasingly diverse in terms of its cultural and racial backgrounds. More than at any time in our past, we are a multicultural society—a mosaic, racially and culturally. Not surprisingly then, researchers have become even more interested in pursuing issues concerning adolescents from African, Hispanic, Asian, and Native American families with questions such as: How do their racial and cultural differences affect these teenagers? What is unique about teenagers from nonwhite families? What are the special concerns of minority adolescents and their families? How much does an adolescent's race matter in our current society? Are there certain benefits for adolescents who belong to one race rather than to another?

RACE AND IDENTITY

Although race is not necessarily the most important factor shaping an adolescent's development, race does have an impact on teenagers' identities. In the case of teenagers who are members of racial minorities, however, the impact of race is usually more complex and more negative than for Anglo teenagers. This is not to say that the family's income, the area of the country in which they live, or the attitudes of their peers and teachers can't reduce the negative impact that race can have on minority adolescents' lives. Nevertheless, race and racism still continue to influence the development of minority teenagers (Fedullo, 1994; Hacker, 1992; Ramirez, 1990; Sanchez, 1993; Sue, 1991; West, 1994).

DEFINING RACISM

If racism is defined as stereotyping and discriminating against people on the basis of skin color, then racism is found throughout the world among people of all races. In every racial group there are those who believe their race is superior, and many of them discriminate and stereotype on the basis of skin color. But racism can be defined in another way. Racism can be applied only to whichever race has the financial, political, and police power in a particular society—the power to cause the most suffering to people from other races. From this viewpoint, Anglo Americans have the most financial and social power and would, therefore, be the most likely to be racist (Hacker, 1992). Whichever definition of racism we use, however, doesn't change the fact that the identities and daily lives of minority teenagers are still affected by various degrees of racism in our society.

RACISM AMONG ADOLESCENTS

Although we have undeniably made progress toward becoming a less racist society, minority adolescents still encounter prejudice on the basis of their physical appearance. Despite the passage of more than 30 years since enactment of the landmark Civil Rights Acts of 1964, we are seeing a rise in racial violence and harassment in many of our public schools. Milder forms of harassment include name calling, graffiti, jokes, and social segregation. But teenage racism also includes physical attacks, destruction of others' property, and violent threats. For example, in Water Valley, Mississippi, trouble started when a group of white high-school students waved the Confederate flag during an African American history program. The incident prompted African American athletes to boycott varsity games. In Falls Church, Virginia, Asian-American students have also been the victims of racial slurs and fights. As one white male student said, "We just don't like them. There's so many of them, you just can't get away from them 'gooks' and 'chinks'" (Viadero, 1989).

In some communities, racial incidents such as these have been attributed to a nationwide rise in hate groups such as the neo-Nazi skinheads. These loosely organized gangs range in age from 13 to 25 and are known for shaving their heads, wearing Nazi insignia, and preaching violence against racial minorities and Jewish people. The Jewish Anti-Defamation League estimated that in 1990 there were about 2,000 skinheads active in at least 21 states—twice as many as 5 years earlier (A.D.L., 1991). Although some people believe that the reversals of much of the civil rights legislation that occurred during the Reagan administration have encouraged the rise in teenage racism, others believe the rapid growth of minorities is at the root of recent upsurges in racial hatred. Whatever the underlying reasons, by the late 1980s a congressional committee reviewing the reports and statistics agreed that racial bigotry and violence are on the rise among high-school students (House Select Committee, 1987).

The rise in racial incidents, however, is not limited only to high-school students. Adolescents enrolled in college have also increased their physical and verbal harassment of black, Hispanic, and Jewish students. These racial incidents include setting fire to crosses in front of blacks' residence halls, putting on blackface musical programs in fraternities and sororities, hanging Confederate flags out the windows of white dorms, and screaming racial insults at minority students. On some campuses, white students have been expelled for racial incidents that interfere with the education of minority students. At many colleges minority students also say they are socially excluded and are made to believe they should be "so grateful" simply for having been admitted that they should not criticize the institution, as if the honor of admittance negates any rights they *might* have. As a result, a number of black high-school students choose to attend predominantly black colleges where they feel less isolated and less resented (Hacker, 1992).

Race can also affect the lives of minority youths in other ways. For instance, minority teenagers are sometimes treated as though they are official representatives for their entire race. Minority teenagers might be asked such questions as: "How do black Americans feel about that?" "Tell me, what are Asian families like?" As one college student explains, "At the end of the term, in a class where I was the only black, we had a discussion. After hearing their comments about the "typical black"—which I didn't know existed—I felt obligated to say something. Before I did, however, I prayed briefly that I would be understood and not just heard" (Garrod, 1992, p. 73).

Some minority teenagers can also be made to believe they are somehow personally responsible for the behavior of all other people of their race: "Why do your people behave like that? Why is it that your race is so involved in drugs and crime?" For example, the only black member of an all white fraternity was asked to "guarantee" them that another black they were considering as a member would turn out to be "good" (Garrod, 1992). In this same fashion, minorities often are compared to one another in ways that are hostile and divisive: "Why hasn't your group made as much progress as their group since you've been in this country longer?" White teenagers, on the other hand, are seldom asked to explain or to defend "the white viewpoint." For example, white adolescents are seldom asked by a person from a racial minority, "Why do whites account for 45% of the people on welfare since you have more than those of us who immigrated more recently?" Likewise, unlike the most well-educated, wealthy members of racial minorities, whites are not as often asked why they aren't "doing more" to help the less fortunate members of their race (Cose, 1993).

Last, but certainly not least, most minority teenagers are aware that their skin color matters most when it comes to dating and sex. Because teenagers' attitudes about socializing with other races are influenced by those of their elders, it's important to examine our society's attitudes toward interracial dating and marriage. For most white Americans, going to school or working with minorities is far more acceptable than dating or marrying them. Without ever having to be told directly, most white teenagers know that their families do not approve of interracial dating—or, if they do, they approve of dating only certain races or only a person whose physical features, skin tone, speech, way of dressing, and social mannerisms are "white enough." Minority teenagers can also get the message from

If you could have chosen your race before you were born, which would you have chosen and why?

their families that they should only date or marry within their race. For instance, when a Chicana marries an Anglo, she might be accused of marrying outside her race in order to gain more social power and status. Or when a Chicano marries an Anglo, he might be accused of finding white women more beautiful and more socially desirable than Chicanas (Blea, 1992; Garrod & others, 1992; Hacker, 1992; Patterson & Kim, 1992; West, 1994).

In terms of marriage, sex, or dating, African American teenagers usually encounter more racism than other minorities. Many specialists in race relations believe this might be due largely to fears and myths surrounding black sexuality—especially the sexuality of black males. The fear that black males are sexually superior to white males seems to fuel an especially intense hostility toward black males' and white females' dating or marrying one another. As one well-known scholar on race relations puts it, "white men face the mythic fear that black men may out-rival them in virility and competence" (Hacker, 1992, p. 62). The scholar and religion professor, Cornel West, agrees: "Black sexuality is a taboo subject in white and black America and a candid dialogue about black sexuality between and within these communities is requisite for healthy race relations" (West, 1994, p.120).

But it doesn't take the scholars' statistics to convince minority adolescents that the social or sexual rejection they often experience is real. And it doesn't take statistics to prove to interracial teenage couples that most Americans don't approve of their relationship. Leaving sex aside, very few adolescents are close friends with someone from another race. When they are, most still see their friend as "exceptions" to their race: "She's not like the rest of them, you see." "He's not like most people from that country." Aside from the bonds that often develop between male athletes, interracial friendships are rare. Interracial dating and marriage are rarer still, as evidenced by the fact that only 2% of all people marry someone of another race (Hart Research, 1992; Larson, 1990; Roberts, 1994).

The issue of interracial dating is perhaps best explored in teenagers' descriptions of their own experiences. "I often had to reconcile within myself the fact that as a black person I belonged to this fraternity that made no effort to include blacks. My relationships with women, or the lack thereof, are a result of my unique situation. It is not fully acceptable to have interracial relationships, especially for those white women who are conscious of their class and position. They care about what their peers will think, as well as their parents" (Garrod, 1992, p. 117). "Laura is not Korean. She is Italian. The topic of interracial marriages happens to be a major issue for my generation of Korean Americans. I consider myself lucky, because my parents never so much as hinted at disapproval of Laura" (Garrod, 1992, p. 103).

Regardless of their race, most adolescents know that racism still exists. In one survey of nearly 1,200 people between the ages of 15 and 24, 80% of the white respondents said they had witnessed racial discrimination (Hart Research, 1992). Among nearly 2,000 high-school students, half had witnessed or participated in a racial incident that involved physical violence. More boys than girls had been involved in racial troublemaking and most of the male troublemakers were from high income families (Lapchick, 1991). In yet another nationwide survey of teenagers and adults, 80% of the whites believed that all other races would rather be on welfare than have a job (Smith, 1991).

RACE AND IMMIGRANT FAMILIES

In contrast to young African Americans, adolescents whose families have recently immigrated to the United States often encounter racial issues of another kind. Although our country is supposedly a melting pot, conflict and ambivalence over immigration sometimes make us more like a boiling pot. Given the mounting costs to taxpayers of supporting immigrant families, we are divided on the issue of U.S. immigration. As jobs for poorly educated adults have become increasingly scarce, immigrants with poor English skills and little education are often unable to support their families without welfare assistance. In 1970 the average immigrant earned about 3% more than a native-born American, but by 1990 was earning 16% less. The 19.3 million legal and illegal aliens who have entered the United States since 1970 used almost $60 billion worth of free government services in 1992. But due to their low wages and high unemployment,

Insert 7–1

The Education of Berenice Belizaire

When Berenice Belizaire arrived in New York from Haiti with her mother and sister in 1987, she was not a happy adolescent. She spoke no English, lived in a small apartment, and left behind a comfortable house, friends, and relatives.

At school she endured teasing, taunting, and food throwing from both the black and the white students. When she pleaded with her mother to go back to Haiti, her mother explained that most of the schools there had been closed due to political and economic turmoil.

A bright and dedicated student, Berenice learned English in two years, graduated as vale-

dictorian of her high school, and enrolled in Massachusetts Institute of Technology where she is preparing for her future in computer design.

As a counselor for many Haitian immigrant students explains, one of the biggest social issues confronting female adolescents such as Berenice is whether their families will go against their traditions by allowing their adult daughters to live away from home before they marry.

Berenice also explains that in high school she and other immigrants used to criticize each other for getting lazy by saying "you're becoming too American."

Source: J. Klein (1993, August 9). The education of Berenice Belizaire. *Newsweek,* p. 26.

they were able to pay back only about $20 billion in taxes. The net burden on taxpayers is about $1,600 per immigrant each year. Especially in those states where the immigrant population is high, the burden on taxpayers contributes to a growing resentment or ambivalence toward immigrant adolescents and their families. As a consequence, adolescents whose families have recently immigrated often feel the effects of racism and prejudice, as the stories in Inserts 7–1 and 7–2 illustrate (Morganthau, 1993).

RACE AND AFRICAN AMERICANS

In comparison to other racial minorities, African Americans have met particularly strong resistance in being assimilated into our society. Among adolescents, for example, those who emigrate from the Caribbean often make a point of distinguishing themselves from African Americans even though their skin color can be as dark or darker. Emphasizing their Caribbean heritage is not intended to fool anyone into seeing them as literally "less black" than any other group, but is intended to protect themselves from being treated like African Americans—a group that has been treated with less respect than any other race in our society. In terms of housing, education, or interracial dating and friendships, African Americans have been, and continue to be, more segregated than any other racial group. Compared to Hispanic and Asian Americans, black teenagers are the least

Insert 7–2

An Immigrant's Story: Breaking the Bonds of Hate

In the jungles of Cambodia I lived in a refugee camp. I have spent half of my life in war. The killing is still implanted in my mind.

When I came to America nine years ago at the age of 10, I thought I was being born into a new life. No more being hungry, no more fighting, no more killing. I thought I had escaped war. But for the immigrant, America presents a different type of jungle. You have to be deceptive and unscrupulous in order to make it. If you're a kid my age, you drop out of school to work because your parents don't have enough money to buy you clothes for school. You may end up selling drugs because you want cars, money, and parties, as all teenagers do.

I hated America because, to me, it was not the place of opportunities or the land of the melting pot, as I had been told. All I had seen were broken beer bottles on the street and homeless people and drunks using the sky as their roof. I couldn't walk down the street without someone yelling out, "You f...ing gook" from his car. I dropped out of school in ninth grade to join a gang. It all came to an abrupt halt when I crashed a car.

I called a good friend of the Cambodian community in Minneapolis for advice. She promised to help me get back in school. And she did. Since then I've been given a lot of encouragement and caring by American friends and teachers who've helped me turn my life around. They opened my eyes to a kind of education that frees us all from ignorance and slavery. Individuals who were willing to help me have taught me that I can help myself.

I'm now a 12th grader. I plan to attend college in the fall. I am struggling to believe I can reach the other side of the mountain.

Source: V. Khiev (1992, April 27). Breaking the bonds of hate. *Newsweek*, p. 8.

likely to be allowed to merge socially, sexually, or geographically into white society (Hacker, 1992; West, 1994).

A few specific examples illustrate the extent of the racism affecting a number of black adolescents in our country today. Blacks are less likely than any other races to live in predominantly white neighborhoods. In fact, when the percentage of African Americans in a neighborhood exceeds 8%, white residents generally start moving out. Nearly 65% of black children also still attend segregated public schools. African American males are also the most likely racial group to be the perpetrators and victims of crime. Racism also seems to affect black males more adversely than black females in terms of income. For instance, unlike black women with college degrees, black college men end up barely ahead of white men who go no further than high school in terms of lifetime yearly incomes. This suggests that black males, perceived as more threatening and more assertive, might be less welcome or given fewer opportunities in the workplace than black females. And as far as getting along together on the job, black and white women tend to mingle more easily and more frequently at work than do black and white men. This is partly because most women tend to feel less tense than men about

How have your racial attitudes changed since
you were a teenager?

race and are better at finding common experiences among themselves as women
that lessen racial differences (Gibbs, 1991; Hacker, 1992).

It has also been pointed out that many white Americans have more hostile or
more ambivalent feelings about African Americans than about other racial minorities. Some believe that blacks have been given enough time and enough opportunity to make more educational and financial advances, especially in comparison to
immigrant groups such as Jewish and Asian Americans. Other white Americans
seem unwilling to confront their own racism regarding blacks because of our
nation's shameful history of slavery. Although some do feel responsible for a system that has enabled whites to profit from the slavery of blacks, others do not
believe they should now be held personally responsible for such discrimination in
the past. Indeed, many employers are quite open about preferring to hire Hispanic
immigrants instead of native-born blacks. Notably, many Americans prefer to go to
a Hispanic or Asian doctor, dentist, or hygienist than to a black dentist or physician. So as we move toward the year 2000, the uncomfortable reality still confronts us: Minority teenagers and their families still have to cope with forms of
prejudice and discrimination that most whites never encounter (Hacker, 1992).

BIAS AND SHORTCOMINGS IN THE RESEARCH

In addition to the resentment or prejudice many minority adolescents experience in their own lives, they are also negatively affected by the way in which much of the social science research has been conducted. The main bias in our research is that most of our data and theories about adolescence are based on white, middle-class, male subjects. For example, until 1978 very few articles had been published in professional psychology journals about Mexican American children and their families (Hispanic Health Coalition, 1978). Given the focus on white male adolescents, we have comparatively little information about female and minority teenagers.

The second bias in much of our existing research is ethnocentrism. **Ethnocentrism** is the belief in the superiority of one's own ethnic or racial group. We are ethnocentric when we interpret another group's behavior, physical appearance, art, music, language, family roles, humor, dress, and other aspects of culture as inferior, less advanced, or less sophisticated than our own. For example, defining beauty as having straight hair, thin lips, rounded eyes, and a tall, skinny body can be seen as ethnocentric if the person doing the defining can't perceive other groups' physical features as equally beautiful. It's also ethnocentric to believe that every family is unstable, dysfunctional, deficient, or disadvantaged unless there are only two or three children living with both biological parents in a home with no other relatives.

Perhaps one of the most powerful examples of ethnocentrism in terms of its impact on public opinion was the 1965 Moynihan Report. This U.S. Senate committee report concluded that African American families were primarily to blame for their own poverty because they were too matriarchal in that the women had too much power over the men. The senate committee told the American public that if African American women were less domineering, African American men would be much better off financially. As Senator Moynihan stated in his committee's report: "The weakness of the Negro family structure is the principal source of most of the aberrant, inadequate, and antisocial behavior that perpetuates poverty and deprivation. The matriarchal structure retards progress of the group as a whole and imposes a crushing burden on the Negro male" (Moynihan, 1965).

In the decade that followed this highly publicized report, many researchers refuted its conclusions and criticized its ethnocentric ways of gathering and interpreting the data. As part of the backlash to the Moynihan report, nearly 500 articles about African American families appeared during the 1960s and 1970s—five times more than in the entire century that preceded the report. First, the critics argued that although many black families are different from white nuclear families, the differences are neither dysfunctional nor pathological. Second, Moynihan's committee failed to mention the racism in our country that contributed to poverty. Nor did it mention that the welfare laws at the time penalized poor women for getting married by withdrawing welfare support no matter how low the married couple's income. As a consequence, many poor women remained single to keep their children fed and sheltered. Third, the committee chose to ignore that white women in low-income families were about as likely as black women in low-income families to be unmarried. Finally the report equated being the head of the household with matriarchy. Matriarchy, however, refers to a society in which women hold more of the financial and political power than men. However, most African American women still earn less money than most black men; and women in our country, regardless of race, have less political power than men. In other words, Moynihan's accusations regarding matriarchy were grossly inaccurate (Ladner, 1971; Staples, 1982).

Reports such as Moynihan's are also criticized for blaming the victim. Blaming the victim is the process of faulting victimized people for problems that actually arise from the attitudes, policies, and institutions of the society. Blaming the victim is a way of rationalizing cruelty, injustice, and discrimination by placing the entire responsibility on the victims rather than on any of the policies or attitudes in the society at large that contribute to their predicament. In blaming the victim, we refuse to place any of the blame for problems, such as poverty, on any defects or characteristics of the dominant group or its policies. In the case of the Moynihan Report, poverty was blamed entirely on the African American family—above all on black women who supposedly emasculated and demoralized black men (Ryan, 1972).

Another common source of bias in the research on minority adolescents and their families is income. Many of our generalizations about minorities are based on research that did not take income into account or didn't compare the minority subjects with people from other racial groups with similar incomes. Because family income is much more closely linked to children's academic and social success than is race, we need to consider an adolescent's economic situation before drawing any conclusions about his or her racial group. For example, a white teenager from a low-income family is much more likely to become pregnant, drop out of school, break the law, or abuse drugs than a nonwhite teenager from a higher-income family. Either the researcher needs to compare adolescents from different racial groups whose families have roughly the same incomes, or the researcher needs to compare adolescents of the same race from several different economic backgrounds. If this hasn't been done, we can't draw valid conclusions about the impact of race on any aspect of the adolescent's life (Fisher, 1991).

Although we might want to believe that ethnocentrism or other forms of bias no longer exist in the research, this is not the case. Because so few researchers and writers are from minorities or from lower-income backgrounds, ethnocentric attitudes toward nonwhite or lower income people still influence our research—what questions are asked, how the data are gathered, the ways in which the results are interpreted, and which results are accepted for publication and dissemination to the public. This is not to say that only white people can be ethnocentric or that all research conducted by whites is biased. Nor is it to say that people who are biased or ethnocentric in conducting their research are intentionally trying to be racist. People of any race can and do have ethnocentric or racist views. Indeed, some social scientists believe a certain amount of racism might be an evolutionary artifact initially designed to protect "us" from "them"— an instinctive reaction to trust people who look the most like us and to fear people who look the least like us (Fox, 1994). Nevertheless, the fact remains that racial minorities and people from lower-income backgrounds do not have nearly the control over gathering and interpreting the data as do most whites. As one social scientist somewhat comically puts it, "even the rat was white" (Guthrie, 1976).Whether we're examining the findings in psychology, sociology, anthropology, or the biological sciences, there has long been a bias against minority adolescents and their families—a bias that has not yet been eradicated (Fox, 1994; Harding, 1993; Schiebinger, 1993).

In this light, as you read the research on minorities, you need to be asking yourself such questions as: Are the questions that this researcher chose to focus on biased toward any particular racial or economic group? Could the data be interpreted in any ways other than how this writer chose? Do I see any evidence of ethnocentric judgments against another group's values? Could these conclusions be viewed any differently if they were interpreted by someone from the group that was studied? Was income factored out before drawing conclusions about these subjects on the basis of their race?

MINORITIES AND INCOME

THE RACIAL INCOME GAP

The biggest single problem now facing most Hispanic, African, and Native American adolescents and their families, however, is lack of money. We can see the vast financial gaps among racial groups in our country by considering five measures—number of families living in poverty, median family incomes, the net worth of families, average individual incomes, and number of families on welfare.

Nearly 20% of the children in our country are poor—the highest percentage since 1964 when President Lyndon Johnson declared his "war on poverty." When we break these statistics down by race, however, the bleakness of the situation is even more clear. The official poverty level determined yearly by the federal government is based on a family's size. The poverty level for a family of four in 1993 was about $14,000 a year. As Figure 7–2 illustrates, only 15% of white and Asian American children were living below that level, compared to nearly 50% of black and 40% of Hispanic and Native American children. A black child's chances of being poor are nearly 1 in 2, a Hispanic child's more than 1 in 3, an Asian-American child's 1 in 6, and a white child's 1 in 8. As recorded by our most recent census, the poorest part of our country is South Dakota's Pine Ridge Indian Reservation where 65% of the families are living in poverty. If the economic patterns of the 1980s are repeated, 25% of the children in our country will be living in poverty by the year 2000 (Fuchs & Reklis, 1992; U.S. Department of Commerce, 1992b).

Another way of looking at race and poverty is to compare median family incomes. Not to be confused with the mean or average income, the median is the income that half of the people in a group make more than and the other half make less than. Keep in mind that 80% of all mothers are now working outside

Figure 7–2

Race and income

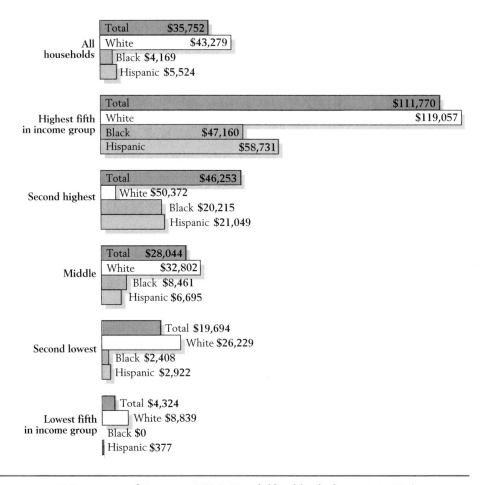

Source: U.S. Department of Commerce (1994). *Household and family characteristics.* Washington, DC: Bureau of the Census.

the home, so most family incomes represent two adults' wages. Considering both married and unmarried adults, half of all white families are living on less than $34,000 a year; half of all Hispanic American families live on less than $22,000; and half of all African American families live on less than $19,000 (U.S. Department of Commerce, 1992b).

We can also compare different racial groups financially by looking at families' net worth (Bane & Ellwood, 1989; Fuchs & Reklis, 1992). **Net worth** is the value of a family's home, vehicles, and investments minus their debts. Nearly 70% of white families own their home in contrast to only 40% of black and Hispanic families. Although half of the Hispanic and white homes are worth more than $75,000, only half of the black homes are worth more than $40,000. Almost a third of white families have a net worth of more than $100,000 compared to only 5% of black and 12% of Hispanic families. We can also see vast racial differences when we compare the average incomes of men and women who are working full-time. Black men working full-time make about 72 cents for every dollar earned by a white man. A black man with a college degree earns only about 75% as much as a white man with the same education. So even when blacks or Hispanics have the same total family income as whites and Asians, that income usually represents the salaries of two working adults. White and Asian American men are more likely to be earning enough money so that their wives do not have to work, or work only part-time. Unemployment rates are also higher among minorities with similar levels of education to whites. For example, black adults with college degrees are more than twice as likely as white graduates to be unemployed (Hacker, 1992).

Finally we can consider how many families in each racial group are on welfare. Although half of all welfare recipients are white, only 10% of all white families are receiving welfare in any given year. In contrast, nearly 40% of black and 30% of Hispanic families receive welfare assistance. Although most families receiving welfare only need this assistance for brief periods of time, white and Asian families are on welfare for the shortest periods of time. To put welfare spending into perspective, however, consider this: 11 times more money is spent on welfare benefits for people over age 65 than for children under 18. To keep every American above the poverty level would cost taxpayers about $5,100 a year for each family—less per year than what we spent in 43 days on the 1991 Persian Gulf War (Roberts, 1994).

So the question is: Why do one fifth of the children in such a wealthy nation live in poverty? One answer lies in the changes that have occurred in our national economy. Although many Americans blame the rise in poverty on fatherless families, the fact is that half of all poor children are living with married parents. Obviously then, out-of-wedlock births do not account for poverty in these families. What has happened is that our economy has moved further away from the production of goods such as steel and automobiles toward jobs in the service industries. In the past, most parents with only a high-school degree, and many who were high-school dropouts, nevertheless could earn a good income in industry. Nowadays, however, most jobs require far more education for far less income. As a result, those parents with the least education—most of whom are members of racial minorities—have fallen fastest into poverty. Especially for parents whose English is poor and for those who never finished high school, well-paying jobs are hard to come by. So even when minority parents have full-time jobs, it is harder for them to keep their families out of poverty. In fact, nearly one fourth of the black parents and one third of the Hispanic parents who work full-time earn incomes below the poverty level (U.S. Department of Commerce, 1992b).

Think of it this way: A male and female with high-school degrees get married, each having a job that pays minimum wage. They have two children. He works full-time and she works part-time—because on their salaries they cannot afford to pay for child-care if they both work full-time. In this situation, their family will be almost $2,000 below the poverty line of $14,000.

Because poverty and race are so closely linked, race becomes an increasingly explosive issue as our economy worsens and poverty rises. For the first time in our country, during the 1960s, we decided to work simultaneously against racism and poverty. Within 8 years, half of America's poor were lifted out of poverty. But in the midst of the financial downturns in our economy during the 1970s and 1980s, many of the laws and policies that were intended to combat poverty have been reversed. As our economy has slumped and most families have become poorer, racial tensions have also risen—as they have historically when there is more competition for fewer jobs and fewer resources (Hacker, 1992; West, 1994).

SINGLE PARENTS, RACE, AND INCOME

In addition to these economic changes, another factor has contributed greatly to poverty, especially among racial minorities—fatherless families. Leaving race aside, about 24% of the children in our society are living in a fatherless family, and half of all poor children come from these homes. Analyzed by race, the numbers are staggering. As shown in Figure 7–3 and Table 7–2, nearly 60% of African American children live with an unmarried mother, compared to 30% of Hispanic and less than 20% of Asian and white children. The Hispanic population shows wide variation. Nearly half of Puerto Rican children live in a fatherless family, but fewer than 20% of Mexican American children do. (Hacker, 1992).

Almost one fourth of all babies are now being born out-of-wedlock—this comprises 17% of white, 23% of Hispanic, and 60% of black births. Among all teenage parents, only 1 in 3 couples is married when their child is born. Among black teenagers, only 1 in 10 mothers are married. So more than a third of African American children under the age of 18 are living with a mother who has never been married—a mother who typically had her first child as a teenager, quit school, and is unqualified for most jobs even at minimum wage. If these trends continue, 40% of all births and 80% of births to minority females will be to unmarried parents within the next 5 years. For the first time in our country's history, almost as many children are now living with a mother who has never been married as with a divorced mother. As a consequence, only 5% of black children and 30% of white children will be living with their married biological parents throughout the first 18 years of their lives by the year 2000 (National Commission on Children [NCC], 1993; Roberts, 1994).

The financial impact of fatherless families is sobering. Regardless of race, a mother's marital status is directly linked to the kind of life-style her children will lead. Whereas half of all married couples have a family income greater than $41,000 a year, half of the divorced mothers have incomes less than $16,000; and half of the mothers who have never been married live on $8,500 a year. Fatherless families are 5 times more likely to be on welfare. But as you can see from Table 7–2, fatherless families are far more common in some races than in others. More

Figure 7–3

Single-parent families

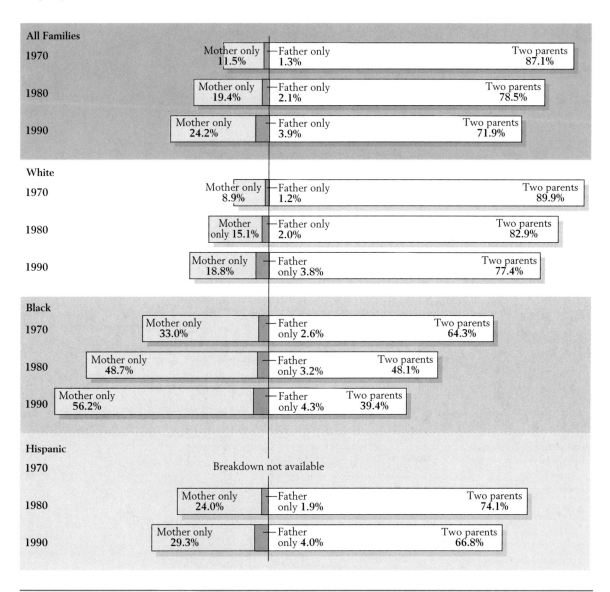

All Families

1970   Mother only 11.5% | Father only 1.3% | Two parents 87.1%

1980   Mother only 19.4% | Father only 2.1% | Two parents 78.5%

1990   Mother only 24.2% | Father only 3.9% | Two parents 71.9%

White

1970   Mother only 8.9% | Father only 1.2% | Two parents 89.9%

1980   Mother only 15.1% | Father only 2.0% | Two parents 82.9%

1990   Mother only 18.8% | Father only 3.8% | Two parents 77.4%

Black

1970   Mother only 33.0% | Father only 2.6% | Two parents 64.3%

1980   Mother only 48.7% | Father only 3.2% | Two parents 48.1%

1990   Mother only 56.2% | Father only 4.3% | Two parents 39.4%

Hispanic

1970   Breakdown not available

1980   Mother only 24.0% | Father only 1.9% | Two parents 74.1%

1990   Mother only 29.3% | Father only 4.0% | Two parents 66.8%

Table 7–2

Families Headed by Unmarried Mothers

Black	60%
Puerto Rican	44%
Native American	40%
Native Hawaiian	21%
Mexican	18%
White	18%
Cuban	16%
Vietnamese	14%
Japanese	12%
Korean	10%
Filipino	10%
Chinese	6%

Source: U.S. Department of Commerce (1992). *Household and family characteristics.* Washington, DC: Bureau of the Census.

children are growing up in fatherless families in the United States than in any other industrialized nation. We also have the highest teenage pregnancy and out-of-wedlock birth rate of any industrialized country. We discuss poverty in Chapter 8, so for now we leave the discussion on this note: Black, Hispanic, and Native American adolescents are the most likely to spend most of their childhood in a low-income family or living in abject poverty, even when their parents are married and employed (Roberts, 1994; U.S. Department of Commerce, 1992b).

MINORITIES AND EDUCATION

PARENTS' EDUCATIONAL ACHIEVEMENTS

Education assumes a special importance in the lives of minority youth in two ways. First, the fact that most Hispanic, Black, and Native American adults are more poorly educated than most white and Asian parents limits their family incomes. Second, family incomes are closely tied to how much children achieve academically. As Figure 7–4 shows, only half of Hispanic Americans have a high-school diploma, compared to about 80% of Asian and white adults. These racial disparities show up even greater when we look at college degrees. More than 20% of white and nearly 40% of Asian adults have college degrees, but the number drops to about one tenth of Hispanic and black adults (Roberts, 1994).

These differences in their parents' educations, in turn, determine adolescents' standards of living while they are growing up. Adults who do not finish high

Figure 7–4

Educational advances and race

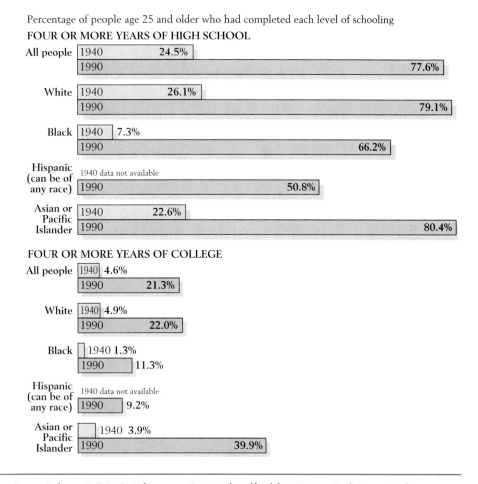

Percentage of people age 25 and older who had completed each level of schooling

FOUR OR MORE YEARS OF HIGH SCHOOL

All people 1940 — 24.5%
1990 — 77.6%

White 1940 — 26.1%
1990 — 79.1%

Black 1940 — 7.3%
1990 — 66.2%

Hispanic (can be of any race) 1940 data not available
1990 — 50.8%

Asian or Pacific Islander 1940 — 22.6%
1990 — 80.4%

FOUR OR MORE YEARS OF COLLEGE

All people 1940 — 4.6%
1990 — 21.3%

White 1940 — 4.9%
1990 — 22.0%

Black 1940 1.3%
1990 — 11.3%

Hispanic (can be of any race) 1940 data not available
1990 — 9.2%

Asian or Pacific Islander 1940 3.9%
1990 — 39.9%

Source: Roberts, S. (1994). *Who we are: Statistical profile of the U.S.* New York: Times Books.

school earn an average of only $11,000 a year; high-school graduates take in about $17,000; and college graduates average about $31,000. Only 7% of the adults who completed high school end up on welfare, in contrast to more than 20% of the adults who never finished high school. For example, only half of Hispanic parents have graduated from high school, and they account for nearly half of the increase in poverty among children since 1980. Lack of education also affects the vicious cycle characteristic of children born out-of-wedlock—so many of their parents are high-school dropouts, and the children are almost inevitably doomed to poverty. Among the nearly 16 million children in fatherless homes, only 9% have a parent who attended college. High dropout rates also help explain why nearly half of the black males between the ages of 25 and 34 are either unemployed or earning a wage below the poverty level (Roberts, 1994).

On a positive note, minority parents are better off educationally than ever before. The number of blacks and Asian Americans who have finished high-school and earned college degrees is 10 times greater than it was 50 years ago. Nevertheless, during the past 20 years, troubling declines have occurred among blacks and Hispanics. For example, since 1970 the proportion of black doctors has declined, and the percentage of black college professors has remained unchanged. During the past two decades, most of the increases in medical and university jobs have been among white women and Asian Americans. Despite educational gains in the 1950s and 60s, African American parents, who constitute only 10% of the work force, still account for nearly 20% of such low-paying jobs as janitors, maids, and security guards and for only 3% of the higher-paying jobs such as biologists, doctors, or lawyers. Although nearly a third of white men have managerial and professional jobs, only 13% of black men do. Likewise, 70% of all migrant workers are Hispanic, and many other Hispanics have low-paying jobs in sweat shops and agriculture (Hacker, 1992; Roberts, 1994).

ADOLESCENTS' EDUCATIONAL ACHIEVEMENTS

Given that their parents are usually better educated and earn higher incomes, it is not surprising that most Asian American and non-Hispanic white students graduate from high school and college at higher rates than do teenagers from other racial groups. Roughly 90% of white and Asian students graduate from high school by age 25. Likewise, nearly 20% of white youths graduate from college, as do nearly 40% of Asian Americans—two times the percentage of whites and four times that of blacks and Hispanics. In contrast, by the time they are 25, only 60% to 70% of the young people from other racial groups graduate from high school and fewer than 10% graduate from college (N.C.E.S., 1994).

Not only are white and Asian students more likely to graduate from high school and college, they also usually have better math, reading, and science skills than other high-school students. We examine these racial differences more closely in Chapter 10, so for now a few examples will illustrate this point. At all grade levels, white and Asian students earn higher scores on national achievement tests. Whereas only a third of all white high-school students have failed a grade, nearly half of African, Hispanic, and Native American students are at least one grade-level behind. Considering gender, only one fourth of all white teenage girls are either behind a grade level or have dropped out of school compared to more than half of all black teenage males. Likewise, nearly 40% of Asian American and 30% of white students are in the highest ability classes in 8th-grade English. But only 15% of black and Hispanic students and 9% of Native American students are in these advanced English classes (National Center for Educational Statistics [NCES], 1991; Roberts, 1994).

Our parents' incomes, however, are not the only factors affecting how far we get academically or financially in our own lives. When we compare Scholastic

Aptitude Test (SAT) scores, Asian American teenagers from the lowest income families still outperform black and Hispanic teenagers from similar economic backgrounds. And even when their parents' incomes and education are similar, Hispanic students earn 66 points more, on average, than black students. In this same vein, even though 43% of Asian American high-school students first learned a language other than English and even when their family incomes are the same as whites', their SAT scores are higher. The same can be said for Jewish Americans. What this means is that factors other than income affect children's academic and financial success—factors we discuss in Chapter 10. Nevertheless, regardless of race, most teenagers with well-educated, higher-income parents turn out to be richer and more well-educated when they are adults. So whether we are comparing parents' education, family income, or children's educational achievements, the races end up ranked in roughly the same order from highest to lowest: Asian, white, Hispanic, black, and Native American (Hacker, 1992; Roberts, 1994; Taylor, 1990).

EDUCATING MINORITY STUDENTS

Recognizing that white and Asian American students usually achieve more than those from other groups, a number of public schools and colleges have made special efforts to improve the skills and graduation rates of Hispanic, black, and

Insert 7–3

Adolescents' Attitudes on Educational Inequities

Student in Ghetto High School

"You can understand things better when you go among the wealthy. People on the outside may think we don't know what it is like for other students, but we visit other schools and we have eyes and we have brains. Most of the students in this school won't go to college. Many will join the military. If there's a war, we have to fight. Why should I go to war and fight for opportunities I can't enjoy—for things rich people value, for their freedom, but I do not have the freedom and I can't go to their schools? The parents of rich children have the money to get them into better schools. The extra things they have are seen like an inheritance. They feel it's theirs and they don't understand why we should question it."

Student in Wealthy High School

"I agree that it's unfair the way it is. But putting them in schools like ours is not the answer. Why not put some advanced placement classes in *their* school. Fix the roof and paint the halls so it will not be so depressing."

Source: J. Kozol (1991). *Savage inequalities: Children in America's schools.* New York: Harper Perennial.

Native American students. (These programs are discussed in Chapter 10.) Issues related to the education of minority students, however, often provoke new sources of racial hostility and conflict. Many of these controversies revolve around college admission policies, minority athletes, the school curriculum, and racial inequalities in the quality of public education (Darder, 1991; Ramirez, 1990; Sue, 1991).

When it comes to college admissions, a number of Asian and white students believe that they are being discriminated against when students from other racial groups with lower grades and lower SAT scores are admitted in their place. Surpassing all other racial groups in grades and in SAT scores, many Asian American students are upset by quotas that limit their admissions to colleges. In California, more than a third of Asian American high-school seniors meet the criteria for being admitted into one of their state's universities. But quotas have been set to limit their admissions despite their qualifications. Other universities also accept minorities with grades and SAT scores lower than other applicants. Of course, having different standards for admission is not new in our country's private high schools or universities. For years virtually all colleges have admitted students with lower grades whose parents are alumni and students who are athletes. Quotas were also used to reject or to limit Jewish students' enrollment in college and in professional schools despite their higher academic qualifications (Hacker, 1992).

It has been a longstanding practice in our society to admit male athletes into college who lack the academic qualifications of other students. Without a doubt, great athletic talent can catapult a minority teenager to fame and fortune even without the help of a college or university. Witness the case of 19-year-old Manny Ramirez. A high-school outfielder and son of a cab driver and a seamstress who had emigrated from the Dominican Republic to the United States, Ramirez was drafted by the Cleveland Indians and signed to a $250,000 contract. But the reality is that only 1 in 10,000 high-school athletes makes it to a professional team. Despite these overwhelming odds, too many black and Hispanic high-school boys, despite the support of their teachers, coaches, and families, fail to develop their academic skills in pursuit of athletic and financial glory. Wherever sports are profitable, college officials admit teenage boys who lack the skills to succeed in college but who can contribute to the school's budget and reputation. Most colleges actively recruit black athletes, many of whom have barely made it through high school. Not surprisingly then, only 25% of black athletes graduate from college and more than 90% of the athletes who are barred from playing during any given year because of low grades are black. Thus the troubling question remains unanswered: How can we help teenage athletes, many from low-income minority families, to focus more on their academic skills in order to have greater financial security as adults (Hacker, 1992)?

Educating minority students also raises difficult questions and causes heated debates about the curriculum in our public schools and colleges (Gates, 1992). There has been widespread debate over making the curriculum more inclusive and less ethnocentric at all levels of education. Like all students, teenagers from racial minorities tend to be more motivated by material that is relevant to their own lives, history, and culture. Yet attempting to make the curriculum more inclusive and expansive raises a number of controversial questions, including: How should the curriculum be updated and expanded to present more information about the literature, history, and culture of nonwhite and female Americans? Who will decide what to include and what to exclude? How are we to create a curriculum for public schools and colleges that reflects the diversity in our society yet also focuses on our commonalities?

Finally, we are still confronted with this painful question: What are we going to do for the black, Hispanic, and Native American students, most of whom are still receiving a poorer education than most Asian and white students? Across the country there are vast differences between not only the quality of teachers, the physical condition of schools, the student–teacher ratio, and school safety, but also access to materials such as computers, library books, and science equipment. The amount we taxpayers spend to educate each public school student ranges from $3,200 to $12,000 a year. But more money is given to those who already have more to begin with—students from wealthier families who live in the richer communities where minorities cannot afford to live. Because school funding largely depends on how much money is collected from property taxes on the residents' homes and businesses, those children who live in poor areas have the least money made available for their educations. Among others who have lamented these gross inequities in our schools, Jonathan Kozol refers to ours as a nation of "savage inequalities" (Kozol, 1991; Roberts, 1994).

Although we like to tell ourselves that our schools offer equal opportunity to all, in reality we have a caste-like system in which students with the richest parents get the best educations. As the U.S. Commissioner of Education concluded 25 years ago: "Our nation does not have a truly public school system in a large part of its communities. It has permitted what is in effect a private school system to develop under public auspices. Equality of educational opportunity throughout the nation continues today to be more a myth than a reality." As one minority teenager puts it, "All that stuff about 'the dream' means nothing to the kids I know in East St. Louis. So far as they're concerned, Dr. Martin Luther King died in vain. He gave his speeches and he died and now he's gone. But we're still here. Go and look into a toilet in this school if you want to know what life is like for students in this city" (Kozol, 1991, p. 80 & 36).

PHYSICAL WELL-BEING

PRENATAL HEALTH AND CHILDHOOD DISEASES

It almost goes without saying that an adolescent's physical well-being is closely connected to his or her family's income. As a consequence of poverty—not race—many babies are born with fetal alcohol syndrome, AIDS, addiction to crack cocaine, and mental or physical defects that could have been prevented by better prenatal care. Poor children also have more preventable diseases and problems with their sight and hearing than those whose parents can afford adequate food, housing, and medical care. In many cases, not having health insurance or not having easy access to medical facilities also deprives poor children of the medical care they need, including rudimentary, basic immunization. Poor children are also the most likely to suffer physical and mental harm due to exposure to such diverse threats as lead poisoning, toxic wastes, raw sewage, contaminated water, and unsanitary food (Children's Defense Fund [CDF], 1992).

Because the problem is related not to race but to lack of money, thousands of white children also suffer from these physical and mental ailments. But because a higher percentage of minority children are poor, proportionately more of them are stricken and afflicted with these preventable problems. For example, in a survey of nearly 14,000 Native American youths, fetal alcohol syndrome—preventable merely by the pregnant woman's abstaining from alcohol—was a major cause of mental retardation and learning problems (Blum, 1992). Likewise, twice as many black as white children suffer from asthma, deafness, and forms of mental retardation that could have been prevented simply with better prenatal care (Gibbs, 1991; Hacker, 1992). And, compared to other races, Native American children are twice as likely to die from heart disease, influenza, and pneumonia, while Latino children have 4 times as much amoebic dysentery, tuberculosis, and hepatitis (Busch-Rossnagel & Zayas, 1991; Young, 1994).

CRIME, DRUGS, AND VIOLENCE

The health risks associated with being black, Hispanic, or Native American go beyond poor prenatal care and childhood disease. Because these adolescents are the most likely to be growing up in poverty, they are also the most likely to live in dangerous, crime-ridden neighborhoods and to attend run-down schools plagued by violence and drugs. Given that so many live in fatherless homes, minority teenagers are also the least likely to get the kinds of adult supervision that can reduce their chances of injury from accidents or neighborhood violence. This means that black, Hispanic, and Native American adolescents are the most likely to be killed or injured as a result of violence and drugs. They are also at higher risk for contracting AIDS and other diseases, such as hepatitis, that come from using drugs.

A few examples serve to illustrate these health risks. Yearly national surveys of almost 78,000 adolescents show that Hispanics use more of the most dangerous drugs—cocaine, crack, heroin, and steroids—than any other race (Johnston, O'Malley, & Bachman, 1993). Among black males, the leading cause of death is murder; and black females are 3 times more likely than white females to be murdered (Hacker, 1992). The infant death rate in New York's Harlem is higher than in Bangladesh. Nearly half of the babies that do survive require hospitalization for physical problems that often lead to mental retardation (Kozol, 1991). Black, Hispanic, and Native American adolescents top the list in deaths, injuries, and diseases related to violence, crime, drugs, and sex (American Psychological Association [APA], 1993).

PSYCHOLOGICAL WELL-BEING

Physical Self-Esteem

Regardless of race, self-esteem is closely connected to how satisfied teenagers feel with how they look. According to what most people in our society consider attractive, we should all want to have a fairly thin nose, lips that are full but not "too thick," eyes that are rounded rather than slanted, thick eyelashes, light skin, straight hair, and a tall, slender build. If we are female, we should also have fairly large breasts, relatively flat buttocks, and long slender legs. If we are male, we should be muscular, tall, broad-shouldered, and hairy-chested.

So how do adolescents feel about themselves when they do not "measure up" to these standards because of their racial features and physiques? Regardless of how well-educated or how financially well-off they are, too many minority teenagers still feel bad about themselves because they believe that their lips or hips are too full, their eyes too slanted, their skin too dark, their breasts too small, their bodies too short, their frame too frail, or their eyelashes too skimpy. Some Asian American teenagers have cosmetic surgery to enlarge their breasts and to make their eyes less slanted. One Korean American teenager recalls some of her classmates' comments: "Do you have eyelashes?" "Flat face, flat face, that's not the only place!" "Yellow face, can you see out of those eyes!?" (Kim, 1991, p. 201). Black Americans have also tried to meet Eurocentric standards by straightening their hair or lightening their skin.

Among others, the renown African American author and professor of religion at Princeton, Cornel West, explains, "much of black self-hatred and self-contempt has to do with the refusal of many black Americans to love their own black bodies—especially their black noses, hips, lips and hair" (West, 1994, p. 122). Likewise, one Hispanic American scholar also maintains that too many Chicano males have internalized white standards of beauty by rejecting Chicana women for Anglos: "White women are held up as the model of beauty; the kind of woman to lust after and sometimes marry. To some Chicano men, attachment to such a woman signifies upward mobility and masculine worth, and it leaves the Chicana outside" (Blea, 1992, p. 67). Too many African, Asian, Hispanic, and Native American teenagers are still made to feel ashamed or embarrassed by the physical features of their own race (Kim, 1991; Morton, 1991; Robinson & Ward, 1991; Wade, 1991).

This is not to say that white adolescents never feel bad about how they look. Many do. Many white teenagers chronically diet, use hair products and cosmetics, have facial or breast surgery, take steroids and pump iron for larger muscles, and take hormones to grow taller in their quests to measure up to our definitions of attractiveness. The situation is different for minority adolescents though, because the physical features they are often made to feel ashamed of are aspects of their race—essential aspects of themselves, their relatives, and their ancestors that are too often ridiculed or caricatured in our society. In terms of racial shame or racial pride, when a white teenager wishes he was taller or wishes she was thinner, it is not the same as when a minority teenager wishes his skin was lighter or wishes her eyes were not slanted.

RACIAL SELF-ESTEEM

As self-esteem can be affected negatively by feeling bad about our ethnic and racial features, so our self-esteem can suffer merely because we feel uncomfortable about being different from the majority. In this sense then, adolescents from racial minorities always carry the additional burden with them of standing out and being noticed instead of simply being able to relax as an indistinguishable part of the crowd. As one adolescent puts it: "I did not want to be different from everybody else. My parents wanted me to not just accept the fact that I was Korean, but to embrace it. I wanted to ignore it" (Garrod & others, 1992, p. 96). Sadly, most minority teenagers are not yet free from feeling a certain degree of discomfort, stress, or stigma associated with not being white, even when their families are well-educated and financially well-off (Blea, 1992; Hacker, 1992; Martinez & Dukes, 1991; Ramirez, 1990; Sue, 1991).

This is not to imply that every teenager's self-esteem is negatively affected simply because he or she is a member of a racial minority. To the contrary, some adolescents feel a great deal of racial or ethnic pride. For example, between 1970 and 1990, the number of people claiming to be of Native American ancestry nearly doubled (Hacker, 1992). Or as one African American college student proudly explains, "Members of my family have always carried themselves with a sense of arrogance and I do not mean this in a bad light. I am a young black man, socialized by elite white institutions, very aware of the racism that surrounds me, yet my perspective on life is one of empowerment and unfettered opportunity" (Garrod & others, 1992, p. 117).

Nevertheless, racism is still a reality that can undermine the self-esteem of even the most well-educated, self-assured minority youth. As one African American college student explains, "If you're called a nigger, you are nothing. You could have eighty million books under your belt, all the degrees in the world. You could be that amazing. And with that word somebody takes it all away from you" (Glickman, 1993, p. 168). And as one of our nation's most renown scholars on racial issues concludes, "No matter how degraded their lives, white people are still allowed to believe that they possess the blood, the genes, and the patrimony of superiority" (Hacker, 1993, p. 217).

RACIAL STEREOTYPES

Although teenagers who are members of racial minorities usually share a lot in common in terms of the factors we've discussed, each group is also unique. More important, there are vast differences within every racial group in how adolescents think and behave based on economic differences. A family's income is usually more closely linked to what adolescents have in common with one another than is race. So before discussing some of the unique aspects of each racial group, it is extremely important that you remember that access to money, not racial issues, is what makes most groups different from each other. That is, adolescents whose families have about the same amount of money usually have more in common with each other than adolescents of the same race from widely different economic backgrounds. As one Native American teenager says, "It wasn't race that made me an outsider. It was poverty" (Garrod & others, 1992, p. 82). Keeping this in mind, let's turn our attention to some of the unique features of African, Hispanic, Native, and Asian American families—features closely linked to each group's general economic situation.

AFRICAN AMERICAN ADOLESCENTS

THE FAMILY

A number of changes have occurred in African American families that have a direct bearing on the lives of black adolescents. Two of the most important are the movement to the cities and the rapid rise in fatherless families (Hacker, 1992; Reed, 1993; Slaughter, 1990).

Unlike teenagers in their parents' generation, many black teenagers are now living in large urban areas rather than in rural communities. Half of all African American teenagers live in the South, constituting more than a third of the population in Mississippi, Louisiana, and South Carolina. But even in the South, more blacks are living in urban areas than ever before. This move to urban areas is unfortunate in that black teenagers are now more likely to live where crime, drugs, unemployment, and violence are the worst. The movement away from rural areas in search of jobs has also brought for many African American parents the hardship of separation from their extended families—a network of adults who offer one another spiritual, emotional, and financial support. Not only have extended families helped unmarried mothers raise their children, they also help married couples survive through hard financial times. Although some urban black parents talk nostalgically about going back home to the rural areas where their older relatives live, the reality is that by the year 2000 the vast majority of African American teenagers will be growing up in urban areas.

A second transformation in black families is the rapid rise in fatherless families. Compared to other races, black teenagers generally start having sex at an earlier age and have more out-of-wedlock babies. Before they are 18, 40% of black girls have become pregnant compared to only 20% of white girls. But half of the white girls terminate their pregnancies compared to only one third of the blacks. As a result, nearly 60% of black children are now living in a fatherless family. Families in which the teenage daughter, her child, and the child's grandmother all live together are becoming increasingly common. Often the grandmother, now only in her 30s, was herself an unmarried teenage mother. Upward of 20% of black adults are now taking care of children other than their own (Hacker, 1992).

Black families at all economic levels, however, are confronted with another problem—the scarcity of black males. Although male babies of all races are more likely than female babies to die from genetic problems or disease, black male infant death rates are among the highest in the country. Black males are also more likely than any other group of men to be murdered, to die from drugs, or to end up in prison. Unlike any other racial group, black females outnumber black males from adolescence on. To complicate matters further, the educational differences between males and females are also greatest among blacks. More than 80% of black females, but only 50% of black males, finish high school. For every 100 black women currently graduating from college, only 67 black men are graduating. In fact there are now more black males in prison than in college. What these differences mean is that black females with high-school diplomas or college degrees do not have as many males to date or to marry as do women of other races. Moreover, a black female has less chance than women from other races of marrying or dating outside her race. Thus most African American girls grow up knowing that their chances of marrying a black male with an education equal to their own are slim (Hacker, 1992; Williams, 1990).

STRENGTHS AND PROGRESS

Despite the many difficulties confronting them, African American families have made great advances. Not only are black adults more educated than ever before, they have shown remarkable persistence and strength coping with racism and economic hardship. Both in urban and rural areas, many African American parents are working together to improve their community and to supervise one another's children. Black mothers have worked together successfully to bring about improvements in their children's run-down urban schools (Winters, 1993). Likewise, a number of black men are not only taking care of their own children, but also are assuming the responsibility of helping to raise other people's children. The African American community has developed a unique form of communal networking referred to as "other mothers"—seeing all children as "our" children and working together as a community to improve all children's lives. Faced with the shortage of black men and poverty, black women have historically been resourceful and self-reliant in taking care of their families (Bell-Scott, 1991; Collins, 1991; Hacker, 1992; Hooks, 1993; Reed, 1993).

One of the chief sources of strength and leadership within the black community has been the church. Compared to other races, most African American teenagers and adults are more actively involved in their churches and turn to their church leaders more often for guidance and support. Black Americans are also the most likely to say they will follow their religious teachings rather than create a code of ethics to suit their own individual needs. Black churches have historically taken an active role in political and social issues, such as voter registration and desegregation, as well as in spiritual matters (Kosmin & Lachman, 1993; Patterson & Kim, 1992).

Finally, it is important to remember that African American families have survived an experience that is unique in scope and scale: Unlike wave upon wave of other immigrants, they did not come voluntarily to this country. They were not seeking fortune, religious freedom, or political opportunity, nor escaping war, fleeing poverty, or avoiding prosecution. African Americans were brought against their will, kidnapped, raped, beaten—then enslaved, if they were still alive. Stolen away from their homelands in vast numbers, they came without any expectation of ever being assimilated into American society. Despite this, black Americans have made remarkable progress. There are now more black political leaders, publicly recognized authors, successful film-makers, renown actors, and professionals than ever before—a reality that can serve as a source of pride and inspiration for their children (Hacker, 1992).

HISPANIC AMERICAN ADOLESCENTS

Most of the available statistics and research do not distinguish between various groups of Hispanic Americans, so you will have to keep this shortcoming in mind as we proceed. Part of the problem for researchers is that the terms *Hispanic*, *Latino*, and *Chicano* obscure the differences among the various groups from Spanish-speaking countries. And although they share a common language, depending on their country of origin, Hispanic Americans are very diverse in terms of their beliefs, values, and life-styles. For example, nearly 45% of Puerto Rican Americans are living in a fatherless family, compared to only 18% of Mexican Americans. Like African American teenagers, however, Hispanic Americans usually share several characteristics—their immigration, their Spanish language, and certain family roles and values (Augenbraum & Stavan, 1993; Blea, 1992; Busch-Rossnagel & Zayas, 1991; Sanchez, 1993).

IMMIGRANTS AND MIGRANTS

As noted at the beginning of this chapter, Hispanic American teenagers are more apt to be confronted with the kinds of racism or resentment associated with newly arriving immigrants. Although many Hispanic families have been in this country as long or longer than any other minorities except Native Americans, the fact that 90% of our immigrants are now from Hispanic countries has created resentment in certain parts of the United States. As a consequence, even teenagers whose families have been in this country for hundreds of years can be treated as though they are newly arrived, unwelcome immigrants. Because most Hispanic families at one time or another emigrated from Mexico, about 75% of these teenagers live in the Southwest. Those whose families are from Puerto Rico and other Caribbean countries live mainly in New York and Florida (U.S. Department of Commerce, 1992a).

Although only a small percentage of Hispanic Americans are involved in migrant work, 80% of all migrant workers are Hispanic. Nearly 800,000 children live in these migrant families. With their unsanitary living conditions, poor diets, low incomes, and the physical demands involved in doing "stoop" labor, these teenagers and their families are among the most poorly educated and physically ill people in our country. The typical migrant worker dies 20 years earlier than the average white American. Because their families move frequently and because they often have to work in the fields and orchards alongside their parents, these teenagers have a hard time keeping up in school. These parents usually are neither native speakers of English nor high-school graduates. So despite a great desire for their children to be well-educated, they often cannot help with school work or offer the kinds of experiences at home that enhance school achievement. In an effort to help these teenagers, some school districts send special tutors to migrant camps and offer toll-free telephone hotlines for counseling and referral services. Nationwide, schools are trying to make better use of computerized records that would enable teachers to keep better track of migrant students' skills and special needs. But with money in short supply, the task of helping migrant teenagers keep up academically is painstakingly slow and arduous (Augenbraum & Stavan, 1993; Sanchez, 1993).

LANGUAGE

Another problem for many Hispanic American adolescents is that English is a second language. Depending on how recently they have immigrated, their English skills range from excellent to nonexistent. For those children who are not bilingual, the language barrier can create social as well as academic problems. Not being able to converse on a level with others their age can leave Hispanic American students feeling socially stigmatized, as well as academically behind most people their age. Students with limited English proficiency are referred to as "**LEP**" students. In most schools they are provided with special instruction from bilingual teachers, but in smaller school systems or rural areas these students' special needs often cannot be met. These language difficulties help to explain why nearly half of our Hispanic teenagers drop out of high school before graduating.

In 1973 the Supreme Court ruled that public schools have to provide special programs for students who can't speak English. Nevertheless, the debate about how best to provide bilingual education continues, leaving politicians and educators disagreeing on such questions as: Should all classes be offered in both English and Spanish? What kind of training does a teacher need to meet the needs of Spanish-speaking students? How should we teach English to adolescents without making the curriculum or the teaching methods seem babyish (National Council of La Raza, 1992; Walsh, 1990)?

THE FAMILY

Most Hispanic American teenagers come from homes in which the family plays a more central role in children's lives than in most non-Hispanic households. Respecting and obeying your elders and yielding to your father's authority are part of the Hispanic family's cultural heritage. The extended family is also usually more involved in one another's lives than are those in many middle-class non-Hispanic families.

This kind of family structure has its benefits and drawbacks. On the positive side, the emphasis on obeying authority helps explain why some Hispanic American teenagers behave well at school and in the community—in order not to shame their family. On the negative side, the family's emphasis on obedience and conformity contributes to foreclosing their identities sooner than other teenagers. Rather than experimenting with different roles and values and defying some of their parents' wishes in order to form an identity of their own, Hispanic American youths tend to adopt their adult roles earlier in life. Especially for teenage girls, the emphasis on becoming a wife and mother can overshadow the development of intellectual and vocational skills. The family's traditional gender roles might also partly explain why Chicanas are less likely to have jobs and more likely to have large families than other females in our society (Augenbraum & Stavan, 1993; Busch-Rossnagel & Zayas, 1991; Sanchez, 1993).

As is true for all minorities, however, the longer Chicanos live in the United States, the more their families and gender roles adapt to the prevailing norms. Two Chicanas and their two mothers exemplify some of these changes. Cynthia's mother divorced her husband, worked in a factory by day, went to school at night, and raised three children. A feminist activist, Cynthia's mother also founded her community's Hispanic Women's Association. Another daughter, Luz, works 30 hours a week to put herself through college. Her mother, a social worker and leader of the local Hispanic Women's group, is upset, though, because Luz does not have a close identification with the Hispanic community. Luz, whose boyfriend is white, is annoyed that her mother is trying to push her closer to her Chicana heritage (Glickman, 1993).

NATIVE AMERICAN ADOLESCENTS

TRIBAL DISTINCTIONS

Native Americans constitute only 1% of our population, and their numbers are not increasing as are Hispanic and African Americans. But as is true for Hispanic Americans who have immigrated from different countries, Native Americans have many differences according to their tribal origin. Just as the terms *Hispanic* and *Chicano* obscure the differences between people who come from Mexico and those who come from Haiti, the term *Native American* obscures the differences between teenagers whose families come from different tribes. The nearly 500 different Indian tribes speak more than 200 separate languages and often have different political and economic concerns (Cornell, 1990).

THE FAMILY

Like other minorities, most Native Americans have moved away from rural areas to live in urban areas where jobs are more plentiful. Only one fourth of the Indian population still lives on reservations, and most of them are elderly people.

How accurate are your images of Native American adolescents?

Nearly half of all Native Americans live in Arizona, New Mexico, California, and Oklahoma—the state with the largest Native American population. Facing economic hardships without benefit of the support of their extended families and rural communities, many of these families have not found a better life in the cities. Almost 45% of Indian children now live in a single-parent household, and their poverty rates are among the highest of any race (U.S. Department of Commerce, 1992a).

Compared to all other races, Native American teenagers are more handicapped in several respects. The average adult has completed only 9 years of school, and nearly one third of the adults are illiterate. Only one fifth of the adult males have a high-school diploma. Not surprisingly then, Native Americans have a higher rate of poverty than any other race in the United States. Nearly 60% of all Native American children also suffer physically, economically, or psychologically from their parents' alcoholism. Nearly 40% of all deaths are alcohol related; nearly one fourth of the babies in some tribes are born with mental and physical defects from fetal alcohol syndrome; and more than half of all Indian teenagers abuse alcohol (Blum, 1992; Young, 1994).

Despite these hardships, many families try to encourage adolescents to adopt more of their traditional Native American ways and values. Traditionally the family has emphasized respect for the elderly, commitment and involvement in the local community, and a less self-centered style of relating to other people than is often found in our society at large. Talking too much about yourself, hurting others in order to get ahead, boasting about your accomplishments, and competing too aggressively at the expense of others are discouraged. While such cooperative, unselfish attitudes are admirable, they have inadvertently put many Indian students at a disadvantage in school. Because most teachers expect students to be outspoken, verbally assertive, competitive, and proud of their accomplishments, Native American students are often misperceived as being disinterested, shy, self-effacing, and lazy. Those educators who have come to understand these cultural differences, however, have designed their classroom activities in ways that do not put Native American students at such a disadvantage (Fedullo, 1994).

Although gender roles have traditionally been very conservative and restrictive, the younger generation is gradually being given more freedom. Exemplifying these changes, one daughter's mother graduated from college and supported her five children after her husband died of alcoholism at the age of 28. Now attending college herself, this daughter explains, "Everyone but the traditionals in the tribe were glad for me. As a young woman, I should have been starting a family. When Grandma told them I was going to college, they'd look away. But in my eyes, going to college wasn't going to make me less Indian or forget where I came from" (Garrod & others, 1992, p. 86).

ASIAN-AMERICAN ADOLESCENTS

THE MODEL MINORITY?

Although only 3% of our teenagers are Asian Americans, they have attracted national attention in most discussions about race and racism. Why? First, Asian Americans have distinguished themselves academically and professionally as one of the most successful groups in our society. Second only to Jewish Americans, Asian Americans as a group have outperformed whites and all other minorities in their educational achievements. In terms of the number of years completed in school, SAT and achievement scores, enrollments in advanced high-school classes, prestigious awards to high-school students, and college and professional degrees, Asian American teenagers are usually number one. This generally holds true even when they come from low-income families and even though nearly 40% of those taking the SAT test didn't speak English as their first language (NCES, 1991; Taylor, 1990).

Most Asian American teenagers live in the West, with almost half living in California and Hawaii. As a consequence of immigration from war-torn countries in Southeast Asia, our Asian American population tripled in size during the 1980s. Given how recently many of these families emigrated from non-English speaking countries, their accomplishments are even more impressive. So the question inevitably arises: Why have Asian Americans, like Jewish Americans, made so many advances in comparison with other minorities and native-born whites? In seeking answers to this question, of course, another question is also being addressed: Is there anything we can do as a society to help other minorities achieve as much as most Asian and Jewish Americans?

How closely is your definition of a "good looking" person based on Caucasian standards?

Before answering these questions, though, it is important to dispel several myths about Asian Americans. First, not all Asian Americans have made as many advances as the Japanese, Korean, and Chinese Americans. Many immigrants from Southeast Asia have not succeeded financially or academically in the United States. At least half of the Southeast Asian immigrants in California are on welfare, as are more than a third of all Vietnamese families nationwide. A number of these adolescents are still struggling to learn English and to overcome the psychological scars from the horrors of war (Ramirez, 1990).

Second, Japanese and Chinese Americans are not "model minorities" when it comes to how they have been treated in the United States. Although most Asian Americans are models of rapid progress and assimilation into our society, during the early part of this century, hostility, violence, and racism grew as the numbers of Japanese and Chinese immigrants steadily increased. During this period, we passed laws preventing these immigrants from owning property, marrying outside their race, attending white schools, and voting. We also harassed and feared them for speaking their native languages and practicing their religions. Following the bombing of Pearl Harbor and the subsequent war with Japan, the U.S. government forced 110,000 Japanese Americans to leave their homes, close their businesses, and move to fenced prison camps that were euphemistically referred to as **"relocation centers."** These Japanese Americans were imprisoned until the end of World War II, leaving most of them bankrupt. Italian and German Americans were not similarly imprisoned, harassed, or persecuted, even though their native countries were also enemies of the United States during the war.

Long Before World War II, in 1924, we banned Asian immigration. Not until long after the war, in 1954, did we allow them to receive citizenship. In short, there is not much that is "ideal" about the way Japanese and Chinese immigrants were treated in our country. Even today, Asian American teenagers still encounter racism in their schools and communities. They often feel discriminated against by colleges that limit their enrollment despite their higher qualifications; and many continue to suffer from the hurtful kinds of racism that other racial minorities also experience (Phillips, 1981).

In regard to education, some Asian American students still encounter another interesting form of stereotyping in their schools—being stereotyped as the quiet, mathematically inclined, "brainy types." Well-meaning teachers too often do a disservice by stereotyping their Asian students as being especially interested or talented in math and science and being weak or disinterested in other areas. Asian American students have shown remarkable talents in a wide variety of disciplines and skills. Since 1981 they have won 20 of the 70 scholarships awarded by the Westinghouse Science Talent Search, our nation's oldest and most prestigious high-school science competition. But they also account for 25% of the enrollment at the world famous Julliard School of the Arts. The point is that racial stereotypes, even when favorable, can create stress for those students who do not fit them. Racial stereotypes can also make Asian students feel socially isolated or ostracized when other teenagers perceive them only as "the brainy, quiet, somber type." As one Korean American teenager explains, "My high-school classmates tended to impute 'brain' status to me. I resented the fact that people saw me as 'quiet' but not much else. If only people really knew me, I thought to myself, they would see me not just as a quiet, smart person, but as a regular three dimensional individual" (Garrod, 1992, p. 96).

THE FAMILY

Part of the explanation for the success of so many Asian American adolescents lies in the values and habits they have learned at home—characteristics associated with being a "model" minority in our society. Raised to be self-disciplined and respectful toward those in authority, many Asian American students have the skills and attitudes that make them successful in school and in the workplace. These children are also made to believe that their accomplishments or failures reflect on their entire family, not only on themselves. Unlike most other teenagers, Asian American students are often motivated to succeed and to be

**Insert
7–4**

Counseling Minority Adolescents

John, an Asian American, has been an excellent student during his first two years in college as an electrical engineering major. He first came to the counseling center because he was failing a course. John is also having headaches, stomach aches, and insomnia. But a physician found no physical cause for his symptoms.

The counselor found it hard to work with John because he wasn't very self-disclosing and responded to most questions with only very short, polite answers. John never expressed his feelings and saw his problem as academic only. After many months, however, John began to open up to his counselor. John admitted that he felt tense and guilty about coming for counseling because he didn't want to embarrass his family.

When the counselor convinced him that other Asian American students had come into counseling feeling the same way, John seemed to relax and become more self-disclosing. As it turned out, John had always felt pressured by his parents to be a top student. Feeling that he wouldn't be loved unless he made straight "A"s, John had spent most of his high-school and college years studying, at a high cost to his social life.

In fact, he feels awkward and far behind his peers socially. He has also harbored secret wishes for many years about becoming an artist, but chose engineering instead in order to please his parents. As his counseling continues, John continues to explore questions of self, race, and family upbringing: Who am I? How do I reconcile my own needs with what my Asian American parents want me to be?

Source: Adapted from D. Wing Sue (1981). *Counseling the culturally different.* New York: Wiley.

well-behaved and law-abiding out of their need not to shame and embarrass their entire family (Phillips, 1981).

Although these aspects of the family are beneficial, other traditional family values can create certain problems for young Asian Americans. Self-discipline and respect are sometimes carried to the extreme by obedient, restrained teenagers who do not feel relaxed enough to express their feelings or opinions to their parents or others in positions of authority. Too much self-restraint can also make it hard to be self-disclosing or physically affectionate with friends. Given the family's emphasis on self-restraint, they can be misperceived as stuck-up, aloof, emotionally distant, uptight, meek, uncaring, overly polite, or submissive. Finding it difficult to be outspoken and assertive can also be a handicap in social, academic, and work situations. As Insert 7–4 illustrates, some Asian American students need help becoming more outgoing, more expressive, and more unrestrained (Ramirez, 1990; Sue, 1991).

CONCLUSION

Nobody wants to be stereotyped on the basis of race. As we read more, meet new people, and expand our horizons, we need to remember not to replace old racial stereotypes with new ones—even though some of the new stereotypes might be positive. At the same time, we also want to appreciate our racial differences and to remember the role that money plays in creating commonalities and differences among people. As we have seen, when it comes to values, achievements, and behavior, adolescents from the same socioeconomic class generally share more in common than adolescents from the same race with widely different socioeconomic backgrounds. Race does play an important role in many aspects of adolescents' lives, however, regardless of income. Sadly, dealing with racism and stereotypes is still a part of many minority adolescents' lives in our society. Finally, those of us who are not members of a racial minority have to continue to recognize and to combat the sources of racism, such as poverty and educational inequities, that are so much a part of our fellow citizens' lives.

Review/Test Questions

1. How has our society changed in terms of race? Cite specific statistics.

2. Explain six ways in which racism affects many adolescents' lives. Give specific examples and statistics.

3. How do adolescents from various racial groups compare in terms of their education? Cite specific statistics from high school and college enrollments, SAT scores, and ability grouping.

4. In terms of percentages, how does each racial group compare in income and marital status?

5. How do various racial groups compare with regard to teenage pregnancy?

6. In what ways and for what reasons is racism against black teenagers unique from racism against other minorities?

7. Using three different economic measures, compare the wealth and the poverty among all racial groups. Then describe at least three different explanations for these economic differences.

8. In what ways are African, Native, and Hispanic American adolescents often unique?

9. What are the unique strengths and the special problems of each racial minority in our society today?

10. Citing specific percentages, how much educational progress has each minority group made in our society?

11. In what five ways are Asian American teenagers not the "model" minority?

12. How does being a recent immigrant affect adolescents and their families?

13. In what four ways is our research biased or inadequate in regard to minority adolescents and their families?

14. What are three pitfalls we need to avoid in studying or generalizing about minority youth?

15. What is ethnocentrism? Provide three specific examples in your explanation.

16. What is "racism?" Provide an example in each area: social, educational, sexual, verbal, physical, and economic.

17. How can race affect an adolescent's self-esteem?

18. What is an "ethnocentric" standard of beauty, and how can this negatively or positively affect adolescents of various races?

19. What are "relocation centers" and what role did they play in the lives of certain Asian American families?

20. How can the "traditional" values in Native, Hispanic, African, and Asian American teenagers' families help and hinder them?

Questions for Discussion and Debate

1. If you had to be of a race other than your own, which would you choose and why? Specifically, how do you think your new race would affect you both positively and negatively?

2. What examples of racism or racial stereotyping did you see around you as an adolescent? How did this affect you?

3. How ethnocentric are your standards of physical attractiveness for males and females? Be specific in terms of eyes, body build, skin color, hair, and facial features.

4. How do you think schools should accommodate students who speak no English or whose English skills are poor?

5. What information or statistics from this chapter made you feel most ashamed or angry? Why?

6. In what ways do you think you have benefited or paid a price for being a member of your race? How has this changed from early adolescence to now?

7. How do you feel about interracial dating, interracial marriage, and being close friends with someone from another race? How have these issues affected you or any of your friends?

8. If you were attending a high school and a college in which only 10% of the students and teachers were your race, how would this affect you? Be sure to consider dating, friendships, grades, the way you behave in class, the way you dress, and how you speak.

9. What do you admire most about each racial group discussed in this chapter? How would you feel about being an adolescent of that race during the 1990s?

10. In what ways have your racial attitudes and your behavior changed since your early adolescence? In what ways are they the same? Why?

Glossary

ethnocentrism, p. 253
LEP, p. 272

net worth, p. 256
relocation centers, p. 277

References

A.D.L. (1991). *Racism in America.* New York: Anti-Defamation League.

Adelson, J. (1980). *Handbook of adolescent psychology.* New York: Wiley.

American Psychological Association. (1993). *Violence and youth.* Washington, DC: Author.

Augenbraum, H., & Stavan, I. (1993). *Growing up Latino.* Boston: Houghton Mifflin.

Bane, J., & Ellwood, D. (1989). One fifth of the nation's children: Why are they poor? *Science, 245,* 1047–1053.

Bell-Scott, P. (1991). *Double stitch: Black women write about mothers and daughters.* New York: Harper Perennial.

Blea, I. (1992). *La Chicana.* Westport, CT: Praeger.

Blum, R. (1992). Indian American youths. *Journal of the American Medical Association, 68,* 135–142.

Busch-Rossnagel, N., & Zayas, L. (1991). Hispanic adolescents. In R. Lerner, A. Petersen & J. Brooks-Gunn (Eds.), *Encyclopedia of adolescence* (pp. 492–498). New York: Garland.

Children's Defense Fund. (1992). *Adolescent and young adult fact book.* Washington, DC: Author.

Collins, P. (1991). The meaning of motherhood in Black culture. In P. Bell-Scott (Ed.), *Double stitch: Black women write about mothers and daughters.* New York: Harper Perennial.

Cornell, S. (1990). *The return of the native: American Indian political resurgence.* Hillsdale, NJ: Erlbaum.

Cose, E. (1993). *The rage of a privileged class.* New York: HarperCollins.

Darder, A. (1991). *Culture and power in the classroom.* Westport, CT: Greenwood Press.

Fedullo, M. (1994). *Light of the feather: A teacher's journey into Native American classrooms and culture.* New York: Doubleday.

Fisher, C. (1991). *Ethics in applied developmental psychology.* New York: Abelex.

Fox, R. (1994). *The challenge of anthropology.* New Brunswick, NJ: Transaction.

Fuchs, V., & Reklis, D. (1992). America's children: Economic perspective & policy options. *Science, 255,* 41–46.

Garrod, A., Smulyan, L., Powers, S., & Kilkenny, R. (1992). *Adolescent portraits.* Boston: Allyn & Bacon.

Gates, H. (1992). *Loose canons: Notes on the culture wars.* New York: Oxford University Press.

Gibbs, J. (1991). Black adolescents. In R. Lerner, A. Petersen, & J. Brooks-Gunn (Eds.), *Encyclopedia of adolescence* (pp. 73–78). New York: Garland.

Glickman, R. (1993). *Daughters of feminists.* New York: St. Martin's.

Guthrie, R. (1976). *Even the rat was white: A historical view of psychology.* New York: Harper & Row.

Hacker, A. (1992). *Two nations: Black and white, separate, hostile, unequal.* New York: Charles Scribner's.

Harding, S. (1993). *The racial economy of science.* Bloomington: Indiana University Press.

Hart Research (1992). *Young Americans' racial views.* Washington, DC: People for the American Way.

Hispanic Health Coalition (1978). *Hispanic mental health bibliography.* Los Angeles: University of California.

Hooks, B. (1993). *Sisters of the yam: Black women and self-recovery.* Boston: South End Press.

House Select Committee (1987). *Race relations and adolescents.* Washington, DC: U.S. Congress.

Johnston, L., O'Malley, P., & Bachman, J. (1993). *National survey results on drug use:*

1975–1992. Rockville, MD: National Institute on Drug Abuse.

Khiev, V. (1992, April 27). Breaking the bonds of hate. *Newsweek*, p. 8.

Kim, H. (1991). Do you have eyelashes? In C. Gilligan, A. Rogers, & D. Tolman (Eds.), *Women, girls and psychotherapy* (pp. 201–213). New York: Haworth.

Klein, J. (1993, August 9). The education of Berenice Belizaire. *Newsweek*, p. 26.

Kosmin, R., & Lachman, S. (1993). *One nation under God.* New York: Harmony.

Kozol, J. (1991). *Savage inequalities: Children in American's schools.* New York: HarperCollins.

Ladner, J. (1971). *Tomorrow's tomorrow: The black woman in America.* New York: Anchor.

Lapchick, R. (1991). *Youth attitudes on racism.* Chicago: Northwestern University Press.

Larson, R. (1990). The solitary life. *Developmental Review, 10,* 155–183.

Martinez, R., & Dukes, R. (1991). Ethnic and gender differences in self-esteem. *Youth and Society, 22,* 318–338.

Morganthau, T. (1993, August 9). America: Still a melting pot? *Newsweek*, pp. 16–26.

Morton, P. (1991). *Disfigured images: The historical assault on Afro-American women.* Westport, CT: Greenwood Press.

Moynihan, P. (1965). *The Negro family: Case for national action.* Washington, DC: Department of Labor.

National Center for Education Statistics. (1991). *Ability grouping by race.* Washington, DC: Author.

National Center for Education Statistics. (1994). *Dropout rates in the U.S. in 1993.* Washington, DC: Author.

National Commission on Children. (1993). *Just the facts: A summary of recent information on America's children and their families.* Washington, DC: Author.

National Council of La Raza. (1992).

Hispanic American youth. Washington, DC: Author.

Patterson, J., & Kim, P. (1992). *The day America told the truth.* New York: Plume.

Phillips, V. (1981). *The abilities and achievements of Orientals in North America.* Beverly Hills, CA: Sage.

Ramirez, M. (1990). *Psychotherapy and counseling with minorities.* Riverside, NJ: Pergamon.

Reed, W. (1993). *Research on the African American family.* Westport, CT: Greenwood Press.

Roberts, S. (1994). *Who we are: Statistical profile of the U.S.* New York: Times Books.

Robinson, T., & Ward, J. (1991). Cultivating resistance among African American female adolescents. In C. Gilligan, A. Rogers, & D. Tolman (Eds.), *Women, girls, and psychotherapy* (pp. 87–104). New York: Hayworth.

Ryan, W. (1972). *Blaming the victim.* New York: Random House.

Sanchez, G. (1993). *Becoming Mexican American.* Hillsdale, NJ: Erlbaum.

Schiebinger, L. (1993). *Nature's body: Gender in the making of modern science.* Boston: Beacon Press.

Slaughter, D. (1990). *Black children and poverty.* San Francisco, CA: Jossey Bass.

Smith, T. (1991). *Racial attitudes: A national survey.* Chicago: University of Chicago.

Staples, R. (1982). *Black masculinity.* San Francisco: Black Scholars Press.

Sue, D.W. (1991). *Counseling the culturally different.* New York: Wiley.

Taylor, D. (1990, October 7). Asian-American test scores. *Education Week*, p. 8.

U.S. Department of Commerce. (1992a). *Population reports: Marital status & living arrangements.* Washington, DC: Bureau of the Census.

U.S. Department of Commerce. (1992b). *General population characteristics: Poverty in the U.S.* Washington, DC: Bureau of the Census.

U.S. Department of Commerce. (1993). *Population estimates by age, sex, race & Hispanic origin*. Washington, DC: Bureau of the Census.

Viadero, D. (1989). Schools witness troubling revival of bigotry. *Education Week, 35*, 1.

Wade, J. (1991). Race and sex differences in adolescent self perceptions of attractiveness and self-esteem. *Personality and Individual Differences, 27*, 552–565.

Walsh, C. (1990). *Pedagogy and the struggle for voice*. Westport, CT: Greenwood Publishing.

West, C. (1994). *Race matters*. New York: Random House.

Williams, C. (1990). *Black teenage mothers: Pregnancy and child rearing from their perspective*. New York: Lexington Books.

Winters, W. (1993). *African American mothers and urban schools*. New York: Free Press.

Young, T. (1994). *The health of Native Americans*. Hillsdale, NJ: Erlbaum.

8

ADOLESCENTS AND THEIR FAMILIES

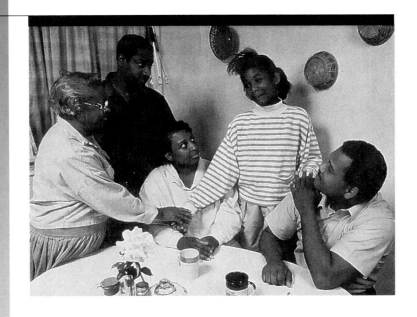

CHAPTER OUTLINE

KEY QUESTIONS ADDRESSED IN THIS CHAPTER

1. How stressful is adolescence for most families?
2. How do fathers and mothers affect their sons' and daughters' development?
3. How does each parent's marital happiness affect adolescents?
4. How alike are siblings and how does family size and birth order affect adolescents?
5. How do our society's traditional beliefs about mothering and fathering affect adolescents?
6. In what ways does a mother's employment affect adolescents?
7. How have changes in our economy affected adolescents?
8. Why are more adolescents living in poverty than ever before?
9. How do most adolescents' relationships with their mothers and fathers differ?
10. What factors contribute to the sexual and physical abuse of children?

Families in our society have changed in at least three ways that have dramatically affected the lives of adolescents. First, most families today are poorer than in the past 40 years (U.S. Dept. of Commerce, 1992). Second, more couples are divorcing and remarrying than at any previous time in our country's history. Third, more mothers have jobs outside the home than ever before. The result of these changes is that teenagers today are more likely than ever to be living in poverty, with their unmarried mother or in a blended family with a stepparent, or in a family headed by two employed adults who are struggling to make ends meet. And virtually all teenagers have grown up in homes with a mother who has always had a job outside the home.

So one question we explore in this chapter and in Chapter 9 is: How have these changes in our society affected adolescents for better or for worse? We also examine two of the most popular questions asked by social scientists about families: How are most adolescents getting along with their parents? How do mothers and fathers influence their sons' and daughters' development during adolescence?

ADOLESCENCE AS A FAMILY CRISIS?

PARENT–ADOLESCENT CONNECTIONS

Many parents worry that their teenage children are going to reject most of their family's values and disconnect emotionally from the family. Many parents also fear that their family is going to have to endure a major upheaval and crisis until the teenage years have passed. Despite these fears, this isn't the reality for most adolescents and their parents.

To begin with, when it comes to values and choices involving education, political views, religion, drug use, future jobs, and prejudice, most adolescents do reflect their parents' values. Even during the 1960s when it was widely believed that college students who were protesting against the Vietnam War were rebelling against their parents, the fact was that most of the protesters reflected the very values their parents had instilled in them (Yankelovich, 1981). It's true, however, that most adolescents are influenced mainly by other teenagers when it comes to such "values" as how they dress, the music they listen to, how they style their hair, and opinions about curfews or borrowing the family car. But even then, most teenagers choose to associate with peers who are from the same kinds of family backgrounds as themselves. It's not as likely for teenagers to be "led astray" by another adolescent who has nothing in common with them as it is for "birds of a feather to flock together." Despite their hairstyles, nose rings, baggy jeans, and other fads that come and go, teenagers' most important choices and values usually turn out to be pretty much like their parents', affirming the old adage that "the acorn doesn't fall far from the tree" (Hartup & Overhauser, 1991; Offer & Church, 1991; Savin-Williams & Berndt, 1990).

The fear that teenage children will disconnect from their parents and stepparents is also generally unfounded. Adolescents don't spend as much time with

What were most meal times like in your family?

their parents as when they were younger, and they are much more private in terms of how much they want to share about their lives. But if they've had close relationships with parents during childhood, they won't necessarily turn away or disconnect emotionally simply because they've become teenagers. In fact, most of us as teenagers have about the same type of relationship with the adults in our families that we had with them as younger children. Becoming more self-reliant and developing an identity of our own doesn't require rejecting our parents or their values. So the bad news is that if a teenager and parent are having a hard time getting along or don't feel especially close to each other, they probably had pretty much the same kind of relationship in the 12 years that preceded adolescence. But the good news is that the vast majority of teenagers and parents or stepparents do get along well and feel loved by one another (Baumrind, 1991; Flannery, Torquati, & Lindemeier, 1994; Harter, 1990; Hauser, Powers, & Noam, 1991; Steinberg, 1990).

Then why do so many of us have the impression that teenagers reject their parents? In part, our misconceptions come from the lasting—yet unfounded—concern from the college protesters in the 1960s and early 1970s that young people are inevitably bound to turn against their elders. Also, most adolescents and their parents do disagree and argue about matters related to their personal habits and social lives. Because these disagreements tend to be most intense in the first year or two of adolescence, adults might fear that things are only going to become worse as their teen grows older. In fact though, adults and teenagers usually get along better in middle and late adolescence. Granted, much of the arguing that takes place is stressful, and these disagreements can leave parents and stepparents feeling that they aren't being respected or appreciated. But the fact remains that most adolescents do feel emotionally connected and loved by the adults in their family (Clark-Lempers, Lempers, & Ho, 1991; Fine, Donnelly, & Voydanoff, 1991).

CAUSES OF ARGUMENTS

Although it's not much fun for anyone, arguing with our parents and stepparents is actually a necessary part of becoming self-reliant and developing an identity of our own (Baumrind, 1991; Hauser, Powers, & Noam, 1991). By asserting and defending our own opinions, differentiating our thoughts from those of our parents, and respecting the rights of others to disagree with us, we're learning how to think for ourselves without cutting our ties to those we love. What are most of us as adolescents arguing about with our parents? Politics and religion? No. Educational decisions and future vocations? No. Our table manners, hairstyles, clothes, curfews, messy bedrooms, rules for dating and using the car, allowance, loud music, and the junk food we eat? Yes. Underlying most of these arguments is the issue of freedom versus responsibility. On the one hand, parents aren't willing to grant teenagers as much freedom as teenagers think they're old enough to handle. On the other hand, most teenagers aren't willing enough to assume responsibility for the consequences of their own decisions (Borrine, 1991; Leaper, 1989; Offer & Church, 1991; Shave & Shave, 1989).

Because most adolescents spend much more time around their mother than their father, they usually argue more with her (Steinberg, 1990; Youniss & Smollar, 1985). Interestingly, when fathers spend more time with their teenage children, they start to argue with them more—yet they say they feel closer to one another because they're spending more time together (Almeida & Galambos, 1991). But regardless of which parent we argue with more, we generally disagree less after the first year or two of adolescence. During early adolescence, families have to put more time into negotiating the new rules and the roles that parent and child will play. Nevertheless, adolescents usually say that most of their stress comes from their peers, not from their parents or stepparents (Clark-Lempers, Lempers, & Ho, 1991; Colten, Gore, & Aseltine, 1991; Compas & Wagner, 1991; Dornbusch & others, 1991; Larson & Asmussen, 1991).

RESOLVING ARGUMENTS

How do most adolescents, parents, and stepparents resolve most of their arguments? Think back to your own adolescence. If yours was like most families, most of your arguments with the adults either ended in a standoff in which nobody won, or somebody walked away without anything being resolved. Most adults try to build the case for their side by arguing for what is socially correct or conventional, and most teenagers see arguments in terms of personal freedom and personal jurisdiction. For example, in an argument about homework and television, the adult is more likely to focus on the issues of hard work and self-discipline: "Why aren't you mature and self-disciplined enough to watch less TV and do what it takes to pull up your grades?" Meanwhile, the adolescent is focused on an altogether different issue—freedom. "My personal freedom is at stake here because I should be given the right to decide what to do with my time." Because adults and adolescents tend to be reacting to entirely different issues, their discussions often get them nowhere. Although they're discussing the same situation, they're not discussing the same issues (Smetana, Yau, Restrepo, & Braeges, 1991).

Most adults also find it easier to resolve conflicts with teenage girls than with teenage boys. Girls are generally more willing to listen, to talk things over, to compromise, and to apologize. So how much stress a family goes through during adolescence might often depend on whether the child is a son or a daughter. For reasons discussed in earlier chapters, boys generally have more trouble than girls getting along with their peers and with their families both during childhood and during adolescence (Asher & Coie, 1990; Lamb, 1994; Petersen, Kennedy, & Sullivan, 1991; Robins & Rutter, 1990).

FATHERS, MOTHERS, AND DISCIPLINE

How well adolescents and their parents or stepparents are getting along also depends on how each adult has disciplined children in the preceding years. Adolescents who are more socially and psychologically well-adjusted and mature have usually been raised by adults who use a democratic style of parenting. Adults who have been loving, yet consistently firm, generally have an easier time relating to their teenagers and enforcing rules than adults who have been dictatorial, indifferent, or indulgent. Remember that democratic parenting also contributes to adolescents' getting along well with their peers, doing well in school, becoming self-reliant, and staying out of serious trouble (Baumrind, 1991; Cooper & Cooper, 1992; Harter, 1990; Hauser, Powers, & Noam, 1991; Steinberg & others, 1991).

When it comes to discipline, in most families fathers have more control than mothers, especially with sons and especially during adolescence. In part this happens because mothers are more likely than fathers to be indulgent or overly protective with children as they're growing up. Mothers are also more likely to become enmeshed and to reverse roles with one of their children—situations stemming from early childhood that lead to a teenager's being immature, dependent, undisciplined, and hard to control. The father's greater control might also come in part from his almost always having more financial power and higher status in the world beyond the family. But for whatever the reason in any particular family, adolescents and their parents usually agree that their father has more control over them than their mother does (Baumrind, 1991; Montemayor & Flannery, 1991; Patterson, Reid, & Dishion, 1992; Steinberg, 1990).

MARITAL HAPPINESS AND ADOLESCENT WELL-BEING

How well adolescents get along with their parents, stepparents, and peers is also linked to the nature of the marriage itself. For instance, adolescents whose parents are happily married are more flexible, more adaptable, and more self-controlled than those living with unhappily married parents (Fleeson, 1991). Adolescents living with adults who relate well to each other are also less hostile, less cynical, less impatient, and less rigid than those whose parents are at odds with each other (McDonough & Cooper, 1994). The parent who is happily married contributes a great deal to a teenager's social, academic, and psychological well-being. In general, adolescents who have been raised by two happily married adults have fewer social, psychological, and academic problems than those raised by unhappily married adults (Blechman, 1990; Cowan & Cowan, 1992; Hinde & Stevenson, 1995; Parke & Ladd, 1992; Robins & Rutter, 1990; Sigel, McGillicuddy, & Goodnow, 1992).

The effects of living with an unhappily married parent appear well before adolescence. For instance, 2-year-olds with unhappily married parents tend to have mothers who are overly involved and overly dependent on them, and fathers who are distant, critical, and punitive. During early childhood, these children are usually more withdrawn, more aggressive, more immature, and more unpopular than children living with happily married parents (Cohn, Patterson, & Christopoulos, 1991; Cowan & Cowan, 1992; Strassberg & others, 1992; Youngblade & Belsky, 1992). But how does marital happiness affect children's development? Why are the two connected? The answers to these questions seem to lie in four areas: the father's withdrawal and punitiveness, the mother's overinvolvement, the strength of generational boundaries, and the mother's mental health.

When parents aren't happily married, they not only tend to react more negatively toward one another, but also they react toward the children in ways that interfere with their development. Fathers tend to withdraw or to become overly critical and overly punitive; and unhappily married mothers tend to be overly critical of the way the husband relates to the children, often openly mocking or disagreeing with him. Thus a father's unhappy marriage often interferes with his establishing close bonds to his children. In fact, one of the best ways to predict how involved a father will be in his children's lives is marital happiness (Biller, 1993; Cowan & Cowan, 1992; Parke & Ladd, 1992; Snarey, 1993; Warshak, 1992).

Meanwhile, the mother is likely to turn to one of her children in search of the intimacy that is lacking in her marriage. Gradually the mother might actually reverse roles with her son or daughter, giving the child the responsibility for being her confidante, best friend, or counselor. When unhappily married mothers become overly involved in their children's lives, the children often become aligned with her against their father—the triangulation discussed in earlier chapters. That is, when a mother isn't happily married, at least one of her children is likely to end up continually siding with her against the father (Hinde & Stevenson, 1995; Minuchin & Nichols, 1994). Not surprisingly, parents who are not happily married also tend to baby their teenage and young adult children and to discourage them from leaving home (White & Edwards, 1990).

These findings on marital happiness apply not only when our parents are married to one another, but also when they're divorced and married to other people. A divorced parent who is happily remarried is usually more helpful and more cooperative in seeing to it that the children have a close relationship with their other parent. But when the divorced parent hasn't remarried or is unhappy in the second marriage, he or she often works against the children's maintaining a good relationship with the other parent. So a parent who isn't happily remarried is at greater risk of having teenagers who wind up feeling distant or totally alienated from one parent—usually their father (Biller, 1993; Furstenberg & Cherlin, 1991; Kalter, 1990; Maccoby & Mnookin, 1993; Snarey, 1993; Warshak, 1992).

Interestingly, marital happiness seems to be more closely related to the son's overall well-being than to the daughter's. Unhappily married parents fight and argue more in front of their son and directly involve him in more of their disagreements. As discussed in more detail later, the son's social and psychological problems also seem to be more closely tied to the mother's moods and happiness than are the daughter's. In this sense then, the quality of the parents' marriage might be even more important for sons than for daughters (R. Emery, 1989; Forehand, 1991; Hetherington, 1991; Maccoby, 1990; Wallerstein, 1991).

Briefly, let's look at one study that illustrates how adolescents are affected by their parents' marital happiness. An ironic pattern was noticed in a group of extremely introverted, socially isolated, submissive teenagers. Away from home these shy, lonely teenagers were meek, quiet, unassuming, and withdrawn. But at home they were generally hostile, outspoken, aggressive, and demanding. Why this "Dr. Jeckyl–Mr. Hyde" behavior? As it turned out, these teenagers had shared several characteristics since early childhood. First, their parents had been unhappily married since the children were very young. Second, their mothers were depressed, chronically unhappy women, often acting as though they were helpless victims of life and powerless martyrs in the marriage—the external locus of control attitudes that characterize depressed people. Third, these teenagers had been relating to their mothers in enmeshed, overly protective ways since they were 3 or 4 years old. Then why were they so hostile and demanding around their mothers? It seems that each mother's depression and portrayal of herself as a victimized, powerless person—particularly in regard to the father—made these children feel responsible from a very early age for making their mother happy and for protecting her somehow from their father. Yet as they were growing up, each child resented being triangulated into these marital problems and resented the mother for being so preoccupied with her own unhappiness. In an effort to make their mothers happy, these shy children withdrew even further from the world outside their families, failed to develop social skills appropriate for someone their age, and became increasingly demanding and hostile at home as a way of getting their mothers to attend to them—an early childhood adaptation to their parents' unhappy marriages, which only worsened as these shy children aged (Waxler & others, 1992).

ADOLESCENTS AND THEIR SIBLINGS

Although our parents' marital happiness is important, our development as teenagers is also affected by our siblings. Three of the questions about siblings that have been popular with social scientists are: How does birth order and the number of children in a family affect a child's development? How are children without siblings different from other children? How alike are siblings?

Does it matter whether you were born first or last in your family? In terms of each child's development, does it matter whether we have one sibling or five? According to confluence theory, the answer is yes. **Confluence theory** maintains that our birth order and the number of siblings we have is related to our intelligence, academic success, and vocational achievements. For example, the oldest child will usually enjoy certain advantages over younger siblings because parents tend to give their first child more attention. Likewise, if parents wait a few years before having another child, the two children will be more alike in terms of their school achievements and later vocational accomplishments. Confluence theorists contend that children born first and children with fewer siblings have better prospects in terms of their IQ scores, grades, and level of education completed, as well as future job status and income (Smith, 1989; Zajonc, 1983).

In large part, these advantages can be explained by their receiving more attention which, in turn, seems to help them develop social and intellectual skills. On the other hand, well-educated, financially comfortable parents usually have fewer children than more poorly educated, lower-income parents. Their children's superior intellectual and social skills, therefore, might primarily be a result of their having had the opportunities that money can buy—music lessons, computers, travel, tutors, and so on—rather than an actual difference in how their parents interacted with them.

So even though we don't really know why, birth order and number of siblings are correlated with school performance and success in the workplace. Some confluence theorists even believe that the ups and downs in our nation's SAT scores are related to increases and decreases in family size. SAT scores rose in the 1980s when students taking the tests came from smaller families than those taking the test in the 1960s and 70s (Zajonc, 1983). But as intriguing as confluence theories are (especially if you're the first-born child from a small family, right?), the statistics on which they're based are only correlational. They can't be used to prove cause and effect.

Adolescents Without Siblings

If, as confluence theory suggests, having too many brothers and sisters is a disadvantage, then what about having no siblings? Is it an advantage to be the only child in a family? In many ways, yes. In terms of IQ scores, grades, achievement tests, and social adjustment, the child without siblings often seems to end up ahead of children with siblings. For example, although many people still assume that a child without siblings is going to be spoiled or socially inept, teenagers without siblings are not more socially immature, self-centered, or difficult to get along with. Although the only child does spend more time playing alone, he or she doesn't report feeling any lonelier. When differences do emerge, teenagers without siblings often come out ahead in terms of their grades, social skills, psychological adjustment, and achievements in school and in the workplace (Boer & Dunn, 1992; Veenhoven & Verkuyten, 1989).

SIMILARITIES BETWEEN SIBLINGS

Social scientists, like most of us, have also been curious about how alike or how different siblings are. These studies show us a few rather surprising things about ourselves and our siblings (Boer & Dunn, 1992; Dunn & Plomin, 1989).

Interestingly, most of us don't have as much in common with our brothers or sisters as we might assume in terms of our personalities, our interests, or our achievements. For example, one way in which siblings are most alike is their intelligence test scores, yet the correlation is a relatively low .35–50. Put differently, the average difference between siblings' IQ scores is 13 points compared to an average of 18 points between strangers. When we look at personality, attitudes, or psychological problems, the similarities between siblings are even fewer.

How can this be? If we're raised in the same home and have the same biological parents, why aren't we more like our brothers or sisters? Part of the answer is that we don't necessarily have much in common genetically with our siblings. Since we get only half of our genes from each parent, and since these genes can combine in countless unique patterns, the odds of our being very similar genetically to our siblings are actually pretty slim. Second, growing up in the same family isn't the same as growing up in the same environment. Our experiences and how we relate to each parent are different, even though we're living under the same roof.

Moreover, as already noted, our personalities at birth do influence the way our parents relate to us and the ways we react to them. For instance, maybe your sister has a genetic predisposition toward hostile, aggressive behavior, but you have a genetic predisposition toward a more laid-back, easy-going temperament. So when your parent comes home and yells at both of you for leaving the kitchen a mess, your sister responds by exploding which, in turn, causes your parent to become even angrier. You, on the other hand, grin sheepishly and clean up your part of the mess; and your parent, in turn, is in a good mood around you for the rest of the evening. But seeing that your parent isn't mad at you anymore, your sister becomes even angrier and sets in motion another different set of experiences for you and her. In any event, we're much less like our siblings than many of us might initially assume.

DEFINING MOTHERS' AND FATHERS' ROLES

What determines how close children will be to their fathers by time they reach adolescence? Why is it that most teenagers know their mother better than their father and feel closer to her? What is it that makes most adolescents' relationships with their mothers and fathers so different? In answering such questions, we might look in four directions: the cultural expectations that affect our laws, traditions, and policies; biased research; the mother's attitudes; and the father's attitudes.

CULTURAL EXPECTATIONS AND POLICIES

One of the reasons why adolescents usually have such different relationships with their mothers and fathers is our society's particular definitions of those roles. Since the turn of the century, we have based our national policies, social customs, policies in the workplace, laws, and our behavior in our families on two pervasive beliefs: The mother's relationship with children is more important than the father's; and the father's chief contribution to his children is money. How do these assumptions filter into our family lives and affect our relationships with our fathers?

First, the assumption about each parent's role shapes the policies and laws we have chosen to establish for ourselves in the workplace: Which parent is typically given the greater freedom to leave work for a sick child or to attend a child's school events? Why are workplaces and work schedules not arranged so that preschool children can be given more care by their fathers? Now turn your attention to our legal system: Which parent has traditionally been awarded custody of children after a divorce? What assumptions about fathers underlie these legal decisions? These same assumptions about fathers are also reflected in our federal legislation: Why haven't we enacted any federal policy, as have other industrialized nations, allowing fathers time off work to attend to their newborns or to care for their sick children?

Second, our expectations for each parent are influenced by the belief that instinct or natural know-how somehow make all females better at caring for the young and all males better at earning money. But if we look at historical and cross-cultural data, the evidence for defining our roles as we do on the argument of instinct or "what nature intended" isn't very convincing. Remember that our society's definitions of the good mother and father are only one among many ways that human beings have chosen to define these two roles throughout time. For example, in many hunting-gathering societies, after weaning the infant, the mother returns to her major adult role in the community as a worker who gathers food. Older boys and girls, not the mother, care for young children. Likewise, in agrarian societies it's considered "natural" that older women in the community, not the child's mother, should provide most of the childcare (Silverstein, 1991).

Third, fathers' and mothers' roles are redefined partly in response to economic changes such as industrialization, wars, and recessions. For instance, in colonial America it was the fathers, not the mothers, who were considered more necessary for the moral and intellectual upbringing of children. Unlike fathers in recent decades, colonial fathers were almost always granted legal custody of their children after a divorce, and books and advice on child rearing were addressed to them, not to the mothers. The father's wisdom in understanding and nurturing the young was generally considered superior to the mother's. But as our country became more industrialized, taking men's work farther from their homes, we began to redefine fathers' and mothers' roles. The good father then became the man who provided most for his children by earning money. And the good mother was the woman who took charge of the children's academic and moral training. As the father's role was redefined by these economic changes, he came to be seen more as the intruding, less-competent parent whose value was determined less by how well he related to his children than by the financial status he achieved in the world beyond his family (Griswold, 1993).

Fourth, each society's expectations for mothers and fathers at any given point in history can be shaped by political or philosophical concerns more than by what's in the best interest of children. For example, in England and in our country, as the birth rate of the white, middle-class began to decline, concerns arose that "civilization" would be jeopardized by the high birth rates of blacks and immigrants from southern and eastern Europe. In reaction, a number of politicians and clergymen began to glorify motherhood in an attempt to encourage white, middle-class women to have more children. The good mother stayed home and the good father stayed away from home making money. Reinforcing these attitudes, childcare experts during the 1960s and 1970s, such as Dr. Benjamin Spock, based their advice to parents on the assumption that what happens to a child is determined mainly by what the mother does or does not do. The idea that mothering is a full-time job or a profession that justifies keeping mothers out of the work force came about as industrialization forced people to move to cities, as the extended family dissolved, and as fears became more prevalent about the white, middle-class having too few children (Silverstein, 1991).

Biased Research

These beliefs about mothers' and fathers' roles also influenced the research in the social sciences—research that affects the advice that counselors, teachers, and friends have given to parents. Until the 1980s, most researchers proceeded on the foregone conclusion that the mother-child relationship was the one that really counted. As a result, very few researchers were collecting data on the impact fathers have on adolescents or younger children, other than to note the effects of growing up without a father in a single-mother household. Only in the 1980s did social scientists really begin to give careful consideration to the father's importance beyond his role as a breadwinner (Lamb, 1989).

Perhaps one of the most damaging results of having ignored fathers for so long has been the tendency to blame mothers for whatever problems their children develop. Because social science research reflected our society's belief that the mother has more power to shape the child's development, she has tended to get not only most of the credit, but also most of the blame, for how the child turns out. For example, a survey of 577 published studies from the 1970s showed that 72 different kinds of psychopathology in children were blamed on mothers and none on fathers. Although the mother's interactions with their children were examined in about 75% of the studies, only about 50% of the studies included any information about the father (Caplan, 1989). More recent surveys indicate only minor improvements in terms of studying the father's impact on his children's development (Phares & Compas, 1992).

Ignoring fathers in our research is especially sad and distressing in light of the research we *do* have, which shows that fathers play an extremely important role in their children's development. Cross-cultural research points to the benefits of the father's active parenting, especially during infancy and early childhood. Societies in which fathers are expected to be actively involved with infants generally have more positive attitudes about the rights of women and children, as well as fewer crimes against property and people, including child abuse and family violence. Societies that exclude fathers from infant care also have more children who grow up overly dependent on their mothers. Boys deprived of their fathers early in life are also likely to engage in rigid, exaggerated forms of masculinity such as delinquency, aggression, and defiance (Biller, 1993; Bozett & Hanson, 1991). But until our research focuses as much on fathers as it does on mothers, we will continue to act as though fathers are less important than mothers, except that men should continue to be the primary breadwinners for their families.

THE MOTHER'S ATTITUDES

The closeness between adolescents and their fathers also depends in part on the mothers' attitudes about mothering and fathering. Almost all women in our country have been socialized to believe that a good mother is the children's primary source of comfort, compassion, intimacy, and nurturance. As a result, many women derive a great deal of self-esteem from how well they, and they alone, meet their children's emotional needs. This is especially true in the socialization of white, middle-class females who usually see mothering in more exclusive, possessive ways than in other socioeconomic or cultural groups. For example, black Americans have a more expansive, less possessive view of mothering—the view that nurturing and raising children is a communal responsibility, not only the biological mother's domain. Indeed, the African American community's concept of "other-mothers" is that many women can and should help nurture "our" children. In comparison to a mother who has been socialized to believe that the children are exclusively or primarily "hers," a woman who has a more expansive attitude is not as likely to be as possessive, competitive, or jealous of the father or of other nurturing adults such as stepmothers (Bell-Scott, 1991).

The point here isn't to criticize white, middle-class women for the way they have been socialized to view their roles as mothers. The point is that many mothers inadvertently push fathers away from greater intimacy with their children. That is, too many women still seem to feel jealous, threatened, or uncomfortable if the father is getting "too close" or is somehow infringing on areas that our society has traditionally believed are "for mothers only." For instance, nearly 25% of the mothers in one recent survey said they didn't want their husband to be more involved with the children. These women seemed to derive most of their feelings of power and self-esteem from their relationships with their children (Pleck, 1989). In the same way that most men believe they aren't good enough fathers if they aren't earning enough money, many women believe they aren't good enough mothers if their children are as close to their father as to her—especially if children confide in their father, instead of in her, on matters having nothing to do with money, school, sports, or work. Either knowingly or unknowingly, mothers who are overly invested in mothering make it more difficult for children to become as close as they might have been to their fathers (Biller, 1993; Corneau, 1991; Marone, 1989; Secunda, 1992; Snarey, 1993; Weiss, 1990).

The mother also affects the relationship teenagers have developed with their father because she continually lets them know how she feels about him. If she thinks the father is doing a good job as a parent, this comes through clearly to their children. But if she's continually criticizing or correcting his parenting, this also comes across. Because most fathers spend so little time with their children, they have fewer chances to modify any negative impressions they might have of him. For instance, if your mother lets you know she thinks your father is cheap, the more time you spend with him the better chance you'll have of making this judgment for yourself (Biller, 1993; Snarey, 1993).

One way of assessing your mother's attitudes is to ask yourself such questions as: How would my mother feel if I phoned home tonight and asked to talk to my father, not to her, about something involving my personal life—not about money, not about my courses, not about my grades, but about my personal life? How would my mother feel if my father and I spent a weekend alone without including her? If you're fortunate, your mother wouldn't mind your having this kind of intimacy with your father. But too many mothers do inadvertently undermine or interfere with the closeness between fathers and children. As one adult daughter put it, "Most of my life I thought the reason my father and I had no relationship was because he just didn't care. But now that I'm older, I realize a lot of it's because of my mother. When I try to get closer to my dad, my mom will suddenly become very distant with me. Funny—I never picked up on that before" (Secunda, 1992, p. 51).

The ways in which the mother's attitudes can affect the relationship between adolescents and their fathers is perhaps most clearly illustrated in the research on divorce. Most teenagers who see their fathers regularly or who live with him part-time after a divorce say they feel closer to him than when their parents were married to each other. How is it that a divorce brings these children and fathers closer? Many divorced fathers tell us this happens because they can finally be nurturing and intimate with their children without the mother interfering, criticizing, or behaving in jealous, competitive ways. Remember too that unhappily married fathers tend to withdraw from their children or to become increasingly harsh and critical. But for whatever the reason in any particular family, many teenagers are closer to their fathers when he is no longer living with their mother (Minuchin & Nichols, 1994; Snarey, 1993; Warshak, 1992; Weiss, 1990).

Many mothers, of course, actively encourage their husbands or ex-husbands to be intimately involved with their children from early childhood on. This seems to be more likely when the mother has a job outside the home than when she is a full-time homemaker during most of the years the children are growing up. In general, adolescents with employed mothers are closer to their fathers than teenagers whose mothers were mainly full-time homemakers. When the mother works, children and fathers usually spend more time together, and fathers spend more time equally with their sons and daughters (Crouter & Crowley, 1990). Although fathers and teenagers argue more when they spend a lot of time together, they also feel closer to one another (Almeida & Galambos, 1991). Fathers also say they feel more relaxed at home with their children when the wife is alleviating some of the financial burdens by working. Moreover, full-time homemakers usually see the father primarily as a breadwinner, not as an equally involved or equally nurturing parent. Then, too, without a focus and source of self-esteem outside the home, full-time homemakers are more apt to become overly involved in their children's lives and to push fathers further away from their children (Biller, 1993; Cowan & Cowan, 1992; Gilbert, 1993; Lerner & Galambos, 1991; Richards & Duckett, 1991).

These findings are also true, by the way, when parents are divorced. Most divorced mothers who worked outside the home while they were married are more supportive of the father and children spending time together and having a close relationship than mothers who were primarily full-time housewives before their divorce. As a leading expert on child development explains, "Many mothers have come to believe that motherhood is their life and crowning glory. For them, the raising of children is a mission above all others. Such women resent active father involvement because it represents a threat to their exclusive parental relationship with the child" (Biller, 1993, p. 31). In contrast, women whose self-esteem isn't based so exclusively on their roles as mothers are more supportive of fathers and their children having close relationships, whether the parents are still married to one another or not (Cowan & Cowan, 1992; Crosby, 1993; Lerner & Galambos, 1991; Warshak, 1992).

THE FATHER'S ATTITUDES

Even if the mother wants the father to be more involved in nurturing and raising their children, the father has to be willing. For example, not all adolescents whose mothers are employed feel closer to their fathers (Paulson, Koman, & Hill, 1990). Obviously factors other than the mother's job and her attitudes about fathering affect how close fathers are to their own children. The father's education can play some role, for example. Some well-educated fathers do seem to communicate better with their teenage children than fathers with less education (Wright, Peterson, & Barns, 1990). Yet men with blue collar jobs tend to spend more time with their children than men with white collar jobs (LaRossa, 1989). What might matter most is not how much education the father has, but which hours he has free to be with his family. For example, blue collar fathers who work night shifts don't get along as well with their children as blue collar fathers whose jobs allow them to be home at night (Barling, 1991).

Even if some fathers are allowed more time with their children, most men haven't been socialized to see the importance of involvement with their children.

Even midway through their lives, many men are trying to come to grips with who their own elusive fathers were, and they lack intimacy with their own children as a consequence of not having been close to their own fathers (Osherson, 1992). Unlike most women, most men have also been deprived of the experiences that teach people how to relate intimately and communicate well with infants and older children. If we want to increase the odds that teenagers and their fathers will feel closer to each other than most now do, we'll need to do more to help

Insert 8–1

Training Boys to be Fathers

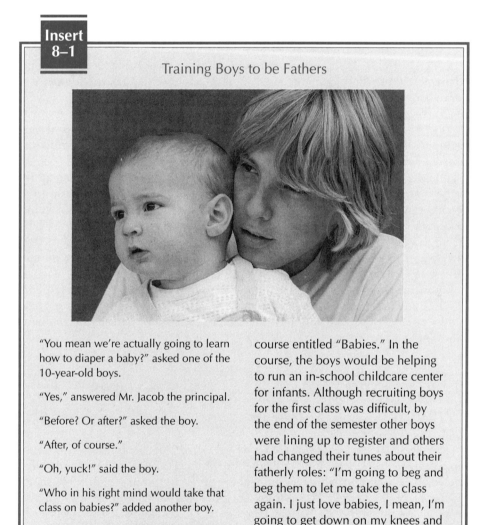

"You mean we're actually going to learn how to diaper a baby?" asked one of the 10-year-old boys.

"Yes," answered Mr. Jacob the principal.

"Before? Or after?" asked the boy.

"After, of course."

"Oh, yuck!" said the boy.

"Who in his right mind would take that class on babies?" added another boy.

In one elementary school, the staff created an elective, boys-only course entitled "Babies." In the course, the boys would be helping to run an in-school childcare center for infants. Although recruiting boys for the first class was difficult, by the end of the semester other boys were lining up to register and others had changed their tunes about their fatherly roles: "I'm going to beg and beg them to let me take the class again. I just love babies, I mean, I'm going to get down on my knees and beg them."

Source: A. Herzig & J. Mali (1980). *Oh, boy! Babies.* Boston: Little Brown & Co.

males feel more comfortable with children. For example, as you can see from Insert 8–1, one elementary school designed a class to teach boys how to nurture, care for, and communicate with infants in hopes of making them more comfortable and better prepared for their future roles as fathers (Herzig & Mali, 1980). Authors, psychologists, and educators are also trying to help fathers interact and communicate more comfortably with their own children (Biller, 1993; Levant & Kopecky, 1995; Marone, 1989).

Bringing fathers and teenagers closer also requires changing certain policies and traditions at the national and local level. For example, Sweden has passed laws enabling fathers to spend several weeks at home with their newborn infants and to take time off from work without loss of income when their children are sick (Lamb, 1989). If we want fathers to have more opportunities to contribute to their children's development, and if we want adolescents to have the chance to get to know more about their fathers, our society is going to have to be more willing to enact similar policies. To date, however, we have been reluctant—to put it mildly—to pass legislation or to adopt policies that could bring fathers and their children closer together. We remain the only industrialized country that doesn't provide federally supported childcare for employed parents or guarantee parents paid leaves when their child is born. And only in 1993 did we finally enact the Family and Medical Leave Act, which entitles both fathers and mothers up to 12 weeks of unpaid leave per year for the birth of babies, adoption, or care of a child or other sick family member. Compared to other industrialized nations, we have a long way to go in enabling fathers to become more actively involved in their children's lives and enabling mothers to help meet their family's financial needs (Berry, 1993; Lamb & Sagi, 1989; Vogel, 1993).

Considering our societal expectations, our laws, and our policies and traditions at home and in the workplace, it's not surprising to find that most teenagers have grown up under-fathered and over-mothered—a situation that is associated with a host of teenage problems (Biller, 1993).

ADOLESCENTS AND THEIR FATHERS

Adolescents' Relationships with Fathers

How well did you know your father when you were an adolescent? How much time did you spend with him, and what did you do together? How comfortable did you feel talking with him about anything other than your school work, sports, the news, or financial matters? Even now, do you know your father's greatest fears, his worst failures, his happiest moments? Do you know what he wishes he could do differently with his life if he were your age? If he's divorced, do you know how the end of his marriage affected him? How comfortable would you feel spending a whole weekend alone with your father, without an athletic event or a television to give the two of you something to do? When you phone home and your father answers, does he quickly say something like: "Oh, just a minute,

I'll get your mother for you," or "What's wrong? Do you need money or are you having some sort of trouble with your grades?" Can you and your father spend an hour simply talking about what's going on in your lives?

If you're like most adolescents in our country, you don't know your father as well as you know your mother—in large part because you didn't spend very much time with him while you were growing up. As young children and as teenagers, most of us say we communicate better, feel more relaxed, and share more personal information with our mother. Although most adolescents feel loved by their father, they spend more time with their mother and believe she understands them better. Not surprisingly, then, most of us know more about our mother's life than about our father's. In fact, many teenagers know so little about their father's life that they cannot even describe his work. He "goes to the office," or "does computer work," or "works at the plant." Father's world is more mysterious than mother's. He is foreign; mother is the known, the familiar. Most adolescents still grow up seeing their father as the chief disciplinarian, the primary breadwinner, and the more worldly wise parent. He is also generally seen as emotionally and intellectually tougher than the mother, as well as more private and more emotionally distant. Indeed, many adolescents see their father as too busy or too tired to spend time with them, unlike mother who is usually considered more approachable and available (Biller, 1993; Lamb & Sagi, 1989; Snarey, 1993).

But haven't contemporary fathers changed a lot in terms of spending more time getting to know their children? Some, yes. Most, no. The overwhelming majority still spend very little time with their children, especially their teenage children. In fact, the typical father doesn't spend much more time with his children than men in his father's generation did. Most fathers still only spend 2 to 3 hours a week on childcare tasks, while those 20% of mothers who are full-time housewives spend 9 to 18 hours a week on childcare. But even in the 80% of families in which both parents earn incomes, the mother still does most of the childcare. In large part this is because most employed mothers don't have jobs that demand as many hours of work as the father's job. But even in families in which the mother has a full-time job, only 10% of the fathers are responsible for the primary care of their preschool children and only 5% are primarily responsible for the care of their school-age children. Sadly, most fathers spend only about 20 minutes a day with their children. On the other hand, the minority of fathers—those who hold less traditional sex role beliefs—spend around 2 hours a day caring for their children. Likewise, when both parents work, fathers have sole responsibility for childcare more than twice as often than when the mother is a full-time homemaker (Snarey, 1993).

How do most adolescents' fathers feel about not having had more time with their children while they were growing up? Most say they wish they had been able to devote less time to their work and more time to their children. And most say they derive a great deal of pleasure from taking care of or being with their children. For example, in a 1991 national Gallup Poll, nearly 60% of the fathers said they got more pleasure from being with their children than from doing a good job at work. Other polls and feedback from fathers also indicate their desire to have less pressure on them to earn money and more time to be with their children (Biller, 1993; Snarey, 1993).

Not only are fathers allowed less time with their children than mothers, when they're together they usually aren't talking much or actually doing something active together. Most of the time fathers and their children are either watching television or watching sports. So, as mentioned, part of the problem is that many fathers need help learning how to relate more intimately with their children. This isn't to say that teenagers aren't ever close to their fathers, or that some aren't closer to him than they are to their mother. Some are—and you might be one of them. But those teenagers and fathers are still the exceptions, not the rule (Biller, 1993; Corneau, 1991; Gilbert, 1993; Griswold, 1993; Silverstein, 1991).

The Father's Impact on Sons and Daughters

Sadly, most of our fathers influence us mainly by virtue of their absence, scarcity, or underinvolvement in our daily lives. Either through choice or through circumstances beyond their control, many fathers are not actively or intimately parenting their own children—a reality that undermines adolescents' maturity and psychological adjustment. What exactly can our fathers contribute by being actively involved in our lives while we're growing up? Or, as is more often the case, how do many fathers fail to contribute to our development because they are absent, scarce, or too uninvolved with us during infancy and childhood? First, let's consider these questions without considering the differences between sons and daughters (Biller, 1993; Cowan & Cowan, 1992; Lamb, 1994; Lamb & Bornstein, 1992; Parke, 1992; Peplar & Rubin, 1994; Snarey, 1993).

In terms of social maturity, psychological health, academic achievements, and future jobs, adolescents who are the most mature and most well-adjusted generally have fathers who have been actively involved in their lives since infancy. Conversely, most adolescents who have trouble getting along with their peers, do poorly in school, or have psychological problems have been under-fathered—or deprived of a father altogether—while they were growing up. The father's behavior is closely associated with the son's psychological problems that manifest as aggressiveness, violence, and lawlessness. For both teenage girls and boys, delinquency is also closely associated with the father's alcohol abuse and physical violence. In contrast, teenage problems such as depression, anxiety disorders, and dependent personality disorders are more closely linked to their mother's depression, or enmeshment, or other emotional problems (Phares & Compas, 1992).

The importance of being raised in a home with a loving, involved adult male is especially easy to see in the research on unmarried mothers and their children. For reasons discussed in the next chapter, these teenagers —especially the boys— are generally the most poorly behaved at home, at school, and in the community, and are the most psychologically, academically, and socially troubled (Asher & Coie, 1990; Biller, 1993; Cherlin & others, 1991; Furstenberg & Cherlin, 1991; Kalter, 1990; Lamb, 1994; Parke & Ladd, 1992; Warshak, 1992).

Part of the father's influence is due to his generally having more power than the mother to make children behave more maturely and less aggressively, especially if the child is male—and especially during adolescence. Furthermore, the father traditionally has been the model for children to learn the skills and attitudes for achievement outside the home. So adolescents who have had a close, loving relationship with their father or stepfather are usually less aggressive, more self-disciplined, more law abiding, and more academically and vocationally successful than poorly fathered teenagers.

These benefits are related to three kinds of behavior that are generally learned from the male parent—self-reliance, assertiveness, and self-discipline. From infancy on, male parents are usually more apt than female parents to encourage our self-reliance, self-control, and assertiveness. Thus an actively involved father can offset a mother's overly protective tendencies, as a mother can offset a father's moving a child too fast toward self-reliance and self-control. Our fathers' insistence on self-reliance and self-discipline is especially beneficial during our teenage and adult years when we need these skills to succeed academically, socially, and vocationally. For example, 40-year-old men and women whose fathers had been actively involved in their lives while they were growing up are more likely to be happily married, successful at work, empathic, tolerant, socially mature, and nonaggressive than those who hadn't spent much time with their fathers and consequently had not received as much discipline at home (Franz, McClelland, & Weinberger, 1991). Even as infants and toddlers, those of us with highly involved fathers are more outgoing, socially mature, self-disciplined, independent from our mothers, eager to explore things around us, and at ease around unfamiliar people than are children who are under-fathered. And these patterns continue throughout our teenage years. Moreover, these connections between fathering and a child's social development are stronger for boys than for girls during both early childhood and adolescence (Biller, 1993; Snarey, 1993).

Two findings stand out from the research on fathering. First, regardless of the behavior or attitude we're considering, adolescents benefit most when their fathers are actively involved in parenting on a day-to-day basis. Second, infancy and the first few years of life are especially important times for fathers to be actively parenting and bonding with their children. For example, adolescents whose fathers were absent or virtually uninvolved in their upbringing during infancy and the preschool years generally have the most trouble getting along with their peers and have the most serious psychological problems—problems that were already apparent by time these children were 5 or 6 years old (Asher & Coie, 1990; Parke & Ladd, 1992). Likewise, infants and preschoolers who become closely bonded to their fathers are generally better off socially and psychologically throughout childhood and adolescence (Biller, 1993; Lamb & Bornstein, 1992).

The ramifications of this research, then, are that most of us are still on the wrong track concerning parenting in early childhood. That is, in contradiction to our prevailing practices, parenting should *not* be turned over almost exclusively to mothers during infancy and the preschool years. We should *not* exclude a father from parenting simply because he's a teenager or because he isn't married to the mother of his child. Even unwed teenage fathers can contribute to their children's social and intellectual development (Lerman & Ooms, 1992). The research clearly supports the old saying that "the hand that rocks the cradle rules the world." So we need to do a much better job seeing to it that the father's hands are equally on the cradle—because, as one leading expert and researcher concludes, "Father neglect is the most prevalent form of child maltreatment in our society" (Biller, 1993, p. 247).

FATHERS AND DAUGHTERS

Although social scientists have historically underestimated the father's importance relative to the mother, this has been especially true in regard to the father-daughter relationship. Researchers and parents too often have assumed that the mother's influence was far more important than the father's, especially during their daughter's adolescence. But more recent research shows that a father has an equally powerful influence over his daughter's development, especially during her teenage years. Let's see what this research is telling us about fathers and their teenage daughters (Biller, 1993; Caplan, 1989; Coulter & Minninger, 1993; Marone, 1989; Phares & Compas, 1992; Secunda, 1992; Snarey, 1993).

Sons Versus Daughters   Compared to sons, do most daughters get their fair share of their father's time? In general, most fathers spend about as much time with their daughters as with their sons during the childhood years. But when there is an imbalance, it almost always favors the son. Also, after a divorce, most fathers spend more time with their sons than with their daughters (Furstenberg & Cherlin, 1991; Kalter, 1990; Warshak, 1992). During adolescence, a father is

How close are you to your father, and how well do you know him?

**Insert
8–2**

How Sexist is Your Father?

How would you rate your father on a 10-point scale on the following? The higher your father's score, the less sexist he is in terms of how he related to his sons and daughters.

1 = strongly disagree   10 = strongly agree

____ 1. My father has basically the same expectations or definitions for a good or successful son as for a good or successful daughter.

____ 2. My father taught his daughters and his sons that there are times when they shouldn't ignore their own needs merely to please other people.

____ 3. My dad does the same types of activities with his sons and daughters.

____ 4. My father is equally supportive of his daughter's athletic activities as his son's.

____ 5. My father has the same attitudes and rules about his children's dating and sexual matters whether it's his son or his daughter.

____ 6. My father didn't focus any more on his daughter's appearance or her weight than he did on his son's appearance or weight.

____ 7. My father showed an equal interest and enthusiasm in his son's and his daughter's school achievements.

____ 8. My dad encouraged his daughter to argue with him as much as he encouraged his son.

____ 9. My father is as willing or unwilling to admit he's wrong or to apologize to his daughter as to his son.

____ 10. My father encourages his daughter to take risks as much as he does with his son.

____ 11. My father wouldn't be more upset if his daughter didn't marry or have children than if his son didn't.

____ 12. My father spends as much time talking about what's going on in his daughter's life as his son's life.

____ 13. My father spent an equal amount of time with his sons and daughters while we were growing up.

____ 14. My father isn't any more likely to make jokes about women, women's appearance, or women's sexuality than he is about men's.

____ 15. My father doesn't behave as though his daughter has to "act like a lady" but his son is allowed to "sow his wild oats."

____ 16. My father encourages his daughter's independence as much as his son's.

also more likely to back away from his daughter emotionally than from his son. Thus, many teenage girls believe they lose much of the closeness they once had with their fathers (Coulter & Minninger, 1993; Secunda, 1992.

This drifting apart is especially sad because fathers seem to have the most positive impact on their daughters when they're actively involved in her teenage years. Why? One reason is that, once girls enter adolescence, they usually start backsliding in intellectual confidence, competitiveness, assertiveness, and self-reliance—the very skills they need for academic and vocational success. Because fathers generally encourage these characteristics more than mothers, teenage daughters benefit greatly from a close relationship with their fathers. A close relationship with her father also helps a teenage daughter pull away enough from her mother to establish an identity of her own. Helping his daughter entails encouraging her self-reliance and her separateness from the family, not smothering, overprotecting, rescuing, or babying her. If a father is overly indulgent or overly involved in his daughter's life, he interferes with her social, academic, and psychological development (Biller, 1993; Snarey, 1993).

Cognitive and Vocational Development   Because most fathers spend much less time with their teenage daughters than do mothers, how is it they still influence her development? First, the father's attitudes about male and female gender roles are clear to his daughter, even if he doesn't spend much time with her. By the ways in which he treats his wife and other women, a father is continually sending his daughter messages about what he feels and believes about females. For example, does the daughter see her father continually interrupting his wife, correcting her opinions, and refusing to yield when she's right and he's wrong? Does the daughter see her father making fun of unattractive females, refusing to do any of the housework, or expecting his wife to serve him after she gets home from work? Fathers who treat their wives in nonsexist ways tend to have daughters who aspire to higher-paying, traditionally male jobs than do fathers who are sexist in their own marriages (Nelson & Keith, 1990).

Unfortunately too many fathers still don't give their daughters as much encouragement as they give their sons in terms of developing her intellectual skills and preparing her to be financially self-reliant. For example, when a family's income falls, parents often lower their educational goals for their daughters but not for their sons (McLoyd, 1989). Trying to be loving and protective, too many fathers inadvertently encourage their daughters to become overly dependent on approval from other people (especially from males), overly cautious about taking risks, and overly focused on their social lives rather than on their intellectual and vocational skills (Biller, 1993; Coulter & Minninger, 1993; Marone, 1989; Secunda, 1992; Snarey, 1993).

Sexual and Social Development   This body of research also shows that the father plays an especially important part in how his teenage daughter feels about her appearance and her sexuality. By acknowledging rather than ignoring his daughter's sexual maturity, by encouraging her romantic relationships, and by helping her enjoy how she looks, a father helps his daughter develop self-confidence and lay the groundwork for fulfilling relationships. But by denigrating or making fun of her body or other women's bodies, a father can instill the embarrassment or shame that undermines his daughter's confidence and respect for her own physical and sexual self. Moreover, some teenage girls who are deprived of good fathering while they're growing up become sexually promiscuous or obsessed with boys as a way of trying to compensate for the affection or attention they never got from their fathers.

Realizing the important role he might play in his daughter's sexual and social development, one father honored his daughter's emergence into womanhood by celebrating her first menstrual period alone with her in a special rite of passage. When she started her period, this father took his daughter on an overnight camping trip during which he told her that he wanted her to have a more positive image of menstruation than our culture generally provided. After telling her about Native American celebrations of menstruation and womanhood, the father told her how he hoped she would welcome her new sexuality and the changes in her body and in her life. He also urged her to listen to her own inner voices and to assume responsibility for developing her talents and designing her own life. "Afterwards, with tears running down my cheeks, I told her how much I loved and cared for her. She cried too. We held each other and I felt such joy for the wonder and blessing of having such a daughter to enrich my life" (Pinkson, 1992, p. 154).

From a psychoanalytic point of view, a father also helps his daughter relate well to teenage boys by helping resolve her Electra complex during early childhood, years before she ever reaches adolescence. As you remember, resolving an **Electra complex** requires the little girl to stop idolizing or doting on her father in ways that would make it difficult for her to eventually relate well to males her age. During adolescence a father further helps his daughter relate to boys by disclosing some of his own imperfections rather than trying to maintain the image of the infallible hero. By helping her see him as a human being rather than as her knight in shining armor, the father is helping her to accept other males as human beings as well. But if a father isn't able to give his daughter a realistic picture of himself, or insists that she continue to see him as her hero, or tries to make her feel guilty for abandoning him emotionally for other males, then he undermines her sexual and social development.

Self-Confidence and Self-Reliance   As the daughter's child-like body matures into that of a young woman and as she seeks more independence, too often the father responds in ways that undermine her self-confidence and self-reliance. Sometimes a father reacts by spending less time with her. Another might react by intrusively prying into her personal life, or by becoming overly controlling and overly vigilant. Some react to their daughter's attempts at independence by doting on her in ways that make her feel guilty for not continuing to rely on "daddy" in the same child-like ways she did as a young girl.

Any of these reactions can leave a teenage girl puzzled and confused, trying to determine how to please her father and how to restore the close relationship they had when she was younger. If her father retreats from her, she might spend years wondering, "What's wrong with me?" If he doesn't support her independence, she might continue to act in dependent, child-like ways with her father, as well as in her romantic relationships. Without the self-confidence that comes from her father's approval, despite her imperfections, the daughter can develop a **false self**—a personality she creates solely to please her father. This false self can be carried to such an extreme that the daughter becomes a **codependent**—an individual who continually ignores what is best for her in order to please and take care of other people. Other daughters become so desperate to please their fathers that they develop eating disorders in their efforts to be "perfect" daughters, or as a way of trying to restore the close relationship they had with their fathers when they were skinny, asexual, little girls.

A father can help his daughter avoid becoming codependent or developing a false self by encouraging her to develop **intentionality**—the ability to direct her energies toward goals of her own choosing and to focus on her own needs, rather than continually seeking the approval of other people. Because most teenage girls lose self-confidence and hold themselves back intellectually, a father can be his daughter's strongest ally in keeping her independent self alive.

Because most fathers love their daughters deeply, we must wonder why these men too often behave in ways that undermine feminine self-confidence, sexuality, and self-reliance. In part, a father might be hurt or angry about having to give up the adoration and attention he once received from his daughter as a young girl. He might not be ready to be dethroned yet, or to give up "his little princess." Without even realizing that he's withdrawing from her, he might redirect his energy elsewhere as he sees her becoming less reliant on him. He also might feel uncomfortable about her sexual maturation, so he inadvertently pulls away from her. Of course, he might also be less involved in her life because he's preoccupied with his own mid-life issues. Finally, a father sometimes has a hard time letting his daughter grow up because he has come to rely on her to meet too many of his own emotional needs—needs that a wife, not a daughter, should be fulfilling (Coulter & Minninger, 1993; Marone, 1989; Secunda, 1992; Snarey, 1993).

Daughters Whose Fathers Have Died   Even when her father is no longer alive, a daughter can still be affected greatly by her feelings for him, or her memory of him. Sometimes the daughter grows up feeling angry at her father for having deserted her by dying. Sometimes she lives under the shadow of believing that her father was a perfect, flawless male that no other male can measure up to. In the first case, the daughter might never feel comfortable trusting males because she fears they will abandon her, as her father did—if not physically, then emotionally. In the second case, by idolizing her dead father, a daughter might never be content with "real-life" males who do have flaws, because she is continually comparing them to the unattainable fantasy of her father. Of course the impact of a father's death affects each girl differently and might not cause any significant problems as she ages. The point is that we shouldn't assume a father's influence on his daughter ends when he dies (Secunda, 1992; Wakerman, 1984).

FATHERS AND SONS

Social and Psychological Development   As mentioned, the effects of under-fathering or of father absence are in certain respects worse for sons. Boys whose fathers have been very involved in their lives since early childhood seem to fend off problems that boys are more likely to develop than girls. In comparison to girls, boys with little or no contact with a father fare more poorly academically, socially, psychologically, and emotionally (Biller, 1993; Corneau, 1991; Gilmore, 1990; Osherson, 1993; Peplar & Rubin, 1994; Phares & Compas, 1992; Pittman, 1993; Snarey, 1993; Warshak, 1992).

One of the easiest ways to underscore the father's special role in his son's life is by examining the research on unmarried mothers. Almost without exception, boys who live with their father rather than with their unmarried mother are more socially and psychologically well-adjusted, more mature and well-behaved, and more successful in school. Even having a close relationship with a man other than the father can benefit a boy who lives with his unmarried mother. For example, preschool boys living with an unmarried teenage mother who have a close rela-tionship with their grandfather are more intellectually mature, less fearful, and less hostile than those without a male relationship (Radin, Oyserman, & Benn, 1991). For reasons examined in the Chapter 9, boys are almost always more adversely affected than girls when they are living with an unmarried mother (Furstenberg & Cherlin, 1991; Kalter, 1990; Warshak, 1992).

What unique contributions can a father make to his son's development? One of the most widely studied questions about fathers and sons has to do with the son's vocational development. How much influence do fathers have over the jobs their sons will have as men? As you might expect, there is a close relationship between the father's and son's educational and vocational achievements—stronger than that between mother and son. In general, a son follows in his father's footsteps in terms of socioeconomic level and the basic values that their jobs reflect. When there are differences, it's usually because the son has chosen a job with more sta-tus and income—a step up the ladder that is a source of pride for most fathers. In fact, most fathers approve of whatever type of work their son chooses as long as the son isn't stepping down the ladder financially in comparison to his father. Interestingly, a father who likes his own job generally has a closer relationship with his son than a father who dislikes his work. This might be because a man who is happy with his work is more relaxed with his children when he's home. It could be that men who like their jobs have personalities that bring them closer to their children. In any event, most fathers do have a significant impact on their sons' vocational and educational achievements (Barling, 1991; Biller, 1993).

A son's control over his aggressive impulses is also closely tied to the nature of the relationship with his father. A father's absence, lack of involvement in his son's life, or his own violent, aggressive, or criminal behavior are clearly linked to his son's potential for aggression, violence, and lawlessness. Lacking a good fatherly influence, many boys act out very exaggerated notions of masculinity, including extreme aggression, sexual promiscuity, and physical abuse of women.

They rape, abuse alcohol, smoke heavily, and break the law. In this sense then, fathers are usually more responsible than mothers for determining whether their son will learn to curb his destructive, aggressive, or violent impulses (Biller, 1993; Bozett & Hanson, 1991; Lamb, 1994; Peplar & Rubin, 1994).

Significance of the Father-Son Bond   Why does father absence or lack of involvement affect boys to a greater degree than girls? One reason is that when a mother is absent, psychologically disturbed, or emotionally distant from her children, another woman usually steps in to offer some support and guidance, especially to the daughter. But when a father is emotionally distant or absent, another man isn't as likely to step in to help the children. Because so many children are now living with a divorced or never-married mother, sons are especially vulnerable to receiving insufficient fathering—either from their own father or from other men. As a result, more teenage boys than girls are suffering the effects of not having a close relationship with an adult of their own gender—a situation that usually hinders boys academically, socially, and psychologically (Biller, 1993; Corneau, 1991; Warshak, 1992).

Boys also usually suffer more than girls from under-fathering or father absence because most mothers have less control over their son's infantile, impulsive, defiant, or aggressive behavior. Especially when she's a single parent, the mother generally has a harder time than the father in setting limits and disciplining her son. Now add to this what we've discussed in earlier chapters: From infancy through adolescence, boys have more social, psychological, and developmental problems than girls. From infancy on, boys outnumber girls in almost every category of psychological disorder, learning disability, or physical condition that can interfere with a child's social and psychological well-being (Ebata, Petersen, & Conger, 1990; Lamb, 1994; Robins & Rutter, 1990). In this sense then, boys may need their fathers more than girls do because they have more problems to deal with at the outset. Because these kinds of early childhood problems set the course for our teenage and adult development, a close father-son relationship seems to be more important during infancy and the first few years of a boy's life than during adolescence (Biller, 1993; Snarey, 1993). Although two actively involved parents are better than one, if one adult is more likely than the other to help their son learn more adaptive, more mature ways of thinking and behaving, it's often the father. In fact, when his father or stepfather is around, a teenage boy not only tends to behave better, he also treats his mother more respectfully (Baumrind, 1991; Patterson, Reid, & Dishion, 1992; Steinberg, 1990).

Finally, when a father is absent or relatively uninvolved in parenting, the son is more apt to wind up in an enmeshed, overly protective, indulgent, or infantile relationship with his mother. As discussed, these indulgent or enmeshed relationships are associated with a number of social problems and psychological disorders for teenage and young adult sons, including schizoid personality disorders, social withdrawal, depression, chronic low self-esteem, hypochondria, sexual dysfunction, and anxiety and dependent personality disorders. As one male therapist explains, a large part of the father's role is to teach his son that, "You can let go of mom; there's a whole world beyond mother that is exciting and interesting and ultimately manageable" (Osherson, 1992, p. 216). Thus, fathers who turn over too much of the parenting to the mothers are more likely to have sons who develop social and psychological problems associated with extreme dependence and enmeshment with their mothers (Biller, 1993; Corneau, 1991; Parker, 1983; Pittman, 1993; Goldstein, 1990)

Conflict, Competition, and Intimacy   It has long been recognized that most sons and fathers are more competitive, more combative, and more jealous of one another than most fathers and daughters. For example, most fathers and sons argue and interrupt one another more than most fathers and daughters (Montemayor & Flannery, 1991). As Insert 8–3 illustrates, these jealous, competitive aspects of the father-son relationship are frequently reflected in mythology, literature, and films. But why is there usually more competition and jealousy between fathers and sons than between fathers and daughters?

First, teenage sons generally spend more time with their fathers than do teenage daughters, so there's simply more opportunity for conflicts to arise. Second, unlike most mothers, most fathers don't tend to give in or back down with their children. Third, in the same way that a mother might behave in jealous or competitive ways with her teenage daughter, the father might behave in jealous, competitive ways with his teenage son. The adolescent son, filled with possibility for the life that lies ahead, might remind some fathers of what they haven't achieved. One adult son makes this point when he finally realizes why his father yells at him over a minor mishap: "Dad, you're not angry at me about the steps. You're mad at me because I am young and I am going away" (Hallowell, 1992). Fourth, a son might be more intent on winning his father's approval for accomplishments during adolescence, whereas daughters might not be as intent on getting this kind of recognition from their fathers until later in their adult lives. So the son might feel more upset when his father doesn't give him the approval he wants in order to feel like a "real man."

Fifth, teenage sons seem to need more emotional distance and more competition with their fathers in order to build their self-confidence, become self-reliant, and fashion identities of their own. Indeed, fathers might be doing the most good by being much more involved in their son's infancy and early childhood and by standing back more passively and silently during the teenage years. But for a daughter, the pattern seems to be reversed in that she benefits more from a close relationship with her father as an adolescent than as a young girl (Biller, 1993; Snarey, 1993). So in contrast to a daughter, a teenage boy seems to need a certain degree of combat and competition with his father—not wanting to feel totally defeated or overshadowed by his father, yet not wanting to believe that his father is so weak that he can be defeated or overshadowed by a teenage boy. As one adult son comments, "I knew at that moment that my son would love me with the same fear and intensity with which I loved my father, for a boy's father is, after all, his first competitor and his eternal enemy" (Wright, 1992). Indeed, even our fairy tales and movies recognize that teenage sons often convert their fathers into

Insert 8–3

Fathers and Sons

"Father! Father! Oh do not walk so fast. Speak, father, speak to your little boy, or else I shall be lost."
William Blake (1789). *Songs of Innocence.*

Consider these movies and fairy tales and ask yourself: What lessons or advice do these movies and myths offer us about fathers and sons?

Star Wars

Luke Skywalker, the idealistic young space hero, is mourning his lost father, a heroic man whom Luke believes has been killed by the evil Empire of his terrifying enemy, Darth Vader (a pun on "Dark Father"). In order to become a Jedi knight, Luke has to become disciplined and selfless enough to attain The Force—the spiritual power that will make him feel manly. Luke's wise old male mentor, Obi-wan Kenobi, also tells him he must learn to trust his feelings if he ever hopes to align with The Force. When he's finally able to follow his mentor's advice, Luke defeats and unmasks the evil Darth Vader, discovering that Darth is his long-lost father—a man who, like the universe, is a combination of both good and evil. At this point Luke is also able to behave nicely toward Princess Leia, who turns out to be his sister.

Field of Dreams

At the beginning of this film, an Iowa farmer played by Kevin Costner tells the story of how

adversaries—a situation that benefits the son but often hurts or perplexes the loving father (Blos, 1989; Erikson, 1968; Freud, 1949).

Sixth, not knowing how to express their love for people as directly and affectionately as most girls do, teenage boys might argue with their fathers as a way of establishing a certain connection between them. For example, wrestling with dad or taunting and provoking him might be the best way to establish intimacy. The son who mocks or berates his dad over the outcome of a sports event might not be arguing with his father as much as he's establishing intimacy in the only way he knows how—an emotional wrestling match that reassures the son that his father still loves him even when the son is being assertive (Osherson, 1992).

his mother died and his father gave up his base-ball career in order to raise the son. But when the son became a teenager, he no longer had time to play catch with his father and, at the age of 17, he left home to protest all the things his father stood for—after which, the father died. Now the son is grown but feels something is missing in his life. He starts hearing voices from his cornfield telling him, "If you build it, he will come." The son believes the voice is telling him to build a baseball diamond so that his father's baseball hero, Shoeless Joe Jackson, will come to play baseball with him. But the voices continue: "Go the distance. Ease the pain." In his quest to understand what the voices are trying to tell him, the son meets another of his father's heroes, the author J. D. Salinger. In the end, the son's father appears in his baseball uniform. They play their final game of catch; and the son is finally at peace.

"Iron John"

One of the fairy tales collected by the Brothers Grimm is entitled "Iron Hans," or "Iron John." In the tale, one of the king's hunters discovers a huge, wild, primitive-looking man living in the forest whose hair is so rust-colored that he is named "Iron" John. The fearful king then imprisons Iron Hans in a cage. Some time later the prince's golden ball rolls into the cage and the son has to strike a deal with the wild man: He will steal the key to free the wild man in exchange for his ball. And where's the key? Under his mother's pillow. Once free, Iron John heads back for the forest. But the son begs Hans to take him along because he fears being punished by his parents for stealing the key and setting loose the wild man. Iron John agrees, but warns the son: "You'll never see your parents again if you go with me." Then he hoists the son onto his shoulders and off they go into the forest.

"Jack and the Bull"

In this fairy tale a young boy is cast out by a mean family of women. Hungry and dispirited, Jack meets a bull who recognizes the boy's plight and tells him to "unscrew my left horn." Making fun of the bull, Jack does what he's told and finds, to his amazement, an endless supply of fresh, warm bread and milk. The powerful, wise bull and the young boy become friends and have a series of wonderful adventures together. After teaching Jack lessons about courage and tenderness, the bull dies; and Jack finds a happy life on a farm with a woman who becomes like a mother to him.

The quality of a teenage son's relationship with his father also seems to be connected to events in the son's early childhood. The minority of teenage boys who are extremely jealous and combative with their fathers usually did not bond closely to their father as preschoolers. Instead, these boys became overly bonded to their mothers and failed to identify with their fathers. When a son doesn't form a solid attachment to his father during the first 4 or 5 years of his life, rivalry and other kinds of conflict with his father become especially intense in late childhood and adolescence (Biller, 1993).

Finally, some psychoanalytic theorists contend that Oedipal issues reappear again for teenage boys in ways they don't for teenage girls (Blos, 1989). That is, even if a boy succeeds at the age of 4 or 5 in giving up overreliance on his mother and becomes bonded to and identified with his father, he might have a resurgence of child-like needs to be taken care of again by his mother as a young teenager. At the same time, the teenage boy feels jealous and competitive toward his father for being intellectually, physically, and financially superior. The father, in turn, is interceding between the mother and son so that his son doesn't become overly reliant in child-like ways on the mother. This psychoanalytic explanation has been offered as one of the reasons why some teenage boys living with an unmarried mother revert back to infantile, dependent behavior rather than develop the self-reliance, self-confidence, and self-discipline appropriate for boys their age. But even when a father or stepfather is present, a teenage son's regression in regard to his mother can become the battlefield on which the married couple fights with one another. Seen from this viewpoint, the father or stepfather has to win the son over from the mother at this point or the son ends up with the tragic fate of Oedipus—emotionally married to his mother and unable to become self-reliant or mature enough to relate well to females his age. As one male psychotherapist puts it, "To become a separate person, the boy must perform a great deed. He must pass a test: he must break the chain to his mother" (Gilmore, 1990, p. 135).

You might not respect or feel comfortable accepting these psychoanalytic interpretations of what goes on between many fathers and sons. If not, perhaps the social learning theories explained earlier seem more fitting. But whichever theoretical explanation you feel more comfortable with, it's interesting to note that once the father-mother-son group ends, some teenage sons do get along better with their fathers. For example, sons in college who don't live at home say they feel closer and communicate better with their fathers than do sons in college who keeping living at home (Montemayor & Flannery, 1991).

Beyond adolescence, when a son eventually feels more confident and secure about his own identity, he becomes freer to establish or to re-establish a less combative, more intimate relationship with his father. In other words, "when a son earns his independence and feels that his own cup is full, then he can raise it to toast his father" (Scull, 1992, p. 57). As two adult sons explain their emotional reunions with their fathers: "I have begun wearing my father's ring. I slip it on, I will sheepishly admit, for its powers," reports one (Brower, 1992). And about the relationship with his father another man says, "After so many years of being buffeted by swirling currents of father-son tensions, intermittent hostilities and redeeming love, why, I mused, does it remain so hard for us—two black men—to just get along? Yet now I want my father to know that with each morning look into the bathroom mirror, I see a little more of his face peering through mine. The years don't carry us away from our fathers—they return us to them" (Marriott, 1992).

ADOLESCENTS AND THEIR MOTHERS

THE MOTHER'S IMPACT ON SONS AND DAUGHTERS

Behaviors and attitudes of mothers, like those of fathers, seem to be closely linked to particular aspects of their adolescent children's development. Our mothers seem to have greater influence than do our fathers over what kind of explanatory styles we develop—how we interpret or explain other people's behavior, the events going on around us, our own behavior, and the situations in which we find ourselves. For reasons discussed in preceding chapters, most teenagers who are psychologically well-adjusted and get along well with their peers have a mother who interprets the world in optimistic, self-motivated, non-hostile ways. Likewise, most teenagers who have trouble getting along with people or are psychologically troubled have a mother who has a pessimistic, passive, helpless, or hostile explanatory style. For example, mothers with helpless, passive, glum styles talk more with their children about negative emotions and negative events than do mothers who aren't depressed—a habit that then seems to encourage a depressed mother's child to grow up focusing most on negative emotions in themselves and in others (Waxler & others, 1992). Fathers' explanatory styles also have some bearing on their children's ways of interpreting the world. But the connections are usually stronger between mothers and children, perhaps because we seem to develop our explanatory styles during early childhood when most of our fathers are the least involved in our lives (Seligman, 1991).

Second, our mother's mental health is often closely connected to how well or how poorly adapted we are as children and as adolescents. Given the impact that the mother's explanatory style seems to have on children, and given the connection between mental health and explanatory styles, it's no surprise that depressed adolescents often have the same negative, helpless styles as their mothers. Not all children in a family, however, are equally influenced by their parents. Whichever child has the most fragile, child-like, or dependent temperament tends to be the most negatively affected by a depressed parent. Likewise, the timing of a mother's depression seems to be important. Mothers who are depressed during their child's early years seem to have a more negative impact than those who become depressed much later in their child's life. The link between teenage depression and the father's mental health is not nearly as strong as between mother and child (Harrington, 1994; Phares & Compas, 1992; Rubin, Lemare, & Lollis, 1990; Waxler & others, 1992).

Third, it seems that mothers have more influence than fathers on the ways we think and behave in relating to people. According to the attachment theorists, the parent who spends the most time with us in early childhood provides the lifelong model both for our expectations of people and for our own behavior in relationships. Thus, if your mother made you feel loved, yet simultaneously taught you to be self-reliant, tolerant, empathic, forgiving, and unselfish, then as a teenager, you're able to establish satisfying relationships with people. But if your mother made you feel unloved or rejected, then as a teenager you will tend to be outgoing, but unable to be intimate with people because you are overly aggressive, defiant, and indifferent. On the other hand, if your mother made you feel loved but was overly protective, indulgent, or enmeshed with you, you will tend to be shy, socially immature, clingy, possessive, overly dependent, demanding, hostile, and self-centered—a pattern most likely to occur if your mother was depressed or chronically unhappy during the first few years of your life (Belsky & Cassidy,

Insert
8–4

The Unresolved Oedipal Complex

What happens to the teenage son who did not identify with his father as a young boy and who remains too dependent on his mother in child-like ways? From the psychoanalytic viewpoint, these sons are at risk of arrested ego development and likely will be extremely immature in social reasoning and social relationships. As adults, these sons might find themselves in a situation similar to that described in the following passage by the therapist of a young man named Eric:

Eric is in his living room: amused, detached, ironic. He has a talent for making fun of everything, but he reserves his greatest scorn for yuppies and their perfect lifestyle. It's noon and he has just got out of bed. His hair is long and tangled. He hasn't shaved for three days. As he looks out the window, he smiles condescendingly at the joggers struggling so hard to keep in shape.

For Eric society is a dark gray mass in which everybody has been pigeonholed. He has chosen not to work regularly for fear a steady job would clip his wings and diminish his precious freedom. He fears a steady relationship for the same reasons. All the girls he goes out with are nice, but . . . there's always a "but": but she's not interested in the arts, etc.

Nothing is ever perfect enough for Eric to get totally involved in it. The "eternal adolescent" doesn't realize that he too is part of society.

At 35 Eric still clings to the illusion that he can become anything he wants. He fantasizes about revealing himself to the world in some dazzling manner. But when reality intrudes and a fascination fades, he crashes. He spends his life dreaming outlandish dreams that never amount to anything. He intends to write a great novel, but never manages to put pen to paper. He can never buckle down to anything requiring self-discipline. Rejecting a world in which love has to be earned, Eric lives in an unreal world. Drugs and alcohol abuse transform him into a cynical and desperate man who perceives the whole world through his narrow, pessimistic view. His attempt to escape from the world of his mother has been directed upward, in a rejection of the world of the flesh and life's necessary compromises. Eric will never belong to any woman other than his mother and will never really be rooted in life. Eric, the eternal adolescent, is still obsessed with the idea of becoming a famous musician. One day when I dared express serious doubts about the possibility he would achieve his dream of fame and fortune, he put an abrupt stop to the therapy, storming out of my office . . . slamming no less than three doors on his way out.

Source: G. Corneau (1991). *Absent fathers, lost sons.* Boston: Shambala, pp. 53–58.

1994; Karen, 1994; Lamb & Bornstein, 1992; Parkes, Stevenson-Hinde, & Marris, 1991; Radke-Yarrow, 1991).

MOTHERS AND SONS

A mother generally seems to influence her son's development in at least four important areas: social maturity, self-reliance, individuation, and certain types of psychological disorders that we will examine in Chapter 15. As we've already discussed, a mother can also have a profound impact on her son's development by affecting the type of relationship he has with his father and by the impressions she gives him of his father. And, as we will see in the next chapter, the mother's influence on her son can be especially powerful when she and his father are divorced.

Self-Reliance and Social Maturity   As mentioned, most teenage boys want the kind of approval from their fathers that enables them to believe they have left their boyhood behind—that they have truly entered manhood. But in order to achieve the self-reliance, self-discipline, and social maturity needed to receive approval from his father, a son has to become increasingly independent from his mother—a feat that psychologists have long believed is difficult for some boys. That is, many teenage boys seem to have an easier time winning the approval of their mothers than the approval of their fathers; but they also have a harder time giving up a child-like dependence on their mothers. Like girls, teenage boys generally respect and admire their fathers more than their mothers, but consider mothers to be the main source of comfort and approval. Yet compared to girls, teenage boys are often more likely to persist in relying on their mothers in overly dependent, demanding, infantile ways. When this happens, the mother has to be wise enough and self-reliant enough to push her son away so that he can develop the social maturity and independence that is appropriate for someone his age. As one psychotherapist has explained, "Mama can give him security that he will be taken care of, but she can't make him feel like a man" (Pittman, 1993, p. 151). In other words, if the son is to mature socially, psychologically, and emotionally, he must not be allowed to remain too reliant on his mother (Biller, 1993; Block, 1971; Blos, 1989; Hauser, Powers, & Noam, 1991; Pittman, 1993; Silverstein & Rashbaum, 1994).

In discussing mothers and sons, it is noteworthy that as an adult, a son is much more likely than a daughter to still be living at home with his mother. Less than one fifth of all single women between the ages of 25 and 35 are living with their mother, compared to more than one third of all single men. It could be that, compared to daughters, sons are more likely to feel financially or emotionally responsible for their mothers—or that mothers are more apt to tolerate their son's dependence and immaturity than their daughter's. It could also be that sons are more socially immature or more psychologically troubled in ways that make them more reliant on their mothers for continued care and attention (Bradsher, 1990).

Individuation and Mental Health   Why might teenage sons become overly involved and overly protective of their mothers in ways that interfere with becoming individuated and forming an identity of their own? One reason may be that our society's gender roles may lead sons to feel they ought to be responsible for their mother's happiness and financial well-being. The attitude that males should be responsible for taking care of females, especially when it comes to money, may lead some teenage boys to become overly involved with their mother's life. In any event, when a son perceives his mother as powerless, weak, needy, or depressed, he's more likely to get overly involved in her life in ways that interfere with individuation and that contribute to social and psychological problems in his own life (Biller, 1993; Hinde & Stevenson, 1995; Minuchin & Nichols, 1994; Silverstein & Rashbaum, 1994).

The research isn't telling us that teenage daughters never become too involved or remain too reliant on their mothers. Some do. But boys seem to be at greater risk of developing these problematic relationships with their mothers. For example, compared to girls, teenage boys' social and psychological problems are usually more closely related to the kind of relationship they have with their mothers and to the mother's mental and emotional problems (Block, 1971; Phares & Compas, 1992; Seligman, 1991; Pianta, Egeland, & Stroufe, 1990). Compared to girls, teenage boys also have more social or psychological troubles that are seemingly related to their not feeling securely loved or not becoming independent enough from their mothers during early childhood (Blos, 1989; Cohn, Patterson, & Christopoulos, 1991; Corneau, 1991; Pittman, 1993). As explained in the next chapter, sons of unmarried mothers are also more likely than daughters to suffer negative consequences. But married or not, the mother who convinces her son while he's growing up that she doesn't need him to take care of her emotionally or financially contributes most to his social and psychological well-being as a teenager. In short, weak, unhappy mothers contribute more than self-reliant, happy mothers to their sons' problems.

Mothers and Daughters

Mothers also have an impact on their daughter's social development, as well as on their self-reliance, sexuality, and vocational plans (Apter, 1990; Brown & Gilligan, 1992; Caplan, 1989; Debold, Wilson & Malave, 1992; Gilligan, Rogers, & Tolman, 1991; Glickman, 1993; Mens-Verhulst, Schreurs & Woertman, 1993).

Self-Reliance and Vocational Development   Most teenage girls don't get as much encouragement as do sons to become self-reliant and intellectually self-confident, either at home or away. For example, although we tend to tease or criticize teenage boys for not being self-reliant or self-confident enough by referring to them as "mommies' boys," there is no equivalent term for girls who remain too reliant on their mothers. The term *mommy's boy* is considered more insulting than *daddy's girl*, which merely implies that the teenage girl is being pampered by her loving father. In any event, the mother-daughter relationship can serve as an important source for encouraging girls to form identities of their own, become more self-reliant, and express their opinions and needs. This is especially true if the father doesn't encourage his daughter's independence or assertiveness.

In regard to her daughter's intellectual development and future financial security, the mother who is employed outside the home while her children are growing up serves as an important source of vocational information and encouragement. In general, daughters whose mothers have always contributed to the family's income end up with more education and higher paying jobs than do the 20% whose mothers were full-time homemakers for most of the years their children were growing up (Lerner & Galambos, 1991). As two grown daughters whose mothers always worked explain: "One thing my mom drummed into my head is have your own money." "It was so weird. You know, my stepmother gets her allowance from my father—like she's still a little kid" (Glickman, 1993, p. 59).

For some teenage daughters, their mother's role as a full-time homemaker creates a source of tension and guilt. Some feel guilty because they don't want a life like their mother's, and others feel angry or disappointed that their mother didn't do more with her life intellectually or vocationally. Still others feel pity for their mother, yet resent feeling they are responsible for making their mother happy. Several daughters explain their feelings this way: "Mom did everything for dad and us kids. I adore her, and that narrowed my vision of what I could be because I didn't learn much about the richness and variety of life choices from her." "I had been my mother's protector for so long that when the time came for me to go to college, I was afraid she wouldn't be able to get along without me" (Caplan, 1989, p. 192 & 196). "I was so happy when my mother went to work. Before, she was so miserable that she made enormous emotional demands on us" (Glickman, 1994, p. 42). This isn't to say that the 20% of mothers who don't earn an income can't be supportive of their daughter's intellectual and vocational development. Obviously some do, and your mother might be one of them. Nevertheless, daughters whose mothers have always had jobs outside the home do generally achieve the most educationally, financially, and vocationally.

Sexuality and Physical Self-Confidence   In a different way than fathers, mothers also affect the way their teenage daughters feel about their appearance and sexuality. When a mother makes clear, by what she says and does, that she enjoys her sexuality and that she likes the way she looks, her daughter is more apt to feel comfortable with her own appearance and enjoy her own sexuality. Although most teenage boys are excited by the changes in their bodies that give them access to greater status and power, many teenage girls feel embarrassed or frightened by their sexuality and physical maturity. Having been through the same experience herself, a mother has a unique opportunity to help her daughter feel excited and comfortable with her sexuality and her body. While teaching her to appreciate and accept the changes associated with sexual maturity, a mother can also teach her daughter not to place too much importance on her own appearance, as our society so often encourages. A mother also has unlimited opportunities to help her daughter grow up without judging herself by unrealistic standards of what women ought to look like (Debold, Wilson, & Malave, 1992; Flaake, 1993; Flax, 1993; Tolman, 1991).

Unfortunately, this research shows us that many mothers feel too uncomfortable or too dissatisfied with their own sexuality, femininity, aging, or appearance to convey positive attitudes to their daughters. Other than menstruation, contraception, and rape prevention, most mothers and daughters never discuss any aspect of female sexuality with one another—sexual desire, passion, excitement, or giving oneself sexual pleasure. Some teenage girls respond to their mother's discomfort or lack of interest in sexuality by trying to ignore or deny their own sexuality—dressing and acting like young, asexual girls or like "one of the guys."

Other daughters exaggerate their femininity and sexuality in an effort to figure out how to incorporate sexuality and femininity into their lives in light of their mothers' negative attitudes. Given this, it's usually other women, such as stepmothers or aunts, who help teenage girls feel more comfortable with the passionate, sexual aspects of their lives.

Latina and Black Mothers and Daughters   When it comes to encouraging their daughters' self-reliance, assertiveness, and self-confidence, many African and Hispanic American mothers seem to be doing a better job in certain regards than many white mothers (Augenbraum & Stavan, 1993; Bell-Scott, 1991; Debold, Wilson, & Malave, 1992; Glickman, 1993).

African American and Latina mothers are more likely than white women to work outside the home while their children are growing up. As a result, their daughters tend to be more aware of the fact that they're going to have to earn an income of their own as women to help support their children and themselves. Compared to a black or a Hispanic girl, a white girl is more apt to be preparing herself for a future in which her husband will supply all, or most, of her financial support. In this regard, African and Hispanic American women seem to be doing a better job of communicating the economic realities of a married, single, or divorced woman's life to their daughters.

Many African American daughters also manage to express themselves and maintain self-confidence during adolescence, more so than many white or Latina girls. In part, African American daughters' strengths seem tied to the nurturance and encouragement of women other than their own mothers—their "other-mothers." These other-mothers not only embody more ways of being women than one mother can provide, they also can help a teenage girl better understand her own mother (Collins, 1991). Especially in comparison to white, middle-class families, many black and Latina daughters are encouraged to form close, supportive relationships with women other than their mothers—aunts, stepmothers, grandmothers, mothers' friends, and teachers. Indeed, a teenage girl can often discuss topics and problems with these women that she doesn't feel comfortable discussing with her mother. Many black mothers are more apt to work with other women in less jealous, less possessive ways than white mothers when it comes to raising their daughters. It also appears that African American and working-class daughters might feel more connected to and more respect for their mothers' strength and self-reliance than many white, middle-class daughters (Bell-Scott, 1991; Debold, Wilson, & Malave, 1992).

Conflict and Intimacy   Regardless of race, most mothers and teenage daughters say they feel close to one another—closer than most mothers and sons feel and closer than most fathers and daughters feel. On the other hand, most mothers and daughters are more jealous, combative, and competitive toward one another than are fathers and daughters or mothers and sons. Why? First, unlike teenage boys, teenage girls generally spend more time with their mothers and less time with their fathers. This gives mothers and daughters more opportunity to find things they disagree about. A teenage girl also tends to avoid potential conflicts with her father by limiting her contact with him, whereas she feels more comfortable or more confident that she'll get her way by arguing with her mother. Some girls argue more with their mothers because they've learned that, compared to arguing with their fathers, they're more likely to persuade mother to see their point of view or to make mom back down.

Second, adolescence is the time when daughters need to begin pulling away from their mothers somewhat in order to become more self-reliant and more self-defined. Although a close relationship with her father during adolescence seems to boost a girl's self-reliance and her intellectual and vocational confidence, some degree of emotional separation from her mother is beneficial. Perhaps this is because girls compare themselves to their mothers in a more competitive way and need more emotional space between them to develop their own values and identities. Most teenage boys seem to have done this sort of separating from their mothers around the age of 4 or 5 in order to bond and identify with their fathers. Stated in psychoanalytic terms, most boys resolve their Oedipal complex as preschoolers, whereas girls may not have to separate from their mothers in this way until adolescence. So part of the mother-daughter conflict might be a result of the daughter's need to pull away from her mother during her teenage years (Biller, 1993; Snarey, 1993).

Third, there is sometimes a certain competitive or jealous dimension to the mother-daughter relationship during adolescence—a negative dimension that usually doesn't exist between fathers and daughters. This might be in part because the daughter's sexuality, physical attractiveness, and options in life make the mother feel bad about her own physical self or the choices she made in her life. Or, if the daughter doesn't believe she's measuring up to her mother's beauty, intellect, or professional achievements, she might feel jealous and competitive. This comparison and competition can also make a teenage girl overly tense or critical about her mother. One daughter's comments illustrate these feelings: "My mother said, 'you'll make me look dowdy when you show up in that.' I couldn't believe it—my mother was jealous of me. Then I got mad at myself, because part of me was glad to outdo her" (Caplan, 1989, p.31).

Some mothers and daughters also become overly critical of each other because each sees herself as a reflection of the other. The tension caused by mothers and daughters seeing themselves as extensions of one another is evidenced by these two separate daughters' comments: "I used to feel that everything my mother did reflected on me. I was embarrassed by her looks, the way she dressed, the way she talked, and I hated her for it. But then I also hated myself for hating her." "My mother wanted me to lose weight for my own sake, sure—but also for her, and I couldn't stand being her route to her club ladies' praise" (Caplan, 1989, pp. 183, 189).

Another source of conflict for some teenage daughters is jealousy or anger toward their mother for treating them differently from their brothers. When a daughter sees that her brother has received most of mother's time and attention, she can feel both betrayed and jealous. Some daughters also see that their mother dotes, excuses, serves, babies, and sets fewer limits on the son. The mother also expects and demands less from him. If this is happening, it can create stress between the mother and daughter. As one daughter comments, "Whenever mama was sick, my brother was nowhere to be found. I was expected to take care of mama. It never felt OK for me to need to be taken care of" (Caplan, 1989, p. 111).

Finally, some daughters feel angry or ashamed when their mothers behave in subservient, child-like, overly dependent, or submissive ways in relationships with men. As a daughter ages, she usually takes more notice of the way her mother relates to the man in her life—either the father, stepfather, or boyfriend. Observing her mother's behavior, the daughter might sometimes feel mad or ashamed that her mother isn't behaving in more self-respecting or self-reliant ways. As one daughter explains: "My otherwise lovely father had a habit of putting my mother down. It tore me apart. I hated him for insulting her, and that made me want to side with her. But I hated her for not standing up for herself" (Caplan, 1989, p. 186). In her day-to-day relationship with a man, the mother is sending her daughter powerful messages about how a woman ought to assert her feelings and opinions, express her anger, and maintain her self-respect and autonomy. For example, some mothers say that when teenage daughters point out continual acquiescence to their husbands, they admit this is an area of struggle in their lives that they are trying to change (Debold, Wilson, & Malave, 1992). Because adolescence is the time when many girls "lose their voices" and become increasingly submissive and self-deprecating, a self-reliant, self-confident mother or stepmother can be one of a girl's most powerful "voice" teachers (Bingham, 1995; Glickman, 1993; Pipher, 1994).

Regardless of the source of the tension or conflict, most mothers and their teenage daughters say they have a close relationship. So although most mothers and daughters do argue or feel tense, conflicted, jealous, disappointed, or angry at each other from time to time, most stay bonded to each other in loving, supportive ways. Whether we're talking about sons and daughters or fathers and mothers, most adolescents don't reject or separate themselves completely from either parent in becoming more self-reliant and self-defined. Adolescents don't need to end a loving, supportive relationship with either parent in order to become autonomous, mature adults. The struggle for teenage sons and daughters and their parents is one of redefining, not cutting, their connections to one another.

MOTHERS' EMPLOYMENT

Statistics and Trends

Mothers also affect their children's development by working outside the home. Given the financial needs of their families, more women than ever have to continue working outside the home after they have children. Some mothers are also keeping their jobs because, like fathers, they enjoy the stimulation and self-esteem that come from earning an income and interacting with other adults. Our high divorce rates have also forced into the work force women who would otherwise prefer to be full-time homemakers. The result is that nearly 80% of all adolescents and 70% of all preschoolers have mothers who work outside the home.

Nearly twice as many teenagers as 20 years ago have grown up in homes in which their mothers have always contributed to the family's income. So when we refer to employed mothers, we're referring to the vast majority of mothers in our country (Department of Commerce, 1992).

CRITICISMS OF EMPLOYED MOTHERS

What impact does a mother's working outside the home have on her children? Because widespread changes in a society are often met with suspicion and fear, it's understandable that as mothers entered the work force in greater numbers, they were met with a barrage of criticism: Why did she have children if she didn't plan to stay home and take care of them? How can she let someone else raise her own children? That poor husband has to do so much baby-sitting for their children. She ought to stay home so their children will have someone there when they get home. She's so selfish, isn't she?

But let us now examine the assumptions that underlie these negative reactions. Perhaps the most important and the most unfounded assumption is that mothers who have jobs have chosen this option over staying home. Too many upper-income people still fool themselves into believing that most mothers could stay home if they wanted to do so. But the reality is that most mothers work for the same reason fathers do—their family needs the money. Look at it this way: 25% of the women who work have a husband who earns less than $10,000 a year, and 35% more two-parent families would fall into poverty if mothers quit work (Bane & Ellwood, 1989; Dodd, 1989).

Another questionable assumption is one that children need to be with their mother more than they need to be with their father—which, as shown throughout this chapter and in earlier chapters, isn't so. Some people assume that nature intended for women to raise the young while men earn the money. The "good" father is still too often seen as the man who provides the most financially, and the "good" mother is still too often seen as having no financial responsibility for their children. Thus, unlike mothers, fathers are seldom criticized or made to feel guilty for earning incomes. Although we often assume that tremendous changes have taken place in the roles of mothers and fathers, we might ask ourselves: Why is the employed father thanked and noticed for helping with housework and child-care, when the employed mother is barely acknowledged for the same contributions? Why are children's problems more apt to be blamed on their mother's having a job than on their father's working?

If our society had arrived at the point where both parents were considered equally important to their children's development, we might expect to hear criticisms like these: Why did that man have kids if he didn't plan to spend more time with them? Why did that woman have kids if she didn't plan to take better care of them financially than she does? How can that mother deprive her children of more time with their father by refusing to relieve him of some of the financial pressure by getting a job herself? Isn't that mother wonderful for helping her husband out with his housework even though she has such a demanding job? We might even ask: Why haven't researchers focused more on the benefits of having a father who devotes less time to his work and more time to his children?

Finally, some well-intentioned people argue that children who are taken care of by anyone other than their own mother will somehow suffer. But this assumption ignores several realities. First, full-time homemakers tend to be more dissatisfied, more depressed, and more emotionally troubled than mothers who have jobs outside the home, which may, in turn, have a negative impact on their children's development. For example, teenagers whose mothers are depressed, chronically unhappy, full-time homemakers tend to have more psychological and social problems than teenagers whose mothers have always worked outside the home (Waxler & others, 1992). Likewise, mothers who go back to work before their children are 2 years old report being happier with their marriages and less depressed than those who stay home (Cowan & Cowan, 1992). Second, decades of exhaustive research have failed to prove that children whose mothers are full-time housewives are any more advanced in terms of their emotional security, self-confidence, attachment to parents, academic achievements, or overall psychological and emotional well-being (Cowan & Cowan, 1992; Crosby, 1993; Lerner & Galambos, 1991). In fact, being cared for by other caring, competent adults often benefits children from troubled or impoverished families (Silverstein, 1991). Third, less than 20% of our preschool children are in childcare centers. Most infants and preschoolers are being taken care of by relatives, friends, or baby-sitters while their parents work (O'Connell, 1993). In short, blaming teenagers' problems on their mothers' working while the children were growing up is both cruel and unsupported (Caplan, 1989).

Given the fact that 80% of all mothers do work outside the home, the lingering objections that some people still raise might seem odd or even pointless. Yet the media continues to project an image of the "typical" mother that is a far cry from reality. Only 30% of mothers in television shows are earning an income—yet, amazingly, almost 90% of their families have a middle-class or higher income. Then again, on television 95% of the families are white (in reality less than 80%), 60% of the single-parent families are headed by men (in reality only 9%), and only 9% of the single-parent families are the result of a divorce (in reality more than 50%) (Moore, 1992).

Benefits for Adolescents

The bottom line is that adolescents who have grown up with mothers who work outside the home usually have advantages that go beyond having a higher standard of living. These adolescents are usually more socially mature, more psychologically well-adjusted, more successful academically, and more open-minded about gender roles than are those whose mothers were full-time homemakers while their children were growing up. Most children whose mothers work are as well off—and often better off—in terms of their self-esteem, close relationships with parents, grades, mental skills, social maturity, future jobs, and educational achievements than are those whose mothers are housewives (Barber & Eccles,

1992; Crosby, 1993; Gilbert, 1993; Lerner & Galambos, 1991). For reasons we will examine in the next chapter, if their parents divorce, adolescents whose mothers were employed throughout their marriage are usually better off emotionally than are those whose mothers were housewives during most of their married lives (Furstenberg & Cherlin, 1991; Maccoby & Mnookin, 1993; Pasley & Ihinger-Tallman, 1994; Warshak, 1992).

Why are adolescents whose mothers work usually better off? Part of the answer is that their mothers are usually happier than are most housewives. Most employed women are more satisfied with their lives, are less depressed, have more self-esteem, have fewer psychosomatic illnesses, and are more satisfied with their marriage than are nonemployed mothers (Crosby, 1994; Gilbert, 1994; Lerner & Galambos, 1991). Perhaps this helps to explain why most full-time housewives say they would choose to have a job, if they had it to do all over again; and why most employed women say they would keep working even if they did not need the money. Most employed mothers also tend to be less overly involved in negative ways with their children than are mothers who stay home. Both the sons and daughters of employed mothers also tend to have more open minded attitudes about gender roles than do housewives' children (Barber & Eccles, 1992; Caplan, 1989; Richards & Duckett, 1991). Then, too, when the wife has a job, the father and children tend to have a closer relationship because they've spent more time together (Almeida & Galambos, 1991; Paulson, Koman & Hill, 1990; Richards & Duckett, 1991).

Disadvantages for Adolescents

However, the research isn't saying that no disadvantages exist for some teenagers when their mothers and fathers both work outside the home. For example, some adolescents see that although their mother resents working, she must continue because of a divorce or her husband's losing his job. In these cases, the mother's stress and anger tend to filter down to her children. But a far more common source of stress when both adults are working is that most fathers or stepfathers don't do their fair share of work at home. Even when both adults work an equal number of hours at their jobs, the mother or stepmother still ends up doing most cooking, cleaning, laundering, shopping, errands, and child-related tasks. Part of the reason is that most fathers and stepfathers work longer hours and earn more money than do their wives. Especially in the first few years of a child's life, mothers are often only working part-time or working at jobs in which they have afternoons or summers free. For reasons already discussed, some fathers are also less involved in their children's lives or in housework because their wives discourage them. On the other hand, when the man and woman have roughly the same incomes, they tend to share childcare and housework more equally. In general, a full-time housewife does 90% of the housework and childcare compared to 60% to 70% for a mother who has a full-time job (Gilbert, 1993; Goodnow & Bowes, 1994).

Another concern when both the man and the woman work is: How will teenagers be affected by no supervision after school or during vacations? It's estimated that 10 to 15 million children, referred to as **latchkey children,** are alone for several hours after they get home from school. Most of these children are white and come from higher rather than lower-income families. The belief that lack of supervision is far more common among single-parent households is a misconception because nearly 7% of two-parent households have children who must look after themselves at least part of the day, compared to 8% of single-mother families. In fact, most children whose parent or parents are still at work when they come home from school are living in relatively safe, middle-class neighborhoods. Moreover, only 10% of all children are alone for more than 2 hours a day, and less than 1% are left alone at night (Lerner & Galambos, 1991).

This isn't to say that having an adult at home after school might not have some value for certain adolescents. For example, in a study of almost 5,000 8th graders, teenagers left alone at home for more than 11 hours a week were twice as likely to skip school, drink, and smoke tobacco or marijuana, regardless of their parents' marital status and income. On the other hand, these unsupervised teenagers were also twice as likely to say they were angry at their parents, which suggests that other factors caused their problems. Those teenagers who had been left to take care of themselves at home during elementary school years also had more serious problems than those who weren't left alone after school until they were teenagers (Richardson, 1989). It's also important to consider what teenagers are doing when they're alone after school. Those who go directly home and stay there until an adult returns don't have more academic or social problems than do teenagers whose parent or stepparent is home every afternoon. The teenagers who get into trouble and make poorer grades are generally those who go off with their friends after school rather than going home (Lerner & Galambos, 1991).

There's also a big difference between leaving teenagers home alone for a few hours after school and failing to supervise them. Employed adults do have to make an extra effort once they get home to keep up with what's going on in their teenagers' lives. But this doesn't imply that an employed couple isn't supervising teenagers as well as families in which the mother is a full-time homemaker. It is true that unmarried mothers generally don't supervise their teenage children as much as married mothers. But this seems more related to the mother being the only adult in the family than to whether she has a job. All in all then, teenagers whose mothers are married and work while the children are growing up are as well off, or better off, than teenagers whose mothers stayed home—even when their married mother went back to work while the children were infants or preschoolers (Lerner & Galambos, 1991).

ADOLESCENTS AND POVERTY

STATISTICS AND TRENDS

Whether or not their mothers are employed, one thing is certain about today's adolescents: more of them are living in poverty or in low-income families than at

Figure 8–1

Who are children living with?

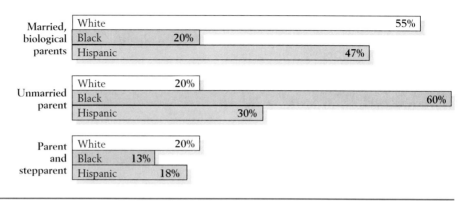

Source: Bureau of the Census (1992). *Current population reports: Family characteristics.* Washington, DC: U.S. Department of Commerce.

any time since the 1960s. Nearly 20% of our children are now growing up poor, a figure that will reach 25% by the year 2000. As if these statistics aren't depressing enough, more than a third of our country's children live in poverty for at least one year. For reasons we've already discussed in Chapter 7, poverty is far worse among minority children than among whites. For example, 90% of the children who live in poverty for more than 10 years are black. Stated differently, only 14% of black children escape poverty altogether while they're growing up. What does "poor" or "poverty" mean in actual dollars? The **poverty level,** determined yearly by federal government economists, is now about $14,000 annually for a family of

Figure 8–2

Marital status and yearly family incomes

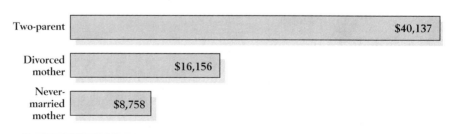

Source: Bureau of the Census (1992). *Marital status and living arrangements.* Washington, DC: U.S. Department of Commerce.

Figure 8–3

Adolescents' economic situations by race

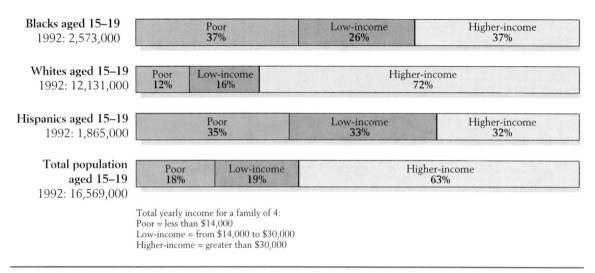

Blacks aged 15–19 1992: 2,573,000	Poor 37%	Low-income 26%	Higher-income 37%

Whites aged 15–19 1992: 12,131,000	Poor 12% / Low-income 16%	Higher-income 72%

Hispanics aged 15–19 1992: 1,865,000	Poor 35%	Low-income 33%	Higher-income 32%

Total population **aged 15–19** 1992: 16,569,000	Poor 18% / Low-income 19%	Higher-income 63%

Total yearly income for a family of 4:
Poor = less than $14,000
Low-income = from $14,000 to $30,000
Higher-income = greater than $30,000

Source: Bureau of the Census (1992). *Current population reports.* Washington, DC: U.S. Department

four. At present, about 12 million of the 64 million children (19%) in our country live in a home where the total income falls below $14,000 a year. More disturbing still, nearly 5 million of these poor children are in families with incomes of less than $6000 a year. Leaving aside these extremely poor families, the typical adolescent today is growing up in a family that is less affluent than a similar family in the 1960s or 1970s. Even with 80% of mothers working outside the home, overall most families have lost 5% to 12% of their incomes since 1970. At present, half of all white families live on less than $37,000 a year, half of all Hispanic families on less than $22,000 a year, and half of all black families on less than $19,000 a year (Bennett, 1994; Census Bureau, 1992; Fuchs & Reklis, 1992; N.C.C., 1993).

THE ROOTS OF POVERTY

Why? Why are so many children in our country now poor or growing up with a lower standard of living than most children in recent decades? Before answering, take a minute to picture your idea of the "typical" poor or low-income family. What do you see? An unmarried, black mother living in an urban area who doesn't have to work because she can support her children on welfare? A Hispanic family living in rural areas as migrant workers? A divorced, white mother who has a full-time job? A Native American family living on a reservation? How many of the adults in your imagined family have jobs? Now let's compare your picture to the statistics. About 45% of all poor children are in white families who live in rural areas. Most receive no welfare benefits. Of these poor white children, nearly half live with two parents. Regardless of race, almost all poor children live in rural areas and small towns. Only 1 in 10 lives in an urban ghetto. Contrary to popular notions, our rising divorce rate isn't the major reason underlying the dramatic increases in childhood poverty. Although divorce does lower the family's standard of living, most divorced mothers remarry within 5 years, thereby raising the family income to an even higher level, in most cases, than before the divorce.

The rise in family poverty is directly related, however, to increasing out-of-wedlock births. Although only 5% of all babies born in 1960 had unmarried mothers, today nearly 30% of babies are born out-of-wedlock. As a result, nearly 30% of black, 10% of Hispanic, and 4% of white children are now living with a mother who has never been married. Among teenage parents, only 10% of blacks, 40% of Hispanics, and 50% of whites are married. Because most teenage parents have too little education to earn decent incomes, it's not surprising that half of their children are living in poverty. Some projections show that by the year 2000, 40% of all births and 80% of minority births will be to unmarried parents. In 1992, for the first time in our country's history, approximately the same number of children were living with a divorced mother as with a mother who had never been married. As a result of divorce and out-of-wedlock births, only 6% of black children and 30% of white children born in 1980 will be living with both parents for all 18 years of childhood (Bane & Ellwood, 1989; Barling, 1991; Johnson, Sum, & Weill, 1988; McLoyd, 1989; NCC, 1993).

Births to unmarried mothers, however, don't explain the other half of all poor children whose mothers are married. Could it be that poverty has risen among these married parents because they are quitting school more often than parents in the past? No. It is true that the higher a parent's level of education, the more money they usually make. But by that logic, families should be better off financially than they are because adults have, on average, more schooling than at any time in our nation's history. For instance, nearly 75% of all mothers now have a high-school diploma in contrast to only 50% in 1960. Simply put, a parent's level of education has less financial payoff today than it once did. For example, college-educated African American parents now earn about a third less than their counterparts in 1973. Likewise, although Hispanic American parents are better educated than ever before, their median incomes have dropped by about a third in the past 30 years. For reasons discussed later in Chapter 11, it now takes more education to earn a good living than it once did.

Then why more poverty among married couples? Could it be that women are partly to blame for having more children than in the past, or for not doing their share of earning money? Or could it be that women are taking jobs away from men so that families actually end up with less money? No. First, married women are waiting longer to have children and are having fewer of them than were women in the 1960s and 1970s. Second, 80% of all women are now working, even before their children start school—almost twice the number who worked in

1970. In fact if women quit their jobs, another 35% of our families would fall into poverty. Third, most women's jobs are service or secretarial jobs—not the jobs most unemployed men want, are qualified for, or would accept (Bane & Ellwood, 1989; Barling, 1991).

So why can't a greater number of married couples earn more than $14,000 a year for their families? A large part of the answer is that certain economic factors beyond any individual's control have thrown lower income families into poverty —hence the new terminology for these families, the **working poor.** After rising substantially during the 1960s, real wages have been almost stagnant since the early 1970s. So although more parents are now working, they have a lower standard of living on the whole than did most parents 25 years ago. For example, between 1973 and 1986 the youngest parents, many of whom had had children as teenagers, suffered a 25% decrease in income—a setback as severe as that of the Great Depression in the 1930s. In large part what has happened is: High-paying jobs that required only a high-school diploma, such as those in the auto and steel industries, have become more scarce as our economy has moved toward service jobs—jobs that pay much less to high-school graduates. So nowadays a parent with a high-school diploma often gets a job that pays only minimum wage and offers few chances for advancement. Think of it this way: A male and female with high-school diplomas get married and have two children. He works full-time at minimum wage, and she works part-time because they can't afford to pay someone to care for their children. This family of four will be almost $2,000 below the poverty line.

Race, Marital Status, Education, and Poverty

So which adolescents are the most likely to grow up in poverty or in a low-income family? As Table 8–1 shows, about 10% of white, 35% of Hispanic, 40% of black, and 40% of Native American children live in families with a total income of less than $14,000 a year—most with an unmarried mother. Although 75% of white children live in a family with a total income of more than $28,000, only 35% of black, Hispanic, and Native American children do. Having a mother who is married, however, is a financial boost in all racial groups. For example, compared to married women of their own race, single white mothers have only about half as much money, and single black and Hispanic mothers have only one-third as much. Clearly then, the mother's race and marital status are two of the best ways to predict which adolescents are living in low-income families or in abject poverty. Some groups, however, have fallen deeper and faster into poverty than others. For example, although only 10% of all children in our country are Hispanic, they account for nearly half of the increase in poverty since 1980. As noted, the parents' education is also related to family income. So the fact that only 30% of Hispanic parents have graduated from high school limits them to the lowest paying jobs. Latino women are also more likely to be full-time homemakers and to have more children than white or black women (Bennett, 1994; NCC, 1993; U.S. Department of Commerce, 1992).

Figure 8–4

Children living in poverty: Parents' marital status and education

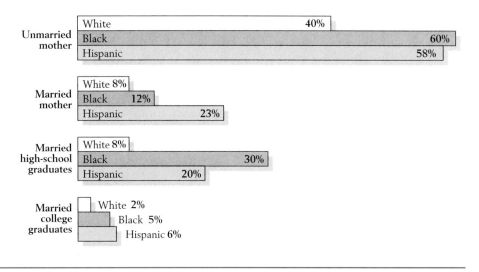

Source: Bureau of the Census (1992). *Current population reports.* Washington, DC: U.S. Department of Commerce.

Another way to think about poverty is to consider how many years a child spends in poverty. If your mother has never been married and is white, the odds are that you will spend 5 of the first 15 years of your life in poverty. But if she's married, the odds are that you will spend only 6 months living in poverty. In contrast, if your mother is black and married, the odds are that you will still spend 3 years of your childhood in poverty. In other words, having an unmarried mother is more harmful financially for black children than for white (Duncan & Rodgers, 1988).

Remember though, for the reasons discussed in Chapter 7, white adults on the whole earn higher incomes than black adults with equivalent levels of education. For example, most black men with college degrees end up only a few dollars ahead of white men with a high-school diploma. Indeed, there is little evidence that more schooling improves the income of blacks relative to whites, although it does improve their income relative to other blacks. Likewise, when economic times get tough and people are fired, minority parents are usually hit harder than white parents. So a parent's race, marital status, and level of education all play a part in determining the likelihood of children growing up in poverty or in a low-income family (Hacker, 1992).

Table 8–1	
Families on welfare	
Race	
Black	40%
White	38%
Hispanic	16%
Asian	2%
Other	3%
Mother's Age	
21 or less	16%
22–29	40%
30–39	31%
40 & older	13%
Fathers	
Unwed	53%
Divorced	34%
Dead	2%
Unknown	2%
Number of Children in the Family	
One	44%
Two	30%
Three	16%
Four	10%

Source: A. Hacker (1992). *Two nations: black, white, separate and unequal.* NY: Charles Scribner's.

SINGLE MOTHERS AND WELFARE

But are most unmarried mothers trying to lift their families out of poverty? Isn't our welfare system enabling or even encouraging these women to have children and get along without having to get a job? The popular belief is that our welfare system makes it easy for women to choose single motherhood and to raise their children on welfare. But this isn't the reality.

Although welfare benefits rose dramatically during the 1960s, since then they have fallen by 25% after adjustments for inflation. **Aid to Families with Dependent Children (AFDC)** is the major source of welfare for mothers and their children. Yet the AFDC eligibility rules have been tightened such that only about half of all poor children are now receiving welfare assistance, in contrast to 80% 20 years ago. Despite these cutbacks, out-of-wedlock births have continued to increase. Moreover, some states with the lowest welfare benefits have the most single mothers and vice versa. So it doesn't appear that welfare is at the root of why so many single women are becoming mothers. In addition, no state pays enough welfare to keep a mother and her children out of poverty. For example, in 32 states welfare pays only $6,000 a year to a family of four. So 90% of mothers receiving welfare still live below the poverty level. In short, our welfare system isn't enabling single mothers and their families to "get by okay" without working (Bane & Ellwood, 1989; Fuchs & Reklis, 1992; Hacker, 1992).

But why don't more of these unmarried mothers have jobs if welfare isn't keeping them out of poverty? Well, first, ask yourself: If a teenage mother finds a job paying minimum wage, who's going to pay for childcare? Given that the average cost of childcare is $3,000 a year per child, and that we are the only industrialized nation on earth without subsidized childcare for the poor, where are these infants and preschoolers going to be while their single mothers are at work? Second, the existing welfare rules discontinue many benefits when the mother gets a job. So a single mother who has a full-time job that pays $6 an hour will have only $1,500 more a year than an unemployed woman on welfare. Moreover, until 1988, 25 states discouraged single mothers from getting married by refusing to give any welfare to two-parent families, regardless of how poor they were. Third, most single mothers are too poorly educated to qualify for even minimum wage jobs. Among single mothers on welfare, 30% dropped out of school in the ninth grade, 75% have no work experience whatsoever, 50% are still teenagers, and 50% have children under the age 6. Even though the 1988 Welfare Reform Bill requires all welfare recipients to participate in a job training or education program, most of these young mothers are qualified for only the lowest paying jobs. And last, but hardly least, most unwed fathers pay no child support. Although some states are now experimenting with programs that withhold child support payments directly from the father's paycheck, many unwed fathers are too young and too poorly educated to hold a steady job (Bane & Ellwood, 1989; Fuchs & Recklis, 1992).

THE IMPACT OF POVERTY

As discussed in preceding chapters, adolescents are generally better off when they grow up in families with no serious financial problems. To summarize briefly: Compared to teens from low-income families, other adolescents make better grades, complete more years in school, and are less likely to get pregnant, be delinquent, or abuse drugs. Because poor children generally grow up without a father or stepfather, many of their problems can be attributed to having been raised by only one adult. Also, given the neighborhoods and privileges that money makes possible, teenagers from more well-to-do families generally go to better schools, have more talented teachers and better medical and psychological care. Poor and low-income children are also more likely to experience stress or danger at home, such as physical violence, rape, drug abuse, and alcoholism. Even when they are fortunate enough to live with a father or stepfather, poor children also experience more stress from long periods of his unemployment. In this vein, it's noteworthy that in 1982 our country experienced its highest rate of unemployment since the Depression. Although unemployment rates have dropped since 1982, changes in our economy have resulted in the parents of millions of adolescents losing their jobs and facing months or years of unemployment (McLoyd, 1989).

Adolescents whose fathers or stepfathers lose their jobs often experience other problems, too. Unemployed men are more apt to become depressed, explosive, and physically abusive. As his family's financial worries mount and the father's self-confidence diminishes, alcohol abuse and physical violence also tend to increase. Their father's losing a job is also associated with teenagers' becoming more moody, hypersensitive, aggressive, depressed, and distrustful. Many of these teenagers also lower their own educational goals and adopt more pessimistic attitudes about their own futures. Many teenagers whose fathers aren't able to find work also begin to suffer more stress-related illnesses, to misbehave at school, and to make poorer grades. Although there's too little data to determine the long-term psychological effects a father's unemployment might have on his children, the short-term effects certainly aren't beneficial (Barling, 1991; McLoyd, 1989).

Homeless Adolescents

Given the extent of poverty in our society, it shouldn't surprise you to learn that homelessness increased four-fold between 1980 and 1990. The federal government now estimates that roughly 600,000 people are homeless, although other experts believe this figure is far too low. Nevertheless, the fact remains that thousands of adolescents and their parents are in such dire situations that they resort to living in shelters or on the streets. Among homeless mothers, 90% had children out of wedlock, 75% are minorities, 50% dropped out of high school, and 30% have mental disorders or are drug abusers. Many of these homeless mothers were physically or sexually abused by their own parents or by a former husband (Jencks, 1994; Kondratas, 1993; Milburn & D'Ercole, 1991).

Homeless adolescents, however, include more than only those whose parents are too poor to provide them with food and shelter. Homeless youth also include teenagers who have run away from home and those whose parents aren't able to take care of them because of problems such as drug abuse, alcoholism, mental disorders, physical and sexual abuse, and imprisonment. If we include all of these categories, about 1.5 million teenagers are now classified as homeless—a three-fold increase in the past 20 years. Among homeless teenagers, about half have run away or been thrown out of their parents' homes, foster homes, or institutions for troubled youth. The shortage of money for public shelters, however, has left many of these homeless adolescents on the street. There are also about 30% fewer foster homes than there were in the late 1980s, and the number of teenagers seeking foster care has increased by 35% (Rotherman, Koopman, & Ehrhardt, 1991).

Insert 8–5

Homeless Adolescents

Elizabeth, age 13, is one of six children living with her single mother. After falling behind on the rent, her family moved to the shelter five months ago. "We had to move out of our house. We got evicted because my mother didn't have enough money to pay rent and because my father wasn't giving us a lot of children support and because he couldn't afford it because he has to give it to three other girls too—his girlfriends from before. My mother was the only one working because my brother quit his job."

Haydn, age 16, came to the shelter with his brother and mother. His parents divorced 6 years ago, and his mother was imprisoned on drug charges. When their mother was recently released from prison, it was decided that they should stop living with their father, stepmother, and six stepsiblings and join their mother in the shelter to help her get back on her feet. "My friends don't really know where I am now. I don't tell because like any kids my age, I'd be ashamed. You just don't want your friends to know that you live in a shelter. All those feelings, I just keep them inside."

Georgia, age 13, has a mother and father who are both alcoholics. Her parents are divorced, and her father is no longer working. Before coming to the shelter, the family was living with her mother's alcoholic boyfriend. "I come from an alcoholic background, with my father and my mother being codependent. I have a deadly fear of alcohol and drugs. My maturity is up a few years. I take care of myself. My father and I are very close now that he's sober for the past five years. But I can't live with him because he lives with four other guys and he only has one room. I don't tell people I live in a shelter. They think that either you're drugged up like you're a major addict, or that your parents are druggies and you're worthless. It's like this big chain."

Barbara, age 17, is pregnant and has been a runaway since she was 11. Both parents were using drugs and her father, a Vietnam veteran, would mix alcohol with his medications then become violent and sexually abusive. "My dad spazzed out and went crazy. It was scary. He's beat up on me and my mother and held guns to us."

April, age 14, lives with her brother, mother and 16-year-old pregnant sister. Their mother is a drug user, and the family was evicted from their lifelong home after a police raid for drugs. "I told my math teacher where I lived and she was like 'oh.' But teachers gossip and tell each other. Sometimes I think teachers think bad of kids in shelters like, 'that's why those kids are acting so bad.'"

Source: M. Walsh (1992). *Moving to nowhere: Children's stories of homelessness.* Westport, CT: Auburn House.

Given their situations, it's easy to understand why most homeless teenagers are at high risk for abusing drugs, getting pregnant, becoming prostitutes, and being victims of violence. Trading sex for drugs or money, homeless teenagers—including boys—are also at high risk for contracting AIDS and other venereal diseases, and for being raped. As for the possibility of a brighter future, nearly half of homeless teenagers have dropped out of school, and nearly half of those that do still go to school have learning or behavior problems. It's no surprise, then, that a third of homeless teenagers have attempted suicide. As Insert 8–5 illustrates, homeless teenagers suffer from a host of social and psychological problems that most of us, even as adults, would find daunting, if not insurmountable (Athey, 1991; Rotherman, Koopman, & Ehrhardt, 1991; Walsh, 1992).

As a society, our feelings about the homeless, welfare, and low-income families are contradictory. In public opinion polls, most of us say the poor do not deserve their poverty. Most of us also say it's unfair that the wealthy get better health care and better education than the poor. At the same time, the majority also say that people are poor because they are lazy, unwilling to make sufficient personal sacrifices, or aren't trying hard enough. When asked who is responsible for helping the poor, most of us answer "poor people." Fewer than 10% of us say we feel any personal responsibility to help the poor, although half of us say that they should be helped (Patterson & Kim, 1992).

PHYSICAL AND SEXUAL ABUSE

Many homeless teenagers have been physically or sexually abused by members of their families. Thousands of other children, however, are still living in situations where a family member is physically or sexually abusing them. Because many cases of physical or sexual abuse are not reported to the authorities, it is estimated that 1.6 million children in our country experience some form of abuse in their families (Widom, 1994). There seem to be several factors in common in these families (Cicchetti & Carlson, 1989; Johnson, 1992; Kurtz, Kirtz, & Jarvis, 1991; Westen, 1990).

First, financial or marital stress increases the likelihood that a child will be physically or sexually abused. Those parents who themselves were abused as children are also more likely to be sexually or physically abusive with their children or stepchildren. The better that parents or stepparents feel about themselves with regard to their own self-esteem, financial status, and marital happiness, the less apt they are to abuse a child. It is far more common, however, for sexual abuse to occur between people who are not biologically related. For example, incest between fathers and daughters is rare compared to incest between stepfathers and stepdaughters. Although most victims of sexual abuse are females, male children are also victims (Lew, 1990). The physical and sexual abuse of children also knows no bounds in terms of race or socioeconomic class (Hooks, 1993).

How does being physically or sexually abused by someone in the family affect a young person? As you might expect, children who have been frequently hit or beaten by a member of the family tend to turn their own anger and aggression toward other people. But the majority of abused children do not become delinquent or violent, nor are the majority of delinquent, violent teenagers victims of abuse. Nevertheless, having been physically or sexually abused appears to increase the risk for developing a range of problems in adolescence, including delinquency, violence, sexual promiscuity, pregnancy, and alcohol and drug abuse

(Cicchetti, 1992; Peplar & Rubin, 1994; Youngblade & Belsky, 1993; Widom, 1994). Likewise, incest victims are more likely than other children to develop psychological disorders later in life (Bass & Davis, 1991; Blume, 1990; German, Habenicht, & Futcher, 1990).

MEMORIES OF OUR FAMILIES

In closing, we return to one of our initial questions: What impact do parents or stepparents have on our teenage development? In answering this question, there is one final factor to consider: How accurate are our memories and perceptions of our families and our childhood? Whether we're in therapy trying to figure out how our families have affected us, or whether a researcher is simply gathering information from us about our families, how trustworthy are our memories? How accurate are our memories and present perceptions of our families?

As you might suspect, memories and perceptions of our families are largely colored by our own temperaments, mental health, and overall quality of our lives. In general, teenagers and adults who are psychologically well-adjusted and have relatively pleasant temperaments remember their families and childhoods more positively than do people with psychological problems or difficult temperaments. For example, in a survey of 600 men and women between the ages of 21 and 96, those who remembered their parents as loving were more extraverted, emotionally stable, and happier with their lives than were those who remembered their parents as rejecting and unloving (McCrae & Costa, 1988). The happier and more psychologically well-adjusted we are, the more favorably we remember our past and the more insightful and forgiving we are in regard to members of our families (Bornstein, 1991; Gilovich, 1991; Halverson, 1988; Howard, 1991).

One of the more common ways in which memories and perceptions of our families are distorted is a defense mechanism referred to as splitting. **Splitting** is an immature, distorted way of viewing the world in which other people, events, and relationships are seen as either "all good" or "all bad," completely gratifying and perfect, or completely unacceptable and disastrous. This process involves "splitting" in the sense that people, events, and human relationships aren't perceived in their entirety by seeing that there is some good and some bad in all of them. Splitting also generally means that we idealize some people and vilify others, both to an extreme. People thus become exaggerated caricatures rather than truly human figures. As a result, we perceive each family member or remember past events in overly exaggerated, distorted ways. Today's saintly or heroic parent quickly becomes tomorrow's marred and fallen hero. Splitting usually occurs when we encounter information that, if squarely faced, would make it difficult or impossible to go on loving someone—especially if that person is one of our parents. For example, a teenager whose parent is an alcoholic or a young person who is the victim of incest may vent all of his or her rage at someone in the family other than the alcoholic or the sexual abuser. Rather than squarely and honestly facing an unpleasant truth about a loved one, we might split and distort reality in order to control or deny our rage and pain (Bowlby, 1988; Miller, 1994).

As a young child, splitting can sometimes be an adaptive strategy for dealing with family problems. Indeed, even as adults, most of us occasionally resort to this defense mechanism. But as teenagers and adults, becoming more willing to accept painful truths about people, including our parents, is an essential part of mental health. One of the most extreme examples of splitting is the teenager with a schizophrenic personality disorder. These teenagers' recollections of the past and their perceptions of family members are so distorted that they bear little, if any, resemblance to actual facts. They have, in fact, "lost touch with reality." When splitting has become a teenager's main way of dealing with pain, anger, and disappointment, serious psychological disorders are usually involved (Bowlby, 1988; Miller, 1994; Weiner, 1992).

Let's look at examples of how some teenagers distort perceptions and memories about their families. Shy, lonely teenagers who have insecure, ambivalent relationships with their parents usually remember childhood and perceive their parents in extremely angry, distorted ways. When asked to talk about their families or the past, these teenagers become incoherent and enraged, lacking insight about themselves or their parents and often idealizing one parent while demonizing the other. Prisoners of their own self-deception and immature social reasoning, these teenagers blame everything on family members without assuming any responsibility for their own unhappy situations. In cases involving enmeshment with one parent, these shy teenagers perceive their parents and remember the past in very infantile ways, even though they also launch into angry outbursts against some family members. Even as adults, these people speak and react as if the hurt or anger they felt toward their families as children were as alive in them today as they were 10 or 15 years ago. In contrast, teenagers and young adults who have felt secure and loved by both parents since early childhood seem to understand and work through anger or disappointments with their families and to remember the past in loving, forgiving ways. Although their childhoods were not trouble-free, well-adjusted teenagers talk about the past and their families without getting into an angry stew and without totally deceiving themselves about each parent's shortcomings. Emotionally healthy teenage and adult children also have enough insight to see their own flaws and responsibilities in relationships with family members (Karen, 1994).

Another way of looking at memory and perception is that each of us develops a particular life story or personal narrative about our lives—a story that becomes the lens through which we see the present, the future, and the past—especially those parts of the past that involve our parents and other family members. Our life story guides our plans, memories, hatreds, dreams, and beliefs about who we think we are and can be. The story each of us lives by is the narrative that provides a more or less unifying theme by which we organize and try to make sense of events in our lives. Even our self-esteem is largely determined by the kind of "life story lens" through which we view our life's history. We literally force our own behavior, the events around us, and other people's actions to fit into our particular story by distorting and rewriting events of the past and present. Thus, we often come to believe what simply isn't true about certain family members and about many aspects of our past (Gergen, 1992; Gilovich, 1991).

Due to our own inborn temperaments and the ways each parent relates to us as infants and toddlers, our life stories take shape. For most of us, our personal narratives are relatively happy, upbeat tales in which we envision and interpret life as though we're winners, survivors, or at the very least, doing about as well as anybody else. But sadly, others of us adopt a relatively bleak life story in which we interpret and envision ourselves, events in our lives, and other people's behavior through a dreary, angry, dark lens. In cases of psychological or emotional disturbance, the person's lens is severely clouded, cracked, or discolored. As one therapist has so aptly put it: "Life is the story we live by, pathology is a story gone mad, and psychotherapy is an exercise in "story repair" (Howard, 1991, p. 194). So in listening to adolescents tell us about their families and their past, we must remember that all of us view the past and create perceptions and memories based on the stories we have *chosen* to live by. Rarely are our stories the whole truth or the reality in terms of what has actually gone on in our families.

CONCLUSION

Families affect our adolescent lives in numerous ways. How happily married our parents were while we were growing up, how each parent related to us, how active our fathers were in our daily lives from infancy on, how psychologically well-adjusted each parent was, whether our mothers worked outside the home, our family's income, the number of brothers or sisters we have, whether our mothers were, or are, married—all are part of the complex interactions and dynamics within our families that contribute to who we are as adolescents. Finally, our own personalities and psychological well-being influence how members of our family have affected us and how we, in turn, have affected them. So who we turn out to be as adolescents and as adults depends not only on our families, but also on our selves. In this vein, a person can be seen as being born three times: born of the mother, born of the father, and finally born of one's own self.

Review/Test Questions

1. How much conflict and distance exist between most adolescents and their parents?

2. How much of a family "crisis" does adolescence create?

3. What do most adolescents argue about with their parents? How are these arguments usually resolved? How do the adolescent's and parent's genders affect their arguments?

4. How is ego development related to arguing and enmeshment?

5. How do the three types of parenting styles differ from each other, and how does each affect adolescents?

6. What is confluence theory, and how does it relate to adolescents?

7. How do adolescents without siblings or those from large families differ from adolescents with one or two siblings? Why?

8. Through what means do we as a society define and restrict the father's role?

9. What type of relationship do most adolescents have with their fathers and with their mothers? Why?

10. How do fathers relate differently to sons and daughters?

11. Specifically, how does a father influence his son's and daughter's development? Consider codependency, the false self, gender roles, vocations, sexuality, self-confidence, and ego development.

12. How can a father's death affect an adolescent girl's development?

13. How do mothers affect their son's and daughter's development during adolescence?

14. How and why do most mothers and daughters relate differently than most fathers and daughters?

15. What accounts for the rising number of children living in poverty?

16. How is poverty related to a parent's marital status, education, and race? Give specific statistics to support your answer.

17. Using specific statistics to support your answer, which adolescents are most at risk of being poor?

18. How does the welfare system affect childhood poverty?

19. Using specific statistics from the present and past, how have families in our society changed with regard to poverty?

20. Why are 1.5 million adolescents homeless, and in what ways are they at greater risk than other teenagers?

21. What are the advantages and disadvantages of a mother's employment?

22. Why do some people oppose a mother's working, and what data support or don't support their views?

23. Citing specific statistics to support your answers, what are some of the biggest changes that have taken place in families in our country during the past 30 years?

24. Citing specific statistics, describe adolescents' families in terms of income and parents' marital status.

25. How and why do our perceptions of each family member and our memories about the past get distorted?

Questions for Discussion and Debate

1. How would you interpret the films and fairy tales described in Insert 8–3?

2. How would you encourage teenage boys to take a greater interest in learning about fathering?

3. How did you feel about your mother's earning an income or being a full-time homemaker? In what ways do you think you benefited from her choices?

4. How well did you get along with each of your parents or stepparents as an adolescent? Why?

5. In what ways has your mother's and father's marital happiness affected your development?

6. If you have an unmarried parent, how has this affected you for both good and bad?

7. How did each of your parent's economic

situations affect you as an adolescent?

8. How have your mother, your father, or your stepparents or other adult relatives affected your development differently? What did each of them contribute to you?

9. How close do you feel to your father and to your mother, and what factors do you think contributed to the kind of relationship you

have with each of them?

10. How accurately and objectively do you think you remember your family's past and each of your parents' behavior toward you? In what ways do you think your perceptions and memories of each parent or stepparent might be somewhat distorted or inaccurate?

Glossary

AFDC, p. 332
codependent, p. 308
confluence theory, p. 292
Electra complex, p. 307

false self, p. 308
intentionality, p. 308
latchkey children, p. 326

poverty level, p. 327
splitting, p. 337
working poor, p. 330

References

Almeida, D., & Galambos, N. (1991). Examining father involvement and the quality of father-adolescent relations. *Journal of Research on Adolescence, 1*, 155–172.

Apter, T. (1990). *Altered loves: Mothers and daughters during adolescence.* New York: St. Martin's Press.

Asher, S., & Coie, J. (1990). *Peer rejection in childhood.* New York: Cambridge University Press.

Athey, J. (1991). HIV infection and homeless adolescents. *Child Welfare, 70*, 517–528.

Augenbraum, H., & Stavan, I. (1993). *Growing Up Latino.* Boston: Houghton Mifflin.

Bane, J., & Ellwood, D. (1989). One fifth of the nation's children: Why are they poor? *Science, 245*, 1047–1053.

Barber, B., & Eccles, J. (1992). Long-term influence of divorce and single parenting on career goals. *Psychological Bulletin, 111*, 108–126.

Barling, J. (1991). Father's employment: Neglected influence on children. In J. Lerner &

N. Galambos (Eds.), *Employed mothers and their children* (pp. 181–209). New York: Garland.

Bass, E., & Davis, L. (1991). *The courage to heal.* New York: Harper & Row.

Baumrind, D. (1991). Parenting styles and adolescent development. In R. Lerner, A. Petersen, & J. Brooks-Gunn (Eds.), *Encyclopedia of adolescence* (pp. 746–758). New York: Garland.

Bell-Scott, P. (1991). *Double stitch: Black women write about mothers and daughters.* New York: Harper Perennial.

Belsky, J., & Cassidy, J. (1994). Attachment: Theory and evidence. In M. Rutter, D. Hays, & S. Baron (Eds.), *Developmental principles and clinical issues in psychology and psychiatry.* Blackwell, England: Oxford University Press.

Bennett, W. (1994). *The index of leading cultural indicators: Facts and figures on the state of American society.* New York: Simon & Schuster.

Berry, M. (1993). *The politics of parenthood.* New York: Viking.

Biller, H. (1993). *Fathers and families: Paternal factors in child development.* Westport, CT: Auburn House.

Bingham, M. (1995). *Things will be different for my daughter.* New York: Penguin.

Blechman, E. (1990). *Emotions and the family.* Hillsdale, NJ: Erlbaum.

Block, J. (1971). *Lives through time.* Berkeley, CA: Bancroft Books.

Blos, P. (1989). *Father and son.* New York: Free Press.

Blume, S. (1990). *Secret survivors.* New York: Harper & Row.

Boer, F., & Dunn, J. (1992). *Children's sibling relationships.* Hillsdale, NJ: Erlbaum.

Bornstein, R. (1991). The temporal stability of ratings of parents. *Journal of Social Behavior and Personality, 6,* 641–649.

Borrine, M. (1991). Family conflict and adolescent adjustment in intact families. *Journal of Consulting and Clinical Psychology, 59,* 753–755.

Bowen, M. (1978). *Family therapy in clinical practice.* New York: Aronson.

Bowlby, J. (1988). A secure base. New York: Basic Books.

Bozett, F., & Hanson, S. (1991). *Fatherhood and families in cultural context.* New York: Springer.

Bradsher, K. (1990, January 17). Single men in their twenties. *The New York Times,* p. C1.

Brower, B. (1992). Remembering. In R. Keyes (Ed.), *Sons on fathers.* New York: HarperCollins.

Brown, L., & Gilligan, C. (1992). *Meeting at the crossroads: Women's psychology and girls' development.* Cambridge, MA: Harvard University Press.

Caplan, P. (1989). *Don't blame mother.* New York: Harper & Row.

Cherlin, A., Furstenberg, F., Lansdale, P., Kiernan, K., Robins, P., Morrison, D., & Teitler, J. (1991). Longitudinal studies of effects of divorce on children in Britain and the U.S. *Science, 252,* 1386–1390.

Cicchetti, D. (1992). Peer relations in maltreated children. In R. Parke & G. Ladd (Eds.), *Family peer relationships* (pp. 345–383). Hillsdale, NJ: Erlbaum.

Cicchetti, D., & Carlson, V. (1989). *Child maltreatment.* New York: Cambridge University.

Clark-Lempers, D., Lempers, J., & Ho, C. (1991). Early, middle, and late adolescents' perceptions of their parents. *Journal of Adolescent Research, 6,* 296–315.

Cohn, D., Patterson, C., & Christopoulos, C. (1991). The family and children's peer relations. *Journal of Social and Personal Relationships, 8,* 315–346.

Collins, P. (1991). The meaning of motherhood in black culture. In P. Bell-Scott (Ed.), *Double stitch: Black women write about mothers and daughters.* New York: Harper Perennial.

Colten, M., Gore, S., & Aseltine, R. (1991). Patterning of distress & disorder in a sample of high school aged youth. In M. Colten & S. Gore (Eds.), *Adolescent stress* (pp. 157–180). New York: Aldine De Gruyter.

Compas, B., & Wagner, B. (1991). Psychosocial stress during adolescence. In M. Colten & S. Gore (Eds.), *Adolescent stress* (pp. 67–92). New York: Aldine De Gruyter.

Cooper, C., & Cooper, R. (1992). Links between adolescents' relationships with parents and peers. In R. Parke & G. Ladd (Eds.), *Family peer relationships* (pp. 135–157). Hillsdale, NJ: Erlbaum.

Corneau, G. (1991). *Absent fathers, lost sons.* Boston: Shambhala.

Coulter, B., & Minninger, J. (1993). *The father daughter dance.* New York: Putnam.

Cowan, C., & Cowan, P. (1992). *When partners become parents.* New York: Basic Books.

Crosby, P. (1993). *Juggling: The advantages of balancing career and home for women and their families.* New York: Free Press.

Crouter, A., & Crowley, M. (1990). School-age children's time alone with fathers. *Journal of Early Adolescence, 10,* 296–312.

Debold, E., Wilson, M., & Malave, I. (1992). *Mother daughter revolution.* New York: Addison Wesley.

Demo, D., & Acock, A. (1993). Family diversity and domestic labor. *Family Relations, 42,* 323–334.

Dodd, C. (1989). *Parental and temporary medical leave act of 1987.* Washington, DC: Congressional Record, 13, 5493–5494.

Dornbusch, S., Mont-Reynaud, R., Ritter, P., Zeng-yin, C., & Steinberg, L. (1991). Stressful events and their correlates among adolescents of diverse backgrounds. In M. Colten & S. Gore (Eds.), *Adolescent stress* (pp. 111–131). New York: Aldine De Gruyter.

Duncan, G., & Rodgers, W. (1988). Longitudinal aspects of childhood poverty. *Journal of marriage & the family, 50,* 1007–1021.

Dunn, J., & Plomin, R. (1989). *Separate lives: Why siblings differ.* New York: Basic Books.

Ebata, A., Petersen, A., & Conger, J. (1990). The development of psychopathology in adolescence. In J. Rolf, A. Masten, D. Cicchetti, K. Nuechterlein, & S. Weintraub (Eds.), *Risk and protective factors in the development of psychopathology* (pp. 308–334). New York: Cambridge University Press.

Emery, E. (1989). Family violence. *American Sociological Review, 44,* 321–328.

Emery, R. (1989). *Marriage, divorce and children's adjustment.* Beverly Hills, CA: Sage.

Erikson, E. (1968). *Identity: Youth in crisis.* New York: Norton.

Fine, M., Donnelly, B., & Voydanoff, P. (1991). Adolescents' perceptions of their families. *Journal of Adolescent Research, 6,* 423–436.

Flaake, K. (1993). Sexual development and the female body in the mother-daughter relationship. In J. Mens-Verhulst, K. Schreurs, & L. Woertman (Eds.), *Daughtering and mothering* (pp. 7–15). New York: Routledge.

Flannery, D., Torquati, J., & Lindemeier, L. (1994). Emotional expression and experience during adolescence. *Journal of Adolescent Research, 9,* 8–27.

Flax, J. (1993). Mothers and daughters revisited. In J. Mens-Verhulst, K. Schreurs, & L. Woertman (Eds.), *Daughtering and mothering* (pp. 145–159). New York: Routledge.

Fleeson, J. (1991). Assessment of parent-adolescent relationships. *Journal of Family Psychology, 5,* 21–45.

Forehand, R. (1991). A short-term longitudinal examination of young adolescents. *Journal of Abnormal Child Psychology, 19,* 97–111.

Franz, C., McClelland, D., & Weinberger, J. (1991). Childhood antecedents of conventional social accomplishments in midlife adults. *Journal of Personality and Social Psychology, 60,* 586–595.

Freud, S. (1949). *An outline of psycho-analysis.* New York: Norton.

Fuchs, V., & Reklis, D. (1992). America's children: Economic perspective & policy options. *Science, 255,* 41–46.

Furstenberg, F., & Cherlin, A. (1991). *Divided families.* Cambridge, MA: Harvard University Press.

Gergen, M. (1992). Life stories: Pieces of a dream. In G. Rosenwald & R. Ochberg (Eds.), *Storied lives.* New Haven, CT: Yale University.

German, D., Habenicht, D., & Futcher, W. (1990). Profile of the female adolescent incest victim. *Child abuse and neglect, 14,* 429–438.

Gilbert, L. (1993). *Two careers, one family.* Beverly Hills, CA: Sage.

Gilligan, C., Rogers, A., & Tolman, D. (1991). *Women, girls and psychotherapy.* New York: Haworth Press.

Gilmore, D. (1990). *Manhood in the making.* New Haven, CT: Yale University.

Gilovich, T. (1991). *How we know what isn't so: The fallibility of human reason in everyday life.* New York: Macmillan.

Glickman, R. (1993). *Daughters of feminists.* New York: St. Martin's.

Goldstein, M. (1990). Family relations as risk factors for schizophrenia. In J. Rolf (Ed.), *Risk* and protective factors in the development of psychopathology* (pp. 408–424). New York: Cambridge University Press.

Goodnow, J., & Bowes, J. (1994). *Men, women, and household work.* New York: Routledge.

Griswold, R. (1993). *Fatherhood in America: A history.* New York: Basic Books.

Hacker, A. (1992). *Two nations: Black and white, separate, hostile, unequal.* New York: Charles Scribner's.

Hallowell, C. (1992). Remembering. In R. Keyes (Ed.), *Sons on fathers* (pp. 259–267). New York: HarperCollins.

Halverson, C. (1988). Remembering your parents. *Journal of Personality, 56,* 434–443.

Harrington, L. (1994). *Depressive disorder in childhood and adolescence.* New York: Wiley.

Harter, S. (1990). Self and identity development. In S. Feldman & G. Elliot (Eds.), *At the threshold* (pp. 352–388). Cambridge, MA: Harvard University Press.

Hartup, W., & Overhauser, S. (1991). Friendships. In R. Lerner, A. Petersen, & J. Brooks-Gunn (Eds.), *Encyclopedia of adolescence* (pp. 378–384). New York: Garland.

Hauser, S., Powers, S., & Noam, G. (1991). *Adolescents and their families: Paths of ego development.* New York: Free Press.

Herzig, A., & Mali, J. (1980). *Oh, boy! Babies.* Boston: Little Brown & Co.

Hetherington, M. (1991). Families, lies and videotapes. *Journal of Research on Adolescence, 1,* 323–348.

Hinde, R., & Stevenson, J. (1995). *Relation between relationships within families.* Cambridge,England: Oxford University Press.

Hooks, B. (1993). *Sisters of the yam: Black women and self-recovery.* Boston: South End Press.

Howard, G. (1991). Culture tales: A narrative approach to thinking, cross cultural psychology and psychotherapy. *American Psychologist, 46,* 187–197.

Jencks, C. (1994). *The homeless.* Cambridge, MA: Harvard University Press.

Johnson, C., Sum, A., & Weill, J. (1988). *Vanishing dreams* Washington, DC: Children's Defense Fund.

Johnson, J. (1992). *Mothers of incest survivors.* Bloomington, IN: Indiana University Press.

Johnston, J., & Campbell, L. (1989). *Impasses of divorce.* New York: Free Press.

Kalter, N. (1990). *Growing up with divorce.* New York: Ballantine.

Karen, R. (1994). *Becoming attached.* New York: Time Warner.

Kondratas, A. (1993). Ending homelessness. *American Psychologist, 11,* 1226–1230.

Kurtz, P., Kirtz, G., & Jarvis, S. (1991). Problems of runaway youth. *Adolescence, 26,* 543–555.

Lamb, M. (1989). *The father's role.* Hillsdale, NJ: Erlbaum.

Lamb, M. (1994). *Adolescent problem behaviors.* New York: Erlbaum.

Lamb, M., & Bornstein, M. (1992). *Development in infancy.* New York: McGraw Hill.

Lamb, M., & Sagi, A. (1989). *Fatherhood and family policy.* Hillsdale, NJ: Erlbaum.

LaRossa, R. (1989). Fatherhood and social change. *Men's Studies Review, 6,* 4–9.

Larson, R., & Asmussen, L. (1991). Anger, worry, and hurt in early adolescence. In M. Colten & S. Gore (Eds.), *Adolescent stress* (pp. 21–42). New York: Aldine De Gruyter.

Leaper, C. (1989). Adolescent parent interactions. *Journal of Early Adolescence, 9,* 335–361.

Lerman, R., & Ooms, T. (1992). *Young unwed fathers.* Philadelphia: Temple University Press.

Lerner, J., & Galambos, N. (1991) *Employed mothers and their children.* New York: Garland.

Levant, R., & Kopecky, G. (1995). *Masculinity reconsidered.* New York: Dutton.

Lew, M. (1990). *Victims no longer: Men recovering from incest.* New York: Harper & Row.

Maccoby, E. (1990). Gender and relationships. *American Psychologist, 45,* 513–552.

Maccoby, E., & Mnookin, R. (1993). *Dividing the child: The Social and legal dilemmas of custody.* Cambridge, MA: Harvard University Press.

Marone, N. (1989). *How to father a successful daughter.* New York: Fawcett.

Marriott, M. (1992). Mixed feelings. In R. Keyes (Ed.), *Sons on fathers* (pp. 140–143). New York: HarperCollins.

McCrae, R., & Costa, P. (1988). Recalled parent-child relations and adult personality. *Journal of Personality, 56,* 417–434.

McDonough, M., & Cooper, C. (1994). Marital relationships and the regulation of affect in families of early adolescents. *Journal of Adolescent Research, 9,* 67–87.

McLoyd, V. (1989). Socialization and development in a changing economy. *American Psychologist, 44,* 293–302.

Mens-Verhulst, J., Schreurs, K., & Woertman, L. (1993). *Daughtering and mothering.* New York: Routledge.

Milburn, N., & D'Ercole, A. (1991). Homeless women. *American Psychologist, 11,* 1161–1169.

Miller, A. (1994). *Drama of the gifted child.* New York: Doubleday.

Minuchin, S., & Nichols, H. (1994). *Family healing.* New York: Simon & Schuster.

Montemayor, R., & Flannery, D. (1991). Parent-adolescent relations in middle and late adolescence. In R. Lerner, A. Petersen & J. Brooks-Gunn (Eds.), *Encyclopedia of adolescence* (pp. 729–734). New York: Garland.

Moore, M. (1992). The family as portrayed on prime time television. Sex Roles, 26, 41–61.

National Commission on Children (1993). *Just the facts: A summary of recent information on America's children and their families.* Washington, DC: Author.

Nelson, C., & Keith, J. (1990). Comparisons of female and male early adolescent sex roles. *Adolescence, 97,* 183–204.

O'Connell, M. (1993). *Who's minding the kids?* Washington, DC: Bureau of the Census, U.S. Department of Commerce.

Offer, D., & Church, R. (1991). Generation gap. In R. Lerner, A. Petersen & J. Brooks-Gunn (Eds.), *Encyclopedia of adolescence* (pp. 397–399). New York: Garland.

Osherson, S. (1992). *Wrestling with love: How men struggle with intimacy.* New York: Fawcett.

Osherson, S. (1993). *Finding our fathers: The unfinished business of manhood.* New York: Fawcett.

Parke, R. (1992). Familial contribution to peer competence among young children. In R. Parke & G. Ladd (Eds.), *Family peer relationships* (pp. 107–134). Erlbaum: Hillsdale, NJ.

Parke, R., & Ladd, G. (1992). *Family-peer relationships: Modes of linkage.* Hillsdale, NJ: Erlbaum.

Parker, G. (1983). *Parental overprotection: A risk factor in psychosocial development.* New York: Grune & Stratton.

Parkes, C., Stevenson-Hinde, J., & Marris, P. (1991). *Attachment across the life cycle.* New York: Tavistock/Routledge.

Pasley, K., & Ihinger-Tallman, M. (1994). *Stepparenting: Issues in theory, research & practice.* New York: Greenwood Publishing.

Patterson, G., Reid, J., & Dishion, T. (1992). *A social learning approach: Antisocial boys.* Eugene, OR: Castalia.

Patterson, J., & Kim, P. (1992). *The day America told the truth.* New York: Plume.

Paulson, S., Koman, J., & Hill, J. (1990). Maternal employment and parent-child relations. *Journal of Early Adolescence, 10,* 279–295.

Peplar, D., & Rubin, K. (1994). *The development and treatment of childhood aggression.* Hillsdale, NJ: Erlbaum.

Petersen, A., Kennedy, R., & Sullivan, P. (1991). Coping with adolescence. In M. Colten & S. Gore (Eds.), *Adolescent stress* (pp. 93–110). New York: Aldine De Gruyter.

Phares, V., & Compas, B. (1992). The role of fathers in child and adolescent psychopathology. *Psychological Bulletin, 111*, 387–412.

Pianta, B., Egeland, B., & Stroufe, A. (1990). Maternal stress and children's development. In J. Rolf, A. Masten, K. Nuechterlain & .W. Weintraub (Eds.), *Risk and protective factors in the development of psychopathology* (pp. 215–236). New York: Cambridge University Press.

Pinkson, T. (1992). Honoring a daughter's emergence into womanhood. In C. Scull (Ed.), *Fathers, sons, and daughters* (pp. 148–155). Los Angeles: Jeremy Tarcher.

Pipher, M. (1994). *Reviving Ophelia: Saving the selves of adolescent girls.* New York: Putnam.

Pittman, F. (1993). *Man enough: Fathers, sons and the search for masculinity.* New York: Putnam's Sons.

Radin, N., Oyserman, D., & Benn, R. (1991). Grandfathers, teen mothers, and children under two. In P. Smith (Ed.), *The psychology of grandparenthood* (pp. 85–89). London: Routledge.

Radke-Yarrow, M. (1991). Attachment patterns in children of depressed mothers. In C. Parkes (Ed.), *Attachment across the life cycle.* New York: Routledge.

Richards, M., & Duckett, E. (1991). Maternal employment and adolescents. In J. Lerner & E. Duckett (Eds.), *Employed mothers and their children* (pp. 85–123). New York: Garland.

Richardson, L. (1989). Children unsupervised after school. *Pediatrics, 43*, 145–149.

Robins, L., & Rutter, M. (1990). *Straight and devious pathways from childhood to adulthood.* New York: Cambridge University Press.

Rotherman, M., Koopman, C., & Ehrhardt, A. (1991). Homeless youths and HIV infection. *American Psychologist, 11*, 1188–1197.

Rubin, K., Lemare, L., & Lollis, S. (1990). Social withdrawal in childhood. In S. Asher & J. Coie (Eds.), *Peer rejection in childhood* (pp. 51–72). Hillsdale, NJ: Erlbaum.

Savin-Williams, R., & Berndt, T. (1990). Friendship and peer relations. In S. Feldman & G. Elliot (Eds.), *At the threshold: The developing adolescent* (pp. 277–308). Cambridge, MA: Harvard University Press.

Scull, C. (1992). *Fathers, sons, and daughters.* Los Angeles: Jeremy Tarcher.

Secunda, V. (1992). *Women and their fathers.* New York: Delacorte Press.

Seligman, M. (1991). *Learned optimism.* New York: Random House.

Shave, D., & Shave, B. (1989). *Early adolescence and the search for self.* New York: Praeger.

Sigel, I., McGillicuddy, A., & Goodnow, J. (1992). *Parental belief systems: The psychological consequences for children.* Hillsdale, NJ: Erlbaum.

Silverstein, L. (1991). Transforming the debate about child care and maternal employment. *American Psychologist, 46*, 1025–1032.

Silverstein, O., & Rashbaum, B. (1994). *The courage to raise good men.* New York: Viking.

Smetana, J., Yau, J., Restrepo, A., & Braeges, J. (1991). Conflict and adaptation in adolescence: Adolescent-parent conflict. In M. Bolten & S. Gore (Eds.), *Adolescent stress* (pp. 43–64). New York: Aldine De Gruyter.

Smith, B. (1989). Birth order and sibling status effects. In M. Lamb (Ed.), *Sibling relationships* (pp. 153–166). Hillsdale, NJ: Erlbaum.

Snarey, J. (1993). *How fathers care for the next generation.* Cambridge, MA: Harvard University Press.

Steinberg, L. (1990). Autonomy, conflict and harmony in the family relationship. In S. Feldman & G. Elliot (Eds.), *At the threshold* (pp. 255–569). Cambridge, MA: Harvard University.

Steinberg, L., Mounts, N., Lamborn, S., & Dornbusch, S. (1991). Authoritative parenting and adolescent adjustment across varied ecological niches. *Journal of Research on Adolescence, 1*, 19–36.

Strassberg, Z., Dodge, K., Bates, J., & Pettit, G. (1992). The relation between parental conflict strategies and children's sociometric standing in kindergarten. *Merrill-Palmer Quarterly, 38,* 477–493.

Tolman, D. (1991). Adolescent girls, women, and sexuality. In C. Gilligan, A. Rogers & D. Tolman (Eds.), *Women, girls, and psychotherapy* (pp. 55–71). New York: Haworth.

U.S. Department of Commerce. (1992). *General population characteristics.* Washington, DC: Bureau of the Census.

Veenhoven, R., & Verkuyten, M. (1989). The well-being of only children. *Adolescence, 51,* 713–725.

Vogel, L. (1993). *Mothers on the job: Maternity policy in the U.S.* New Brunswick, NJ: Rutgers University Press.

Wakerman, E. (1984). *Father loss.* New York: Doubleday.

Wallerstein, J. (1991). The long term effects of divorce on children: A review. *Journal of American Academy of Child Psychiatry, 30,* 349–360.

Walsh, M. (1992). *Moving to nowhere: Children's stories of homelessness.* Westport, CT: Greenwood Press.

Warshak, R. (1992). *The custody revolution: The fatherhood factor and the motherhood mystique.* New York: Poseidon.

Waxler, C., Denham, S., Iannotti, R., & Cummings, M. (1992). Peer relations in children with a depressed caregiver. In R. Parke & G. Ladd (Eds.), *Family peer relationships* (pp. 317–344). Hillsdale, NJ: Erlbaum.

Weiner, I. (1992). *Psychological disturbance in adolescence.* New York: Wiley.

Weiss, R. (1990). *Staying the course: Men who do well at work.* New York: Fawcett.

Westen, D. (1990). Physical and sexual abuse in adolescent girls with borderline personality disorder. *American Journal of Orthopsychiatry, 60,* 55–66.

White, L., & Edwards, J. (1990). Emptying the nest and parental well-being. *American Sociological Review, 55,* 235–242.

Widom, C. (1994) Childhood victimization. In R. Ketterlinus & M. Lamb (Eds.) *Adolescent problem behaviors* (pp. 127–165). Hillsdale, NJ: Erlbaum.

Wright, D., Peterson, L., & Barns, H. (1990). The relations of parental employment and contextual variables. *Journal of Early Adolescence, 10,* 382–398.

Wright, L. (1992). Reunion. In R. Keyes (Ed.), *Sons on fathers* (pp. 150–154). New York: HarperCollins.

Yankelovich, D. (1981). *New rules.* New York: Random House.

Youngblade, L., & Belsky, J. (1992). Parent child antecedents of five-year-olds' close friendships. *Developmental Psychology, 1,* 107–121.

Youngblade, L., & Belsky, J. (1993). The social and emotional consequences of child maltreatment. In R. Ammerman & N. Herson (Eds.), *Children at risk: Factors contributing to child abuse and neglect.* New York: Plenum.

Youniss, J., & Smollar, J. (1985). *Adolescent relations with mothers, fathers and friends.* Chicago: University of Chicago Press.

Zajonc, R. (1983). Validating the confluence model. *Psychological Bulletin, 93,* 457–480.

9

ADOLESCENTS IN SINGLE-PARENT AND BLENDED FAMILIES

Chapter Outline

Key Questions Addressed In This Chapter

1. How does divorce affect adolescents?
2. How have families in our society changed during the past three decades?
3. How does living with a single mother affect adolescents?
4. How does living in a blended family affect adolescents?
5. Which factors influence how well adolescents adjust to their parents' divorce & remarriage?
6. In comparison to girls, how do teenage boys respond to divorce, living with a single mother, and living in a blended family?
7. What are the shortcomings of the research on adolescents living with divorced and single parents?
8. Which factors determine how living with a single parent will affect an adolescent?
9. How do mothers' and fathers' reactions to divorce and remarriage affect adolescents?
10. What changes in our society might help adolescents adjust better to their parents' divorce and remarriage?

CHANGES IN ADOLESCENTS' FAMILIES

During the 1980s, children in the United States were affected by dramatic increases in three aspects of our society: poverty, divorce, and out-of-wedlock births. As shown in the preceding chapter, the increase in poverty has hurt teenagers in many ways. In this chapter, we examine how the increases in divorce and out-of-wedlock births have affected millions of adolescents. To start, let's compare today's families with those of the supposed "good old days" when children grew up with both of their happily married parents—or did they? The historical facts paint a far less rosy picture of the past (Coontz, 1989; Phillips, 1989; Skolnick, 1991).

Insert 9–1

The Family: Facts and Fictions

How much do you know about the families in our society?

True or false?

_____ 1. Nearly 80% of all mothers are employed outside the home.

_____ 2. By the year 2000, only 25% of teenagers will be living with both biological parents.

_____ 3. Nearly 30% of all teenagers now live with an unmarried mother.

_____ 4. Roughly 60% of all first marriages end in divorce.

_____ 5. After a divorce, men paying child support pay about $3,000 a year.

_____ 6. About 90% of the babies born to black teenagers are born out-of-wedlock.

_____ 7. Low-income mothers marry sooner after a divorce than other mothers.

_____ 8. Nearly 50% of black children are now living in poverty.

_____ 9. Nearly 20% of all children are living in a blended family.

_____ 10. Nearly 20% of our society's children are living below the poverty line.

_____ 11. Most poor children are white and live in rural areas.

_____ 12. Out-of-wedlock births are increasing faster among whites than minorities.

_____ 13. About 15% of our children live with adoptive parents, foster parents, or grandparents.

_____ 14. Almost as many teenagers are living with a divorced mother as with a mother who has never been married.

_____ 15. About half of all children in our country are living with both biological parents.

All of the above are true.

Figure 9–1

Adolescents' families

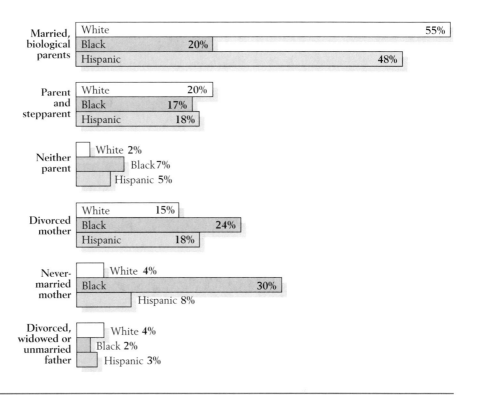

Until World War II, the majority of adolescents did not grow up with both parents. Because men frequently deserted their families, parents commonly died young, and couples were often separated for years because of economic reasons, nearly as many American children were living in single-parent and blended families in 1800 as in 1960. In fact, for a child to live with at least one parent is more likely today than it was in 1940. In 1993, only one out of every 25 children was living with someone other than a parent; but in 1940, the ratio was 1 in 10. Looking even further into history, we can see that premarital pregnancies are not exclusively a modern social trend. During the late 1700s in rural New England, one bride in three was pregnant before the wedding. And with regard to divorce, we shouldn't jump to the conclusion that couples of yesteryear stayed together more often simply by working harder at their marriages than we do today. Yes, it's true that divorce was rare in colonial America. But it's also true that because so many adults died young—especially young mothers—the average marriage lasted only 12 years.

Nevertheless, our rates of divorce and out-of-wedlock births are higher than ever before. So the number of adolescents growing up in single-parent and blended families is steadily increasing. One way to appreciate the effects of divorce and out-of-wedlock births on many adolescents is to take the quiz in Insert 9–1 and to study the statistics in Figure 9–1. As you can see, a third of our children (nearly 22 million) live with an unmarried parent—nearly three times as many as in the 1960s and 1970s. Another 20% are living with a parent and step-parent (U.S. Department of Commerce, 1992).

ADOLESCENTS LIVING WITH UNMARRIED MOTHERS

Among the 30% of children living with single mothers, nearly a third were born out-of-wedlock and the rest have parents who are divorced. In other words, 10% of teenagers have never lived with their father. In the past, most unmarried, pregnant women got married. But as times have changed, so have attitudes, including those about raising children born out-of-wedlock. From 1940 to 1985, out-of-wedlock births in our country increased by 725% among whites and 300% among nonwhites. Black children, however, have born the brunt of this dramatic change. Until the 1950s, black and white Americans married and divorced at about the same rates. Nowadays, almost 90% of white women, but only 65% of black women, have been married by time they are 30. The average white woman is married for nearly half of her life; but the average black woman is married for one-fourth of hers. As a result, nearly 90% of black children are living with their unmarried mother (U.S. Department of Commerce, 1992; 1993). A word of caution is needed here with regard to Hispanic American families because they differ greatly. For example, single-parent families are three times more common among Puerto Rican Americans than among Cuban and Mexican Americans (Ahlburg & DeVita, 1992). Unfortunately, most of our statistics for Hispanic Americans are not broken down into these subgroups—a shortcoming you need to bear in mind.

As for the divorce statistics, if we include couples who are not yet legally divorced but who live separately, 65% of us who say "I do" eventually say "I don't"—a three-fold increase since 1960. Most children's parents get divorced within the first 10 years of their marriage. Parents with low incomes, the least education, and the highest incidence of having become parents as teenagers are the most likely to divorce. For example, white children whose mothers were high-school dropouts are twice as likely to have divorced parents as those whose mothers attended or graduated from college. Yet a black woman who attends college, delays marriage until in her 20s, and avoids premarital pregnancy is still twice as likely as a white woman with a similar background to end up divorced. Since divorced parents usually wait a few years before remarrying, 50% to 70% of white children live for at least 1 year with their unmarried mothers. For black children, the figures reach 85% to 95%. Perhaps more startling, it is estimated that by the year 2000 only 25% of white teenagers and 10% of black teenagers will be living with both biological parents by age 18 (U.S. Department of Commerce, 1992; Hernandez, 1989).

If you believe television provides an accurate reflection of society, you might think that a fairly large number of adolescents in single-parent families are living with their fathers. Of the single-parent families depicted on television, 50% are headed by the father—who's usually raising the children alone because their mother is dead (Moore, 1992). But 90% of American children in single-parent families live with their mother. And virtually all of the 2 million children living with their unmarried fathers have mothers who are alive (U.S. Department of Commerce, 1992).

ADOLESCENTS IN BLENDED FAMILIES

Even though the majority of marriages end in divorce, 80% of adults remarry within 2 to 3 years. Consequently, almost 20% of adolescents live with their parent and stepparent. Each day in our country alone, 1300 new blended families are formed. Almost 4 million children are living with their parent and stepparent, and another 6 million have stepparents they aren't living with. Divorced mothers who are well-educated or who have relatively high incomes generally wait the longest before remarrying. Well-educated fathers with good incomes, however, remarry sooner than less-educated fathers with low incomes. Race also affects an adolescent's likelihood of having a stepparent. Compared to other mothers, black mothers are the least likely to remarry. So, more than 80% of white children are living in a blended family within 4 years after their parents' divorce compared to only 30% of black children. If current trends continue, more than a third of American children will be living in a stepfamily before the age of 18. Unfortunately, half of these marriages will also end. Unlike poorer, less well-educated women, women who waited until their 20s before becoming mothers and who attended college have about a 50-50 chance of divorcing in either their first or second marriage. In fact, college-educated women are somewhat more likely to stay married to their children's stepfather than to their father (Cherlin, 1992).

FINANCIAL IMPACT OF SINGLE PARENTING

Whether their mother is divorced or has never been married, teenagers living with an unmarried mother generally share one thing in common: a low standard of living. As shown in Figure 9–2, regardless of your race, if your mother is married you will almost always have a much higher standard of living than if she's single. For example, the average family income for married, white mothers is $36,000 a year, compared to only $17,000 for single, white mothers. The situation is even poorer for unmarried Hispanic and African American mothers whose families live on an average income of just more than $9500. As a point of reference, half of all American families have a total income greater than $37,000; and the poverty level for a family of four is about $14,000. Another way to appreciate the relationship between a mother's race and marital status and her children's lifestyle is to compare family assets—the value of the vehicles, house, real estate and other investments after deducting the family's debts. Only

Figure 9–2

Family incomes by race and marital status

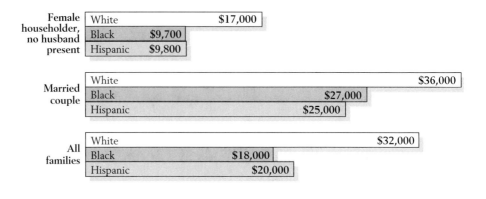

Source: U.S. Department of Commerce (1991). *Family characteristics and marital status.* Bureau of the Census.

half of all unmarried Hispanic and black mothers have assets worth more than $750; but of all married Hispanic and black mothers, half are in families with assets worth more than $16,000. Among whites, only half of the unmarried women have assets worth more than $22,000, but half of the married women's family assets are worth more than $62,000 (U.S. Department of Commerce, 1992).

Why is it that most children are stuck in such lousy financial situations when their mothers are single? First, employed women earn an average of 30% less than do employed men. Second, women's jobs offer fewer chances for advancement. Third, some women make choices early in life that hurt career choices later. They come from the group of women lucky enough to have husbands whose incomes enable them to choose homemaking over a career. Of course, nearly 60% of black men and 30% of white men make too little money to support a family without their wives' incomes. So although they account for less than 20% of all mothers, those who choose not to work outside the home while they are married run the risk of building up no marketable skills or work experience. Thus, if forced to get jobs due to divorce, these mothers—even though they might be highly educated—are less qualified than other women their age with similar educations and long work histories. Remember, though, more than 80% of all American mothers are employed throughout their marriage; more than half go back to work within a year after each child's birth; and married mothers bring in about a third of the family's income (Wilkie, 1991).

Another reason why most children with unmarried mothers are so poor is that so many of their fathers pay little—or no—child support. Of the 10 million divorced mothers, nearly 60% should be receiving child support. But only 50% receive the full amount due, and another 25% receive nothing at all. In 1990, divorced fathers owed about $25 billion in unpaid child support. The more educated the father and the more often he sees his children, the more likely he is to be sending them money. Still, most divorced fathers pay only $3000 a year; and only 5% pay as much as $5000. In other words, the average divorced mother has to earn 90% of the money to support her children (Children's Defense Fund [CDF], 1994; U.S. Department of Commerce, 1991; Center for Law & Social Policy [CLSP], 1994).

Poverty in single-parent families is also more common in our country than in other industrialized nations, in part because of our national welfare policies. Unlike most other advanced nations, the United States has not enacted the legislation necessary to create programs, such as national health care and day-care, that financially protect unmarried mothers and children (Edelman, 1992; Hewlitt, 1992). So in terms of their standard of living, it's best for adolescents to have parents who get married and stay married. A close second is for the mother to remarry fairly soon after a divorce. In fact, children whose mothers remarry often find their standard of living better than before the divorce (Hetherington & Jodl, 1994; Maccoby & Mnookin, 1993). Worse off are children whose mothers don't remarry; but the most financially deprived children are those whose mothers have never been married.

FACTORS INFLUENCING THE IMPACT OF DIVORCE AND LIVING WITH A SINGLE PARENT

LIMITATIONS OF THE RESEARCH

The financial impact of living with a single mother is much easier to assess than the emotional or psychological effects of the parents' divorce or remarriage. Unfortunately most researchers who have gathered and interpreted data on single-parent and blended families have done so from a biased viewpoint. The general assumption has been that single-parent and blended families are worse for children than are families with two biological or adoptive parents. As a result, researchers have failed to explore the beneficial aspects of these families. Furthermore, too much information comes from individuals with ongoing problems in single-parent or blended families. Although valuable, these studies don't provide a clear picture of adolescents who are happy and well-adjusted in these families. Most researchers have also overlooked such variables as family income and the child's gender, which influence how well children adjust to divorce and blended families. Finally, very few studies have compared children's behavior and mental health before and after their parents divorce or remarry. Consequently, the idea that young people with ongoing problems must be reacting to their parents' divorce or remarriage is an assumption that simply went unchallenged. Fortunately, more researchers are considering these shortcomings and their work is yielding fuller explanations about why some adolescents adapt better to divorce, single parenting, and blended families.

CHILDREN'S WELL-BEING BEFORE AND AFTER DIVORCE

Concerning the effects of a parent's divorce or remarriage on adolescents, the most obvious issue is how well-adjusted the child was during the parents' marriage. Researchers typically look at the child's school performance, peer relationships, psychological health, and behavior at home and at school. We're learning that those teenagers who have serious or long-lasting problems after their parents divorce or remarry almost always had the same problems while their parents were married. Even when their parents are married to each other, children with difficult personalities or with psychological or social problems react the most negatively to any stress or family change—boys moreso than girls (Parke & Ladd, 1992; Robins & Rutter, 1990). When parents divorce or remarry, these are the children who have the most trouble adapting. In short, a parent's divorce or remarriage often intensifies, but rarely causes, a teenager's ongoing problems (Booth & Dunn, 1994; Emery, 1992; Furstenberg & Cherlin, 1991; Hetherington & Jodl, 1994; Kalter, 1990; Pasley & Ihinger-Tallman, 1994; Wallerstein, 1991; Warshak, 1992).

Two impressive longitudinal studies illustrate this point. In a 10-year study that began when children were 3 to 4 years old, boys whose parents eventually divorced were making poor grades, were hard to control, and had trouble getting along with their peers years before the divorce. Unlike the sons, the daughters' behavior and school performance were generally unrelated to whether their parents eventually divorced (Block & Gjerde, 1989). Similarly, in a longitudinal study involving nearly 12,000 British and 2280 American children, boys having academic, social, or emotional problems after the divorce had these problems years before their parents separated. In fact, once the behavior and grades before the divorce were taken into account, the rating of the impact of the divorce itself fell almost to zero. Once again, the girls' behavior and grades were unrelated to their parents' divorces. Oddly enough, those teenage girls whose parents divorced actually had fewer academic and behavior problems than did the girls whose parents were still married (Cherlin & others, 1991).

PARENTS' CONFLICTS

Adolescents who adapt best to their parents' divorces or remarriages are those exposed to the least anger and hostility between their parents—both while they were married and after they stop living together. As mentioned in preceding chapters, one reason boys generally have the most problems after their parents divorce might be because parents fight and argue more around boys than around girls. Unhappily married parents also stay together longer before divorcing when they have sons, exposing sons to more of their arguments and fights (Emery, 1992; Forehand, 1991; Greene & Leslie, 1989; Hetherington & Jodl, 1994; Wallerstein, 1991).

As you would expect, however, most people don't get along well after their divorce. Thus, the vast majority of divorced parents try to have as little to do with each other as possible (Ahrons, 1994; Buehler & Ryan, 1994; Furstenberg & Cherlin, 1991; Maccoby & Mnookin, 1993). Of course, it's not feasible to avoid all contact with each other if the father plans to stay in contact with his children. Being dragged into their divorced parents' conflicts, however, does more damage to teenagers than does any other single factor except falling into poverty. The research is remarkably consistent on this point, and the damage extends to children's grades, social development, antisocial behavior, and mental health. Again and again the research shows that the adult who does the greatest damage is the one who vents anger against the other parent or stepparent in front of the child or who involves a child in the adults' rivalries and animosities (Ahrons, 1994; Buchanan, Maccoby, & Dornbusch, [forthcoming]; Furstenberg & Cherlin, 1991; Hetherington & Jodl, 1994; Kalter, 1990; Maccoby & Mnookin, 1993; Martin & Martin, 1992; Pasley & Ihinger-Tallman, 1994; Wallerstein, 1991; Warshak, 1992). Although divorced parents act out their anger and jealousy in countless ways, three areas that commonly harm their children involve ongoing money problems, perceptions of the marital past, and custody or living arrangements.

Financial Conflicts   Considering the financial plight of most divorced mothers, it's not surprising that their children can be upset or damaged by continuing animosity between their parents regarding money. Because of the meager child support most fathers pay, many children hear or sense their mother's resentment and financial suffering. Yet even the small group of teenagers whose fathers are sending enough money to pay for most, or even all, of their needs can still be upset by their parents' ongoing financial conflicts. Even with a well-educated mother who is receiving ample alimony and child support, and earning a good income of her own, children have no guarantee of being spared their parents' financial battles. For example, in an attempt to alienate her children from their father, a financially well-off mother might try to convince them that no matter how much money their father sends, "it isn't enough" or that "it isn't fair that he makes more money than I do." Even a well-educated mother who didn't want to hold a job while she was married might say or imply such potentially damaging things as: "If it hadn't been for your father, I would have had a great career, so he ought to pay 100% of your expenses until you graduate from college," or "Your father didn't do anything to raise you, so I shouldn't have to use any of my income to help support you kids now" (Beer, 1992; Einstein, 1994; Grief, 1990; Jones & Schiller, 1992). In fact, divorced women who didn't have to work because their husbands earned high incomes can be more resentful and angrier than divorced lower-income women who did have to work. Why? The wealthier woman experiences the greater drop in her standard of living (Furstenberg & Cherlin, 1991).

Adolescents can also be upset by hearing their fathers complaining about financial matters related to the divorce. Fathers often believe they are unfairly burdened by having to send money that indirectly benefits the woman they no longer love, especially if the ex-wife refused to get a job while they were married, or if she contributes little or nothing of her own salary to support their children after the divorce. Some teenagers are also caught in the middle when the father complains that their mother is spending or saving part of the child support money for herself, is making teenage children pay for items that should come from the child support checks, and is deceiving the children into believing she is unselfishly giving them everything she has. As one father's friend explained, "They kick sand in his face and then he lets them dance all over him financially" (Jones & Schiller, 1992, p. 168). Many fathers who are fulfilling, or even exceeding, their child support obligations believe that their ex-wife, and even their own children, continue to badger and exploit them for more—extra clothes, tuition, gas money, sports equipment, and other costly items that are legally supposed to come from the father's child support checks—in return for granting him their affection or visitation "rights" (Beer, 1992; Depner & Bray, 1993; Grief, 1990; Martin & Martin, 1992; Seltzer, 1991).

Even when their parents aren't divorced, teenagers are more apt to become stressed and depressed when their parents continually subject them to their financial worries (Compas & Wagner, 1991; Conger, 1991; Dornbusch & others, 1991; Patterson & others, 1992). No child should be burdened with a parent's financial worries, and divorced parents should make extra efforts to avoid doing so. As two divorced mothers explain: "Whenever I was in a funk about money, I'd start wondering aloud whether I should have gotten divorced. That wasn't good for the kids." "I could have avoided much of my anger at my former husband and what I put the kids through if I had chosen to be more financially self-sufficient throughout the years of my marriage" (Crytser, 1990, pp. 97, 104). Sadly, many teenagers are upset, or end up alienated from one of their parents, as a consequence of the financial conflicts after the divorce (Beal & Hochman, 1991; Emery, 1992; Everett, 1993; Furstenberg & Cherlin, 1991; Kalter, 1990; Maccoby & Mnookin, 1993).

Although it might sound odd, in one respect most adolescents in this country have a factor in their favor with regard to the financial aspects of divorce: Most teens generally adjust better to their parents' divorce when their mother was earning an income while she was married—and, as we know, that applies to 80% of all American mothers. But why is this so? In part, the answer might involve the mother's anger and jealousy over her ex-husband's financial advantages. The lower the mother's income compared to the father's while they are married, the angrier and more resentful she tends to be after their divorce. That is, if the husband earns a high salary that enables his wife to be a full-time homemaker, she has a greater drop in her standard of living after a divorce than if both she and her husband were employed throughout their marriage. When their parents' incomes are more equal throughout the marriage, children seem to be caught in less financial warfare after their parents' divorce (Furstenberg & Cherlin, 1991; Haynes, 1988; Johnston & Campbell, 1989). As one divorced mother says, "I get a great deal of satisfaction out of knowing that I am supporting myself and my daughter" (Crosby, 1993, p. 107). Teenagers might also adapt better when their mothers were employed throughout their marriage because these fathers and children tend to be closer to one another than are those in homes where the mother is a full-time homemaker (Biller, 1993; Paulson, Koman, & Hill, 1990; Richards & Duckett, 1991; Snarey, 1993). Also, full-time homemakers not only tend to be more depressed than do employed mothers, they also become enmeshed with one or more of their children more often—which might explain why these children don't adapt as well after a divorce (Cowan & Cowan, 1992; Crosby, 1993; Lerner & Galambos, 1991). So the small group of teenagers whose mothers were full-time homemakers tend to have more trouble adapting, both to divorce and to remarriage, than do children whose mothers earned an income of their own (Biller, 1993; Emery, 1992; Maccoby & Mnookin, 1993; Warshak, 1992).

Conflicts Regarding the Marital Past   Adolescents can also be damaged by the ongoing tension related to each parent's feelings about the divorce. A divorce puts an end to living together, but it doesn't erase the painful memories and emotions that can continue to make life difficult for children, even years after their parents' divorce. Because children do not understand much of what has gone on in their parents' marriage and divorce, they can easily be caught up in harmful or painful situations regarding their parents' marital past. For example, most children certainly aren't aware that most divorces begin when one parent falls in love with someone else (Gigy & Kelly, 1992; Kitson & Holmes, 1992; Reibstein & Richards, 1993; Vaughan, 1990). So without understanding the reasons for each parent's feelings, these teenagers typically see an ongoing anger in the parent who was betrayed and an ongoing guilt, unhappiness, or ambivalence about the divorce in the other parent (Ahrons, 1994; Ambert, 1989; Kitson & Holmes, 1992). Although children are subjected to less conflict when the parent who fell in love with someone else accepts responsibility for the divorce and apologizes, such apologies sometimes never occur (Ahrons, 1994).

Moreover, most adolescents don't understand that the parent who initially wanted the divorce usually spent months or years vilifying and demoralizing the other long before they separated. As one parent explains, "My wife would tell me about her boyfriend to impress on me that she didn't love me. I was devastated. She was merciless and showed no sign of compassion. Finally, I just couldn't take it anymore and I had to move out, leaving my home and my children" (Vaughan, 1990, p. 175). In order to rationalize leaving marriages and to ease the guilt, parents who want a divorce typically vilify their spouse in an attempt to convince themselves that their spouses are unlovable and unloving—an act of self-deception that sometimes involves trying to convince the children of these untruths as well (Ahrons, 1994; Guttman, 1993; Reibstein & Richards, 1993; Vaughan, 1990). Neither parent wants to look like the bad guy in the children's eyes—especially not the parent who wanted to leave the marriage.

Most adolescents are also unaware that mothers usually initiate divorces and that women are more apt to leave a marriage because they have fallen in love with someone else (Ahrons, 1994; Gigy & Kelly, 1992; Kitson & Holmes, 1992; Reibstein & Richards, 1993; Ripps, 1994). Unknown to most children, fathers are more likely to say they still love their spouse at the time of the divorce (Guttman,

1993; Kitson & Holmes, 1992). Even older teenagers might be unaware that whichever parent rejected the other tends to want to remain friends, is more ambivalent about the divorce even years later, and often winds up being the most depressed in the long run (Kitson & Holmes, 1992; Vaughan, 1990). This situation can be especially confusing to children when they want their parents to reconcile. For example, teenagers might see one parent refusing the other's request to celebrate birthdays and holidays together, as if they were still a family, or to date each other even after the divorce (Ahrons, 1994; Vaughan, 1990). Not understanding that the parent who left the marriage is usually the one who is friendlier and more ambivalent afterward, teenagers can misinterpret the rejected parent's anger or unfriendliness as signs of meanness or insensitivity (Vaughan, 1990). Especially when the rejected parent starts dating or falls in love, teenagers often see the parent who initiated the break either begin to act willing to renew the marriage or become very angry and depressed (Ahrons, 1994; Vaughan, 1990). As one parent admits, "Even though I was the one who wanted the divorce, I couldn't stop myself from being depressed by continually comparing myself to the woman he married" (Savage & Adams, 1989, p. 90). Because children so rarely understand the realities and dynamics involved in their parents' divorce, they sometimes form very inaccurate impressions about which parent is the "unselfish, fragile, powerless" one and which is the "powerful, self-confident, tough guy." The irony is that some teenagers end up pitying and defending the parent who has the most power and who inflicted the most pain during the divorce (Ahrons, 1994; Berman, 1992; Vaughan, 1990).

Teenagers can also be stressed or damaged when hearing distorted, accusatory stories about why their parents got divorced. Although men are more likely than women to accept partial responsibility for their divorce, very few couples agree on why they got divorced and most blame the ex-spouse rather than assume any responsibility themselves (Kitson & Holmes, 1992). As time passes, however, the parent who adjusts well to the divorce subjects the children to fewer accusatory stories about the former spouse. As one divorced father explains, "My ex was the most emotionally demanding, critical, negative person I've ever met. But now I see that she was emotionally starved her whole life and I blame that on her parents who hated each other and took it out on her" (Vaughan, 1990, p. 174). However, teenagers are likely to hear the unhappy or guilt-ridden parent continue to blame or criticize the former spouse. Especially when a parent is still feeling guilty, as is often the case when he or she fell in love with someone else while still married, teenagers are apt to be surrounded by lies, criticisms, secrets, and a "rewriting of history" about the past. Both parents—but especially the one who feels guilty for ending the marriage—often invent whatever "facts," memories, or stories they need to help them live with their shame, pain, anger, or regrets (Guttman, 1993; Kitson & Holmes, 1992; Vaughan, 1990).

How likely is it that adolescents will discover the unpleasant truths surrounding their parents' divorce? The answer depends almost entirely on the character of their parents and stepparents (Beal & Hochman, 1991). In some cases, teenagers are emotionally devastated or alienated from a parent by an angry or jealous adult's divulging information about the marriage and divorce. For example, one adolescent's father told her about the affair her mother had during the marriage, which caused the daughter to turn against her mother (Pipher, 1994). No matter how they try to rationalize why they disclosed upsetting information about each other to the children, those parents or stepparents who resort to such selfish, vengeful tactics are often jeopardizing the psychological well-being of their children or stepchildren (Ahrons, 1994; Guttman, 1993; Martin & Martin, 1992). As one expert puts it: "Missiles aimed at an ex-spouse or stepparent will more readily lodge in the hearts of the children" (Kalter, 1990, p.14).

Other attempts to influence the children might involve less volatile—even trivial—aspects of the marital history, but can easily cause problems for adolescents. For example, arguments over who did the housework and the childcare during their marriage can contribute to teenagers' stress after their parents divorce (Maccoby & Mnookin, 1993). By trying to make children believe that the other parent did little or nothing to raise them, some parents are trying to force a sense of indebtedness on the children toward the "good" parent, or to force a bond that results in alienation from the "bad" parent. In an attempt to present themselves as being "the more loving" or the "self-sacrificing" parent who was "always there," some divorced parents literally cut out the former spouse's image from the family's old photographs. In fact, one company called "Divorce X" exploits this urge by using computer technology to erase former spouses from photographs and to replace the gap with a new person's picture (Kantrowitz, 1994). In any event, most teenagers hear very different stories from each divorced parent about who raised them and did the housework while they were married—with mothers usually less willing than fathers to give the other credit (Hetherington & Jodl, 1994; Maccoby & Mnookin, 1993).

Conflicts over Living Arrangements and Custody   Another common source of stress for adolescents is their parents' continuing arguments over visitation schedules or living arrangements. Many angry or jealous custodial parents limit the children's contact with the other parent by restricting the number of days they can spend together each month. Some parents also resort to more subtle methods for making teenagers feel guilty, uncomfortable, or stressed when they're going to be with their other parent. For example, the mother might act as though she is "only being concerned for your happiness" when she tells her daughter, "it's a shame that your father lives so far out of town that you won't be able to see your friends when you're there." And the father might continually arrive late to pick the children up at their mother's, or insist on having a "flexible" schedule such that he grants himself the power to interfere with the mother's plans, routines, and social life. Not understanding that prearranged, consistent schedules are necessary in order for adults to meet their responsibilities, run an organized home, and fulfill their own social and vocational activities, teenagers can be manipulated into believing that the parent or stepparent who insists on establishing and honoring dependable schedules is "not spontaneous enough," "uptight," and "inflexible." Immediately before delivering them to their other parent for a visit, a parent might also create stress for teenage children by looking sad or saying such things as: "I'm going to miss you so much this week. It's so lonely without you around." In fact, teenagers generally react to the transitions between their parents' homes in the way the parent they are leaving reacts. So when a teenager seems especially upset by these transitions, one or both of their parents are often making them feel guilty, depressed, insecure, or worried (Ahrons, 1994). In general, mothers who were full-time homemakers while they were married seem to have the most difficulty with the children spending time with their father, especially if he has remarried (Emery, 1992; Johnston & Campbell, 1989; Maccoby & Mnookin, 1993; Warshak, 1992). The unselfish, loving adult minimizes children's stress by adhering to a fixed schedule and making the transitions between households as well-organized, low-key, matter-of-fact, and cheerful as possible (Ahrons, 1994; Buchanan, Maccoby, & Dornbusch, forthcoming; Furstenberg & Cherlin, 1991; Maccoby & Mnookin, 1993).

Finally, teenagers can be damaged by being placed on the custody battlefield. Some parents agree to **joint custody** in which they are legally allowed to each have a say on major decisions concerning such matters as their children's education, religion, and medical care. More commonly, only the mother is awarded custody. Unfortunately, when custody and visitation issues are being negotiated, too many parents put their own needs, including the need for revenge, ahead of their children's best interests (Maccoby & Mnookin, 1993; Paquin, 1990).

Regardless of whether their parents are arguing about the children's living arrangements, custody, money, or the events surrounding their divorce, adolescents can be caught in the cross-fire in two ways (Buehler & Ryan, 1994). First, one or both parents can engage in an openly hostile assassination of the other's character. In these post-divorce war games, teenagers can be used as spies, allies, weapons, and hostages. Second, one or both parents can take the more sly, passive-aggressive approach of gradually trying to separate the children from the other parent by behaving in ways that send such messages as: "I didn't do anything wrong, so I don't know why your other parent is doing this . . ." or "I sacrificed the most to raise you, therefore . . ." and so on. Whichever strategy their parents use, most teenagers in these situations fare more poorly socially and psychologically after the divorce than those whose parents don't denigrate each other in front of the children and don't try to align child against parent (Buchanan, Maccoby, & Dornbusch, [forthcoming]; Furstenberg & Cherlin, 1991; Guttman, 1993; Kalter, 1990; Maccoby & Mnookin, 1993; Pasley & Ihinger-Tallman, 1994; Robinson, 1993).

MOTHER'S FINANCIAL SITUATION

Many negative consequences of divorce virtually disappear if the unmarried mother has enough money or raises her children's standard of living by remarrying. For example, in a study involving nearly 11,000 adolescents, when family incomes were equal, the mother's status as single, married, or remarried made almost no difference on 22 different measures of her children's academic achievements, mental health, and social behavior (Marsh, 1990). Likewise, adolescents whose single mothers have adequate money tend to marry later and live at home longer than those living with low-income mothers (Kiernan, 1992; Tasker & Richards, 1994). In short, whether their mother is single or married, teenagers with similar family incomes do about the same in terms of their grades, high-school and college graduation rates, teenage pregnancies, drug and alcohol abuse, mental health, social maturity, and delinquency (Amato, 1994; Barber & Eccles, 1992; Dornbusch & others, 1991; Hetherington & Jodl, 1994; Levin, 1989; McLanahan, Astone, & Marks, 1993; Mednick, Baker, & Reznick, 1990; Smith, 1990).

MOTHER'S EMOTIONAL WELL-BEING

The mother's mental and emotional condition is also closely connected to the effects on children of living in a fatherless home. For instance, even when their parents are still married, a teenager's depression is more closely tied to the mother's depression and gloomy styles of thinking than to the father's (Harrington, 1994; Phares & Compas, 1992; Seligman, 1991; Waxler & others, 1992). Likewise, regardless of whether our parents are divorced, how they respond to the stress in their lives is often related to how we react and how well we cope with change and stress in our own lives (Sigel, McGillicuddy, & Goodnow, 1992). For example, teenagers who grow up with a parent who is often in a bad mood tend to act in a similar way (Blechman, 1990). Likewise, even when their parents are still married, teenagers are more apt to be depressed and to drink heavily when their parents continually express their worries about financial matters around the children (Compas & Wagner, 1991; Conger, 1991; Dornbusch & others, 1991; Patterson & others, 1992). Especially for the teenager who has a difficult temperament or emotional or psychological problems, a parent's moods and stress level can have a considerable impact on the teenager's moods and behavior (Harrington, 1994; Parke & Ladd, 1992; Seligman, 1991). In short, teenagers need to see that both parents can take care of themselves financially and emotionally, regardless of whether they are divorced.

Because most children live with their mothers and because children tend to be more closely bonded to their mother than to their father, the more content and psychologically stable she is, the better off these teenagers are after her divorce. When the single mother seems relatively calm, upbeat, and content, her children tend to follow suit. But when the mother seems gloomy, fragile, helpless, upset, and overwhelmed, the more likely it is that one of her children will develop academic, social, or psychological problems—especially the child who had problems before the divorce. Think about the influence of your own parents' moods and emotional well-being as you were growing up. It shouldn't surprise you that a mother's adjustment to divorce and single parenting is closely linked to her children's academic, social, and psychological well-being (Ahrons, 1994; Furstenberg & Cherlin, 1991; Furstenberg & Teitler, 1993; Hetherington & Jodl, 1994; Kalter, 1990; Maccoby & Mnookin, 1993; Mednick, Baker, & Reznick, 1990; Pasley & Ihinger-Tallman, 1994; Robinson, 1993).

MOTHER'S ORGANIZATIONAL AND DISCIPLINARY SKILLS

The way a single mother manages the household and disciplines her children also affects her teenagers. Many single mothers are not able to monitor and control their children, especially teenage sons, as well as most married couples. The lax discipline and lack of supervision characteristic of many single-parent families can contribute to teenagers' poor grades, delinquency, truancy, aggressiveness, and poor self-control (Furstenberg & Cherlin, 1991; Hetherington, 1991; Krein & Beller, 1988; McLanahan, Astone, & Marks, 1993; Patterson, Reid, & Dishion, 1992; Sessa & Steinberg, 1991).

Moreover, a single parent tends to have a more difficult time than does a couple in establishing a well-organized household. Household organization includes such things as eating the evening meal together, keeping up with the grocery shopping, maintaining the home, and establishing schedules and routines. Teenagers in poorly organized households are less likely to acquire the attitudes and habits that help them succeed at school and at work—how to work with those in authority, organize their personal lives, and achieve goals through self-discipline. Moreover, a well-organized household seems to be more closely related to how well boys adjust after their parents divorce than it does to how well girls adjust (Furstenberg & Cherlin, 1991; Hetherington, 1991; Pianta, Egeland, & Stroufe, 1990). Likewise, those adolescents who generally adjust best to having a stepparent are those whose mothers maintained the upper hand and ran a well-organized household as single parents (Beer, 1992; Hetherington, 1991; Jones & Schiller, 1992; Papernow, 1993). Overall, a well-organized household helps any adolescent, but seems particularly beneficial for those in single-parent families (Brooks-Gunn, 1994; Furstenberg & Cherlin, 1991; Hetherington, 1991; McLanahan, Astone, & Marks, 1993; Nock, 1988; Wallerstein, 1991; Weiss, 1994).

GENERATIONAL BOUNDARIES IN THE SINGLE PARENT FAMILY

A single parent's lack of control over a teenage child sometimes reflects a more serious problem—the collapse of generational boundaries and role reversals. Remember that a generational boundary is an unwritten, yet clearly understood, set of rules and expectations that lets children know the adults have the ultimate power, control, and authority in the family. In other words, the parents do not permit any of the children to behave as their peers. As emphasized in preceding chapters, teenagers do better academically, socially and psychologically when their parents and stepparents consistently maintain and enforce these generational boundaries. Although some unmarried mothers do an excellent job in this regard, boundaries will most likely collapse in fatherless families. In these families, the mother becomes overly dependent on at least one of her children. As a consequence, the teenager assumes the role of a parent or spouse—a damaging situation referred to as role reversal. For example, a teenager might control the mother's social life, including whether she can ask her boyfriend over for dinner or when she can remarry. Usually it is the son who reverses roles with his mother, thus being elevated to a position of power over the household (Guttman, 1993; Silverstein & Rashbaum, 1994; Snarey, 1993; Warshak, 1992). Regardless of gender or age, however, children need parents who take care of their own adult emotional needs through adult relationships instead of allowing their children to become their peers, confidants, or financial and emotional caretakers (Bowen, 1978; Hinde & Stevenson, 1995; Johnston, 1990; Minuchin & Nichols, 1994; Silverstein & Rashbaum, 1994).

Generational boundaries are also important because they prevent teenagers from becoming too involved or enmeshed in their single parent's life. Until she remarries, a mother and child are at more risk of developing these enmeshed or peer-like relationships with each other. Believing they are responsible for their mothers can interfere with teenagers' own social and emotional development (Guttman, 1993; Hinde & Stevenson, 1995; Minuchin & Nichols, 1994; Wallerstein, 1991; Weiss, 1994). It can also sometimes further alienate teenagers from their fathers. Unable to see their fathers except through the eyes of their divorced mother, these teens turn against or pull away from their fathers (Berman, 1992; Bowen, 1978; Corneau, 1991; Kalter, 1990; Minuchin & Nichols, 1994; Warshak, 1992). If that happens, many later turn against their mothers as well (Guttman, 1993; Hetherington & Jodl, 1994; Karen, 1994; Wallerstein, 1991; Warshak, 1992).

TIMING OF THE DIVORCE

Researchers have also wondered about the significance of a child's age and developmental period at the time of the divorce: Does a child's age matter when the parents divorce? Does it matter how long a child lives in a fatherless home? On the one hand, teenagers who lived with an unmarried mother during the first 5 or 6 years of their lives seem to have more academic and behavioral problems than do those in a single-parent home later in childhood (Ahlburg & DeVita, 1992; Krein & Beller, 1988; McLanahan, Astone, & Marks, 1993). Moreover, the longer children live with a single mother, the more likely they are to suffer in areas such as grades, future income, delinquency, drug use, high-school or college graduation, teenage pregnancy, and their own divorce rates (Krein & Beller, 1988; Nock, 1988). On the other hand, teenagers who were between the ages of 8 and 13 when their parents divorced may have the hardest time adjusting because these seem to be the ages at which children are the most likely to be manipulated by one of their parents in ways that cause them to turn against their other parent—most often their father (Guttman, 1993; Hetherington & Jodl, 1994; Smith, 1990; Wallerstein & Blakeslee, 1989).

THE INFLUENCE OF SIBLINGS

Does having brothers or sisters make it any easier for children to adapt to their parents divorce? Generally, yes. Judging from grades, behavior at school, and overall stress, a child with siblings seems to recover more quickly than does an only child. Perhaps that's because children with siblings are less likely than an only child to become enmeshed in a parent's life or to get caught in the middle of the ongoing conflicts between their divorced parents. Yet, most siblings disagree with each other about their perceptions of the divorce and how they feel about what's gone on in the family (Monahan, Buchanan, Maccoby, & Dornbusch, 1993). Also, boys are generally more demanding, more aggressive, and more competitive than are girls for a single mother's attention (Boer & Dunn, 1992; Hetherington & Jodl, 1994). Nevertheless, teenagers with a brother or sister often do better than does an only child after parents divorce (Boer & Dunn, 1992; Kempton & others, 1991; Wallerstein & Blakeslee, 1989).

CONTACT WITH FATHERS

Time spent with fathers can also influence how children adjust to the divorce and life with a single mother. Unfortunately, most children don't see much of their father after their parents divorce. For example, half of the 2,200 children in one survey hadn't seen their father in a year and only 15% had spent time with him every week. Although sons saw more of their fathers than daughters, nearly a quarter of these children hadn't seen their father in 5 years (Furstenberg & Cherlin, 1991). On a happier note, more recent surveys show that many divorced fathers are trying to maintain contact with their children (Guttman, 1993). For example, in a sample of 1,100 families in Northern California, only about 15% of the children hadn't seen their father during the past year (Maccoby & Mnookin, 1993). And in another survey of almost 1,400 fathers, 25% of the men saw their children every week (Seltzer, 1991). Indeed, the number of fathers legally arranging for their children to live with them full-time or part-time after a divorce has almost doubled in the past 20 years (U.S. Department of Commerce, 1992). Moreover, most fathers say the most painful part of their divorce is being deprived of living with their children (Grief, 1990; Guttman, 1993; Kitson & Holmes, 1992).

So if it hurts so much, why don't more fathers spend time with their children after divorce? Since most fathers pay little or no child support, the main reason seems to be financial. That is, not providing any money, these fathers don't feel entitled to see their children or are no longer welcomed by the children or their mother. But those fathers who are paying child support also spend very little time with their children. Most of these fathers say it is extremely difficult to remain close to their children when they are only allowed to spend 4 nights a month together and when they are no longer part of their children's day-to-day lives (Depner & Bray, 1993; Dudley, 1991; Furstenberg & Cherlin, 1991; Grief, 1990; Guttman, 1993).

But the reasons most fathers give for not seeing more of their children involve their ex-wives. Usually the father believes his ex-wife either makes it difficult for him to see the children or that she actively works to undermine the father–child bond. For example, some mothers won't allow the children to be with their father for even a few days without intruding—taking the children to do errands during their brief stays with their father, or dropping by the father's home to spend time with the children before he gets home from work. Likewise, nearly 40% of the divorced mothers in one study complained that the father was spending too much time with their children (Pearson & Thoennes, 1990). Most mothers are also more opposed than most fathers to letting the children live part-time with each of them after their divorce (Maccoby & Mnookin, 1993). Having to ask an ex-wife's permission to see his children, or surviving the dramas involved in picking up and delivering the children, can be demeaning and heart-wrenching experiences for a father. For example, the ex-wife might consistently delay having the children ready when their father arrives, taking the opportunity to air grievances against him in front of the children. Worse still, as he waits for his children, the mother might put her ex-husband through such ordeals as inviting him inside to see the Christmas tree or bringing up the possibility of reconciling. Reduced to having "visitations rights" and having to interact with his ex-wife can be so painful and humiliating that many fathers withdraw from their children (Biller, 1993; Depner & Bray, 1993; Dudley, 1991; Furstenberg & Cherlin, 1991; Guttman, 1993; Maccoby & Mnookin, 1993; Seltzer, 1991; Warshak, 1992).

On the other hand, a number of mothers are upset because their ex-husbands aren't involved enough with the children. As mentioned, mothers who earned incomes while married are usually more supportive of their children's spending time or living part-time with their father than are mothers who were full-time homemakers (Ambert, 1989; Emery, 1992; Johnston & Campbell, 1989; Maccoby & Mnookin, 1993; Warshak, 1992). When the ex-wife remarries, some fathers also reduce the time they spend with their children because they feel like outsiders or strangers now that another man has stepped into their children's lives. In contrast, the father's getting remarried usually has very little, if any, impact on how much time he spends with his children (Buehler & Ryan, 1994; Furstenberg & Cherlin, 1991; Kitson & Holmes, 1992; Maccoby & Mnookin, 1993).

Some fathers also say they stay away because their children seem so angry, critical, or insensitive. Because most children live with their mother, they might hear only her versions of the marriage and divorce stories and witness only her emotional and financial struggles. As discussed, most children are not in a position to understand the dynamics of divorce, particularly when adultery was involved. In addition, most adolescents are not aware that a woman tends to stay unhappy or resentful longer than does a man, even when she is the one who wanted the divorce (Ambert, 1989). Nor do most teenagers understand that fathers generally experience more depression, more physical illness, and more psychological problems after a divorce than do mothers. Contrary to the image of the carefree, swinging playboy, most divorced fathers feel extremely lonely, depressed, disoriented, and powerless—mainly because they have lost so much contact with and so much influence over their own children (Grief, 1990; Depner & Bray, 1993; Guttman, 1993; Martin & Martin, 1992; Seltzer, 1991).

Some teenagers, of course, are sensitive and astute enough to recognize their father's feelings or powerlessness. For example, one 15-year-old son who knew that his mother had divorced his father for another man said to his father's therapist, "Dad is just too nice and Mom takes advantage of him" (Martin & Martin,

1992, p. 190). Many other teenagers, however, push their fathers away because they hold him responsible for the divorce, as well as for their mother's ongoing problems, anger, or unhappiness (Beal & Hochman, 1991; Berman, 1992; Depner & Bray, 1993; Wallerstein & Blakeslee, 1989; Warshak, 1992). Children may also incorrectly assume that their mother is totally "powerless" and pitiable because their father generally has the greater financial clout. In reality, however, most mothers wield tremendous power by shaping how children feel about their father and by determining how much time they spend with him (Ahrons, 1994; Furstenberg & Cherlin, 1991; Depner & Bray, 1993; Guttman, 1993; Kalter, 1990; Maccoby & Mnookin, 1993; Wallerstein, 1991; Warshak, 1992).

Recognizing the suffering of fathers does not negate the suffering of mothers. And, of course, it's natural for teenagers to be angry with the father who pays no child support or spends very little, if any, time with his children. The fact remains, however, that many adolescents don't realize the extent of their father's suffering, if for no other reason than that they see so little of him. Many teenagers do not understand why their father might find it difficult or painful to spend time with them—for reasons related to seeing his former wife, being back in a home he had to leave, or wondering how his child support money is being spent. As a society we could do a better job helping children and their fathers maintain close relationships by dispelling the sexist assumption that a mother is always the "victim" and a father is always the "bad guy" when a marriage ends. We might also help teenagers understand that, if either parent is still unhappy or angry years after their divorce, it isn't necessarily the other parent's fault. For example, the parent who was in love with someone else at the time of the divorce often ends up the most depressed and discontent years later—perhaps because most people in extramarital relationships never marry each other (Kitson & Holmes, 1992; Reibstein & Richards, 1993). In any event, some teenagers' relationships with their parents would probably improve if they could understand that both adults must take control of their own lives and assume responsibility for their own happiness after a divorce.

Regardless of the reasons why many divorced fathers spend so little time with their children, most of these teenagers report feeling sad, upset, and rejected (Beal & Hochman, 1991; Berman, 1992; McGuire, 1989; Rosenberg, 1989). But can we measure the importance of the time children spend with their fathers after a divorce? Exactly what are the effects of his absence? Well, we do know that the small percentage of adolescents who spend a lot of time or live part-time with their fathers after the divorce usually benefit in several areas. Not only are they less likely to abuse drugs and alcohol, they also have more self-confidence, make better grades, and are less aggressive, less depressed, and less involved in delinquency than teenagers who see little or nothing of their fathers (Biller, 1993; Warshak, 1992). Nevertheless, this doesn't mean that all children who have no contact with their father develop academic, emotional, or social problems (Emery, 1989; Furstenberg & Cherlin, 1991; Wallerstein, 1991).

Nowadays, divorced fathers often request more visitation days and more joint-custody agreements, or outright custody of their children (Warshak, 1992).

Historically our legal system automatically granted custody to fathers because men were considered better suited to raise, educate, guide, and protect children. Not until the 1920s did our custody laws start reflecting the assumption that it was in children's best interests to live with their mother (Friedman, 1994). More recent changes in our custody laws, however, are based on our growing awareness that children need both parents active in their daily lives after a divorce.

LIVING WITH SINGLE PARENTS

CHARACTERISTICS OF SINGLE FATHERS

Because less than 3% of American teenagers live with an unmarried father, we don't have as much information about these families as we do about the 30% who live with single mothers (U.S. Department of Commerce, 1992). What we have learned about these adolescents and their fathers, however, might surprise you.

Contrary to popular belief, single fathers are usually just as nurturing and committed to their children as are single mothers (Biller, 1993; Dudley, 1991; Pruett, 1992; Snarey, 1993; Van Wert, 1992; Warshak, 1992). In fact, some teenagers rate their single fathers as more nurturing than do teenagers in two-parent families when rating either parent (Hanson, 1986). Why are men whose children live with them part-time or full-time after a divorce usually more nurturing than are other divorced fathers? In part, it might be because these fathers are somewhat better educated than fathers whose children do not live with them. But more importantly, most active fathers have been as involved—in some cases more involved—than the mother in raising the children since they were born. Yet these teenagers often hear a different story from their divorced mothers. That is, mothers are more likely than fathers to claim all of the credit for raising the children, even when the father contributed as much or more—not an occasional token gesture, but regularly performing such tasks as changing diapers, tending crying infants at night, preparing meals, doing laundry, working the garden, canning food, baking birthday cakes, carpooling to school, making school lunches, and keeping house (Buchanan, Maccoby, & Dornbusch, [forthcoming]; Hetherington & Jodl, 1994; Maccoby & Mnookin, 1993).

Many adolescents' fathers say they feel more comfortable and more self-confident with their children once the ex-wife isn't around to criticize their fathering (Ahrons, 1994; Guttman, 1993; Kalter, 1990; Warshak, 1992; Maccoby & Mnookin, 1993). Indeed, teenagers who live equally with both parents after a divorce more often hear their mother criticize their father's parenting than vice versa (Maccoby & Mnookin, 1993). Nevertheless, many adolescents and fathers report feeling closer to one another after the divorce than before. Some fathers believe that their ex-wives interfered with and disapproved of the ways they related to their children. Others believe the mother was, and still is, jealous of the father–child bond. For example, one mother offered to return half of the father's child support money if he would spend less time with their children (Pruett,

1992). But, as one father explains, "I finally realized after my divorce that I had more patience and tolerance with my kids when I was doing it myself." His ex-wife also noticed: "I was so moved seeing what was going on between my ex and the kids because he was so soft and involved with them. I felt it was crazy that we were divorced" (Minuchin & Fishman, 1981, p. 205).

Of course not all single fathers are happy that their children are living with them. And not all single fathers are attentive or committed to their children. When a father believes he has "gotten stuck" with his children because their mother isn't able or willing to care for them, he might not be as loving and committed as the father who has volunteered or fought a legal battle to have his children live with him. It is also important to note that 20% of single fathers and their children are living in poverty, which means they are faced with many of the same problems as impoverished single mothers (Meyer & Garasky, 1993).

SINGLE PARENTS AND SONS

On the whole, adolescents are as well-off living with their unmarried father as with their unmarried mother (Warshak, 1992). "On the whole," however, ignores the question of the child's gender. Boys who live with their fathers generally fare better than do those who live with their mothers in terms of their educational achievements, mental health, social maturity, self-discipline, self-confidence, and ego development. One leading expert on child custody summarizes the research in this way: "It's not divorce that gives boys a harder time than girls. It's mother custody" (Warshak, 1992, p.139). Unlike girls who live with their unmarried fathers, boys who live with single mothers are usually more aggressive, defiant, immature, hostile, and have poorer grades and poorer peer relationships (Amato & Keith, 1991; Biller, 1993; Furstenberg & Cherlin, 1991; Hetherington & Jodl, 1994; Kalter, 1990; Wallerstein, 1991; Zaslow, 1989; Zill, 1994; Zimiles & Lee, 1991).

So the question is: Why do boys who live with their fathers generally fare better? To begin with, boys have more psychological and social problems than girls as they're growing up, even when their parents aren't divorced (Asher & Coie, 1990; Ebata, Petersen, & Conger, 1990; Ketterlinus & Lamb, 1994). So perhaps boys need—especially during adolescence—the discipline, supervision, and control that fathers or stepfathers generally provide better than mothers (Andrews & Dishion, 1994; Biller, 1993; Warshak, 1992; Snarey, 1993). Not surprisingly then, many teenage boys do behave better and are more well-adjusted after their mother remarries (Astone & McLanahan, 1991; Furstenberg & Cherlin, 1991; Pasley & Ihinger-Tallman, 1994; Warshak, 1992).

Second, until the mother remarries or creates a happier life for herself as a single woman, the son seems to be more adversely affected by her bad moods, her depression, and her conflicts with his father than does the daughter (Capaldi, Forgatch, & Crosby, 1994; Colten, Gore, & Aseltine, 1991; Emery, 1992; Forehand, 1991; Pianta, Egeland, & Stroufe, 1990). For example, in two separate longitudinal studies, teenage sons—even 6 years after the divorce—showed more stress, hostility, and social and psychological trouble associated with their mother's emotions and moods than did daughters (Hetherington & Jodl, 1994; Wallerstein, 1991). Then too, when girls live with their unmarried fathers, other women generally step in to help and to serve as female models. Rarely, however, do men step in to help single mothers raise their sons. So boys almost always lose more than girls because they no longer have daily contact or a close relationship with an adult male (Biller, 1993; Warshak, 1992).

Sons are also more likely than daughters to be negatively affected by being too involved or enmeshed with the mother and by reversing roles with her. As a consequence, the son believes he has the right to an equal or greater say than his mother, while simultaneously feeling responsible for her care and protection (Silverstein & Rashbaum, 1994; Snarey, 1993; Stroufe, 1989; Warshak, 1992). When a father or stepfather is around, a son isn't as likely to reverse roles with his mother or to behave in demanding, aggressive, infantile ways—at least not for long. This may help to explain why teenage sons are more likely than daughters to leave home when their mother remarries (Kiernan, 1992). In any case, it is not the strong, self-reliant, single mother who reverses roles or becomes enmeshed with her son, but the weak, dependent, or depressed mother (Pianta, Egeland, & Stroufe, 1990; Pittman, 1993; Silverstein & Rashbaum, 1994). After a divorce then, sons in particular need to see that their mothers can take care of themselves emotionally, socially, and financially—or, at the very least, that their mother relies on another adult, not on one of her children, to help her. Boys between the ages of 9 and 13 when their parents divorce also seem to have an especially hard time adjusting. Not only do a number of these boys become progressively more hostile—especially toward their fathers—and more psychologically troubled as they age, many are profoundly angry at their mother for reasons having to do with the divorce, although they remain strongly identified or enmeshed with her (Hetherington, 1991; Kalter, 1990; Guttman, 1993; Wallerstein & Blakeslee, 1989).

On the other hand, many single mothers keep the upper hand and maintain generational boundaries regardless of how many sons they have. Why? Part of the answer might be that parents who feel especially guilty about the divorce or who believe they aren't "good enough" parents are the most apt to hand over too much power and authority and to discipline too little (Bowen, 1978; Hinde & Stevenson, 1995; Miller, 1994; Silverstein & Rashbaum, 1994). Another part of the answer might lie in the mother's own background. For example, one divorced mother who continually catered to her angry, demanding teenage son admitted to her therapist that she had always felt inadequate as a mother and was trying to make it up to her son by tolerating his infantile, irate behavior (Silverstein & Rashbaum, 1994). Women who reverse roles with their children, or who are overly dependent on a child for emotional intimacy and self-esteem, often have a history of angry, distant relationships with men, including their own fathers, as well as a history of depression and low self-esteem (Ainsworth & Eichberg, 1991; Miller, 1994; Minuchin & Nichols, 1994; Patterson, Reid, & Dishion, 1992; Pianta, Egeland, & Stroufe, 1990). So not only is the single mother's relationship with her son usually more problematic than with her daughter, but the way she relates to him is also linked to aspects of her personality and life other than her divorce.

Another reason teenage boys might have a harder time is that boys generally catch more of the anger the mother still feels toward the father. Divorced mothers are more apt to criticize their sons than their daughters for being "just like your father" (Greene & Leslie, 1989; Hetherington & Jodl, 1994; Wallerstein, 1991). By not remarrying or by not seeming especially interested in a sexual, intimate relationship with a man, an unmarried mother can also inadvertently contribute to her son's discomfort with his own masculinity and sexuality (Berman, 1992; Pianta, Egeland, & Stroufe, 1990). Mothers also more often criticize or mock their former husbands in front of their sons. For example, the mother might continually tell the son that his father is cheap and selfish because he won't send more money than the amount agreed to in their divorce settlement. As one expert sums up the research: "Most mothers would never deliberately undermine their sons' self-esteem. They just don't seem to realize that to encourage a son to turn against his father is to encourage him to turn against himself. A mother's negative opinion of her former spouse, if conveyed to her son, can do more harm to his gender identification and his self-esteem than the lack of contact with his father. Rarely does a boy hold a negative opinion of his father without holding the same opinion of himself" (Warshak, 1992, p.163). Too many sons who are alienated from their fathers lack self-confidence, are socially immature and emotionally troubled, and have trouble relating to females socially or sexually—if they relate to them at all. Moreover, the son might eventually turn against his mother for contributing to his alienation from the father (Biller, 1993; Bowen, 1978; Corneau, 1991; Kalter, 1990; Minuchin & Nichols, 1994; Pittman, 1993; Warshak, 1992). As one adult son who wants his father to forgive him for driving him away explains, "I remember I hurt my dad over and over again. I think I did it because Mom filled me with so many ideas that he was a bad person. I feel so sorry about that now" (Wallerstein & Blakeslee, 1989, p. 193).

SINGLE PARENTS AND DAUGHTERS

As is true for boys, a daughter generally fares best when she lives part-time with each of her parents after their divorce—or, at the very least, if she maintains a close relationship with both (Blau, 1995; Buchanan, Maccoby, & Dornbusch, [forthcoming]). Nevertheless, the daughter who lives with her unmarried father is generally better off in terms of academic, social, or psychological adjustment than the son who lives with his unmarried mother (Kalter, 1990; Warshak, 1992).

Why is it important for a daughter to maintain a close relationship with her divorced father? For reasons we discussed in Chapter 8, fathers have a significant impact on their daughter's development during adolescence—perhaps even more than during her early childhood (Biller, 1993; Secunda, 1992; Snarey, 1993; Warshak, 1992). The father seems to have a special impact on how his daughter feels about her sexuality and her femininity and how she relates to boys. Daughters who live with their unmarried mothers and spend little or no time with their fathers tend to date, go steady, have sex, leave home, and get married at a much earlier age than do daughters who remain close to their fathers

(Hetherington, 1991; Kiernan, 1992; Tasker & Richards, 1994). The father who affirms his daughter's femininity, feels comfortable with her sexuality, and demonstrates in his own life how much he respects and appreciates self-reliant women is helping his teenage daughter learn to relate to males in healthy ways. This seems to be especially true when the mother has not remarried and there is no model for the daughter of an intimate, adult relationship in the home (Ahrons, 1994; Biller, 1993; Debold, Wilson, & Malave, 1992). Indeed, some daughters become anorexic partly in reaction to being separated from their fathers after divorce. As one of these anorexic daughters says, "I felt guilty all the time—guilty because I was angry with Mom for needing me so much—guilty for wanting more time with Dad" (Maine, 1993, p. 116). For all of these reasons then, the most loving mother is the one who encourages and supports the daughter and father having a close relationship, especially when the parents are divorced (Debold, Wilson, & Malave, 1992; Maine, 1993; Minninger & Goulter, 1993; Pipher, 1994; Secunda, 1992).

Of course the single mother also influences the daughter's attitudes, especially in regard to financial self-reliance. When the single mother is earning most or all of the money to support herself and her children, as most do, the daughter is learning that financial self-reliance is just as important for women as for men. On the other hand, if a divorced mother acts as though her working outside the home is a burden that has been wrongly or unfairly forced upon her, or acts as though none of her income should be used to help support or educate the children, the daughter is learning that women shouldn't be financially responsible for themselves or their children. For example, most divorced mothers in one recent survey were encouraging their teenage daughters to marry a man who would support them, rather than encouraging them to take care of themselves financially (Girls Count Project, 1993). Fortunately, most teenage girls living with divorced mothers seem to be learning the importance of becoming financially self-reliant (Barber & Eccles, 1992; Darmody, 1991; Glickman, 1993).

The single mother also influences the daughter's attitudes about sexuality, femininity, and male–female relationships. If the mother makes clear to her daughter that she is enjoying her own sexuality and is expressing her sensuality in an intimate relationship, then the daughter is likely to feel increasingly comfortable with her own body, sexuality, and romantic relationships. On the other hand, if the single mother seems relatively uninterested in sex, romance, or intimacy with another adult, then the teenage daughter often behaves in one of two ways. Either the daughter tries to conceal or deny her sexuality and her femininity by dressing and acting in boyish, child-like ways—ridiculing and avoiding girls who dress and act in sexier, more feminine ways and withdrawing from dating or from becoming emotionally intimate with boys. Or the daughter goes overboard in the other direction—dressing and acting in extremely provocative ways and being overly focused on dating, having sex, or getting married at an early age. Either way, many of these daughters have an unmarried mother who doesn't appear to enjoy her own sexuality, to have passion in her own life, or to derive much pleasure from an intimate, romantic relationship with another adult (Debold,

Wilson, & Malave, 1992; Gilligan, Rogers, & Tolman, 1991; Glickman, 1993; Mens-Verhulst, Schreurs, & Woertman, 1993; Wallerstein & Blakeslee, 1989).

Some teenage girls also have trouble becoming emotionally intimate with males or becoming self-reliant because their unmarried mothers inadvertently discourage them from growing up, asserting themselves, or leaving home. When a mother isn't married, she is more likely to behave in ways that make her daughter feel guilty, disloyal, or "selfish" for trying to establish an independent life for herself or for expressing any needs or feelings—above all anger—that might make her mother sad, angry, or uncomfortable (Guttman, 1993; Hetherington, 1991; Pipher, 1994). As one expert on daughters of divorce puts it, "This stickiness binds her in a web of love and guilt to her mother. She has trouble moving out into the world and making a life separate from her mother's" (Wallerstein & Blakeslee, 1989, p. 98). For example, Wallerstein cites the case of a daughter who left for college but was unable to break free from her needy mother who still had not created a happy life for herself 10 years after her divorce. After college, the daughter moved back to be near her mother and rebuffed her supportive, loving father out of loyalty to her mother (Wallerstein & Blakeslee, 1989, p. 99). Moreover, if the daughter perceives her divorced mother as an unhappy woman who hasn't had much success or happiness with men or in the world of work, she may hold herself back academically, vocationally, or socially in an attempt to avoid feeling guilty about surpassing her own mother (Wallerstein & Blakeslee, 1989). In this vein, unmarried African American mothers seem to do a better job than unmarried white mothers encouraging their daughters to grow up, become self-reliant, express their anger, and challenge their mothers (Bell-Scott, 1991; Debold, Wilson, & Malave, 1992). In any event, the struggle to separate from a needy or depressed mother may partly explain why many white daughters say their relationships with their divorced mothers become more distant and stressful as time passes (Berman, 1992; Wallerstein & Blakeslee, 1989; Zill, Morrison, & Coiro, 1993).

SINGLE PARENTS' LIVE-IN PARTNERS

What if the teenager's divorced parent decides to live with someone rather than get married? A few studies give us a glimpse into these families (Isaacs & Leon, 1988; Maccoby & Mnookin, 1993). Interestingly, teenagers seem to disapprove more of their mother having a live-in boyfriend than of their father having a live-in girlfriend. In fact, when the mother brings her boyfriend to live with them, teenagers start spending more time at their father's place. In contrast, the father's live-in girlfriend doesn't seem to have much impact on the time his children spend with him. It may be that teenagers have a double standard when it comes to each parent's sexual arrangement. It may also be that the mother and boyfriend who don't get married have certain problems of their own that affect how the children feel about them. Then too, it's possible that teenagers are angry or confused when a man who supposedly loves their mother won't marry her. Some of these teenagers might ask themselves: "If this guy supposedly loves my mother, then why isn't he marrying her and helping with some of her financial problems? What am I going to tell my friends about why my mom and her boyfriend aren't married yet?" But for whatever reasons, many teenagers don't seem keen on the idea of living with their mother and her boyfriend.

LIVING IN A BINUCLEAR FAMILY

Although most teenagers of divorced parents live with their mothers, about 10% live about equal time with each parent. These are referred to as **dual residency** or **binuclear families.** Although these families are still relatively rare, recent research is giving us a clearer picture of these adolescents and their parents. One surprise is that the parents in these binuclear families don't get along much better with each other than other divorced adults. In fact, the majority of these parents have as little to do with each other as possible. Although these parents tend to have somewhat higher incomes and more education than other divorced couples, they are only somewhat more likely to be cooperative in matters related to their children. The main thing that sets binuclear families apart is that the fathers insist on their children living with them part-time, and the mothers agree. Nevertheless, mothers are generally more opposed to dual residency than fathers, especially if they were full-time homemakers before the divorce (Buchanan, Maccoby, & Dornbusch, [forthcoming]; Maccoby & Mnookin, 1993; Pearson & Thoennes, 1990; Warshak, 1992).

Given the anger and pain most divorced couples feel, how do these couples make the binuclear family work? First, each parent must disengage emotionally and assume a strictly business-like attitude toward the other. In order to minimize conflict and stress for their children, most of these parents limit their contact with each other to brief phone conversations or to letters in which they discuss only child-related matters. For their children's sake, each parent has to establish clear boundaries between their two households, adhere to fixed schedules, and abide by a consistent, unchanging routine for transporting the children from one home to the other. Dual residency is easier to manage with teenagers than with young children, when there are only one or two children, and when neither parent has remarried. Parents and adolescents seem to prefer dual residency to a life with one parent. It isn't necessary that the parents get along with each other, or even converse much with each other. It is essential that each parent keeps the children out of their adult conflicts (Ahrons, 1994; Blau, 1995; Buchanan, Maccoby, & Dornbusch, [forthcoming]; Maccoby & Mnookin, 1993; Robinson, 1993).

The Stanford Custody Project offers some of the best research comparing teenagers in binuclear families with those living primarily with one parent. The Stanford researchers have followed children from more than 1,000 families for 5 years after their parents' divorce. Overall, the findings show that the parent with whom teenagers live most of the time has less effect on their grades, depression, and stress than do other factors. First, as we've seen repeatedly, those teenagers who do best are the ones whose parents do not drag them into their conflicts. In this regard, the mother's behavior usually has more influence than does the father's. However, once drawn into the adults' problems, children in binuclear families are usually more stressed than those living with one parent. Second, teenagers are better off when the parents limit their interactions with each other than when they continue a conflicted relationship. Thus, as children grow older and each parent begins the process that leads from dating to remarriage, most parents in binuclear families try to maintain the peace by disengaging from each other. Third, when their parents disagree about each other's contributions to raising the children when they were married, teenagers are usually exposed to more conflict and stress. If either parent tries to claim credit for having raised the children, more conflict results than if both parents let their children know that they each contributed a great deal. Fourth, compared to children living with only one parent, teenagers in binuclear families feel closer to their parents and are more satisfied with their living arrangements. Moreover, those teenagers who feel equally close to both parents are not more troubled or stressed than those who feel much closer to one parent than to the other (Buchanan, Maccoby, & Dornbusch, [forthcoming]; Maccoby & Mnookin, 1993).

LIVING IN A BLENDED FAMILY

Most teenagers living in binuclear families have at least one parent who has remarried. So not only are they members of a binuclear family, they are members of a blended family in at least one of their parent's homes. A **blended family** is any family in which a biological parent and his or her spouse are living with children from one or both of their former marriages. Although almost 20% of all teenagers are now living in a blended family, fewer than 2% are living with their father and stepmother. Yet nearly a third of all Americans are members of a stepfamily, even though many of them have never actually lived together (Cherlin, 1992).

BENEFITS

Most children, even as adults, report that their parents' divorce was one of the most difficult, stressful experiences of their lives (Beal & Hochman, 1991; Berman, 1992; Pasley & Ihinger-Tallman, 1994; Teyber, 1994). Fortunately, when children begin living in a blended family within a few years after their parents divorce, their lives often improve. Most children do as well or better in terms of their grades, social behavior, and peer relationships when their parent remarries (Astone & McLanahan, 1991; Dornbush & others, 1990; Mednick, Baker, & Reznick, 1990; Nielsen, 1993; Richards & Duckett, 1991; Zimiles & Lee, 1991). Teenagers living in a blended family also tend to have somewhat less psychological and emotional stress and to use less alcohol and drugs than those living with a single parent (Foxcroft & Lowe, 1991; Flewelling & Bauman, 1990; Turner, Irwin, & Millstein, 1991). They also tend to wait longer before having sex or getting

Insert 9–2

Adolescents' Feelings about Divorce and Stepparents

"When my parents were married, I hardly ever saw my dad because he was always busy working. Now I've gotten to know him more because I'm with him every weekend. Mom got remarried and divorced again, so I've gone through two divorces so far. The one thing I really worry about is that I think my dad and his new wife want to have a baby. Then it could be a lot like what happened with my dog Spunker. I've said I'll never love any dog as much as I love him. Well, a year ago I picked up a little black puppy from the pound, and now I'm not as friendly with Spunker as I used to be."

"Now that I'm older I do think it would be good for my mother to find someone—I mean, I feel sorry for her because I'm always going out on weekends and she hardly ever goes out. It's as if she's spending all her time with us kids because she can't seem to break the emotional tie."

"I think that if parents are going to divorce and not scar their children for life, they should keep them out of what's going on as much as possible. I'm not saying parents should lie to kids, but they shouldn't make them suffer for what they've done and they don't have to give them the details of what went wrong or try to make them hate the other parent or stepparent."

"My little sister had just been born, so their divorce seems especially weird. I mean, God, it's so hard for me to imagine how people who've just had a baby can turn around and split up."

"It's a shame, but my sister and brother thought that loving our stepmom meant they were being disloyal to our natural mother. At times they were so hard on our stepmother that I got furious. I think they felt guilty getting attached to her because our mother said bad things about her."

"The hardest part is the constant going from one parent's house to the next. Half the time I'm not sure where I'll be. While my stepdad's very nice, he's not perfect—especially when he nags me. Also, he can be strict. At the dinner table, he insists we kids have good manners."

"Another problem was not liking how Mom and he acted together. During the years it was just her and me, Mom always came into my room to kiss me goodnight. Now that she was affectionate with Daniel, too, I was jealous. But the longer I lived with my stepfather, the more attached we became."

Sources: J. Krementz (1984). *How it feels when parents divorce.* New York: Knopf.
M. Rosenberg (1990). *Talking about stepfamilies.* New York: Bradbury Press.

married than do those in single-parent homes (Kiernan, 1992; Tasker & Richards, 1994). In many ways then, teenagers in blended families are often very similar to teenagers whose parents have never divorced (Booth & Dunn, 1994; Emery, 1992; Furstenberg & Cherlin, 1991; Levin, 1989; McLanahan, Astone, & Marks, 1993; Pasley & Ihinger-Tallman, 1994). On the other hand, a child with serious psychological, academic, or social problems rarely improves, and may even get worse, when the parent remarries (Booth & Edwards, 1992; Ganong & Coleman, 1994a; Martin & Martin, 1992). Since most children do not have serious psychological or social problems, however, living with a parent and stepparent is generally better than living with an unmarried parent—especially for sons (Amato, 1994; Beer, 1992; Biller, 1993; Emery, 1992; Furstenberg & Cherlin, 1991; Guttman, 1993; Hetherington & Jodl, 1994; Kalter, 1990).

NEGATIVE STEREOTYPES

Despite the many benefits of blended families, negative stereotypes about stepparents and stepchildren are still alive and well in the 1990s (Ganong & Coleman, 1994a; Crosbie-Burnett, 1994; Pasley, Ihinger-Tallman, & Lofquist, 1994). People who have never lived in a blended family generally have the most negative images of stepparents and stepchildren, despite the fact that most teenagers and their stepparents say they get along well together and feel close to one another (Ahrons, 1994; Booth & Dunn, 1994; Ganong & Coleman, 1994b; Fluitt & Paradise, 1991; Furstenberg & Cherlin, 1991; Parish, 1991). For example, a number of teachers and counselors still believe that students from blended families are going to make poorer grades and have more emotional problems, despite the grades and statements of the children in their classes that refute these negative beliefs (Crosbie-Burnett, 1994). Indeed, most schools ignore blended families in the curriculum, as well as in their practices and policies. For example, when a couple arrives at a school function or a teacher conference, most teachers automatically address them as if they were the student's biological parents—a situation that can be especially embarrassing or stressful if the adolescent is present. It is not so much that school personnel actively work to create negative stereotypes of blended families—in general, the existence of stepparents is simply ignored. This insensitivity is especially irksome, and often saddening, for families with a stepparent who is intensely involved with a teenager's academic work and future goals (Crosbie-Burnett, 1994; Nielsen, 1993).

It's been difficult to get a clear picture of blended families because researchers have traditionally lumped all blended families together without considering their differences. For instance, adolescents usually take longer to adjust to the blended family that includes a new baby or stepsiblings, as is the case for about half of these teenagers (Beer, 1992). So before trying to gauge how well any particular adolescent might adapt to a blended family, we need more information on such questions as: Is the adolescent's stepparent male or female? Is there a new baby in the blended family? What's the family's income and how well do the divorced parents get along? Researchers have only recently begun gathering data on these kinds of questions, so we need to keep this shortcoming in mind. Let's see what the research tells us about the 4 million teenagers in the United States who live in blended families.

In spite of the benefits, it takes time for adolescents to adjust to life in a blended family. In the first year or so, everyone must come to grips with how they're supposed to act and their obligations to one another. There are no easy ways to establish these roles and rules ahead of time. Only by living together, talking about problems as they arise, and learning through trial and error does each blended family arrive at its own answers. Because most divorced fathers remarry sooner than their ex-wives, the first stepparent in most teenagers lives is their father's new wife. But because so few children live with their fathers after a divorce, the stepparent that most teenagers live with is a stepfather. Whichever parent remarries first, three factors generally determine how well adolescents get along with their stepparents: (1) the other parent's reactions to the new marriage, (2) the boundaries between each parent's households, and (3) the adolescent's gender and mental health.

THE FORMER SPOUSE'S REACTIONS

A good way to predict adolescent adjustment with their stepparents is to ask: How has the other parent reacted to the former spouse remarrying? Because fathers usually remarry first, much of the research focuses on how teenagers' relationships with their fathers and stepmothers are affected by their mother's reactions. Unfortunately, most children sense or are directly told that their mother isn't happy about their father remarrying—most commonly when the mother is still single (Ahrons, 1994; Ambert, 1989; Emery, 1992; Furstenberg & Cherlin, 1991; Johnston & Campbell, 1989). Yet even when both parents have remarried, most teenagers see that the mother has the harder time accepting the former spouse's marriage and the new stepparent—even when the mother is the one who wanted the divorce (Ahrons, 1994; Beer, 1992; Buehler & Ryan, 1994; Furstenberg & Cherlin, 1991; Robinson, 1993). As we've also discussed, teenagers are seldom aware that the parent who had an extramarital affair or who wanted to leave the marriage typically has the most trouble accepting the former spouse's new marriage. As one teenager's mother put it, "I kept wishing they'd have a disaster. If his marriage fails, then I'll know I was right to leave him" (Ahrons, 1994; p. 220). The situation can be especially difficult when teenagers aren't happy about the remarriage of the parent who was rejected or betrayed in the former marriage. As one of these rejected parents who finally found happiness in a second marriage says, "After all the pain I've been through, you'd think my kids would be a little bit happy for me" (Ahrons, 1994, p. 223).

Many adolescents pick up their parent's feelings about the other's marriage and the new stepparent from nonverbal reactions, as well as from what is directly said. A parent's tone of voice, sarcasm, tearful expressions, and heavy sighs are powerful forms of communication. For example, a mother might let her teenage son see her crying when his newly remarried father returns belongings of hers that he had been storing in his house. Without saying a word, the mother has sent the teenager a potentially damaging message: "Your father and stepmother are being mean to me." Likewise, a father might tell his daughter that "after our divorce, your mom and I got along fine until your stepfather came along;" or the mother might say, "Your father has gotten so cheap, inflexible, and mean since he married her!" A parent might also tell the children not to list the stepparent on school records as a person to contact in case of emergencies. Repeated often enough, such simple acts can affect how well teenagers get along with their stepparents—especially those children who have had the most trouble adapting to their parents' divorce and those with emotional or psychological problems (Beer, 1992; Einstein, 1994; Martin & Martin, 1992; Pasley & Ihinger-Tallman, 1994; Robinson, 1993).

Rather than admitting that they are jealous of the new stepparent or that they regret having divorced, some parents try to make their children feel guilty or uncomfortable for liking their stepparent. One common method is to portray the newly remarried couple as far more powerful and fortunate, or to imply that the stepparent is somehow responsible for the misfortune and unhappiness in the unmarried parent's life. Basically this is a game of "poor me, the innocent victim"—a ploy that sometimes continues well into children's adult lives (Beal & Hochman, 1991; Berman, 1992). The game goes like this: "Poor me, I don't have . . . like your other parent and stepparent do." "Poor me, if it wasn't for your stepparent, I could have . . . ." "Poor me, I work so hard but don't get to go on nice vacations or have a big house like they do." When a parent behaves in these ways, adolescents have a harder time establishing close relationships with their stepparents without feeling guilty or disloyal (Booth & Dunn, 1994; Furstenberg & Cherlin, 1991; Robinson, 1993; Visher & Visher, 1991). In the end, however, these "poor me" strategies sometimes backfire when the teenager who has served as the ally and protector of the supposedly victimized, helpless parent eventually recognizes the ploy. In such cases, the teenage or adult child turns against the manipulative, deceitful, or jealous parent who has played the role of innocent martyr and helpless victim for so many years (Corneau, 1991; Guttman, 1993; Hetherington & Jodl, 1994; Pittman, 1993; Visher & Visher, 1991).

FAMILY AND GENERATIONAL BOUNDARIES

Teenagers also get along better with their stepparents when their divorced parents have established clear boundaries between their households. By maintaining boundaries, divorced parents are reassuring their children that they are no longer involved in each other's lives except as needed to conduct child-related business. The parent who violates the former spouse's new family boundaries is doing and saying things that send children the destructive message that their parents are still in a family together. For example, the father might enter the mother and stepfather's home uninvited when he comes to pick up the children; or the mother might phone her children regularly at their stepmother's, yet get very agitated in front of the children when their stepmother phones them. A parent might even go so far as to ask his or her child for a "tour" of the blended family's home while the stepparent and former spouse are absent. Through such unkind acts, a parent can make it difficult, if not impossible, for some teenagers to live with or relate well to their stepparents (Beer, 1992; Blau, 1995; Booth & Dunn, 1994; Furstenberg & Cherlin, 1991; Pasley & Ihinger-Tallman, 1994; Robinson, 1993; Visher & Visher, 1991).

Some teenagers are placed in these stressful situations because their parent regrets the divorce and wants to see their former spouse's new marriage fail. For example, mothers who continually contact their ex-husbands to discuss minor matters not essential to their children's well-being are often unhappy with their boyfriends or having second thoughts about the divorce (Johnston & Campbell, 1989). The divorced father generally seems to be better than his ex-wife in establishing boundaries between their households and private lives (Furstenberg & Cherlin, 1991; Maccoby & Mnookin, 1993). But regardless of which parent does the better job establishing boundaries, teenagers adapt best to blended families when they see the emotional ties and household connections between their parents forever broken (Ahrons, 1994; Bray, Berger, & Boethel, 1994; Cissna, Cox, & Bochner, 1994; Hetherington & Jodl, 1994; Robinson, 1993; Visher & Visher, 1991).

Some teenagers also have trouble adjusting to the blended family because one or both divorced parents allowed generational boundaries to collapse in their single-parent homes (Beer, 1992; Hetherington & Jodl, 1994; Jones & Schiller, 1992; Papernow, 1993). For example, one therapist reported that a teenage client was continually criticizing her father for "having changed and gotten less flexible" since he had remarried. In reality, however, the father had finally begun to establish the appropriate generational boundaries in relation to his daughter, unlike the mother whom the daughter considered "flexible" because she inappropriately allowed her daughter to relate to her as a peer or roommate (Minuchin & Nichols, 1994). In other words, if children have been granted too much power and control by either of their divorced parents, they are likely to have a difficult time accepting the adults' authority and boundaries in the blended family. As you remember from preceding chapters, socially mature and psychologically well-adjusted teenagers generally come from homes in which the adult or adults have ultimate authority and control. Unfortunately some teenagers believe their parent and stepparent are "selfish" or "mean" for establishing boundaries and a hierarchy. Thus these teenagers may want, or may choose, to live with the unmarried parent who relates to them much like a peer.

Marital Intimacy

In order for the blended family to succeed, the teenagers involved need to understand that the adults' marriage must come first for the benefit of everyone. Although the children are loved and cared for, the central hub of any healthy family is a strong, intimate marriage—a relationship that assumes top priority for both the husband and the wife. Some teenagers, however, have a hard time accepting the fact that a marriage is the central, pivotal relationship around which a well-adjusted family revolves. Because so many divorced parents lacked intimacy in their marriage, the blended family is the first opportunity some teenagers have to see a marriage that is intimate, romantic, affectionate, sexual, and separate from the children's lives. Moreover, in many marriages that end in divorce, one or both parents was more emotionally intimate and involved with the children than with their spouse (Bowen, 1978; Cowan & Cowan, 1992;

Hinde & Stevenson, 1995; Minuchin & Nichols, 1994). If this was the case in their parents' former marriage, teenagers might feel intensely jealous or angry when they see their parent and stepparent deriving most of their intimacy from each other and making their marriage the main priority. As one adult son puts it, "I can't recall ever seeing my parents hug or kiss while they were married. So I couldn't help noticing the ways my father and his new wife were around each other. Ultimately, being around them was the best thing that could have happened to me "(Berman, 1992, p. 130).

Especially when a teenager opposes the divorced parent's remarriage, the couple must maintain the strength and intimacy of their bond to each other. As two different couples explain, "If you don't come right out and lock hands and say, 'Look, kids, you're not splitting us up. If you want to leave, leave. But we're here to stay so it's your option.'" "The tensions in our blended family didn't subside until I made my teenage daughter realize where my loyalty was going to be, even though I loved her" (Cissna, Cox, & Bochner, 1994, p. 265–266). To make matters worse for some teenagers, the other parent might imply, or even say, that the remarried parent and stepparent have no right to put their marriage first or that the new marriage is a replacement for the parent–child relationship. That is, a jealous or vengeful parent might try to convince the children that "now that your other parent has a new spouse, surely you see that I need you and love you more." A mother might say that the father and stepmother are being "selfish" or "unloving" to take vacations or to share activities together that don't always include the children. Likewise, a father might try to convince his children that their mother is being "disloyal to you by putting your stepfather ahead of you children." The fact remains, however, that the most well-adjusted teenagers usually live with adults whose marriage is their top priority (Ganong & Coleman, 1994a; Papernow, 1993; Hinde & Stevenson, 1995; Minuchin & Nichols, 1994; Visher & Visher, 1991).

It is fortunate for most adolescents, therefore, that their parent's second marriage is usually more emotionally intimate, more sexually satisfying, and more fulfilling than the first marriage (Beer, 1992; Ganong & Coleman, 1994a; Jones & Schiller, 1992). For example, divorced fathers often describe their second wives as more intelligent, achievement-oriented, sexual, self-confident, communicative, and nurturant than their ex-wives (Schuldberg & Guisinger, 1991). Likewise, divorced mothers often describe their second husbands as more compromising and more willing to do more housework than their ex-husbands (Hobart, 1991). Except for those adults who married for the first time as teenagers—who, as we know, are usually the most poorly educated, the poorest financially, and the most likely to have had children at a very young age—second marriages are actually less likely than first marriages to end in divorce (Ganong & Coleman, 1994a).

Adolescents' Gender and Mental Health

A teenager's gender and mental health also influence relationships with stepparents and other members of the blended family. Sons often create more stress than daughters for adults in blended families (Giles-Sims & Crosbie-Burnett,

1989; Guisinger, Cowan, & Schulberg, 1989; Verner, 1989). This might help to explain why a son is more likely than a daughter to leave home after the mother remarries (Kiernan, 1992). Interestingly, the divorced parent's relationship with each other is also more strained when they have a son (Ahrons & Rogers, 1987). Given the gender differences in ego and social development and that divorce affects boys more negatively than girls, this should come as no surprise. Compared to girls, boys' interpersonal skills and social reasoning are usually less advanced; and boys are generally more hostile and angrier after their parents' divorce (Capaldi, Forgatch, & Crosby, 1994; Cherlin et al., 1991; Colten, Gore, & Aseltine, 1991; Hetherington & Jodl, 1994; Kalter, 1990; Wallerstein, 1991). Boys also tend to have more psychological and emotional problems than girls before their parents' divorce, which can put more stress on everyone in the blended family (Asher & Coie, 1990; Ebata, Petersen, & Conger, 1990; Harrington, 1994; Robins & Rutter, 1990).

A teenager's mental health can also affect how well he or she adapts to the blended family. Since only a small percentage of teenagers have serious psychological disorders, most adapt fairly well to living with their stepparents. A small group, however, have serious mental problems, such as schizoid personality disorders or clinical depression, that underlie the intense anger and chronic hostility they continue to display even years after their parents divorce or remarry. These troubled teenagers tend to invent things that never happened, to twist what is said or done in ways that bear almost no resemblance to reality, and to dismiss or ignore certain facts and events that might make the parent they are most dependent upon or enmeshed with look "bad" or "evil." Moreover, psychologically disturbed teenagers tend to see every person as either "all good" or "all evil," rather than as a mixture of both—a defense mechanism referred to as "splitting." Commonly these teenagers vent their rage on the most convenient scapegoat—their stepparent or whichever parent they are least bonded to. Indeed, psychologists have pointed out that even fairy tales allow children to vent the anger they feel toward their own mothers onto the "wicked" stepmother (Bettelheim, 1976). By distorting, exaggerating, and obsessing on the scapegoat's flaws and mistakes, psychologically disturbed teenagers are often trying to avoid confronting certain painful truths about the parent to whom they are most bonded (Bowlby, 1988; Halverson, 1988; Miller, 1994; Weiner, 1992).

For instance, depressed teenagers who have an extremely negative view of themselves and of the world around them tend to focus consistently on the negative aspects of their stepparents and their parents' divorce. Whenever things aren't going well in their lives, these teenagers tend to blame their stepparents (Fine & Kurdek, 1994). Likewise, the teenage boy who is extremely hostile or aggressive toward his stepfather often has an enmeshed relationship with his mother that has contributed to severe social and emotional problems throughout his childhood (Capaldi, Forgatch, & Crosby, 1994). As one stepmother of a suicidal teenager explains, "My stepson is determined to prove that his father and I have ruined his life. Everything he does to destroy his life is his father's fault and nobody can persuade him otherwise" (Jones & Schiller, 1992, p. 32). In any event, unless they undergo intensive therapy, psychologically disturbed teenagers seldom improve, and may even get worse, when a parent remarries (Booth & Dunn, 1994; Ganong & Coleman, 1994a; Martin & Martin, 1992).

Adolescents and Their Stepfathers

Fortunately, however, most teenagers get along pretty well with their stepfathers, although many are not especially close to him (Beer, 1992; Ganong & Coleman, 1994b; Hetherington & Jodl, 1994). Those teenagers closest to their stepfather have usually lived with him since they were young children and tend to have seen very little, if any, of their own father (Bray, Berger, & Boethel, 1994; Emery, 1992; Furstenberg & Cherlin, 1991). Nevertheless, the stepfather is usually far less active in disciplining or interacting with his stepchildren than is the mother (Astone & McLanahan, 1991; Beer, 1992). Teenagers whose stepfathers are predictable, even-tempered, and easy-going have better relationships with him than those whose stepfathers are punitive, erratic, quick-tempered, or overly critical (Pasley & Ihinger-Tallman, 1994; Robinson, 1993; Rosen, 1989). In fact, some teenagers say they like their stepfather more than their own father (Fluitt & Paradise, 1991). On the other hand, a number of stepfathers become increasingly distant and disengaged as the years pass because their stepchildren continue to reject them (Bray, Berger, & Boethel, 1994; Hetherington & Jodl, 1994). Interestingly, if their stepfather makes more money than their mother, or if he is helping to support them financially, stepchildren grant him the most decision-making power (Giles-Sims & Crosbie-Burnett, 1989). So it seems that a certain Golden Rule might be operating: "He who has the gold is allowed to makes the rules." Teenagers also seem closer to their stepfather when he doesn't have any biological children of his own (Crosbie-Burnett & Giles-Sims, 1994; Ganong & Coleman, 1994a). In part this may be because a stepfather with biological children often feels disloyal or guilty if he gives too much or gets too close to his stepchildren (Clingempeel, Colyar, & Hetherington, 1994; Einstein, 1994).

Who gets along best with their stepfather—the teenage boy or the teenage girl? As mentioned, boys generally create more stress than girls whether they are living with a stepmother or with a stepfather. Teenage boys do, however, usually get along better than teenage girls do with their stepfathers (Ganong & Coleman, 1994b; Hetherington, 1991; Pasley, Ihinger-Tallman, & Lofquist, 1994). This seems to be especially true when the son has a close relationship with his biological father (Warshak, 1992). Why? Part of the reason might be that teenage girls have more reason to feel uncomfortable around their mother's husband for sexual reasons. That is, girls have more reason to feel embarrassed or worried about forms of touching, hugging, or interacting that might have sexual overtones. And although very few stepfathers sexually harass or molest their stepdaughters, incest is far more common between girls and their stepfathers than between girls and their fathers (Bass & Davis, 1991).

In general, adolescents seem to feel more comfortable around their stepfathers than their stepmothers. Why? Well, remember that unlike the stepmother, the stepfather usually has the stage all to himself because the majority of fathers see so little of their children after a divorce. Second, most stepfathers and fathers have much less interaction and are less threatened by each other than most mothers and stepmothers, for reasons discussed shortly. As a result, teenagers aren't as likely to be negatively affected by the competition, conflicts, or jealousies between their father and stepfather (Ahrons, 1994; Fine & Kurdek, 1994). Perhaps because of the men's more nonchalant attitudes toward each other, spending time with their father generally does not interfere with children's relationships with their stepfather, which is not as true with regard to mothers and stepmothers. That is, being close to your stepfather is usually not any more difficult if you're also close to your father (Ahrons, 1994; Furstenberg & Cherlin, 1991; Hetherington & Jodl, 1994; Pasley & Ihinger-Tallman, 1994). Also helping the stepfather is the fact that the children's father generally doesn't disapprove of his ex-wife remarrying as much as she does if he remarries. In fact, the father might appreciate the stepfather for assuming some of the financial responsibilities for the mother and children, especially if the father no longer has to pay alimony when his ex-wife remarries. Finally, because men usually remarry before women, the stepmother usually comes along when children are living with a divorced mother who hasn't yet remarried—a situation that can make teenagers feel sorry for their mother and resentful of their stepmother. So the stepmother often blazes a trail that makes life easier for a future stepfather. Indeed, when their mother finally remarries, teenagers, their stepmothers, and their fathers often say they feel happier, more relaxed, and more comfortable with one another (Ambert, 1989; Emery, 1992; Furstenberg & Cherlin, 1991; Pasley & Ihinger-Tallman, 1994; Wallerstein & Blakeslee, 1989).

Adolescents and Their Stepmothers

Although most adolescents don't live with their stepmother, the quality of their relationship seems to be influenced primarily by three factors: our society's ideas about mothering, their mother's feelings about the stepmother, and the adults' financial conflicts.

For reasons discussed in Chapter 8, middle- and upper-class white families in our country tend to define a mother's role in very possessive, restrictive ways (Bell-Scott, 1991; Biller, 1993; Collins, 1991; Debold, Wilson, & Malave, 1992; Warshak, 1992). Even when parents are still married to each other, some mothers believe the father is intruding on "her territory" when he is nurturing or involved with their children. This restrictive view of who is and isn't entitled to nurture and love children can contribute to much of the conflict and tension that teenagers experience when a stepmother enters their lives. As one mother said about her children's stepmother, "When Ann, who is extremely concerned about the welfare of my children, suggests something for their benefit, my immediate reaction is to get angry and accuse her of intruding. The truth is that I feel jealous and guilty that I, the real mother, didn't think of it first" (Maglin & Schniedewind, 1989, p. 313). And, as one stepmother comments after having lived with her stepchildren for years, "When I answer the phone, their mother doesn't even acknowledge who I am. She acts like I'm not involved in any way in her kids' lives even though they live with us part-time" (Ahrons & Rogers, 1987, p. 172). By defining motherhood in such restrictive ways, many of us have inadvertently made it more difficult for some teenagers to create close relationships with their stepmothers.

As a society then, we could do a better job relieving some stress for adolescents by creating less restrictive, less possessive attitudes about mothering, as African American families have historically done (Collins, 1991; Debold, Wilson, & Malave, 1992; Lewis & Crosbie-Burnett, 1993). These more open-minded attitudes about mothering are based on a belief that children benefit from close relationships with as many women as possible—women who nurture, love, and advise them without arousing the biological mother's jealousy, fear, or anger. Within many African American communities, women gladly share the responsibilities of mothering and feel a communal responsibility for raising "our" children. As one African proverb says, "It takes a whole village to raise a child." If this attitude were more generally accepted in our society, some teenagers might feel less disloyal and more comfortable having close relationships with their stepmothers. For example, unlike stepfathers, stepmothers are portrayed in very negative ways in our fairy tales and in children's literature (Dainton, 1993; Noy, 1991; Salwen, 1990; Schectman, 1991). Some recent children's books, however, are presenting much more positive, more loving images of stepmothers (Leach, 1993; Martin, 1994; Zakhoders, 1992).

Because most teenagers' attitudes about their stepmothers are powerfully affected by their mother's feelings and behavior, it is fortunate that some mothers do make life easier for their children by reassuring them that loving or being friends with their stepmother isn't an act of disloyalty or betrayal. As one teenager's mother says: "It really isn't worth it to program my kids to hate their stepmother or to be angry and defensive when she seems to be out-parenting me" (Crytser, 1990, p.61). In general, mothers who were earning an income of their own before their divorce are more supportive of their children's stepmothers than mothers who were full-time homemakers (Ambert, 1989; Emery, 1992; Johnston & Campbell, 1989). Remember though that teenagers whose mothers were employed before their divorce tend to have an easier time adjusting to their parents' separation even before a stepmother enters the scene (Emery, 1992; Hetherington, Cox, & Cox, 1981; Kinard & Reinherz, 1986; Warshak, 1992). What seems to be happening is that employed mothers are more likely than homemakers to have interests and sources of self-esteem other than their children, which may make the stepmother seem less threatening (Gilbert, 1993; Lerner & Galambos, 1991; Repetti, Matthews, & Waldron, 1989).

The fear or jealousy that many mothers feel is especially sad and ironic when we consider how most stepmothers feel. Most stepmothers aren't interested in being second mothers to their husband's children, especially not when his children are already teenagers or when the stepmother has a fulfilling career or children of her own. On the other hand, most stepmothers do work harder than stepfathers to become close friends with their stepchildren (Beer, 1992; Crosbie-Burnett & Giles-Sims, 1994; Fine & Kurdek, 1994; Fine & Schwebel, 1992; Martin & Martin, 1992). And although stepfathers tend to be closest to their stepsons, stepmothers tend to be closest to their stepdaughters—a situation that might be especially threatening or upsetting to the mother (Maglin & Schneidewind, 1989; Quick, McKenry, & Newman, 1994). Unfortunately for most teenagers, their mothers do not encourage them to be close friends with, let alone to love, their stepmothers (Ahrons, 1994; Artlip, Artlip, & Saltzman, 1993; Beer, 1992; Crytser, 1990; Einstein, 1994; Jones & Schiller, 1992; Keenan, 1992; Maglin & Schneidewind, 1989; Martin & Martin, 1992; Quick, McKenry, & Newman, 1994; Smith, 1990).

Sadly, many teenagers hear their mother criticize their stepmother for an assortment of "evils" and shortcomings. If the stepmother doesn't "do enough" for her stepchildren, she can be accused of being indifferent or unloving. Yet if she is "too close" or does "too much," she can be criticized for over-stepping her bounds. The generous, good-hearted stepmother with a good income of her own who buys nice gifts or vacations for her stepchildren is sometimes accused of "bribing" or trying to "buy" affection (Jones & Schiller, 1992). And the stepmother with children of her own is often criticized for playing favorites (Crytser, 1990; Jones & Schiller, 1992; Maglin & Schneidewind, 1989). On the other hand, if the stepmother has no children, she is sometimes portrayed by the mother as someone who doesn't like children, doesn't know how to relate to them, or is too ambitious and career-oriented to be a loving stepmother (Morell, 1994). As one divorced mother explains, "I kept hoping my daughter's stepmother would lose her temper or do something to make Janie like her less. I felt I was competing for my own daughter's love" (Crytser, 1990, p. 27). And as one stepmother explains, "Their mother bad-mouthed me, but I never knew exactly what she said, so I couldn't defend myself" (Jones & Schiller, 1992, p. 51). In many cases then, the closer adolescents are to their stepmother, the more hostile their mother becomes toward their father and his wife—even when the mother divorced the father for another man (Ahrons, 1994; Hetherington, Cox, & Cox, 1981; Jones & Schiller, 1992; Artlip, Artlip, & Saltzman, 1993; Einstein, 1994; Smith, 1990).

Many adolescents are also stressed by ongoing financial conflicts between their mother and stepmother. It is extremely rare for teenagers to have a stepmother who has enough money of her own to take no money from their father for herself or for her children. As one fortunate teenager's stepmother explains, "I adore my husband and I don't care about his money because I have my own" (Jones & Schiller, 1992, p.83). But since very few mothers and stepmothers are financially well-off on their own, most teenagers hear one or both women complaining that the other is taking too much of the father's money. Many teenagers hear their mother complain that the stepmother or her children are getting too much from the father—including college tuition and future inheritance. Even when their mother is doing well financially and their father is exceeding his child-support obligations, teenagers can still be made to believe that their father and stepmother are not entitled to their higher standard of living or are mistreating the mother or them financially. Many teenagers also hear their stepmothers complain about the money being sent to their mothers: "I don't think my husband's kids deserve a penny from us after the way they've treated us. If they're part of our family enough to get tuition, they should be part of it enough to visit, communicate, and be responsible to other members of the family." "My stepkids blame me for every problem their mother has. Supposedly I even prevent their dad from giving her more money." "His ex-wife teaches his kids that Dad is supposed to pay for everything" (Jones & Schiller, 1992, p. 77 & 109). Especially if money is in short supply, if the stepmother or mother resents having to earn an income to help pay the bills, or if the mother is contributing little or nothing to support the children, teenagers are likely to get caught in the middle of these financial wars (Ahrons, 1994; Artlip, Artlip, & Saltzman, 1993; Beer, 1992; Einstein, 1994; Jones & Schiller, 1992; Martin & Martin, 1992; White, 1994).

Some adolescents are fortunate to have a stepmother who understands how society's attitudes about mothering and a mother's own feelings and problems contribute to difficulties with her stepchildren. For example, the stepmother may understand that the mother is a depressed person with a stress-related illness who does not have a fulfilling relationship with her boyfriend or her new husband. An understanding stepmother might also recognize how the mother's insecurities and unhappiness are motivating her to lie to the children or to alienate them against her and their father (Ephron, 1986; Maglin & Schneidewind, 1989; Robinson, 1993). Given the special nature of difficulties they confront, most teenagers' stepmothers feel more unappreciated, disliked, stressed, and criticized than do their stepfathers (Ahrons, 1994; Beer, 1992; Crytser, 1990; Dainton, 1993; Ganong & Coleman, 1994b; Hetherington & Jodl, 1994; Jones & Schiller, 1992; Quick, McKenry, & Newman, 1994; White, 1994).

FORGIVENESS AND RECONCILIATION

Given the battles, the sadness, the secrets, and the confusion surrounding their parents' divorces and remarriages, it isn't surprising that there are teenagers who carry their anger at parents or stepparents into their adult lives. As we've discussed throughout this chapter, young people are usually most angry toward and alienated from their father, especially if he paid no child support, if their mother didn't remarry, or if their mother continues to display her jealousy or resentment of their father or stepmother. The children whose anger is usually most intense and long-lived are those whose parents' divorce involved adultery, those with an enmeshed or depressed parent, and those who have serious emotional or psychological problems. Indeed, teenagers and adults who sustain a prolonged, intense hatred for a parent or stepparent are often suffering from serious psychological problems such as schizoid personality disorders or clinical depression. In these cases, the sustained rage and hostility are consequences of their mental disorder, not of their parents' divorce or remarriage (Weiner, 1992). But unless intensely angry children eventually come to understand their parents' divorce more fully and to view past events more honestly, they often repeat their parents' mistakes in their own marriages and remain permanently estranged from one or both parents. Thus, forgiveness and reconciliation with parents and stepparents can be both a healing and a transforming experience (Berman, 1992; Bloomfield & Kory, 1994; Halpern, 1990). So what can teenage or adult children do to improve their relationships with a parent or stepparent?

First, the person has to *want* to let go of the anger. That is, if you hold your parent or stepparent responsible for almost all of the failures, disappointment, and misery in your own life year after year, then you are probably trying to avoid dealing with your own shortcomings and responsibilities. As one young man put it, "I finally had to realize that I had been using their divorce as an excuse for any and every failing in my life and that it was time to stop" (Berman, 1992; p. 234).

Second, if a teenage or adult child continually focuses anger at only one parent or stepparent, he or she might be avoiding the unpleasant realities of the other parent's life and character. Using scapegoats to deny the truth about a parent is especially common when that parent has engaged in upsetting behavior like adultery, physical or sexual abuse, or alcoholism (Miller, 1990; 1994). Indeed, most of us are far more likely to blame and vent anger at our stepparents than at our parents—especially mothers (Bowlby, 1988; Karen, 1994; Main, 1993; Miller, 1990; 1994; Minuchin & Nichols, 1994). Nevertheless, most older teenage and adult children become more willing to hear both parents' side of the divorce story and to confront the painful realities they have denied for years (Berman, 1992; Bloomfield & Kory, 1994; Weiner, 1992). But resolving intense anger means learning what we are denying about the past and why we have been denying it—a painful journey that often requires a therapist's help because "it's harder to let go of a good enemy than to let go of a good friend."

Third, resolving intense anger means a willingness to re-examine certain "facts" about each parent, their marriage, and their divorce—including memories of what we believe happened in the past. Indeed, many childhood memories are based on what each parent has told us, not on what we ourselves actually saw or heard (Halverson, 1988). Moreover, if a child is enmeshed in either parent's life, he or she will judge and remember the other parent and the stepparent in very biased, negative ways (Karen, 1994; Main, 1993; Miller, 1994; Minuchin & Nichols, 1994). Given these biases, we sometimes need professional help to dismantle the untrue stories we created or were manipulated into believing. In gaining a more objective, more mature understanding of our family's past, we may see that the "weak, powerless" parent we felt sorry for was manipulating us through lies, secrets, and half-truths. And we may discover that the parent we felt most "bonded" to actually had us in "bondage." On the journey toward dismantling anger and rebuilding relationships, new images often emerge in regard to which parent or stepparent was actually the most loving, unselfish, financially generous, honest, and flexible. And on this journey, we must often confront our own mistakes and unkindness and offer our apologies. As one daughter explains, "I finally wrote a letter to my stepmother apologizing for my reactions to her and saying that I wanted to work my way back into their family" (Berman, 1992, p. 251). As we come to see our family's past more clearly, we can learn to view our parents and stepparents as fallible human beings—people who, like ourselves, deserve compassion and forgiveness.

CONCLUSION

So we see that most adolescents do better in a blended family than with an unmarried parent—especially boys living with an unmarried mother. However, an adolescent's successful adjustment to living either with an unmarried parent or in a blended family depends on many factors—the teenager's personality and gender, the parents' financial situations, parents' conflicts before and after the divorce, contact with their father, their mother's emotional state, disciplinary skills, and household organization, the timing of the divorce, generational and family boundaries, and the teenager's mental and social well-being before the divorce. When divorced parents are content with their own lives, their children generally have an easier time and are better adjusted than when either parent continues to display jealousy, anger, or resentment. Although we cannot change the fact that single-parent and blended families have become the norm in our society, perhaps we can learn enough to help many of these children from being subjected to so much unnecessary stress and hardship.

Review/Test Questions

Cite specific statistics or research findings to support your answers whenever possible.

1. How have families in our society changed during the past 20 years?
2. Which adolescents are most likely to have parents who never married or parents who are divorced and remarried?
3. What is the financial impact of single parenting on various racial groups?
4. What are the limitations of our research on divorce, remarriage, and single parenting?
5. What factors affect children's adapting to life with a stepparent?
6. How does conflict between parents before and after divorce affect children?
7. What are three sources of conflict for parents after a divorce?
8. Why do many adolescents' parents stay angry at each other years after their divorce?
9. Why do divorce and remarriage generally have a more negative impact on boys than on girls?
10. How much contact do most adolescents and their divorced fathers have? Why?
11. Why does a parent's remarriage often create stress for adolescents?
12. How can each of these situations create problems for adolescents after their parents divorce: family and generational boundaries, enmeshment, and role reversals?
13. What aspects of living with an unmarried parent can have a negative impact on adolescents?

14. How does gender and age affect children's adjustment to divorce and remarriage?

15. How might our society make divorce and remarriage easier on children?

16. Why might the mother's remarriage affect sons and daughters differently?

17. In what ways is a teenager generally affected when the mother remarries?

18. How does living with a single father differ from living with a single mother? Why?

19. How do adolescents' relationships with stepmothers and stepfathers usually differ? Why?

20. What are the advantages and disadvantages of living in a binuclear family?

Questions for Discussion and Debate

1. If your parents are divorced or remarried, which parts of this chapter were most relevant and most upsetting to you? Why?

2. How much should parents tell teenagers about their divorce and marriage?

3. If you have a stepparent, how easy or difficult was it for you to become his or her friend? Why?

4. How do you feel about binuclear families and joint custody? What is the best living arrangement for children after a divorce?

5. What would be hardest about being a stepparent or about having your own children live part-time with a stepparent?

6. How have you or your friends been affected by divorce or by living in a single-parent or blended family?

7. Watch one television program about a single-parent family and another about a blended family. How realistic were these families?

8. If you or any of your friends have half-siblings or stepsiblings, what have these relationships been like?

9. Given that out-of-wedlock births and divorce are very common in our country, what could our society do differently for the benefit of children in these families?

10. What do you think your own parents, stepparents, or siblings would find most interesting and most upsetting in this chapter? Why?

Glossary

binuclear family, p. 375
blended family, p. 376
dual residency, p. 375
joint custody, p. 362

References

Ahlburg, D., & DeVita, C. (1992). New realities of the American family. *Population Bulletin, 47,* 15.

Ahrons, C. (1994). *The good divorce.* New York: Harper Collins.

Ahrons, C., & Rogers, R. (1987). *Divorced*

Families. New York: Norton.

Ainsworth, M., & Eichberg, C. (1991). Effects of mother's unresolved loss of an attachment figure. In C. Parkes, J. Hinde & P. Marris (Eds.), *Attachment across the life cycle* (pp. 160–183). New York: Routledge.

Amato, P. (1994). Implications of research on children of divorce. In A. Booth & J. Dunn (Eds.), *Stepfamilies* (pp. 81–88). Hillsdale, NJ: Erlbaum

Amato, P., & Keith, B. (1991). Parental divorce and adult well being. *Journal of Marriage and the Family, 53,* 43–58.

Ambert, A. (1989). *Ex-spouses and new spouses.* Greenwhich, CT: JAI Press.

Andrews, D., & Dishion, T. (1994). Mircosocial underpinnings of adolescent problem behavior. In R. Ketterlinus & M. Lamb (Eds.), *Adolescent problem behavior* (pp. 187–209). Hillsdale, NJ: Erlbaum.

Artlip, M., Artlip, J., & Saltzman, E. (1993). *The new American family.* Lancaster, PA: Starburst Publishers.

Asher, S., & Coie, J. (1990). *Peer rejection in childhood.* New York: Cambridge University Press.

Astone, N., & McLanahan, A. (1991). Family structure, parental practices and high-school grades. *American Sociological Review, 94,* 130–152.

Barber, B., & Eccles, J. (1992). Long-term influence of divorce and single parenting on career goals. *Psychological Bulletin, 111,* 108–126.

Bass, E., & Davis, L. (1991). *The courage to heal.* New York: Harper & Row.

Beal, E., & Hochman, G. (1991). *Adult children of divorce.* New York: Delacourte.

Beer, W. (1992). *American stepfamilies.* New Brunswick, CT: Transaction Press.

Bell-Scott, P. (1991). *Double stitch: Black women write about mothers and daughters.* New York: Harper Perennial.

Berman, C. (1992). *A hole in my heart: Adult children of divorce speak out.* New York: Simon & Schuster.

Bettelheim, B. (1976). *The uses and abuses of enchantment.* New York: Knopf.

Biller, H. (1993). *Fathers and families: Paternal factors in child development.* Westport, CT: Auburn House.

Blau, R. (1995). *Successful coparenting.* New York: Simon & Schuster.

Blechman, E. (1990). *Emotions and the family.* Hillsdale, NJ: Erlbaum.

Block, J., & Gjerde, P. (1989). The personality of children prior to divorce. *Child Development, 57,* 827–840.

Bloomfield, H., & Kory, R. (1994). *Making peace in your stepfamily.* New York: Hyperion.

Boer, F., & Dunn, J. (1992). *Children's sibling relationships.* Hillsdale, NJ: Erlbaum.

Booth, A., & Dunn, J. (1994). *Stepfamilies.* Hillsdale, NJ: Erlbaum.

Booth, A., & Edwards, J. (1992). Starting over: Why remarriages are more unstable. *Journal of Family Issues, 13,* 179–194.

Bowen, M. (1978). *Family therapy in clinical practice.* New York: Aronson.

Bowlby, J. (1988). *A secure base.* New York: Basic Books.

Bray, J., Berger, S., & Boethel, C. (1994). Role integration & marital adjustment in stepfather familes. In K. Pasley & M. Ihinger-Tallman (Eds.), *Stepparenting* (pp. 69–87). Westport, CT: Greenwood.

Brooks-Gunn, J. (1994). Research on stepparenting families. In A. Booth & J. Dunn (Eds.), *Stepfamilies* (pp. 167–189). Hillsdale, NJ: Erlbaum .

Buchanan, C., Maccoby, E., & Dornbusch, S. (forthcoming). *The divided child: Adolescent adjustment after parent divorce.* Cambridge, MA: Harvard University Press.

Buehler, C., & Ryan, C. (1994). Former spouse relations during family transitions. In K. Pasley & M. Ihinger-Tallman (Eds.), *Stepparenting* (pp.

127–151). Westport, CT: Greenwood.

Capaldi, D., Forgatch, M., & Crosby, L. (1994). Affective expression in family problem solving with adolescent boys. *Journal of Adolescent Research, 9,* 28–49.

Center for Law & Social Policy. (1994). *Ending poverty: Child support enforcement.* Washington, DC: Author.

Cherlin, A., Furstenberg, F., Lansdale, P., Kiernan, K., Robins, P., Morrison, D., & Teitler, J. (1991). Longitudinal studies of effects of divorce on children in Britain and the U.S. *Science, 252,* 1386–1390.

Cherlin, A. (1992). *Marriage, divorce and remarriage: Changing patterns in the U.S.* Cambridge, MA: Harvard University Press.

Children's Defense Fund. (1994). *Enforcing child support.* Washington, DC: Author.

Cissna, K., Cox, D., & Bochner, A. (1994). Relationships within the stepfamily. In G. Handel & G. Whitchurch (Eds.), *The psychosocial interior of the family* New York: Aldine De Gruyter.

Clingempeel, G., Colyar, J., & Hetherington, M. (1994). Stepchildren and biological children loyalty conflicts. In K. Pasley & M. Ihinger-Tallman (Eds.), *Stepparenting* (pp. 151–175). Westport, CT: Greenwood.

Collins, P. (1991). The meaning of motherhood in Black culture. In P. Bell-Scott (Ed.), *Double stitch: Black women write about mothers and daughters.* New York: Harper Perennial.

Colten, M., Gore, S., & Aseltine, R. (1991). Patterning of distress & disorder in a sample of high-school aged youth. In M. Colten & S. Gore (Eds.), *Adolescent stress* (pp. 157–180). New York: Aldine De Gruyter.

Compas, B., & Wagner, B. (1991). Psychosocial stress during adolescence. In M. Colten & S. Gore (Eds.), *Adolescent stress* (pp. 67–92). New York: Aldine De Gruyter.

Conger, R. (1991). Family economic pressure & early adolescent alcohol use. *Journal of Early Adolescence, 11,* 430–449.

Coontz, S. (1989). *The way we never were: American families & the nostalgia trap.* New York: Basic Books.

Corneau, G. (1991). *Absent fathers, lost sons.* Boston: Shambhala.

Cowan, C., & Cowan, P. (1992). *When partners become parents.* New York: Basic Books.

Crosbie-Burnett, M. (1994). Stepparent families and the schools. In K. Pasley & M. Inhinger (Eds.), *Stepparenting* (pp. 199–217). Westport, CT: Greenwood.

Crosbie-Burnett, M., & Giles-Sims, J. (1994). Adolescent adjustment and stepparenting styles. *Family Relations, 43,* 2–15.

Crosby, F. (1993). *Juggling: Advantages of balancing career & home for women and their families.* New York: Free Press.

Crytser, A. (1990). *The wife-in-law trap.* New York: Simon & Schuster.

Dainton, M. (1993). Myths and misconceptions of the stepmother identity. *Family Relations, 42,* 93–98.

Darmody, J. (1991). Adolescent personality, formal reasoning and values. *Adolescence, 26,* 731–742.

Debold, E., Wilson, M., & Malave, I. (1992). *Mother-daughter revolution.* New York: Addison Wesley.

Depner, C., & Bray, J. (1993). *Nonresidential parenting: New vistas in family living.* Newbury Park, CA: Sage.

Dornbusch, S., Mont-Reynaud, R., Ritter, P., Zeng-yin, C., & Steinberg, L. (1991). Stressful events and their correlates among adolescents of diverse backgrounds. In M. Colten & S. Gore (Eds.), *Adolescent stress* (pp. 111–131). New York: Aldine De Gruyter.

Dornbush, S., Ritter, P., Mont-Reynaud, R., & Chen, Z. (1990). Family decision making and academic performance in a diverse population. *Journal of Adolescent Research, 5,* 143–160.

Dudley, J. (1991). Increasing our understanding of divorced fathers who have custody. *Family*

Relations, 40, 279–285.

Ebata, A., Petersen, A., & Conger, J. (1990). The development of psychopathology in adolescence. In J. Rolf, A. Masten, D. Cicchetti, K. Nuechterlein & S. Weintraub (Eds.), *Risk and protective factors in the development of psychopathology* (pp. 308–334). New York: Cambridge University Press.

Edelman, M. (1992). *The measure of our success.* Boston: Beacon.

Einstein, E. (1994). *The stepfamily.* Ithaca, NY: Einstein.

Emery, E. (1989). Family violence. *American Sociological Review, 44,* 321–328.

Emery, R. (1992). Parental divorce & children's well-being. In N. Haggerty (Ed.), *Risk and resilience in children.* London, England: Cambridge University Press.

Ephron, D. (1986). *Funny sauce: Us, the ex, the ex's new mate, the new mate's ex, and the kids.* New York: Viking.

Everett, C. (1993). *Divorce and the next generation.* New York: Haworth Press.

Fine, M., & Kurdek, L. (1994). A model of stepfamily adjustment. In K. Pasley & M. Ihninger-Tallman (Eds.), *Stepparenting* (pp. 33–51). Westport, CT: Greenwood.

Fine, M., & Schwebel, A. (1992). Stepparent stress. *Journal of Divorce and Remarriage, 17,* 1–15.

Flewelling, R., & Bauman, K. (1990). Family structure as a predictor of initial substance use. *Journal of Marriage and the Family, 52,* 171–181.

Fluitt, J., & Paradise, L. (1991). The relationship of current family structures to young adults' perceptions of stepparents. *Journal of Divorce and Remarriage, 15,* 159–174.

Forehand, R. (1991). A short-term longitudinal examination of young adolescents. *Journal of Abnormal Child Psychology, 19,* 97–111.

Foxcroft, D., & Lowe, G. (1991). Adolescent drinking and family factors. *Journal of Adolescence, 14,* 255–273.

Friedman, D. (1994). *Towards a structure of indifference: Origins of maternal custody.* New York: Aldine De Gruyter.

Furstenberg, F., & Cherlin, A. (1991). *Divided families.* Cambridge, MA: Harvard University Press.

Furstenberg, F., & Teitler, J. (1993). Reconsidering the effects of marital disruption. *Adolescence, 66,* 127–135.

Ganong, L., & Coleman, M. (1994a). *Remarried family relationships.* Beverly Hills, CA: Sage.

Ganong, L., & Coleman, M. (1994b). Adolescent stepchild-stepparent relationships. In K. Pasley & M. Ihinger-Tallman (Eds.), *Stepparenting* (pp. 87–105). Westport, CT: Greenwood.

Gigy, L., & Kelly, J. (1992). Reasons for divorce. *Journal of Divorce & Remarriage, 18,* 169–187.

Gilbert, L. (1993). *Two careers, one family.* Berkeley, CA: Sage.

Giles-Sims, J., & Crosbie-Burnett, M. (1989). Adolescent power in stepfather families. *Journal of Marriage and the Family, 51,* 1065–1078.

Gilligan, C., Rogers, A., & Tolman, D. (1991). *Women, girls and psychotherapy.* New York: Haworth Press.

Girls Count Project. (1993). *Girls count in America's future.* Denver, CO: Author.

Glickman, R. (1993). *Daughters of feminists.* New York: St. Martin's.

Greene, R., & Leslie, L. (1989). Mothers' behavior and sons' adjustment following divorce. *Journal of Divorce, 12,* 235–251.

Grief, G. (1990). *The daddy track and the single father.* Lexington, MA: Lexington Books.

Guisinger, S., Cowan, P., & Schulberg, D. (1989). Changing parent and spouse relations in the first years of remarriage. *Journal of Marriage and the Family, 51,* 445–456.

Guttman, J. (1993). *Divorce in psychosocial perspective.* Hillsdale, NJ: Erlbaum.

Halpern, H. (1990). *Cutting loose: An adult guide to coming to terms with your parents*. New York: Bantam.

Halverson, C. (1988). Remembering your parents. *Journal of Personality, 56*, 434–443.

Hanson, S. (1986). Parent child relations in single father families. In R. Lewis & B. Salts (Eds.), *Men in Families*. Beverly Hills, CA: Sage.

Harrington, L. (1994). *Depressive disorder in childhood and adolescence*. New York: Wiley.

Haynes, J. (1988). Power balancing. In J. Folberg & A. Milne (Eds.), *Divorce Mediation* (pp. 277–296). New York: Guilford.

Hernandez, D. (1989). Demographic trends and the living arrangements of children. In E. Hetherington & J. Arasteh (Eds.), *Impact of divorce, single-parenting & stepparenting on children* (pp. 3–22). Hillsdale, NJ: Erlbaum.

Hetherington, M. (1991). Families, lies and videotapes. *Journal of Research on Adolescence, 1*, 323–348.

Hetherington, M., Cox, M., & Cox, R. (1981). Effects of divorce on parents and children. In M. Lamb (Ed.), *Nontraditional Families* (pp. 233–287). Hillsdale, NJ: Erlbaum.

Hetherington, M., & Jodl, K. (1994). Stepfamilies as settings for development. In A. Booth & J. Dunn (Eds.), *Stepfamilies* (pp. 55–80). Cambridge, MA: Harvard University.

Hewlitt, S. (1992). *When the bough breaks: The cost of neglecting our children*. New York: Basic.

Hinde, R., & Stevenson, J. (1995). *Relation between relationships within families*. Cambridge, England: Oxford University Press.

Hobart, C. (1991). Conflict in remarriages. *Journal of Divorce & Remarriage, 15*, 69–86.

Isaacs, M., & Leon, G. (1988). Remarriage and its alternative following divorce. *Journal of Marital and Family Therapy, 1*, 163–173.

Johnston, J. (1990). Role diffusion and role reversal. *Family Relations, 39*, 403–413.

Johnston, J., & Campbell, L. (1989). *Impasses of divorce*. New York: Free Press.

Jones, M., & Schiller, J. (1992). *Stepmothers: Keeping it together*. New York: Carroll Publishing.

Kalter, N. (1990). *Growing up with divorce*. New York: Ballantine.

Kantrowitz, B. (1994, October 24). If only it were so easy in real life. *Newsweek*, 6.

Karen, R. (1994). *Becoming attached*. New York: Time Warner.

Keenan, B. (1992). *When you marry a man with children*. New York: Pocket Books.

Kempton, T., Armistead, L., Wierson, M., & Forehand, R. (1991). Presence of a sibling as a potential buffer following divorce. *Journal of Clinical Child Psychology, 20*, 434–438.

Ketterlinus, R., & Lamb, M. (1994). *Adolescent problem behaviors*. New York: Erlbaum.

Kiernan, K. (1992). Impact of family disruption on transitions to adult life. *Population Studies, 46*, 213–234.

Kinard, E., & Reinherz, H. (1986). Effects of marital disruption on children's school achievement. *Journal of Marriage and the Family, 48*, 285–293.

Kitson, G., & Holmes, W. (1992). *Portrait of divorce*. New York: Guilford.

Krein, S., & Beller, A. (1988). Educational attainment of children from single parent families. *Demography, 25*, 221–234.

Leach, N. (1993). *My wicked stepmother*. New York: Macmillan.

Lerner, J., & Galambos, N. (1991). *Employed mothers and their children*. New York: Garland .

Levin, M. (1989). Sequelae to marital disruption in children. *Journal of Divorce, 12*, 25–80.

Lewis, E., & Crosbie-Burnett, M. (1993). Use of African American family structure to address the challenges of European American postdivorce families. *Family Relations, 42*, 243–248.

Maccoby, E., & Mnookin, R. (1993). *Dividing the child: The Social and legal dilemmas of custody*. Cambridge, MA: Harvard University Press.

Maglin, N., & Schneidewind, N. (1989). *Women in stepfamilies*. Philadelphia, PA: Temple University Press.

Main, M. (1993). *A typology of human attachment organization*. New York: Cambridge University Press.

Maine, M. (1993). *Father hunger: Fathers, daughters and food*. New York: Gurze Books.

Marsh, H. (1990). Two parent, stepparent and single parent families. *Journal of Educational Psychology, 82,* 327–340.

Martin, A. (1994). *Karen's stepmother*. New York: Scholastic.

Martin, D., & Martin, M. (1992). *Stepfamilies in therapy*. San Francisco: Jossey Bass.

McGuire, P. (1989). *Putting it together: Teenagers talk about family breakup*. New York: Delacorte Press.

McLanahan, S., Astone, N., & Marks, N. (1993). The role of mother-only families in the reproduction of poverty. In A. Huston (Ed.), *Children in Poverty*. New York: Cambridge University Press.

Mednick, B., Baker, R., & Reznick, C. (1990). Long-term effects of divorce on adolescent academic achievement. *Journal of Divorce, 13,* 69–88.

Mens-Verhulst, J., Schreurs, K., & Woertman, L. (1993). *Daughtering and mothering*. New York: Routledge.

Meyer, D., & Garasky, S. (1993). Custodial fathers. *Journal of Marriage & the Family, 55,* 73–89.

Miller, A. (1990). *Banished knowledge: Facing childhood injuries*. New York: Doubleday.

Miller, A. (1994). *Drama of the gifted child*. New York: Basic Books.

Minninger, J., & Goulter, B. (1993). *The father–daughter dance*. New York: Putnam's Sons.

Minuchin, S., & Nichols, M. (1994). *Family healing*. New York: Simon & Schuster.

Monahan, S., Buchanan, C., Maccoby, E., & Dornbusch, S. (1993). Sibling differences in divorced families. *Child Development, 64,* 152–168.

Moore, M. (1992). The family as portrayed on prime time television. *Sex Roles, 26,* 41–61.

Morell, C. (1994). *Unwomanly conduct: The challenges of intentional childlessness*. New York: Routledge.

Nielsen, L. (1993). Students from divorced and blended families. *Educational Psychology Review, 5,* 177–200.

Nock, S. (1988). The family and hierarchy. *Journal of Marriage and the Family, 50,* 957–966.

Noy, D. (1991). Wicked stepmothers in Roman society and in imagination. *Journal of Family History, 16,* 345–361.

Papernow, P. (1993). *Becoming a stepfamily*. San Francisco, CA: Jossey Bass.

Paquin, G. (1990). Mediators' perceptions of couples. *Journal of Divorce and Remarriage, 14,* 79–90.

Parish, T. (1991). Ratings of self and parents by youth. *Adolescence, 26,* 105–112.

Parke, R., & Ladd, G. (1992). *Family-peer relationships:Modes of linkage*. Hillsdale, NJ: Erlbaum.

Pasley, K., & Ihinger-Tallman, M. (1994). *Stepparenting: Issues in Theory, Research & Practice*. Westport, CT: Greenwood .

Pasley, K., Ihinger-Tallman, M., & Lofquist, A. (1994). Remarriage and stepfamilies. In K. Pasley & M. Ihinger-Tallman (Eds.), *Stepparenting* (pp. 1–15). Westport, CT: Greenwood.

Patterson, C., Griesler, P., Vaden, N., & Kupersmidt, J. (1992). Family economic circumstances, life transitions, and children's peer relations. In R. Parke & G. Ladd (Eds.), *Family peer relationships* (pp. 385–424). Hillsdale, NJ: Erlbaum.

Patterson, G., Reid, J., & Dishion, T. (1992). *A social learning approach: Antisocial boys*. Eugene, OR: Castalia.

Paulson, S., Koman, J., & Hill, J. (1990). Maternal employment and parent–child relations. *Journal of Early Adolescence, 10,* 279–295.

Pearson, J., & Thoennes, N. (1990). Custody after divorce. *American Journal of Orthopsychiatry, 60,* 233–249.

Phares, V., & Compas, B. (1992). The role of fathers in child and adolescent psychopathology. *Psychological Bulletin, 111,* 387–412.

Phillips, R. (1989). *Putting asunder.* Cambridge, England: Cambridge University Press.

Pianta, B., Egeland, B., & Stroufe, A. (1990). Maternal stress and children's development. In J. Rolf, A. Masten, K. Nuechterlain & W. Weintraub (Eds.), *Risk and protective factors in the development of psychopathology* (pp. 215–236). New York: Cambridge University Press.

Pipher, M. (1994). *Reviving Ophelia: Saving the selves of adolescent girls.* New York: Putnam.

Pittman, F. (1993). *Man enough: Fathers, sons and the search for masculinity.* New York: Putnam's Sons.

Pruett, K. (1992). Divorce and the nurturing father. In C. Scull (Ed.), *Fathers, sons and daughters* (pp. 171–179). Los Angeles: Jeremy Tarcher.

Quick, D., McKenry, P., & Newman, B. (1994). Stepmothers and their adolescent children. In K. Pasley & M. Ihinger-Tallman (Eds.), *Stepparenting* (pp. 105–127). Westport, CT: Greenwood.

Reibstein, J., & Richards, M. (1993). *Sexual arrangements: Marriage and infidelity.* New York: Macmillan.

Repetti, R., Matthews, K., & Waldron, I. (1989). Employment and women's health. *American Psychologist, 44,* 1394–1401.

Richards, M., & Duckett, E. (1991). Maternal employment and adolescents. In J. Lerner & E. Duckett (Eds.), *Employed mothers and their children* (pp. 85–123). New York: Garland.

Ripps, S. (1994). *Passion for more: American wives reveal their affairs.* New York: St. Martin's Press.

Robins, L., & Rutter, M. (1990). *Straight and devious pathways from childhood to adulthood.* New York: Cambridge University Press.

Robinson, M. (1993). *Family transformation during divorce & remarriage.* New York: Routledge.

Rosen, M. (1989). *Stepfathering.* New York: Simon & Schuster.

Rosenberg, M. (1989). *Talking about stepfamilies.* New York: Bradbury.

Rubenstin, J., & Feldman, S. (1993). Conflict resolution in adolescent boys. *Research on Adolescence, 3,* 41–66.

Salwen, L. (1990). The myth of the wicked stepmother. *Women and Therapy, 10,* 117–125.

Schectman, J. (1991). *The stepmother in fairy tales.* New York: Sigo Press.

Schuldberg, D., & Guisinger, S. (1991). Divorced fathers describe their former wives. *Journal of Divorce & Remarriage, 14,* 61–87.

Secunda, V. (1992). *Women and their fathers.* New York: Delacourte Press.

Seligman, M. (1991). *Learned optimism.* New York: Random House.

Seltzer, J. (1991). Relationship between fathers & children who live apart. *Journal of Marriage & the Family, 53,* 79–101.

Sessa, F., & Steinberg, L. (1991). Family structure and the development of autonomy. *Journal of Early Adolescence, 11,* 38–55.

Sigel, I., McGillicuddy, A., & Goodnow, J. (1992). *Parental belief systems: The psychological consequences for children.* Hillsdale, NJ: Erlbaum.

Silverstein, O., & Rashbaum, B. (1994). *The courage to raise good men.* New York: Viking.

Skolnick, A. (1991). *Embattled paradise.* New York: Harper Collins.

Smith, D. (1990). *Stepmothering.* New York: Ballantine.

Smith, T. (1990). Parental separation and adolescents' academic self-concepts. *Journal of Marriage and the Family, 52,* 107–118.

Snarey, J. (1993). *How fathers care for the next generation*. Cambridge, MA: Harvard University Press.

Stroufe, A. (1989). Relationships and relationship disturbances. In A. Sameroff & R. Ende (Eds.), *Relationship disturbances in early childhood* (pp. 97–124). New York: Basic Books.

Tasker, F., & Richards, M. (1994). Adolescents' attitudes toward marriage after parental divorce. *Journal of Adolescent Research, 9*, 340–462.

Teyber, E. (1994). *Helping children cope with divorce*. New York: D.C. Heath.

Turner, R., Irwin, C., & Millstein, S. (1991). Family structure and experimenting with drugs. *Journal of Research on Adolescence, 1*, 93–106.

U.S. Department of Commerce. (1991). *Who's helping out*. Washington,DC: Bureau of the Census.

U.S. Department of Commerce. (1992). *Population reports: Marital status & living arrangements*. Washington,DC: Bureau of the Census.

U.S. Department of Commerce. (1993). *Fertility of American women*. Washington,DC: Bureau of the Census.

Van Wert, W. (1992). The transformation of a single parent. In C. Scull (Ed.), *Fathers, sons and daughters* (pp. 190–196). Los Angeles: Jeremy Tarcher.

Vaughan, D. (1990). *Uncoupling*. New York: Vintage.

Verner, E. (1989). Marital satisfaction in remarriage. *Journal of Marriage and the Family, 51*, 713–725.

Visher, E., & Visher, J. (1991). *How to win as a stepfamily*. New York: Brunner Mazel.

Wallerstein, J. (1991). Long term effects of divorce on children. *Journal of American Academy of Child Psychiatry, 30*, 349–360.

Wallerstein, J., & Blakeslee, S. (1989). *Second chances*. New York: Ticknor & Fields.

Warshak, R. (1992). *The custody revolution: The fatherhood factor and the motherhood mystique*. New York: Poseidon.

Waxler, C., Denham, S., Iannotti, R., & Cummings, M. (1992). Peer relations in children with a depressed caregiver. In R. Parke & G. Ladd (Eds.), *Family peer relationships* (pp. 317–344). Hillsdale, NJ: Erlbaum.

Weiner, I. (1992). *Psychological disturbance in adolescence*. New York: Wiley.

Weiss, R. (1994). A different kind of parenting. In G. Handel & G. Whitchurch (Eds.), *The psychosocial interior of the family*. New York: Aldine De Gruyter.

White, L. (1994). Stepfamilies over the life course. In A. Booth & J. Dunn (Eds.), *Stepfamilies* (pp. 109–137). Hillsdale, NJ: Erlbaum.

Wilkie, J. (1991). Decline in men's labor force participation and changing structure of family support. *Journal of Marriage & the Family, 117*, 41–49.

Zakhoders, B. (1992). *The good stepmother*. New York: Simon & Schuster.

Zaslow, M. (1989). Sex differences in children's response to parental divorce. *American Journal of Orthopsychiatry, 59*, 118–141.

Zill, N. (1994). Understanding why children in stepfamilies have more learning and behavior problems. In A. Booth & J. Dunn (Eds.), *Stepfamilies* (pp. 97–108). Hillsdale, NJ: Erlbaum.

Zill, N., Morrison, D., & Coiro, M. (1993). Effects of divorce on parent–child relationships, adjustment and achievement in young adulthood. *Journal of Family Psychology, 7*, 91–103.

Zimiles, H., & Lee, V. (1991). Adolescent family structure and educational progress. *Developmental Psychology, 27*, 314–320.

ADOLESCENTS AND THE SCHOOLS

CHAPTER OUTLINE

KEY QUESTIONS ADDRESSED IN THIS CHAPTER

1. What are the major problems in our high schools today?
2. How well are most adolescents performing academically?
3. What factors affect academic performance?
4. What changes are being made in some schools to improve student achievement?
5. How do adolescents' academic skills affect the national economy?

OUR NATION'S SCHOOLS

Since the passage of legislation in the 1940s requiring all American children to stay in school until the age of 16, our schools have played an increasingly larger role in adolescents' lives. Not only do schools try to provide the skills that adolescents will need later in life, but the school experience is also the hub of most adolescents' social lives. Aside from the family, schools play a larger role throughout our childhood and teenage years than any other single institution or activity. In examining adolescents and their schools, countless questions arise: How well are most adolescents doing academically? What determines who does well and who does poorly? What do adolescents think about their schools? What do their teachers think? What are the major problems facing our schools, and what is being done about them? How does education affect a person's life beyond adolescence?

THE STUDENT POPULATION

Teenage students today differ in many respects from their counterparts of former decades. First, the student population is much more racially diverse than ever before. Nearly 25% of all public school students are members of a racial minority. Within the next 20 years, more than one in three students will be a member of a racial minority. Indeed, white students already are in the minority in many public school systems. For example, only 15% of the students in the public schools in Phoenix, Chicago, Birmingham, San Antonio, and San Francisco are non-Hispanic whites (National Center for Education Statistics [NCES], 1993; U.S. Department of Commerce, 1992).

Second, teenagers nowadays cope with problems at school that preceding generations never faced. More violence and physical harassment occur at school than ever before. Most teachers in urban schools say that violence and gang-related activities are their most pressing concerns. Even outside the central cities, one fifth of the teachers believe violence is the leading problem in their school. From 1985 to 1990, 65 students and six teachers were killed in shootings, with 200 more severely wounded at school. Most of these shootings occurred in California, New York, and Florida. Although 93% of the shooters were male, 25% of the victims were female (Council of the Great City Schools [CGCS], 1993; Center to Prevent Handgun Violence [CPHV], 1992).

Third, high-school students are more likely than ever to have part-time jobs during the school year (Barton, 1989; Mortimer, 1991). Nearly 5 million students from ages 13 to 17 were working in 1990—twice as many as in 1950. Nearly 70% of juniors and seniors work; and by the time they are seniors, 90% of all high-school students have had a job. Although most students work only 10 to 15 hours a week, 15% of them work more than 20 hours a week. Teenage girls are nearly as likely as boys to have jobs. The implication for school administrators is that most students have commitments after school that compete with homework—a reality that teachers have had to take into account in making assignments and setting standards.

Fourth, the parents and stepparents of contemporary teens are better educated than ever before. Although only 50% of Americans older than 65 have high-school diplomas, nearly 85% of teenagers' parents are high school graduates. Moreover, nearly one in five teenagers have parents with a college degree, compared to fewer than one in 10 only 30 years ago. This is good news for teachers. The better educated the parents, the more likely the student is to get help with schoolwork and encouragement to foster good academic habits at home (U.S. Department of Commerce, 1994).

But the bad news is that the discrepancies between parents' educational levels are greater than ever. So high-school teachers are more likely to have students whose families have widely different academic skills. One reason is that before the law required all children to stay in school until age 16, parents with poor educations usually quit school at a relatively early age and went to work. The second reason is the rapid growth in our immigrant population. Many teenagers whose families recently immigrated to the United States have parents with poor English skills and very little formal education. For example, nearly half of all Latino students live with parents who have not graduated from high school, in contrast to only about 5% of white and Asian American students. Because immigrant students compose the fastest growing group in our public schools, teachers increasingly are confronted with students who have few English skills and often are not able to get help at home with their assignments (U.S. Department of Commerce, 1994).

Fifth, unprecedented numbers of teenage students complain about being dissatisfied with school. Accustomed to being entertained by movies, television, videos, computers, and other fast-paced technology, most teenage students have the same complaint about school: It is b-o-r-i-n-g. Students in college-bound classes are generally not as bored as those in vocational or general classes. But even among the college-bound, most complain that the curriculum and the teaching are boring and irrelevant (Boyer, 1983; Fernandez, 1993; Fiske, 1992; Goodlad, 1983).

ADOLESCENTS' TEACHERS

Teachers, too, differ in many ways from those who once taught adolescents. Virtually all teachers now have college degrees; and nearly half have a graduate degree. Although many schools were once run only by one female teacher, today about 30% of adolescents' teachers and 95% of their principals are male. The typical high-school teacher is 37 years old, has about 13 years of teaching experience, and earns approximately $30,000 a year. Nearly half have held a part-time job during their teaching career (NCES, 1993).

Although they are not as well-paid as most adults with similar levels of education, most adolescents' teachers say they enjoy their work. Their chief complaint is that so few of their students are enthusiastic, well-disciplined, or self-motivated. In inner-city schools, teachers also worry a great deal about violence and gang

Table 10–1		

High-school teachers' greatest concerns

	Teachers in urban schools	Teachers in non-urban schools
Violence and gang activity	83%	18%
Lack of parental involvement	70%	45%
Bilingual education for non-English speaking students	65%	13%
Restructuring the school curriculum & practices	60%	20%
Need for more early childhood education	40%	12%
Need for more money	36%	35%
Increasing the skills of all students	30%	0%
AIDS education	30%	17%
Gender or racial equity	29%	14%

Source: Council of the Great City Schools (1993). *Critical educational trends: America's urban schools.* Washington, DC: Author.

activities. Understandably, most teachers want parents to be more involved in their children's education and to impose higher standards for doing homework, reading, and developing self-discipline. Most teachers also want to be given more power to develop the curriculum, to choose their textbooks, and to redesign their schools to better fit students' needs (CGCS, 1993).

Although virtually all high-school teachers are college graduates, very few of them have received the training necessary to meet teenage students' needs. Most colleges do not provide the students in teacher-training programs with up-to-date methods for motivating or for disciplining adolescents. Too theoretical and eth-nocentric, most teacher-education programs are outdated. Although many college graduates are creative and insightful enough to develop skills on their own after they have been teaching awhile, most are at a loss when confronting the problems so pervasive in schools today. In fact, experts have long argued that one of the best ways to improve discipline in our schools and to raise students' achievement levels is to improve our teacher education programs (Goodlad, 1990; Seymour & Seymour, 1993; Sizer, 1992; Tyson, 1994).

NATIONWIDE INEQUITIES

The quality of an adolescent's education, of course, depends on more than the teachers' qualifications and attitudes. A large part of what a teenager experiences and learns at school depends on the amount of money that is being spent on his or her education—not the families' costs of clothing and feeding students, but the per-student allotment each school has for buying supplies and paying teachers. All students should have access to resources such as stimulating texts, computers, and library materials in clean, safe facilities. We also need to provide individualized instruction and smaller classes much more often than we do. On average, we taxpayers spend about $5,000 a year on each public school student (U.S. Department of Education, 1994). Although this might seem an exorbitant sum to some people, in many ways it is not much. After adjustment for inflation, we are spending only about 10% more to educate our young people than we did a decade ago. Certainly, more money is spent for ventures that can be considered less deserving than education. For example, the $8 billion spent on public education in 1990 was about 1% of the national budget.

Remember that taxpayers end up paying far more in the long run to support those young people who do not become well educated. We spend roughly

Figure 10–1

Inequities in educational spending

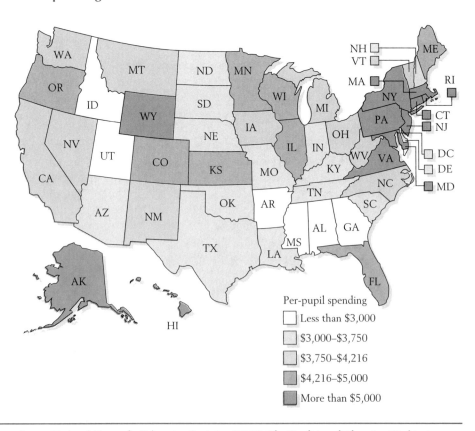

Source: National Center for Education Statistics (1993). *The Condition of Education.* Washington, DC: Author.

$18,000 a year for each young person who ends up in prison and millions of dollars in welfare benefits for parents who are too poorly educated to support themselves or their children. Nearly 90% of the male inmates in New York City's prisons are high-school dropouts whose upkeep costs the local taxpayers nearly $60,000 a year per prisoner. For every $1 spent on education and early prevention of learning problems, we would save $5 in costs now spent for remedial education, welfare, and imprisonment (Berlin & Sum, 1988; Economic Policy Institute [EPI],1989; Kozol, 1991; NCES, 1993).

Unfortunately, some students have far less money spent on them than others throughout their 12 years in school. The amount of money spent on a student depends on three things: the amount given equally to all states by the federal government from our national budget, a state supplement decided upon by each legislature from its state budget, and a local allotment voted by taxpayers in each school district. Because states and local communities differ in how much they are willing to invest in education, the per-student spending varies greatly from district to district, state to state. As Figure 10–1 illustrates, students in some states receive two to three times more than do students in other states. For instance, New Jersey students have three times more money spent on their education than do students in Alabama. Moreover, we spend seven times as much to educate the 25% of students planning to attend college as to educate the 75% in general and vocational classes. As the U.S. Commissioner of Education concluded 25 years ago, "We have a caste society that violates American democracy. The nation does not have a truly public school system in a large part of its communities; it has permitted what is in effect a private school system to develop under public auspices. Equality of educational opportunity is more a myth than a reality" (Kozol, 1991, p. 80). In short, we do not provide equal opportunity to a good education; and the least likely to receive that opportunity are teenagers from poor families, many of whom are minorities. Furthermore, these financial inequities do not escape the notice of adolescents in our poor, run-down schools (Kozol, 1991; NCES, 1993).

These financial inequities also affect the quality of teachers who interact with our children; and they help explain why the quality of teaching differs so widely among school districts. Both inner-city and rural schools have a harder time attracting highly qualified teachers. Teachers in rural areas tend to be younger, less experienced, and less well-educated than those in the better parts of town in more urban areas. This, in turn, can affect the course options available to students. For instance, a calculus course is available in only half of rural high schools, but is offered in 90% of urban schools (CGCS, 1993; Hodgkinson, 1994). An odd side note to school finances involves the junk-food vending industry. A growing number of educators, health care officials, and politicians want to ban vending machines from all public schools due to the high fat content and low nutritional values of these snack foods. But many teachers and principals oppose such laws because the vending machines generate a great deal of income for their schools. Some schools add as much as $40,000 a year to their budget from their percentage of the sales from vending machines—money that is used to buy materials and services for students. Despite opposition, West Virginia passed a state law in 1994 banning any vending machine food with more than 8 grams of fat per 1-ounce serving (Miller, 1994).

LEVELS OF EDUCATION

HIGH-SCHOOL DIPLOMAS AND COLLEGE DEGREES

Obviously, the perceptions that students and teachers have about the importance of school might influence the dropout rate. But let's leave perceptions aside for now and focus on the numbers. How many years of schooling do most adolescents eventually complete? Well, nearly 85% of all young people graduate from high school by time they are 25, and about 20% graduate from college. However, as you can see from Table 10–2 and Figure 10–2, these statistics vary with race and family income (Mortenson, 1991; Mullis, 1992; U.S. Department of Commerce, 1994).

Owing to the link between family income and race, it might come as no surprise that African and Hispanic American students generally achieve the least. Because a parent's education and marital status are also closely linked to race and income, any one of these factors can usually influence how far an adolescent will go in school. Non-Hispanic white and Asian American adults are the most likely to have good educations and to make higher incomes; and their children are the most likely to finish high school and graduate from college. Notice from Table 10–3 that Asian and non-Hispanic white parents are also the most likely to be married. In other words, these children usually have the benefit of two incomes and two adults to supervise or tutor them. In a sense, these statistics illustrate a principle we might call the "survival of the children of the fittest—the economically fittest." Those students whose parents have the most education and the most money usually end up at the top of the educational heap.

Table 10–2

Race, gender, income, and education

	Asian		Black		Hispanic		White	
	male	female	male	female	male	female	male	female
Living in poverty	8%	8%	50%	50%	45%	45%	10%	10%
Graduating high school	75%	87%	90%	90%	50%	82%	45%	50%
Graduating college	20%	21%	41%	39%	7%	11%	9%	10%

Poverty level = $14,000 for a family of 4

Source: U.S. Department of Commerce (1992, 1994). *School enrollment and characteristics of students: Poverty in America.* Washington, DC: Bureau of the Census.

Table 10–3

Adolescents at greatest risk of academic failure

	Parent unmarried	Parent high-school dropout	Family income less than $15,000
All teenagers	25%	11%	20%
Asian	15%	8%	17%
Black	50%	15%	50%
Hispanic	25%	50%	40%
Cuban	25%	15%	20%
Mexican	20%	40%	40%
Puerto Rican	35%	30%	45%
Native American	35%	15%	45%
White	18%	6%	15%

Source: U.S. Department of Commerce (1994). *Poverty in America.* Washington, DC: Bureau of the Census.

Although 80% of African Americans graduate from high school by time they are 25, fewer than 10% finish college. In contrast, nearly 90% of Asian American students graduate from high school and nearly half finish college—twice the percentage of whites and four times that of blacks and Hispanics. Between these extremes, about 85% of non-Hispanic whites graduate from high school and 20% graduate from college. On average, Asian and white students also have higher skills in math, reading, writing, and science at all grade levels. Whereas only a

Figure 10–2

Race, family income, and high-school graduation

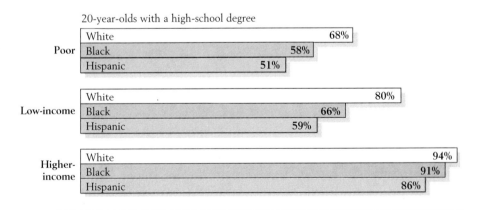

Source: U.S. Department of Commerce (1992). *Current population reports.* Washington, DC: Bureau of the Census.

What was most memorable about your
graduation from high school?

third of all white or Asian high-school students have failed a grade, nearly half of
the students from other racial groups are at least one grade-level behind. Keep
this in mind though: Regardless of race, fewer than 25% of all teenagers go on to
eventually graduate from college. The vast majority of teenagers enter the work
force or a job training program after graduating from high school. Another 15%
drop out of school and start looking for work without a high-school diploma.

Racial differences also emerge concerning college majors, as Table 10–4 shows.
Because Asian Americans represent only 2% to 3% of our population, it is especially noteworthy that they earn more than 5% of the degrees in medicine, 3% of
all doctorates, and almost 4% of all undergraduate degrees. In contrast, African
Americans, who represent about 12% of the population, earn only 5% of the
degrees in medicine, 4% of the doctorates, and 6% of the undergraduate degrees.
Likewise, Latino students, constituting about 10% of the population, earn only
3% of the undergraduate, medical, or doctoral degrees. Between these extremes,
non-Hispanic white students, who represent nearly 75% of the population, earn
about 85% of the undergraduate degrees, 90% of the doctorates, and 86% of the
degrees in medicine (Hacker, 1992).

EDUCATION: WHAT IT'S WORTH

Most adolescents are so bored with school that many wonder, at least occasionally: Is it worth it? So let's examine what a high-school diploma is actually
worth. From the perspective of taxpayers, businesses, and the national economy,
graduating from high school and college is worth quite a lot. High-school and college graduates cost taxpayers less because they usually can support themselves
and their children without needing welfare; and they are able to pay more taxes

Table 10–4

Race, college degrees, and college majors

	Asian	Black	Latino	White
Degrees				
Bachelor, 1977	1.5%	6.5%	2.1%	90.0%
Bachelor, 1991	3.8%	6.0%	3.2%	86.0%
Doctorate, 1977	2.2%	4.3%	1.8%	91.0%
Doctorate, 1991	3.1%	3.8%	2.9%	89.0%
Law, 1990	2.0%	5.0%	3.0%	90.0%
Medicine, 1990	5.3%	5.0%	3.0%	86.0%
Majors				
Area/ethnic studies	0.7%	0.4%	0.5%	0.3%
Business	18.0%	26.0%	23.0%	25.0%
Education	4.0%	7.0%	8.0%	9.0%
Health/nursing	5.0%	7.0%	5.0%	7.0%
Science/engineering	34.0%	18.0%	17.0%	16.0%
Social sciences	13.0%	18.0%	13.0%	15.0%
Language/literature	4.0%	4.0%	6.0%	6.0%
Others	22.0%	20.0%	26.0%	22.0%

Source: A. Hacker (1992). *Two nations: Black and white.* New York: Charles Scribner's.

into the national coffer than less well-educated citizens. A male high-school dropout will contribute about $80,000 less in taxes over his lifetime than a male high-school graduate. Most teenagers who do not graduate from high school will also eventually need welfare to support their own children, since high-school dropouts are 10 times more likely than college graduates to live in poverty (U.S. Department of Commerce, 1994).

In short, education pays. As Figure 10–3 shows, the more education a person has, the more money he or she usually earns. The average high-school dropout earns 60% less than the average high-school graduate. A college graduate earns nearly three times as much as a high-school dropout and two times as much as a high-school graduate over the course of a lifetime. The average male high-school dropout will earn $260,000 less and a female will earn $200,000 less than their counterparts with high-school diplomas. In terms of yearly incomes, those without a high-school diploma earn about $11,000, high school-graduates about $17,000, college graduates about $32,000, and people with more than four years of college about $43,000 (Kirsch, 1993; Roberts, 1994; U.S. Department of Commerce, 1990, 1994).

The skills that students acquire in high school and college are also worth something to the nation's economy. High-school graduates who have mastered skills in

Figure 10–3

Average monthly incomes and educational levels

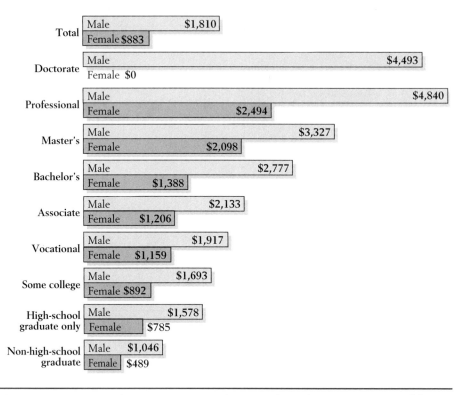

Source: U.S. Department of Commerce (1991). *What's it worth?* Washington, DC: Bureau of the Census.

reading, math, and science enable us to keep up with the competition at an international level. Our fastest growing occupations need young workers with much higher math, language, and reasoning skills than ever before—and with higher skills than most young Americans presently have. Now more than ever, we must compete in an international marketplace in which the skills of each country's work force are pitted directly against one another. Unfortunately, our workers fall far behind those of most other industrialized countries. Estimates indicate that 14 million Americans do not have the basic academic or vocational skills needed to do most of the jobs now available in our society. U.S. companies spend nearly $210 million a year to train and upgrade their workers whose basic academic skills are too poor to keep up with the demands of their jobs (National Alliance of Business [NAB], 1990).

ACADEMIC SKILLS

How poor are teenagers' academic skills? Very. How do our high-school students' academic skills compare to those of high-school students in other industrialized nations? Not well. Compared to our teenagers of 20 years ago and to those in other industrialized nations today, we are not in good shape. As a national commission concluded in 1982: "If an unfriendly, foreign power had attempted to impose on America the mediocre educational performance that exists today, we might well have viewed it as an act of war. As it stands, we have allowed this to happen to ourselves. We have, in effect, been committing an act of unthinking, unilateral educational disarmament" (National Committee on Excellence in Education [NCEE], 1983).

COLLEGE-BOUND STUDENTS

But what about our college students? Surely they are as academically skilled as college students in other countries, right? In general, no. As the president of our largest teachers' association puts it: "About 95% of the kids who go to college in the United States could not be admitted to college anywhere else in the world" (Innerst, 1990). Since the late 1980s, many colleges report a 10% to 30% increase in remedial courses for incoming freshmen; and most faculties report that freshmen lack basic skills in reading and writing (Carnegie Foundation, 1994). Yet college-bound teenagers are earning only half as many "C"s in high school as they did during the 1960s. By 1990 more than 20% of the teenagers entering a public college and more than half entering a private college had graduated from high school with an "A–" average (Cooperative Institutional Research Program [CIRP], 1991). In other words, even though college-bound teenagers are receiving more "A"s and "B"s, most of these students are not as well prepared or as knowledgeable as college-bound students once were. The most popular way of assessing college-bound students' skills is by comparing their Scholastic Aptitude Test (SAT) scores to those of students in previous decades. Unfortunately our SAT scores do not paint a very rosy picture. Since the early 1960s, the national average for the SAT has declined by nearly 75 points. Although female math scores have improved slightly during the past 20 years to an average score of 450, the average male math score of 500 has not improved. Meanwhile, average verbal scores have fallen to an all-time low of 422 points. The other bad news is that, after improving from 1960 to 1990, black and Latino scores have not improved since. Nearly a third of the approximately 1 million students who take the test each year are minorities; and although Native Americans' scores continued to increase slightly, black and Hispanic students' scores fell in 1990. Moreover, the gap between the highest and lowest scores has widened (College Exam Board [CEB], 1992).

HIGH-SCHOOL STUDENTS

The poor performance of students on their SATs makes sense, though, in light of high-school students' performances on national achievement tests. The

Figure 10–4

Adolescents' reading skills

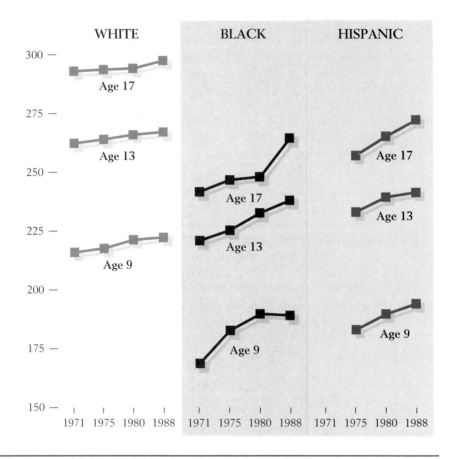

Source: I. Mullis, E. Owen, & G. Phillips (1990). *Accelerating academic achievement: Summary of findings of 20 years of NAEP.* Washington, DC: U.S. Department of Education.

National Assessment of Educational Progress (NAEP) periodically tests a nationwide random sample of 9-, 13-, and 17-year-olds to assess their skills in math, reading, writing, geography, history, government, and science. The NAEP also compares our students' scores with the scores of students from other industrialized countries. So what do these tests reveal about academic performance during the past 20 years? They show that we are not as smart as many of us think we are—especially not in comparison to students in other advanced countries. On the whole, our teenagers' achievement levels are not much better than they were 20 years ago. Although minority students' skills have improved in virtually all subject areas since 1970, they still perform below Asian and non-Hispanic whites

Figure 10–5

Adolescents' math skills

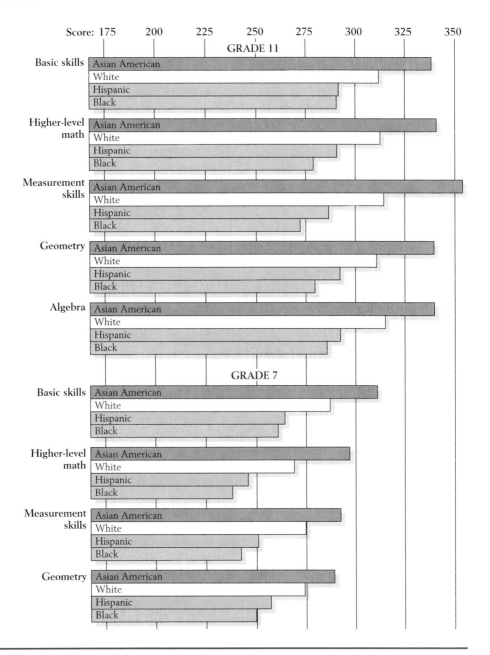

Source: I. Mullis, E. Owen, & G. Phillips (1990). *Accelerating academic achievement: Summary of findings of 20 years of NAEP.* Washington, DC: U.S. Department of Education.

Figure 10–6

Adolescents' science skills

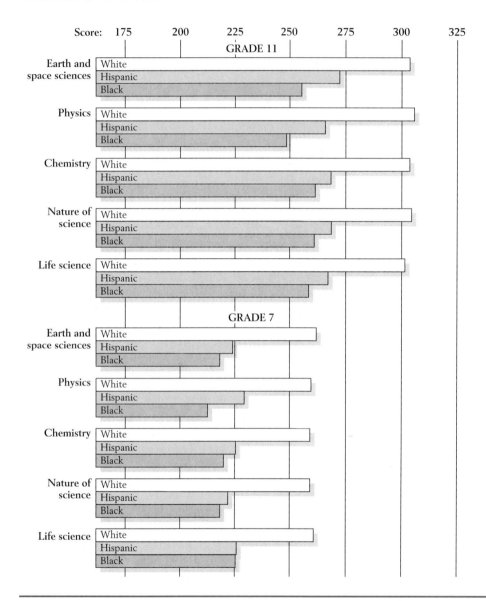

Source: I. Mullis, E. Owen, & G. Phillips (1990). *Accelerating academic achievement: Summary of findings of 20 years of NAEP.* Washington, DC: U.S. Department of Education

in all subjects. As shown in Figures 10–4, 10–5 and 10–6, adolescents' academic skills vary considerably according to race (Mullis, 1992).

Reading and Writing   With regard to language and reading skills, most high-school students can read only at a superficial level. They might get the gist of the material, but they can't analyze it. The good news is that black and Hispanic students and teenagers living in poor communities have made sizable improvements in reading since the 1970s. But the bad news is that most African and Hispanic American 17-year-olds read only about as well as most white and Asian American 13-year-olds. Regardless of race, most teenagers write even more poorly than they read. Assigned to write a paragraph expressing a point of view on a simple topic, two-thirds of high-school seniors tested in 1992 could not do so. More than one-third wrote contradictory and unsupported responses when asked to defend their viewpoint in writing. According to a survey sponsored by the U.S. Department of Education, half of the young people who graduated from high school in 1992 scored in the lowest fifth on literacy. Even more distressing, 4% of the college graduates also scored in the lowest fifth on this national survey of literacy (Kirsch, 1993).

Math and Science   By the end of high school, half the students cannot solve moderately challenging math problems. Only half of seniors do an adequate job solving problems with decimals, fractions, and percents in problems such as: "Is 87% of 10 greater than 10, less than 10, or equal to 10?" Only 6% of the seniors can solve the more difficult math problems that require some understanding of algebra and multiple-step problem solving, such as: "Suppose you have 10 coins, with at least one quarter, a dime, a nickel, and a penny. Which is the least amount of money you could have: 41¢, 47¢, 50¢, or 82¢?" Nearly one-fourth of the 7th graders cannot adequately solve problems in addition, subtraction, multiplication, and division. On a more positive note, girls' math skills have improved during the past 20 years. In fact, girls outperform boys until the age of 13, falling only slightly behind boys by age 17. Nevertheless, the average Japanese student not headed for college is better at math than the top 5% of our college-bound students. Yet somehow most of our students have gotten a very inflated sense of their abilities. Two-thirds say they are "good at math."

   In the study of science, our teenage students are in even worse shape. In international rankings against people their age in other industrialized countries, our teenagers scored last. Fewer than 10% of our seniors had specialized knowledge in any area of science. Nearly one-fifth cannot answer questions that require basic scientific information, such as: "In an ordinary light bulb with a screw-type base, which is the part that glows to produce the light: the thin wire, a special gas, the type of glass, or the special paint that coats the bulb?" Although math scores have changed very little since the early 1970s, our science scores have gone steadily downhill. Only 5% of our seniors can qualify to enroll in a college-level science course. Although teenage males' and females' reading skills have become more alike during the past 20 years, the gender gap has not narrowed in science—

neither has the racial gap. In science skills, the average African and Hispanic student is 4 years behind the average white and Asian American student.

History and Geography   So how are our students doing in history, civics, and geography? Not so well there either. Most seniors know less about civics than students did in the 1970s. Fewer than half of the seniors can put historical events in the correct chronological order. Most do not know the central ideas embodied by our most important documents, such as the Constitution and the Bill of Rights. Only 50% of the seniors know that religious freedom is guaranteed in the Constitution; and although most know how Lincoln died, only one-fourth of eighth graders know any of the goals of the Civil War. Likewise, when seniors are asked to contrast the powers of the president today with those of the first president, only 40% can come up with at least two answers.

So, yes, the percentage of Americans who finished high school increased by more than half from 1970 to 1990; and the percentage who finished at least 4 years of college doubled. Yet considering our SAT scores and the results of the NAEP, it's clear that, as a people, we are not necessarily better educated. Therefore, we must wonder why. Why are so many teenagers and young adults achieving less than people their age did 2 decades ago?

FACTORS AFFECTING ACADEMIC ACHIEVEMENT

FAMILY INCOME

As mentioned, the best indicator of how well an adolescent will do in school or how much education he or she will eventually complete is family income. Regardless of race, adolescents from low-income families almost always do more poorly academically than their classmates from wealthier families. So let's see which cities have the highest percentage of students living in poverty with a family income of less $14,000 for a family of four: New Orleans (45%), El Paso (35%), Baltimore (31%), New York and Philadelphia (tied at 30%), Detroit (28%), Boston and San Antonio (tied at 27%), Memphis (25%), and Washington (24%) (U.S. Department of Commerce, 1992).

The parents' educational levels and marital status are closely related to family income. In general, adults with the best educations have the highest incomes; and in general, married mothers have far more money than unmarried mothers. Because certain races are more poorly educated and have more unmarried mothers than others, race and marital status are also fairly reliable ways of predicting most teenagers' success in school. For example, nearly half of all African American teenagers live in a low-income family with an unmarried mother; and only half of Latino teenagers have parents who have graduated from high school. Only about half of the young males from these two groups finish high school. Table 10–5 shows which teenagers are the most likely to graduate from high school and

Table 10–5

Race and education: Population under age 30

	White		Asian		Black		Hispanic	
	male	female	male	female	male	female	male	female
High-school graduates	75%	87%	90%	90%	50%	82%	45%	55%
College graduates	20%	21%	41%	39%	7%	11%	9%	10%

Source: U.S. Department of Commerce (1992). *Household and family characteristics.* Washington, DC: Bureau of the Census.

those who have the most social forces working against them (U.S. Department of Commerce, 1994).

Why does the family's income usually make such a difference? First, the poorest families generally live in school districts where students receive the worst educations. Children from poorer families are also the least likely to attend private schools and preschool programs. Four times as many children from families with incomes greater than $40,000 attend private schools than from families making less than $20,000. More than half of the children from families with incomes greater than $35,000 attend preschool programs. For families earning less than $15,000, the figure drops to fewer than 20%. Regardless of their race, students from poor families are the least likely to have these educational advantages (O'Connell, 1993; Roberts, 1994).

Another disadvantage of coming from a low-income family is being unable to afford a college education. Many teenagers whose grades and SAT scores would qualify them for admission to college cannot afford to go or can afford to attend only junior college. To be sure, loans and grants for low-income students increased during the 1980s—while college costs nearly doubled. The cost for attending college has increased more than 100% during the past 10 years. The average cost of a private college is now about $16,000 per year and about $6,000 for a public college. Meanwhile, federal aid to college students has been cut by more than 60%, to about half the amount available in 1980. As a result, fewer qualified students from low-income families are going to college—a financial setback that has hit blacks and Latinos especially hard. Only about 10% of white college students come from families with incomes less than $20,000; but nearly 40% of black students come from families at that income level. Here's another way to look at it: White college students are twice as likely as black students to come from families with incomes greater than $60,000 (American Council on Education [ACE], 1992; Astin, 1990; Hansen, 1993).

Low family income can also affect academic achievement by having a negative impact on a student's physical health. Students from low-income homes are the most likely of all students to have their school performance impaired by physical problems, including: lead poisoning, asthma, typhoid, cholera, dysentery, and ear and eye problems. Drowsiness or inattentiveness due to poor nutrition is also very common. For example, in East St. Louis, where 98% of the residents are black, nearly 30% of the families live on less than $7,500 a year, and 75% are on welfare. This community not only has one of the highest rates of childhood asthma in the United States, but also other health problems resulting from contact with raw sewage and lead in the soil in their neighborhoods. Cholera, lead poisoning, and typhoid attack a number of these students. As one mother says, as she bails raw sewage from her sink, "It's a terrible way to live" (Kozol, 1991, p. 94; Needleman, 1990).

A family's income is also linked to the stress a student faces at home. In general, when there is enough money, the environment at home is less stressful than when money is scarce. For example, during the recession of the 1980s, relationships between teenagers and parents became more strained in families that fell into financial hard times. Many of these adolescents' grades fell during these lean years (Flanagan, 1990). Likewise, a survey of nearly 8,000 teenagers showed that family income was more closely related to their grades than was their parents' marital status (Dornbusch & others, 1991). Once again, family incomes are usually fairly reliable predictors of teenagers' grades and their high-school and college graduation rates.

FAMILY VALUES

So is family income all that matters? No. Don't some teenagers from poor families do well in school despite their economic disadvantages? Yes. Clearly, factors other than money affect teenagers' academic achievements. You can see from Figure 10–7 that on the SAT black students whose parents earn from $50,000 to $60,000 score below Asian teenagers from families in the $10,000 to $20,000 range. Even when family incomes are similar, Hispanic students also score an average of 70 points more than black students. Even though more than 40% of Asian American teenagers taking the SAT first learned a language other than English, and even when their family incomes are the same, their scores are higher than other races' scores. So although a family's income is the best single indicator of an adolescent's academic success, other factors are also at play (CEB, 1992; Jencks, 1994; Taylor, 1990).

One primary influence is the home environment. The values and habits that students learn at home can either help or hinder them academically. Some students excel in school, despite low family-incomes, because of the habits and attitudes their families have instilled in them. Notably, Asian American and Jewish families value education, self-discipline, hard work, and persistence. As a result, these teenagers generally surpass others academically, even when their families do not have much money. Regardless of race or heritage, teenagers from families that place a high value on education, that read instead of watch television, and that supervise children's schoolwork generally achieve more than those from less involved, less educationally oriented homes. It is extremely important to

Figure 10–7

Race, income, and average SAT scores

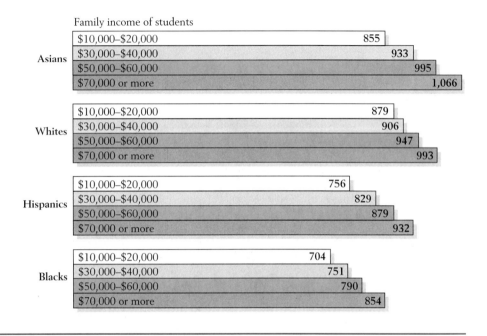

Family income of students

Asians	$10,000–$20,000	855
	$30,000–$40,000	933
	$50,000–$60,000	995
	$70,000 or more	1,066
Whites	$10,000–$20,000	879
	$30,000–$40,000	906
	$50,000–$60,000	947
	$70,000 or more	993
Hispanics	$10,000–$20,000	756
	$30,000–$40,000	829
	$50,000–$60,000	879
	$70,000 or more	932
Blacks	$10,000–$20,000	704
	$30,000–$40,000	751
	$50,000–$60,000	790
	$70,000 or more	854

Source: The College Board (1992). *Scholastic Aptitude Performance.* Princeton, NJ: Author.

understand that income isn't all that dictates the kinds of habits and values students acquire at home. For example, in a survey of more than 5,000 teenagers and their parents, minority students and parents from lower-income families were as likely to value good grades and a college education as wealthier white families (Indiana Youth Institute, 1994). Merely because a student comes from a wealthy family does not mean that he or she has been taught to value education, hard work, and self-discipline. And merely because parents are poor or uneducated does not mean that their children have not learned to value education or to work hard in school (Barton & Coley, 1992; Weiner, 1992; White, 1993).

HOMEWORK AND TELEVISION

One of the most beneficial habits we can learn at home is to discipline ourselves to read and study every day. Most students' grades and their national achievement test scores relate closely to how much time and effort they put into their schoolwork. As Insert 10–1 demonstrates, those teenagers who excel in a particular area are not magically blessed with talents at birth that guarantee

Insert 10–1

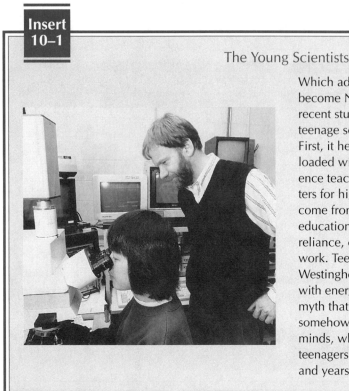

The Young Scientists

Which adolescents are the most likely to become Nobel Prize-winning scientists? A recent study of our nation's most talented teenage scientists helps answer this question. First, it helps to come from New York—a state loaded with special science schools, gifted science teachers, and many science research centers for high-school students. It also helps to come from an immigrant family that values education and to have parents who foster self-reliance, curiosity, self-discipline, and hard work. Teenagers who have won the prestigious Westinghouse Science Talent Awards bubble with energy and enthusiasm. But contrary to the myth that these talented young people are somehow blessed at birth with special scientific minds, what sets most of them apart from other teenagers is their self-discipline, dedication, and years of hard work.

Source: J. Berger, (1993). *The young scientists.* Reading, MA: Addison Wesley.

success. Those who excel are the hard-working, self-disciplined, self-motivated students who spend countless hours perfecting their talents (Berger, 1993). As is true in most other endeavors in our lives, academic success and excellence are the results of 1% inspiration and 99% perspiration. So how much "perspiration" are most teenage students putting out? Judging from national statistics and comparisons to students in other industrialized countries, most of our teenagers clearly are not working up much of a sweat over their homework. Most American students put most of their time and energy into their part-time jobs, television, and their friends. Each week the typical American high-school student spends about 20 hours watching television, 20 hours with friends, and 6 hours doing homework. Fewer than 15% of our students spend as much as 20 hours a week studying. Students who attend nonreligious, private schools tend to study more than students in public or Catholic schools. The typical 8th grader in a private, nonreligious school spends about 14 hours a week watching television and 11 hours doing homework. But 8th graders in Catholic and public schools spend nearly 22 hours watching television and only 6 hours studying (NCES, 1990). Even college-bound seniors do far more socializing and television watching than studying.

Before we go blaming teenagers for their addiction to television and their aversion to studying, however, we need to consider what their role models are doing: Most American adults watch 32 hours of television a week (Barton & Coley, 1992; Bence, 1991; CEB, 1992; Mullis, 1992; Nielsen, 1988).

In addition to our addiction to television, another part of the problem is that most schools require so little of our teenage students. Not only do we spend fewer days in school each year than students in most other industrialized nations, but we also spend 2 to 3 hours less in school each day and take far fewer academic courses. The average American high-school student spends only 3 hours a day in academic classes for a total of about 1,450 hours during all four years of high school. By 11th grade, only about half of our students are still taking a science course; only 10% of high-school graduates study biology for at least 1 year; and fewer than 20% study physics. By the time they graduate, for example, high-school students in Germany, Japan, and France spend twice as many hours in their academic classes as we do (National Education Commission on Time & Learning, 1994). Compared to other nations, we also assign very little homework. Only about 40% of our high-school seniors are asked to write anything about what they have read each week or are asked to do more than 15 minutes of math homework a day. Only 15% of our seniors have been asked to write weekly reports of at least three pages in their history or civics classes. And only about half of our high-school students do experiments in their science classes on a regular basis (Mullis, 1992). Compared to Japanese and Chinese students, our teenagers spend much less time studying and much more time sleeping, playing sports, watching television, dating, being with their friends, and earning spending money for themselves at their part-time jobs. Nevertheless, most Japanese and Chinese students have very well-rounded lives playing sports, spending time with friends, and watching television. In other words, studying does not restrict Asian teenagers to the hum-drum, boring, stressful existence many of us envision when rationalizing our own academic laziness (Fuligni & Stevenson, in press; Juster & Stafford, 1991; White, 1993).

THE CURRICULUM AND TEACHING TECHNIQUES

Most American teenagers invest very little time in schoolwork, and very few are motivated by what they *are* asked to study. Time and again teachers tell us that their most difficult job is motivating their students to do the work. Most students say they do not do their work because "it's boring." In other words, if our students do not find the material entertaining, most simply don't do the work. As a consequence, many schools are trying to improve students' basic skills by updating and redesigning the curriculum and teaching methods (Boyer, 1983; CGCS, 1993; Fiske, 1992).

A few specific examples illustrate some of these attempts to motivate teenage students. A small regional high school in Maine has abolished its system of grouping students according to ability and has formed a committee of teachers, the principal, and the custodians to set the direction for reform efforts. The school also bought 90 computers for teachers and for students to take courses by satellite from state universities. The teachers are also being taught new teaching and grading methods based on cooperative learning—a system in which students are taught in mixed-ability groups without having to compete against one another at each other's expense (Viadero, 1992). In the city of New York, where half of all teenagers quit school, the school system in 1991 was beginning to create 15 small, theme-oriented high schools, including one for environmental studies, one for performing arts, and one for science and technology studies. With enrollment limited to fewer than 500 students, these schools are designed to offer more personal attention. One of the schools, the Metropolitan Corporate Academy, is housed in a former office building and is provided with computers and furniture by an investment firm that plans to help the students find jobs after they graduate (Bradley, 1992).

Another idea is pairing teenagers from low-income families with adult mentors who agree to make tax-deductible contributions to the students' college educations. In some cases a sponsoring corporation puts up the money for college and asks its employees to volunteer as mentors. The mentors must agree in writing to contact the students at least once a month for 5 years. The fifth year is included because the first year of college is such an important transitional step for most low-income students. During the 5 years, the sponsor helps with homework, takes the student to his or her place of work, and offers advice on how to succeed at school and at work. A sponsor may request a certain type of student, such as someone who speaks Spanish or someone who is an athlete. The sponsor, the student, and the parents sign a legally binding pledge that outlines their commitments. If the student drops out of school, is suspended, or fails a grade, his or her contract becomes void. Sponsor-a-Scholar is a spinoff of a project begun in New York by a philanthropist and businessman who has promised to pay the college expenses for an entire 6th-grade class, if they finish high school (Lawton, 1991).

Some creative, outspoken school superintendents have also taken the lead in reforming some of our nation's worst schools. Among them is Joseph Fernandez, who has served as superintendent of two of the largest school systems in our country—the districts for the city of New York and Dade County, Florida. Fernandez raised many students' achievement scores and lowered dropout rates by implementing school-based management and shared decision making. These programs give teachers more control over the curriculum, allowing them to develop and implement more innovative teaching techniques (Fernandez, 1993).

In our effort to help more teenagers succeed in school, it is also important to evaluate the effects of preschool programs. Federally funded preschool programs, most notably Head Start, were designed during the 1960s to help poor children catch up with middle-class children before starting to school. Researchers have begun comparing the performances of the original Head Start students, now adolescents and young adults, with those of other poor children who did not attend these preschool enrichment programs. On the whole, the teenagers who were in Head Start have been in fewer special education classes, had higher graduation rates, and had lower rates of delinquency and pregnancy than poor teenagers who were not in preschool programs (Washington, 1991).

TRACKING

Another factor affecting teenagers' academic skills and progress is the widespread practice known as tracking. In almost all schools, students are assigned to a particular type of curriculum or "tracked" before they reach adolescence. In elementary school a student is placed in a higher or lower track, usually based on reading ability. By adolescence, most students are well aware of their track—college-bound, general, vocational, or special education. Within each track, most students are further segregated on the basis of their supposed abilities into higher and lower levels of each academic course. Despite the problems associated with this form of segregation—which have been known for many years—tracking remains the norm in virtually all of our schools. Once students have been assigned to a track, whether officially or not, they rarely move to a higher track. This is good news for the 25% who are presumed bright enough for the college-bound track. But the other 75% assigned to the general, vocational, or special education tracks are essentially trapped in a curriculum that limits their future job options and their circle of friends. Moreover, the more creative, enthusiastic, intelligent, and experienced teachers are usually assigned to the high-track students—students who generally come from the more well-to-do, well-educated families. Hispanic, black, Native American, and poor white children are more likely to be assigned to the lower tracks, even though some of them are capable of doing better work. Not surprisingly, students in lower tracks usually come to view themselves as "dummies" or "retards." At the very least, they often see themselves as "dumber" than students in the academic track. Long before they reach high school, most students, as well as many of their teachers and prospective employers, have come to see the vocational and general tracks as the place for losers (Games, 1991; NCES, 1991; National Education Association [NEA], 1988; Rosenthal & Jacobsen, 1968; Wheelock, 1993).

Another problem with tracking is that this form of segregation seldom raises the academic skills or improves the social behavior of students in the lower tracks. The strongest argument in support of tracking is that students in the lower tracks will make more progress because their teachers will individualize the instruction to their needs and give them more personal attention. But this promise seldom materializes. Indeed, students from the lower tracks can improve when allowed into classes with college-bound students as a result of peer tutoring, more engaging materials and teaching methods, and the teachers' higher expectations. Why, then, despite the mounting evidence against tracking, does tracking continue in virtually all schools? First, many teachers are reluctant to try teaching students of different abilities in the same class. They worry that this break from tradition will create problems for them, as well as for their students. But most objections come from the parents of the 25% of students who are headed for college. Many of these well-educated, higher-income parents fear that their children will somehow be held back by being taught in the same classes with students from lower-income families or students with lesser academic skills. Thus, most adolescents remain on the same old track—still separate, still unequal (Wheelock, 1993).

RACE AND GENDER

Like many other Americans, many teachers, counselors, and principals treat students differently on the basis of skin color and gender. Most educators are becoming more aware of the harmful effects of inadvertent sexism and racism. Nevertheless, racism and sexism at most schools still prevail in the curriculum, teaching methods, teachers' behavior and attitudes, standards and methods of punishment, grading, and counseling (ACE, 1992; Darder, 1991; Kozol, 1991; National Council of La Raza, 1992; Sadker & Sadker, 1993; Walsh, 1990).

Insert 10–2

Shortchanging Female Students: Sexism in the Schools

Which of the following are true?

1. Male students talk more than females in high-school and college classes.
2. Male students generally have more self-confidence academically than female students.
3. High-school and college instructors call on male students more often.
4. Most high-school and college textbooks focus on male accomplishments.
5. In high school and college, female students often achieve more in all-female classes than in coed classes.
6. Before adolescence, girls are ahead of or equal to boys on almost all academic skills.
7. By the time they reach high school, most girls have fallen behind most boys in achievement and self-esteem.
8. Males receive more college scholarships than females.
9. Male students receive more time from their high-school and college teachers than do female students.

10. Teachers are twice as likely to praise girls as boys for following the rules, being neat, and being quiet.
12. Teachers usually give boys more time to answer questions in a discussion than they give girls.
13. Boys are more than twice as likely as girls to argue with a teacher whom they think is wrong.
14. As they progress through high school and college, most female students become quieter in class, but male students become more vocal.
15. Teachers are more likely to name a male than a female as their most outstanding student.
16. Girls in single-sex schools generally have higher self-esteem than girls in coeducational schools.

Each of the preceding is true.

Source: Based on data from: M. Sadker & D. Sadker (1994). *Failing at fairness: How America's schools cheat girls.* New York: Charles Scribner's.

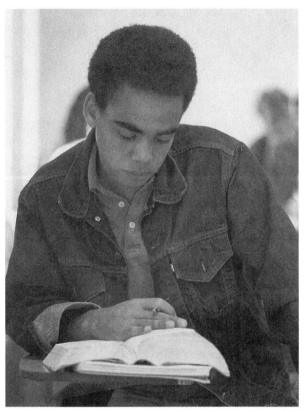

How have your race and gender affected your education?

A few examples illustrate the kinds of sexism and racism that remain in many adolescents' schools. Both male and female students who are on school athletic teams are less likely to drop out of school, become delinquent, abuse drugs, or become teenage parents. Nevertheless, very few schools offer female students the same athletic opportunities, encouragement, or funding as they offer male students (Diegmueller, 1994). With regard to race, one case under investigation by the U.S. Justice Department in 1994 involved an Alabama principal who allegedly threatened to cancel the senior prom if any interracial couples planned to attend. The principal also allegedly told a sophomore student with a black father and a white mother that she was "a mistake" and that he wanted to prevent other couples from doing what her parents had done—an act for which the courts required the school system to pay $25,000 in damages to the student (Walsh, 1994).

In terms of the curriculum and school policies, many school systems need an overhaul to keep pace with demographic changes. For example, Minnesota's minority population has increased by 75% since 1980; and the number of low-income students has risen dramatically. Accordingly, Minnesota's schools have been pressed to do a better job of enforcing their racial harassment policies and making their curriculum more inclusive for minority and low-income students (Richardson, 1994). Fortunately, a growing number of schools are dedicated to treating minority and female students more equitably. In specific areas such as math and science, in which female and minority students are furthest behind, more appropriate teaching methods and materials are being introduced. Because their self-defeating attitudes about math and science often hinder minority and female students, many of these newer approaches are based on building self-confidence. Teachers are presenting more role models of females and minorities who enjoy their careers in science and math. Teachers and counselors are also encouraging all students to see math and science as skills that everyone can and should acquire. When such methods are tried, female and minority students do become more interested in their courses and in future jobs that require a math or science background (Campbell, 1991; Clewell, 1991; Fennema, 1990; Frederick & Nicholson, 1992).

Textbook authors and publishers have been asked for years to include more information about females and racial minorities. But progress has been slow. Most high-school and college textbooks still focus on white, male contributions, subjects, and illustrations. In two prominent high-school history textbooks published after 1990, fewer than three of the 800 pages featured women. In 1990, most books used in high-school music and chemistry classes focused almost exclusively on male contributions and male examples; and none of the five leading science textbooks included a single picture of a female scientist (Darder, 1991; Gates, 1992; Sadker & Sadker, 1993; Walsh, 1990).

Given what happens in most coeducational classrooms, perhaps it is not surprising to find that many female students achieve more in all-female schools or all-female classes. Both at the high-school and college levels, girls in single-sex schools generally achieve more and become interested in less sex-stereotyped subjects than do girls in coeducational schools. Without boys in their classes, many girls are more outspoken, more assertive in defending their points of view, more willing to try challenging problems, and more actively engaged with their teachers. Similar results are not found for male students in all-male classes. As Insert 10–2 illustrates, in high school and in college, male students generally dominate the discussions and receive much more of their teachers' time and attention. This surely helps explain why female students' self-confidence and academic achievements generally fall behind the males' by the time they reach high school, even though girls start out ahead of boys academically in elementary school (Holland & Eisenhart, 1991; Lee & Marks, 1990; Sadker & Sadker, 1993).

Too many female students also say they are confronted with another problem—sexual harassment, both from teachers and from fellow students. This is not to say that male students are never harassed or sexually coerced by their teachers or fellow students. Nevertheless, girls generally encounter more of such harassment. Some evidence also suggests that girls who are members of racial minorities encounter more sexual harassment than non-Hispanic white girls. But regardless of race, many female students report having been sexually harassed in ways that interfere with their schoolwork and make them tense and uncomfortable about going to school or being in certain classes. Sexual harassment ranges from having their breasts or thighs touched without permission, being grabbed at, and having lewd remarks made to them, to being coerced into having sexual intercourse with a teacher, coach, or professor. Before they graduate from high school, most girls have been touched, grabbed, or spoken to lewdly by male students or a male teacher or coach. When confronted, most teachers, coaches, and professors defend themselves by saying they were "only teasing" or "flirting." When teachers or fellow students are confronted with having sexually harassed a female student, the disciplinary actions are often a mockery, not a serious effort to punish or to educate the offenders. The National Education Association, the National Association of School Boards, and the American Association of University Women, however, do not see any form of sexual behavior toward male or female students as harmless fun or joking. The nation's largest teachers' union recommends that students participate in a series of classes on sexual harassment to teach them how to prevent and report these incidents in school and in the workplace. Among others, these professional organizations have taken a stand against any teacher, professor, coach, counselor, or administrator who relates to male or female students in any sexual way. In 1992 the Supreme Court also ruled against sexual harassment in our public schools and colleges. When a high-school sophomore took her economics teacher to court for forcing her to have sex with him, the Supreme Court ruled in her favor by stating that monetary compensation can be awarded for damage caused by a teacher's or a fellow student's sexual harassment or sexual coercion (American Association of University Women, 1993; Deich & Weiner, 1986; Gittins, 1990; Paludi, 1991; Stein, 1994; Stein, Marshall, & Tropp, 1993).

LEARNING DISABILITIES

In addition to issues related to race and gender, some teenagers are not doing well in school owing to physical impairments referred to as learning disabilities. **Learning disabilities** are conditions resulting from dysfunctions in the central nervous system that impair spatial perception, visual-motor coordination, memory, written or spoken language, or abstract reasoning. For example, students who have the learning disability known as **dyslexia** perceive certain letters and numbers backwards. A "b" might be seen as a "d" or a "3" as an "E." Teenagers who have been identified as learning-disabled students can be helped with special teaching techniques and special classroom materials.

A second category of learning disabilities, now referred to as **attention deficit hyperactivity disorders** (ADHD), was once called minimal brain dysfunction (MBD) or hyperactive child syndrome. The main characteristic of ADHD is a severe discrepancy between a student's grades and his or her intellectual abilities, most commonly determined by an IQ test. It is widely agreed that ADHD first begins to create problems in early childhood when the child's inattentive,

Insert 10–3

Attention Deficit Hyperactivity Disorder

Unlike a child who is simply bored or unmotivated, the student with attention deficit hyperactivity disorder has a history of poor grades and academic failure that began in elementary school. In order to be diagnosed, a teenager must demonstrate most of the following traits over a period of months or years at home, at play, and at school from early childhoon on:

Inattentive

_____ often fails to pay attention to details and makes careless mistakes

_____ has trouble paying attention when playing

_____ does not seem to listen to what is being said directly to him or her

_____ often fails to follow directions or complete schoolwork and chores

_____ usually has trouble organizing tasks and activities

_____ often avoids and dislikes sustained mental effort

_____ often loses things

_____ easily distracted when working

_____ often forgetful in daily activities

Hyperactive

_____ often fidgets or squirms

_____ often leaves seat in class

_____ often runs around and climbs on things when such behavior is inappropriate

_____ has trouble playing quietly

Impulsive

_____ often blurts out answers to questions in class

_____ often has trouble waiting in line or waiting for his or her turn

Source: APA Task Force (1994). *Diagnostic and statistical manual of mental disorders.* Washington, DC: American Psychiatric Association.

impulsive, defiant, hyperactive behavior creates serious problems at home and at school. Because they have such serious problems keeping up and getting along with other students, virtually all teenagers with ADHD are identified as having this neurological problem by the first or second grade in school. Restless, impulsive, easily distracted, and often aggressive, students with ADHD have made poor grades or failed courses since early elementary school. They are slow to complete their homework and tests, often fail to remember things, and have a hard time following directions. Because they are often quite impulsive, defiant, hyperactive, and excitable, most ADHD students are also fairly unpopular with classmates and teachers. Students with ADHD make poor grades, seldom get along well with

How comfortable would you feel having deaf or blind students in your classes?

their peers, and often suffer from low self-esteem, in some cases becoming clinically depressed. As explained in Chapter 15, ADHD is now believed to contribute to the aggressive, defiant, impulsive, and violent behavior that many delinquents have displayed since early childhood (Achenbach & McConaughy, 1992; Farrington, Loeber, & VanKammen, 1990; Weiner, 1992).

One question about ADHD, however, continues to be debated: Do some students have a type of attention deficit disorder that does not involve hyperactivity, aggression, or poor grades? Some psychologists believe that a few students with ADHD have not been properly diagnosed because they are not hyperactive or defiant and because their grades are relatively good. On the other hand, their IQ test scores suggest that these students are capable of making better grades. Some researchers believe this indicates a variant of attention deficit disorder. They say such students might seem lazy or unmotivated when in fact they are doing their best. Through hard work coupled with their high intelligence, these learning disabled students supposedly still manage to earn high grades and to succeed in college (APA Task Force, 1994; Weiner, 1992).

Psychological and Emotional Problems

Some teenagers' failures and frustrations at school are also a consequence of psychological and emotional problems—problems that have very little to do with the school. Most psychological and emotional problems have a negative impact on teenagers' grades and on their behavior around their teachers and classmates. A sudden drop in grades or chronically poor grades are two of the most common symptoms of mental or emotional problems. Because psychological problems are discussed in Chapter 15, for now we only briefly mention a few disorders that are commonly associated with poor school attendance and poor grades (Achenbach & McConaughy, 1992; Harrington, 1994; Weiner, 1992).

Dependent Personality and Anxiety Disorders   Teenagers who frequently complain of feeling sick or regularly invent excuses for not going to school are referred to as "school phobic." Most school phobic students make fairly good grades and want to do well. Nevertheless, these teenagers frequently convince one or both of their parents to let them stay home because of their supposed headaches, stomach pains, nausea, or sore throats (or an unfair teacher, a long bus ride, the boring work, unfriendly classmates, and so forth). Although their aches and pains might be real, they stem from the student's emotional problems, not from a physical dysfunction. One of the clues to the cause of school phobia is the parent's compliance with such excuses. Many school phobic teenagers are suffering from extreme shyness and a lack of self-confidence around people their age—a psychological condition known as an **anxiety disorder.** Other school phobic teenagers are extremely immature, overly protected children who have been allowed to remain too dependent on one or both of their parents—a mental condition known as a **dependent personality disorder.** In either case, most school phobic teenagers have been nervous about going to school and uncomfortable leaving home since early childhood. Many of these school-phobic teenagers are extremely dependent on their mothers. Owing both to their overinvolvement in the child's life and to their own psychological or marital problems, these mothers have acquiesced to and made excuses for the child since very early childhood. The school-phobic teenager demands attention through various ailments, temper tantrums, crying, and sulking. By whatever means, these teenagers learned early in life how to get their mothers to give in to their demands. Meanwhile, many of the fathers permitted their wives to baby these children and remained too detached and uninvolved in the children's lives to foster self-reliance. These fathers often vacillate between being angry at their wives for pandering to the children year after year and withdrawing even further from the children. Given their family situations, the key to helping teenagers overcome school phobia is teaching them to become more self-reliant, more assertive, more outgoing, more socially mature, and more separated from the parent they are so dependent on (Weiner, 1992).

Passive Aggression Toward Parents

Some teenagers also underachieve or fail at school as a way of expressing anger at their parents. In these families, children are not allowed to express their anger,

Insert 10–4

Dropouts Talk about Quitting School

Brent, Age 18

"I was a senior when I dropped out. I used to get harassed by the teachers and the whole student body because I was different. The problem is the dropouts who don't know why they dropped out. I know why I dropped out, so I'm not a problem."

Sara, Age 15

"If you're looking for why we're dropping out to make sense, forget it. The young, gifted, middle-class, and bored. Fits me well."

Sheila, Age 17

"In the 9th grade I really started f_ _ _ ing up. The school was threatening my mom. If I didn't go to school, they were going to fine her 50 days in jail or something. My dad used to beat me up pretty bad. I had bruises. I wouldn't go to school because I was afraid. They got me a social worker. I told them, "Don't say anything to my dad until you get me out of the house." They said, "Okay." But the motherf_ _ _ _ _ s told him. He came home and beat the s_ _ _ out of me."

Carrie, Age 17

"We need something like Dropouts Anonymous, where teachers, students, parents, administrators, and family members all get to talk about it. Because when you think about it, kids don't really drop out because of the school. They drop out because there's some other personal problem that is affecting the way they come to school."

Source: A. Sheffield & B. Frankel (1989). *When I was young I loved school: Dropping out and hanging on.* New York: Children's Express Foundation.

resentment, or jealousies; so they try to punish their parents by doing poorly at school. In some cases, a teenager believes that one or both parents expect too much and set standards that are impossible to achieve. In other cases, the teenager feels insecure, angry, or jealous because another sibling has been such a success at school that the child fears being unable to measure up. Others underachieve academically because they are unintentionally intimidated or pressured by the exceptional intelligence or success of one or both parents. At the other extreme are those students who hold themselves back academically because they are afraid of outdoing their parents. If neither parent has gone to college, done well financially, or succeeded in school, a bright teenager can worry about how his or her successes might affect family relationships. Still others refuse to work hard at school as a way of letting parents know how upset they are about such matters as divorce, or remarriage, or the birth of a new baby (Weiner, 1992).

CONCLUSION

Some adolescents do much better than others academically; some drop out of school altogether; and others continue on to graduate from college. The factors that influence these educational differences include: the family's income, the habits and attitudes instilled at home, inequities in educational spending, racism, sexism, tracking, learning disabilities, psychological and emotional problems, and the student's own unique personality. The costs of being poorly educated are evident not only in individual incomes, but also in the national economy. It is in all of our best interests, therefore, to do a better job than we are doing to educate our young people. As explained in the next chapter, our success or failure in preparing teenagers for their future jobs ultimately affects us all.

Review/Test Questions

Use statistics and findings from specific studies to support your answers.

1. How has the student population changed in recent years?
2. What do most high-school teachers consider to be the major problems in our schools?
3. How do most teenage students feel about school?
4. Which adolescents are the least likely to graduate from high school or college?
5. Which factors influence an adolescent's academic performance? Which influence how much education he or she will probably complete?
6. In what ways are our nation's school not providing equal educations for all students?
7. How have college and high-school graduation rates changed in recent decades?

8. In percentages, what are the high-school and college graduation rates of adolescents from various racial groups?
9. How do race and gender affect academic achievement?
10. In what ways do most schools treat male and female students differently?
11. How do our teenagers' academic skills compare to those of teenagers in other industrialized countries?
12. How much is a high-school and college education worth in terms of salary?
13. Describe the typical high school teacher in terms of age, income, race, and education.
14. What is tracking and how does it affect students?
15. How does their family's income affect students' academic achievement?
16. Why do some teenagers from wealthy families not succeed in school while some teenagers from very poor families do?

17. How have financial aid and college expenses changed in the past 15 years?
18. What are learning disabilities, and how do they affect academic achievement?
19. What are the symptoms of attention deficit disorder and dyslexia?
20. How can emotional or psychological problems affect academic achievement?
21. Describe the ways the typical American high-school student spends time.

22. How have teenagers performed on various sections of the NAEP tests during the past 20 years?
23. How do adolescents' academic skills affect taxpayers and the national economy?
24. What are some schools doing to try to improve students' skills?
25. In what ways are many schools racist and sexist?

Questions for Discussion and Debate

1. What creative ideas do you have for improving teenagers' academic skills?
2. How do you feel about tracking? Why?
3. If you were a high-school teacher, what would you do differently from what your own teachers did?
4. Who was the best teacher you ever had, and what specifically did he or she do to motivate and encourage students?
5. Why would you or wouldn't you be a teacher in a poor school?
6. During a typical week, how did you spend your time as a high-school student? How did this affect your schoolwork?
7. Given that only 20–25% of teenagers eventually graduate from college, what do you think the schools' goals should be for the other 75–80%?
8. Which values from your own family helped and hindered you most as a student?

9. How would you encourage a potential dropout to stay in high school?
10. How did your own family's economic situation affect your academic goals and achievements?
11. How has your race and gender affected the way you have been educated?
12. Have you or anyone you know ever been sexually harassed or sexually exploited by a teacher or professor? How was the situation resolved?
13. How do you feel about the financial inequities in our nation's schools, and what would you do to redress these inequities if you had the power?
14. How have learning disabilities affected your life or the life of anyone you know?
15. What examples of sexism and racism have you encountered in your high-school and college experiences?

Glossary

anxiety disorder, p. 430
attention deficit disorders, p. 427

dependent personality disorder, p. 430
dyslexia, p. 427

learning disabilities, p. 427

References

Achenbach, T., & McConaughy, S. (1992). Taxonomy of internalizing disorders of adolescence. In W. Reynolds (Ed.), *Internalizing disorders in childhood and adolescence.* New York: Wiley.

American Association of University Women. (1993). *Hostile hallways: Sexual harassment in America's schools.* Washington, DC: Author.

American Council on Education. (1992). *Status report on minorities in education.* Washington, DC: Author.

APA Task Force (1994). *Diagnostic and statistical manual of mental disorders.* Washington, DC: American Psychiatric Association.

Astin, A. (1990). *The Black undergraduate.* Los Angeles: Higher Education Research Institute.

Barton, P., & Coley, R. (1992). *America's smallest school: The family.* Princeton, NJ: Educational Testing Services.

Barton, P. (1989). *Earning and learning.* Princeton, NJ: Educational Testing Service.

Bence, P. (1991). Television and adolescents. In R. Lerner, A. Petersen, & J. Brooks-Gunn (Eds.), *Encyclopedia of adolescence* (pp. 1123–1126). New York: Garland.

Berger, J. (1993). *The young scientists.* Reading, MA: Addison Wesley.

Berlin, G., & Sum, A. (1988). *Toward a more perfect union.* New York: Ford Foundation.

Boyer, E. (1983). *High school.* New York: Harper & Row.

Bradley, A. (1992, April 1). NYC to create theme oriented high schools. *Education Week,* p. 5.

Campbell, J. (1991). The roots of gender inequity in technical areas. *Journal of Research in Science Teaching, 28,* 251–264.

Carnegie Foundation. (1994). *The academic profession: An international perspective.* Ewing, NJ: California/Princeton Fulfillment Services.

Center to Prevent Handgun Violence. (1992). *Caught in the crossfire: Gun violence in our nation's schools.* Washington, DC: Author.

Clewell, B. (1991). Minority and female participation in math and science. In R. Lerner, A. Petersen, & J. Brooks-Gunn (Eds.), *Encyclopedia of adolescence* (pp. 647–657). New York: Garland.

College Exam Board. (1992). *College-bound seniors.* Princeton, NJ: Author.

Cooperative Institutional Research Program. (1991). *The American freshman.* Washington, DC: Author.

Council of the Great City Schools. (1993). *Critical educational trends: America's urban schools.* Washington, DC: Author.

Darder, A. (1991). *Culture and power in the classroom.* Westport, CT: Greenwood Press.

Deich, B., & Weiner, L. (1986). *The lecherous professor.* Urbana: University of Illinois.

Diegmueller, K. (1994). Efforts to boost girls' participation in sports urged. *Education Week, 13,* 8.

Dornbusch, S., Mont-Reynaud, R., Ritter, P., Zeng-yin, C., & Steinberg, L. (1991). Stressful events and their correlates among adolescents of diverse backgrounds. In M. Colten & S. Gore (Eds.), *Adolescent stress* (pp. 111–131). New York: Aldine De Gruyter.

Economic Policy Institute. (1989). *Shortchanging education.* Washington, DC: Author.

Farrington, D., Loeber, R., & VanKammen, W. (1990). Long term criminal outcomes of hyperactivity-impulsivity-attention deficit and conduct problems in childhood. In L. Robins & M. Rutter (Eds.), *Straight and devious pathways* (pp. 62–81). New York: Cambridge University Press.

Fennema, R. (1990). *Math and gender.* New York: Teachers College.

Fernandez, R. (1993). *Tales out of school.* New York: Little Brown.

Fiske, E. (1992). *Smart schools, smart kids: Why do some schools work?* New York: Simon & Schuster.

Flanagan, C. (1990). Families and schools in hard times. *New Directions for Child Development, 46,* 7–26.

Frederick, J., & Nicholson, H. (1992). *The explorers' passage: Studies of girls and math, science and technology.* Indianapolis: Girls National Resource Center.

Fuligni, A., & Stevenson, H. (in press). Time use and achievement among American, Chinese and Japanese high-school students.

Games, P. (1991). Educational achievement and tracking in high school. In R. Lerner, A. Petersen, & J. Brooks-Gunn (Eds.), *Encyclopedia of adolescence* (pp. 291–294). New York: Garland.

Gates, H. (1992). *Loose canons: Notes on the culture wars.* New York: Oxford University Press.

Gittins, N. (1990). *Sexual harassment in schools.* Washington, DC: National School Boards.

Goodlad, J. (1983). *A place called school.* New York: McGraw Hill.

Goodlad, J. (1990). *Teachers for our nation's schools.* San Francisco: Jossey-Bass.

Hacker, A. (1992). *Two nations: Black and white, separate, hostile, unequal.* New York: Charles Scribner's.

Hansen, J. (1993). *College costs and financial aid.* New York: College Board.

Harrington, L. (1994). *Depressive disorder in childhood and adolescence.* New York: Wiley.

Hodgkinson, H. (1994). *The invisible poor: Rural youth in America.* Washington, DC: Institute for Educational Leadership.

Holland, D., & Eisenhart, M. (1991). *Educated in romance: Women, achievement and college culture.* Chicago: University of Chicago.

Indiana Youth Institute. (1994). *High hopes, long odds.* Gary, IN: Author.

Innerst, C. (1990, July 5). Schools really bad. *The Washington Times,* p. 44.

Jencks, C. (1994). *The homeless.* Cambridge, MA: Harvard University Press.

Juster, F., & Stafford, F. (1991). The allocation of time. *Journal of Economic Literature, 29,* 471–522.

Kirsch, I. (1993). *Literacy in America.* Washington, DC: U.S. Department of Education.

Kozol, J. (1991). *Savage inequalities: Children in America's schools.* New York: HarperCollins.

Lawton, M. (1991, September 18). Program pairs adult mentors with teenagers. *Education Week,* 6–7.

Lee, V., & Marks, H. (1990). Sustained effects of single sex secondary school experience. *Journal of Educational Psychology, 82,* 578–592.

Miller, L. (1994). Proposal urging schools to ban junk food. *Education Week, 13,* 19.

Mortenson, T. (1991). *Equity of higher educational opportunity for women, Black, Hispanic and low income students.* Iowa City, IA: American College Testing.

Mortimer, J. (1991). Employment. In R. Lerner, A. Petersen, & J. Brooks-Gunn (Eds.), *Encyclopedia of adolescence* (pp. 311–318). New York: Garland.

Mullis, I. (1992). *Trends in academic progress.* Washington, DC: U.S. Department of Education.

National Alliance of Business. (1990). *The business roundtable participation guide.* New York: Author.

National Center for Education Statistics. (1993). *The Condition of Education.* Washington, DC: Author.

National Center for Education Statistics. (1990). *Profile of the American 8th grader.* Washington, DC: Author.

National Center for Education Statistics. (1991). *Ability grouping by race.* Washington, DC: Author.

National Center for Education Statistics.

(1994). *Dropout rates in the U.S.: 1993.* Washington, DC: Author.

National Committee on Excellence in Education. (1983). *A nation at risk.* Washington, DC: Author.

National Council of La Raza. (1992). *Hispanic American youth.* Washington, DC: Author.

National Education Association. (1988). *Ability grouping: A research summary.* Washington, DC: Author.

National Education Commission on Time & Learning. (1994). *Prisoners of time.* Washington, DC: Author.

Needleman, H. (1990). The long term effects of exposure to low doses of lead in childhood. *New England Journal of Medicine, 322,* 83–88.

Nielsen, A. (1988). *Nielsen report on television.* Northbrook, IL: Nielsen Company.

O'Connell, M. (1993). *Who's minding the kids?* Washington, DC: Bureau of the Census.

Paludi, M. (1991). *Ivory power: Sexual harassment on campus.* Albany: State University of New York.

Richardson, J. (1994). Report urges St. Paul to address diversity in schools. *Education Week, 13,* 3.

Roberts, S. (1994). *Who we are: Statistical profile of the U.S.* New York: Times Books.

Rosenthal, R., & Jacobsen, L. (1968). *Pygmalion in the classroom.* New York: Holt Rinehart and Winston.

Sadker, D., & Sadker, M. (1993). *Failing at fairness: How America's schools cheat girls.* New York: Macmillan.

Seymour, D., & Seymour, T. (1993). *America's best classrooms.* New York: Peterson's Guides.

Sizer, T. (1992). *Horace's school.* Boston: Houghton Mifflin.

Stein, N. (1994). *Flirting or hurting?* Washington, DC: National Education Association.

Stein, N., Marshall, N., & Tropp, L. (1993). *Secrets in public: Sexual harassment in our schools.* Wellesley, MA: Wellesley College.

Taylor, D. (1990, October 7). Asian-American test scores. *Education Week,* p. 8.

Tyson, H. (1994). *Who will teach the children?* New York: Random House.

U.S. Department of Commerce. (1994). *Current population reports: Household and family characteristics.* Washington, DC: Bureau of the Census.

U.S. Department of Commerce. (1990). *What's it worth?* Washington, DC: Bureau of the Census.

U.S. Department of Commerce. (1992). *School enrollment and characteristics of students.* Washington, DC: Bureau of the Census.

U.S. Department of Education. (1994). *School expenditures: 1994–95.* Washington, DC: Author.

Viadero, D. (1992, April 2). Throwing out the traditional school model at Piscataquis High. *Education Week,* pp. 21–23.

Walsh, C. (1990). *Pedagogy and the struggle for voice.* Westport, CT: Greenwood Publishing.

Walsh, M. (1994). Justice department seeks to oust Alabama principal. *Education Week, 13,* 1.

Washington, V. (1991). Preschool programs' impact on adolescence. In R. Lerner, A. Petersen, & J. Brooks-Gunn (Eds.), *Encyclopedia of adolescence* (pp. 833–838). New York: Garland.

Weiner, I. (1992). *Psychological Disturbance in Adolescence.* New York: Wiley.

Wheelock, A. (1993). *Crossing the tracks.* New York: New Press.

White, M. (1993). *The material child: Coming of age in Japan and America.* New York: Free Press.

11

WORK AND VOCATIONAL DEVELOPMENT

Chapter Outline

Key Questions Addressed In This Chapter

1. What are adolescents' attitudes toward work?
2. How does having a part-time job affect adolescents?
3. What kinds of jobs are adolescents preparing for?
4. What factors influence adolescents' vocational choices?
5. How effective is high-school vocational education?
6. How does chronic unemployment affect young people?
7. How do race and socioeconomic class affect vocational development?
8. How does gender affect vocational development?
9. What are some of the creative vocational education high-school programs that have been developed?
10. What is the financial worth of a high-school or college education?

During adolescence most of us become increasingly focused on our future jobs and incomes. Especially as we approach that final year in high school, we are confronted with such concerns as: What kind of work would I like to do after I get out of high school or college? How do I go about preparing myself to get that job? Will I be happy at that particular work? How do I go about finding a job? How do I know what kind of work I would be good at? What are the odds that I can find the job I want? What's going to happen to me if I can't find a job, or if I don't like the jobs I find? How do I decide what kind of work I want to do for the rest of my life? How much choice am I really going to have about the work I end up doing?

Yet the study of vocational development extends beyond adolescents' concerns with their own futures. Teenagers' vocational development also affects schools, businesses, and the national economy, raising such controversial questions as: What should schools and businesses be doing to help prepare adolescents for their future jobs? Why are our young people much less prepared for the workplace than their counterparts in other industrialized countries? Who should pay to train teenagers entering the work force—the businesses that will eventually hire them or the taxpayers who support the schools? What should be done to help the growing number of poor teenagers who can't find jobs after graduating from high school? How can we get teenagers, especially teenage girls, to make wiser vocational choices than many of them are making? Considering the forecasts for the future, what kinds of jobs should adolescents be preparing themselves for? Vocational questions also involve teenagers' part-time jobs: Do the benefits of part-time jobs outweigh the risks? What are most teenagers learning at their jobs? Are our teenagers too much concerned with earning money and too little concerned with their schoolwork?

ADOLESCENTS' PART-TIME JOBS

CHANGES AND TRENDS

In no other industrialized country do as many teenagers work as in the United States. So let's start by examining the changes and trends in teenagers' part-time jobs (Barton, 1989; Mortimer, 1991). Most adolescents in our society clearly want to earn money while they are still in school. Nearly 5 million teenagers from ages 13 to 17 are working—twice as many as in 1950. Only about 7% of high-school seniors have never had a part-time job; and 50% to 70% of 16-and 17-year-olds are working. Roughly 15% of our teenagers are working more than 20 hours a week during the school year. More girls work than ever before. During the past 30 years the number of teenage boys with part-time jobs has increased by about 10%, but the number of girls with jobs has doubled. Teenage girls are now almost as likely as boys to be working part-time, and most high-school students are working about 15 hours a week.

Figure 11–1

Percent of adolescents with jobs

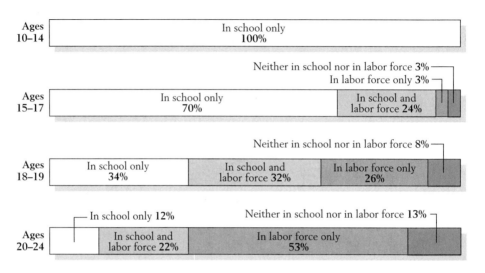

Source: U.S. Department of Commerce (1992). *Current population reports.* Bureau of the Census.

As adolescents age, more of them get part-time jobs, and they work longer hours. In part this happens because the **Fair Labor Standards Act** prohibits employers from allowing teenagers younger than 16 to work more than 15 hours a week or to work after certain hours at night. These federal laws also prohibit hiring young adolescents for jobs involving physical risks, such as operating heavy machinery or working around dangerous chemicals. Not until teenagers are 18 are they allowed to work unrestricted hours. Older adolescents are also more interested in having a part-time job because they want the money for dating, cars, and entertainment with their friends.

Most teenagers today, however, are working for different reasons than most teenagers used to work. During the 1950s and 1960s, most teenagers worked to help their parents make ends meet or to save money to go to college. Nowadays most teenagers work only to buy things for themselves. Very few employed teenagers save any of their money, contribute any of it to the family, or put any of it aside for college. Oddly enough, the teenagers most likely to have a job are those from middle-income families, not those from the poorest families who need the money for basic necessities. In other words, having a part-time job isn't something most teenagers are motivated to do because their parents are poor.

Teenagers from low-income families, however, are more likely than those from richer families to be working more than 20 hours a week during the school year. Because teenagers from upper middle-class families are usually planning to go to college, working more than 20 hours a week might lower their grade-point average. This isn't a risk that college-bound teenagers need to take since working 10 to 15 hours a week provides them with enough spending money. But the 75% who are not going on to college do not need to be as concerned with their grade point average because they will be entering the job market directly after graduation. In fact, their part-time jobs can often lead to better paying full-time jobs after graduating from high school. So only about 10% of college-bound high-school students work more than 20 hours a week, compared to 25% of their classmates.

The likelihood of having a part-time job also depends partly on the teenager's race. Although they work fewer hours, white students are more likely to have part-time jobs than black or Hispanic students. Hispanic males, however, are more likely than black males to be working part-time. Why these racial differences? First, the kinds of part-time jobs that teenagers are qualified for are usually harder to find in inner-city and poor areas where so many minority youth live. Second, black and Hispanic girls are more likely than their white classmates to have children out-of-wedlock, which results in less free time after school hours for a part-time job.

ATTITUDES TOWARD WORK

How do adolescents feel about their part-time jobs and what are they learning? As is true for adults, much depends on the kind of job a teenager has. Those whose jobs allow them a certain degree of independence and respect enjoy working more than those with boring jobs who are treated like robots or servants. Teenagers whose jobs help them develop new skills or challenge them intellectually enjoy their work more than those who are doing less gratifying tasks such as sweeping floors, cleaning tables, or washing cars. Like adults, adolescents' perceptions of work also depend on the bosses they have and the people they work with. Regardless of our age, when we are treated with respect and work with friendly, cooperative people, we're happier and more motivated to do well. Being sexually harassed by the boss or other co-workers can also make working a tense, unpleasant ordeal. Given the kinds of boring jobs that most teenagers have, too many of them develop negative, cynical attitudes about work. Although most teenagers are glad to be working because of the money, most say their jobs are fairly boring (Cole, 1983; Greenberger & Steinberg, 1986; Lewko, 1987; Stern, 1990).

As shown in Table 11–1, most adolescents work in the service industry, mainly in fast food restaurants. Most teenagers also work in jobs traditional for their gender. Notice that more than a third of teenage girls do secretarial or clerical work. Likewise, almost one fourth of boys are doing nonfarm labor. One of the reasons these gender differences are important is that part-time jobs should help teenagers acquire skills that can help them later. Yet most teenage girls are getting experience only in clerical work, and very few are receiving any training for higher paying jobs such as craft work, operating equipment, or transporting goods (U.S. Department of Labor, 1993).

Insert 11–1

How Adolescents Perceive Their Jobs

Charlotte, age 16

"The job I had wasn't like I expected it to be. They treated me like I was a nobody. I was trained to work on a cash register, but as time passed they had me taking out trash, mopping the floor, and cooking. They embarrassed me many times so I decided to leave."

Kevin, age 18

"I work for a carpet cleaning company. My pay is good and my co-workers are real nice. I'm treated like an adult and a partner."

Jason, age 17

"Among my friends, maintaining a nice car is the main reason for having a job. Others have jobs so they can get out of the house and away from mom and dad for a while. My parents never let me have a job during school. They say that they would rather give me an allowance than for me to be distracted from my studies. So far it has worked. My grade point average is about 3.8, and I have been able to participate in forensics, debate, and the school plays. Education and experiences in high school are much more important and valuable than the little bit of spending money from minimum wage slave labor."

Kim, age 17

"Teenage workers' biggest problem is that their employers don't treat them with enough respect. One of my managers is constantly making plays at me. When I stand up for myself, he threatens me with my job."

Sunni, age 15

"I have a job training and showing horses for different farms. Getting there on time, making sure all my horses are healthy, and doing well is my way of being independent. It's not just the money. It's more or less the way I try to earn respect for being responsible."

Brian, age 16

"I think it's great to work. In my case, I have to. My mother and father are divorced, and I have to help my mom any way I can. So my brother and I got jobs. We both make good money and we never have to ask her for money."

Source: Glenbard East Echo. (1984). *Teenagers themselves.* New York: Adama Books.

ADVANTAGES AND DISADVANTAGES

Five million teenagers worked during the 1990–1991 school year. But aside from the money they earn, what are teenagers achieving by working? What are they learning from their experiences at work? Are their jobs interfering with their school work? Do the benefits of working outweigh the costs?

One benefit is that some part-time jobs teach teenagers habits, attitudes, and skills that will help them later, including: getting to work on time, dressing

Table 11–1				

Adolescents' and young adults' jobs

	Male		Female	
	16–19 years	20–24 years	16–19 years	20–24 years
Professional/technical	2%	10%	2%	14%
Managers/administrators	1%	6%	1%	5%
Sales workers	6%	6%	12%	6%
Clerical workers	7%	8%	36%	42%
Craft workers	12%	21%	1%	2%
Operatives & transport	18%	22%	7%	10%
Nonfarm laborers	23%	11%	2%	2%
Household workers	.2%	0%	5%	1%
Service workers	24%	10%	30%	17%
Farm workers	6%	3%	1%	.5%
Total Employed	4,016,000	7,255,000	3,590,000	6,360,000

Source: U.S. Department of Commerce (1993). *Current population reports: Individual incomes by race and gender.* Washington, DC: Bureau of the Census.

appropriately, cooperating with co-workers, assuming responsibility for getting a job done, and learning to interact with a boss. Some working teenagers also become more self-confident, more socially mature, and more self-reliant. As mentioned, the right part-time job can also be an important stepping stone for the 75% of adolescents who are not headed for college. A part-time job with the right company sometimes leads to a much better full-time job after graduating from high school. Perhaps no company better illustrates this than McDonald's (Mabry, 1989). The largest corporate employer of adolescents, McDonald's employs more than 400,000 people under the age of 20 and a higher than average number of minority youth. Unlike most other large corporations, McDonald's tends to promote its employees more on the basis of skill and hustle than academic credentials. Only half of its corporate executives are college graduates, and most managers and owners have worked their way up through the organization to positions with excellent benefits and high salaries. For many low-income youth, such part-time jobs can lead to lifelong careers in a company. All in all then, teenagers who are lucky enough to get the right part-time job can benefit in ways other than immediate money (Cole, 1983; Greenberger & Steinberg, 1986; Lewko, 1987).

Nevertheless, this same research shows that a part-time job doesn't always work to a teenager's advantage—even with a company like McDonald's. On the whole, teenagers work at very boring jobs that do not require special skills or involve much interaction or cooperation with their co-workers. Most teenagers are not given much independence, authority, chance for advancement, or challenge. Most spend a large part of their time at work alone with no supervisor, customers, or co-workers around. Some teenagers even become more cynical and negative about working after having had a part-time job. Almost all workers, of course, enter the workforce at entry-level positions and have to work their way up to more interesting jobs. But the point is that many teenagers aren't profiting from their jobs in terms of learning valuable habits or lessons.

Another concern is whether jobs interfere with teenagers' grades. Fortunately for most students, working 10 to 15 hours a week does not interfere with their school work. But students who work more than 20 hours a week do make lower grades and tend to use more drugs, to drink more, and to smoke more than other teenagers. Boys who work more than 20 hours a week are also more likely to be delinquent. However, adolescents who choose to work more than 20 hours a week usually are not good students to begin with. So their long hours at work might not contribute as much to their poor grades as do their disinterest in school and weak academic skills. But working long hours does mean less parental supervision, more freedom to make decisions on their own, and more chances to associate with people their parents might not approve of. As a result, teenagers who work more than 10 to 15 hours a week are more likely than those who work less to make bad decisions and associate with people who encourage them to get into trouble (Bachman & Schulenberg, 1993; Greenberger & Steinberg, 1986; Manning, 1990; Steinberg & Dornbusch, 1991; Yamoor & Mortimer, 1990).

Another concern is that employed teenagers might not be acquiring realistic or practical lessons about work and money. It would be nice if having to earn money themselves would help teenagers appreciate the value of a dollar and learn to manage money well. Unfortunately, most teenagers are allowed to spend all of their money solely on themselves for their own immediate pleasure and entertainment. Very few are made to save any of what they earn, to contribute anything to charity, or to share any with their families. American teenagers have more buying power than teenagers anywhere else in the world—$95 billion per year. And what most of our adolescents do with their money is what virtually no adults can ever do—spend it all on themselves while their food, shelter, and education is provided for by someone else. This "premature affluence" that many of our teenagers enjoy also seems to foster great disillusionment and resentment when they eventually get out into the real world and learn how money, spending, and saving really work (Bachman & Schulenberg, 1993).

Finally, as odd as it might seem in light of so many parents encouraging their children to get a job, perhaps we should discourage more teenagers from working. Given that our childrens' academic skills lag far behind those of teenagers in other industrialized countries, maybe we should look to Tokyo, where half of the high schools prohibit students from having part-time jobs. While nearly 80% of our high-school students work, only one fourth do in China or Japan (Fuligni & Stevenson, 1994). In fact, many of our teachers say they have to cut back on homework and expect less work in class because so many students have part-time jobs. Maybe our teenagers, like those in most other industrialized countries, should be spending more of their time studying, participating in extracurricular activities, interacting with their families, and developing personal interests and identities. Maybe our teenagers would also be better off financially in the long run and better prepared for their adult jobs if they spent more time studying and less time flipping hamburgers and selling tacos after school (Waldman & Springen, 1992).

FACTORS INFLUENCING VOCATIONAL PATHS

Aside from their part-time jobs, high-school students have to confront a more serious vocational question: What kind of work am I going to do once I leave school? Approximately one in five adolescents eventually graduates from college, and nearly that many drop out of high school. The other 60% graduate and either start to work immediately or enroll in a program for additional vocational training. The 20% who drop out are usually unemployed or only able to obtain part-time work. What determines the vocational path an adolescent will take? What factors influence how far an adolescent will eventually go vocationally and financially? Which young people are the most likely to end up unemployed or working in the lowest paying, least satisfying, menial jobs? Which teenagers have the best chance of earning high incomes and working at a job they enjoy as adults? The answers lie primarily in four areas: the amount of education and income the adolescents' parents and stepparents have, the adolescent's gender and race, certain aspects of the adolescent's personality, and economic factors operating in the society.

SOCIOECONOMIC STATUS AND RACE

Let's begin with factors in the adolescent's family. Adolescents who come from families with more education and higher incomes are the most likely to graduate from high school and from college. As a result, they are the most likely to end up with the better paying, more enjoyable jobs as adults. In other words, teenagers generally follow in the footsteps of their parents and stepparents in terms of their future financial success and job status. Accordingly, non-Hispanic white, Jewish, and Asian American teenagers are the most likely to end up with the most education and, as a result, with the best paying jobs. This is why it is so important to narrow the racial and gender differences in high school and college graduation rates. The more education young people complete, the greater their future earning power and the lower their odds of being unemployed. The average American adult with a college degree who works full-time earns about $42,000 a year—a figure that drops to $26,000 for the adult with only a high-school diploma (Samuelson, 1992).

For reasons discussed at length in preceding chapters, race, education, and income are closely connected for most adults in our society. As a result, race is closely connected to most adolescents' vocational paths. Race also affects adolescents in the work force because racial discrimination still affects hiring, firing, and promoting in our society. Many employers and co-workers still feel uncomfortable working with African Americans, especially with black males. It seems that the stereotype of blacks as aggressive, outspoken, hostile, or angry too often hurts their chances of being hired or promoted. Some employers are also reluctant to hire black Americans for fear that blacks will be hard to get along with, "have a chip on their shoulder," or be overly sensitive about racial issues. Indeed, many employers are quite open about preferring to hire immigrants instead of black Americans. Moreover, in occupations such as dentistry and medicine, where physical contact occurs, black professionals still encounter prejudice (Hacker, 1992).

Let's consider a few specific examples to illustrate these links between race, education, incomes, and job status. Because only half of black teenage males graduate from high school, and only about 7% graduate from college, their job choices and incomes as adults are more restricted than the job options and incomes of black females. Given their limited educations, many African and Hispanic American youths eventually end up in the least desirable, lowest paying jobs. Although representing 12% of all workers, African Americans represent only 3% of the doctors, lawyers, or engineers but 25% of the maids, janitors, orderlies, and cab drivers. At the other extreme, more than 40% of Asian American teenagers eventually graduate from college. As a result, they usually end up with higher incomes and more prestigious jobs than other racial groups, with the exception of Jewish Americans. Although Asian Americans constitute only 2% of population, they earn more than 2% of the college degrees, especially in lucrative fields such as medicine, science, and engineering (Hacker, 1992).

So if we had to pick one single factor that usually predicts an adolescent's future job and income, it would be family income. On the other hand, our adult jobs and incomes depend on more than just how rich or how poor our families were. Most of us know of someone from a low-income family with poorly educated parents who has nonetheless become a financial success. And most of us also know of someone from a wealthy, well-educated family who has not achieved much despite the advantages he or she has been given. Why?

FAMILY ROLES AND ATTITUDES

As we're growing up, we become aware of the kinds of work our parents and stepparents do, how much or how little they work, and what their attitudes are about matters related to work and money. Aside from how much money or how much education the adults in our families have, they are continually conveying information to us as children about such matters as: What does a person need to do in order to find work they enjoy? Who or what is ultimately responsible for how well people do financially? What does it take to advance or to be well-liked at work? How important is it for a woman to have a job?

Of course we have no way of predicting what attitudes any particular adolescent is learning at home about work-related issues. But we can examine some of the vocational habits and attitudes of a nationally representative sample of 2,000 adults—attitudes and habits that are surely filtering down in some way to the adolescents in their families. According to these adults, petty theft, indifference, sexual harassment, lying, and laziness are the norm where they work. Most frankly admitted that they spend more than 7 hours a week goofing off at work. Almost half admit calling in sick regularly when they aren't. And most believe people at work get ahead through politics and cheating, not through dedication and hard work. Only 10% like their jobs; 70% feel no loyalty to their employer; and 75% do not give work their best effort. Most don't believe what their managers tell them, and 25% would compromise their personal beliefs in order to get ahead at work (Patterson & Kim, 1992).

Although we do not know how many teenagers share these kinds of beliefs and habits, we do know that the attitudes of the adults in a girl's family influence her vocational path. As girls are growing up, they acquire attitudes that affect their later vocational decisions. What girls see and hear at home does affect their future vocational decisions: Do they see the women in the family earning an income? If so, how do the women feel about working? Do they hear their mothers or stepmothers complaining about having to work or criticizing their husbands for not supporting the entire family? Does a girl see that her mother went to work only because a divorce forced her to?

In general, girls who grow up seeing the women in their families earning an income achieve more vocationally and financially than girls from homes in which only the men earn the money. Girls whose stepmothers and mothers have always taken their own jobs or careers seriously tend to prepare themselves for higher paying jobs than housewives' daughters. Because so few women have husbands who earn enough money to enable them to be full-time homemakers, most teenage girls are accustomed to seeing the women in their families go to work— at least part-time. But a woman's working, in and of itself, might have less influence on her daughter or stepdaughter than does the attitude she communicates about having a job. Some employed women make clear to the girls in their families that the husband or former husband should be providing all or most of the money. Even though her mother or stepmother works, a girl can be raised to believe that a woman's "real" job should only be to raise the children and that any income she earns is a favor, not a responsibility, to the family. As a consequence, many teenage girls still fail to prepare themselves adequately for a future job, assuming instead that a man will, and ought to, take care of them financially. In one 1990 survey of high-school girls, 80% were planning not to be employed after they got married, even though most of them had divorced mothers who had to work in order to keep the family afloat (Girls Count Project, 1994). So if the women in her family are either housewives or workers who resent having to hold jobs, a girl is less likely to consider her own future in the work force seriously (Barber & Eccles, 1992; Glickman, 1993; Gustafson, 1991; Lerner & Galambos, 1991).

Fathers and stepfathers also can influence a girl's vocational path, especially during the girl's adolescence. They can encourage or discourage her self-reliance, her seriousness about a future job, and her plans for economic independence. In general, women who are the most vocationally and financially successful were encouraged by their fathers or stepfathers to be assertive, ambitious, and financially self-reliant (Biller, 1993; Coulter & Minninger, 1993; Marone, 1989; Secunda, 1992; Snarey, 1993).

Fathers and stepfathers also influence boys' vocational paths. The men in a family usually have a greater impact than the women on a son's vocational decisions and attitudes. The teenage boy who usually gets the furthest in his future job and income is the one who has a father or stepfather who is actively involved in his life, especially during early childhood. In terms of their adult achievements, the most fortunate sons have fathers or stepfathers who are hard-working, self-disciplined, and self-motivated, even if they didn't get as far financially or vocationally as they would have liked in their own lives. These men help their sons by enforcing clear standards for mature, self-reliant behavior. Living with an adult male also seems to benefit both male and female children because the man teaches them, through the way the family functions, valuable lessons about authority and hierarchy—lessons they carry with them later into the workplace. That is, teenagers who live with an unmarried mother are less likely to learn how to control their aggressive and immature behavior, how to obey authorities, how to function in a hierarchical organization, and how to set limits and achieve goals on their own (Nock, 1988). As a result, teenagers who have grown up in fatherless families usually achieve less vocationally and financially, even when their mothers have a decent income and a good education (Biller, 1993; Corneau, 1991; Pittman, 1993; Snarey, 1993).

By observing how the adults approach their own jobs and by talking about work-related matters, adolescents are influenced by the adults they live with. For example, the educational and vocational achievements of nearly 3,000 young adults closely matched the expectations that their parents had for them 10 years earlier as high-school seniors. The parents' expectations were even more strongly linked to the son's accomplishments than to the daughter's (Poole, 1991). Likewise, 600 adults who as teenagers had planned to enter a job similar to their father's had usually accomplished this goal (Trice, 1991).

TEMPERAMENT AND EXPLANATORY STYLES

Another factor influencing an adolescent's future job and income is his or her temperament. As discussed in preceding chapters, from early childhood on, we each have certain characteristics that make it easier or more difficult for us to get along well with people. Those of us who are basically outgoing, calm, optimistic, lively, easygoing, even-tempered, self-disciplined, and self-reliant get along with co-workers, clients, customers, and bosses better than those of us who are introverted, moody, somber, pessimistic, overly excitable, aggressive, or impulsive. These aspects of our dispositions also affect how well we prepare ourselves for our future jobs and how we go about making our vocational decisions. Those of us who are extremely volatile, aggressive, or introverted tend to interpret situations, make decisions, and react to people in ways that interfere with our vocational success. For example, in job training programs, during job interviews, or on the job, we tend to fly off the handle too easily, overreact to criticism, adapt poorly to change and uncertainty, and behave in childish or aggressive ways when we get frustrated (Block, 1981; Chess & Thomas, 1993; Halverson & Kohnstamm, 1994; Kagan, 1989).

Some of us also have more problems at work as a result of our helpless or hostile explanatory styles. As you remember, explanatory styles are our ways of interpreting or explaining why good and bad things happen to us. Those of us with internal locus of control attitudes generally believe that we are responsible for most of the good and the bad that happens in our lives. Our ways of reasoning enable us to accept our fair share of the blame for what is not going well at work and to change things about ourselves in order to improve our situations. In contrast, those of us with external locus of control attitudes, or helpless ways of interpreting the world, blame other people and circumstances beyond our control for most of what happens to us. Given our cynical, helpless, or pessimistic styles of interpreting people and events, we are less self-motivated, less aware of our own shortcomings, and less willing to change aspects of ourselves in order to improve our situations or our relationships. At work, as well as at school and in our personal lives, those of us with these helpless patterns of thinking do not fare as well as those of us who have more honest, more accurate ways of interpreting what is happening in our lives (Bandura, 1991; Seligman, 1991).

Two specific examples illustrate these links between disposition, explanatory style, and vocational success. In a study that followed 171 people from early adolescence to the age of 40, those individuals with the most difficult temperaments achieved less, got along more poorly with people, and were more dissatisfied with their adult jobs than those who were more extroverted, emotionally stable, and easygoing. What is especially important is that these individuals were from upper, middle-class families, which suggests that their dispositions had as much or more influence than their parents' socioeconomic status (Block, 1971; 1981). Teenagers and young adults who have relatively internal locus of control attitudes also report being happier with their jobs and with their lives as full-time college students than do those with more helpless, pessimistic attitudes (Michalos, 1991; Strack & Argyle, 1990).

EGO DEVELOPMENT

In addition to temperament, an adolescent's level of ego development can also affect his or her vocational success. Two teenagers the same age with the same general intelligence can reason and behave in very different ways depending on their levels of ego development. Those with more mature egos generally reason and behave in ways that appeal to other people—people like job interviewers, employers, supervisors, and co-workers. The more advanced a person's level of ego development, the better he or she usually gets along with people. Compared to teenagers who might be very well educated, but who have immature ego development, teenagers whose egos are more mature have ways of thinking that help them get ahead at school and at work, including being able to: consider perspectives other than their own, recognize other people's motives, and accept advice or information that contradicts their own opinions. Young people with mature ego development are also better at admitting their own shortcomings and gaining at least some understanding of the motives underlying their own behavior. So even though an 18-year-old comes from a highly educated, high-income family, he or she might reason and behave in very immature, irrational, self-centered ways at work. And even though an 18-year-old comes from a poorly educated, lower-income family, he or she might be very mature and insightful about work-related matters (Damon & Hart, 1988; Gullotta, Adams, & Montemayor, 1990; Harter, 1990; Hauser, Powers, & Noam, 1991).

Remember, too, that our ego development during adolescence and early adulthood is partly determined by how each parent has related to us since early childhood. Even well-educated and financially successful adults might relate to a child in ways that interfere with ego development; and even adults with very little education or income can behave in ways that help their children reach very advanced levels of ego development. For example, a person with a master's degree in psychology might be too protective and indulgent as a parent, having undermined his or her teenage child's social maturity and ego development since early childhood. Regardless of income or education, adults who consistently refuse to tolerate a child's immature, aggressive, overly dependent, or impulsive behavior increase the odds of the child's eventual academic, social, vocational, and financial success (Asher & Coie, 1990; Baumrind, 1991; Marcia, 1991; Minuchin & Fishman, 1981; Parker, 1983).

The kinds of relationships we had with our primary caretaker and with other children when we were preschoolers are also pretty good indicators of our eventual success at work. Many teenagers and adults who do not get along well with people at work, or who do not live up to their intellectual potential, have been socially immature, withdrawn, and overly dependent on their mothers since early childhood. Young children who are allowed to remain overly dependent on either parent, or who are not taught the social skills necessary for getting along well with other children, often grow up to have the most problems with their employers and co-workers. Likewise, teenagers who have had an enmeshed relationship with either parent tend to have more problems at work as a result of their lack of initiative, over-reliance on others, poor self-discipline, and social immaturity. Many teenagers and young adults with difficult dispositions, as well as those who have an overly dependent relationship with either parent, lack an understanding of what makes themselves and others tick. They are generally unable to recognize or to understand the motives that underlie their own behavior or the behavior of the people they work with (Chess & Thomas, 1993; Franz, McClelland, & Weinberger, 1991; Kagan, 1989; Karen, 1994; Parkes, Stevenson-Hinde, & Marris, 1991).

For example, one study showed that teenage boys who were shy, irritable, explosive, impulsive, or ill-tempered achieved less financially and vocationally by the age of 40 than men who were more outgoing, calm, self-controlled, flexible, and easygoing as teenagers. Even when physical attractiveness and socioeconomic backgrounds were taken into account, the boys with the better dispositions came out ahead vocationally. Even at the age of 40, the males with the difficult dispositions lacked insight into their own behavior, withdrew from any mildly frustrating situation, and misinterpreted other peoples' suggestions as criticisms and demands—exactly as they had as teenagers (Caspi, Elder, & Herbener, 1990). Likewise, grown men and women who deal poorly with stress, uncertainty, or challenges at work often revert back to the ways they were allowed to behave with their mothers as young children—throwing temper tantrums, withdrawing, sulking, making themselves physically sick, or getting mad at others for what is actually their own fault (Karen, 1994; Parkes, Stevenson-Hinde, & Marris, 1991).

SOCIETY'S GENDER ROLES

As explained in preceding chapters, adolescents' vocational paths are profoundly influenced by gender roles, sexism, and gender stereotypes. At the high-school and college levels, most males are still preparing themselves for the jobs that males in our society have traditionally held—jobs that usually offer higher salaries and more chance for advancement than those most girls are preparing themselves for. At all age levels, nearly 80% of all women are still in "female" jobs as secretaries, sales clerks, teachers, and nurses. As shown in Table 11–1, most teenage and young adult workers are still entering gender-typed jobs. Even though females are more likely than males their age to graduate from high school, they still lag far behind in job status and incomes as adults. Women working full-time still earn only about 70 cents for every dollar men earn—about the same

How has your gender influenced your choice of jobs?

wage gap that existed 40 years ago. Even now, a woman with a college degree earns about as much over the course of her lifetime as a male with only a high-school diploma. The average female high-school graduate earns less than a male high-school dropout during her lifetime. Although more women and girls are now working than ever before, only 25% of them earn more than $20,000 a year, compared to nearly 50% of employed males (Faludi, 1991).

Why? The main reason is that teenage girls continue to prepare themselves for those jobs that pay the least and offer the fewest chances for advancement. Nearly 40% of all women and girls work in clerical jobs—a higher percentage than in the 1970s. Nearly 70% of the lowest paying jobs with our nation's largest employer, the federal government, are also held by females—a number that increased during the 1980s. During the same period, the percentage of women in the best paid government jobs declined to less than 1%. Female workers have made progress in many occupations, such as insurance adjustors, branch bank managers, and pharmacists; however, the pay and status of these jobs have fallen, and male workers are bailing out. Although more teenage girls are preparing for jobs as doctors, lawyers, and other higher paying professions, women's numbers in these professional jobs increased by only about 5% during the 1980s. For instance, male students still earn 75% of the doctoral degrees in business and 91% in engineering; and 75% of all college professors are male (Faludi, 1991; Sadker & Sadker, 1993).

Recent surveys from the 1990s show that many teenage girls still do not take their future roles as wage-earners seriously enough. Many are still preparing for life primarily as wives and mothers, not wage-earners. Regardless of race or socioeconomic class, a number of high-school and college girls consider getting a job much less important than being wives and mothers. Many still say they plan to work only "until I get married," or "until my first child is born." Many see themselves working only part-time "just to help out a little" or working only "after all of my children are grown up" (Girls Count Project, 1994; Holland & Eisenhart, 1991; Sadker & Sadker, 1993; Schulenberg & Goldstein, 1991; Sidel, 1990).

The point is not whether girls have the right to feel this way or whether they ought to value working as much as being wives and mothers. The point is that their feelings and their expectations about work, motherhood, and marriage do not fit the realities that lie ahead for virtually all of them. Too many young women and girls are ignoring the irrefutable statistics showing what awaits them: More than 50% of their marriages will end in divorce. Most of their ex-husbands will not pay any child support. Most of their children will live in poverty on only the mother's income. More than 80% of them will have to work in order to support themselves and their children, whether they are married or not. And unmarried mothers and their children have fallen faster into poverty than have other Americans during the past 20 years (U.S. Department of Commerce, 1994).

So the central question is: How can we do a better job of getting teenage girls to take their future roles as wage-earners more seriously? As shown in the preceding chapter, much more could be done in our schools. Teachers and counselors can do more to encourage female students to take their intellectual development more seriously, teach girls to be more outspoken and assertive, and see to it that female students catch up to the males in areas such as computer technology, math, and science. Our schools could also do a better job helping male and female students change their stereotypes about gender and work. For instance, when students are asked to "draw a picture of a scientist," the result is almost always a picture of a male. And in recent surveys of science and music textbooks, almost 70% of the pictures are of male scientists and musicians. Most college textbooks are also heavily biased toward presenting male accomplishments and male role models. At the high-school and college level, our schools still have a long way to go in terms of helping female students develop their skills and plan more realistically for their futures as wage-earners (American Association of University Women, 1992; Mortenson, 1991; Sadker & Sadker, 1993).

Beyond the schools, we also could do more to help young people envision and implement more expansive vocational and more realistic options for themselves. As mentioned in Chapter 6, Mattel Toys' talking Barbie had, among its prerecorded repertoire, this inspirational message: "Math class is tough." (Sadker & Sadker, 1993). In and of itself, of course, one math-phobic Barbie doll is not likely to change many little girls' lives. But toys are merely one of the hundreds of ways that we send sexist messages to young people about their future jobs. Reaching more Americans than any other single medium, television continues to feed young people inaccurate information about work, gender, and money. Just as a number of parents and teachers protested with letters to Mattel, so must all concerned individuals be vigilant and respond to inaccurate portrayals in the media. For instance, 80% of all women have jobs; more than 50% of marriages end in divorce; most families cannot get by on just one adult's income; and 90% of all single-parent families are headed by a woman—very few of whom are widows. But on prime-time family shows in the 1990s, young people see this picture: only 20% of the women have jobs; 60% of the single-parent families are headed by men; most single parents are widowed; and most families enjoy—on only the husband's salary—a middle- or upper-class lifestyle (Moore, 1992). Even though most teenagers see that their own families and their friends' families don't fit these television models, they are nonetheless being presented with distorted information about what work, money, and family life should, or could, or might be, "if only"—if only I marry the right man, if only I get the right job, if only I get lucky, if only I didn't have to . . .

PREPARING YOUTH FOR THEIR FUTURE JOBS

How can we do a better job preparing young people for their future jobs? How can we help the millions of young people who are too poorly educated or too unskilled to hold a steady job? How can we help those fortunate young people with a good education decide what kinds of jobs they are best suited for?

CHRONIC UNEMPLOYMENT

Especially among racial minorities living in our inner cities, unemployment has become a way of life for thousands of young people—many of whom have children of their own, even though they are still teenagers themselves. Most of these unemployed young people are high-school dropouts. Yet many have graduated from high school with such poor skills in math, writing, and reading that they are not qualified for even the simplest, lowest paying jobs. More than a third of African and Hispanic American teenagers who want a job cannot find work, compared to only 13% of the teenagers from other racial groups (U.S. Department of Labor, 1993).

Not only does their chronic unemployment result in the sapping of national resources, these young people pay a high emotional consequence as well. Unable to find work or keep a steady job, many young people turn to drugs and alcohol. Others become clinically depressed in their state of hopeless despair. As self-esteem falls, frustration rises along with violence, physical abuse of children and spouses, and crime. Young people who are unemployable or who have so few skills that they are permanently stuck in dead-end, low paying jobs are the most likely not only to commit crimes, but also to be the victims of violence. Lacking the self-esteem that comes from having a good job, young black males are especially prone to try to build self-respect by fathering children or becoming involved in the violent culture of street life (Anderson, 1992). To make matters worse, many unemployed young people are too embarrassed or too demoralized to seek help from those agencies or programs that might help them find work, while others do not realize that such programs or agencies even exist (Kieselbach, 1991).

VOCATIONAL EDUCATION AND JOB TRAINING

Fortunately, many innovative programs are succeeding in re-educating and retraining our least employable young people. Unfortunately, these programs are too few and far between to be reaching all but a few who need them. Examining a few of these exemplary programs, however, can at least give us a glimpse of what is possible.

Among the earliest and most creative vocational education programs that connected teenagers directly to the local business community was the Foxfire project in Rabun Gap, Georgia. As Insert 11–2 explains, Foxfire was one of the first programs to integrate the high-school curriculum with vocational projects in the community (Wigginton, 1985). Another model for integrating the high-school curriculum with "real life" experiences in the community is project REAL in North Carolina. Project REAL was designed to provide teenagers with an alternative to duplicating their parents' careers as poor miners, farmers, and mill workers. These students learn about business, math, and finances by developing a plan for establishing a small business of their own. Under the direction of school supervisors and local business people, the students set up businesses that fill real

Insert 11–2

The Foxfire Project

The Foxfire Project was founded in a small, Appalachian community in the mountains of Georgia during the 1960s as a way of getting high-school students more motivated to improve their reading and writing skills. The project initially began by having English students interview and photograph older citizens, then writing down the stories to preserve local history and folklore.

The result was the stunningly successful series of *Foxfire* books. Through the years, the students have established a furniture making business, written three more best sellers, and recorded an album of Appalachian music.

This outstanding vocational program has indeed lived up to it's name, Foxfire—a tiny organism that glows in the darkness of shaded mountain coves.

needs in the community and contribute to the community's economy. The start-up money for their businesses is provided by the school system. Once the business is on its feet, the students or the school can buy the company back and run it for their own profit. The oldest REAL project is the "Way Off Broadway Deli," owned by the four former high-school students who established it during their school days. Other businesses include a T-shirt shop, a boat rental business, a childcare center, a pig farm, and an ice cream parlor (Mathis, 1989).

In a more urban setting in Rochester, New York, Wegman's supermarket chain helps teenagers graduate from high school, learn job skills, earn money, and stay off

What experiences or people in your life have had an impact on your vocational plans?

drugs. Wegman's gives part-time jobs to those students who are at high risk for dropping out of school and gives them their own on-the-job mentor—a person who advises them on personal matters, drives them to and from work, helps them with their homework, and teaches them what they need to know at work. In return, the students promise to attend school regularly and not to use drugs. Those who stay in the program until they graduate are also awarded a $5,000 a year scholarship to any accredited college in the state (W.T. Grant Foundation, 1988).

The nation's largest shopping mall in Minneapolis-St. Paul is also being used as a vocational education center. The school system's original hope was to locate an elementary and high school in the mall itself, as it was being built. By locating the schools at the mall, it was hoped that adults coming to shop would also take classes to help them finish their own educations or advance their job skills. The idea was that adult students could leave their children in a childcare center operated by the high-school students. High-school students could also integrate their part-time jobs and their classes more easily if both were housed in the same complex. Although the idea fell through, a small area of the mall was built for classrooms for teenagers to attend business, economics, and vocational classes. After class they step out into the mall, have a quick snack, and head off for their internships in the mall under the direction of a shop manager (Walsh, 1994).

Unfortunately, the vocational programs in most of our high schools involve nowhere near the creativity or the connection to the real world of these programs. Poorly funded and understaffed, most of our vocational programs are run with outdated materials and equipment. Moreover, school districts where the poorest students live and youth unemployment is highest generally have the worst vocational programs. To help with the demands and the expense of state-of-the art job training materials, other countries, notably Japan and Germany, have reached out to their local businesses and industries. Like teenagers in these countries, more teenagers in our society could be trained in the places where they might eventually be employed—going into hospitals, offices, factories, restaurants, and other places of work as a routine part of school.

Of course, another major obstacle in vocational training programs is that most of our high-school students have such poor reading, writing, and math skills. Furthermore, three of every four jobs now require a worker with training beyond high school. In short, our young, poorly educated work force is a threat to the national economy because our ability to compete successfully in the world market is jeopardized. Yet we continue to spend nearly seven times more money to educate the 25% who are planning to attend college than to educate the 75% who are going directly into the work force. When it comes to helping teenagers make the transition from high school to work, we have been doing a pretty lousy job, especially in comparison to other advanced countries (Berlin & Sum, 1988; Educational Testing Service, 1990).

Realizing the gravity of the situation, in 1994 the U.S. Congress approved the School to Work Act—a bill that allocates $300 million a year for vocational and job training programs for young people. Top priority is to be given to those programs that link the school curriculum more directly to on-the-job training. This

Vocational Types and Job Choices

Artistic

____ creative, intuitive, expressive

____ prefers unstructured situations

____ independent and introspective

____ dislikes conformity

Suitable jobs: dancer, actor, musician, artist, author, stage director, composer.

Realistic

____ practical

____ rugged and robust

____ physically strong, well-coordinated, or athletic

____ weak in verbal or interpersonal skills

____ mechanically inclined

____ prefers solving concrete, not abstract, problems

____ not especially creative

Suitable jobs: engineering, farming, construction, tool designing, mechanic.

Intellectual

____ introspective and task oriented

____ unconventional

____ not especially sociable, maybe even shy

____ prefers thinking through problems to acting

____ intellectually self-confident

____ works well independently

____ reserved, curious and analytical

Suitable jobs: technical writer, researcher, scientist, psychologist.

Enterprising

____ verbally skilled and sociable

____ high energy level

____ assertive and outgoing

____ self-confident

____ enjoys power, status, and leadership

____ dislikes long periods of intellectual work

Suitable jobs: real estate agent, salesperson, political or business manager, television production.

Social

____ sociable and verbally skilled

____ group oriented and humanistic

____ likes to solve problems through feelings

____ avoids physical exertion and intellectual problem solving

____ enjoys training or advising others

____ idealistic, helpful and understanding

Suitable jobs: teacher, social worker, therapist, missionary.

Conventional

____ prefers well-structured environment

____ does not enjoy leading others

____ dislikes ambiguity

____ conscientious, obedient, orderly and calm

____ values status and money

Suitable jobs: book-keeper, clerical worker, financial analyst, traffic manager, banker

Source: J. Holland (1985). Making vocational choices. Englewood Cliffs, NJ: Prentice Hall.

legislation is specifically intended to improve the vocational skills of the 75% of high-school students who do not go on to college. The hope is that this new legislation will help our youngest workers catch up to people their age in other industrialized countries (Olson, 1994).

IDENTIFYING VOCATIONAL INTERESTS

Clearly, most teenagers and young adults do not have a great deal of choice in the jobs they eventually get. Nevertheless, a minority of young people are fortunate enough to have the family backgrounds and sufficient education to make a number of choices about their eventual life's work (Vondracek, 1991).

At the high-school and college levels, written tests are available than can help students identify their vocational skills and interests. These tests help students match their personalities, talents, and interests with the requirements of particular types of jobs. One of the most popular tests is the **Strong-Campbell Interest Inventory** (Campbell, 1974). A similar approach is to take a test that categorizes your interests by occupational type and then identifies particular jobs that should be well-suited for you. Perhaps the most well-known is **Holland's occupational types.** According to the formulators of these tests, answers to questions about personalities and interests can be used to identify one of six occupational categories: realistic, intellectual, enterprising, artistic, social, or conventional. As Insert 11–3 shows, once your personality or occupational type is identified, you can prepare yourself for certain types of jobs and steer away from others (Holland, 1985).

CONCLUSION

The jobs and incomes most of us end up with as adults are influenced by much more than our preferences or childhood fantasies. In part our vocational paths are influenced by aspects of our personalities, explanatory styles, and levels of ego development. Our paths are also affected by factors in our families over which we have little or no control as we are growing up: each parent's income and educational level, the relationship with our primary caretaker during preschool years, the limits and standards each parent reinforced, and our parents' expectations of us from early childhood onward. Finally, our vocational paths are affected by the quality of our vocational programs and by factors operating in the society at large such as racism and sexism. So even though adolescence might be the first time in our lives that we give serious thought to our future jobs, our vocational paths have been influenced by many forces throughout our childhood. Still, we must ask: How can we do a better job providing young people with the academic and vocational skills they will need to meet our country's economic challenges?

Review/Test Questions

1. In what ways does a family's socioeconomic situation affect its adolescents' vocational development?
2. What are the advantages and disadvantages of adolescents having part-time jobs?
3. How do race and gender affect adolescents' vocational choices and attitudes?
4. How is an adolescent's level of ego development related to his or her vocational development?
5. How can explanatory styles and temperament affect a young person's vocational path?
6. In what ways have adolescents' part-time jobs changed during recent decades?
7. What societal factors affect adolescents' vocational development?
8. How and why are most males' and females' vocational paths different?
9. How do the vocational roles and attitudes of each of the adults in an adolescent's family affect his or her vocational path?
10. What are some of the more creative approaches being implemented in vocational education and job training?
11. How do the educational skills of young workers affect the nation?
12. How does the quality of our young work force compare with that of other nations?
13. How does chronic unemployment affect young people?
14. What are occupational types, and how are they determined?
15. What is an interest inventory, and how is it used to help adolescents?
16. What are the Fair Labor Standards Act and the School to Work Act, and how do they affect adolescents?
17. In what ways can television affect teenagers' vocational choices and attitudes?
18. What are the best ways of guessing an adolescent's eventual job and income as an adult?
19. How much is a high-school or college education worth?
20. Concerning their education and vocational training, how have we treated students bound for college and those not bound for college?

Questions for Discussion and Debate

1. What factors influenced your vocational attitudes and choices? Be sure to take account of each of these: your early childhood relationship with your parents, your ego development, your race and gender, each parent's vocational path, and your family's socioeconomic situation.
2. How did your mother, stepmother, or other female relatives incorporate work into their lives? How did this affect your choices and attitudes?
3. As you were growing up, how did your favorite television programs portray the world of work, including men's and women's vocational roles?
4. How would you design a vocational curriculum for high-school students if money were no object?
6. What were the most beneficial vocational experiences you had as a teenager?

7. What were the advantages and disadvantages of your part-time job as a teenager? If you didn't have a job, how did that affect you?

8. Are you following the vocational path you thought you would follow when you were 14? Why or why not?

9. How would you categorize yourself on the basis of Holland's occupational types? How closely is your present career course matched to your type?

10. How have your explanatory style, temperament, race, and gender affected your vocational choices and attitudes? What do you wish had been different?

Glossary

Fair Labor Standards Act, p. 440

Holland's occupational types, p. 458

Strong-Campbell Interest Inventory, p. 458

References

American Association of University Women. (1992). *How schools shortchange girls.* Washington, DC: Author.

Anderson, E. (1992). *Streetwise.* Chicago: University of Chicago.

Asher, S., & Coie, J. (1990). *Peer rejection in childhood.* New York: Cambridge University Press.

Bachman, J., & Schulenberg, J. (1993). How part-time work relates to drugs use, problems behavior, and satisfaction among high-school seniors. *Developmental Psychology, 29,* 220–235.

Bandura, A. (1991). Self-efficacy, impact of self-beliefs on adolescent life paths. In R. Lerner, A. Petersen, & J. Brooks-Gunn (Eds.), *Encyclopedia of adolescence.* New York: Garland.

Barber, B., & Eccles, J. (1992). Long-term influence of divorce and single parenting on career goals. *Psychological Bulletin, 111,* 108–126.

Barton, P. (1989). *Earning and learning.* Princeton, NJ: Educational Testing Service.

Baumrind, D. (1991). Parenting styles and adolescent development. In R. Lerner, A. Petersen, & J. Brooks-Gunn (Eds.), *Encyclopedia of adolescence* (pp. 746–758). New York: Garland.

Berlin, G., & Sum, A. (1988). *Toward a more perfect union.* New York: Ford Foundation.

Biller, H. (1993). *Fathers and families: Paternal factors in child development.* Westport, CT: Auburn House.

Block, J. (1971). *Lives through time.* Berkeley, CA: Bancroft Books.

Block, J. (1981). Some enduring and consequential structures of personality. In A. Rabin (Ed.), *Further explorations in personality.* New York: Wiley.

Campbell, D. (1974). *The Strong-Campbell interest inventory.* Palo Alto, CA: Stanford University Press.

Caspi, A., Elder, G., & Herbener, E. (1990). Childhood personality and the prediction of life course patterns. In L. Robins & M. Rutter (Eds.), *Straight and devious pathways from childhood to adulthood* (pp. 13–36). New York: Cambridge University Press.

Chess, S., & Thomas, A. (1993). Continuities and discontinuities in temperament. In R. Robins & M. Rutter (Eds.), *Straight and devious pathways from childhood to adulthood* (pp. 205–220).

New York: Cambridge University Press.

Cole, S. (1983). *Working kids on working.* New York: Lothrop, Lee & Shepherd.

Corneau, G. (1991). *Absent fathers, lost sons.* Boston: Shambhala.

Coulter, B., & Minninger, J. (1993). *The father daughter dance.* New York: G.P. Putnam's Sons.

Damon, W., & Hart, D. (1988). *Self-understanding in childhood and adolescence.* New York: Cambridge University Press.

Educational Testing Service. (1990). *From school to work.* Princeton, NJ: Author.

Faludi, S. (1991). *Backlash: The undeclared war against American women.* New York: Crown.

Franz, C., McClelland, D., & Weinberger, J. (1991). Childhood antecedents of conventional social accomplishments in midlife adults. *Journal of Personality and Social Psychology, 60,* 586–595.

Fuligni, A., & Stevenson, H. (in press). Time use and achievement among American, Chinese and Japanese high-school students.

Girls Count Project. (1994). *Girls count in American's future, in tomorrow's work force.* Denver: Author.

Glenbard East Echo. (1984). *Teenagers themselves.* New York: Adama Books.

Glickman, R. (1993). *Daughters of feminists.* New York: St. Martin's.

Grant Foundation, W.T. (1988). *The forgotten half.* New York: Author.

Greenberger, E., & Steinberg, L. (1986). *When teenagers work.* New York: Basic Books.

Gullotta, T., Adams, G., & Montemayor, R. (1990). *Developing social competencies in adolescence.* Newbury Park, CA: Sage.

Gustafson, S. (1991). *Female life careers.* Hillsdale, NJ: Erlbaum.

Hacker, A. (1992). *Two nations: Black and white, separate, hostile, unequal.* New York: Charles Scribner's.

Halverson, C., & Kohnstamm, G. (1994). *The developing structure of temperament and personality from infancy to adulthood.* Hillsdale, NJ: Erlbaum.

Harter, S. (1990). Self and identity development. In S. Feldman & G. Elliot (Eds.), *At the threshold* (pp. 352–388). Cambridge, MA: Harvard University Press.

Hauser, S., Powers, S., & Noam, G. (1991). *Adolescents and their families: Paths of ego development.* New York: Free Press.

Holland, D., & Eisenhart, M. (1991). *Educated in romance: Women, achievement and college culture.* Chicago: University of Chicago Press.

Holland, J. (1985). *Making vocational choices.* Englewood Cliffs, NJ: Prentice Hall.

Kagan, J. (1989). *Unstable ideas: Temperament, cognition and self.* Cambridge, MA: Harvard University Press.

Karen, R. (1994). *Becoming attached.* New York: Time Warner.

Kieselbach, T. (1991). Unemployment. In R. Lerner, A. Petersen, & J. Brooks-Gunn (Eds.), *Encyclopedia of adolescence* (pp. 1187–1198). New York: Garland.

Lerner, J., & Galambos, N. (1991). *Employed mothers and their children.* New York: Garland Publishing.

Lewko, J. (1987). *How children and adolescents view the world of work.* San Francisco: Jossey Bass.

Mabry, M. (1989, December 18). Inside the golden arches. *Newsweek,* pp. 46–48.

Manning, W. (1990). Parenting employed teenagers. *Youth and Society, 22,* 184–200.

Marcia, J. (1991). Identity and self-development. In R. Lerner, A. Petersen, & J. Brooks-Gunn (Eds.), *Encyclopedia of adolescence* (pp. 529–534). New York: Garland.

Marone, N. (1989). *How to father a successful daughter.* New York: Fawcett.

Mathis, N. (1989, June 7). Way off Broadway. *Education Week,* p. 15.

Michalos, A. (1991). *Life satisfaction and happiness: Global report on student well-being.* New

York: Springer Verlag.

Minuchin, S., & Fishman, H. (1981). *Family therapy techniques.* Cambridge, MA: Harvard University Press.

Moore, M. (1992). The family as portrayed on prime time television. *Sex Roles, 26,* 41–61.

Mortenson, T. (1991). *Equity of higher educational opportunity for women, Black, Hispanic and low income students.* Iowa City, IA: American College Testing.

Mortimer, J. (1991). Employment. In R. Lerner, A. Petersen, & J. Brooks-Gunn (Eds.), *Encyclopedia of adolescence* (pp. 311–318). New York: Garland.

Nock, S. (1988). The family and hierarchy. *Journal of Marriage and the Family, 50,* 957–966.

Olson, L. (1994). President signs school-to-work transition law. *Education Week, 13,* 1.

Parker, G. (1983). *Parental overprotection: A risk factor in psychosocial development.* New York: Grune & Stratton.

Parkes, C., Stevenson-Hinde, J., & Marris, P. (1991). *Attachment across the life cycle.* New York: Tavistock/Routledge.

Patterson, J., & Kim, P. (1992). *The day America told the truth.* New York: Plume.

Pittman, F. (1993). *Man enough: Fathers, sons and the search for masculinity.* New York: G.P. Putnam's Sons.

Poole, M. (1991). A contextual model of professional attainment. *Counseling Psychologist, 19,* 603–624.

Sadker, D., & Sadker, M. (1993). *Failing at fairness: How America's schools cheat girls.* New York: Macmillan.

Samuelson, R. (1992, August 31). The value of college. *Newsweek,* p. 75.

Schulenberg, J., & Goldstein, A. (1991). Gender differences in adolescents' career interests. *Journal of Research on Adolescence, 1,* 37–61.

Secunda, V. (1992). *Women and their fathers.* New York: Delacorte Press.

Seligman, M. (1991). *Learned optimism.* New York: Random House.

Sidel, R. (1990). *On her own: Growing up in the shadow of the American dream.* New York: Viking.

RELIGIOUS DEVELOPMENT

CHAPTER OUTLINE

KEY QUESTIONS ADDRESSED IN THIS CHAPTER

1. How religious are American adolescents and their parents?
2. How is an adolescent's religious affiliation associated with education, income, region, race, and gender?
3. Which factors influence adolescents' religious beliefs and practices?
4. How much influence does religion have on adolescents' social behavior and attitudes?
5. In what ways have adolescents' religious beliefs and practices changed in recent decades?
6. What are many religious organizations doing in order to better meet the needs of adolescents and their families?
7. How do adolescents cope with death and dying?
8. How do religious beliefs and practices typically change from childhood through adolescence?

ADOLESCENTS AND RELIGION

How religious are adolescents today? What influence does religion have on their behavior? Are adolescents any more or less religious than teenagers were in the past? How do adolescents' conceptions of, and ideas about, spirituality and morality differ from those of young children?

LIMITATIONS OF THE RESEARCH

Questions such as these, intriguing as they are, have been difficult for researchers to answer. Most of our information about religious views and practices have come from adults or college students, seldom from adolescents and even more rarely from young children. When we do gather information from adolescents, what often emerges is more a picture of their parents' religious beliefs and practices and less a picture of the adolescent's. Until children are old enough to leave home, they are often obliged to adopt the religious practices of older family members. Some parents require their teenage children to attend religious services even when they have made clear that they don't want to. Consider, for example, surveys in which teenagers report attending religious ceremonies weekly, an indication that might lead us to believe that they are quite committed to their religion. However, such attendance might reflect their parents' rules or values more than it does the teenagers' commitments or beliefs. So gathering information from young adults or older teenagers who are no longer living at home probably yields a truer picture of how young people feel and behave with regard to religion (Benson, Donahue, & Erickson, 1989).

Several other factors also make it difficult to answer questions about adolescents and religion. Researchers have not studied the same group of children as they age to see how their religious views change. Nor do we know what kinds of experiences or which factors influence how children and adolescents perceive religious matters. Not many studies have addressed how our family incomes, education, race, or friends' beliefs affect our religious views as we age. And very little has been determined regarding the effects of geographical location, school, or personality on one's religious views. It would be interesting to know how adolescents' religious beliefs and practices are related to their overall intelligence, self-esteem, and maturity in social and moral reasoning—none of which we presently know. On the whole, we have been limited to asking adolescents which religion they belong to, how often they attend activities or services sponsored by a religious institution, and how often they pray or think about spiritual matters. Moreover, we have not had reliable ways of checking to see how closely their answers on surveys match their actual behavior. Most of us probably tend to exaggerate our religious commitment in ways that flatter us around researchers and surveyors. All and all then, very few studies have focused on children's or adolescents' religious beliefs and practices (Benson, Donahue, & Erickson, 1989).

CHANGES FROM CHILDHOOD THROUGH ADOLESCENCE

On the basis of the limited information we do have, it seems that our religious views do change as we move through childhood and adolescence. Many of these changes reflect our more mature ways of reasoning about moral and social issues during adolescence and early adulthood (Kohlberg, 1984; Kohn, 1990; Kurtines & Gewirtz, 1991; Piaget, 1965).

Most adolescents have more abstract notions about God and spirituality than they did as young children. Most teenagers no longer envision God as an actual person who exists in some physical space somewhere out in the heavens. Our moral reasoning enables most of us as teenagers to grasp more abstract principles, such as justice and mercy, and also enables us to grasp the concept of a spirit or a spiritual guide that has no physical form. Most young children, however, envision God in very concrete, physical terms. Indeed even those children who say there is no god are able to draw pictures of what a god would look like if there was one. And their drawings are quite diverse and creative—white gods, black gods, big gods, large handsome gods, and ugly, tiny gods. Although young children envision God in very concrete, human terms, most of them can speculate about a number of complicated spiritual questions such as: Where did God come from? How long will the world will last? Also noteworthy is that not all young children envision God as big and strong. Children who are worried or depressed discuss and draw pictures of God as weak, small, hostile, or vulnerable (Coles, 1990).

When asked why they believe there is a God, young children also reason in less abstract ways than do adolescents. Young children rely more on what those in authority tell them to believe. Many say they believe in a deity because "the Bible says so" or "because my daddy says there is." But adolescents rely on more rational thinking and less on what authorities tell them. So a teenager might decide to believe in God because "the universe is too orderly and too complex to have just happened this way by accident." During adolescence most of us are also modifying our religious beliefs as we talk with people and encounter information that contradicts our childhood notions. By the end of adolescence, most of us are also less involved in religious activities than we were as young teenagers (Benson, Donahue, & Erickson, 1989; Fowler, 1981).

These religious changes reflect the changes in reasoning that occur as we age. Most adolescents think in more complex, more mature ways about moral and social issues than they did as young children. Insert 12–1 summarizes some of these differences in the moral and social reasoning of children and adolescents. As our reasoning skills become more advanced, we get better at discerning complex issues, as well at judging them from more than only one perspective. Rather than merely agreeing with what authorities say, most of us as adolescents are more willing to question religious authority. So as our moral reasoning advances, we are more willing to reject certain aspects of our religious upbringing and to embrace aspects of other religions. As teenagers, we are usually less willing to naively accept the rules and punishments handed down by those in power without examining the contradictory and complex assumptions underlying them (Kohlberg, 1984; Piaget, 1965).

Given their different levels of social and moral reasoning, some adolescents are better than others at being empathic and tolerant toward people with different religious views. Teenagers with arrested ego development or with certain personality disorders are seriously impaired in their ability to reason about moral or social matters. Those teenagers with arrested ego development typically think and respond in ways that are self-centered, narrow-minded, inflexible, judgmental, and self-righteous. Confronted with information that contradicts their beliefs,

Insert 12–1

Immature Moral Reasoning

According to the work of Jean Piaget and Lawrence Kohlberg, the following characteristics describe adolescents whose general ways of reasoning and behaving are egocentric and child-like. These ways of thinking and behaving are referred to as **arrested ego development, moral realism,** or **preconventional reasoning.**

Absolutist or Dualistic

Interpret situations, solve problems, or pass judgment in terms of direct opposites and absolutes

Close-Minded

Reject information or opinions that contradict theirs without considering new data

Defensive

Rationalize and use defense mechanisms rather than admit mistakes or apologize

Egocentric (Self-Centered)

Inconsiderate of other people's feelings

Inflexible: Brittle Ego

Adapt poorly to new or changing circumstances or to new information

Intolerant or Critical

Expect others to live up to their high ideals but quick to reject, punish, and criticize others

Judgmental or Punitive

Quick, harsh in judging or punishing others without considering the situation, motives, past or overall patterns of behavior

Naive or Gullible

Unable to recognize the motives underlying other people's behavior

Self-Righteous or Hypocritical

Unwilling to judge self by high standards applied to others

Single-minded or Simplistic

Unable to see more than one solution or perspective

Stereotyped Reasoning

Judge and categorize people on basis of stereotypes and isolated incidents

Stubborn

Refuse to listen to others' opinions or beliefs

Unempathic or Insensitive

Unable to consider others' feelings and perspectives

Unforgiving

Judge others by rigid, high standards; reluctant to forgive

these adolescents usually react defensively and cling to their beliefs even more desperately. Their immature reasoning skills make them quick to stereotype people, slow to recognize their own faulty reasoning, and uncomfortable with anyone or anything that calls their own beliefs or behavior into question.

In contrast, teenagers with more mature reasoning can respond from a more tolerant, forgiving, compassionate, and open-minded position. Instead of reasoning in dualistic, absolutist ways as many children do, more mature teenagers can see the shades of gray, the "what ifs," and the "maybes," in discussing or acting upon religious matters. As Insert 12–2 illustrates, in religious or spiritual matters, teenagers

---

Insert 12–2

How Mature is Your Moral Reasoning?

According to psychologists who study moral development, the following statements represent the least mature moral reasoning. The higher your score, the more immature your moral reasoning. How would you rate yourself in terms of your behavior and attitudes as a 16-year-old?

1 = very much like me   10 = not at all like me

_____ 1. I obey rules mainly because I'm afraid of being caught and punished.

_____ 2. I respect and obey those in authority without questioning them.

_____ 3. I think about myself first, others second.

_____ 4. I obey rules mainly to get rewarded or recognized.

_____ 5. I uphold the rules of society or religious institutions even when they contradict my beliefs.

_____ 6. I live my life mainly by trying to live up to other people's expectations.

_____ 7. I make moral decisions mainly on what others believe and approve.

_____ 8. I basically try to avoid changing the established order of things.

_____ 9. I put the individual's needs second to the society's.

_____ 10. I believe that no matter what society you live in, the rules for right and wrong should be the same.

_____ 11. I think that society's laws should be the ultimate moral authority.

_____ 12. I do not find it difficult to integrate my religion's moral teachings with my own ideas about ethical or moral matters.

_____ 13. I believe there is a clear "right" or "wrong" morally if you just study the situation carefully enough.

_____ 14. I do not believe it is all right to break laws simply because they violate one of my ethical principles.

_____ 15. I think the motives for a person's crimes or sins are irrelevant to how they should be punished.

with the most mature levels of reasoning are tolerant, broad minded, and willing to judge themselves and other people by the same set of standards.

RELIGIOUS AFFILIATION AND INVOLVEMENT

DENOMINATIONS

The major Protestant faiths are Baptist, Methodist, Episcopal, Presbyterian, and Lutheran. The term **evangelical** refers to those conservative Protestant denominations that adhere to a very literal translation of the Bible. Among these evangelical denominations are the Assemblies of God, Brethren, Church of Christ (Christian Scientists), Holiness, **Jehovah's Witnesses,** Pentecostal, and Seventh Day Adventists. At the other extreme are the **Unitarians,** who are among the most socially liberal, well-educated worshipers in the United States. Their members are Christians, non-Christians, and agnostics who believe in religious tolerance and who accept a wide range of personal lifestyles. Finally there are two groups who identify themselves as nonreligious. The **agnostics** do not believe that the existence of a god or an afterlife can either be proved or disproved; and the **atheists** are convinced that neither a god nor an afterlife exists (Kosmin & Lachman, 1993. Unless otherwise cited, all statistics and information in the remainder of this chapter are from this source).

Within certain religions are groups referred to as sects, rather than as denominations. A **sect** is a dissenting religious group that tries to preserve its spirituality by isolating its members from outside influences. Sect members believe in a fixed, unquestionable set of truths handed down and interpreted by a small, select group of leaders. A sect usually exercises close control over its members. Among others, the **Seventh Day Adventists** and the **Amish** are sects that usually educate their children from kindergarten through high school in their own schools and live, work, and socialize only within their own community.

As shown in Figure 12–1, nearly 90% of American teenagers and their families consider themselves to be Christians. Of these Christians, about 25% are Catholics and the rest Protestant. The largest Protestant denomination is the Baptist church with nearly 1.2 million members in the United States. Another 7% to 8% of American youth claim to be agnostics or atheists. Approximately 3% are Jewish, and 5% are Hindus, Muslims, or Buddhists. Contrary to the notion that large numbers of people belong to "New Age" groups, these churches attract no more than 28,000 Americans. So if you had a nationally representative group of 10 teenagers, five would be Protestant, three Catholic, one non-Christian but a member of a religion, and one agnostic or atheist.

As explained in preceding chapters, most teenagers adopt their family's values (Benson, Donahue, & Erickson, 1989). This holds true with religion—the percent of adolescents in each religious faith or denomination closely mirrors that of the adult population. A teenager's religion and denomination are usually closely

Figure 12–1

Adolescents' religious affiliations

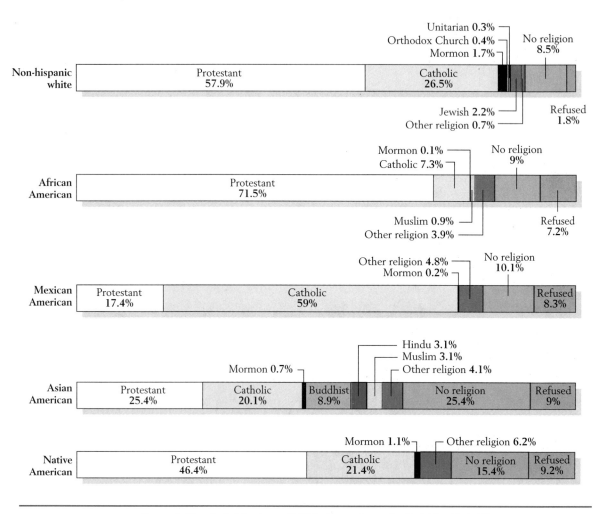

Source: R. Kosmin & S. Lachman (1993). *One nation under God.* New York: Harmony.

associated with four factors: where they live, the family's educational and financial status, family's social values, and family's political views.

REGIONAL DIFFERENCES

Although our society is diverse, our religious faiths are not evenly dispersed across the country. Members of the two largest religious faiths, Roman Catholics and Baptists, live primarily in two parts of the country. Most Baptists live in the South and most Catholics live in New England. The concentrated strength of the Baptists in the South contrasts with their relative lack of power in other regions of the country. The Baptist influence in the South, however, exerts considerable influence on adolescents living in the region, regardless of their religion. Perhaps most obvious is the influence on public education, which extends to such areas as textbook adoptions and the curriculum—particularly to sex education. As practiced in the South, Christianity is a relatively distinct religion based on an evangelistic, fundamentalist heritage that generally supports a literal translation of the Bible and a relatively conservative moral code. Most adolescents who are members of evangelical religions live in a southern state. Like most of their parents, most adolescents living in the South are more church oriented than are those in other sections of the country, hence the region's nickname—the "Bible Belt." Even beyond the South, however, families living in rural areas are usually more actively involved in their religions and more religiously conservative than are families in the suburbs and cities.

The denomination most evenly spread throughout the country is Methodist. Most other religions are, like the Baptist denomination, more or less concentrated in certain areas of the country. For example, most Lutherans live in North Dakota, South Dakota, and Minnesota. The most clustered are the Latter Day Saints, or **Mormons,** who comprise 70% to 80% of Utah's population. The 8% who are agnostics and atheists live mainly in the sparsely populated regions of the Pacific Northwest and the Southwest—Oregon having the highest percentage at 17% of its population.

EDUCATIONAL AND FINANCIAL DIFFERENCES

As you can see from Table 12–1, families from different religious groups often differ greatly in terms of wealth and education. For example, almost 50% of all Jewish and Unitarian adults are college graduates, but the figure drops to 5% of Jehovah's Witnesses and Pentecostals. Among our nation's two largest religious groups, twice as many Catholics as Baptists have college degrees. Because education and income usually go hand in hand, the rankings are similar for family income. Financially, teenagers from agnostic, Unitarian, Episcopal, Presbyterian and Jewish families are the most well-off, and those from Baptist and evangelical families are among the least well-off. In fact, in our society a person's religion is usually a better predictor than race of his or her educational achievements. For example, African American Catholics are 40% more likely to be college graduates than are African Americans Protestants. Perhaps surprising for a country where religious freedom has been a fundamental issue, the better educated, wealthier families are also the most likely to be agnostics.

On the whole then, teenagers who are the most religious and those with the most conservative views come from poorer, less well-educated families. Why? In part, low-income families tend to join more conservative churches because the economic instability and insecurity in their lives seems to attract them to more

| Table 12–1 |

Religion, education, and income

	Education	Employment	Income
	Percent college graduates	Percent working full-time	Median annual household income (in thousands of dollars)
Agnostic	36.3	63.5	33.3
Assemblies of God	13.7	48.8	22.2
Baptist	10.4	52.3	20.6
Brethren	11.4	46.2	18.5
Buddhist	33.4	59.4	28.5
Roman Catholic	20.0	54.3	27.7
"Christian"	16.0	51.8	20.7
Christian Science	33.1	40.1	25.8
Churches of Christ	14.6	47.2	26.6
Congregationalist	33.7	49.7	30.4
Disciples of Christ	39.3	55.4	28.8
Eastern Orthodox	31.6	55.1	31.5
Episcopal	39.2	52.6	33.0
"Evangelical"	21.5	47.0	21.9
Hindu	47.0	64.1	27.8
Holiness	5.0	49.9	13.7
Jehovah's Witnesses	4.7	44.1	20.9
Jewish	46.7	50.1	36.7
Lutheran	18.0	50.0	25.9
Methodist	21.1	49.6	25.1
Mormon	19.2	49.9	25.7
Muslim	30.4	62.5	24.7
Nazarene	12.5	48.5	21.6
No religion	23.6	60.5	27.3
New religious movements	40.6	63.4	27.5
Pentecostal	6.9	52.8	19.4
Presbyterian	33.8	48.8	29.0
"Protestant"	22.1	49.3	25.7
Seventh Day Adventist	17.9	46.0	22.7
Unitarian	49.5	52.7	34.8

Source: R. Kosmin & S. Lachman (1993). *One nation under God.* New York: Harmony.

structured, more authoritative religious groups. Also, middle- and upper-income families seem to be less interested in religions that emphasize highly emotional services and rituals that may appear odd to people in more mainstream religions. Lower-income families are more likely to join religious groups whose services include personal testimonies before the entire congregation, highly emotional baptism rituals, miracle cures fostered by "the laying on of hands," communication from a spirit via "speaking in tongues" (glossolalia), or demonstrations of faith by handling poisonous snakes.

SOCIAL AND POLITICAL DIFFERENCES

On the whole, adolescents from the most well-educated families are also raised with the most liberal social and political attitudes—attitudes reflected in whichever religious beliefs they hold. For example, the most well-educated groups, Jewish Americans and agnostics, are also the most likely to register to vote, to support pro choice, and to favor legal rights for gays. Evangelical Protestants are among the most poorly educated and are more likely to oppose movements such as gay rights, ordination of women clergy, or pro choice. Remember, though, within almost any religion some congregations are much more liberal than others.

Religious groups also differ concerning gender roles, not only within the religion but also within the family and society. Teenage girls whose families belong to the more conservative faiths are the most likely to forgo higher education and high-status jobs in order to be full-time housewives and mothers. For example, Jewish girls and women are generally more well-educated than are Protestant girls and women. Girls who are members of conservative religions generally marry younger and have more children than do girls from less religious families. Each religion's rituals also reflect the roles it espouses for males and females. Two of our society's most liberal religions, the Unitarians and Quakers, ordain heterosexual and lesbian women. At the other extreme, Catholics and Orthodox Jews refuse to ordain women, regardless of their sexual orientation.

RACIAL DIFFERENCES

As shown in Figure 12–1, race also plays a large role in adolescents' religious affiliations. Some of these differences might surprise you. Contrary to many stereotypes, most Asian, Irish, and Native American teenagers are Protestants. African American adolescents are the most overwhelmingly Protestant of any racial group. Like their elders, almost half of all black teenagers are Baptists, and another 15% are members of evangelical Protestant faiths. Nearly 80% of black adults are church members who regularly attend services and who believe that religion plays a very important part in their daily lives. Fewer than 5% consider themselves nonbelievers. In contrast, only 50% of white adults report this degree of religious commitment, and nearly 20% of Asian and Native Americans consider themselves nonreligious.

The commitment of so many black adolescents and their families to their church, however, is easy to understand given the role the church has played historically in these communities. Compared to other Christian faiths, the black church has played the most overt role in political struggles. Black church leaders led the way in the Civil Rights Movement and voter registration drives. During the 1960s, at least 93 black southern churches were bombed or burned because of their pastor's or members' involvement in desegregation and voter registration. In many poor, inner-city neighborhoods, the church remains a strong political institution that often provides day care for the young and the elderly, emergency food distribution, and literacy programs.

African Americans have also become more involved than have other races in the Islam or **Muslim** faith. The religious movement known as the Nation of Islam was led to prominence during the 1960s by the son of a black Baptist minister from Georgia, Elijah Muhammad. Although the membership is only 30,000 nationwide, its influence is especially strong with young black males living in inner cities. The black Muslims have often come to the public's attention through such renown members as Muhammad Ali, the rap group Public Enemy, and the films *Malcolm X* and *Do the Right Thing.* Part of the appeal to these young men seems to be the subservient roles that Muslim women are expected to assume toward men. This doctrine, in turn, seems to offer young black males, especially those living in poverty, a certain boost in self-esteem. The Muslim faith also demands, however, that its followers give up alcohol and pray three times a day—expectations perhaps lost on some of its younger members. In any event, nearly 1% of African American teenagers, mainly males, are black Muslims.

In contrast to African Americans, most Hispanic American teenagers are Catholic, like their parents. However only about one fourth of these teenagers actually practice their faith. Part of the reason is that the Catholic Church in the United States is often very different from Catholicism as practiced in their home countries. Another reason is that Protestantism has such a strong following in the United States that many Hispanics opt to downplay or to relinquish their Catholicism (Gonzalez & LeVelle, 1988). Hispanic adolescents whose families are from Caribbean countries have a somewhat unique religious tradition, although most officially identify themselves as Catholics. The Caribbean tradition includes elements of non-Western religions and a clergy of men and women who combine the skills of priest, social worker, herbalist, and psychotherapist. One such practice, "Santeria," is a folk religion often linked with voodoo. It is estimated that there are several hundred thousand U.S. followers, most of them near Miami, Florida. Needless to say, these Santerias have found it easier to be accepted by simply labeling themselves "Catholics."

Many Caribbean immigrants also have something in common with Native American adolescents—concealing their traditional religious beliefs and practices. Many ancestral tribal religions were considered "pagan" by white Americans, and Native Americans were persecuted for practicing them. As a consequence, many Native Americans claimed to have stopped practicing their native religions, although they continued worshiping in secrecy. Although 70% of young Native Americans identify themselves as Christian, nearly a third claim no religious affiliation or say they are members of an undefined religion.

Asian American adolescents are more likely than teenagers from other racial groups to be agnostics or atheists. As noted, the most well-educated and most financially well-off Americans are generally the least religious. With the exception of Jewish Americans, Asian Americans have the highest educational and financial status of any group. These two groups are also the least likely to be religiously active. Many Asian Americans also have a Buddhist heritage in which gods, the supernatural, and the belief in an afterlife are not considered essential to living a religious, spiritual life. Although fewer than 10% of Asian Americans are Buddhist, this ancestral tradition might help explain their more secular approach to spirituality in the United States.

Jewish adolescents and their families also have a unique cultural and religious heritage. Many Jewish American teenagers come from well-educated families that describe themselves as culturally Jewish, but as agnostic or nonreligious. Nearly half of all Jewish Americans who married after 1980 married a non-Jewish person, and nearly a third of their children are being raised as members of neither parent's religion. Only one fourth of the children in Jewish-Gentile homes are being raised in **Judaism,** and nearly 40% are raised as Christians. Because a number of these Jewish-Christian marriages are second marriages, some of these adolescents are growing up in families where siblings or stepsiblings practice different religions.

Gender Differences

Among all Christian faiths in the United States, females are generally more involved in religion than are males. Christian females not only attend religious services more often than do Christian males, but are also more likely to believe in translating the Bible literally, to pray, and to say that religion plays an important part in their daily lives. Likewise, nearly twice as many males as females say they are agnostics. Among Jewish and other non-Christian religions, however, the males slightly outnumber the females. These gender differences are not especially surprising, though, since the children's religious upbringing is usually the woman's responsibility in most families in our society. Most females are also socialized to take more interest in those matters that involve serving or doing good or being connected to others. In this sense then, "masculinity," at least as our culture has defined it, makes it more difficult for many boys and men to embrace religious doctrines that call for submissiveness, humility, and emotionality.

Religious Involvement

Although most American teenagers say they are Christians, there is often quite a gap between being affiliated with a particular religion and actually practicing that religion (Bachman & O'Malley, 1992; Kosmin & Lachman, 1993).

Since most teenagers adopt their families' religious practices, let's examine adults' religious habits. More than 90% say they believe in God; more than half say they pray at least once a day; and 40% say they attend a worship service every week. Nearly 50% report being modestly or nominally religious, and another 20% describe themselves as committed to their religions. Yet, in follow-up studies, researchers find far fewer worshipers in the pews than were indicated on the surveys. Apparently many of us exaggerate our activity levels in church when answering the pollsters. Like adults, teenagers today are less likely than were teenagers in the 1970s to attend religious services, read scripture, pray, or participate in a religious organization. In a 1980 nationwide survey of high-school seniors, nearly 45% said they attended a religious service once a week, compared to only 30% in 1990. In 1990, 15% of the seniors had never attended a religious service of any sort (Bachman & O'Malley, 1992).

Those adolescents who actually do make a formal commitment to a religious organization usually participate in a public service or ritual that serves as an initiation and celebration. These initiations usually involve attending special classes for several months prior to the service in order to learn beliefs and ritual procedures. Catholic and Lutheran adolescents attend Catechism classes in preparation for their **confirmation** service. Jewish adolescents attend classes to study Hebrew and the Torah (the first five books of the Bible) with their rabbi in preparation for their **bar mitzvah** (son of the commandment). In many religions, these rituals have been altered to allow teenage girls to participate equally with boys. For example, except among Orthodox Jews, girls are allowed to prepare and participate, like boys, in a **bat mitzvah** (daughter of the commandment).

Because most adolescents practice as their families do, it is noteworthy that most adults in our society have undergone religious changes in recent years. Compared to adults in earlier decades, many adolescents' parents and stepparents see religious institutions and the clergy as less essential for having a spiritual life. More adults now believe they can find spiritual guidance and comfort on their own without attending religious services or asking advice from the clergy. In other words, most of us believe we can be religious without attending services and without being actively involved in a religious organization. The result is that more teenagers have grown up in homes with adults who practice their own private kinds of spirituality. Most teenagers also see that the adults they live with do not turn to religious leaders for advice on personal issues such as divorce, contraception, or abortion. Women are also more likely than ever before to question or to leave their religion over such issues as refusing to ordain women or objecting to a woman's right to choose whether to terminate a pregnancy. Adults also do more "shopping" before joining a church or synagogue; and they are more willing to switch faiths or congregations if they are dissatisfied. In fact, nearly a third of Americans switch denominations during their lifetime (Kosmin & Lachman, 1993).

In response to these changes, the clergy has generally become more casual and down to earth, both in dress and in conducting services. Giving up clerical collars and robes for more casual, more secular clothes, many members of the clergy have also tried to make their services more entertaining and less ritualized. Music during services has become more contemporary, and services are designed so that the audience is more actively involved. Some churches have also used technology and advertising more to their advantage. Some "mega-churches" attract as many as 14,000 people to their entertaining weekend services. Some of these churches' brochures offer creative programs for children, teenagers, single adults, unmarried parents, and the elderly. One such church in Florida allows latecomers to hear the start of the service from outdoor speakers in the parking lots. This church also features choirs accompanied by orchestras and well-known Christian musicians who are well-paid from the church's multimillion dollar budget (Kosmin & Lachman, 1993).

All in all, most adolescents are growing up in families that don't emphasize or publicly practice religion as in former years. We might well wonder then: How does religion, or the lack of it, affect adolescents' behavior? Are religious teenagers less likely to use drugs, commit crimes, cheat in school, or have sex than their nonreligious peers?

RELIGION AND ADOLESCENT BEHAVIOR

SOCIAL BEHAVIOR

As mentioned, the teenagers most involved in a church and its religious practices generally come from lower-income homes, live in rural areas, and have less well-educated parents. This being the case, it is difficult to say whether being religious, in and of itself, is the underlying reason for any differences we might find in their behavior. For example, religious teenagers do not use as many hard drugs or drink as much as nonreligious teenagers (Benson, 1990; Brownfield & Sorenson, 1991). But alcohol and hard drugs are also harder to come by and harder to use without getting caught in rural areas. Hard drugs and alcohol also cost money, which is scarce in lower-income families. In other words, it is hard to sort the influence of religion itself from the influences of family incomes, rural or urban settings, and adult supervision. With this in mind, let's look at some particular teenage behaviors and attitudes that do seem to be related to religion.

In general, teenagers who regularly attend religious services are somewhat less likely to have sex than are other teenagers. The exception is African American teenagers, whose rates of church attendance and teenage pregnancy are both high. Religious teenagers also seem to drink less and use fewer drugs than do those who rarely or never attend religious services. On the other hand, the connections between religion and behavior are not especially strong in many cases. For example, in a survey of 3,000 teenagers who reportedly attended church weekly, fewer than half were virgins and nearly a third had been "binge drinking" (more than five drinks during a brief span of time) within the past 2 weeks (Benson & Eklin, 1990). On the whole, religion is not as strong a predictor of drug, alcohol, or tobacco use, delinquency, or sexual activity as are family income and race (Benson, 1990; Benson, Donahue, & Erickson, 1989).

Perhaps part of the reason why the links between religion and behavior are not stronger is that so few religious institutions directly address issues such as sex, alcohol, and drugs. Many African Americans have urged their church leaders to take a more aggressive role against teenage pregnancies and out-of-wedlock births (Stevenson, 1990). Yet among all races, most religious institutions are apt to ignore those social issues that most concern teenagers. In one survey of 3,000 church-going adolescents, half said they had spent less than 2 hours in all their years at church discussing any issue related to sex, alcohol, or drugs (Benson & Eklin, 1990).

KNOWLEDGE AND TOLERANCE

We might also wonder how religion affects adolescents' tolerance for people who do not share their particular religious beliefs. "America for Americans" has often meant "America for Protestants." Like many of their elders, many adolescents are at least moderately intolerant of religious differences. As the statements of the 16-year-old author in Insert 12–3 testify, some adolescents have a difficult time tolerating or understanding others' religious views (Shoenberger, 1993). Some religions are also much more zealous and insistent than are others in recruiting new members (Collings, 1991; Kosmin & Lachman, 1993).

Insert 12–3

An Adolescent's Views on Religious Ignorance and Intolerance

This summer I was one of 20 teens who spent five weeks at the University of Wisconsin at Superior studying acid rain with a National Science Foundation Young Scholars program. Represented among us were eight religions. It was amazing, given the variety of backgrounds, to see the ignorance of some of the smartest young scholars on the subject of other religions.

On the first day, one girl mentioned that she had nine brothers and sisters. "Are you Mormon?" asked another girl, who I knew was a Mormon herself. The first girl, shocked, replied, "No, I dress normal!" She thought Mormon was the same as Mennonite, and the only thing she knew about either religion was the Mennonites don't, in her opinion, "dress normal."

My friends, ever curious about Judaism, asked me about everything from our basic theology to food preferences. "How come, if Jesus was a Jew, Jews aren't Christian?" my Catholic roommate asked me in all seriousness. Nobody was deliberately rude or anti-Semitic, but I got the feeling that I was representing the entire Jewish people through my actions. I realized that many of my friends would go back to their small towns thinking that all Jews like Dairy Queen Blizzards and grilled cheese sandwiches.

The most awful thing for me, however, was not the benign ignorance of my friends. Our biology professor said that they had to make sure the EPA got its money's worth from the study—he "wouldn't want them to get Jewed." I was astounded. The professor had a doctorate, various other degrees, and seemed to be a very intelligent man. What scares me about my whole visit was that I never met a real anti-Semite or a malignantly prejudiced person.

Many of the people I met had been brought up to think that Jews, or Mormons, or any other religion that's not mainstream Christian were different and that difference was not good. Difference in America is supposed to be good. Ignorance was the problem I faced this summer. By itself, ignorance is not always a problem, but it leads to misunderstandings, prejudice and hatred.

—Chana Schoenberger, age 16, Bethesda, MD

Source: C. Shoenberger (1993, September 20) Getting to know about you and me. *Newsweek*, p. 8.

CONVERSION EXPERIENCES

Some older adolescents who have not been religious throughout their teenage years undergo what is known as a **conversion experience.** These adolescents may reject their family's religion and join a sect, such as the Hare Krishna, that sometimes involves moving to a members-only community. Other teenagers and adults, suddenly convert back to their family's Christian faith, an experience sometimes referred to as being **"born again."** Most conversion experiences are relatively sudden, intense, or abrupt—changes that are highly charged with emotion and zeal. Most conversions also occur after other young members of the sect or religion have encouraged the adolescent to convert (Collings, 1991).

Conversion experiences are not new. In fact, conversion is one of the most studied topics in religious research. In general, adolescents who have conversion experiences are troubled by some unresolved conflict or crisis in their lives. In the midst of their troubles, the new religion and its members offer guidance and solace. Most conversion experiences occur during a time when the person can find no meaning in life or when troubles seem insurmountable. By "making a decision for Christ" or by adopting a new religion, these adolescents are usually attempting to resolve intense conflicts in their lives (Collings, 1991).

DEATH AND BEREAVEMENT

Part of the reason why many young people and their families are not more religious may be the failure of many religious institutions to help people deal with their day-to-day problems. Ironically, these often involve death and dying. That is, the focus of most religious institutions regarding death and dying is the afterlife, rather than the questions that trouble adolescents: How do I deal with knowing that I am going to die from this fatal disease? How do I relate to my dying parent? How do I deal with my brother's suicide? How can I deal with my anger over my best friend's having been killed by a drunk driver? Often our religious institutions do too little to help young people with issues related to death or dying (Becker, 1973; Kosmin & Lachman, 1993).

Most adolescents first encounter death by having to deal with the loss of a family member or a friend. But thousands of adolescents with life-threatening or fatal conditions have to deal with death and dying at another level—having to face and prepare for their own impending death. Although we do not have a great deal of research on the topic, the few studies that are available offer us important information about how teenagers deal with death and dying.

DEATH OF A LOVED ONE

As Insert 12–4 illustrates, many adolescents are forced to confront death when a parent or sibling dies. The ways in which these teenagers react to death or terminal illness are as varied as their situations and their personalities. No single,

Insert 12–4

Living With Your Parent's Death

"I am my mother's slow moving footsteps as she walks down to the hospital to get her cancer check-up, her utter despair as she finds the results, and her trouble finding the words to tell Dad. I am the slow and reluctant boy who takes a couple of Mom's things to the hospital where she will stay before the operation. I am Mother's loneliness in her hospital bed as she patiently awaits Father's next visit. I am her joy to find us with him as he walks near her bed, her curiosity to learn of the day's events, and her sorrow as a very short visiting period ends. I am my mother's frail, ever-weakening body as she slips into a coma. I am the sparkling tear that runs down her stiff face as the words of a friend's letter roll out. I am the disbelief of everyone as the news reaches us that Mom has died. I am not the pounds of make-up that hide the painful expression on her cold, still face, nor am I her whole shell that lies in an open casket, but I am her spirit walking, somewhere about the room. I am the sorrow of all as the casket is being lowered into the ground. I was my mother. I am her spirit."

—16-year-old son

Source: J. Krementz (1982). *How it feels when a parent dies.* New York: Knopf, p. 80.

predictable pattern applies to dying, grieving, or recovering. Some become withdrawn and depressed in ways that are obvious to all concerned. Others become angry, acting out their grief in hostile, defiant ways. As they grieve, many teenagers develop physical symptoms of stress, such as insomnia or chronic headaches. Still others seem to rebound and recover too quickly, acting within weeks of the death as if nothing had ever happened. Years later, however, many of these young people relive the experience and grieve intensely (Balk, 1994; Cook & Oltjenbruns, 1989; Harris, 1991; Krementz, 1982).

An adolescent's reaction also partly depends on the circumstances of the loved one's death. If a friend or family member dies from a fatal illness, the adolescent lives with the knowledge of the impending death for months or years. In these situations, it's possible to say goodbye in intimate, loving ways, to take time to make amends or apologize for past misunderstandings, and to discuss ways to cope with the impending death. Adults who were teenagers when their sibling died from cancer report that the prolonged illness and death gave them a special maturity and drew the family closer together (Martinson & Campos, 1991). Other teenagers whose friends have died from cancer say their lives are profoundly changed by the maturity and insight they developed while their friend was dying. Ironically, some teenagers say that a friend's death matured them in ways that set them apart and made them feel more withdrawn around other teenagers. Most teenagers who have experienced someone's death also say they have a deeper appreciation of life and closer bonds with people afterward (Davies, 1991; McNeil, 1991; Oltjenbruns, 1991).

On the other hand, a death that comes after a prolonged illness can also leave adolescents feeling guilty. Some adults, who were teenagers when their sibling died from a prolonged illness, still feel guilty years later for not having treated their brother or sister better before they died (Fanos & Nickerson, 1991; Harris, 1991). In most families the child who is sick for months or years before dying consumes parents' time and attention, leaving the other children feeling neglected or jealous. When a terminally ill child finally dies, the other siblings sometimes feel a certain relief when the all-consuming task of attending to the dying child is, at long last, over. But these short-lived feelings of relief are often replaced later by guilt or shame. Therapists and family members need to reassure these teenagers that their feelings of resentment or jealousy are not evil, hateful, or unloving. Their reactions are understandable, predictable responses to the end of the arduous task of caring for a dying member of the family (Klein & Schleifer, 1993; Weiss, 1994).

When a friend or family member dies in an accident, is murdered, or commits suicide, adolescents are usually left with a different set of issues to deal with. In these cases, adolescents are often guilty or troubled for not having set things straight or for having been angry, or inattentive, or unkind before the person died. Unexpected death leaves no time to say goodbye or make amends. Suicides are especially troubling for the many adolescents plagued by a lingering guilt that they might somehow have prevented the loved one's death (Weiss, 1994).

When someone dies, the adolescent must not only cope with the death itself, but also with the somewhat strange and uncomfortable reactions of other people. After someone in an adolescent's family dies, friends and other people often act in ways that make the grieving teenager feel even worse. At one extreme, people can respond by being overly solicitous and overly sensitized to the death in ways that leave the teenager feeling like an emotional cripple. In their efforts to be kind, friends might behave as though the bereaved teenager will have a break-down at the slightest remark linked to the deceased. They might shower the youth with such questions as: "Are you okay?" "Do you feel up to doing this with us?" "Do you feel up to doing this homework yet?" Although a certain amount of sensitivity is certainly in order, too much continual concern or pampering can make bereaved teenagers feel excruciatingly self-conscious. At the other extreme, teenagers and other people can feel so uncomfortable around someone whose loved one has died that they withdraw. As one teenager whose father died explains, "I guess my friends didn't know what to say because they felt kind of embarrassed, so they'd just look at me and no one would say hello. Then it got to be a little too much—like no one would say the word 'father' around me. So I finally transferred to a different school"(Krementz, 1982). In a society in which coping with death and dying are talked about so little in religious institutions and families, most of us are poorly prepared for helping adolescents deal with this aspect of living.

ADOLESCENTS WITH FATAL ILLNESSES

Society in general, and religious institutions in particular, seem even less equipped to deal with terminally ill adolescents. It is difficult enough to help teenagers deal with the death of a loved one. But it is even more difficult for many of us to realize that some teenagers need our help preparing for, and living with the knowledge of, their own impending death. Modern medicine and technology have enabled us to keep children with fatal illnesses and life-threatening conditions alive for longer periods of time. As a result, many children who otherwise would have died shortly after birth or in early childhood are now reaching adolescence before they die. For most dying teenagers, the illness or condition has been part of their lives for many years and they are fully aware that death is pending. Teachers, friends, and family members are also living with the reality that the teenager they love is facing death.

Perhaps no one has been as helpful as Dr. Elisabeth Kubler-Ross in providing us with information about dying patients. In her years of work with dying patients, Kubler-Ross found that dying children and their families usually experience a cycle of feelings as they come to terms with the impending death. Most people's first reaction to the news that they, or their loved one, is going to die is denial: "The doctors must have made a mistake." "This can't be happening to me." Once the reality settles in, the next reaction is usually anger: "This isn't fair! Why me? What did I do to deserve this?" The dying person's anger, of course, can be extremely hard on family members and friends who are trying to be understanding and comforting. Once the anger subsides, depression and withdrawal often set in. Resigned to the impending death, not only the patient, but also the family and friends, usually go through a period of depression in which they pull away from one another in their grief and confusion. During this time, the dying adolescent is the most vulnerable to feeling isolated and abandoned. This can also be the hardest time for their teenage friends or family members to reach out and reaffirm they're standing by. Before dying, the teenage patient and the family usually reach the final emotional stage—acceptance. When this occurs, a certain peacefulness replaces the tension, depression, and anger.

It is during this final stage that dying adolescents, their relatives, and their teenage friends often discuss such matters as what the patient wants at his or her funeral. Rather than skirting these issues or pretending they are not dying, teenagers whose families encourage them to discuss these issues without embarrassment seem most at peace. When the family is not denying the reality, dying teenagers often discuss such matters as who they want their special belongings given to and what they want done at their funeral. Most dying teenagers also want honest, straightforward answers to questions about the details of their death: "How much will it hurt? How will I know when death is near? What will happen to my body?" If there is honesty and openness about what is happening in this final stage, these adolescents and their families and friends have the chance to express their anger, to make their apologies, and to express their sadness in ways that help them grieve and go on with life (Kubler-Ross, 1969, 1983; Powell, 1982).

DEATH EDUCATION

Given the secrecy, discomfort, and silence that usually surround death and dying in our society, some public institutions are trying to educate young people in ways that religious institutions have failed to do. Among others, Kubler-Ross advocates giving young children and adolescents honest information about death and dying. Most adolescents are relatively naive when it comes to such questions as: What happens to a body after death? How do different societies bury and grieve for their dead? How should we behave around someone when a member of their family dies? What does a dead body look like? What are you supposed to say or do at a funeral or a wake? Kubler-Ross is also among those who believe that children and adolescents should be more involved in the realities of death as they age. For example, when someone they know dies, young children should be encouraged to say their farewells to the dead person in private, view the body at the funeral home, and be at the graveside along with everyone else while the casket is lowered into the earth. Cultures in which children are more directly involved in these kinds of experiences as they are growing up generally are more at ease with death and dying than in a society like ours where death and dying are dealt with so much less openly (Cook & Oltjenbruns, 1989; Kubler-Ross, 1983).

Aside from religious institutions and families, schools can help adolescents and younger children learn more about death and dying. Some high schools are exploring these issues within the regular curriculum through specially selected readings, films, and guest speakers. Other schools offer special workshops and discussion groups through the school's guidance office on such topics as coping with a death and talking to a relative of a suicide victim (Hetzel, 1991).

Another option is that pursued by the Boston Children's Museum, which put together the first exhibit to offer young children and teenagers an array of experiences focused on death and dying. Young children had to be accompanied by a parent, and the more explicit sections were preceded by descriptions that allowed the parent and child to choose whether to view those particular exhibits. The exhibit included an open coffin, funeral music from around the world, tombstones, a videotape of a dead mouse's body being eaten by insects, embalming chemicals, and burial clothes. As a general theme, the exhibit tried to dispel myths about death. As one puppet in a videotaped show said, "Dying isn't like a vacation. It's not like going to visit your grandmother. You don't come back again." As you might expect, given the level of discomfort with death and dying in our society, many parents were very critical of the exhibit: "How dare you present this topic in a children's museum!" Others, however, were appreciative: "Thank you for being brave enough to do this." Children themselves also evaluated the exhibit: "I hate thinking about death." "I liked this exhibit because I love my grandmother and the doctor said she might die and I don't want her to, but this makes it a little easier" (Weld, 1984).

CONCLUSION

Religion does play some part in most adolescents' lives—at least to the extent that most teenagers identify themselves with a particular religion. However, most teenagers are not especially active in religious organizations. The role religion plays in an adolescent's life depends largely on the family's practices, the part of the country the family lives in, the family's income, the parents' educations, and the adolescent's race and gender. In general, teenagers whose families are the most well-educated and most well-off financially have the most liberal religious views. But regardless of their socioeconomic class, most adolescents' religious views and practices mirror those of their parents and stepparents.

Many religious institutions are not addressing the needs of most adolescents. Issues such as sex, drugs, dying, suicide, and grieving are often ignored in our churches, temples, and synagogues. All in all, there is still much to be done in terms of meeting the spiritual needs of young people in our society.

Review/Test Questions

Cite specific statistics or research findings to support your answers.

1. How religious are today's adolescents?
2. How is an adolescent's religious affiliation associated with education, income, geographical region, and race?
3. What could account for most females being more religiously active than are most males?
4. How much does religion influence adolescents' social behavior?
5. What are four or five specific ways in which adolescents' religious practices or beliefs have changed in recent decades?
6. How are some religious organizations trying to better meet adolescents' needs?
7. To what religions do most adolescents belong?
8. Which adolescents are most likely to be atheists or agnostics? What do these terms mean?
9. How does our religious thinking relate to our social, moral, and ego development?
10. What do these terms mean and give a specific example of each: evangelical, conversion experience, and sect.
11. What are a "bar mitzvah" and a "bat mitzvah"?
12. How do our religious beliefs and practices generally change from childhood through adolescence? Why?
13. How do adolescents react to death and dying?
14. What are some of the suggestions that have been made for helping adolescents cope better with death and dying?
15. Which adolescents are the most likely to have conversion experiences?

Questions for Discussion and Debate

1. How are your religious or spiritual beliefs different from what they were when you were a teenager?
2. What accounts for the changes in your religious beliefs since you were a young child?
3. What influence did your religion or your spiritual beliefs have on your behavior as a teenager?
4. In what ways might religious institutions attract more adolescents?
5. How much of a role has religion played in your life since you were 12? Why?
6. As an adolescent, how did you react to religious beliefs and practices that differed from your own?
7. What experiences have caused you to question some of your own religious beliefs or practices?
8. How have your views about funerals, death, or fatal illnesses changed as you have aged? Why?
9. As an adolescent, what were your views or thoughts on death and dying?
10. If you have ever known someone who died, what impact did his or her death have on you?

Glossary

atheist, p. 469
agnostic, p. 469
Amish, p. 469
bar mitzvah, p. 476
bat mitzvah, p. 476

born again, p. 479
conversion experience, p. 479
evangelical, p. 469
Jehovah's Witness, p. 469
Judaism, p. 475

Mormon, p. 471
Muslim, p. 474
sect, p. 469
Seventh Day Adventist, p. 469
Unitarian, p. 469

References

Bachman, J., & O'Malley, M. (1992). *Monitoring the future.* Ann Arbor: University of Michigan Social Research Institute.

Balk, D. (1994). Death and adolescent bereavement. *Journal of Adolescent Research, 24,* 37–44.

Becker, E. (1973). *The denial of death.* New York: Macmillan.

Benson, P. (1990). *The troubled journey: Portrait of 6th–12th grade youth.* Minneapolis, MN: Lutheran Brotherhood.

Benson, P., Donahue, M., & Erickson, J. (1989). Adolescence and religion: Review of the literature from 1970–1986. *Research in the Social Scientific Study of Religion, 1,* 153–181.

Benson, P., & Eklin, C. (1990). *Effective Christian education: National study of Protestant congregations.* Minneapolis, MN: Search Institute.

Brownfield, D., & Sorenson, A. (1991). Religion and drug use among adolescents. *Deviant Behavior, 12,* 259–276.

Coles, R. (1990). *The spiritual life of children.* Boston: Houghton Mifflin.

Collings, J. (1991). *The cult experience.* New York: Thomas.

Cook, S., & Oltjenbruns, K. (1989). *Dying and grieving.* New York: Holt, Rinehart and Winston.

Davies, B. (1991). Long term outcomes of adolescent sibling bereavement. *Journal of Adolescent Research, 6,* 83–96.

Fanos, J., & Nickerson, B. (1991). Effects of sibling death during adolescence. *Journal of Adolescent Research, 6,* 70–82.

Fowler, J. (1981). *Stages of faith.* New York: Harper & Row.

Gonzalaz, R., & LeVelle, M. (1988). *The Hispanic Catholic in the U.S.* New York: Northeastern Pastoral Center.

Harris, E. (1991). Adolescent bereavement following the death of a parent. *Child Psychiatry and Human Development, 21,* 267–281.

Hetzel, S. (1991). Loss and change: New directions in death education for adolescents. *Journal of Adolescence, 14,* 323–334.

Klein, S., & Schleifer, M. (1993). *It isn't fair: Sibling of children with disabilities.* Westport, CT: Greenwood Press.

Kohlberg, L. (1984). *The psychology of moral development.* New York: Harper & Row.

Kohn, A. (1990). *The brighter side of human nature: Altruism and empathy.* New York: Basic Books.

Kosmin, R., & Lachman, S. (1993). *One nation under God.* New York: Harmony.

Krementz, J. (1982). *How it feels when a parent dies.* New York: Knopf.

Kubler-Ross, E. (1969). *On death and dying.* New York: Macmillan.

Kubler-Ross, E. (1983). *On children and death.* New York: Macmillan.

Kurtines, W., & Gewirtz, J. (1991). *Moral behavior and development.* Hillsdale, NJ: Erlbaum.

Martinson, I., & Campos, R. (1991). Adolescent bereavement. *Journal of Adolescent Research, 6,* 54–69.

McNeil, J. (1991). Helping adolescents cope with the death of a peer. *Journal of Adolescent Research, 6,* 132–145.

Oltjenbruns, K. (1991). Positive outcomes of adolescents' experience with grief. *Journal of Adolescent Research, 6,* 43–53.

Piaget, J. (1965). *The moral judgment of the child.* New York: Free Press.

Powell, C. (1982). *Adolescence and the right to die.* Washington, DC: American Psychological Association.

Shoenberger, C. (1993, September 20). Getting to know about you and me. *Newsweek,* p. 8.

Stevenson, H. (1990). The role of the African American church in education about teenage pregnancy. *Counseling and Values, 34,* 130–133.

Weiss, M. (1994). *Conditional love: Parents' attitudes toward handicapped children.* South Hadley, MA: Bergin & Garvey.

Weld, E. (1984, October 3). Seeing death as part of life. *The Boston Globe,* p. 15.

13

DATING AND SEXUALITY

CHAPTER OUTLINE

KEY QUESTIONS ADDRESSED IN THIS CHAPTER

1. How do dating, having sex, and getting married affect adolescents' lives?
2. How do physical abuse and date rape affect adolescents?
3. How sexually active and sexually responsible are most adolescents?
4. Which factors influence an adolescent's sexual behavior and decisions?
5. What are the negative consequences for many sexually active teenagers?
6. How can we reduce teenage pregnancy, sexually transmitted diseases, and out-of-wedlock births?
7. How is the psychological and physical development of gay and lesbian adolescents different from that of heterosexual teenagers?

Perhaps no other topic receives as much attention or creates as much conflict and confusion in our society as teenage sexuality. As a nation, we have reached general agreement about the ages we believe young people are ready to get a driver's license, go to college, get a job, get married—even go to war. Legal requirements or restrictions apply to all these activities. Determining when a child is ready to leave home or become a parent is less formally recognized, even though some legal ramifications still apply. Nevertheless, most of us recognize that by their late teens most people should be able to live on their own, and we firmly believe "standing on their own two feet" for at least *some* period should precede their starting families.

But agreeing on the age at which a young person is old enough to have sex, buy contraceptives, or abort an unwanted pregnancy is much more difficult. To be sure, teen pregnancy is nothing new. Unfortunately, what is new is the astonishing increase in unwed teenage parents. Yes, adolescents have been having sex and conceiving babies since time immemorial. But for thousands of years in most societies, taboos and traditions against unwed motherhood have pressured most pregnant girls to get married. Others secretly terminated their pregnancies or left their communities long enough to conceal the pregnancy and arrange a quiet adoption. Compared to the "good old days," however, in our society more teenagers than ever engage in premarital sex. Predictably enough, the results are higher than ever numbers of out-of-wedlock babies and correspondingly high levels of sexually transmitted diseases—diseases that affect not only the infected mothers, but also can damage their babies. In turn, our society is confronted with social, moral, and legal issues that we have not been able to resolve.

Adolescent sexuality also raises a number of disturbing and controversial issues in regard to dating and steady relationships: What are the risks involved in going steady as very young adolescents? What are we going to do about physically abusive boyfriends and date rape among teenagers? How are teenage boys supposed to learn when "No" means "No," and how can girls learn to avoid risky dating situations? Teenage sexuality also draws our attention to sexual orientation: Why are some adolescents gay? How does being gay affect an adolescent's development? Why are some teenagers so hostile or abusive toward their gay and lesbian peers? To consider such questions, let's begin with the research on dating and adolescents' attitudes about cohabitation, marriage, and parenthood.

ADOLESCENT DATING

DATING AND COURTSHIP

Dating during adolescence is an essential part of healthy development in our society. Not only does dating help us become more socially skilled, it gives us opportunities to learn how to be sexually and emotionally intimate with another person. By dating we are able to develop aspects of our identities that otherwise would not be discovered or cultivated. By being emotionally, romantically, and sexually

Adolescents' Sexual Experiences

| **Adolescent Males** | **Adolescent Females** |

Adolescent Males

"When I was in junior high school I found that my fantasies were a lot more pleasurable than the reality. In my imagination I could make things work perfectly and be with just who I wanted. But the reality wasn't anywhere near as great. I was awkward with girls and had trouble getting it on with them."

"Everyone's going around wondering why they aren't having the greatest sexual experiences in the world and nobody's saying anything about it."

"It's like a game. My male friends told me that when a girl says "no," she doesn't really mean it. So if she doesn't yell out loud or hit me over the head with it, I'm not supposed to listen."

"My girlfriend and I were very mature for 14-year-olds. She brought a willingness to explore our sexuality together while I encouraged her to think of our relationship as a long-term thing. Together we said "I love you" for the first time and together we made love for the first time. I remember almost backing out when we were about to have sex, and she told me straight out that she wanted me to make love to her."

Adolescent Females

"When I was 16 I learned about sex all the wrong ways. I never knew what I was doing and never got any pleasure out of it. I had to get drunk and stoned to get me through it."

"The first time I had sex I was lying there thinking: You mean this is it? Am I supposed to be thrilled by this? It wasn't that it hurt or anything because it didn't. It just didn't feel like anything to me. I figured there must be something wrong with me, so I didn't say a word to him."

"He had a good girl/bad girl complex where only bad girls wanted, enjoyed, and pursued sex. But here I was, as virginal as could be, and being very insistent about the fact that I wanted sex and lots of it."

"I couldn't believe I'd just had sex with someone. My parents never talked about sex, except my mother's innuendoes about it being bad. So I thought I was the worst person in the world."

Sources: R. Bell (1988). *Changing bodies, changing lives.* Boston: Random House.
A. Garrod & others (1992). *Adolescent portraits.* Boston: Allyn & Bacon.

involved with someone our age, we expand ourselves beyond what is possible through our relationships with family members and friends (Garrod & others, 1992; Miller, 1990; Padgham & Blyth, 1991; Savin-Williams & Berndt, 1990).

Before most of us start dating, we generally go through a period of having crushes on people we really don't know well. Our crushes are idealized fantasies that enable us to explore the possibilities of dating at a safe distance (Adams-Price & Greene, 1990). By age 15, however, most of us have started dating; and by 18, we have usually had at least one serious romantic relationship. However, the dating of early adolescence usually differs in several respects from that of late adolescence. Most young teenagers go on dates in small groups or with several other couples. But as they age, get drivers' licenses, and gain more freedom, fewer curfews, and more responsibilities, most teenage couples spend increasing amounts of time by themselves. In fact, older teenagers say they feel happiest and most satisfied with their lives when they are alone with their boyfriend or girl-friend. As they mature, teens increasingly make decisions about who they want to date more on the basis of personality and less on added status or popularity. In other words, as we age, most of us care less what other people think about who we date (Padgham & Blyth, 1991; Paul & White, 1991; Savin-Williams & Berndt, 1990).

Although very few teenage romances endure beyond adolescence, these rela-tionships are neither frivolous nor unimportant. Teenage couples can have a pro-found impact on each other's lives. They can also break one another's hearts in ways that teach them important lessons about themselves, about love, and about life. Indeed, teenagers say that problems with their boyfriends or girlfriends generally create more stress than events related to their families (Dornbusch & others, 1991). Tragically, the end of a romantic relationship can sometimes result in the deeply depressed or psychologically disturbed teenager's considering, attempting, and even accomplishing suicide (Harrington, 1994; Kaczmarek & Backlund, 1991).

Because dating is such an essential part of teenage development, not dating at all can be a symptom of serious psychological or emotional problems. Indeed, a number of older adolescents who have never dated have been found to be clini-cally depressed, or to have severe personality disorders or other emotional and developmental problems that require intensive therapy (Bornstein & Bruner, 1993; Weiner, 1992). Along these lines, the teenagers who never date or who have the most difficulty dating are those who have had problems in their social development throughout childhood. These teenagers often have too little self-confidence, social maturity, and self-reliance to even begin dating, let alone to maintain a steady dating relationship (Asher & Coie, 1990; Main, 1993; Parke & Ladd, 1992; Parkes, Stevenson-Hinde, & Marris, 1991; Savin-Williams & Berndt, 1990;).

So who do teenagers date? In general, they date those people with whom they have the most in common in terms of race, age, physical attractiveness, and fam-ily background. In other words, although interracial dating or dating someone from a very different economic background does occur, these couples are actually quite rare—which perhaps explains why they attract our attention. Moreover, most adolescents grow up in homes in which interracial dating and marriage are frowned upon. As discussed in Chapter 7, white, Hispanic, Asian, and Native American teenagers are more likely to date one another than they are to date black teenagers. Regardless of race, however, most teenagers grow up knowing that their families would rather they date and marry within their race. So despite all the efforts to reduce racism, when it comes to dates, sex, or marriage, very few of us socialize outside our race as adolescents or as adults (Hacker, 1992; Hallinan & Williams, 1989; West, 1994).

The next ingredient in the dating mix is physical appearance. Those girls and boys who look sexually mature at an early age tend to start dating somewhat sooner than other people their age. In part this might be because their hormones arouse interest in sex, and in part because people treat them as if they're old enough to start dating simply because they look older than they are (Padgham & Blyth, 1991; Phinney, 1990). Likewise, those teenage boys who are extremely short tend to date somewhat later than taller boys—partly because they tend to be less self-confident around girls and partly because females in our society tend to be more attracted to males of at least average height (Martel & Biller, 1987). On the other hand, unless a teenager is extremely unattractive, appearance does not prevent having close friends or dating (Adams, 1991; Coie, 1993).

Certain factors within the family are also related to adolescents' dating patterns. Teenagers who live with an unmarried parent tend to start dating and to go steady sooner than those who live with two married adults. This might be because their own parents started dating or got married at an especially early age. It might also be that the drawbacks of living with an unmarried parent, such as cramped or poor living space, motivate these teenagers to start dating at an early age as a way of getting away from home (Tasker & Richards, 1994). The family's cultural background can also influence when an adolescent starts dating. For example, Hispanic American teenagers tend to start dating later, but then marry earlier, than white teenagers; whereas African American teenagers tend to start dating earlier but marry later than Hispanics or whites (Augenbraum & Stavan, 1993). Finally, how satisfied parents and stepparents are with their own lives partially determines their reactions to the adolescent's dating. Parents who enjoy their own lives tend to be less bothered and less worried by their adolescent's dating than do parents who are unhappy (Lerner & Galambos, 1991; Silverberg & Steinberg, 1990).

Girls' attitudes about dating can also be affected by the way their parents integrate sex and romance into their adult relationships. Girls whose mothers and stepmothers obviously enjoy the sexual, romantic aspects of their own lives generally date and are relatively at-ease around boys without being too focused on dating at an early age. In contrast, those girls whose mothers seem embarrassed by or disinterested in the sexual, romantic aspects of their own lives tend to follow other paths. Some of these daughters become excessively focused on dating and marriage at an early age. Others continue dressing and behaving like young children who aren't interested in dating (Debold, Wilson, & Malave, 1992; Flaake, 1993; Tolman, 1991). The same generally holds true for girls and their fathers or stepfathers. If a man is comfortable with the sexual and romantic aspects of his life, and also approves of his daughter's or stepdaughter's dating, then the daughter is apt to feel more comfortable about dating and sexuality (Coulter & Minninger, 1993; Marone, 1989; Secunda, 1992).

Girls, however, are generally more interested than boys in the emotional than in the sexual aspects of dating. This tends to be true among gay and lesbian youths as well as among heterosexuals. This isn't to say that girls aren't interested in sex or that a girl isn't sometimes more interested in the sexual aspect of dating than her partner. But even among gay and lesbian youth, most girls are more interested than boys in creating emotional intimacy. And girls are usually more interested than boys in exchanging details about their lives and in expressing and examining feelings with the people they care about (Brown & Gilligan, 1992; Gilligan, Lyons, & Hanmer, 1990; Josselson, 1992; Maccoby, 1990; Richards, 1991).

MARRIAGE AND COHABITATION

Although most of us first date, fall in love, and have sex as teenagers, very few of us want to get married, become parents, or live with our boyfriend or girlfriend until we're older. Only 12% of teenage girls and 3% of teenage boys are married. The males also tend to wait longer to marry, and girls usually date and marry boys who are several years older than themselves. Hispanics are the most likely to marry as teenagers, and blacks are the least likely. Nearly one fourth of Hispanic girls marry before 20, compared to only 12% of white and 5% of black girls. More than half of older teenagers think it's a good idea to live with the person you love before getting married. Only 4% of all teenage girls, though, were living with their boyfriends in 1990. More than 80% of all teenagers are planning to get married and have children someday. But most males wait until they are 26, and most females until they are 24—which is 3 or 4 years later than most people married during the 1950s. Typically, the first baby comes 2 years after the wedding (Alan Guttmacher Institute [AGI], 1994).

RAPE AND PHYSICAL ABUSE

Date and Acquaintance Rape   One of the most devastating aspects of dating for too many teenage girls is being forced or coerced into having sex by a date, boyfriend, or male acquaintance. Teenage girls are raped by dates or boyfriends more often than any other age group. In fact, a female is four times more likely to be sexually assaulted by someone she knows when she is between the ages of 15 and 20 than at any other time in her life—typically by a male several years older than she (Levy, 1991). Estimates show that nearly one fourth of all teenage and college-aged women are forced into having sex against their will by someone they know (Smith, 1994). On college campuses, freshmen women are most often the victims of date rape (Bohmer & Parrot, 1993).

Certain teenage girls, however, are more at risk than others (Levy, 1991; Parrot, 1991; Warshaw, 1988). In general, girls who date many different boys and who engage in heavy drinking on their dates are most at risk of being sexually assaulted. Date rape is also more common among those who date athletes and members of all-male social organizations. In fact, on college campuses, fraternity pledges are the most likely of all male students to force a woman they know into having sex against her will. It is unclear whether this is because too many of these teenage males—most of whom are only a few months out of high school—

**Insert
13–2**

Date and Acquaintance Rape

"I was in my first semester in college. This guy was a football player. There was a party in our dorm with kegs and stuff. Even though I wasn't quite 18, they let me into the party. When he asked me to come back to his room—which was right down the hall from where all of us were—I thought there would be other people there. I kept telling him to stop and I was crying. He had a hand over my face. I was scared. Afterwards, I felt ashamed and dirty. He came to my room the next day and wanted to go out with me. Who would believe me?"

"Wait—time out!" This is not what I want!" And he said something like "this is what you owe me" because he had made me dinner."

"I was afraid to tell because there were so many places where I felt I could be judged. Why did I go with him? Why didn't I drive my own car? Why didn't I scream? Why didn't I know that he was this kind of guy?"

Source: R. Warshaw (1988). *I never called it rape.* New York: Harper & Row.

somehow feel pressured to prove a twisted concept of manhood, or whether it is because so much heavy drinking goes on in fraternities. Women who date college athletes are also more likely than those who do not date athletes to be sexually assaulted. Especially in situations where everyone is drinking, young athletes sometimes take advantage of their status on campus by assuming they have a right to have sex with any woman they please. Of the documented cases of gang rape by college students from 1980 to 1990, 55% were committed by fraternity members and 40% by athletes (O'Sullivan, 1991). This is not to say that a young woman should automatically feel safe simply because her date is not a fraternity member, athlete, or drinker. Nor is it fair to stereotype all fraternity members, or athletes, or drinkers as potential rapists.

Most young men who force a woman they know to have sex against her will do not believe that what they did was rape. To some, forcing a woman to have sex is rape only if the woman is beaten, fights back physically, or screams for help. Other males consider their behavior purely sexual, not as an act of violence or aggression. Still others rationalize their assault by saying that once a woman gets a man sexually aroused beyond a certain point, it isn't possible for him to stop himself. Others defend their assaults on the grounds that they had spent a lot of money on her or told the victim they loved her. Then, too, some say they were only acting the way men "are naturally supposed to act" whenever a woman says "No." Others claim to have become "confused" because their date dressed in a sexy outfit, acted flirtatious, or enjoyed foreplay, but then said she didn't want to go any further. Moreover, if the woman has ever voluntarily had sex with him before, a young man can be under the false impression that he cannot be found legally guilty of raping her on any of their future dates (Bohmer & Parrot, 1993; Grauerholz & Koralweski, 1991).

As a way of reducing date rape, many high schools and colleges have implemented education programs (Bohmer & Parrot, 1993; Deich & Weiner, 1986). These approaches include teaching female students how to avoid dangerous situations, especially those that involve heavy drinking or drug use, and how to convince a date that "No" means "No." These programs are also trying to teach young men how to distinguish among flirting, arousal, and consent. Among the most radical attempts to stop date rape is the "Sexual Offense Policy" at Antioch College, written by students in 1992. Its purpose is to empower female students to become equal partners in determining sexual behavior. For example, the policy states that if sexual conduct is not mutually and simultaneously initiated, then the person who is initiating the activity is responsible for getting the other person's verbal consent. Asking "Do you want to have sex with me?" is not enough. Consent must be granted for each specific act as the level of intimacy increases (Antioch College, 1992). Although its critics believe that Antioch's program is carrying "sexual correctness" too far, the fact remains that most teenage and young adult couples need more guidance in order to reduce the number of sexual assaults among dating couples.

Physical Abuse   In addition to being sexually abused by a date or boyfriend, too many teenage girls are also physically abused by their boyfriends—a nationwide problem that affects women of all ages. A male beats up his present or former girlfriend or wife every 12 seconds in the United States. And in 1992, 3,000 women were murdered by their current or former boyfriends and husbands (Jones, 1993). Teenage girls who are physically abused by their boyfriends generally share several traits. In most cases, the boyfriend's abusive behavior begins as verbal outbursts of jealousy—insulting and screaming at her for such things as talking to another boy, wearing her skirt too short, or going off with her girlfriends without first asking his permission. A girl who eventually is physically abused, for example, might first be forbidden by her boyfriend to wear anything but baggy sweat clothes or be kept under surveillance by his cruising around her home during the evening to make sure she isn't out with anyone except him. A physically abusive boyfriend typically drinks a lot, talks in demeaning ways about women, and is physically aggressive toward people other than his girlfriend. Although the girl is frightened or concerned early on in their relationship by his verbal outbursts, she often blames herself for his bad temper or excuses his verbal assaults by telling herself that his jealousy comes from his loving her so much. Unfortunately, these girlfriends too often end up "loved to death" (Jones, 1993; Levy, 1991).

SEX AMONG TEENAGERS

Sexual Behavior

Fortunately, most teenagers' romantic relationships do not involve sexual or physical abuse. Most, however, do involve sex. By the age of 20, only 20% of all teenagers are still virgins. More than 50% of all girls and almost 75% of all boys have sex before their 18th birthday. It is true, then, that there has been a "sexual revolution"—but the revolution is mainly female. In the mid-1950s, roughly 75% of all 20-year-old women were still virgins, in contrast to only 20% in 1990. Moreover, male teenage virgins might be somewhat more common today than they used to be (Hayes & Hofferth, 1987). As shown in Figure 13–1, the group whose sexual behavior has changed the most during the past 30 years is white teenage girls. Nowadays only 25% of white 20-year-old women are virgins, and only 4% are still virgins when they get married. By way of comparison, during the 1950s, 60% of white 20-year-old men and women were virgins; and 25% remained so until marriage. Nevertheless, teenage girls are still more likely to be virgins than are teenage boys (AGI, 1994. All statistics and information in the remainder of this chapter are from this source unless otherwise referenced).

Simply because so many more young women have had sex as teenagers, however, does not mean that teenagers are sexually wild and reckless. First, most adolescents wait until they are at least 17 to have sex. Nearly half are still virgins at the age of 17, and only 15% have had sex as 13-year-olds. In addition, many of these very young teenage girls say they were forced into having sex against their will. Remember, too, that one in five people do not have sex as teenagers. Second, teenage girls are still not as sexually active as boys their ages. So when addressing teenage sexuality, we must heed differences between genders. Most females today first have sex about 7 years before they marry, most males about 10 years. Throughout the teenage years, the number of males who have had sex at any given age approximates the number of females a year older who have had sex. In other words, girls wait longer than boys to lose their virginity. Thus, the old double standard: Most boys feel more comfortable about, or more pressured into having sex as teenagers than do most girls.

You might also be surprised to learn that most teenagers do not move in wanton abandon from one lover to the next. Half of all teenagers wait 18 months after first having sex before they have sex with another person. Those teenagers who start having sex at a very early age, however, do move more quickly from one partner to the next and do have sex with more people than teenagers who wait

Figure 13–1

Teenage sex before marriage

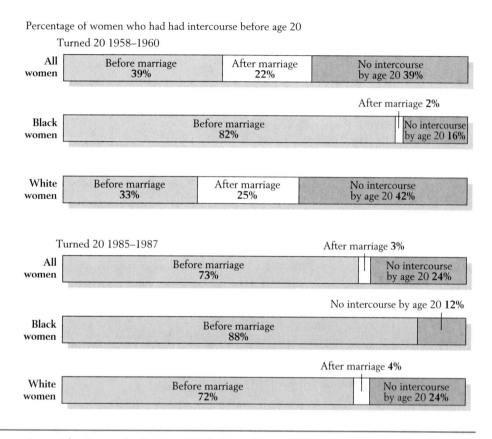

Percentage of women who had had intercourse before age 20

Source: Alan Guttmacher Institute (1994). *Sex and America's teenagers.* New York: Author.

until later in adolescence to lose their virginity. But even by their 20s, 40% of all women have had sex with only one or two people. Likewise, only one fourth of all 15- to 17-year-old girls have had sex with more than two people. Moreover, teenage girls who are sexually active are no more likely than older unmarried women to have sex with more than one man in a given period of time. As of 1990, only about 10% of unmarried women between the ages of 15 and 30 had had sex with two or more partners during the past 3 months. On the other hand, teenage and young adult males have had more sexual partners than most women their age, mainly because they started having sex earlier in their lives.

Figure 13–2

Teenage contraceptive use

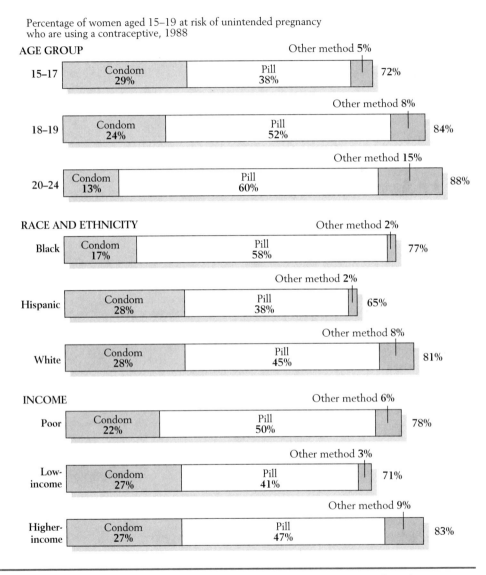

Percentage of women aged 15–19 at risk of unintended pregnancy
who are using a contraceptive, 1988

Source: Alan Guttmacher Institute (1994). *Sex and America's teenagers.* New York: Author.

CONTRACEPTIVE USE

Because the vast majority of older teenagers are having sex, we might well worry and wonder: How well are they doing in preventing pregnancy? Surprisingly, most teenagers use contraceptives as effectively as do unmarried adults. Nearly two thirds of all sexually active teenagers use some form of birth control the first time they have sex—usually a condom. During the 1980s, the number of teenagers using condoms the first time they had sex nearly doubled in all races and income groups. The older the teenagers, the more likely they are to use birth control the first time and to use it regularly thereafter. About half of those teenagers who do use contraceptives use the pill; and about 30% use condoms. As shown in Figure 13–2, as adolescents age, they are more likely to use birth control pills than to rely on condoms.

If today's teenagers are better at using contraceptives, then why do 1 million American teenage girls still get pregnant every year? The reasons vary, depending on the couple. First, slightly more than one third of sexually active adolescents don't use any contraceptive. Others use unreliable methods such as withdrawal and the rhythm method. Second, too many teenagers who rely on condoms or birth control pills use them incorrectly. Only 30% of the teenagers and only 40%

AN EXTRA SEVEN POUNDS COULD KEEP YOU OFF THE FOOTBALL TEAM.

Become a father before you're ready and you may always wonder what else you could have been.
THE CHILDREN'S DEFENSE FUND

of the adults using condoms use them every time they have sex. Likewise, too many teenage girls and older women do not correctly follow the directions for taking their birth control pills, especially women and girls from low-income families and very young adolescents. Couples who don't use any contraceptive, or who use one incorrectly, have a 90% chance of conceiving a child during a year of sexual activity; thus, 1 in 5 sexually active girls get pregnant each year.

Racial and Economic Differences

On the whole then, most adolescents wait to have sex until after age 17, and most do about as well as unmarried adults in using contraceptives. However, race and family income considerably influence the situation. Regardless of race, teenagers living in poverty or in low-income families are the most likely to have sex, become sexually active at a young age, use no birth control, and get pregnant. Half of male teenagers from families with annual incomes less than $20,000 have sex before their 16th birthday—6 months sooner than males from higher-income families. Likewise, half of low-income girls have sex before age 17, nearly 6 months sooner than do other girls their age. Low-income adolescents are also the least likely to terminate an accidental pregnancy. As a consequence, more than 80% of teenage parents are from poor or low-income homes. In other words, most teenagers who come from well-educated, well-to-do families reduce their odds of getting pregnant by using contraceptives properly or by waiting until they are older before having sex. If they do get pregnant, most of them opt to end the pregnancy rather than become parents or place the baby for adoption.

The connection between teenage pregnancy and family income is especially disturbing in light of the number of teenagers who live in poor or low-income families. Remember that nearly 20% of all teenagers were living below the poverty level in 1992. An additional 20% were in families whose annual incomes ranged from $15,000 to $28,000. That white teenagers are the least likely to get pregnant reflects their economic advantages. That is, slightly more than 10% of white teenagers live below the poverty level, compared to almost 40% of Hispanic and black teenagers (U.S. Department of Commerce, 1992).

Race, however, is even more closely related than family income to adolescents' sexual behavior and decisions. In general, black adolescents are more sexually active at an earlier age than are other teenagers. Half of all black males have had sex by age 15, and half of black females by 16. Hispanic and white teens do not reach this level of sexual activity until nearly 2 years later, at about age 17 or 18. Moreover, black males usually do not marry—if they marry at all—until nearly 20 years after first having sex, compared to only 10 years for other males their age. Similarly, black females generally have sex 12 years before they get married, compared to only 7 years for other women their age. Black teenagers also have the highest rates of out-of-wedlock births. In contrast, pregnant Hispanic girls usually get married: one in four Hispanic girls marries as a teenager—a higher ratio than any other group. Race is also related to the contraceptives adolescents use. Birth control pills are the most popular among black teenagers, but the least popular among Hispanics. Compared to other teens, Hispanics rely less on birth control pills and more on condoms as they move from early to late adolescence (Blea, 1992; Gibson & Lanz, 1991; Padilla & Baird, 1991).

Also, remember that teenagers from the lowest-income families are the most likely to have parents who oppose abortion and who started having sex at early ages, had children out-of-wedlock, and quit high school. These parents are also the most likely to abuse drugs and alcohol, to have sexually transmitted diseases, and to be in trouble with the police. In general then, those teenagers who have children out-of-wedlock are those who—like their own parents—have the poorest grades, quit school, abuse drugs and alcohol, and have been arrested. In other words, becoming a teenage parent tends to go hand-in-hand with other academic and social problems (Ketterlinus, Lamb, & Nitz, 1994).

FACTORS INFLUENCING SEXUAL BEHAVIOR

Race and family income are not the only factors related to adolescents' sexual decisions. Among the many other factors are: (1) the age at which they enter puberty; (2) their use of alcohol and drugs; (3) the degree of communication with the adults in their family about sex; (4) the behavior and attitudes these adults model; (5) the friends they choose; (6) the amount of accurate information they have about sex and contraception; (7) their self-esteem and future plans; and (8) society's sexual attitudes and policies.

TIMING OF PUBERTY

Other factors such as family income being equal, most children who become physically mature at an early age become sexually active sooner than other people their age. In part, the dramatic increases in their hormones contribute to the early maturer's being more interested in sex. But at least as important is that other people relate to them in more sexual ways because they look older. Not only do the most physically mature teenagers start dating earlier than their peers, but also they associate with older teenagers who are often already sexually active. Unfortunately, the sooner adolescents start dating and having sex, the more often they fail to protect themselves against pregnancy and sexually transmitted diseases. For example, a 13-year-old boy isn't as likely as a 17-year-old boy to have condoms with him the first time he has sex. The youngest teenagers also tend to have sex with more people, which increases their chances of contracting sexual diseases. Because most girls date boys several years older than they are, the youngest teenage girls are forced, coerced, or persuaded to have sex against their will more often than girls who start dating at a later age. Nearly 75% of the girls who had sex before age 14 say they were forced into it, compared to only 7% of the sexually active girls between the ages of 18 and 22. If young teenagers are not physically forced, they might nonetheless be pressured by their partner or by their friends into having sex (AGI, 1994; Flannery, Rowe, & Gulley, 1993; Phinney, 1990).

FAMILY COMMUNICATION

How well they communicate with their parents about sexual issues also influences adolescents' sexual decisions. Adolescents whose families are relatively relaxed and open about discussing sexual topics generally use contraceptives and condoms more reliably and make other sexual decisions more carefully than other teenagers. At the other extreme, very religious adults who try to frighten their children away from having sex by condemning premarital sex as sinful usually don't succeed. For example, approximately 55% of the girls from fundamentalist Protestant families have sex as adolescents, as do 60% from more liberal Protestant families and 48% from Catholic families (AGI, 1994). On the whole, teenagers from very religious families have sex and get pregnant about as often as teenagers from less religious families (Benson, Donahue, & Erickson, 1989; Caldas, 1993; Jones, 1986). Teenagers, though, are not unique in this regard. Religious adults are also about as likely as the less religious to commit adultery, employ prostitutes, and engage in other kinds of sexual behavior that are commonly labeled sinful or deviant (Kosmin & Lachman, 1993; Patterson & Kim, 1992).

In any event, teenagers who receive the most accurate, explicit sexual information at home usually make the most responsible, mature sexual decisions. When adults in a family talk about such matters as how to say "No," why a person shouldn't have sex too young, how to decide when to have sex, and how to use contraceptives reliably, the odds of a teenager's getting pregnant or catching a sexually transmitted disease decrease. Unfortunately, though, very few teenagers learn much about sex from the adults they live with. Most of what young people learn about sex comes from their friends or from television. For instance, nearly one third of 15-year-old girls report that neither of their parents has talked to them about pregnancy, birth control, or sexually transmitted diseases. And because our society still holds females responsible for birth control, boys generally receive even less sexual information at home than girls (AGI, 1994).

FAMILY ROLE MODELS

The way adults in the family conduct their own sexual and social lives also has an impact on what adolescents do. Have the men and women in the family had babies out-of-wedlock or married young because they were expecting a child? Have the adults terminated unplanned pregnancies and waited until they were adults to become parents? Did the adults start dating and having sex at an early age? Have the men in the family practiced birth control and been opposed to fathering babies at a young age? In these matters, teenagers generally do what the adults' in their families have done (AGI, 1994; Caldas, 1993; Ketterlinus, Lamb, & Nitz, 1994; Tasker & Richards, 1994).

Because teenage girls face bigger risks—pregnancy and physical or sexual abuse, for instance—than do boys, the women in a girl's family can play an especially important role in her sexual values and decisions. Mothers, stepmothers, or other women who assume a nurturing role in a girl's life influence her sexual decisions by what they say and do with their own lives. Without ever discussing the topic with her directly, these women continually convey attitudes about female sexuality and sexual relationships. If she is fortunate, as she's growing up a girl sees these women enacting very positive attitudes about sex and romantic relationships. From a very early age, a girl can observe that the women she loves have sexual dimensions to their lives—facets they clearly value and enjoy. These women can also demonstrate through their own relationships that no woman should use sex as bait for a relationship or as a method to bolster low self-esteem. By observing how the women in her family embody positive attitudes, a girl can develop self-confidence, assertiveness, and appreciation for her own sexuality.

Unfortunately, many mothers and other female relatives conceal these aspects of their lives from their daughters, too often limiting conversations about sex to the basic physical facts of menstruation and pregnancy. A mother's silence on such topics as sexual desire, sexual passion, and love-making conveys to her daughter that female interest in these matters is too embarrassing, unimportant, or shameful to merit even a conversation. Worse, some mothers and female relatives act as if female sexuality should revolve exclusively around pleasing a man, holding onto a relationship, and competing with other women. As a consequence, these daughters may learn to deny their own sexual feelings and needs, including the choice to say "No." So either by ignoring sex altogether or by defining female sexuality exclusively in terms of male desires, a mother's discomfort with—or lack of respect for—female sexuality can be passed on to her daughter. In turn, the daughter might either try to postpone growing up by avoiding boys or, at the other extreme, become overly focused on pleasing boys and being perceived as sexy (Flaake, 1993; Tolman, 1991; Debold, Wilson, & Malave, 1992).

Several daughters explain how their own sexual decisions were affected by the way their mothers and stepmothers lived their own lives. The daughters of two feminist mothers say: "Men have said to me, 'Why won't you sleep with me? Aren't you a liberated woman?' And I say, 'I won't sleep with you *because* I'm a liberated woman and I do what I want to do.'" "When I was 16, my mother told me that sex complicates a relationship and she helped me figure out for myself whether I really wanted to have sex with Robert" (Glickman, 1993, p. 126, 136). And one stepdaughter says, "My divorced mother had a boyfriend for 10 years. But she never showed any real passion or sexual or romantic interest in him. They acted like brother and sister. Without realizing it at the time, I patterned myself after my stepmother who clearly enjoyed the sexual, romantic aspects of her life with my father" (Nielsen, in progress).

PEERS

A teenager's sexual decisions also are influenced by the sexual behaviors of peers. Teenagers whose friends are having sex are more likely to have sex than are those whose friends are still virgins. Likewise, when teenagers believe their friends are using contraceptives, they themselves are also more likely to use them.

Conversely, when they believe that their friends disapprove of virginity or of contraceptives, teenagers tend to follow suit. On the other hand, as stated repeatedly in preceding chapters, teenagers usually choose to associate with people they have the most in common with. As is true with substance abuse and smoking, teenagers who are sexually active, or who are interested in becoming so, tend to choose friends like themselves. On the bright side, the vast majority of teenagers say they are not pressured into having sex by their friends (AGI, 1994; Caldas, 1993).

ALCOHOL AND DRUGS

Drinking heavily and using drugs are also related to what teenagers do sexually. Adolescents who are high on drugs or alcohol run the highest risks of getting pregnant, catching diseases, and being raped or otherwise physically abused. At whatever age, when we're high, we are less likely to protect ourselves against pregnancy and disease and more likely to make poor choices regarding our sexual partners and behavior. For example, older teenage males engage in more anal sex, use condoms less often, and have sex with more people when they are drinking heavily or using drugs than when they are sober—all of which puts them at higher risk for contracting AIDS and other venereal diseases. Thus, many programs designed to reduce teenage pregnancy and sexually transmitted diseases try to help young people appreciate the connection between risky sexual behavior and drinking or using drugs (Clapper & Lipsitt, 1991; Jemmott & Jemmott, 1993).

SELF-ESTEEM AND FUTURE PLANS

Adolescents' plans for the future also influence their sexual decisions. Generally, teenagers who have their hearts set on getting a good education and a good job are better at postponing sex and at using contraceptives than are those who have very few plans for the future. Teenagers with higher educational and career plans are also more likely to terminate an accidental pregnancy. In contrast, young people with low self-esteem and with the least hope of accomplishing much in the future more commonly get pregnant and decide to have children out-of-wedlock. For example, one reason why so many young black males father children is to boost their egos in a world of poverty and unemployment that offers them few other sources for self-esteem (Anderson, 1992). Similarly, teenage girls with low self-esteem who are unhappy about their appearance have sex with more boys than do girls with higher self-esteem who are happier with the way they look (Fisher, 1991). Likewise, girls who have boosted their self-esteem by playing on a school athletic team are less likely to get pregnant than are girls with similar family backgrounds who do not play sports (Diegmueller, 1994). In general then, the higher an adolescent's self-esteem and plans for the future, the more effort he or she puts into preventing a pregnancy (Caldas, 1993).

SEX EDUCATION

Given equivalent factors in family income, age, and race, the adolescents least likely to conceive a child or catch a sexually transmitted disease are those who have accurate information about pregnancy and disease prevention. Especially when their peers or their parents have given them incorrect information, sex education classes can be especially effective ways to reduce pregnancy and disease. For many teenagers, however, sex education classes come too late and offer too little explicit information about contraception to do much good. As one teenager, pregnant with her third child, says: "I was scared to take birth control pills cause my momma always told me they give you breast cancer, cervic cancer, something like that. The doctor was always telling me it wouldn't do that to me, but I'm listening to my momma" (Musick, 1993, p. 213).

Contrary to what some adults fear, sex education classes do not cause virgins to abandon their values and suddenly decide to have sex. Some virgins actually postpone having sex even longer after having had a sex education course than virgins who have never had such a course. Part of the reason is that the most effective sex education courses do more than merely teach adolescents how to use contraceptives. The best programs teach students how to decline sex, how to postpone sexual activities until they are older, and how to avoid situations, such as heavy drinking, that lead to risky sexual behavior (AGI, 1994; Eisen, Zellman, & McAlister, 1990; McKinney & Peak, 1994).

SOCIETY'S ATTITUDES

Finally, the ways in which our society deals with sex influences young people's sexual decisions. About one third of American adults report that they think sex outside marriage is morally wrong, regardless of the participants' ages. The majority of us, however, do not disapprove of premarital sex on moral grounds—a dramatic shift since the 1960s, when 75% of American adults disapproved of sex before marriage. Nowadays most of us are worried primarily about the negative consequences of having sex as a teenager—namely, unwanted pregnancies, out-of-wedlock births, and disease (AGI, 1994).

Despite our concerns, we have not done nearly as much as other industrialized countries to help teenagers avoid these negative consequences. Although teenagers in other advanced nations are as sexually active as are ours, their teenage pregnancy and birth rates are far lower. Why? Part of the answer is that we have far more children growing up in poverty (20%), and poverty is related to teenage pregnancy. But the answer goes beyond poverty. Other countries offer their children more thorough sex education—well before adolescence—and make contraception and abortions affordable and accessible. Other advanced nations are also more open about sex, less condemning of teenage sex, and more relaxed about advertising contraceptives on television and providing contraceptives and sex education in their schools. As Insert 13–3 shows, our supposedly "liberated" society is far more uptight and uncomfortable about teenage sexuality than the supposedly conservative Japanese (Jones, 1986; White, 1993).

> **Insert 13–3**
>
> ### Japanese Teenagers and Sex
>
> Why do many of us have the impression that Japanese teenagers are more sexually conservative than American adolescents? In reality, two thirds of Japanese girls have had sex by the age of 15, and nearly 90% of all teens report that they masturbate more than twice a week.
>
> In Japan, sex among teenagers is much more openly approved of than in the United States. Japanese children are not taught that sex is immoral or dirty, and sex is treated more explicitly and more straightforwardly. Teenage magazines for males and females routinely carry articles on how to use contracep-
>
> tives, how to please your partner sexually, how to achieve orgasms, how to learn from sex in movies, and how to arrange a visit with your girlfriend or boyfriend to a "love hotel."
>
> In fact, it isn't even necessary to be dating someone before having sex with him or her. Unlike the public displays of affection between American teenagers, however, the Japanese keep their sexual feelings and behavior more private. Moreover, for most Japanese, having sex as a teenager is of far less importance than performing well in school, preparing for a future job, and making close friends.

Source: M. White (1993). *The material child: Coming of age in Japan and America.* New York: Free Press.

Our ambivalent feelings about teenage sexuality are particularly well illustrated in the way we handle sexual issues in the media, especially on television. Keep in mind that the average teenager watches 24 hours of television a week and that many rank television as an important source of information about sex (Bence, 1991). Although the major networks finally agreed to air public service announcements about using condoms as protection against AIDS, they refuse to advertise condoms or any other product as a contraceptive. By way of comparison, in the African nation of Zaire, where AIDS is raging among heterosexuals, television advertising helped to boost the yearly sale of condoms from 900,000 to 18 million in only 3 years. Similarly, in our own country, television campaigns against drunk driving, cigarette smoking, and drugs have helped to reduce these behaviors, especially among the young (Alter, 1994). Nevertheless, although we are willing to advertise a wide variety of feminine hygiene products and pregnancy testing kits on television, we have yet to advertise a single contraceptive. Meanwhile, we bombard adolescents with sexual messages that say virtually nothing about the possible negative consequences (AGI, 1994).

In a similar vein, the advertising industry continually uses sex to entice teenagers into buying a wide array of products. As Insert 13–4 illustrates, we even use sex to sell provocative clothing for little girls (Talbot, 1993). Moreover, many teenage magazines, movies, romance novels, song lyrics, television programs, and advertisements send the message that having sex is one of the surest ways to achieve love, romance, and excitement. Sadly then, too many girls have sex in hopes of achieving the artificially romanticized experiences we have immersed them in. And too many boys have sex in an attempt to live up to the media's images of masculinity and sexiness (Holland & Eisenhart, 1991; Peirce, 1990; Smith, 1990; Thompson, 1990).

Our society's contradictory messages about teenage sex also come through in the way we handle sex education in our schools. Fifty states require that students be given information about AIDS, but only 46 require sex education programs. More important, most sex education programs provide very little, if any, explicit information about disease or pregnancy prevention. The average student receives

Insert 13–4

Showing Too Much Too Soon?

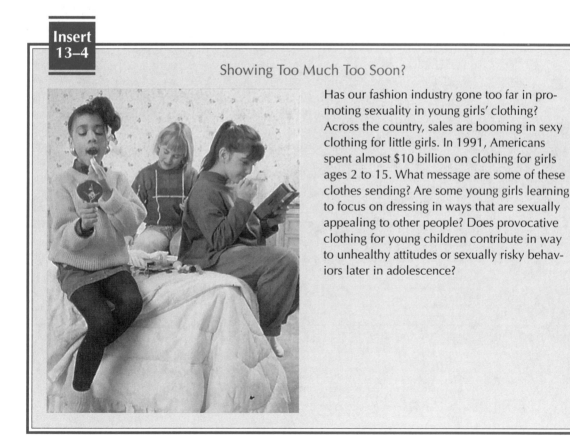

Has our fashion industry gone too far in promoting sexuality in young girls' clothing? Across the country, sales are booming in sexy clothing for little girls. In 1991, Americans spent almost $10 billion on clothing for girls ages 2 to 15. What message are some of these clothes sending? Are some young girls learning to focus on dressing in ways that are sexually appealing to other people? Does provocative clothing for young children contribute in way to unhealthy attitudes or sexually risky behaviors later in adolescence?

Source: M. Talbot (1993, April 26). Showing too much, too soon. *Newsweek*, p. 59.

less than 11 hours of instruction from 7th through 12th grade on birth control or sexually transmitted disease, most of which they get after they have already started having sex (McKinney & Peak, 1994).

In short, we American adults are still extremely conflicted, confused, and hypocritical about teenage sexuality. Like it or not, 80% of our teenagers have sex before the age of 20. Yet unlike other industrialized nations, we persist in denying our young people explicit information about or easy access to contraceptives, abortion, and testing or treatment for sexually transmitted diseases. We also aren't doing a very good job giving adolescents the specific skills they need to say "No" or to withstand peer pressure (AGI, 1994; Lawson & Rhode, 1993).

SEXUALLY TRANSMITTED DISEASES

PREVALENCE AND PREVENTION

Contracting a sexually transmitted disease is one of the risks of having sex. As shown in Figure 13–3, adults catch more **sexually transmitted diseases (STDs)** than do teenagers. Nevertheless, every year nearly 3 million teenagers—about one in four of the sexually active—are infected with one or more STDs. Bacterial STDs, such as chlamydia, and incurable viral diseases, such as genital warts, are especially common among sexually active teenagers, regardless of race or socioeconomic class. Teenage girls catch these diseases more easily than boys because anatomical differences make it easier for these viruses, bacteria, and fungi to be spread to females. In fact, a teenage girl is nearly twice as likely as a boy to catch gonorrhea, chlamydia, or hepatitis by having sex with an infected person without using a condom. Teenage girls might also have a higher risk of getting certain infections than do adult females because their cervix is still undergoing age-related changes, and their bodies have fewer protective STD antibodies (AGI, 1994; Ketterlinus, Lamb, & Nitz, 1994).

The best protection for the 80% of all teenagers who have sex before age 20 is using condoms each time they have sex. Limiting the number of people they have sex with also reduces the odds of getting a disease. The problem with this

Figure 13–3

Sexually transmitted diseases and age

Estimated new cases of STDs, 1992: 12 million

Ages 19 and younger 25%	Ages 20–24 41%	Ages 25 and older 34%

Source: Centers for Disease Control and Prevention (1993). *Annual report.* Atlanta: Author.

approach, though, is that having only one sexual partner does not necessarily limit you to exposure to that one person's diseases. If your lover has had sex with other people, you are, in effect, having sex with all of them—and whomever they've had sex with—in terms of exposure to untreated diseases.

As is true with pregnancy, STDs are more common among teenagers from poor and low-income families and those who have not received enough information about how STDs are contracted and prevented. As a result, black, Hispanic, and homeless teenagers contract more STDs than other people their age. Because poor teenagers generally start having sex earlier, have more partners, and use condoms less regularly, they're more likely to catch a sexual disease than are more well-to-do teens (Boyer & Hein, 1991b; Rotheram & Koopman, 1991).

VARIETY AND CONSEQUENCES

The likelihood of contracting and curing STDs varies widely. As shown in Table 13–1, three of the most common STDs among teenagers and adults are chlamydia, trichomoniasis, and gonorrhea. Though curable, these diseases, if left untreated, can cause infertility, increase the risk of catching AIDS, and cause premature births. Untreated gonorrhea can cause permanent damage to the heart, brain, joints, and eyes. Though still rare, syphilis has more than doubled since the mid-1980s among teenagers and can, if untreated, sometimes be fatal.

Other viruses cause more serious sexual diseases for which no cure has been found. Among the rarest, but most frightening and always fatal, is **HIV**—the virus that causes AIDS. Although AIDS is still rare among teenagers, about 20% of the cases are diagnosed when people are in their 20s. Because it usually takes about 8 years for the symptoms to appear, these people probably contracted the virus as teenagers. Moreover, the rate of HIV infection among adolescents more than doubled between 1991 and 1994. Compared with adult victims, a greater proportion of adolescent victims are female. Because the AIDS virus can also be contracted by sharing a hypodermic needle, teenagers who use intravenous drugs—many of whom are from low-income families—are at high risk (Rotheram & Koopman, 1991; Ketterlinus, Lamb, & Nitz, 1994).

Other sexually transmitted viruses, however, infect far more teenagers than does the human immunodeficiency virus—most notably the viruses that cause genital warts, **HPV,** and genital herpes. Genital warts look like small growths or raised, rough little patches of skin on the male or female genitals, anus, inside the throat, or cervix. This virus can develop into cancer at any of these locations. One strain of the herpes virus causes chicken pox, shingles (a painful skin disease), and cold sores around the mouth. The other strain causes genital herpes, which erupts into painful blisters on the genitals, increases a woman's chances of developing cervical cancer, and can be passed on to a baby during birth.

Because adolescents often do not know enough about the symptoms of these diseases, infected teens frequently ignore the signs of infection, going untreated for months, or years. Being unable to recognize the symptoms also means that many teenagers' have sex with an infected person without first stopping to notice the

Table 13–1			

Sexually transmitted diseases

Disease and annual incidence	Consequences for the infected person		
Curable, nonviral diseases	**Woman**	**Man**	**Fetus and newborn**
Chlamydia 4 million	Pelvic inflammatory disease Ectopic pregnancy Chronic pelvic pain Infertility Increased risk of HIV if exposed	Epididymitis Infertility Increased risk of HIV if exposed	Premature delivery Pneumonia Neonatal eye infections
Trichomoniasis 3 million	Increased risk of HIV if exposed	Increased risk of HIV if exposed	Premature delivery
Gonorrhea 1.1 million	Pelvic inflammatory disease Ectopic pregnancy Infertility Infection of joints, heart valves, or brain Increased risk of HIV if exposed	Infertility Infection of joints, heart valves, or brain Increased risk of HIV if exposed	Blindness Meningitis Septic arthritis
Syphilis 120,000	Serious damage to many body systems Mental illness Increased risk of HIV if exposed	Serious damage to many body systems Mental illness Increased risk of HIV if exposed	Stillbirth or neonatal death Active syphilis Damage to heart, brain, or eyes
Chancroid 3,500	Increased risk of HIV if exposed	Increased risk of HIV if exposed	Unknown
Noncurable, nonviral diseases	**Woman**	**Man**	**Fetus and newborn**
HPV 500,000–1 million	Cancer of cervix, vulva, vagina, or anus	Cancer of penis or anus	Warts in throat that can obstruct air passages

continued

Disease and annual incidence	Consequences for the infected person		
Noncurable, nonviral diseases	Woman	Man	Fetus and newborn
Genital herpes 200,000–500,000	Increased risk of HIV if exposed	Increased risk of HIV if exposed	Premature delivery Brain damage Death
Hepatitis B 100,000–200,000	Cirrhosis Liver cancer Immune system disorders	Cirrhosis Liver cancer Immune system disorders	Liver disease Liver cancer
HIV 40,000–50,000	Immune system disorders Increased risk of other STDs Immune system disorders	Immune system disorders Increased risk of other STDs	Immune system disorders AIDS

Sources: Centers for Disease Control and Prevention (1992, Table 6). Projections of the number of persons diagnosed with AIDS and the number of immunosuppressed HIV-infected persons, United States, 1992–1994. *Morbidity and Mortality Weekly Report, 41,* 18–19.

visible signs of infection. With better sex education and more use of condoms, the risk of catching or transmitting these diseases would be considerably reduced, as they have been in other countries (Boyer & Hein, 1991a; Jones, 1986).

TEENAGE PREGNANCY

PREGNANCY TRENDS

In addition to disease, sexually active teenagers need to worry about pregnancy. When a teenager gets pregnant, the couple has four options: get married and have the baby, have the baby without getting married, put the baby up for adoption, or terminate the pregnancy. Which choice do most couples make, and what are the consequences? How have teenagers' decisions changed during the past 20 years? The news is both good and bad (AGI, 1994; U.S. Department of Commerce, 1993; Donovan, 1992).

The good news is that because teenagers are using contraceptives more effectively, their pregnancy rate has decreased by almost 20% in the past 20 years. The bad news is that 1 million teenage girls still get pregnant every year. Nearly one in four young women have been pregnant by the time they turn 18; one in two by

Figure 13–4

Outcomes of teenage pregnancies

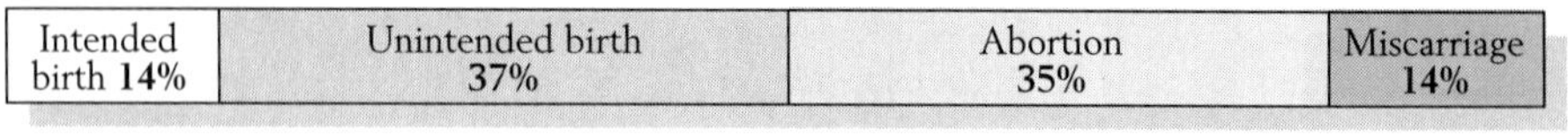

Intended birth 14%	Unintended birth 37%	Abortion 35%	Miscarriage 14%

Source: National Center for Health Statistics (1993). *Monthly vital statistics report, 41.* Washington, DC: Author.

age 21. Analyzed by race, the statistics are even more alarming. Nearly 25% of black teenage girls become pregnant every year, compared to 13% of Hispanics and 8% of whites.

Contrary to some people's beliefs that many of these teenage women secretly want to have a child, nearly 85% of their pregnancies are unplanned. As Figure 13–4 illustrates, only 14% of all pregnant teenagers planned to conceive. Most who do get pregnant, however, are older teenagers. Nearly two thirds of all pregnant teenagers are at least 18 years old. Fewer than 10% are younger than 15. Because girls usually date boys who are 2 to 3 years older than they are, about 40% of the males involved in a teenage pregnancy are older than 20. Moreover, the younger the father, the more likely the couple is to abort the pregnancy. As a result, only 4% of the children born to teenage mothers have a father younger than 20.

ABORTION AND OUT-OF-WEDLOCK BIRTHS

Of the 1 million teenage women who become pregnant each year, almost 15% of their pregnancies end as a consequence of a spontaneous miscarriage (about the same as adult rates). One third of all pregnant teens terminate their unplanned pregnancies, but nearly half of unmarried pregnant teenagers do so. Only one in five teenage mothers, however, is married. So nearly 60% of the white and 90% of the black teenagers have their children out-of-wedlock. Of those teenagers who are married, about a third are pregnant or already mothers when they become brides.

On a more positive note, adolescents account for only 30% of all out-of-wedlock births, down from 50% in 1970. Unfortunately though, this decrease in the teenage percent occurred because so many more adult women are having babies out-of-wedlock. The most dramatic increase has been among white adult women. Figure 13–5 shows that out-of-wedlock births have risen most among well-educated women and women in high paying professional jobs. Nevertheless, more than at any other time in our nation's history, teenage girls who decide to become mothers aren't getting married. Among teenagers, Hispanics have had the greatest increase in out-of-wedlock births. Noteworthy, however, is that Mexican and Puerto Rican Americans are three times more likely than Cuban Americans—

Figure 13–5

Never-married mothers

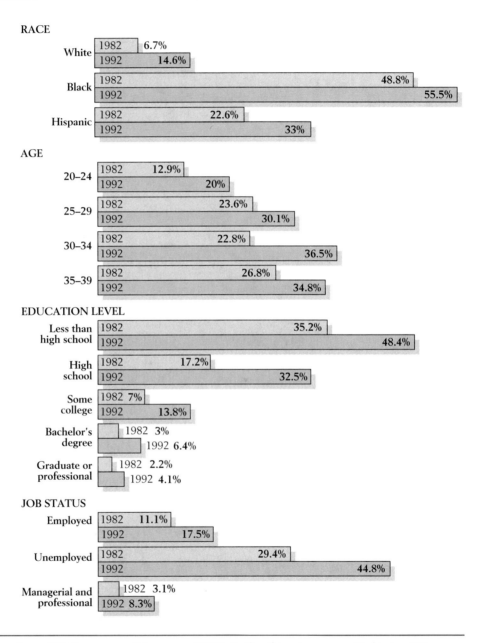

Source: U.S. Department of Commerce (1993). *Fertility of American women.* Washington, DC: Bureau of the Census.

who, on the whole, are far better off financially—to have children out-of-wedlock as teenagers. Only 3% of Cuban American girls are teenage mothers, compared to about 10% of Mexican and Puerto Rican Americans. Still, out-of-wedlock births are the most common among black teenagers, even though their rates have been declining.

How has legalized abortion affected young couples' decisions about pregnancy? In the 12 months following legalized abortion in 1973, teenage abortion increased considerably. Since 1980, however, teenage abortion rates have steadily declined. In part this is because fewer teenagers are getting pregnant, and in part because more girls are deciding to have babies out-of-wedlock. Most girls who choose to abort an unplanned pregnancy are from wealthier families with better educated parents and stepparents. These girls are generally those who have future plans that would be undermined or ended by becoming teenage mothers.

More than 80% of all teenage mothers are from poor or low-income families. Nearly 60% of white teenagers choose abortion, compared to fewer than 50% of black and Hispanic teenagers. Because most girls from low-income families are also the least well-educated, teenage mothers have the fewest academic and job skills. Nearly half of all unwed mothers are high-school dropouts, but only 6% are college graduates.

Young women from low-income families are also the least likely to have abortions, in part, because Medicaid will not pay for the procedure. Because the average cost of an abortion is $250, poor girls and their boyfriends usually cannot afford to end an unwanted pregnancy. Girls from more well-to-do families can either pay for an abortion on their own, with their boyfriend's help, or with help from their family. About half the young women's boyfriends help them pay for the abortion. One fourth of the women pay for the abortion themselves, and the rest get money from their families. Most girls tell one or both of their parents and discuss the decision with their boyfriends. Only Connecticut, Maine, Wisconsin, and the District of Columbia allow minors to terminate a pregnancy without parental consent. In 21 states a teenager must either get her parent's consent or notify her parents before terminating her pregnancy. The remaining states are silent on the issue of parental involvement.

Although those who oppose abortion want teenage girls to have their babies and then put them up for adoption, very few are willing to do this. Thirty years ago almost 20% of white teenage mothers put their babies up for adoption, in contrast to only 3% today. Black teenagers have historically been far less willing to let people adopt their children—only 1% today compared to only 2% in 1965. In short, adoption has never been a very appealing option to pregnant teenagers and their boyfriends.

Race is the best predictor of whether a couple will terminate a pregnancy. Even when family incomes are equal, white teenagers have more abortions or get married before they have the baby far more often than blacks. Regardless of age, family income, or education, having children without getting married is most common among black women. For example, a black mother earning more than $75,000 a year is 10 times more likely never to have been married than a white mother with a similar income. Among women aged 18 to 44, slightly more than 55% of the black women have children without ever having married, compared to only 15% of the white women and 33% of the Hispanic women their age. During adolescence, one in four black women and one in seven white women become mothers. Among males, 15% of blacks, 11% of Hispanics, and 6% of whites have fathered a child by the age of 19 (U.S. Department of Commerce, 1993).

TEENAGE MOTHERS AND THEIR CHILDREN

What is life like for teenage mothers and their children? In general, it is not good (AGI, 1994; Field, 1991; Musick, 1993). Nearly 60% live in poverty with the teenage mother's mother—a young grandmother who herself was often an unwed mother as a teenager. Given their poor educations and young age, most teenage mothers rely on welfare. Approximately half of the welfare money given for children goes to women who became mothers as teenagers, at a cost to taxpayers of about $20 billion a year. If all teenagers were now to start waiting until they were at least 20 before having a child, taxpayers would save about $2 billion a year (Center for Population Options, 1989).

The cost to the mothers themselves is also great. Although 90% of all women finish high school before age 40, only 70% of those who became mothers as teenagers do so. Girls who have babies as teenagers usually live in a poor family and make bad grades or have already dropped out of school before getting pregnant. In other words, having a baby as a teenager is not the main reason why these mothers are so far behind educationally and financially. On the other hand, having a baby as a teenager makes it nearly impossible for these poorly educated young women to escape poverty. To complicate matters further, one fifth of teenage mothers have another baby within 2 years. And of those who do get married, a third are divorced within 5 years—more than twice the divorce rate of women who wait until they are in their 20s to marry.

Despite these hardships, not all teenage mothers regret their choice. As shown in Insert 13–5, some teenage women believe their lives have been enriched by becoming mothers. Having few other sources of self-esteem or intimacy, some teenagers seem to be more satisfied with their lives after their babies are born (Musick, 1993; Williams, 1990).

Despite the satisfaction some mothers express, however, children of teen mothers usually pay a price that goes well beyond growing up in poverty, including: premature birth and poorer health than babies born to older mothers, and more academic and social problems related to forms of mental retardation that could have been prevented by better prenatal care. Moreover, teenage mothers are more likely than older women to abuse drugs and alcohol and to smoke while pregnant. So more of their babies are born with problems such as fetal alcohol syndrome and addiction to crack cocaine (Corser & Adler, 1993; Marques & McKnight, 1991). Because they usually spend most of their childhood and adolescence in a poor, fatherless family, these children have more than their share of

Insert 13–5

Teenage Mothers

"After the baby came out of me, the doctor put him on my stomach. I yelled at that doctor, 'Get that messy thing off me!' I know he ain't a baby doll, but he don't yet seem like he's a real baby."

"I have a wonderful and healthy son. He has made me a better and stronger person. I love taking care of his needs. I'm looking forward to graduating from high school this year."

"One thing I'll never do is get married. No way. Too much divorce in my family. I'll have plenty of boyfriends, but no husbands. Women got to be careful of men. I won't let no man just barge in here and start ordering me around."

"When I was about 11 or 12, I was very lonely so I went to having sex and got pregnant. That's the best thing I have in this world and that's my kids."

"Today I did something I felt bad about. I hit my daughter in the face because she was crying and I couldn't take it anymore. Ever since she was born she been like this crying for everything. Now I am having another baby but I didn't want her to feel alone or not loved."

"It is the most beautiful thing in my life to have a child. Many people think it is OK to have an abortion. We think God will punish us."

"My fiancee don't want me to breastfeed. He don't think that these belong to the baby. They belong to him."

"My baby has brought my life to a stop so I can look back on it so I can raise her like I would have liked to been raised. My father used to beat the hell out of me. If I ever start that I will get help."

"I go to college, work, and take care of my house for my son and boyfriend. I am starting to look better physically so I'm feeling better mentally—a little."

Sources: D. Frank (1983). *Deep blue funk and other stories.* Chicago: Ounce of Prevention Fund.
J. Messick (1993). *Young, poor, and pregnant.* New Haven, CT: Yale University Press.

problems at school, encounters with the police, drug and alcohol abuse, and out-of-wedlock births as teenagers (AGI, 1994; Field, 1991).

YOUNG, UNWED FATHERS

What about the fathers of the children born to teenage mothers out-of-wedlock? Who—and where—are they? As mentioned, most men involved in a teenage pregnancy are in their early 20s. Young men who get their girlfriends pregnant without marrying them are usually those with the least self-esteem, the least money, and the poorest educational backgrounds. As is true for unwed mothers, unwed fathers generally come from poor, fatherless families. They are more apt to be involved in delinquency and drug abuse than other males their age. About half of these unwed fathers see the mothers and children regularly during the first year after a child is born. As the child ages, though, these fathers show up less and less often. And only one third send any money to support their children. Most men who become fathers at a young age also marry more times and have more children than men who wait until they are older before becoming fathers for the first time (Elster, 1991; Lerman & Ooms, 1992; Neville & Parke, 1991).

Because out-of-wedlock births are extremely high among African American youth, considerable attention has been devoted to these young fathers. One of the most frequent explanations for why so many of these young men are fathering children without marrying the mother is poverty. Compared to other young men in our country, more young black males are unemployed or working in dead-end, low paying jobs. More young black fathers have also grown up in fatherless homes. Moreover, as the job market collapsed for black men who were employed in industries, it opened for young black women who were graduating from high school and going to college in greater numbers than were black males their age. So although black women now earn, on average, about the same as white women, black men earn only 69 cents for every dollar earned by white men—a situation that is likely to worsen because more black males now drop out of high school than at any time in the past 20 years. As unemployment has risen, our welfare system has also enabled unwed fathers to escape their financial responsibilities to their children. In short, young black men are less able to support their children than ever before—a crisis that many black Americans are worried about and trying to resolve (Anderson, 1992; Hacker, 1992; Lamann, 1991).

Unfortunately many young fathers choose to get their girlfriends pregnant with no intention of marrying them or of supporting their children. Easier access to contraceptives or better sex education would probably not have prevented these intentional pregnancies. Instead, what is needed is some way to convince more young men that becoming a father carries financial and emotional responsibilities. How do we instill that, though? The words of one young, unwed father illustrate how deeply entrenched these irresponsible attitudes about fathering are: "I'll use a condom with four of my girlfriends, but pregnancy is for your real girl. Marriage is a big step. I want everything to be right. I have a baby with my girlfriend, but I haven't found Miss Right" (Waldman, 1994).

Solutions and Recommendations

So how should we go about reducing teenage pregnancy, STDs, and out-of-wedlock births? How can we best help those teenagers who have already become parents? It goes without saying that the solutions and recommendations are both complex and controversial. As shown in Insert 13–6, we cannot even reach an agreement on much simpler matters, such as whether pregnant cheerleaders should be allowed to stay on the squad (Annin, 1993).

Insert 13–6

Pregnant Cheerleaders: Off the Squad or Not?

If a high-school cheerleader is pregnant, should she be kicked off the squad as an example to other students? If it is widely known in a school that one of the cheerleaders terminated a pregnancy, should she be allowed to continue serving as a representative for her school? Does it matter if the pregnant cheerleader plans to get married? If the cheerleader who terminates her pregnancy is white, but the cheerleader who decides to have her baby out-of-wedlock is black, does this complicate matters? What

about the teenage father-to-be? If he's on the football or basketball team, or if he's the president of the student government, should he be removed from his position as well?

In the fall of 1993, these are exactly the questions that faced the school board in one small town in Texas. In a state where high-school football is taken very seriously, a heated debate spread through community when the school board suspended three cheerleaders from the squad because they were pregnant. It was common knowledge that the three suspended black cheerleaders were pregnant and that a fourth, a white cheerleader who had an abortion, was allowed to remain on the squad.

The ban, which the school board hopes will encourage pregnant students to take care of their children, also applies to other extracurricular activities and continues after the babies are born. Despite the controversy, one of the suspended Texas cheerleaders was not upset by her school board's decision: "I've got other things to worry about than some old cheerleader stuff."

Source: P. Annin (1993, October 18). The day the cheering stopped. *Newsweek*, p.76.

Sex Education   One of the most obvious recommendations is to provide better sex education in our schools and to provide it long before students become sexually active. The vast majority of American adults are in favor of sex education in the schools. The problem is that sex education means different things to different people.

At one extreme are those who advocate giving students explicit information about birth control, including a clinic in school to distribute free condoms and provide free contraceptives. This is the approach taken by most other industrialized nations (Jones, 1986). For example, in Baltimore, where teenage pregnancies and out-of-wedlock births are among the highest in the country, some school clinics are now offering Norplant. The **Norplant** system consists of six thin capsules implanted in a woman's upper arm. The capsules automatically release hormones that prevent pregnancy for up to 5 years. Few side effects are known, and the capsules can be removed at any time if the woman wants to get pregnant. At a cost of about $500, Norplant is one of the least expensive and most reliable contraceptives now on the market. It has the added advantage, of course, of not having to plan ahead before having sex or not having to remember to take birth control pills every day. Like all other contraceptives except the condom, however, Norplant offers no protection against disease (Cowley, 1990; Kantrowitz, 1992).

At the other end of the spectrum are those who advocate the "just-say-no" approach to sex education. This requires encouraging students to abstain from having sex by teaching them ways to resist peer pressure. One such program seems to be working in Atlanta, where junior-high-school girls are learning how to say "No" to their boyfriends and how to use contraceptives if they decide to say "Yes." What's especially intriguing about this program is that older teenagers teach the younger girls. The girls who have taken this 10-hour course are four times less likely to become sexually active as eighth graders and one third less likely to become pregnant by the time they graduate from high school than are other girls in their school (Klein, 1994). Unfortunately, programs that rely only on the "say-no" approach and withhold information about birth control are seldom successful in reducing pregnancy. In fact, teenagers who have been in sex education programs in which abstinence is the only option presented might be at a higher risk of becoming pregnant than teenagers who receive information about contraceptives. In short, most students do not change their sexual behavior or increase their use of contraceptives unless their sex education program gives them specific information about preventing pregnancy and disease, and unless the teachers establish good rapport and trust in these sex education classes (AGI, 1994; McKinney & Peak, 1994).

In order to provide young people with more accurate sexual information, as adults who offer them advice we also need to stay well-informed. As the quiz in Insert 13–7 demonstrates, your own sexual knowledge might not be as accurate or as up-to-date as it needs to be if you are to serve as a reliable source of information for sexually active teenagers.

Programs for Teenage Parents   Once teenagers have already become parents, other approaches are needed to help them and their children. Two of the most popular approaches have been to help teenage parents graduate from high school and to teach them parenting skills. By helping them graduate, it is hoped that more young parents can find jobs that pay enough to support themselves and their children. Because most teenage parents know very little about child development, a number of programs have attempted to teach unwed mothers how to relate to their babies and toddlers. The hope has been that these programs will help the children of teenage parents have fewer mental and social problems. In order to have much impact, however, these interventions have had to be very intensive and ongoing, thus very costly. More discouraging still, even the best programs seem to have less long-lasting effects than was hoped (AGI, 1994; Field, 1991).

Insert 13–7

How Sexually Knowledgeable Are You?

True or false?

_____ 1. A girl can get pregnant even if she has not yet started menstruating.

_____ 2. You can have herpes without having any visible genital sores.

_____ 3. Some sexual diseases can be contracted through oral sex.

_____ 4. The most reliable contraceptive is the birth control pill or Norplant.

_____ 5. Raised patches of skin on the genitals can be signs of genital warts.

_____ 6. Urinating before and after sex decreases the chances of getting pregnant.

_____ 7. Douching after sex reduces the chances of getting pregnant.

_____ 8. Most contraceptives protect against sexually transmitted diseases.

_____ 9. If the visible symptoms of a sexually transmitted disease disappear without medication, it means the disease is cured.

_____ 10. Gays and lesbians cannot contract sexually transmitted diseases other than AIDS.

(See answers on page 530.)

Societal Changes   On a larger scale, our society could adopt a number of changes that have reduced teenage pregnancy and STDs in other nations. First, we should continue trying to convince teenagers to postpone having sex. Second, we should provide more explicit, accurate information about contraception before they become sexually active. Young couples need more consistent messages from us at home, in the media, and in our religious institutions in order to better protect themselves against pregnancy and STDs. Because American males are more opposed to using condoms than men in other advanced nations, we need to do a much better job changing young men's attitudes about this form of birth control, which has the added advantage of protecting couples against STDs (AGI, 1994; Jones, 1986).

Third, we could make contraceptives more effective, cheaper, and easier to buy—something we don't do as well as most other advanced countries. Not only do other governments make contraceptives less expensive and less difficult to obtain, they also encourage family planning and subsidize part of the expense for contraceptives. For instance, couples in Europe can choose from a wide selection of contraceptives, including monthly injections. Despite their Roman Catholic heritage, French schools provide sex education programs in which contraceptives and abortion are candidly discussed. Likewise, the United States was far slower than Britain and France in providing the public with access to **RU-486**—the "morning after" pill that prevents pregnancy by causing the menstrual period to start regardless of whether the woman has conceived. The legal and social disputes in our country, however, are not so much about abortion or contraception as they are about our sexual values. We are a strange and somewhat hypocritical blend of sexuality and prudery, obsessing on sex while remaining skittish about giving our young people the information they need to avoid pregnancy and disease (Population Crisis Committee, 1991).

Fourth, we can address the connection between poverty, low self-esteem, and teenage pregnancy by expanding efforts to provide teenagers with the skills they need to find good jobs. By helping teenagers graduate from high school and get good jobs, we can boost their self-esteem and expand their options in ways that can make becoming a teenage parent less appealing.

Fifth, we need to make young men understand the ramifications of pregnancy so they can better decide about becoming fathers and accept responsibility once they do. Recent changes in welfare laws might cause teenagers to think twice before becoming parents—especially those young men who purposely get their girlfriends pregnant and then walk away from their financial responsibilities after their babies are born. President Clinton's 1994 welfare reform program proposes to cut off welfare to unwed mothers after 2 years so that these fathers would no longer be able to count on taxpayers to take care of their children indefinitely. The plan would also withhold welfare benefits to any unmarried mother who refuses to identify the father of her child. This would then enable states to threaten unwed fathers with such tactics as suspending their driver's licenses or garnishing child support payments from their paychecks. The plan would also allow states to refuse a mother more money if she has a second child while still on welfare (Waldman, 1994).

By using a combination of all of these approaches, we might reduce the rates of teenage pregnancy, out-of-wedlock births, and abortions in our society. Regardless of their race, gender, religion, or economic background, most adolescents begin to have sex in their middle to late teens. Even if we are not comfortable with this reality, we have to do a better job helping our young people avoid the negative, life altering effects of teenage pregnancy and disease.

GAY AND LESBIAN YOUTH

Most concerns and disagreements about teenage sexuality focus on the 90 to 95% who are heterosexual. Although gay and lesbian youth do have a somewhat different set of concerns, they also share much in common with their heterosexual counterparts. Although about half of all teenage boys engage in some homosexual activity, only about 8% of adult males and 3% of adult females are exclusively homosexual. These numbers, by the way, have remained basically unchanged since the statistics first started being collected during the 1940s (Rotheram & Koopman, 1991).

Like other teenagers, gay and lesbian youth have experiences and deal with issues that revolve around romance and sexuality: dating, falling in love, getting over a broken heart, deciding which relationships are and aren't good for them, wondering when or whether to have sex, and protecting themselves against sexually transmitted diseases. And like heterosexual teenagers, homosexual youths must decide how much of their romantic or sexual lives they want their families to know about. But beyond these common experiences and concerns, virtually all gay and lesbian teenagers are confronted with a unique set of concerns and situations.

HOMOPHOBIA AND DISCRIMINATION

First, of course, gay and lesbian teenagers are confronted with the reality that most people do not approve of their sexual orientation. Long before they realize that they are gay, young people who are not heterosexual realize that our society is uncomfortable with, and often extremely hostile and violent toward, homosexuals. In their mildest forms, these attitudes are reflected in children's jokes and insults about "queers," "fags," and "lesbos." More extreme forms of **homophobia**— an irrational fear, hatred, or distorted perceptions of homosexuals—have caused gays to be killed, physically beaten, deprived of the custody of their children, evicted from their homes, fired from their jobs, arrested for having sex in their own homes, and denied the right to serve in the military (Blumenthal, 1992; Herek, 1992; Wells, 1993).

Homophobia and discrimination against gays have existed historically in many countries other than our own. For example, the Nazis imprisoned and killed homosexuals, whom they branded by having them wear an inverted pink triangle (Plant, 1986). More recently in our own society, violence and hate crimes against gays have increased in a number of high schools and colleges, as well as in the larger community (Herek, 1992). Although it is not against the law to be a homosexual, nearly half of the states have laws that make it illegal for any adult to engage in oral or anal sex. These laws are rarely enforced, of course, because they apply to heterosexual couples as well. But when they are enforced, it is almost always in cases involving gay males. Despite efforts to reduce homophobia and discrimination, gay and lesbian teenagers grow up knowing that homophobia is still very widespread in our country (Savin-Williams, 1992).

Gay and lesbian youth also learn that certain people tend to be more intensely homophobic than do others. Both among teenagers and adults, heterosexual males are generally more uncomfortable and more hostile toward gays than are heterosexual females. Most males are also more homophobic toward gay males than toward lesbians. It has been suggested that some heterosexual males who are extremely hostile toward gay males might be trying to conceal their own

Insert 13–8

Gay and Lesbian Adolescents' Experiences

"The only other gay guys I knew in my high school were both jocks—real macho, on the football team and all that. I was clearly not as masculine as they were. It's one thing to be gay and macho, and another to be gay and effeminate. I felt really isolated."

"Just about when I was graduating from high school, I looked at myself and just accepted the fact that I was gay. It's funny because a lot of people think that being a homosexual robs a guy of his manhood. But for me, admitting my own homosexuality gave me my manhood."

"In a straight person's mind, getting a homosexual guy in bed with a girl is going to be all he needs to make a miraculous change. It's funny. Some people think the only reason you're gay is because you had a bad experience with a woman. Like a woman laughed at you or something."

"I cried about it a lot at first. I said to myself, 'You're a homosexual.' And I didn't want to be, not then anyhow. I called myself all sorts of names: 'You're a fag, you're a freak.' Where was my belief in God? Where was my future with a spouse and kids?"

"After people at school found out that I was gay, a lot of them kind of kept a distance from me. I think they were scared I was going to do something to them. I guess that was one of the reasons why I didn't come out sooner. I was afraid they would be scared of me."

"My mother said, 'You didn't need to tell me because I knew all the time.' But I wanted to tell her, because it was coming from me. I've always been proud that I wasn't embarrassed about being a lesbian. I always enjoyed being able to open up other people's minds about it. Being different for me was a way of teaching people to respect others."

Source: R. Bell (1988). *Changing bodies, changing lives.* New York: Random House.

homosexual feelings or experiences. Likewise, people who are politically conservative and less well-educated tend to be more homophobic than well-educated and politically liberal people. People who know someone gay are usually more comfortable about homosexuality than people who are not aware that someone they know is gay. Finally, it's noteworthy that among teenagers, whites are usually more homophobic than blacks or Hispanics (Blumenthal, 1992; Crawford & Robinson, 1990; Herek & Glunt, 1993; Suraci, 1992).

In addition to encountering fear, hostility, or discomfort with their peers, gay teenagers also encounter these responses from some of their teachers and counselors. Some teachers and counselors publicly condemn or joke about homosexuals. Others perceive everything about gay teenagers exclusively in terms of their sexual orientation. Although some gay teenagers' problems are directly related to

What are your feelings about homosexuality?

their homosexuality, too many counselors and teachers automatically assume that all of their problems are related to being gay. For example, in seeking help to improve their grades or to get along better with their siblings, the fact that a teenager is gay might be irrelevant. Yet some counselors and teachers, knowing that a teenager is gay, inadvertently obsess on this one trait. Likewise, much of our existing research has focused too much on the problems associated with being gay and not enough on the normal adjustment of millions of gay people. As is true with too many of the rest of us, researchers and authors have tended to overlook factors or situations other than sexual orientation in searching for explanations for a gay person's problems or behavior. For example, too much research has failed to compare gay people with heterosexuals who have similar family backgrounds or similar problems. Even among professionals, homophobia inadvertently slips into the research and the practices that affect gay and lesbian teenagers (Herek & others, 1991).

On a more positive note, however, the mental health profession no longer considers homosexuality to be a mental illness. In 1973 the American Psychiatric Association (APA) removed homosexuality from its list of mental illnesses. This change came about largely as a result of pioneering research studies by a heterosexual female in the 1950s that demonstrated no significant differences between the mental health of gays and heterosexuals. The findings ultimately led to the APA's removal of homosexuality from the list of mental disorders that need "curing" (Marcus, 1993).

THE CAUSES OF SEXUAL ORIENTATION

Another way gay and lesbian teenagers sense or recognize homophobia is the intense interest so many people have in wanting to know: What causes homosexuality? Obsessing on this question often reflects the homophobic questions that underlie it: What can we do to eliminate or to "cure" homosexuality? How can we "make them normal?" Regardless of why someone might want to know, we can't provide a definitive answer—no one really knows what determines a person's sexual orientation. Both hereditary and environmental factors have been implicated to varying degrees, without consensus among the experts. What we do know is that gay and lesbian teenagers can no more change their sexual orientation than can heterosexuals. Being surrounded by heterosexual teachers, friends, media, and literature does not make a gay person "straight." And gay teachers, friends, parents, and literature do not make a heterosexual person gay (Marcus, 1993; Remafedi, 1991; Savin-Williams, 1992).

In the same vein, homosexuality is not related to a person's economic class, race, or religion. Gay and lesbian teenagers come from all backgrounds (Balka, 1989; Beck, 1989; Marcus, 1993). Gay teenagers come from very poor and from very wealthy families. Nor is being gay related to parental influence. Some gay teenagers, just like some heterosexual teenagers, have parents who are feminists, divorced, gay, overbearing, or inattentive—all of which have been "blamed" for homosexuality at one time or another. The fact is that gay teenagers almost always have heterosexual parents who are no more likely to be different in any special way from the parents of heterosexual children. In other words, virtually all gay parents have heterosexual children, and virtually all gay children have heterosexual parents (Barret, 1990; Falk, 1989; Martin, 1993; Raafkin, 1990).

Contrary to what some insist, people do not "choose" their sexual orientation. What many gay teenagers do choose, however, is to try to fit into a heterosexual world by dating, or even having sex with people of the other sex. But these efforts do not change a gay adolescent's sexual orientation any more than having some

What are your best and worst memories of dating and falling in love?

homosexual experiences makes a heterosexual gay. Moreover, bad experiences with boys do not "make" heterosexual girls into lesbians; and bad experiences with girls do not "make" heterosexual boys into gays. Nor do gay adults try to recruit heterosexuals into being gay. As many gay adults have put it, "Why would I choose to be something that horrifies my parents, that could ruin my career, that my religion condemns, and that could cost me my life if I dare to walk down the street holding hands with the person I love? Can you imagine how gay and lesbian life might be advertised to potential recruits: You, too, can be a member of a despised minority" (Marcus, 1993, p.90).

Not only is being homosexual not a choice, but being gay is not necessarily any measure of one's femininity or masculinity. Gay teenagers grow up in the same heterosexual culture as everyone else—a culture in which girls are socialized to behave and to value "feminine" ways, and boys are socialized to behave and to value "masculine" ways. Yes, some lesbians look and act more masculine than the average teenage girl—and some heterosexual girls look and act more masculine than do many lesbians. And, yes, some gay males are effeminate, but many gay males look and act far more masculine than the average heterosexual male (Marcus, 1993; Pallone, 1990).

SPECIAL CONCERNS AND PROBLEMS

Besides struggling to adapt to a homophobic, heterosexual world, gay and lesbian teenagers have to negotiate the same situations as heterosexuals—how to go about meeting people to date, how and when to express themselves sexually, how to have a satisfying social life, and so on. Other issues and situations, however, set gay teenagers apart from their heterosexual peers: the process of recognizing they are gay and "coming out" to family and friends, the stress of having to hide their sexual and romantic lives, the fear of contracting AIDS, and the struggles involved in dating and forming romantic relationships in a predominantly heterosexual world (Marcus, 1993; Remafedi, 1991; Savin-Williams, 1992).

Virtually all gay people go through their adolescent years trying to determine whether they are "really" gay. Many teenage boys and a small percentage of teenage girls have homosexual experiences as a normal part of growing up. So it's no small wonder that most gay teenagers go through a confusing period of wondering whether they are just "going through a phase." Although most gay adults say they felt "different" from their peers even at a very young age, the certainty of being gay usually doesn't become clear until they are at least in their 20s. Beyond the alienation of "feeling different" or aside from the confusion of being told they'll "outgrow it," gay teenagers often get the message that what they feel is immoral or "sick."

Confused, yet striving to fit in socially, most gays date and have heterosexual experiences as teenagers. As adults, however, they slowly realize that their heterosexual experiences were attempts to fit in socially and to avoid the ostracism, shame, or discomfort they would have encountered by openly admitting to themselves or to other teenagers that they were gay. Therefore, the act of "coming out" to close friends or family members usually takes place in a series of small realizations—not in a sudden bolt of awareness. Although many gay people tell a few friends or family members about themselves during their 20s, others take years to fully realize that they are gay—sometimes after having been married and having had children and grandchildren.

When gays and lesbians do start becoming more open about their sexuality with family or friends, they generally say they feel better about themselves. On the other hand, "coming out" is usually a slow and painful ordeal, especially with parents. At least initially, most parents have a hard time accepting or even acknowledging their child's homosexuality. For example, those who eventually let their families meet their boyfriends or girlfriends are often told that they should not "flaunt" their feelings for each other. The message is that although it is perfectly acceptable—in fact, desirable—for heterosexual couples to do such things as hold hands or rub one another's shoulders in public, gay couples are "flaunting their sexuality" or "hanging all over each other" for showing any physical affection for one another. For example, when her son first told her he was gay, one mother made a nervous joke about interior decorating, then gently asked him if he was worried that he might be attracted to his younger brother's friends. Later, appalled by her own behavior, she wrote a book about their family's eventual acceptance of the son's homosexuality (Dew, 1994).

Given that most gay teenagers do not fully realize they are gay until they are adults, it should be no surprise that many try to deny their homosexuality by buying into the pretense that their behavior is merely a "passing phase" or a way of "experimenting" with bisexuality. As a result, unlike older men who are more apt to use condoms during anal sex with other males, most teenage boys who engage in male anal sex often do not use condoms. These boys are sometimes trying to reassure themselves they aren't gay by not wearing condoms because they tell themselves that only gays can catch AIDS. Although this convoluted thinking might sound farfetched, it's no more irrational than the attitudes about contraceptives held by the thousands of heterosexual couples who become teenage parents (Marcus, 1993).

Given these additional sources of stress in their lives, gay and lesbian teenagers are at a greater risk of developing certain kinds of emotional and psychological problems. Having adopted the deeply rooted taboos against homosexuality, too many of these young people feel a self-loathing or shame that contributes to depression or social withdrawal. Those who are religious also have to adapt somehow to the reality that most religions either condemn their behavior as immoral or refuse to address the issue of homosexuality in any way. A number of gay teenagers cope with these difficult situations by withdrawing from their peers and family, isolating themselves in their own lonely world. Others are driven to more self-destructive alternatives. Gay and lesbian youth are more apt to become clinically depressed, to attempt to suicide, and to abuse drugs or alcohol. Gay teenagers commit suicide at two to three times the rate of heterosexuals, and some studies show that 40% of homosexuals make attempts on their lives when they're young (Marcus, 1993).

As our society gradually becomes more tolerant, some changes are occurring that enable gay and lesbian youth to lead less stressful lives and to experience more of the pleasures that most heterosexual teenagers enjoy. In some communities, the creation of gay social organizations and places to gather socially have enabled these teenagers to have a more normal social life. Some high-school administrations are also becoming more sensitive toward gay students. For instance, in 1994 one Los Angeles school district became the first in the nation to sponsor a senior prom for gay couples (Flaake, 1994). In contrast, in 1980, Aaron Fricke sued his high school for the right to take his male date to the senior prom and later wrote an account of his experiences as a gay teenager (Fricke, 1981).

Some school systems are also offering programs designed to make heterosexual students more aware of their own homophobia and insensitivity toward their gay classmates. In New York City, the Harvey Milk School has been established for gay students who suffered physical or emotional abuse in their former high schools. Our country's largest public school teachers' union has also developed a training course to help teachers talk about homosexuality. The organization has also recommended that all schools have counselors who are trained to meet the needs of gay students. At the college level, several prestigious universities have established gay and lesbian studies departments, and many others offer courses in gay and lesbian literature and history (Marcus, 1993).

One of the most controversial efforts to introduce homosexuality into the school curriculum and to reduce homophobia is a program which was established in New York City in the early 1990s. The curriculum, called "Children of the Rainbow," stresses tolerance for all forms of diversity—racial, cultural, religious, and sexual. Of the 460 pages in the curriculum guide, two paragraphs refer to gay and lesbian parents. In reaction, some parents vigorously objected to the new curriculum on the grounds that it accentuated the positive aspects of being gay. The "Rainbow" curriculum was partially responsible for the superintendent's eventually firing, as was his program for dispensing condoms in those schools where teenagers were most at risk of contracting AIDS and becoming pregnant (Fernandez, 1993). Nevertheless, efforts like the "Rainbow" program in school are enabling many gay and lesbian students to cope better with a hostile, homophobic society. Such efforts also enable gay teenagers to lead happier, more productive lives and to develop a healthier sense of self.

CONCLUSION

We need to do more in our society to reduce our high rates of pregnancy, STDs, and out-of-wedlock births among teenagers and young adults. We also have a long way to go in eliminating homophobia and helping gay, lesbian, and bisexual teenagers adapt to a predominantly heterosexual world. And efforts must continue to stop date rape and physical abuse among heterosexual couples.

Clearly we have made progress in certain areas, such as increasing teenagers' use of condoms and other contraceptives and providing homosexual teenagers with more options for a healthy sexual and social life. On the other hand, we haven't made much progress in terms of publicizing the risks associated with being a sexually active teenager or giving teenagers more explicit information about sexual issues before they become sexually active. Although a number of adults might wish it were different, the reality is that very few young people abstain from having sex as teenagers and that not all teenagers are heterosexual. As a society, we need to take a less ambivalent, less conflicted stand in regard to teenage sexuality. Rather than fooling ourselves into believing that any single variable controls teenagers' sexual decisions, or that a single best method will be found to reduce the negative consequences for sexually active teenagers, we need to take a broader, more realistic view—as have most other advanced nations.

Review/Test Questions

Cite specific statistics or research findings to support your answers.

1. How do most young people feel about getting married or living with a lover as teenagers?

2. What part does dating play in most adolescents' lives?

3. How does dating usually change from early to late adolescence?

4. How common are date rape and physical abuse among teenage couples?

5. How sexually active are most adolescents?

6. Which variables influence teenagers' sexual decisions?

7. What are the most important ways of predicting which adolescents will have sex, get pregnant, or become teenage parents?

8. How do adolescents' sexual activities and the outcomes of sex differ by race and family incomes?

9. How effective is sex education?

10. What are the controversies surrounding sex education?

11. Which forms of contraceptives do most adolescents use? How does this differ by age and race?

12. How effective are adolescents at preventing pregnancy and STDs?

13. What are some of the most common STDs and their consequences?

14. Which STDs have no cures, and what are the consequences?

15. How common are teenage pregnancy, out-of-wedlock births, marriage, and abortion in different racial and economic groups?

16. What are the trends in teenage pregnancy, adoption, abortion, and marriage?

17. How do teenage mothers and young fathers differ from others their age who wait until later in life to become parents?

18. What problems are unique to gay and lesbian teenagers?

19. In what ways can society make life less stressful for gay and lesbian teenagers and young adults?

20. What possible solutions and recommendations have been made for reducing teenage pregnancy, STDs, and out-of-wedlock births?

Questions for Discussion and Debate

1. How did your own dating and sexual experiences affect your development as an adolescent? What do you wish you had done differently and why?

2. When do you think a person is "old enough" to have sex, legally terminate an unwanted pregnancy, live with a boyfriend or girlfriend, get married, and become a parent?

3. How would you try to convince young adolescents to wait until they were older before having sex or becoming parents?

4. What kinds of sexual risks have you taken, and what might have made you behave more responsibly?

5. If you or anyone you know has been physically abused or sexually assaulted by someone they were dating, how did this affect you?

6. What do you think about the Antioch College Sexual Policy? How would you

advise high schools and colleges to go about reducing date rape?

7. After keeping notes for 1 week on the sexual themes and images in prime-time television advertisements, what messages and recurring themes struck you?

8. If you or anyone you know is gay or lesbian, how did being gay or lesbian affect your or their adolescent development?

9. How comfortable do you feel about rooming, being best friends, being in a social club, or being on a team with someone homosexual? What experiences have shaped your feelings? How do your feelings now compare with how you felt as a teenager? Why?

10. Considering the kinds of problems that sexually active teenagers encounter, as well as your own experiences, what sexual advice would you give to teenagers and why? How would your advice differ based on the teenager's age and gender?

Glossary

HIV, p. 509
homophobia, p. 522
HPV, p. 509

Norplant, p. 518
RU-486, p. 521
STD, p. 508

Answers to the quiz in Insert 13–7:
Statements 1 through 5 are true;
the rest are false.

References

Adams, G. (1991). Physical attractiveness and adolescent development. In R. Lerner, A. Petersen, & J. Brooks-Gunn (Eds.), *Encyclopedia of adolescence* (pp. 785–789). New York: Garland.

Adams-Price, C., & Greene, A. (1990). Secondary attachments and adolescent self-concept. *Sex Roles, 22,* 187–198.

Alan Guttmacher Institute (1994). *Sex and America's teenagers.* New York: Author.

Alter, J. (1994, January 17). The power to change what's cool. *Newsweek,* p. 23.

Anderson, E. (1992). *Streetwise.* Chicago: University of Chicago.

Annin, P. (1993, October 18). The day the cheering stopped. *Newsweek,* p. 76.

Antioch College. (1992). *Sexual offense policy.* Yellow Springs, OH: Author.

Asher, S., & Coie, J. (1990). *Peer rejection in*

childhood. New York: Cambridge University Press.

Augenbraum, H., & Stavan, I. (1993). *Growing up Latino.* Boston: Houghton Mifflin.

Balka, C. (1989). *Twice blessed.* New York: Beacon Press.

Barret, R. (1990). *Gay fathers.* New York: Macmillan.

Beck, E. (1989). *Nice Jewish girls.* New York: Beacon Press.

Bence, P. (1991). Television and adolescents. In R. Lerner, A. Petersen, & J. Brooks-Gunn (Eds.), *Encyclopedia of adolescence* (pp. 1123–1126). New York: Garland.

Benson, P., Donahue, M., & Erickson, J. (1989). Adolescence and religion: Review of the literature from 1970–1986. *Research in the Social Scientific Study of Religion, 1,* 153–181.

Blea, I. (1992). *La Chicana.* Westport, CT: Praeger.

Blumenthal, W. (1992). *Homophobia: How we all pay the price.* Boston: Beacon Press.

Bohmer, C., & Parrot, A. (1993). *Sexual assault on campus.* New York: Lexington Books.

Bornstein, M., & Bruner, J. (1993). *Interaction in cognitive development.* Hillsdale, NJ: Erlbaum.

Boyer, C., & Hein, K. (1991a). Sexually transmitted diseases in adolescence. In R. Lerner, A. Petersen, & J. Brooks-Gunn (Eds.), *Encyclopedia of adolescence* (pp. 1028–1041). New York: Garland.

Boyer, C., & Hein, K. (1991b). AIDS and HIV infection in adolescents. In R. Lerner, A. Petersen, & J. Brooks-Gunn (Eds.), *Encyclopedia of adolescence* (pp. 37–43). New York: Garland.

Brown, L., & Gilligan, C. (1992). *Meeting at the crossroads: Women's psychology and girls' development.* Cambridge, MA: Harvard University Press.

Caldas, S. (1993). Current perspectives on adolescent pregnancy. *Journal of Adolescent Research, 8,* 4–20.

Center for Population Options. (1989). *Teenage pregnancy: Cost to taxpayers.* Washington, DC: Author.

Clapper, R., & Lipsitt, L. (1991). Risk taking and alcohol-mediated unprotected intercourse. *Journal of Substance Abuse, 3,* 91–96.

Coie, J. (1993). Toward a theory of peer rejection. In S. Asher & J. Coie (Eds.), *Peer rejection in childhood* (pp. 365–413). New York: Cambridge University Press.

Corser, K., & Adler, F. (1993). *When the bough breaks: Pregnancy and the legacy of addiction.* Portland, OR: New Sage Press.

Coulter, B., & Minninger, J. (1993). *The father daughter dance.* New York: Putnam.

Cowley, G. (1990, December 24). A birth control breakthrough. *Newsweek,* p. 68.

Crawford, I., & Robinson, L. (1990). Adolescents and AIDS. *Journal of Psychology of Human Sexuality, 3,* 25–33.

Debold, E., Wilson, M., & Malave, I. (1992). *Mother daughter revolution.* New York: Addison Wesley.

Deich, B., & Weiner, L. (1986). *The lecherous professor.* Urbana: University of Illinois.

Dew, R. (1994). *The family heart: A memoir of when our son came out.* New York: Farrar, Straus & Giroux.

Diegmueller, K. (1994). Efforts to boost girls' participation in sports urged. *Education Week, 13,* 8.

Donovan, P. (1992). *Our daughters' decisions: The conflict on abortion.* New York: Alan Guttmacher Institute.

Dornbusch, S., Mont-Reynaud, R., Ritter, P., Zeng-yin, C., & Steinberg, L. (1991). Stressful events and their correlates among adolescents of diverse backgrounds. In M. Colten & S. Gore (Eds.), *Adolescent stress* (pp. 111–131). New York: Aldine De Gruyter.

Eisen, M., Zellman, G., & McAlister, A. (1990). Evaluating a sexuality and contraceptive education program. *Family planning perspectives, 22,* 262–271.

Elster, A. (1991). Teenage fathers. In R. Lerner, A. Petersen, & A. Brooks-Gunn (Eds.), *Encyclopedia of adolescence* (pp. 360–364). New York: Garland.

Falk, P. (1989). Lesbian mothers. *American Psychologist, 44*, 941–947.

Fernandez, R. (1993). *Tales out of school.* New York: Little Brown.

Field, T. (1991). Adolescent mothers and their children. In R. Lerner, A. Petersen, & J. Brooks-Gunn (Eds.), *Encyclopedia of adolescence* (pp. 669–674). New York: Garland.

Fisher, M. (1991). Eating attitudes and health risk behaviors. *Journal of Adolescent Health, 12*, 377–384.

Flaake, E. (1994, June 1). The same magic. *Education Week*, p. 4.

Flaake, K. (1993). Sexual development and the female body in the mother-daughter relationship. In J. Mens-Verhulst, K. Schreurs, & L. Woertman (Eds.), *Daughtering and mothering* (pp. 7–15). New York: Routledge.

Flannery, D., Rowe, D., & Gulley, B. (1993). Impact of pubertal status and age on adolescent sexual experience and delinquency. *Journal of Adolescent Research, 8*, 21–40.

Fricke, A. (1981). *Reflections of a rock lobster: A story about growing up gay.* Boston: Alyson Press.

Garrod, A., Smulyan, L., Powers, S., & Kilkenny, R. (1992). *Adolescent portraits.* Boston: Allyn & Bacon.

Gibson, J., & Lanz, J. (1991). Hispanic teenagers' attitudes toward birth control. *Child and Adolescent Social Work Journal, 8*, 399–415.

Gilligan, C., Lyons, N., & Hanmer, T. (1990). *Making connections.* Cambridge, MA: Harvard University Press.

Grauerholz, E., & Koralweski, M. (1991). *Sexual coercion.* New York: Lexington Books.

Hacker, A. (1992). *Two nations: Black and white, separate, hostile, unequal.* New York: Charles Scribner's Sons.

Hallinan, M., & Williams, R. (1989). Interracial friendship choices in secondary schools. *American Sociological Review, 54*, 67–78.

Harrington, L. (1994). *Depressive disorder in childhood and adolescence.* New York: Wiley.

Hayes, C., & Hofferth, S. (1987). *Risking the future: Adolescent sexuality, pregnancy and child-bearing.* Washington, DC: National Academy Press.

Herek, G. (1992). *Hate crimes: Violence against lesbians and gay men.* Newbury Park, CA: Sage.

Herek, G., & Glunt, E. (1993). Interpersonal contact and heterosexuals' attitudes toward gay men. *Journal of Sex Research, 45*, 33–43.

Herek, G., Kimmel, D., Amaro, H., & Melton, G. (1991). Avoiding heterosexist bias in psychological research. *American Psychologist, 46*, 957–963.

Holland, D., & Eisenhart, M. (1991). *Educated in romance: Women, achievement and college culture.* Chicago: University of Chicago.

Jemmott, J., & Jemmott, L. (1993). Alcohol and drug use during sexual activity. *Journal of Adolescent Research, 8*, 41–57.

Jones, A. (1993). *Next time, she'll be dead: Battering & how to stop it.* Boston: Beacon Press.

Jones, E. (1986). *Teenage pregnancy in industrialized countries.* New Haven, CT: Yale University Press.

Josselson, R. (1992). *The space between us.* San Francisco: Jossey-Bass.

Kaczmarek, M., & Backlund, B. (1991). The loss of an adolescent romantic relationship. *Adolescence, 26*, 253–259.

Kantrowitz, B. (1992, December 14). A silver bullet against teen pregnancies? *Newsweek*, p. 42.

Ketterlinus, R., Lamb, M., & Nitz, K. (1994). Adolescent nonsexual and sex related problems and behaviors. In R. Ketterlinus & M. Lamb (Eds.), *Adolescent problem behaviors* (pp. 17–41). Hillsdale, NJ: Erlbaum.

Klein, J. (1994, June 13). Learning how to say

no. *Newsweek*, p. 29.

Kosmin, R., & Lachman, S. (1993). *One nation under God.* New York: Harmony.

Lamann, N. (1991). *The promised land.* New York: Random House.

Lawson, A., & Rhode, D. (1993). *The politics of pregnancy.* New Haven, CT: Yale University Press.

Lerman, R., & Ooms, T. (1992). *Young unwed fathers.* Philadelphia: Temple University Press.

Lerner, J., & Galambos, N. (1991). *Employed mothers and their children.* New York: Garland.

Levy, B. (1991). *Dating violence: Young women in danger.* Seattle: Seal Press.

Maccoby, E. (1990). Gender and relationships. *American Psychologist, 45,* 513–552.

Main, M. (1993). *A typology of human attachment organization.* New York: Cambridge University Press.

Marcus, E. (1993). *Is it a choice?* San Francisco: HarperCollins.

Marone, N. (1989). *How to father a successful daughter.* New York: Fawcett.

Marques, P., & McKnight, J. (1991). Drug abuse among pregnant adolescents. *American Journal of Drug and Alcohol Abuse, 17,* 399–413.

Martel, L., & Biller, J. (1987). *Stature and stigma: Biopsychosocial development of short males.* Lexington, MA: Lexington Books.

Martin, A. (1993). *The lesbian and gay parenting handbook.* New York: HarperCollins.

McKinney, D., & Peak, G. (1994). *School based and school linked health centers.* Washington, DC: Center for Population Options.

Miller, K. (1990). Adolescents' same sex and opposite sex relations. *Journal of Adolescent Research, 5,* 222–241.

Musick, J. (1993). *Young, poor, and pregnant.* New Haven, CT: Yale University Press.

Neville, B., & Parke, R. (1991). Adolescent fathers. In R. Lerner, A. Petersen, & J. Brooks-Gunn (Eds.), *Encyclopedia of Adolescence* (pp.

354–359). New York: Garland.

Nielsen, L. (in progress). *Stepmothering: A feminist approach.*

O'Sullivan, C. (1991). Acquaintance gang rape on campus. In A. Parrot & L. Bechhofer (Eds.), *Acquaintance rape* (pp. 140–156). New York: John Wiley & Sons.

Population Crisis Committee. (1991). *Contraception in America.* Washington, DC: Author.

Padgham, J., & Blyth, D. (1991). Dating during adolescence. In R. Lerner, A. Petersen, & J. Brooks-Gunn (Eds.), *Encyclopedia of adolescence* (pp. 196–198). New York: Garland.

Padilla, A., & Baird, T. (1991). Mexican American adolescent sexuality. *Hispanic Journal of Behavioral Sciences, 13,* 95–104.

Pallone, D. (1990). *Behind the mask: My double life in baseball.* New York: Viking.

Parke, R., & Ladd, G. (1992). *Family-peer relationships: Modes of linkage.* Hillsdale, NJ: Erlbaum.

Parkes, C., Stevenson-Hinde, J., & Marris, P. (1991). *Attachment across the life cycle.* New York: Tavistock/Routledge.

Parrot, A. (1991). *Acquaintance rape: The hidden crime.* New York: John Wiley & Sons.

Patterson, J., & Kim, P. (1992). *The day America told the truth.* New York: Plume.

Paul, E., & White, K. (1990). The development of intimate relationships in late adolescence. *Adolescence, 25,* 375–400.

Peirce, K. (1990). A feminist perspective on the socialization of teenage girls through *Seventeen* magazine. *Sex Roles, 23,* 491–500.

Phinney, V. (1990). The relationship between early development and sexual behaviors in adolescent females. *Adolescence, 25,* 321–332.

Plant, R. (1986). *The pink triangle: Nazi war against homosexuals.* New York: Henry Holt.

Raafkin, L. (1990). *Different mothers: Sons and daughters of lesbians.* Pittsburgh: Clia Press.

Remafedi, G. (1991). Adolescent homosexuality. In R. Lerner, A. Petersen, & J. Brooks-Gunn (Eds.), *Encyclopedia of adolescence* (pp. 504–507). New York: Garland.

Richards, M. (1991). Adolescent personality in girls and boys. *Psychology of Women Quarterly, 15,* 65–81.

Rotheram, M., & Koopman, C. (1991). AIDS and adolescents. In R. Lerner, A. Petersen, & J. Brooks-Gunn (Eds.), *Encyclopedia of adolescence* (pp. 29–36). New York: Garland.

Savin-Williams, R. (1992). Lesbian, gay male, and bisexual adolescents. In A. D'Augelli, & C. Patterson (Eds.), *Lesbian and gay identities across the lifespan.* New York: Oxford University Press.

Savin-Williams, R., & Berndt, T. (1990). Friendship and peer relations. In S. Feldman & G. Elliot (Eds.), *At the threshold: The developing adolescent* (pp. 277–308). Cambridge, MA: Harvard University Press.

Secunda, V. (1992). *Women and their fathers.* New York: Delacourte Press.

Silverberg, S., & Steinberg, L. (1990). Psychological well-being of parents with early adolescents. *Developmental Psychology, 26,* 658–666.

Smith, L. (1990). *Becoming a woman through romance.* New York: Routledge.

Smith, S. (1994). *Child rape victims.* Annapolis, MD: Bureau of Justice Statistics.

Suraci, P. (1992). *Male sexual armor.* New York: Irvington.

Talbot, M. (1993, April 26). Showing too much, too soon. *Newsweek,* p. 59.

Tasker, F., & Richards, M. (1994). Adolescents' attitudes toward marriage after parental divorce. *Journal of Adolescent Research, 9,* 340–462.

Thompson, S. (1990). Putting a big thing in a little hole: Teenage girls' accounts of sexual initiation. *Journal of Sex Research, 27,* 341–351.

Tolman, D. (1991). Adolescent girls, women, and sexuality. In C. Gilligan, A. Rogers, & D. Tolman (Eds.), *Women, girls, and psychotherapy* (pp. 55–71). New York: Haworth.

U.S. Department of Commerce. (1992). *General population characteristics: Poverty in the U.S.* Washington, DC: Bureau of the Census.

U.S. Department of Commerce. (1993). *Fertility of American women.* Washington, DC: Bureau of the Census.

Waldman, S. (1994, June 20). Taking on the welfare dads. *Newsweek,* pp. 34–38.

Warshaw, R. (1988). *I never called it rape.* New York: Harper & Row.

Weiner, I. (1992). *Psychological disturbance in adolescence.* New York: Wiley.

Wells, M. (1993). *Exclusion: Homosexuals and the right to serve.* New York: Regnery Gateway.

West, C. (1994). *Race matters.* New York: Random House.

White, M. (1993). *The material child: Coming of age in Japan and America.* New York: Free Press.

Williams, C. (1990). *Black teenage mothers: Pregnancy and child rearing from their perspective.* New York: Lexington Books.

14

ADOLESCENTS AND DRUGS

Chapter Outline

Key Questions Addressed In This Chapter

1. How and why have adolescents' attitudes and habits changed during the past 20 years in regard to drugs?
2. Which drugs do the most damage to adolescents today?
3. Which factors influence adolescent drug use and abuse?
4. What are the effects and consequences of using various drugs?
5. What are the most effective ways to prevent and to treat drug abuse?

Due to the widespread coverage in the popular media, it comes as no surprise to most of us that too many adolescents use and abuse drugs. What might be surprising, however, is learning which drugs cause the most damage and which adolescents abuse these drugs. Many of us might also be surprised to learn that teenagers and young adults are not using more drugs than ever before. Moreover, the two drugs that have consistently caused the most widespread damage to adolescents—alcohol and nicotine—seem to cause less alarm among young and old than do the more highly publicized drugs such as crack cocaine and LSD. This chapter addresses the following questions: How involved are adolescents in drug use? Which adolescents are the most likely to use or to abuse drugs? What are the effects and consequences of drug use? How can we prevent drug abuse and rehabilitate those who need help?

FACTORS INFLUENCING DRUG USE AND ABUSE

USE VERSUS ABUSE

Before beginning any discussion about drugs, it is important to understand several aspects of drug use. First, substances such as nicotine, alcohol, and diet pills are drugs. Merely because these substances are legal and widely used in our society does not mean they "aren't really drugs" in terms of their physical or their psychological impact. Second, drug use differs from drug abuse. Third, drug use and abuse usually progress in fairly predictable stages (Grilly, 1992; Kandel, 1991; Weiner, 1992).

Drug abuse is when the frequency and dosage is sufficient enough to interfere with daily activities, at which point the person's physical and mental health—and probably both—are in jeopardy. Drug abuse usually entails physical dependency and tolerance to the substance. Tolerance means that the person has to take increasingly larger doses in order to achieve the same high, or effect, as was provided by the initial doses. For example, instead of being able to get high on three or four beers, the person must drink at least a six-pack. A person who uses a drug regularly or in heavy doses usually builds up this kind of tolerance. Adolescents who use any drug, including nicotine and alcohol, on a regular basis in ways that interfere with their performance or their thinking are abusing that drug. For example, adolescents who smoke a pack of cigarettes every day are drug abusers. Not only are they physically addicted to nicotine, they experience physical withdrawal symptoms if they are deprived of their drug. In contrast, the adolescent who gets drunk two or three times a year at a party or who experiments a few times with marijuana is not considered a drug abuser.

Given these definitions, most adolescents are drug users, but very few are drug abusers. Those teenagers who move on to use drugs other than alcohol and nicotine typically proceed through predictable stages. Most who enter the world of drugs as adolescents do so either by smoking cigarettes or by drinking wine and beer. Then many progress to drinking hard liquor. More than half go beyond this and try marijuana a few times. Yet, most give up marijuana in favor of alcohol. Only a small number smoke marijuana regularly and advance to experimenting with cocaine, a hallucinogen, or heroin. Notice, however, that drinking, smoking, or trying marijuana in these progressive stages does not necessarily lead to use of harder drugs or to drug abuse in general. During adolescence and in adulthood, the vast majority of us limit ourselves to drinking, and we drink in moderation. Although a number of us try marijuana once or twice, we usually give it up altogether in favor of alcohol. What the stages of drug use do tell us, however, is that adolescents do not suddenly start using or abusing drugs, such as cocaine or LSD, without first having tried nicotine, alcohol, and marijuana.

The reasons why some young people progress from alcohol to marijuana to harder drugs, but others don't, are not fully understood. We do know that certain factors are closely associated with which drugs we use and how frequently we use or abuse them: our society's habits, our parents' behavior, genetic predisposition to addiction, certain aspects of our personalities, the people we choose to be around, and our race and gender (Cohen, 1991; Kandel, 1991; Rauch & Huba, 1991).

SOCIETAL INFLUENCES

Drug use is widespread among Americans. Indeed, virtually all of us use one drug or another to wake up, go to sleep, calm down, lose weight, be alert, build muscles, or to relax. As Table 14–1 illustrates, we use a wide array of drugs—prescription drugs such as Valium and Librium; legal drugs such as diet pills, nicotine, and alcohol; illegal drugs such as cocaine and LSD; and ordinary household products, such as glue and paint thinner, that we inhale in order to get high. Regardless of race, gender, or income, most of us are drug users. And, as a society, we pay a hefty price for our drug use. Death, accidents, lost work time, and poor health from drug use cost us nearly $25 billion in the workplace every year—and that doesn't include the losses due to alcohol abuse, another $43 billion annually. Nicotine alone is responsible for more deaths and illness than any other substance or disease (Centers for Disease Control [CDC], 1994; Rauch & Huba, 1991).

We have also had trouble making up our minds, as a society, how to deal with certain drugs. Some drugs that are at one time legal and socially acceptable are later declared illegal and looked down upon socially. As our opinions shift, so do our laws and policies. For instance, during the 1800s cocaine was not only legal, but also was considered a helpful stimulant and tonic. For a brief period, cocaine was one of the ingredients in the carbonated beverage that later, without cocaine, became the globally popular Coca-Cola. During the Roaring Twenties we also had a change of heart about alcohol and passed laws banning its use. Having failed to break ourselves from our drinking habits, however, we emerged from this Prohibition Era with new laws that restricted alcohol to adults, with the various states imposing specific age limits. More recently we have been arguing over what kinds of laws to pass regarding our society's second most popular drug—nicotine. As was true for alcohol, as our opinions about nicotine have changed, we have

Table 14–1

America's favorite drugs

Name	Alternative Terms	Source	Intake Method
Alcohol	Booze, juice, shot	Fruits, grains	Swallowed
Methaqualone	Quaaludes	Synthetic	Swallowed
Barbiturates	Blue devils, downers, yellow jackets, reds, goofballs, phenies, blue heavens	Synthetic	Swallowed, injected
Tranquilizers	Valium, Librium	Synthetic	Swallowed
Heroin	Horse, smack, scag, stuff, scat	Opium	Injected, sniffed, smoked
Codeine	Cough syrup	Opium	Swallowed
Demerol		Synthetic	Swallowed, injected
Morphine	White stuff	Opium	Swallowed, injected
Methadone	Dolly, meth	Synthetic	Swallowed, injected
LSD	Acid, sugar, cubes	Semi-synthetic	Swallowed, absorbed through skin, eye drops
PCP	Angel Dust, tic-tac, hog	Synthetic	Swallowed, injected, smoked
Mescaline	Mesc	Peyote	Swallowed
Psilocybin	Magic mushroom	Mushrooms	Swallowed
Amphetamines	Speed, uppers, bennies, pep pills, dexies, hearts	Synthetic	Swallowed, injected
Cocaine	Snow, coke, flake, Bernice, stardust, crack	Coca leaves	Injected, swallowed, sniffed
Caffeine		Coffee beans	Swallowed
Nicotine	Smoke, chaw	Tobacco leaves	Chewed, smoked
Marijuana	Mary Jane, grass, pot, hash, tea, dope, reefer, joint	Cannabis plant	Smoked, swallowed
Glue, gasoline, paint thinner, lighter fluid, toluene		Synthetic	Sniffed

raised the legal age for buying cigarettes, banned advertising cigarettes on television, and have now passed so many laws limiting its use in public areas that various "smokers' rights" groups have begun counter-legislation efforts.

Given our widespread use of drugs and our changing opinions about them, it is easy to understand why most teenagers in the U.S. use drugs. Like their elders, adolescents use far more alcohol and nicotine than all other drugs combined. Also like some of their elders, some teenagers regularly use or experiment with the various kinds of drugs described in Table 14–1.

FAMILY AND GENETIC FACTORS

In addition to society's values and habits, our families influence our attitudes and behavior. This "monkey-see, monkey-do" pattern of conduct makes it likely that parents who drink or smoke will have children who do so, too. Likewise, the teenage children whose parents use illegal drugs, such as cocaine and marijuana, are more likely to use these drugs than are children whose parents don't. So the best way to predict which teenagers will smoke, drink, or use illegal drugs is to identify which of these substances their parents use (Chassin, Rogosch, & Barrera, 1991; Cohen, 1991; Kandel, 1991; Rauch & Huba, 1991).

Our families can also influence our drug use through what they transmit to us genetically. At least in the case of alcohol, some children are born with a genetic predisposition to become alcoholics. Especially when the father is an alcoholic, there is a strong link between the parent's alcoholism and the teenager's (Chassin, Rogosch, & Barrera, 1991; Corser & Adler, 1993).

Drug use is also tied to how religious an adolescent is—a factor determined largely by the adolescent's family. As you recall, most adolescents adopt their family's religious views and habits. Like their older family members, those adolescents who are religious are less likely to use or to abuse drugs than are teenagers and adults in less religious families. The one exception is nicotine. Religious teenagers and adults are not less likely to smoke or to chew tobacco than are less religious people their age. Because low-income families are the most likely to be religious, and because low-income people are also the most likely to smoke, religion and smoking are highly correlated. However, religious teenagers and their parents and stepparents tend to use fewer illegal drugs (Benson, 1990; Brownfield & Sorenson, 1991; Kosmin & Lachman, 1993).

Another important factor is how familiar the parents are with their adolescent's circle of friends and how well they keep up with where and how they spend their free time. Well-supervised adolescents use and abuse fewer drugs than poorly supervised teenagers. Having too much freedom and too little supervision can be a problem in wealthy families as well as in poorer families. Nevertheless, teenagers from low-income families are more likely to be poorly supervised because they are more likely to come from fatherless homes where the unmarried mother usually can't supervise teenage children as well as two adults can. Regardless of whether their families are rich or poor, teenagers in fatherless homes are more likely to use and to abuse drugs and to begin using them at earlier ages than others do. Teenagers living with their unmarried mothers are also at a higher risk of abusing drugs because a father or stepfather is usually better at putting a stop to the kinds of behavior that lead teenagers into drug-related troubles. This is especially true for teenage boys (Flewelling & Bauman, 1990; Foxcroft & Lowe, 1991; Turner, Irwin, & Millstein, 1991; Weiner, 1992).

As you might expect, adolescents who are closely bonded to both parents have a lower risk of abusing drugs than those who do not get along well with their parents. Teenagers who are close to both parents, however, are usually self-confident, well-adjusted, and likable enough to have friends, make fairly good grades, and stay out of trouble with teachers and the police. It's not surprising, then, that those teenagers who get along at home seldom develop serious drug problems. In contrast, teenagers who use drugs regularly tend to spend much less time at home and to have more troubled relationships with their parents and teachers (Johnson & Pandina, 1991; Shilts, 1991).

One way of appreciating the importance of adult supervision is to notice how teenagers' part-time jobs are related to drug use. As you recall, high-school students who work more than 20 hours a week usually smoke, drink, and use more illegal drugs than teenagers who work only 10 to 15 hours at their jobs. At face value, we could misinterpret these findings to indicate that working too many hours causes students to use more drugs. Looking more carefully, however, we see that those teenagers who choose to work 20 hours a week generally make poorer grades, come from low-income families, and have been in trouble at school or with the police before they started working. Those teenagers who choose to work long hours each week are also usually the least well-supervised by the adults at home. In other words, factors other than the number of hours the student works each week are more closely related to his or her drug use (Bachman & Schulenberg, 1993; Steinberg & Dornbusch, 1991; Turner, Irwin, & Millstein, 1991).

PERSONALITY AND PEERS

As with other aspects of our adolescent lives, our decisions about drugs are influenced by more than family or society's attitudes and behaviors. Our decisions are influenced by our own personalities as well. In general, young children who are extremely aggressive, have poor impulse control, and do not get along well with their peers are more likely to use or abuse drugs as teenagers than those whose personalities are less aggressive and more self-controlled. Teenagers who have psychological and emotional problems are also more likely to use or abuse drugs than psychologically well-adjusted adolescents. For instance, teenagers who are clinically depressed and those who have attempted suicide generally use more drugs than other people their age (Doherty & Needle, 1991; Kandel, 1991; Shedler & Block, 1990; Weiner, 1992).

Also, it's probably no surprise that teenagers with low self-esteem use and abuse drugs more often than more self-confident, socially successful teenagers. For example, extremely lonely teenagers who have trouble making friends drink more than do teenagers who have an active, satisfying social life (Page & Cole, 1991). Likewise, teenagers who are already drinking heavily by seventh grade were making poor grades and having trouble getting along with their classmates before they started drinking (Ellickson & Hays, 1991). Those teenage girls who have low self-esteem and are extremely unhappy because they think they are overweight also smoke, drink, and use illegal drugs more often than more self-confident girls who are fairly satisfied with how they look (Fisher, 1991). Whatever our age, we are less likely to abuse drugs when we feel good about ourselves and are relatively satisfied with our lives.

A youngster's personality also influences the kinds of people he or she chooses to associate with. Psychologically and socially well-adjusted youngsters almost always choose to spend their time with those teenagers who, like themselves, get along fairly well with their parents, teachers, and peers. Although most well-adjusted teenagers do occasionally drink and some experiment with marijuana, their main reason for being friends or getting together is not to use drugs. Although most drink, very few of these well-adjusted teenagers abuse alcohol or use any other illegal drug. Although they might encourage each other to drink or to smoke a joint, they disapprove of using any drug in excess or on a regular basis. For those who do try marijuana, their decision is motivated mainly by curiosity, not by a personal problem or by feeling alienated from their parents or from society.

Teenagers with psychological, social, family, or academic problems also choose to associate with people like themselves. As a result of problems that existed in their lives before they ever tried drugs, these teenagers are the most likely to become frequent users or abusers of drugs. When these teenagers are together drinking or doing drugs, they are more concerned with getting high or getting drunk than with interacting with one another. Their friendships are primarily centered around drugs. Some of these teenagers eventually end up drinking or doing their drug—or both—without anyone else around, a habit that usually indicates they have become addicted (Kandel, 1991; Weiner, 1992).

The bottom line is that a "bad group" seldom leads a well-adjusted adolescent into abusing drugs. It is highly unlikely that a relatively happy, self-confident teenager who is doing fairly well in school and gets along with his or her parents will end up abusing drugs. On the other hand, it is also highly unlikely that adolescents who have low self-esteem, make poor grades, have serious psychological or family problems, or break the law, will be able to escape drug-related problems.

DRUG INFORMATION

Providing information about drugs in the right manner can also decrease teenage drug use. One of the clearest examples of the impact of drug education is the change in adolescents' use of nicotine, cocaine, and marijuana. Widespread publicity about the dangers of these drugs has resulted in more adolescents avoiding them. In and of itself, merely giving teenagers information about the harmful effects of drugs is not enough to change their behavior. And trying to scare them with gory details seldom works either (Rauch & Huba, 1991; Tobler, 1986).

We have been able to change the habits and attitudes of many teenagers and adults, however, by combining information about drugs with other strategies. Extensive media coverage of the drug-related deaths of famous athletes and rock musicians, for example, has helped to decrease our use of cocaine. Anti-smoking laws and raising the drinking age have also reinforced the information we are giving young people about the dangers of nicotine and alcohol. Because many adolescents get most of their information about drugs from television, anti-drug ads or commentaries by teenage role models are especially important (Mirzaee, 1991). Yet by whatever means the message gets through, teenagers who abstain and those who refrain from abusing a drug say they control themselves because they fear the consequences—both for themselves and for friends who may be with them when they are under the influence of a drug (Newcomb, Gahy, & Skager, 1990; Schwartz, 1991).

A prime example of the impact of not giving teenagers enough information is the slight increase now occurring in the use of LSD. Having experienced the 1970s when LSD became widely known as a dangerous drug, many adults have made the mistake of assuming that everyone knows about its dangers. Thus, we inadvertently failed to educate young people about the dangers of this drug, focusing attention instead on newer drugs such as crack and PCP. Consequently, more teenagers now believe that LSD is a safe drug, and its popularity is increasing. Also noteworthy is that the increased use of LSD has occurred most among teenagers who are not going to college. This might suggest that college-bound students' parents—many of whom were in college themselves during the 1960s and early 1970s when LSD was popular—have given their children information about the dangers of "tripping" with this dangerous hallucinogen (Johnston, O'Malley, & Bachman, 1993).

RACE, GENDER, AND LOCALE

Race and gender also are related to the motivation, frequency, and variety of drug use. In general, white adolescents drink, smoke, and use more inhalants, hallucinogens, amphetamines, and barbiturates than do other racial groups. Although about as likely as whites to use marijuana and inhalants, Hispanics use more heroin and cocaine than do all other teenagers. Second only to Asian Americans, black teenagers use the fewest drugs. Males of every race, however, use more of every drug, except diet pills, than do females (Johnston, O'Malley, & Bachman, 1993).

The area of the country and the size of the community is also related to drug use. Teenagers living in the West and in the Northeast and those living in large urban areas are the most apt to use drugs. This might partly be explained by the higher rates of poverty, easier access to drugs, and greater drug use among the adults in these areas. But adolescents living in rural areas are not insulated from drugs. Although rural teenagers are somewhat less likely to use marijuana and heroin, they use slightly more crack cocaine than do teenagers in large cities (Cohen, 1991; Johnston, O'Malley, & Bachman, 1993; Kingery, 1991; Pruitt, 1991).

As shown in Insert 14–1, no simple reason explains why some adolescents become drug abusers. Race, gender, family problems, trouble at school, low self-esteem, genetic predisposition, emotional problems, loneliness, poor social skills—all play a part in teenage drug abuse.

Adolescents Who Abuse Drugs

Why might these adolescents have abused drugs?

Steven at 14

When his mother arranged to have him admitted to a psychiatric hospital against his will, Steven was 14. Drinking, smoking pot, and skipping school, Steven was defiant and rebellious, and had already been arrested once for driving without a license. He had recently been in a car accident in which his best friend, sitting next to him, had been killed. His father had also died within the past year from a sudden heart attack. The hospital's therapists eventually discovered that Steven had been a difficult child to control since early childhood. Even as a preschooler, he had shown very little emotion, was unresponsive to punishment, and was determined to do things his own way, even though he continually got into trouble at home and at school. He had been making poor grades and stealing since first grade. He also had always had trouble making close friends.

Moreover, both of his parents had used marijuana regularly. A physically mature boy, Steven looked older than his age. The therapists concluded that Steven's drug abuse and his aggressive, defiant behavior were mainly the consequences of his having an antisocial personality, not a consequence of the deaths of his father and friend.

Male college student, describing his adolescence

"I'm an only child, the son of parents who had to get married when they were 18 because my mother was pregnant. By time I was 12 or 13, my responsible nature had won me a bigger share of independence than my friends enjoyed. My parents didn't question most of the decisions I made. At the age of 14, I was the youngest employee at a movie theater where almost everyone was 4 or 5 years older than me. They became my friends. I was an intelligent young man who spoke easily to adults. I began to explore marijuana when I was 15 and

PRESENT USE AND TRENDS

The Good News

Our most reliable source of information about the drug use of adolescents and college students are the national surveys that have been conducted annually for nearly 20 years by the Monitoring the Future project. Based on information from approximately 17,000 high-school students in private and public schools across the country, these statistics provide valuable information about drug use and trends. In recent years, Monitoring the Future has also been collecting data from college students. So for many drugs, we can compare high-school and college student usage, as well as that of college students to college-age people who are not in college. The good news is that teenagers and college students are now

smoked throughout high school, while I continued to be an Honors student. Since no on caught on, I became more and more involved in marijuana. I used to get stoned before I did almost anything. Get stoned and play basketball. Get stoned and go to classes. Get stoned and lie in the sun. Get stoned for no reason at all. By the time I started college, I began to see it as a problem. Since I had a friend network in which pot smoking was a regular activity, I was afraid that smoking less would mean losing my friends. Finally I decided to go and see a counselor. By the end of my sophomore year in college, I knew that marijuana was something I would have to work on, like an alcoholic, for the rest of my life."

Native American College Student, describing her adolescence

"I grew up in North Dakota. My parents met through a relocation program which was attempting to assimilate Native Americans into urban life from their reservation or tribal communities. My father began drinking when I was born. He died at 28 from alcoholism when I was 7. In seventh grade I went to an affluent college prep school. Poverty, not my race, made me an outsider. Kids were mean there. My mom finished college, but keeping up with the bills was hard because there were four of us kids. In high school I was involved in sports. It was a time when my brother and I numbed ourselves to being poor and to forgetting the Cheyenne and Blackfoot ways. Once I went to college, I thought people would be wise and mature. I was wrong. My first term, I drank whenever I could. I would sit in front of a computer and, for the life of me, couldn't think of a damned thing to say about Conrad's imagery in the *Heart of Darkness*. Second term I got suspended for bad grades. Back home I didn't feel like doing anything. I started to drink on the sly. I'd drink when there wasn't anything for me to do or just to liven things up. Mom finally said, 'Jean, you can't do this to me. This happened to your dad. Why are you doing this?' I didn't know what to say."

Sources: Adapted from A. Garrod, L. Smulyan, S. Powers, & R. Kilkenny (Eds.) (1992). *Adolescent portraits.* Boston: Allyn & Bacon. I. Weiner (1992). *Psychological disturbance in adolescence.* New York: Wiley.

using fewer drugs than people their age have used during the past 20 years. (Johnston, O'Malley & Bachman, 1993. All statistics for the remainder of this chapter are from "Monitoring the Future" unless otherwise cited).

The number of high-school seniors using any illegal drug has fallen to 27%— half the peak level in 1979. Both cocaine and marijuana usage are continuing a long decline. The number of high-school seniors who have used cocaine within the past year has fallen from a high of almost 4% in 1987 to about 1%. Only about 6% of all high-school seniors had tried cocaine in 1992, and fewer than 1% had used it within the preceding month. Likewise, only 25% of all high-school seniors had tried marijuana. Only 6% had used marijuana within the preceding month, and fewer than 2% of 12th graders smoked it daily. These figures represent a huge reduction from the peak level of more than 50% who had tried marijuana and 10% who smoked it daily in 1979. As shown in Table 14–2, cocaine and marijuana are not popular among college students either.

Table 14–2

Drug use: High-school seniors and college students

	Have tried it		Have used within past month	
	Seniors	College	Seniors	College
Alcohol	88%	92%	50%	70%
Been drunk	65%	NA	30%	NA
Drink daily	—	—	3%	4%
Nicotine	65%	NA	28%	23%
Smoke daily	—	—	17%	9%
Chew tobacco	33%	NA	11%	NA
Marijuana	33%	26%	12%	4%
Use daily	—	—	3%	2%
Inhalants	17%	14%	2%	1%
Stimulants	14%	10%	3%	1%
LSD	8%	10%	2%	2%
Cocaine	6%	8%	1%	1%
Crack	3%	2%	.6%	.1%
Ice	3%	.6%	.5%	0%
PCP	2%	NA	.6%	NA
Tranquilizer	6%	7%	.5%	1%
Barbiturates	5%	4%	1%	.7%
Ecstasy	NA	3%	NA	.4%
Steroids	2%	NA	1%	NA
Heroin	1%	.5%	.3%	0%

NA = data not available

Source: L. Johnston, P. O'Malley, & J. Bachman (1993). *National survey results on drug use from Monitoring the Future.* Rockville, MD: National Institute on Drug Abuse.

Stimulants, **barbiturates** (tranquilizers and sleeping pills), and hallucinogens have also lost popularity since the late 1970s. By 1992, the number of high-school and college students using stimulants had fallen from a high of 20% to approximately 7%. The use of amphetamines and other pills to stay awake doubled during the 1980s to the point that nearly one fourth of all high-school and college students were using them. Nowadays only about 12% of all college and high-school students have used them. The use of tranquilizers and sleeping pills has also declined by about two thirds. In 1992 fewer than 3% of all students had used them within the preceding year. Only 2% of the high-school seniors had tried PCP, and only 8% had ever tried LSD in 1992. As has been the case for the past 20 years, heroin and steroids are rarely used by teenagers or college students. Only 1% of high-school seniors had tried heroin, and only 2% had used steroids in 1992. Even fewer used these drugs on a regular basis.

The Bad News

Unfortunately not all of the news from Monitoring the Future is this good. Let's look first at our most popular drug—alcohol. Despite the fact that it is illegal for virtually all high-school students and most college students to buy alcoholic beverages, almost all of them drink. As shown in Table 14–2, only 12% of high-school seniors and 8% of college students have never had a drink. By time they are seniors in high school, half have been drunk and nearly a third have had a drink within the preceding month. Not only do most of us drink as teenagers, but we drink too much in social situations on the weekends. More than 40% of college students, 30% of 12th graders, and nearly 15% of 8th graders reported having five or more drinks in a row on at least one occasion during the past 2 weeks. Most of us cut down on our heavy drinking after our early 20s. Yet even in this age bracket, one third of us have still had five or more drinks in a row during the past 2 weeks. On the brighter side, 12th-grade drinking has fallen. The number of seniors who reported having had a drink within the past month fell from a high of 75% in 1980 to about 50% by 1992. Daily drinking has also fallen from a peak of 7% to roughly 3% in the same period. Nevertheless, as teenagers and adults, we still drink more and drink more often than people in other industrialized countries.

The other bad news concerns nicotine. Although teenage smoking rates dropped dramatically from 1977 to 1981, they have not dropped much since then. Nearly 30% of high-school seniors still smoke, 17% of them daily. The numbers of 8th- and 10th-graders currently smoking has actually risen since 1990 to 16% and 22%, respectively. About half of our young adolescents and nearly a third of our high-school seniors don't believe that heavy smoking poses any serious threats to a person's health. Chewing tobacco also remains fairly popular with white, male teenagers. Nearly a third of these boys have tried chewing tobacco, and almost 15% use it regularly.

Another disturbing finding is that LSD and inhalants have become more popular. Since 1990, the number of eighth graders who have tried LSD has increased from 1.7% to 2.1%. Although virtually all of the increase has taken place among those who are not going on to college, 8% of our teenagers have tried LSD. The use of inhalants is also on the rise. This class of drugs includes common household substances such as glues, aerosols, butane, and solvents, which are sniffed or inhaled to get high. Nearly 10% of 8th graders and 8% of 12th graders have used inhalants within the past year—a three-fold increase since the mid-1970s.

Collegiate and Noncollegiate Differences

How does drug use compare among teenagers planning to go to college, students already in college, and the 75% in this age range who are not in college? In general, college-bound teenagers use fewer drugs than their classmates who are not headed for college. High-school seniors who are not college-bound are twice as likely to drink or use marijuana every day as the 25% who are college-bound. Teenagers who are not going to college are also the ones who have increased their use of LSD. The differences are especially dramatic in regard to cigarette smoking. Fewer than 10% of college-bound teenagers and college students smoke, in contrast to nearly 30% of other people their age who do smoke. On the other hand, once teenagers begin college, they start drinking more. As a result, young people who are in college and those who aren't drink about the same. Compared to other people their age, however, college students drink less on a daily basis and do more heavy, binge drinking on weekends.

But aren't these differences probably because most college students come from families with the higher incomes? Although many of us might assume that teenagers from higher income families are less likely to use drugs, this is usually not the case. Rich and poor teenagers are about as likely to use marijuana, alcohol, and cocaine. During the late 1970s and early 80s, the high price of cocaine did allow the rich greater access to cocaine than was available to the poor. But once the less-expensive form of cocaine, crack, became available in the mid-80s, these income differences disappeared. The two exceptions are nicotine and heroin—both of which are used more by teenagers from low-income families.

RACIAL DIFFERENCES

Unlike family income, race is related to adolescent's drug choices and their motivation for using drugs. Contrary to most people's stereotypes, white and Hispanic teenagers use more drugs than black teenagers. Also contrary to stereotypes, Asian American teenagers whose families have recently immigrated to the U.S. are using more drugs than the average teenager. As shown in Table 14–3, the racial differences show up especially well when each drug is considered separately (Johnston, O'Malley, & Bachman, 1993; McKenry, 1991).

Table 14–3

Race and high-school seniors who have used drugs

	Black	Hispanic	White
Alcohol	80%	90%	80%
Been drunk	36%	65%	70%
Nicotine	5%	25%	28%
Smoke daily	4%	12%	20%
Marijuana	23%	40%	36%
Inhalants	7%	17%	20%
Hallucinogens	1%	9%	11%
Cocaine	2%	12%	7%
Crack cocaine	1%	6%	3%

Source: L. Johnston, P. O'Malley, & J. Bachman (1993). *National survey results on drug use from Monitoring the Future.* Rockville, MD: National Institute on Drug Abuse.

With regard to cocaine and marijuana, African American teenagers are about half as likely to have used these drugs as other teenagers. Although teenagers from lower-income families are the most likely to smoke or chew tobacco, black teenagers are the least likely to use nicotine. Almost one third of white and Hispanic teenagers smoke, compared to only about 5% of black teenagers. And although approximately 5% of Hispanic and white eighth graders have used hallucinogens, only 1% of the black students have tried them. White and Native American teenagers top the list for alcohol use, followed by Hispanic, black, and Asian youths. The number of white and Hispanic seniors who have been drunk is twice that of their black classmates. Not only do white teenagers smoke and drink the most, they also use more inhalants, hallucinogens, barbiturates, amphetamines, and tranquilizers.

Several findings are especially disturbing with regard to Hispanic teenagers. First, Hispanic students have higher dropout rates than blacks or whites, which means that their drug use is underestimated by researchers who are gathering data from students.. It is important, therefore, to look at their drug use in the 8th grade. By 8th grade nearly 20% of the Hispanic students have already tried marijuana—twice the number of whites, and three times that of blacks. Nearly 20% have also tried inhalants and engaged in binge drinking within the preceding 2 weeks—twice the rate of either blacks or whites. Certain groups within the Hispanic population also use drugs more often than others. For example, Hispanic and white students are about as likely to have tried marijuana and to have used it within the preceding month. But Mexican American teenagers are twice as likely to use marijuana and 14 times as likely to use inhalants as other teenagers. Finally, Hispanic students who do stay in school use more of the most dangerous drugs than other teenagers—cocaine, crack, heroin, and steroids. All in all then, Hispanic students have very high rates of drug use in 8th grade, and they use as dangerous a variety of drugs as older adolescents do.

Race also seems to influence the reasons adolescents use drugs. These differences might be because black, Hispanic, and Native American teenagers are much more likely than white or Asian Americans to be living in abject poverty, in fatherless families, and in neighborhoods ravaged by crime and drugs. Black, Native American, and Hispanic teenagers, therefore, usually use drugs to escape the harsh realities of their day to day lives. In contrast, white and Asian teenagers are more apt to use drugs to cope with problems such as feeling lonely, having trouble with a boyfriend or girlfriend, or trying to relax in a social situation (McKenry, 1991; Williams, 1991).

Gender Differences

Besides race, gender is also related to drug use. Males of all races use more drugs and use them more often than do females their age. The only exceptions are smoking cigarettes and taking tranquilizers, which both genders do about equally. The other exception is diet pills. Nearly 12% of teenage girls use them, in contrast to only 4% of the boys. Given our society's obsession with female thinness, this finding is hardly shocking. Fortunately only a third as many teenage girls are using diet pills now as were using them in the early 1980s. As many girls are raised to believe that being thin is part of being feminine, so many boys are still raised to believe that being masculine requires daring and fearlessness—or at least never showing fear. "Real men" take risks and accept challenges without backing down. It hardly comes as a surprise, then, that most males use more drugs and use them more excessively and more often than most females.

A few specific examples highlight these gender differences. By 12th grade, males are one to two times more likely than females to have used drugs. For instance, only .1% of high-school girls have used steroids compared to slightly more than 2% of the boys. Males are also much more likely to use drugs frequently and in excessive amounts. For example, 12th grade boys are almost three times more likely than girls to use marijuana daily and five times more likely to drink daily. Unlike smoking tobacco, chewing tobacco is almost exclusively a male activity. More than 20% of senior boys chew tobacco compared to only 2% of the girls.

Looking back over the past 20 years, we can see that males and females have grown more alike in regard to most street drugs. Nowadays they are basically alike as far as having tried marijuana, smoking cigarettes, and using tranquilizers. Girls are also now as likely as boys to drink, although boys still drink more heavily and more often. Beer, not hard liquor or wine, accounts for most of this gender difference.

ATTITUDES TOWARD DRUGS

As mentioned, teenagers convinced of the dangers of a particular drug are more likely to avoid it. So which drugs do teenagers fear most? Which are they most likely to disapprove of their friends using? How well is information about the harm of drugs getting through to most teenagers? The good news is that most adolescents fear and disapprove of their friends using most drugs. The bad news is that a number of teenagers, especially seventh and eighth graders, are still not convinced of the dangers of smoking or chewing tobacco, binge drinking, or experimenting with other illicit drugs.

Fortunately, virtually all high-school seniors disapprove of using or of trying any drug—with the exception of alcohol. Like most American adults, most teenagers approve more of drinking, smoking cigarettes, and trying marijuana than of using any other illicit drug. Approximately 75% of the seniors disapprove of even trying marijuana or smoking cigarettes. Compared to 10 years ago, adolescents are also more disapproving of drinking. Widespread publicity about drugs, and such acts as raising the drinking age to 21, seem to be changing teenagers' attitudes.

Some of their other attitudes, however, are not as wise and well-reasoned. Most 12th graders believe that having one or two drinks a day is worse than having five or more drinks in a row on the weekend or at a party. This attitude is disturbing because binge drinking is responsible for so many teenage deaths and injuries, especially in motor vehicle accidents. Many teenagers' beliefs about nicotine are also troubling. Unlike their attitudes about other drugs, teenage attitudes about nicotine have not changed much during the past 10 years, especially among the third who smoke. Nearly 50% of the 8th graders and 30% of the 12th graders still refuse to believe that heavy smoking poses a serious hazard to a person's health. Despite all of our anti-smoking laws, policies, and publicity in the past decade, we have failed to convince a number of teenagers that nicotine is an extremely harmful, addictive drug. Very likely, the $4 billion a year that the tobacco industry spends on advertising and promoting cigarettes has helped to maintain the image that smoking is cool, sexy, harmless, and fun. Smoking harms far more people than marijuana through the direct effects of the toxic agents in the cigarette on the smokers and through the indirect effects of second-hand smoke and fumes on nonsmokers. Only half of 12th graders believe we should ban cigarette smoking in certain public places; but 80% favor a similar ban on smoking marijuana (CDC, 1994; Johnston, O'Malley, & Bachman, 1993).

Do adolescents' attitudes toward drugs differ much from their parents' attitudes? For most drugs, no. Most adolescents and the adults in their families agree about which drugs they most approve and disapprove. In the late 1970s and early 1980s, adolescents and their parents disagreed far more than they do today. In 1979, for example, 85% of parents, but only about 30% of the teenagers, disapproved of smoking pot. Today, however, adolescents are only somewhat less likely than are their parents to disapprove of marijuana. On the other hand, teenagers and adults still disagree more about using marijuana than any other drug (Johnston, O'Malley, & Bachman, 1993).

DRUG EFFECTS AND CONSEQUENCES

Regardless of the drug, teenagers who are using any substance regularly or using fairly large doses are the most likely to get into fights, carry weapons, attempt suicide, commit crimes, quit school, and engage in risky sexual behaviors. Whether they are abusing nicotine, alcohol, or any other drug, these teenagers are the most apt to get pregnant, contract venereal diseases and AIDS, die or be injured and disfigured in car accidents or fights, break the law, and make bad grades. Young people who frequently use any drug in excess are the least likely to go to college or to do well in high school and, therefore, the most likely to end up in low paying, dead-end jobs as adults. It is not so much that abusing the drug causes these types of problems to develop. It is more often the case that the teenager who is abusing a drug generally has the kind of personality, family situations, and the academic, social, or psychological problems that contribute to various kinds of maladaptive behavior (Kandel, 1991; McKenry, 1991; Weiner, 1992).

ALCOHOL

As it is for most adults, alcohol is most adolescents' favorite drug. In terms of financial, physical, and psychological losses, alcohol costs adolescents and their families more than all other drugs combined. Most teenage injuries and accidents are related to alcohol abuse, especially among males. Heavy drinking is also linked to teenage violence, delinquency, sexual promiscuity, date rape, and the physical abuse of girls by their boyfriends (Boyd, Howard & Zucker, 1994; Cohen, 1991; Kandel, 1991; McKenry, 1991; Weiner, 1992).

Alcohol abuse also affects many adolescents before they are born. The babies of pregnant women who drink heavily are likely to be born with fetal alcohol syndrome—a condition that permanently retards a child's mental and physical development. For example, in a survey of nearly 14,000 Native American teenagers, many had learning problems and forms of mental retardation that could have been prevented if their mothers had not abused alcohol when they were pregnant (Blum, 1992; Corser & Adler, 1993; Light, 1988).

Even those adolescents who have never had a drink can be negatively affected by alcohol, as a consequence of their parents' drinking problems. If either parent drinks excessively, there is more physical, emotional, and sexual abuse in the family. Parents with drinking problems are also the most likely to have trouble finding and keeping good jobs. As a result, their families suffer needless economic hardships. Indeed, many children on welfare and those living in shelters for the homeless have an alcoholic parent (Jencks, 1994; Watts & Roosevelt, 1989).

Regardless of a family's income, adolescents with an alcoholic parent suffer a number of social and emotional problems. As teenagers and as adults, even when they are no longer living with the alcoholic parent, the children of alcoholics run a higher risk of developing drinking problems and of marrying alcoholics or drug abusers. An alcoholic's children often lack self-confidence, are unable to trust people, and have trouble forming emotionally intimate relationships. Having to take care of or cover up for the alcoholic parent, these teenagers are often unable to develop their own social skills, their own identities, and healthy relationships with people outside the family. As shown in Insert 14–2, growing up in a home filled with lies, secrets, denial, a lack of intimacy, and abuse, usually forces children to subjugate their own development to the needs of the alcoholic parent (Ackerman, 1989; Ryerson, 1985).

Nicotine

Although not nearly as popular as alcohol, nicotine is still used by nearly a third of all teenagers. More than 3 million adolescents smoke and more than 1 million chew tobacco. In several respects nicotine is unique among drugs (CDC, 1994; Johnston, O'Malley, & Bachman, 1993). First, unlike other drugs, nicotine attracts the most users during the early years of adolescence. Although many of us do not start drinking or experimenting with marijuana or cocaine until late adolescence or early adulthood, virtually all smokers take up their habit before the age of 16. Those teenagers who begin smoking at the earliest ages are the heaviest smokers and are the least likely to ever quit smoking. Interestingly, many teenage smokers say their friends did not pressure them into smoking. On the other hand, most smokers' friends do not actively discourage their habit and most

Insert 14–2

Responses from children of alcoholics

Denial

"My mother used to drink and as a teenager I'd come home from school and she'd be passed out. To me, she was napping and that's how I denied for years that my mother was an alcoholic."

Emotional Neglect

"I wish I could have had real parents. I've always wondered what it would have been like to have someone care about me and share my deepest hurts and secrets and successes."

Anger

"When our father used to get us up in the middle of the night and march around the house singing, 'Onward Christian Soldiers,' it would be a school night and we would think that we should be able to sleep like normal kids."

"In my own recovery I found that I slowly experienced and found ways to express anger at Dad for his various abusive rampages while he was drunk. The surprise was that I had seen my mother as a victim all those years and never held her responsible for the hell my brothers and I went through."

Insecurity and Uncertainty

"As a child it seemed like my alcoholic mother was almost always either extremely angry or extremely loving. I never knew when I came home which it would be. It was scary to live in a house like that. I never really knew why. I thought it was me."

Absence of Role Models

"Mom was a closet drinker. I always knew something was wrong, yet couldn't place my finger on it. How could I use her as a role model when I knew she had a problem?"

Emotional Incest

"My alcoholic mother rejected Dad sexually in their mid-40s, so Dad and I became emotionally incestuous. Now I need to learn to set emotional and sexual boundaries with men. I need to learn to be assertive with my needs toward men and not fear losing them."

Sexual Abuse

"The sexual abuse started when I was 12. I thought I was doing something to cause what was happening. My father told me if I did not keep quiet, he would leave my mother. When I was 13 he came home drunk again one night and came into my room. I pulled a gun from under the covers and shot him."

Source: R. Ackerman (1989) *Perfect daughters.* Deerfield, FL: Health Communications.

teenage smokers have friends who smoke. Second, nicotine is the only drug other than heroin that is closely related to socioeconomic class. Teenage smokers are usually from low-income families where the adults generally smoke too.

Third, since the mid-1980s teenagers have not been responding to the widespread publicity against smoking, even though they have responded with regard to other drugs. Although teenagers in 1992 were using fewer of all street drugs than they did in the 1970s and 1980s, they were using as much nicotine. Teenagers now account for one fourth of the $476 million spent each year in our country for cigarettes. In short, our anti-smoking laws and campaigns have not been as successful as similar laws and publicity against other drugs.

Teenage smokers are also unique in that most of them refuse to believe the drug is dangerous. Somehow it has not gotten through to them that smoking is the chief preventable cause of disease and death in our country. Not only is smoking linked to lung cancer, but to heart disease, emphysema, breast and uterine cancer, birth defects, and miscarriages. The effects of breathing other people's smoke are also being documented. Infants, young children, friends, and co-workers of smokers have more pulmonary diseases and allergic reactions than do people in smoke-free environments. Teenagers who chew tobacco instead of smoking it are also at risk for developing cancers of the mouth, throat, and lungs. Because teenagers' attitudes and smoking habits have not changed much since the mid-1980s, our anti-smoking campaigns are probably being offset by the $4 billion spent yearly by the tobacco industry on advertising and promotions.

Marijuana

As is true with tobacco, frequent smoking of marijuana can cause lung cancer and other pulmonary diseases. Other side effects include loss of memory, fragmented speech, inattentiveness, and lower testosterone levels, which contribute to male infertility. As is true with most other drugs, the sensations adolescents have after smoking dope partly depend on what they expect to happen, the kind of setting they are in, and the people they are with. Also like alcohol, using marijuana is linked to many motor vehicle accidents resulting in death or injury (Grilly, 1992).

Several factors set marijuana apart from alcohol. After using marijuana, some young people experience panic or anxiety attacks, and others feel the after-effects for as long as 24 hours. Although marijuana is less physically addictive than alcohol, teenagers can and do become psychologically addicted. Compared to teenagers who drink, those teenagers who use marijuana regularly are more likely to have problems getting along with their parents and to feel alienated from society and school (Grilly, 1992; Kandel, 1991; Rauch & Huba, 1991).

Cocaine and Amphetamines

Unlike marijuana, which is a relaxant, cocaine is a stimulant. Generally the body responds to cocaine much as it does to **amphetamines**—the class of stimulants that includes stay-awake pills, diet pills, speed, and Ice. In fact when cocaine and amphetamines are administered intravenously without the person knowing which has been injected, the effects are identical except that cocaine wears off in about 30 minutes but amphetamines last 2 to 3 hours. The form of cocaine known as crack was introduced to the American market in the mid-1980s. **Crack** is cocaine that has been converted from its powdery, white form into a crystalline substance that resembles large crystals of salt. Although more addictive and more potent than powdered cocaine, crack's cheaper price per unit made it more popular with teenagers and adults during the 1980s (Grilly, 1992; Johnston, O'Malley, & Bachman, 1993).

Whether in powdered or crystallized form, low to moderate doses of cocaine improve physical quickness and strength, as well as performance on cognitive tasks that require sustained attention, such as detecting objects on a radar screen. Conversely, cocaine interferes with physical tasks that require smooth and accurate movements. Therefore, swimmers, football players, and runners find cocaine more appealing than might golfers and tennis players. In high doses, cocaine interferes with alertness and causes depression, social withdrawal, and paranoia. Excessive use can lead to violent behavior. Sudden death can also occur from brain hemorrhages, convulsions, and heart attacks. Approximately 10% of the people who start out as recreational users end up addicted. Most teenagers who use cocaine on a regular basis have social, emotional, academic, or family problems that existed before they started using it (Grilly, 1992; Williams, 1991).

Like cocaine, in low to moderate doses amphetamines speed up the body physically and increase mental alertness. And like cocaine, amphetamines also can be physically addictive. The negative effects of amphetamines can be as mild as the nervousness, headaches, and hyperactivity that come from drinking too much coffee, using diet pills, or consuming stay-awake pills. The negative effects can also be extreme, such as those experienced by people using the drug known as **Ice.** A drug with a high that lasts from 8 to 24 hours, Ice is as addictive as crack cocaine. Unlike cocaine, derived from the leaves of the coca plant, Ice is a synthetic drug. Prolonged use can cause fatal lung and kidney disorders and birth defects, as well as psychological problems lasting up to 2 years after usage. Although its popularity in the United States has primarily been limited to the West Coast, Ice has now replaced cocaine and marijuana as a popular drug for young people in Hawaii (Johnston, O'Malley, & Bachman, 1993).

HALLUCINOGENS: LSD, PCP, AND MDMA

Though rarely used by teenagers, the three most popular hallucinogens are **LSD ("Acid"), PCP ("Angel Dust"),** and **MDMA ("Ecstasy").** Among the hallucinogens, LSD is popular for its relatively cheap price and the duration of the high. In 1990, a hit that lasted up to 12 hours cost only about $5, compared with $70 for a quarter ounce of market-grade marijuana and $50 for a half gram of cocaine. Hallucinogens usually produce pleasurable hallucinations by intensifying and distorting sounds, images, taste, and tactile sensations. Good "trips" can also supposedly make a person more insightful. Some therapists who have used MDMA therapeutically claim that it helps their patients communicate more honestly and gain greater insights into their psychological problems. Timothy Leary, the nationally famous LSD advocate who urged Americans to "turn on, tune in, drop out" more than 20 years ago, was still using LSD in 1991—at the age of 71—pursuing what he calls "noble, spiritual purposes" (Seligman, 1992). However, so-called "bad trips" can involve frightening hallucinations that might lead to paranoia, violence, or even suicidal behavior. Moreover, the effects of a bad trip can be suddenly and unexpectedly relived years after having used the drug—experiences referred to as "flashbacks" (Grilly, 1992; Seligman, 1992).

DRUG PREVENTION AND REHABILITATION

Prevention

Given the harm that most drugs do, we have tried to determine the most effective ways of preventing young people from using and abusing them. As long as so many American adults drink and smoke, it is not probable that we are going to convince young people never to use these drugs. What we can aim for, however, is further reducing the number of teenagers who use them and teaching teenagers how to drink more moderately and more safely. As mentioned, making changes in our society such as passing anti-smoking laws, banning cigarette advertising on television, and raising the drinking age have helped to reduce teenage drinking and smoking. Nevertheless, we have to find more effective ways to change the habits of those teenagers who are drinking, smoking, and chewing tobacco. We also must find better ways to convince teenagers of the dangers of heavy drinking, especially when they or their friends are driving under its influence.

In regard to all other drugs, our attempts to educate young people have obviously had some positive impact. Not only do teenagers use fewer drugs than in the late 1960s, they are also more disapproving of their friends using them. The fact that far fewer girls are using diet pills also suggests that we might be convincing them that there are safer ways to lose weight than with amphetamines. On a more pessimistic note, the slight increases in LSD use among teenagers not bound for college suggests that we need to focus more on disseminating information about its dangers.

Merely trying to scare teenagers away from drugs by giving them information about the harmful side effects, however, is not effective. Merely preaching against the evils of drugs or using scare tactics has seldom worked. Instead, we need to do more of what has seemed to work—combining information with widespread coverage of drug-related deaths of the people teenagers identify with, changing our laws about who is old enough to buy drugs such as cigarettes and alcohol, and setting a better example in our films and on television of people who do not abuse drugs. Notably, the publicity surrounding the deaths of several famous athletes and rock musicians does seem to have had an impact on teenagers' perceptions of cocaine (Johnston, O'Malley, & Bachman, 1993; Newcomb, Gahy, & Skager, 1990; Tobler, 1986; Weiner, 1992).

REHABILITATION

Once adolescents have begun abusing a drug, recovery involves more than overcoming the physical addiction. Giving up the drug is not enough. Rehabilitation also has to teach adolescents more effective skills for coping with life's inevitable problems and new skills for relating to people. Because so many teenage drug abusers have low self-esteem and poor academic skills, staying off drugs often requires teaching them ways to build their self-confidence and improve their grades. The most effective recovery programs also include counseling the adolescent's family so that all involved can learn better ways to relate to each other and to resolve their differences. Self-help groups such as Narcotics Anonymous and Alcoholics Anonymous also provide ongoing support for adolescents after they leave a drug rehabilitation program.

Unfortunately most drug rehabilitation programs for teenagers are not very successful. Why? First, many programs have placed too much emphasis on trying to scare teenagers away from using drugs again by giving them additional information about the hazards of drugs. By itself, this approach rarely works. Moreover, most rehabilitation programs have not taught teenagers specific skills they can use once they return to the real world—skills such as how to study, how to improve their grades, how to make friends without relying on drugs, how to build their self-confidence, and how to solve problems with family members, teachers, and employers. Some rehabilitation programs have also helped adolescents stay off drugs by involving them in a daily exercise program. Their physical activities not only give them something to do with their free time, but also build their self-confidence by improving appearance and physical skills. Extensive individual and family counseling, support groups, and special skills training have succeeded in helping many adolescents remain drug-free (Collingwood, 1991; Tobler, 1986; Weiner, 1992).

CONCLUSION

On the one hand, we can feel relieved that teenagers are using fewer drugs than ever before. On the other hand, millions of adolescents over-use and abuse drugs—above all, alcohol and nicotine. Given the popularity of these two drugs in adult society, we probably cannot convince most teenagers not to use them. We can, however, do a far better job limiting their use of these two drugs and helping young people exercise more self-control and better judgment in using them. As for other drugs, we can only maintain the progress we have made since the 1960s if we continue to educate children about the dangers of drugs well before they reach adolescence. Above all, we need to heed an extremely important lesson from our own past: Merely trying to scare young people away from using drugs is not enough. We need to combine this information with the legislation and widespread publicity that convince young people to avoid certain drugs altogether and to use others more cautiously.

Review/Test Questions

1. How have adolescents' attitudes and use of drugs changed in the past 20 years?
2. What accounts for the changes in adolescents' drug use?
3. Which adolescents are most likely to use and abuse drugs?
4. Which drugs do the most harm to the largest number of adolescents? How?
5. What makes nicotine unique?
6. How can each of the drugs in Table 14–1 affect adolescents?
7. How is drug use different from drug abuse?
8. How do the children of alcoholics often suffer from their parent's drinking problems?
9. In what ways do college-bound teenagers and college students use drugs differently from other people their age?
10. How does alcohol use among college students differ from other people their age?
11. How does race, gender, and family income affect drug use?
12. Using specific statistics on particular drugs to support your answer, what is the "good news" and the "bad news" with regard to drug use among teenagers and college students?
13. In what ways do the family, gender roles, and society affect teenage drug use?
14. What are the most effective ways of changing adolescents' attitudes about drugs?
15. What are the most effective ways of helping adolescents overcome drug abuse?

Questions for Discussion and Debate

1. In what ways did drugs affect you or your friends as teenagers? Remember, nicotine and alcohol are drugs.
2. How would you go about convincing more adolescents not to smoke and not to drink so carelessly?
3. Which information in this chapter surprised you the most? Why?
4. Why do you think white teenagers drink and smoke more than others?
5. What have you seen on television or encountered in school that has most influenced your feelings about drugs?
6. Which aspects of your own life do you think accounted for the ways you used, or refused to use, certain drugs as an adolescent?
7. How has being in college affected your use of drugs? Include alcohol!
8. Which drugs do you think do the most harm? Why?
9. If you or any of your friends has lived with an alcoholic parent, what effect did it have on you or them?
10. How do your attitudes about drugs compare with those of the adults in your family?

Glossary

Acid, p. 555
amphetamines, p. 554
Angel Dust, p. 555
barbiturates, p. 546

crack, p. 555
Ecstasy, p. 555
Ice, p. 555

LSD, p. 555
MDMA, p. 555
PCP, p. 555

References

Ackerman, R. (1989). *Perfect daughters: Adult daughters of alcoholics.* Deerfield, FL: Health Communications.

Bachman, J., & Schulenberg, J. (1993). How part-time work relates to drug use, problem behavior, and satisfaction among high-school seniors. *Development-al Psychology, 29,* 220–235.

Benson, P. (1990). *The troubled journey: Portrait of 6th–12th grade youth.* Minneapolis, MN: Lutheran Brotherhood.

Blum, R. (1992). Indian American youths. *Journal of the American Medical Association, 68,* 135–142.

Boyd, G., Howard J., & Zucker, R. (1994). *Preventing alcohol abuse among adolescents.* Hillsdale, NJ: Erlbaum.

Brownfield, D., & Sorenson, A. (1991). Religion and drug use among adolescents. *Deviant Behavior, 12,* 259–276.

Centers for Disease Control. (1994). *Preventing tobacco use among young people.* Atlanta, GA: Author.

Chassin, L., Rogosch, F., & Barrera, M. (1991). Substance use and children of alcoholics. *Journal of Abnormal Psychology, 100,* 449–463.

Cohen, P. (1991). Predictors and correlates of adolescent drug use. In R. Lerner, A. Petersen, & J. Brooks-Gunn (Eds.), *Encyclopedia of adolescence* (pp. 268–271). New York: Garland.

Collingwood, T. (1991). Physical fitness effects on substance abuse risk factors. *Journal of Drug Education, 21,* 73–84.

Corser, K., & Adler, F. (1993). *When the bough breaks: Pregnancy and the legacy of addiction.* Portland, OR: New Sage Press.

Doherty, W., & Needle, R. (1991). Psychological adjustment and substance use among adolescents. *Child Development, 62,* 328–337.

Ellickson, P., & Hays, R. (1991). Antecedents of drinking among young adolescents. *Journal of Studies on Alcohol, 52,* 398–408.

Fisher, M. (1991). Eating attitudes and health risk behaviors. *Journal of Adolescent Health, 12,* 377–384.

Flewelling, R., & Bauman, K. (1990). Family structure as a predictor of initial substance use. *Journal of Marriage and the Family, 52,* 171–181.

Foxcroft, D., & Lowe, G. (1991). Adolescent drinking and family factors. *Journal of Adolescence, 14,* 255–273.

Grilly, D. (1992). *Drugs and human behavior.* Boston: Allyn & Bacon.

Jencks, C. (1994). *The homeless.* Cambridge, MA: Harvard University Press.

Johnson, V., & Pandina, R. (1991). Effects of family environment on adolescent substance use. *Journal of Drug and Alcohol Abuse, 17,* 71–88.

Johnston, L., O'Malley, P., & Bachman, J. (1993). *National survey results on drug use: 1975–1992.* Rockville, MD: National Institute on Drug Abuse.

Kandel, D. (1991). Drug use. In R. Lerner, A. Petersen, & J. Brooks-Gunn (Eds.), *Encyclopedia of adolescence* (pp. 262–271). New York: Garland.

Kingery, P. (1991). Rural communities near metropolitan areas. *Journal of Health Behavior, 15,* 39–48.

Kosmin, R., & Lachman, S. (1993). *One nation under God.* New York: Harmony.

Light, W. (1988). *Alcoholism and women.* New York: Charles Thomas.

McKenry, P. (1991). Minority youth and drug use. In R. Lerner, A. Petersen, & J. Brooks-Gunn (Eds.), *Encyclopedia of Adolescence* (pp. 265–267). New York: Garland.

Mirzaee, E. (1991). Source of drug information. *Journal of Drug Education, 21,* 95–106.

Newcomb, M., Gahy, B., & Skager, R. (1990). Reasons to avoid drugs among teenagers. *Journal of Alcohol & Drug Education, 36,* 53, 81.

Page, R., & Cole, G. (1991). Loneliness and alcoholism risk in late adolescence. *Adolescence, 26,* 925–930.

Pruitt, B. (1991). Peer influence & drug use among adolescents in rural areas. *Drug Education, 21,* 1–11.

Rauch, J., & Huba, G. (1991). Adolescent drug use. In R. Lerner, A. Petersen, & J. Brooks-Gunn (Eds.), *Encyclopedia of adolescence* (pp. 256–261). New York: Garland.

Ryerson, E. (1985). *When your parent drinks too much.* New York: Warner.

Schwartz, S. (1991). Decision factors and preferences of drug-using & non-using students. *Journal of Drug Issues, 21,* 527–541.

Seligman, J. (1992, February 9). The new age of Aquarius. *Newsweek,* pp. 66–67.

Shedler, J., & Block, J. (1990). Adolescent drug use and psychological health. *American Psychologist, 45,* 612–630.

Shilts, L. (1991). Easy adolescent substance use and extracurricular activities, peer influence & personal attitudes. *Adolescence, 26,* 613–617.

Steinberg, L., & Dornbusch, S. (1991). Negative correlates of part time employment during adolescence. *Developmental Psychology, 27,* 304–313.

Tobler, N. (1986). Meta analysis of 143 adolescent drug prevention programs. *Journal of Drug Issues, 16,* 537–568.

Turner, R., Irwin, C., & Millstein, S. (1991). Family structure, family processes and experimenting with drugs. *Journal of Research on Adolescence, 1,* 93–106.

Watts, T., & Roosevelt, W. (1989). *Alcoholism in minority populations.* New York: Charles Thomas.

Weiner, I. (1992). *Psychological disturbance in adolescence.* New York: Wiley.

Williams, T. (1991). *The cocaine kids.* Reading, MA: Addison Wesley.

15

Externalizing and Internalizing Disorders

KEY QUESTIONS ADDRESSED IN THIS CHAPTER

1. Which factors contribute to delinquency and teenage aggression?
2. What are some of the most successful approaches to decreasing teenage crime and violence?
3. What are the symptoms of depression, schizophrenia, and borderline personality disorders?
4. Which factors contribute to teenage depression and suicide?
5. Why do some adolescents develop eating disorders, and how can they be helped?

As seen throughout this book, the vast majority of adolescents are well-adapted and get along relatively well with their families and their peers. Most teenagers' personalities and ways of relating to people remain basically unchanged from early childhood on. For most of us, adolescence is not a major overhaul in our personalities or in our family and peer relationships. Instead, our teenage years are usually a time for modifying and fine tuning certain aspects of ourselves and our relationships.

For a minority of teenagers, however, the personalities and the problems they have had throughout childhood become especially troublesome during their teenage years. It is not that their problems wait until adolescence to appear. It is that their problems have taken on forms that are increasingly destructive to themselves and to other people. One category of problems is referred to as "externalizing disorders," meaning that the teenager's behavior results in harm to other people and property. Juvenile delinquency, aggression, and violence are externalizing disorders. These disorders run the gamut from being verbally aggressive to stealing and murdering. The second category of teenage problems is referred to as "internalizing disorders"—behavior that is self-destructive, but generally does not physically harm others. This chapter addresses the four most common internalizing disorders—

Table 15–1

Adolescent problems in perspective

Problem	Adolescents Affected
Poverty	
Native American	50%
African American	40%
Hispanic American	35%
White & Asian American	11%
School dropouts	
Native American	40%
African & Hispanic	20%
White & Asian American	12%
Physical or sexual abuse	30%
Smokers	25%
Obesity	25%
Delinquency	10%
Pregnancy	10%
Psychological disorders	10%
Chronic illness	5%
Anorexia & bulimia	1%
Murder victims	1%
Suicide victims	.002%

schizophrenia, borderline personality disorders, depression, and eating disorders—and the externalizing disorders of delinquency and violence.

Before continuing, however, remember that most adolescents do not have these kinds of problems. Moreover, other problems—namely poverty and pregnancy—affect far more teenagers than do depression, suicide, eating disorders, schizophrenia, or delinquency. As shown in Table 15–1, nearly 20% of all teenagers live in poverty and 10% become pregnant. By way of comparison, only 1% have anorexia and far less than 1% commit suicide. This is not to say that one problem is better or worse than another. If, say, your brother or sister is one of the teenagers who has committed suicide, it isn't much consolation to know that 20 times as many teenagers are the victims of poverty. Nonetheless, knowing how many teenagers are affected by various kinds of problems prevents us from believing such unfounded statements as: "Suicide is the major cause of death among teenagers" or "Delinquency and violence are widespread among teenagers."

DELINQUENT AND VIOLENT BEHAVIOR

PREVALENCE AND CONSEQUENCES

Delinquent acts range in severity from major crimes, such as murder or armed robbery, to relatively minor offenses, such as vandalism or disorderly conduct. When we refer to a teenager as a "delinquent," we can also mean that he or she has committed a **status offense,** which is an act that is only illegal because the person is under the age of 18 or 21. For example, running away from home, skipping school, or buying beer are status offenses. Because the term *delinquent* refers to such a variety of behaviors and offenses, it is very difficult to determine the extent of "juvenile delinquency." Moreover, the official statistics on delinquency are based only on the number of teenagers who are caught and arrested. With these shortcomings in mind, consider the statistics in the following paragraphs (Federal Bureau of Investigation [FBI], 1994; National Center for Health Statistics [NCHS], 1991: All delinquency information is from these sources unless otherwise referenced).

About 5% of all teenagers appear in juvenile court each year for offenses other than traffic violations. When questioned by researchers, however, nearly 80% of teenagers report having committed an act for which they could have been arrested had they been caught. No significant differences between racial or economic groups emerge from these self reports. White and well-to-do teenagers are about as likely to break a law as are minority or poor teenagers. Based on those who do get caught and arrested, however, minority and low-income teenagers seem far more delinquent than do white or higher-income teenagers. In other words, race and income don't influence who breaks the law as much as they influence who gets caught and arrested. White and upper-income teenagers are the least likely to get caught and, once caught, the least likely to be prosecuted.

Teenage boys are also more likely to be arrested than girls who have committed the same offense, outnumbering female arrests by 4 to 1. The police and courts are sexist in that they generally treat boys more harshly than they treat girls. Likewise, teenagers from lower-income families are arrested and sentenced to jail more often than wealthier teenagers who commit similar crimes. Girls and wealthier teenagers are also more commonly sent to a psychiatric hospital or ordered by the court to undergo intensive therapy for the same offenses for which boys and poor teenagers are sent to jail.

What kinds of crimes do most teenagers commit? Most are arrested for stealing or for vandalizing property, not for attacking people. In fact, adolescents are less likely than are adults to commit crimes that involve physical harm to another person. Among those teenagers who are arrested, only 4% are charged with a violent crime. Teenagers account for nearly half of the arrests for vandalism, car theft, arson, and burglary, but for less than one hundredth of the arrests for murder. About 1,500 teenagers are arrested each year for murder and 4,000 for rape, versus 500,000 for property damage and 500,000 for theft and robbery. Moreover, most teenagers do not repeat their offense. Only 6% of those teenagers

How did delinquency or poverty affect the lives of anyone you knew as a teenager?

who are arrested are caught breaking the law again. More important, this 6% is responsible for almost half of all teenage arrests and convictions. So it is not true that violence or major crime are widespread among teenagers. What is true is that 5% to 6% of our teenagers repeatedly break the law, harming both people and property without much evidence of remorse or rehabilitation.

Why do we have the impression, then, that crime and violence are major problems among our nation's youth? One reason is that although only 12% of all teenagers have ever been arrested, the crimes and lifestyles of the 6% who are repeat offenders capture the media's attention. In addition, violent crime has been increasing at a rapid rate within this small group of teenagers. Since 1987, teenage arrests for murder have increased by 85% and for carrying weapons by 60%.

Many of those arrested are members of gangs who have seized the national spotlight by terrorizing their neighborhoods with intimidation, violence, and murder. All too often their victims are bystanders or children inside their own homes. Gang arsenals can range from the merely deadly to the super lethal, sometimes including such military-grade weapons as grenades and automatic rifles. Moreover, these weapons are often bought with money made from the drug trade that often puts this group of teenagers in contact with older, more violent, hardened criminals and drug traffickers. Another reason for the focus on teenage lawbreaking is that, although teenagers account for only 9% of the population, they represent 20% of all arrests. Proportionately then, teenagers are arrested for breaking the law at a higher rate than adults.

As a consequence of the hard-core crime and drug trafficking in our nation's poorest neighborhoods, poor adolescents are twice as likely as poor adults to be the victims of a violent crime. Nearly a third of the teenagers arrested for murder have killed someone younger than 18. As shown in Figure 15–1, each year in our country 16,000 people between the ages of 15 and 20 die—50% from accidents, 20% from murders, 13% from suicide, and the rest from natural causes and disease. Solely in terms of the number of deaths, we should be much more concerned about the traffic accidents that kill two and a half times more teenagers than are murdered. Yet analyzed by race, certain groups of teenagers emerge as being much more seriously at risk of being murdered. Because black, Hispanic, and Native American teenagers are the most likely to be living in poor, drug and

Figure 15–1

Causes of teenage death

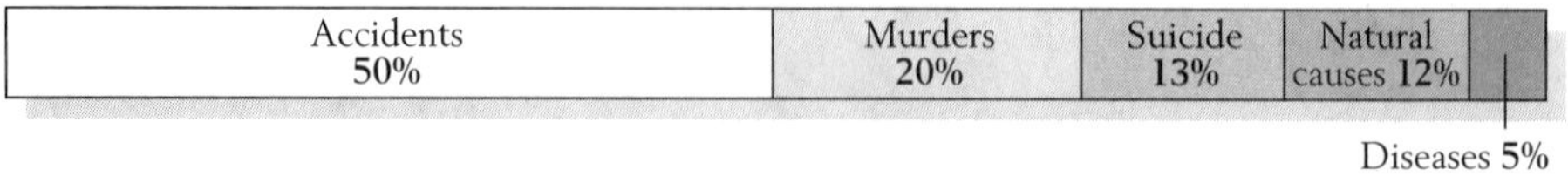

Accidents 50%	Murders 20%	Suicide 13%	Natural causes 12%	

Diseases **5%**

Source: National Center for Health Statistics (1992). *Health and morbidity statistics.* Washington, DC: Author.

crime-ridden areas, they are far more likely than white or Asian American teenagers to be murdered. Murder is now the leading cause of death for black teenage males. Nearly half of the black males who die as teenagers are murdered—seven times the rate of white and Asian males. Black teenage girls are also four times more likely than are white girls to be murdered. The murder rates for American Indians and Hispanic teenagers are also much higher than that of white and Asian Americans.

Environmental Factors

The least aggressive and least destructive delinquent is referred to as the "neurotic" delinquent. These law-breakers are usually cordial, conforming, unaggressive teenagers. Breaking a law is usually their way of trying to get their parents' attention or of forcing their family to deal with a problem at home. These teenagers almost always manage to get caught, even if it requires them leaking word of what they've done. In fact, getting away with their "crime" defeats the purpose for committing it—to get their family's attention. Some of these delinquents are clinically depressed and break the law as a way of getting psychological help. For example, a quiet, meek teenager might steal something from the next door neighbor in order to get her divorced parents to see how upset she is by their constant bickering. The best treatment is to get these "delinquents" and their families into counseling. If these teenagers are depressed, individual therapy can also help eliminate the concerns that motivated them to break the law. When most of us think of juvenile delinquents, we probably don't picture this particular type of law-breaker. When these teenagers are caught, they generally are not arrested or prosecuted. Instead, some sort of agreement is usually reached whereby they receive counseling. Nevertheless, when these teenagers are officially arrested and prosecuted, they do become part of our official delinquency statistics (Weiner, 1992).

More serious crimes are usually committed by "socialized" delinquents. These teenagers either associate with a small group of teenagers who reinforce each other for breaking the law, or they live in poor neighborhoods where a violent, drug and crime-ridden street culture reinforces teenage and adult crime. Most of their law-breaking takes place in the presence of their friends. In its mildest form, socialized delinquency might occur when a group of teenagers gets together, has too much to drink, and decides to vandalize their school. These teenagers generally have good relationships with their families and rarely commit a crime by themselves without their friends along to reinforce the behavior. This type of delinquency frequently occurs when teenagers are not well-supervised by the adults in their families. This is one of the reasons why teenagers living with an unmarried mother tend to be arrested more often than those living with two adults. As mentioned in preceding chapters, the single mother generally cannot provide as much supervision as can two adults, especially not for teenage boys. Even in middle-class and wealthy families, teenagers in fatherless families tend to get into more trouble with the police and school officials (Weiner, 1992).

Another group of socialized delinquents, however, commits far more serious crimes. These teenagers grow up in low-income, crime and drug-infested neighborhoods characterized by high unemployment and easy access to drugs. In this environment, teenage groups and organized gangs can literally run the neighborhoods, terrifying children and adults alike. Frustrated by poverty, desperately searching for self-esteem, teenage males in inner-city ghettos are especially prone to this type of delinquency. The message they receive from friends as they're growing up is: "Watch your back. If somebody messes with you, you got to pay them back. If someone disses [insults, hassles, or otherwise shows disrespect] you, you got to straighten them out." In this milieu, a violent death is preferable to allowing an insult to pass without retribution. As shown by the true story in Insert 15–1, the peer group, the media, poverty, and drugs are among the many factors contributing to this form of socialized delinquency (Anderson, 1992; McCall, 1994).

Insert 15–1

"Makes Me Wanna Holler"

The Autobiography of a Teenage Criminal

In his first-person account of how an intelligent, black teenage male from an intact family descended into a life of crime, Nathan McCall describes the lure of money, drugs, and rage in the making of a street criminal. After serving three years of his 12-year sentence for armed robbery, McCall eventually graduated from college with honors and became a journalist. Several excerpts from McCall's book, give us glimpses into his teenage life:

The main reason we hustled and stole so hard was to pick up money to buy clothes. Among the cats who hung in the streets, we had a tradition of slick dressers. Babes flocked to guys who ragged hard.

When I thought about my life, it seemed there was no future in anything. I wondered how I could make something of myself in the white man's world.

I always marveled at how the toughest cats whimpered and begged for their lives when I stuck the barrel into their faces. Adults who ordinarily would have commanded my respect were forced to follow my orders like obedient kids.

Superfly deeply affected me. I came out of that movie more convinced than ever that the white man and I were like oil and water. I never even knew much about snow (cocaine) until I saw that movie.

At age 17, I had a crumb-snatcher (baby) on the way. If anything, I felt fear. How was I going to guide a new life when I couldn't even direct my own?

I got accepted at all three of the colleges I'd applied to. But my parents couldn't afford for me to live away from home. So there was no choice but to enroll locally. After that first year (in college), which I finished on the honor roll, my motivation dropped. Soon I was back on the streets.

That song was the only thing that came close to explaining the frustration churning inside me: "Makes me wanna holler, the way they do my life. This ain't livin.'"

Source: N. McCall (1994). *Makes me wanna holler.* New York: Random House.

PSYCHOLOGICAL DISORDERS

Unlike socialized delinquents, "characterological" and "psychotic" delinquents are defiant, aggressive, or violent as a consequence of having severe psychological problems that have been with them since early childhood. Many of these delinquents have mental problems referred to as **antisocial, conduct,** or **defiant personality disorders.** As shown in Insert 15–2, these aggressive, defiant teenagers neither empathize with nor respect the rights of others. They feel neither guilt nor remorse for the damage and suffering they inflict. Teenagers with these mental disorders believe they are justified in behaving as they do, no matter what price other people have to pay. Burdened with their aggressive, defiant, or violent personalities, these delinquents often do poorly at school and are hard to get along with—and have been since they were very young children. They are often loners who don't have close friends. When they break the law, they usually act on their own rather than being egged on by others (American Psychiatric Association [APA], 1994; Weiner, 1992).

Virtually all teenagers whose delinquency stems from such serious psychological disorders have been aggressive and defiant since early childhood. So one of the best ways of predicting who has the highest odds of becoming an aggressive or violent delinquent is to look at the behavior of preschool children. Preschoolers who are extremely defiant, physically aggressive, hot-tempered, out-of-control, and unkind toward other children or animals are the most likely to be physically abusive, violent, and delinquent as teenagers. Most aggressive, assaultive, or violent behavior does not suddenly appear during adolescence without any prior symptoms or warnings (Asher & Coie, 1990; Cicchetti, 1992; Kagan, 1989; Parke & Ladd, 1992).

PARENTS' BEHAVIOR

So the question arises: What causes some children to become so aggressive or so violent? As you might expect, there is much we don't know about the causes of human aggression and violence. What we do know is that both family experiences and genetic factors play a part.

As you might expect, most aggressive or violent teenagers have at least one parent who behaves in the same way. One or both parents have often been arrested for illegal or violent activities. Sons who commit violent, aggressive crimes commonly have fathers with police records for violent, aggressive crimes. Drug abuse, alcoholism, physical abuse, and incest are also common in these families. Extremely aggressive or violent teenagers have rarely received the kinds of attention and affection at home that bond them to their parents or that foster a sense of trust or empathy toward people. Some aggressive delinquents have been raised by parents who are harsh and abusive disciplinarians. Others have parents who were so indifferent that they seldom set any limits on their children's aggressive or abusive behavior (APA, 1993; Cicchetti, 1992; Peplar & Rubin, 1994; Phares & Compas, 1992; Patterson, Reid, & Dishion, 1992; Weiner, 1992).

Even when these extreme forms of abuse and pathology do not exist in the family, a number of delinquents seem to have learned very aggressive, hostile

Insert 15–2

Mental Disorders Associated with Aggressive, Violent, and Defiant Behavior

Antisocial Personality Disorder

An ongoing disregard for other people that appears before the age of 15:

____ failure to conform to social norms

____ irritability and aggressiveness, repeated physical fights

____ irresponsibility in social, financial, or work matters

____ impulsive and disorganized

____ deceitfulness, repeated lying

____ reckless disregard for safety of self or others

____ lack of remorse, indifference to others' pain

Oppositional Defiant Disorder

A persistent pattern of negative, hostile, defiant thinking and behavior:

____ often loses temper

____ often argues with adults

____ often defies or refuses to obey adults

____ deliberately does things to annoy people

____ often blames others for his or her mistakes

____ easily annoyed or touchy

____ often angry and resentful

____ often spiteful or vindictive

Conduct Disorder

A persistent pattern of violating rules and disregarding others:

____ bullies, threatens, or intimidates others

____ often initiates physical fights

____ has used a weapon

____ has stolen something that involved confrontation with another person

____ physically cruel to people or animals

____ has forced someone into sexual activity

____ often lies or breaks promises

____ often stays out late at night against parent's orders

____ sets fires with intent to cause serious damage

____ deliberately destroys others' property

____ frequently runs away from home

____ often truant from school

____ has broken into someone's house or car

Source: Adapted from *Diagnostic and Statistical Manual of Mental Disorders* (1994). Washington, DC: American Psychiatric Association.

ways of interpreting the world from their parents. As discussed at length in the preceding chapters, each of us has characteristic ways of interpreting or explaining the events in our lives. Unfortunately, some children learn to interpret the world as though everything bad or hurtful that happens to them is intentionally planned ahead of time by another person in order to hurt, or embarrass, or insult them. This **hostile attribution bias** is especially common in physically aggressive and violent teenagers. Never far from flashpoint because of their hostile style of thinking, these teenagers are quick-tempered and trigger-happy both with their fists and with weapons because they interpret even the most minor incidents as intentional insults. One or both parents also generally have these hostile styles of interpreting and reacting to the world. It seems that, as very young children, some teenagers may learn hostile, overly defensive styles of thinking at home (Asher & Coie, 1990; MacKinnon & others, 1992; Parke & Ladd, 1992).

GENETIC INFLUENCES

For some delinquents, genetic factors also seem to contribute to their defiant, aggressive behavior. How? First, genes might contribute to neurological problems that make a child more physically aggressive and more defiant than other children their age. Specifically, aggressive behavior in delinquents has been associated with the neurological disorder known as **hyperactivity** or **attention deficit hyperactivity disorder** (ADHD). Once referred to as "minimal brain damage," attention deficit disorders typically cause inattentive, hyperactive, somewhat defiant behavior that begins in early childhood. Because a number of delinquents have been found to have attention disorders, part of their delinquency might be related to such a neurological problem (Farrington, Loeber, & VanKammen, 1990; Werner, 1987).

Genes might affect teenage aggression in another way—through hormones that are related to aggressive behavior. For example, some delinquents have been found to have higher than normal levels of testosterone—the hormone that contributes to physical aggression. On the other hand, it is possible that their highly aggressive behavior elevated their testosterone levels rather than the other way around (Dabbs & Morris, 1990; Olweus, Block, & Radke-Yarrow, 1985). Other aggressive teenagers have been found to have abnormal levels of dopamine, a neurotransmitter associated with the ability to control impulses. Scientists pursuing this possibility are trying to learn whether aggressive or violent people might be less able to control their behavior or to delay gratification because of a chemical imbalance (Kramer, 1993). Along these same lines, a child's genetic make-up is responsible for a particular variation of epilepsy that causes explosive outbursts of angry, assaultive, antisocial behavior (Weiner, 1992). In short, some teenagers' violent or aggressive behavior might be influenced, at least in part, by genetic factors (Carlson, 1986; Peplar & Rubin, 1994).

AGGRESSION, VIOLENCE, AND GENDER

Because teenage boys are far more likely than teenage girls to physically assault or murder, we must ask what role gender plays in juvenile crime. Why are males' crimes more physically violent than females' crimes?

Part of the reason is that males in our society are socialized to behave in more physically aggressive ways throughout childhood. As discussed in preceding chapters, male children are raised to be more aggressive, both verbally and physically. Unlike most girls, most boys are socialized to deal with disagreements by arguing, fighting, and yelling. They refuse to give in, seek revenge, and storm off without resolving anything more often than do girls. For too many boys, physical aggression and brute force are acceptable ways for a "real man" to deal with people. So unfortunately, it's not especially surprising that the crimes males commit are generally more aggressive and more violent than those most females commit (Miedzian, 1991; Pleck, Sonnenstein, & Ku, 1993). Throughout childhood and adolescence, males have more psychological disorders that are associated with assaultive, violent, abusive behavior than do females. At whatever age, males also generally have more trouble than females getting along well with people and controlling their destructive or abusive behavior (Asher & Coie, 1990; Ebata, Petersen, & Conger, 1990; Lamb, 1994; Petersen, Kennedy, & Sullivan, 1991; Robins & Rutter, 1990; Rolf & others, 1993).

Also noteworthy is the connection between aggression and depression in males. When males are depressed, they generally express their depression by lashing out against other people. In contrast, depressed females generally turn their depression inward against themselves—developing eating disorders, or becoming clinically depressed, or even committing suicide. For example, teenage girls who are upset by their parents' divorce act depressed, whereas teenage boys act in hostile, aggressive, angry ways toward other people (Colten, Gore, & Aseltine, 1991; Guidubaldi, 1988; Wallerstein, 1991). Likewise, depressed girls with low self-esteem are excessively critical of themselves, even years later as adults. In contrast, depressed boys with low self-esteem become less self-critical and more hostile and aggressive toward other people as they age (Koestner, Zuroff, & Powers, 1991). In other words, males are more likely than females to become aggressive toward other people when they feel depressed or bad about themselves (Block & Gjerde, 1991; Harrington, 1994; Peplar & Rubin, 1994; Safyer & Hauser, 1994).

PREVENTION AND REHABILITATION

Because the factors that contribute to delinquency are so varied, no single approach has been developed for preventing it or for rehabilitating these delinquent teenagers. Preventive measures for young children with certain neurological disorders include drugs that reduce their aggressive, impulsive, or abusive behavior. For others, their parents need help overcoming their own drug and alcohol problems and learning how to discipline children without resorting to physical abuse. Because most poor, unmarried mothers are less able to supervise their children, and because their families usually live in the worst neighborhoods, lifting more families out of poverty and reducing the numbers of unmarried mothers also has an indirect impact on reducing delinquency (Weiner, 1992).

Given what we know about male aggression and crime, a strong case can also be made for developing special programs for young boys who are having problems getting along well with other children. Because these young boys are hard to control at home as well, programs need to help their parents learn better ways of teaching them self-control. In a similar vein, elementary school teachers and school counselors could offer more help for those boys who seem depressed, angry, withdrawn, or friendless. Likewise, because the images of manhood presented to males in our society so frequently focus on physical assertiveness and aggression, we need to offer less violent, more compassionate images of masculinity through such mediums as television, music, sports, and toys.

Rehabilitation, for those who already have been arrested, is even more difficult than prevention. As mentioned, neurotic delinquents usually can be helped through individual and family counseling. Other delinquents, however, need more intensive rehabilitation programs. Unfortunately, we have had very little success rehabilitating the repeat offenders, those who commit the most violent and most damaging crimes. With backgrounds that include severe psychological problems, extremely abusive, dysfunctional families, and abject poverty amid

---

Insert 15–3

Teenagers Who Kill

In 1989 the Supreme Court ruled that people younger than 18 and people who are mentally retarded can be sentenced to death for murder. In our country approximately 1,300 young people under the age of 18 are arrested each year for murder. The United States is one among only 4 countries who have executed a teenage murderer since 1979. Do you think the Supreme Court's ruling is "cruel and unusual punishment" for teenage murderers?

Arthur Bates, 14

Arthur was planning only to rob the house, but once inside, he raped his 60-year-old victim and strangled her to death. He then helped himself to some butter pecan ice cream from her freezer. Before he was 4 years old, Arthur's mother had asked welfare workers for help with her troubled son. By the age of 10, he had been taken over as a ward of the state as an abused child, spending time in detention centers and mental hospitals. The state of Texas had provided Arthur with $113,000 worth of private psychiatric care for 2 years. Nevertheless, he was released to the custody of his stepmother shortly before he committed the murder. When he was arrested an hour after the crime, Arthur immediately confessed and added, matter-of-factly, "You can't do anything to me. I'm just 14."

Janet Weaver, 15

Janet had an argument with her 17-year-old sister, Yvette. Later in the day, Janet and her 22-year-old girlfriend stabbed Yvette to death in her own bedroom. For the next 3 days Janet sat in front of the television set watching cartoons while police combed the house looking for clues. When the two girls were eventually charged with the murder, Janet repeated her sister's last word: "Why?"

Source: G. Hackett (1988, January 1). Kids: Deadly force. *Newsweek,* p. 32.
   A. Press (1986, Nov. 24) Children who kill. *Newsweek,* p. 21.

crime-ridden neighborhoods, these hard-core delinquents have so many problems that keeping them out of trouble after they're released from jail, half-way houses, or juvenile detention centers is extremely difficult. Most of the programs that have succeeded in helping these young people require skilled professionals, and operating costs are high—though not as high as the $18,000 per year required to keep a person in jail (Weiner, 1992).

Some programs include job training or academic help so that delinquents can graduate from high school. Such approaches are aimed at keeping these teenagers off the streets and away from people who will draw them back into breaking the law. The most successful rehabilitation programs offer intensive individual therapy, job training, and programs for drug and alcohol abusers. Some of the most effective programs also teach less-aggressive, less-hostile ways of interpreting and responding to other people's behavior. These are designed to change attributional styles (Asher & Coie, 1990; Peplar & Rubin, 1994; Weiner, 1992).

Three especially unique programs illustrate the creativity and commitment involved in rehabilitating juvenile delinquents. Some teenage felons in Los Angeles are required to work with handicapped children as part of their probation. The idea is simple: rehabilitation through good deeds. Rather than being allowed to return to their former schools and hangouts, these delinquents attend school then work 2 hours every day educating, exercising, and feeding disabled children. The program isn't perfect. After 18 months, about one fifth of the participants in 1990 were expelled. The majority, however, are graduating from high school, making better grades, and acting less hostile and aggressive. Not only are these delinquents learning that other people have greater problems than they do, but they have a chance to build self-confidence and show others that they can be loving and compassionate. Says one 17-year-old former trigger-prone gang member, "Now I really feel like I can do something" (Murr, 1990).

Using a different, somewhat preventive approach, some delinquents in Tulsa, Okla., are sentenced to spend 150 hours on patrol with a police officer. The idea is that the police can be good male role models and that the delinquents might become more empathic by viewing crime from the victims' perspectives. The plan is limited mainly to 12- to 14-year-olds, in hopes that they can be helped before their crimes become more serious. Again, the program isn't perfect, as evidenced by the fact that one teenager viciously attacked and robbed someone after having spent 5 months in the program. Nevertheless, the vast majority have not repeated their crimes, have gone on to finish high school, and have remained friends with their police buddy. "He's cool, he's OK," says one teenage participant. His police partner agrees: "He's like a kid brother. There's nothing we won't talk about—drugs, booze, sex—and if he gets in trouble, he'll have to deal with me" (Woodbury, 1991).

Another approach is to have delinquents live on a beautiful, serene, private school campus—without gates, guards, psychologists, or social workers. At Pennsylvania's Glen Mills "reform" school, 750 male delinquents attend modern, academic classes where computers read aloud what they have written and where gold stars—which can be cashed in for food—are awarded for each book a student reads. All students are also taught a marketable trade. Many of their teachers are brawny, former college athletes. Although not required to, students are encouraged to participate in a team sport in order to gain more cooperative attitudes and boost self-esteem. Each new student is assigned a big brother who acts as his guide and supervisor. All students also share responsibility for their environment and for each other's behavior. For instance, if a student sees someone else throw trash on the ground and ignores it, the witness is also held accountable. And in class, everyone loses their break if one person misbehaves or doesn't work. The student governing body discusses troublesome students and handles virtually all discipline problems without involving the staff. The school's philosophy is to educate students and give them job skills, not to counsel them. Since the program began, nearly 230 students have gone on to college and 50% have avoided further trouble with the police—a success rate far higher than that of most rehabilitation services. As one student says, "Here you learn to take the time to figure out what the consequences are going to be before you act" (Diegmueller, 1994).

SCHIZOPHRENIC AND BORDERLINE PERSONALITY DISORDERS

Although some teenagers' aggressive or violent behavior is related to the kinds of disorders described in Insert 15–2, a lack of self-control and angry behavior can also be symptoms of schizophrenia and borderline personality disorders. Despite their commonalities, however, schizophrenic and borderline disorders are different in many regards (APA, 1994; Goldstein, 1990; Hanson, Gottesman, & Heston, 1990; Perry, Frances, & Clarkin, 1990; Weiner, 1992).

SCHIZOPHRENIA

A gradual breakdown in rational, objective thinking, **schizophrenia** makes it difficult, if not impossible, for its victim to relate well to other people or to function adequately at school or at work. The central feature of a schizophrenic disturbance is a pattern of distorted thinking that separates the person from reality. Of course all of us think irrationally and unrealistically from time to time. But for the schizophrenic teenager, extremely distorted ways of thinking are the norm, not the exception. As shown in the list in Insert 15–4, schizophrenic thinking affects virtually all aspects of the afflicted teenager's life.

Unlike other psychological disorders, schizophrenia usually is not diagnosed until late adolescence or early adulthood, when the symptoms become too severe to ignore any longer. Unfortunately, many schizophrenic teenagers are initially misdiagnosed as being depressed or as having some less serious condition. Many families also refuse to accept that their child is schizophrenic until adolescence ends and the "strange" moods and behavior steadily worsen. Although schizophrenia affects only about 1% of the population, it is one of the most debilitating and most difficult to cure of all psychological disorders. In several respects, schizophrenia has a more negative impact on males than on females. Schizophrenia in males generally appears at an earlier age, often in late adolescence. Most male schizophrenics are also more abusive and violent and less likely to recover from the disorder or to learn how to reduce its recurrences. In large part this might be because males, especially teenage males, are less willing to go to a therapist for help. Regardless of their sex, however, most schizophrenics do not receive the drugs and therapy they need during adolescence—the period in their lives when treatment could often prevent their disorder from becoming completely debilitating. It is extremely important, therefore, that we recognize schizophrenic tendencies as early as possible in a child's life, especially if the child is male.

BORDERLINE PERSONALITY DISORDERS

Only 1% of all teenagers have such severely distorted ways of thinking and behaving that they are classified as having a fully developed case of schizophrenia. A larger number, however, have personality disorders that include milder forms of schizophrenic thinking. A **borderline personality disorder** is exhibited when extremely maladaptive ways of thinking and behaving become enduring characteristics of the individual's personality. As the term "borderline" suggests, these teenagers are able to function adequately as long as they can confine themselves to situations that are relatively free of stress, familiar, unchallenging, and predictable. The problem, of course, is that life is stressful and filled with the unfamiliar, the challenging, and the frustrating. Thus, teenagers with borderline disorders are prone to having psychotic breakdowns periodically throughout their lives. For example, going away to college or trying to live away from home for the first time often bring on their first major breakdowns.

Borderline disorders that involve schizophrenic thinking are referred to as **schizoid disorders** or **borderline schizophrenia.** People with full-blown schizophrenia cannot hold jobs and must usually be institutionalized and heavily medicated, unlike those with schizoid or borderline disorders who can function—although poorly—under certain conditions.

SYMPTOMS AND CONSEQUENCES

Although schizophrenia is the far more serious illness, schizoid teenagers and those with borderline disorders do have certain things in common with schizophrenics. What distinguishes the schizophrenic teenager is the severity of the symptoms.

Denying Reality   Exactly what do we mean when we say a teenager's thinking is schizophrenic? The most obvious symptom is that these teenagers often draw conclusions, have opinions, pass judgments, and make decisions that are far removed or disconnected from facts and actual experiences. They frequently base their conclusions on minimal or circumstantial evidence and overlook or reject the facts that are obvious to everyone else around them. They twist and distort what is said or done until it bears little or no resemblance to what actually happened. They distort the facts, their experiences, and the past so that everything is forced to fit what they want to believe—the unreal. When anyone confronts them with evidence that contradicts the false realities they have created for themselves, they not only refuse to see the flaws in their logic but frequently become infuriated.

Of course, the reality of schizophrenia is serious and grim for its sufferers and their families. So the following joke is not offered as any attempt at humor, but rather for its illustrative purpose: A schizophrenic has convinced herself that she is dead, so the psychiatrist tries to trick her into accepting the reality that she is alive by asking, "Tell me, do dead people bleed?" "No," answers the patient. The psychiatrist then pricks her with a pin, drawing blood, whereupon the schizophrenic proclaims: "Well, how about that! Dead people do bleed!" Interacting with a schizophrenic teenagers is much like this. No matter how you present the reality of a situation, they steadfastly, often angrily, cling to their illogical, "unreal" conclusions. In the most severe cases of schizophrenia, teenagers hear voices and have hallucinations that cause them to create a world of their own so far removed from reality that the only recourse is to institutionalize them.

Splitting is another schizophrenic way of denying and distorting reality. Also known as **displacement,** this disordered thinking results in the victim's perceiving the self, other people, and all experiences only in terms of extreme opposites— "all good" or "all bad," "all saint" or "all sinner," "absolutely brilliant" or "completely stupid." In order to create these unreal images of people, the teenager grossly exaggerates and caricaturizes what other people say and do. Thus, the people, activities, or ideas they love and enjoy one minute might be suddenly tossed away with scorn and ridicule the next.

Especially as very young children, almost all of us use splitting at some point to enable us to cope with realities that are painful, shocking, frightening, or unnerving. Teenagers with borderline or schizophrenic disorders, however, consistently distort reality in this way instead of developing more mature, more realistic ways to deal with the painful aspects of their lives. Splitting is especially common when the painful realities involve one of their parents—above all, the parent who has tried hardest to convince everyone that he or she is the "perfect" one who is never responsible for anything that has gone wrong in the family. For example, a teenager who grew up with a father who fixed most of the meals, bathed and read to the young children every night, walked the children to school every day, cleaned the house, and spent hours with the family after work every night, might use splitting to explain why his mother, who was home all day long, didn't do these things. By mentally rewriting the family history, the troubled teenager creates the fantasy that "my mother raised me while my father ignored us and built his career." Likewise, splitting can occur if the parent who has worked to create an image as "the unselfish saint" is discovered to have committed adultery or to have spent money that was supposed to be saved for the children. In situations such as these, teenagers with schizophrenic and borderline disorders often twist the facts in order to vent their rage at someone other than the person who has, in reality, hurt

> **Insert 15–4**
>
> ## Symptoms of Schizophrenic or Schizoid Disorders
>
> Schizophrenia is a gradual breakdown in a person's ability to think logically, objectively, and rationally. As a consequence, the person cannot maintain a close relationship with anyone and might behave in very hostile, aggressive, or violent ways. The following patterns characterize schizophrenic thinking and behavior:
>
> ### General Style of Thinking
>
> ____ misjudges and misinterprets other peoples' feelings, motives, and behavior
>
> ____ develops views of the world and of people not founded in reality
>
> ____ draws false conclusions from minimal or circumstantial evidence
>
> ____ overlooks the most obvious, objective facts or aspects of a situation
>
> ____ reasons very immaturely and illogically
>
> ____ refuses to change opinions despite objective, contradictory evidence
>
> ____ shows little or no insight about own or others' behavior
>
> ____ steadfastly refuses to see any flaws in own thinking or conclusions
>
> ____ blames external factors and other people for own problems
>
> ____ construes criticism or disagreement as total rejection
>
> ____ fails to consider the consequences of own actions
>
> ____ has delusions or hallucinations
>
> ____ disorganized, incoherent speech
>
> ### General Behavior, Moods and Self-Image
>
> ____ often seems angry, irritable, and hostile without apparent reason
>
> ____ overreacts and lacks self-control

them most. If these disturbed teenagers were to face the truth about the parent they are protecting, the pain would be intense and profoundly upsetting because this is typically the parent to whom they are most bonded. Unfortunately, unless a therapist is able to help these teenagers confront the painful realities they have been trying to deny, they rarely recover from their mental disorder (Bowlby, 1988; Gergen, 1992; McCrae & Costa, 1988; Miller, 1990).

Intense Anger and Lack of Self-Control   Teenagers with schizophrenia or borderline disorders are typically very angry, irritable, and hostile for no apparent reason. They have very little self-control. They fly off the handle easily and are prone to sudden outbursts of verbal or physical abuse, especially around the people they know best. Their lack of self-control and their intense anger, however,

_____ often has sudden outbursts of verbal or physical abuse

_____ extremely negative, critical, sarcastic, argumentative, and impatient

_____ hyperactive and physically agitated or extremely immobile (catatonic)

_____ has many stress-related ailments (migraines, allergy attacks)

_____ tries to shut out the world

_____ unable to sustain enthusiasm for any activity or person

_____ generally seems depressed

_____ prone to severe bouts of anxiety and self-hatred

_____ develops far-fetched ideas (good and bad) about self

_____ occasionally creates grandiose self-image not reflecting reality

_____ sets unreasonable goals and makes unrealistic plans for the future

Relationships with People

_____ lacks close friends, socially isolated

_____ excessively shy and withdrawn, yet angry

_____ shows little or no interest in sex or dating

_____ lacks genuine intimacy with anyone

_____ relates in superficial, immature ways

_____ has unrealistic expectations for people and relationships

_____ becomes increasingly alienated from family members

_____ emotionally cold, distant, indifferent, aloof

_____ pompous, self-righteous, self-centered

_____ seems indifferent to most people's praise or criticism

might not be apparent to people outside the family because many schizoid teenagers are extremely shy, mild-mannered, and obedient away from home.

Another category of schizophrenics includes those who are outwardly angry, aggressive, and defiant away from home as well as with their families. This group, unlike schizoid teenagers, is the most likely to break the law and the most prone to physical violence. Yet even the shy, schizoid child generally becomes much more aggressive, abusive, and hostile as a teenager—especially schizoid boys. Unlike teenagers with antisocial personality disorders, those with schizophrenic or borderline disorders almost always direct their anger and aggression at the people they know best, not at strangers and authority figures. Nevertheless, the anger and violence of teens with schizophrenic or borderline disorders can be frightening—screaming obscenities at people, smashing their own fists through walls, destroying valued possessions, or physically attacking people.

Disturbed Relationships   Harboring far-fetched ideas about other people and the world around them, teenagers with schizoid or borderline disorders seem unable to anticipate the consequences of their own behavior, make realistic decisions for themselves, or make accurate judgments about other people. They generally misjudge and misinterpret other people's feelings, motives, and behavior, often in the hostile ways associated with negative attribution bias. Compared to other people their age, they think and behave extremely immaturely, showing a profound lack of insight into their own behavior or into the behavior of others. Instead of taking an honest look at themselves, they blame other people and factors beyond their control for virtually all of their problems and for their anger and unhappiness. With such hostile attitudes, they come across as exceedingly critical, pompous, and self-righteous.

Understandably, these teenagers have a long history of not getting along well with people—usually from early childhood on. Even with the people they know best, they are unable to establish an intimate relationship. For instance, they might say, "I love my parents, but I don't care how they feel or what they do." Because their expectations of other people and their ideas about relationships are so self-centered and unrealistic, nobody is able to make them happy—at least not for long. They might occasionally have a friend with whom they share a single activity, like playing basketball or watching television. Yet, even then, they relate in superficial, immature, self-centered ways. Not surprisingly, they date very little, if at all, and might show almost no interest in sex.

In trying to relate to people, these teenagers vacillate between one of two unpleasant extremes. Sometimes they isolate themselves completely and try to shut out the world. At other times they interact in ways that are exceedingly possessive, clingy, child-like, and dependent. They make excessive demands on other people, craving a level of such intense, unwavering attention and devotion that ultimately no one can please them. Indeed, some of these teenagers are so self-centered and childishly demanding that they can't even accept the fact that their parents want to have a private, intimate relationship with one another. For example, the teenager might pout for days or literally become enraged when parents take a vacation by themselves or show any physical affection for one another. Harder still on those who know them, these teenagers give back very little, if anything. They are takers. Insensitive to others' needs, they frequently berate and criticize the people who love them for not giving or not doing enough. Yet the more someone gives, the more unreasonable their demands and expectations become. Whenever anyone disappoints or hurts them in any way—which is often, of course—they become enraged, sometimes to the point of being so consumed by hate that they go on despising certain people for years for no rational reason.

Despite their many problems, some teenagers with schizophrenic and borderline disorders are very bright, creative people. As shown in Insert 15–5, those whose schizophrenic tendencies are not too severe can graduate from college and have careers. Nevertheless, the ways they think and behave continue to create problems that require psychiatric help. So often wrong in their judgments and opinions of people, and so critical, possessive, self-centered, touchy, quick-tempered, and

Insert 15–5

Schizophrenic, Schizoid, and Borderline Personality Disorders

Schizophrenia

Bruce had always been a quiet, shy boy with few friends. As a teenager he never dated and was very uncomfortable around anyone other than his immediate family. A very poor student, he dropped out of high school in the 11th grade after having been briefly hospitalized for depression. Bruce also had two mentally ill brothers. After quitting school, he lived with his divorced mother and worked at a simple, low paying job. As a teenager, he occasionally had hallucinations in the form of flashing lights. At 21, he was hospitalized again for depression. Eventually diagnosed as schizophrenic, Bruce was put on medications that enabled him to be released on an outpatient basis to go back to live with his mother.

Schizoid Personality Disorder

Rebecca was always a shy, introverted, perfectionist. All through high school she was an excellent student, but she had very few friends and never dated. After graduating from college, she worked as a performing artist. At 25, after her boyfriend broke up with her, she starting drinking heavily and consequently lost her job. Although there was no history of mental illness in her family, she developed more serious schizophrenic symptoms and appeared to be living in a dream world. She was eventually hospitalized for symptoms of depression. Although she never had hallucinations or disordered thinking, she was eventually put on med-ication and released from the hospital with a diagnosis of schizoid personality disorder.

Borderline Personality Disorder

Joseph was a sophomore in college when he sought help for his social problems. His father was a bitter, emotionally distant man; and his mother had always been overly protective and overly involved in Joseph's life. At age 9 Joseph had an unsettling experience of being rejected by some boys at school, so he withdrew completely from his peers. For the next two years he left home only to go to school or accompany his parents. When he was 11, he made a friend and had a reasonably normal friendship until he was 13. But when his friend dropped him for a new best friend, Joseph withdrew from people again. In college whenever he was attracted to a girl, he would fall suddenly and deeply in love and, like a child, insistently demand her total attention and complete devotion in return. If any girl or any friend disappointed him in any way, he would become enraged and would obsess on how much he hated the person. As his anger and his outlandish demands on people grew worse, people avoided him altogether. He was so demanding, touchy, irritable, and angry that he made life miserable for anyone who became involved with him. Whenever he talked about anyone who had "done him wrong," he would become infuriated, even years after the incident occurred.

Source: Adapted from D. Hanson, I. Gottesman, & L. Heston (1990). Long range schizophrenia forecasting. In J. Rolf (Ed.), *Risk and protective factors in the development of psychopathology* (pp. 408–444). New York: Cambridge University Press. Weiner, B. (1992). *Psychological disturbance in adolescence*, (pp. 192–196). New York: Wiley.

angry, teenagers with schizophrenic and borderline disorders only become more alienated from people and from their families as they age.

Contributing Factors

The kinds of thinking and behavior that are characteristic of schizophrenia and schizoid or borderline disorders are almost always apparent within the first few years of a child's life. Indeed, some symptoms have been identified even in infants. These disorders also run in families. On the other hand, some teenagers without any history of these disorders in their families sometimes develop them; and, some well-adjusted teenagers have relatives with these disorders. The general consensus is that schizophrenia and borderline or schizoid disorders are determined by a combination of the child's genetic disposition and the kinds of experiences he or she has within the family.

So what is it about some families that contributes to schizoid, schizophrenic, and borderline disorders? Although no single factor is always found in their families, certain dynamics are relatively common. First, the mother is often too protective and enmeshed with the child, while the father is too uninvolved or too critical. Second, the parents usually lack intimacy in their marriage, which weakens the generational boundaries and makes role reversals between parent and child common. Third, the child might feel insecurely attached to the parents during early childhood and thus develop aberrant ways of relating to people. Fourth, the parents communicate with each other and with their children in very dishonest, indirect, and contradictory ways. Fifth, the mother tends to have depressed, negative ways of viewing the world and interacting with people.

These connections among poor ego development and enmeshment, weak generational boundaries, and the parent's unhappy marriage are explained in preceding chapters. In the families of many teenagers with schizophrenic or borderline personality disorders, at least one, if not all, of these aspects of family life have gone awry (Bowen, 1978; Hanson, Gottesman, & Heston, 1990; Hinde & Stevenson, 1995; Goldstein, 1990; Karen, 1994; Parker, 1983).

Remember that the situation known as **enmeshment** occurs when parent and child become too involved in one another's lives in ways that prevent the child from becoming independent and mature enough to relate well to people. In these families the mother is often unhappily married, depressed, and chronically dissatisfied. And the father, in his efforts to encourage independence and social maturity in the child, becomes increasingly outspoken and critical of the child's infantile behavior. His efforts, however, are perceived by the mother and child as pushing too hard and being too critical. Unfortunately, when either parent tolerates or excuses the teenager's excessively immature, self-centered, clingy, demanding, petulant, or abusive behavior, schizophrenic and borderline patterns become much worse, not better (Weiner, 1992).

Moreover, because the mother is turning to the enmeshed child for her main source of emotional intimacy, the child begins to feel responsible for protecting her and for making her happy—a situation referred to as **role reversal.** Unable to break this intense focus on the mother, the child interacts less with other children and fails to learn more mature, realistic ways of thinking about relationships. The father becomes decreasingly involved in the child's life, thus allowing the mother and child to become the central couple around which the family revolves. Overprotected and underdisciplined, enmeshed children believe life revolves around their whims, continuing to cling to mother and relate to people in very infantile ways—even as adolescents and adults.

Many teenagers with schizophrenia and borderline or schizoid disorders also learned these self-centered attitudes and behaviors because the **generational boundaries** were weak or nonexistent in their family. One or both parents have allowed the child to have power and privileges equal to that of the adults. These generational boundaries are especially apt to collapse in a marriage that lacks intimacy. In its most extreme form, these children end up being allowed to literally dictate to parents what they may or may not do in their own lives.

Also noteworthy are the several other connections among enmeshment, schizophrenia, and borderline personality disorders. The first concerns the child's gender. Why is it that more teenage males than females are diagnosed with schizophrenic and borderline disorders? Part of the reason might be because mothers tend to get more enmeshed with their sons than with their daughters. Any why might this happen? Partly because boys have more chronic childhood illnesses than girls which, in turn, encourages more overly protective, enmeshed relationships with the mother. Then too, the father's emotional distance and underinvolvement seem to have a more debilitating effect on a son's mental health than on a daughter's, especially during early childhood (Biller, 1993; Elicker, Englund, & Stroufe, 1992; Ebata, Petersen, & Conger, 1990; Snarey, 1993). In other words, the schizophrenic and borderline disorders of enmeshed boys may be as much a consequence of underfathering as of overmothering (Biller, 1993; Bowen, 1978; Cohen, 1990; Goldstein, 1990).

The second connection is that enmeshed children tend to be extremely angry as teenagers and as young adults. Angry at whom? Why? Well, because the father has yielded most of the "parenting power" to the mother, some of these teenagers feel anger at their father for having been too weak, ineffective, and uninvolved in their lives. The greater anger, however, is usually leveled at the mother. Before late adolescence, many enmeshed children realize more clearly how their development has been undermined by having been babied, overly protected, and enmeshed. Remember, too, that these teenagers have usually used splitting to deny certain realities of their family life—above all, to deny certain truths about the parent with whom they are enmeshed. When they start to confront these realities, therefore, they often react with intense anger. Because they lack the insight, maturity, and compassion of most people their age, they either vent their anger directly on the parent or on everyone else in their lives. Indeed, even as adults, many enmeshed children become physically enraged when they discuss their families or their past. Rather than assuming any responsibility themselves, these enmeshed teenagers and young adults launch into angry diatribes, blaming everyone in the family except themselves (Goleman, 1985; Karen, 1994; Main, 1993; Parker, 1983).

Insert 15–6

Symptoms of Borderline Personality Disorders

Emotional Intensity and Anger

_____ subject to intense anger

_____ often seems bristling with rage and hostility

_____ irritable, petulant, argumentative, sarcastic, and critical

_____ prone to intense anxiety and depression

_____ rarely displays any emotion in a mild form

Poor Self-Control

_____ sudden, unjustified outbursts of anger and violence

_____ intolerant of frustration

_____ runs away from home or is truant from school

_____ breaks the law or engages in physically risky activities

_____ engages in self-destructive behavior

Functions Adequately only Within Limits

_____ cannot tolerate challenging tasks or frustration

_____ functions only in predictable, familiar, easily manageable situations

_____ cannot tolerate stress, uncertainty, or ambiguity

_____ marked under-achievement in relation to abilities

Strained Relationships

_____ cannot create or sustain intimacy

_____ exceedingly possessive, clingy, and dependent

_____ excessively demanding and draining

_____ demands unwavering loyalty and constant attention

Teenagers with schizophrenic or borderline disorders also often seem to have been insecure and poorly bonded to their parents as very young children. Being bonded does not mean being tied to the parent. Good bonding means that the child feels secure enough and is encouraged enough to venture more independently into the world beyond the family. Teenagers with a parent who was rejecting or unloving can be quite outgoing, yet physically aggressive and hostile toward people—the pattern associated with violent or physically aggressive psychological disorders. In contrast, teenagers with a parent who was loving, but too protective or too enmeshed in their lives, tend to be excessively shy but infantile and very demanding—the characteristic pattern of schizoid teenagers. As teenagers, both groups have the unusually high levels of anger and hostility that characterize people with schizophrenic and borderline disorders. So there does seem to be a relationship between early childhood relationships with parents and development of these mental disorders later in life (Belsky & Cassidy, 1994; Greenberg, Cicchetti, & Cummings, 1990; Karen, 1994; Main, 1993; Parkes, Stevenson-Hinde, & Marris, 1991).

Teenagers with these mental disorders tend to come from families in which the communication is extremely dishonest, contradictory, and deceitful. For example,

_____ constantly testing another's love or loyalty

_____ continually demands and takes without reciprocating

_____ self-centered and insensitive to others' needs

_____ always unsatisfied with and critical of what others give

_____ becomes enraged whenever someone disappoints him/her

_____ rarely forgives others or forgets past mistakes

Frequently Uses "Splitting"

_____ sees every person, situation or event as either "all good" or "all bad"

_____ either idealizes or demonizes a person

_____ shifts from one extreme judgment of a person to the other extreme

_____ caricatures people rather than seeing them realistically

_____ passes judgment and makes choices too hastily

_____ sees self as "all good" or "all bad"

_____ all-or-none attitudes and decisions

Self-Satisfied and Resistant to Help

_____ sees own thinking and behavior as normal

_____ satisfied and comfortable with own behavior, demeanor

_____ considers own anger and reactions absolutely justified

_____ becomes enraged if anyone suggests therapy or change

Source: B. Weiner (1992). *Psychological disturbance in adolescence.* New York: Wiley.

a mother might continually tell her son how much she loves him and his father, but the child sees that her behavior shows otherwise: If mother is as happy as she says she is, then why does she cry a lot, look so sad and downtrodden, have so many of those headaches, and act so unhappy around my father? Likewise, the father might send his daughter contradictory messages by continually telling her how proud he is of her while berating, criticizing, and ridiculing her. In such families, children grow up continually witnessing or sensing large discrepancies between what their parents say and what they do. When children continually receive these contradictory messages or sense that something is very false in the family, schizophrenic thinking is more likely to develop.

Frequently these disturbed patterns of communication occur because the parents are trying to hide certain truths about themselves from the children. As a result, everyone is being coerced into living up to two unwritten family rules: We all have to agree that there is nothing at all wrong with anything going on in our family—and we all have to promise not to tell anyone anything about what goes on here! Although all parents keep certain truths from their children, the very fabric of these families is woven with lies. For example, even though the children are teenagers, everyone might still be lying about a parent's alcoholism, or about the reasons for the parents' divorce, or about a sibling's suicide attempt. Beyond a certain age, when children are lied to about such important aspects of their families, they are more likely to begin reasoning in schizophrenic ways—ignoring all data that refute the family lies, distorting experiences until they fit the family myths, and denying realities about their parents. Rather than learning to accept imperfections in their family members, these children are learning to reason and relate to people in schizophrenic ways so that everyone in the family can fool themselves into believing "I'm perfect; you're perfect; in this family, we're all perfect" (Bowlby, 1988; Goleman, 1985; Hinde & Stevenson, 1995; Miller, 1990; Weiner, 1992).

Finally, teenagers with borderline and schizophrenic disorders are more apt to have mothers who are depressed or extremely unhappy with their lives—especially during the first few years of the child's life. Although the mother might not literally tell the child she is depressed, her overall demeanor, her facial expressions and tone of voice, and her general behavior convey an image of someone who is extremely fragile, helpless, victimized, and pitiable. Very often the depressed mother tells the children how much she has suffered and sacrificed for them, thus trying to bind them to her through guilt and pity. What seems to happen is that the mother's depressed, negative, helpless ways are adopted by whichever child is born with the most troublesome disposition. This child also tends to become enmeshed with the depressed mother, mirroring her moods and taking on her problems for years to come. In general, a mother's depression is linked to teenagers' borderline and schizophrenic disorders, and a father's mental problems are linked to teenagers' aggressive and violent disorders (Phares & Compas, 1992; Radke-Yarrow, 1991; Rubin, Lemare, & Lollis, 1990; Seligman, 1991; Waxler & others, 1992).

Before we blame these mothers, however, it's important to remember that their own family backgrounds are usually far less than ideal. Many depressed mothers, as well as those who are either rejecting or enmeshed with their children, did not feel loved by their own parents and came from families in which honesty and intimacy were rare. For example, a woman who was emotionally or sexually abused by her father tends to become enmeshed with her son rather than being intimate with her husband (Stroufe, 1989). Similarly, a mother with distant, rejecting parents is often unable to be sexually or emotionally intimate with anyone. She develops very superficial, self-centered styles of relating to people that she inadvertently passes on to one of her children (Ainsworth & Eichberg, 1991). A son's disturbed ways of relating to people seem to be more closely related to his mother's relationship problems than the daughter's (Pianta, Egeland, & Stroufe, 1990). All in all then, the more troubled the mother's family was, the more commonly one of her children develops the severely disturbed behavior associated with borderline and schizophrenic disorders (Ainsworth & Eichberg, 1991; Main, 1993; Parkes, Stevenson-Hinde, & Marris, 1991; Patterson, Reid, & Dishion, 1992).

FACTORS OUTSIDE THE FAMILY

Remember, though, that these kinds of family dynamics do not, in and of themselves, cause children to develop schizophrenia or borderline disorders. These disorders run in families, which suggests that some children inherit a predisposition to develop these problems. Among the other factors that are beyond either parent's control, three are commonly related to schizophrenic and border-line disorders: the child's innate disposition, the child's gender, and early child-hood illnesses.

Each child is born with a unique disposition—some with an excessively fear-ful, anxious, introverted, dependent, volatile, or aggressive disposition. These chil-dren are likely to have trouble developing a mature ego which, in turn, is linked to schizophrenic and borderline disorders (Lamb, 1994; Robins & Rutter, 1990; Rolf & others, 1993).

Children who have chronic illnesses, such as asthma or epilepsy, tend to have more disturbed relationships and less mature ego development than do healthy children. They are more likely to be enmeshed, babied, or overprotected by one or both parents. Also, because of the child's poor health, some infants and mothers do not become securely bonded to each other. For example, mothers whose young children have severe asthma have been found to be less closely bonded than are mothers with healthy children (Madrid & Schwartz, 1991). Some mothers are also angry because their child is so sick. Thus, they try to com-pensate with overprotection and overinvolvement with the sickly child (Parker, 1983). A chronic illness also makes it more difficult for a young child to interact with other children, which then gives them fewer chances to develop psycholog-ically healthy ways of relating to people (Cohen, 1990; Madrid & Schwartz, 1991; Miller & Wood, 1991; Minuchin, 1988; Sholevar & Perkel, 1990).

For reasons not altogether clear, a child's gender is also linked to schizophrenic and borderline disorders. Boys have more psychological disorders than do girls—with the exception of depression—throughout childhood and adolescence. Beginning in adolescence, girls outnumber boys in cases of depression (Asher & Coie, 1990; Ebata, Petersen, & Conger, 1990; Harrington, 1994). Also, as he moves from early childhood to adolescence, a boy's psychological problems are less likely to improve than are a girl's. This is why it's extremely important to pay careful attention to the social and emotional problems boys have during their preschool years (Block & Gjerde, 1991; Kagan, 1989; Kupersmidt, Coie, & Dodge, 1993; Petersen, Kennedy, & Sullivan, 1991). As already mentioned, boys tend to be more enmeshed with their mothers and have more childhood illnesses and neurological disorders than girls. Boys are also more apt than girls to become angry and hostile in response to stress within the family. So when relationships in the family are strained, especially the parents' marriage, boys generally suffer more than girls in terms of developing psychological problems (Robins & Rutter, 1990; Rutter, Hays, & Baron, 1994; Wallerstein, 1991).

The average teenage boy is also socialized to take out more of his anger and hostility on other people than the average teenage girl. For example, teenage boys who have low self-esteem are angry and critical of other people, whereas girls with low self-esteem don't tend to mistreat other people but do tend to be "quietly" depressed and highly critical of themselves (Block & Gjerde, 1991; Koestner, Zuroff, & Powers, 1991; Safyer & Hauser, 1994). In fact, one reason why fewer boys than girls are diagnosed as being clinically depressed is that depressed boys seldom feel free act sad, tearful, and withdrawn. Instead, the depressed boy generally lashes out at those around him. As a result, teenage boys might have more schizophrenic and borderline disorders in part because males are socialized to lash out angrily at others whenever they are hurt, or sad, or upset, or frightened, or feeling bad about themselves (Colten, Gore, & Aseltine, 1991; Harrington, 1994). In sum, whichever aspects of the family are dysfunctional will have the most negative impact on the child who is born with a difficult disposition, a male child, and the child with a chronic illness.

Prevention and Treatment

The first step toward reducing the incidence of schizophrenia and borderline personality disorders is for potential parents to be honest with each other about their family histories. Both parents need to know if anyone in the other's family has a schizophrenic or borderline disorder. With this knowledge, both parents can be on the lookout for any early symptoms in their own children. For example, parents should seek help if their 4-year-old son is extremely shy, seems continually irritable, is extremely hard to please, and clings excessively to one of his parents if his uncle has a schizophrenic disorder. Not only do they seek the help of a professional therapist, but these wise parents make every effort to teach their son the social skills he needs to interact independently and maturely with other children. The knowledgeable therapist advises them not to baby their son, not to encourage his infantile dependence, and not to make excuses for his immaturity, his excessive shyness, or his extremely demanding behavior. The parents also try to avoid interactions with one another and with their children that are associated with these disorders. For example, if either parent is depressed or is having marital problems, they seek further professional help in order to prevent these problems from contributing to any psychological disorders in their children.

When mentally troubled teenagers are still living at home, therapists typically work with the entire family to try to change their unhealthy ways of relating to one another. The most progress is made when the therapist is able to get both parents to stop making such excuses as: "Oh, but he has such low self-esteem and he's so sensitive and immature that we just have to be more loving and accepting when he behaves like that" or "My daughter just doesn't feel good enough about herself for me to encourage her to do that!" The therapist must also teach the teenager more mature social skills, specific ways to control anger, and better ways of testing reality. The parents must be made to understand that the angry, abusive, self-righteous behavior only worsens when they are sweet and accommodating. The teenager perceives such tolerance and "acceptance" as evidence of the adults' being too disinterested, or too weak or frightened to defend themselves, or too stupid to recognize insults and manipulation, or too dishonest to admit feeling angry or hurt. Both the therapist and the adults need to challenge the young person's distorted thinking and set strict limits regarding hurtful, angry, or destructive behavior (Bowen, 1978; Hinde & Stevenson, 1995; Minuchin & Fishman, 1981; Weiner, 1992).

When enmeshment and generational boundaries are part of the problem, the therapist attempts to disentangle the enmeshed relationship and reconstruct marital and generational boundaries. In these families, the therapist is not trying to help parents become more supportive or more understanding of their teenage child. To the contrary, the therapist is trying to teach one or both parents to *stop* being so understanding and accepting of their adolescent's demanding, infantile behavior. The therapist is also trying to get parents to focus less on their teenage child's problems and more on those aspects of their own marriage that are negatively affecting the child.

Because teenagers with schizophrenic and borderline disorders tend to be very hostile, angry, and verbally abusive, their recovery involves intensive therapy with someone who is able to tolerate a great deal of verbal and emotional abuse. Unfortunately, one of the major roadblocks to helping young people with these particular disorders is their refusal to go for help. Once they can be convinced to go, however, the therapist must be someone who is confrontive and direct—someone who is not reluctant to challenge the teenager's distorted thinking, incorrect conclusions, and inappropriate behavior. The therapist's two most important goals are to teach the teenager better ways of reality testing and more mature social skills.

Unfortunately, disorders involving schizophrenic thinking are extremely difficult to treat. About 25% of all schizophrenics seem to recover completely, another 25% improve but suffer occasional relapses, and the remaining 50% make little or no progress and require ongoing residential care. Complete recovery, or learning to reduce the number of relapses, involves intensive counseling and drug therapy. Generally, the most progress is made by those who begin therapy as teenagers, and those with no schizophrenic relatives. The hardest to help are those young people who seem unconcerned about their condition and who persist in believing that nothing is really wrong with them. In this sense, it's actually good news when people with schizophrenic symptoms become so confused or so upset that they agree to get professional help as teenagers. These young people have made the most crucial step toward recovery—realizing that their thinking and behavior are not normal (Weiner, 1992).

Another goal in therapy is to teach family members how to communicate more directly and more honestly with one another. Unfortunately, the young person's thinking and behavior can be so distorted that he or she can no longer relate to the family. In these cases, the therapist helps the family understand the nature of the young person's disorder and helps them adjust to the situation. Because these disorders can require hospitalization or lifelong residential care, many families must be helped to accept these unhappy realities.

AFFECTIVE DISORDERS

SYMPTOMS AND VARIETIES OF DEPRESSION

Affective disorders are what we commonly refer to as depression. Whereas schizophrenic disorders are primarily disorders of thinking, affective disorders are primarily disorders of mood. When we use the term to refer to a psychological disorder, however, *depression* does not mean merely being extremely sad or

When did you feel most depressed as a teenager?

unhappy. Clinical depression is primarily a feeling of emptiness and an inability to derive pleasure from relationships or activities—a condition referred to as **anhedonia** (APA, 1994; Harrington, 1994; Reynolds, 1992; Weiner, 1992. All information on suicide and depression are from these sources unless otherwise referenced).

From 3% to 8% of all teenagers show signs of being clinically depressed. This does not mean, though, that their primary problem is depression. Depression in young people tends to occur along with many other psychiatric problems—most often an anxiety disorder, but also schizophrenic and borderline disorders. Depressed teenagers are also more apt than other teenagers to have problems related to drug and alcohol abuse. About one fourth use drugs, and they are four times more likely than nondepressed teenagers to be heavy drinkers.

As shown in Insert 15–7, depressed teenagers fit one of three basic patterns. The first is a **depressive episode,** which refers to a 2- to 3-week period during which the teenager thinks and acts in depressed ways most of the time. During an episode, the sufferer derives very little, if any, pleasure from any activity or relationship. Even when things happen that should make them happier, such teens remain disinterested, irritable, or listless. They typically have trouble

Insert 15–7

Symptoms of Depression

Depressive Episode

At least five symptoms are present during a period of 2 to 3 weeks:

1. depressed mood most of the day almost every day
2. cannot sustain excitement or interest in anything or anyone
3. significant weight loss or weight gain
4. insomnia or excessive sleeping
5. physically agitated, restless, hyperactive
6. fatigued or loses energy nearly every day
7. feels worthless, low self-esteem
8. has difficulty concentrating at school or work
9. recurrent thoughts of death

Dysthymic Disorder

Depressed or irritable mood for most of the day on most days for at least 2 years.

1. low self-esteem
2. feelings of hopelessness and pessimism
3. loss of interest or pleasure

4. social withdrawal, no close friends
5. chronic fatigue and stress-related illnesses (headaches, stomach aches)
6. feelings of guilt or brooding about the past
7. excessive anger and hostility toward others
8. decreased activity or productivity at school, work, or home
9. difficulty in concentrating, poor memory or indecisiveness

Manic Depression (Bipolar Depression)

Although chronically depressed most of the time, the manic-depressive occasionally has periods in which at least three of the following appear:

1. inflated self-esteem and grandiose thinking
2. decreased need for sleep
3. extremely talkative
4. flights of ideas or experiences that are racing
5. easily distracted
6. increase in activity, hyperactive behavior
7. excessive involvement in pleasurable, often risky activities

Source: American Psychiatric Association (1994). *Diagnostic & statistical manual of mental disorders.* Washington, DC: Author.

concentrating at school and at work. They might either sleep a great deal or have difficulty sleeping. Often they either lose or gain weight. Usually they seem physically agitated and restless, feel extremely tired, and talk about how empty and worthless they feel. They can also be extremely irritable, angry, and hostile—especially depressed boys. Although depressed teenagers might have suicidal thoughts, this isn't necessarily a part of clinical depression. Frequent headaches, digestive problems, allergy attacks, and other stress-related illnesses are also common among depressed teenagers. Above all, they feel helpless and hopeless about improving their situations or their moods.

The second category of depression is referred to as a **dysthymic disorder.** These teenagers show somewhat milder symptoms of depression, but their symptoms last for years. They are seldom free from their symptoms for more than a few weeks at a time. Because they are depressed for such a long period of time, their hopeless, pessimistic ways of thinking and behaving seem to have become permanent aspects of their personalities. They seldom have friends, are terribly lonely, and spend most of their time alone at home. Dysthymic teenagers are usually more hostile, more irritable, and much angrier than are teenagers who are only experiencing a depressive episode.

The third pattern of depression is referred to as **manic** or **bipolar depression.** As the term bipolar (two poles) suggests, these adolescents fluctuate between two different extremes of behavior. When they are in their depressed phase, which is most of the time, they behave like other depressed people. Periodically, however, their depression will suddenly seem to vanish. Then for a brief time, they will think and behave in ways that are referred to as manic. When they are **manic,** their low self-esteem is replaced with an overly inflated sense of importance and self-worth; and their pessimistic thinking becomes unrealistically optimistic and grandiose. For example, when she is in her manic phase, the depressed teenager who has made failing grades all year is suddenly telling everyone about her plans to apply to an Ivy League college next year. In the manic phase, the depressed teenager becomes physically hyperactive, is easily distracted, sleeps very little, talks almost incessantly, and is literally bursting with energy. Both mind and body seem to race along in hyperdrive. Manic teenagers are much more lively and outgoing than usual, even when their behavior isn't appropriate to the situation. Their thoughts flow so quickly and so incoherently that they lose track of the points they are trying to make or forget what they said only seconds before. During the manic phase, the teenager also overdoes it by indulging in risky, exciting, pleasurable activities. For example, they may steal a parent's car and go joyriding late at night or take a credit card and go on a shopping binge. In the end, however, their manic phase ends and they return to acting depressed. Manic depression affects about 1% of the adult population and begins during adolescence for about half of them.

Gender Differences

Most teenagers who are diagnosed as depressed are girls. Part of the reason is that, when boys are depressed, they tend to become hostile, aggressive and verbally or physically abusive. Depressed boys, therefore, are often diagnosed as having a disorders such as those described in Insert 15–2. Another reason might be that girls are socialized not to express their anger by directing it toward other people. Thus, when a girl is angry with someone, she turns her anger inward and harms herself more than she harms others. Girls are also socialized to look within themselves for the source of their problems and to blame themselves when something isn't going well. Boys, on the other hand, tend to blame their problems on someone or something other than themselves. So when a boy feels depressed, he angrily blames everyone except himself (Allgood, Lewinsohn, & Hyman, 1990; Jack, 1991; McGrath & others, 1990; Nolen-Hoeksema, 1990; Peterson, Sarigiani, & Kennedy, 1991).

One 15-year study illustrates these gender differences quite well. In this study following more than 100 children from the age of 3 to 18, the boys who were depressed at the age of 18 behaved in much angrier, more hostile, more antisocial ways than did the depressed girls. The depressed girls acted sad, introspective, and ruminative; but the boys were self-indulgent, physically and verbally aggressive, and very critical and insensitive toward other people. The trait that best predicted which young boys would be depressed as 18-year-olds was hostility. For girls, the best predictors were being highly intelligent, self-critical, and overly introspective (Block & Gjerde, 1991).

GENETIC INFLUENCES

As is true with schizophrenic and borderline disorders, affective disorders run in families. Again, both genetic and environmental factors affect the likelihood of a child's becoming clinically depressed. Manic depression and depression that begins early in a child's life seem to be more influenced by genetic factors than do other depressive disorders. Genetic factors seem to influence depression primarily in two ways—through the child's inborn disposition and through chemical imbalances in the brain. As discussed in Chapter 5, some children are born with dispositions that are melancholic, moody, somber, pessimistic, touchy, and socially withdrawn. These aspects of a child's inborn disposition make fertile ground for developing depressed ways of viewing and interacting with the world. Children born with these **neurotic dispositions** are more likely to become clinically depressed than are children born with more outgoing, upbeat, stable dispositions. Neurotic children also handle stress more poorly than do those with more stable, outgoing dispositions (Chess & Thomas, 1993; Kagan, 1989; Magnusson, 1988; McCrae & Costa, 1986).

Our inborn dispositions are partly affected by what we inherit from each parent's side of the family. As a result, children who have a parent or other close relative with an affective disorder are at higher risk of becoming depressed than are those who do not have these disorders in their families. For example, studies of adopted children whose relatives were depressed have shown them to have a higher incidence of depression (Weiner, 1992).

Genes also contribute to certain chemical imbalances in the brain that have been linked to depression. Neuropsychologists study the effects of the body's chemicals on our moods and behavior. These scientists have found links between depression and certain chemicals in the brain called neurotransmitters. Thanks to **psychopharmacology,** the science of developing drugs that change human behavior and moods, some teenagers have become less depressed by taking antidepressant drugs that affect their neurotransmitters. Not only can these drugs decrease depression, but some seem to boost self-esteem and make the person more sociable and less neurotic. **Prozac** is one of these antidepressant drugs, boasting worldwide sales of more than $1 billion a year. Many other antidepressants, however, have been used successfully to treat depressed teenagers. The fact that these antidepressants have alleviated many people's depression supports the idea that certain forms of depression are influenced by biological factors (Kramer, 1993).

ENVIRONMENTAL INFLUENCES

On the other hand, what children inherit is shaped and influenced by what happens to them after they are born. Because a child is born with a very moody, melancholic disposition doesn't mean that the parents and other experiences can't shape the child's behavior for the better. So what kinds of experiences or situations increase the odds that a child will develop an affective disorder? The most important seem to be: having dysfunctional relationships within the family, learning helpless or hostile explanatory styles from a parent, having a depressed mother, lacking the skills to make close friends, and experiencing a loss.

Family Dynamics   Because many teenagers who are diagnosed as depressed also have schizophrenic or borderline disorders, it's not surprising that all three groups often have similarities in their family backgrounds. Compared to psychologically well-adjusted teenagers, depressed teenagers are more likely to have unhappily married parents, to be enmeshed with their mothers, and to have weak generational boundaries at home. Many depressed youngsters were also insecurely attached to their parents in early childhood. If a child is born with a neurotic disposition, the odds are even greater that these family dynamics will contribute to depression later in his or her life (Belsky & Cassidy, 1994; Bowlby, 1988; Greenberg, Cicchetti, & Cummings, 1990; Karen, 1994).

Helpless or hostile explanatory styles   At the heart of depression is the belief that "I can't do anything to make things better for myself." These hopeless, helpless, passive attitudes are referred to as **external locus of control** or "learned helplessness." As is true with many who have schizophrenic and borderline disorders, depressed teenagers often blame their feelings on other people or on factors external to themselves. Many depressed teenagers also have the hostile attribution biases discussed in preceding chapters (Asher & Coie, 1990). Even among teenagers who are not clinically depressed, those who have pessimistic, helpless ways of interpreting life are lonelier and less self-confident than those with more optimistic styles of thinking. These pessimistic, hostile attitudes, of course, further undermine the depressed teenager's low self-esteem and social relationships (Bandura, 1991; Seligman, 1991; Strack & Argyle, 1990; VanBuskirk & Duke, 1991).

Depressed Mother   In general, the depressed teenager's attributional style is more like the mother's than the father's. In fact, one of the most reliable ways of predicting whether a child will become depressed later in life is whether the mother is depressed—especially during the first few years of the child's life. (Phares & Compas, 1992; Radke-Yarrow, 1991; Seligman, 1991; Sigel, McGillicuddy, & Goodnow, 1992; Waxler & others, 1992).

Lack of Friends   Perhaps it isn't surprising that depressed teenagers generally have poor social skills compared to other people their age. They tend to be lonely people who have no close friends. It might be that a child becomes depressed and subsequently fails to learn the kinds of social skills and behavior that attract people and build friendships. But if depression is tied to a child's inborn temperament, then children with difficult dispositions might become depressed as they age because they have so much trouble making friends. Many depressed teenagers had trouble getting along with their peers even as preschoolers. Although it's not clear which comes first—their depression or their social problems—depressed teenagers generally lack the social maturity and social skills to become intimate with people or to succeed socially.

Experiences of Loss   The onset of depression, or an increase in the severity of the symptoms, usually occurs when a person experiences a profound loss. Sometimes the loss involves another person—the death of a loved one, a divorce that ends the child's contact with a parent, a break-up with a girlfriend or boyfriend, the end of a friendship. Other times the loss involves social status or self-esteem—being kicked off a team, not being chosen for a particular award or honor, not getting a job, not being invited to join in other teenagers' activities, failing a course, and so on. Then too, the loss can be physical—having to give up hope for a career as an athletic career because of an injury, being crippled after a car accident, or having a severe case of acne that leaves disfiguring scars. The loss can also involve an ideal or an image—losing faith in a parent that you discover has committed adultery, or losing the feeling of security after a storm demolishes your family's home, or losing spiritual faith after incidents that call your religious beliefs into question.

This does not mean, however, that any of these kinds of loss cause a teenager to become depressed. The reality is that virtually all of us experience such losses without becoming clinically depressed. In other words, a well-adjusted teenager rarely develops an affective disorder only because tragic or difficult situations arise. Of course, tragedies such as a friend's death or a parent's divorce can cause even the most well-adjusted teenager to feel profoundly sad, angry, and frustrated. Indeed, when people are grieving over a loss, it is normal for them to act in ways that resemble depression. In the wake of sad or tragic experiences, some teenagers might need a therapist's help to deal with their feelings. Remember, though, acting sad and feeling disheartened are not the same as being clinically depressed. Even after a parent dies, it is rare for children to develop the self-hatred, the hopelessness, or the profound pessimism of a depressed person. Life's tragedies and setbacks are "the straws that break the camel's back" mainly for those teenagers who have had problems managing stress and relating to people throughout childhood.

Moreover, how teenagers react to troubling situations is closely connected to how their parents react. Teenagers whose parents are divorced provide an excellent example. Because 90% of children involved in divorce live with their mother afterward, researchers have compared children's depression with their mother's adjustment to the divorce. The better the mother adjusts emotionally to the divorce, to getting remarried, and to their father's remarriage, the less likely it is that any of the children will develop a psychological disorder. When teenagers see their divorced mother dealing relatively well with stress, they absorb and mirror her attitudes. But when the divorced mother continually seems sad, downtrodden, fragile, and so forth, the teenage child with the least resilient disposition is likely to develop psychological problems, especially an affective disorder (Furstenberg & Cherlin, 1991; Hetherington, 1991; Kalter, 1990; Pianta, Egeland, & Stroufe, 1990; Robinson, 1993).

These connections between teenagers' depression and their parents' reactions to tragedy are also found when families are victims of natural disasters such as hurricanes and floods. The effects of the disaster on the parents' mental states are the strongest predictors of whether their children develop psychological problems (Harrington, 1994). So whether we're talking about hurricanes or divorce, a parent who reacts to stress by acting profoundly depressed, helpless, and victimized often passes these tendencies on to children—above all to the child who has the most social and emotional problems to begin with (Sigel, McGillicuddy, & Goodnow, 1992).

Suicide

One of the major concerns that we have about depressed teenagers is that they will try to kill themselves. Approximately 16,000 people ages 15 to 20 die each year in our country. Accidents claim 50%, murder 20%, suicide 13%, and the rest die of natural causes or disease. For all American teenagers, this means that only .002% kill themselves every year. Although 80% to 90% of suicide attempts are by girls, 75% of those who kill themselves are boys. Because suicidal boys generally shoot themselves, but suicidal girls use slower methods, such as an overdose of sleeping pills or gas, girls are saved more often before they die. Race also plays a role. White teenagers are twice as likely to kill themselves as are Hispanic or black teenagers. But Native American youth are twice as likely as whites to commit suicide. The good news is that teenagers are less likely to kill themselves than are older people. Only 7% of all suicides are teenagers, whereas 20% are people in their 20s, and 25% are people older than 60. Likewise, older teenagers are much more likely than are young teenagers to commit suicide. But the bad news is that the teenage suicide rate has increased by 20% since the 1960s. Moreover, estimates show that as many as 1 in 20 teenagers try to kill themselves, even though they fail (NCHS, 1991).

Besides race, sex, and age, how can we predict which teenagers are the most likely to kill themselves? Unfortunately no single symptom is a reliable, fail-safe warning signal. And it still isn't clear whether teenagers who succeed in killing themselves are basically similar to or basically different psychologically from those whose suicide attempts fail. Despite what we don't know, several warning signs and traits are common to teenagers who kill themselves (Berman & Jobes, 1991; Lehnert, Overholser, & Spirito, 1994; Slaby & Garfinkel, 1994; Weiner, 1992).

Insert 15–8

Suicide: Who's at Highest Risk?

Psychological Factors

____ being clinically depressed or schizophrenic

____ having a borderline personality disorder

____ feeling angry and hopeless

____ having no close friends

____ having had trouble relating to people for years

____ having been sexually or physically abused

____ having problems related to being gay

____ being a heavy drinker or drug user

____ feeling unattached to parents

Situational Factors

____ being a Native American

____ being male

____ being an older adolescent or young adult

____ having a suicidal relative

____ leaving home to attend college or to get a job

____ having experienced a recent loss

Warning Signs

____ threatening to kill self

____ dramatic changes in eating or sleeping habits

____ spending increasingly more time alone

____ giving away valued possessions

____ asking questions about death and after-life

____ continually complaining about being tired

____ seeming extremely restless or agitated

Teenagers who succeed in committing suicide usually have made previous attempts or threats to do so. A suicide attempt is also typically preceded by some frustrating or disappointing event, such as breaking up with a boyfriend or girlfriend or failing at school. Rarely is the act sudden, impulsive, or unplanned. Virtually all suicidal teenagers have long-standing psychological problems, especially depression, schizophrenia, and borderline personality disorders. Roughly 15% of those diagnosed as depressed or schizophrenic commit suicide (Clarizio, 1994). Suicidal teenagers also are people who have convinced themselves that they have no power to improve their situations or to influence their own destinies. Those depressed people who drink heavily or use drugs are also more prone to suicide. Suicidal youth have usually convinced themselves that their parents are unaware of or indifferent to their problems. In contrast, depressed teenagers who have someone to confide in rarely harm themselves. Sadly though, parents of some suicidal teenagers have discouraged them from forming close attachments to anyone outside the family by babying them too much. Most teenagers' suicide attempts are made at home, often while their parents are there.

One of the reasons that suicide is more common among older adolescents and people in their 20s is that this is the time when children are leaving home and attempting to live on their own. Going to college or going out into the world to look for a job often means that those young people with serious social and psychological problems can no longer escape the severity of their problems. Too old to keep hiding under a parent's protective wing or to burrow deeper into the family nest, older teenagers and young adults who have not resolved their psychological problems too often resort to suicide.

Several commonly held beliefs about suicidal teenagers, however, are not justified. First, having divorced parents, coming from a low-income family, or living with an unmarried parent are not associated with higher suicide rates. Second, although having a relative who has committed suicide does put a teenager at higher risk, the vast majority of suicidal teenagers have no family history of suicidal behavior. Third, most suicidal teenagers want to end their lives because of problems related to their social lives, not because of problems within the family. A 19-year-old is much more likely to be suicidal because she hasn't had any real friends for years and has never been on a date than because she doesn't get along well with someone in her family. Given the importance of our social and sexual lives in the later years of adolescence, it is not surprising that these aspects of our lives create more stress and unhappiness for us than our families do, even when we are not suicidal (Clarizio, 1994; Dornbusch & others, 1991; Larson & Asmussen, 1991).

PREVENTION AND TREATMENT

Because many depressed and suicidal teenagers also suffer from other mental disorders, the ways to prevent and treat their problems are similar to those used with teenagers who have schizophrenic and borderline disorders. The most successful approaches include: changing certain dynamics within the family, improving social skills, using antidepressants, and teaching more optimistic, more objective ways of interpreting the events in their lives. Therapists aim at teaching everyone better ways of communicating, untangling enmeshed relationships, and teaching parents ways of dealing with their personal, marital, or post-divorce problems without involving their children. The most effective therapists also teach depressed teenagers the specific kinds of social skills they need to make friends, date, and build closer bonds to people outside the family. These social successes, in turn, reduce depression and suicidal thinking. When used in conjunction with intensive therapy, antidepressant drugs can alleviate depressive thinking and self-destructive tendencies. Some teenagers also have reduced their stress and depression by becoming physically active. Daily physical exercise seems to help in two ways—first, by boosting self-esteem because exercise generally improves the person's physical appearance and strength, second by increasing the level of endorphins, which are the body's natural mood elevators (Brown & Siegel, 1988; Tucker, 1990; Tuckman & Hinkle, 1988).

Because depression and suicidal thinking are related to external locus of control attitudes and anger, therapists also work at teaching these teenagers more optimistic ways of thinking about the situations in their lives. Those who have hostile attribution biases and helpless, pessimistic styles of thinking can be taught more objective, more optimistic ways of testing their opinions and conclusions. Because depressed people tend to personalize everything that happens to them, to exaggerate and overgeneralize, and to think in absolute, dichotomous ways, they are taught to subject their own feelings and conclusions to certain "reality testing" exercises: "What is the evidence for your conclusion? What are some alternative explanations or interpretations? Besides what's just been said, why else might that person have behaved that way?" Depressed teenagers might also be asked to record each of their enjoyable activities. The idea is to get them to pay more attention to positive things, thereby focusing less on negative aspects of their lives. This daily recording also helps teenagers make the connections between their moods and the activities they choose. Using such techniques, cognitive therapy seems to be particularly effective at reducing future episodes of depression.

Certain teenagers have a better chance than others of recovering from their suicidal and depressive thinking. In general, the earlier in life the depression started, the more difficult to cure. Likewise, teenagers with a family history of psychological disorders usually make less progress than those without seriously disturbed relatives. Those whose families also make changes and those who get into therapy sooner also stand better chances of recovering. Even after they have overcome their depressive or suicidal episodes, the people who have the fewest relapses are those who continue to see a therapist, especially during periods when they feel especially stressed or vulnerable.

EATING DISORDERS

As is true with suicide, very few adolescents are affected by the eating disorders known as anorexia and bulimia—only 1% of the population aged 12 to 25. Far more overeat. Nearly 25% of all teenagers are obese. Unlike anorexia, however, obesity cannot kill adolescents—at least not until much later in their lives when their excessive weight creates problems for their hearts and overall health (Fisher & Brone, 1991).

In any event, the eating disorder that has generated the most concern from a psychological viewpoint is anorexia nervosa. **Anorexia nervosa** is a psychological disorder in which the person becomes so intensely afraid of gaining weight that he or she basically stops eating and can eventually die from self-starvation. The disorder begins with excessive dieting, then typically progresses to using laxatives or self-induced vomiting so that the calories do not have time to be absorbed by the body—activities referred to as **purging.** Many anorexics are also **bulimic,** meaning that they have episodes of binge eating during which they consume enormous quantities of food in a very short period of time. Binge eating is often followed by purging. Although virtually all anorexics and bulimics are females, some males also develop these disorders (APA, 1994).

How have you contributed to the idea that an "attractive" female has to be extremely thin?

Why certain adolescents become anorexic or bulimic is not altogether clear. The theories and evidence basically follow four lines of thinking. The first is that our society's overemphasis on female beauty and thinness encourages girls to believe that they can never be too thin. Especially for girls who have low self-esteem and very traditional notions about femininity, this kind of societal pressure encourages excessive dieting and anorexic attitudes. In fact, many girls with eating disorders do have low self-esteem and hold very sexist views about how women ought to please men—views that center around a woman's appearance (Bordo, 1993; Fisher, 1991; Newell, 1990; Wolf, 1992).

Another line of thinking is that young people develop eating disorders primarily because they come from dysfunctional families. Many anorexics and bulimics do feel tremendous pressure to be perfect children—perfection that includes having enough self-discipline not to get fat or not to eat at all. These anorexics come from families in which too much emphasis has been placed on self-discipline, perfection, and pleasing the parents. Moreover, many anorexic teenagers are enmeshed with one or both of their parents and have been overly protected and babied while growing up. This suggests that their psychological disorder might be the consequence of not having developed lives independent enough from their parents. Indeed, many of these adult daughters are still being treated as if they are little girls, rather than being encouraged to become mature, self-reliant women. By losing enough weight so that they stop menstruating and begin looking like sexless children, some young women are trying to avoid sexuality and to remain someone's "little girl." Also, in a number of these families, the parents have been working out their own marital unhappiness through the child who eventually develops an eating disorder (Fisher & Brone, 1991; Rodin, 1990; Woodbury, 1991).

Other anorexics, however, seem to have developed their eating disorder as part of their reaction to other forms of stress and trauma. African American, Latina, and lesbian women point out that racism and homophobia contribute to their eating disorders (Thompson, 1995). Some evidence also suggests that eating disorders might be linked to hormonal imbalances. Proving causality is difficult, however, because the chemical imbalances are from measures taken after the person has already developed an eating disorder (Fisher & Brone, 1991; Sigman & Flanery, 1992).

With regard to males with eating disorders, the pattern is somewhat different. Like females, these young men tend to develop their disorders at crucial points of separation from their parents—going away to college, starting a new job, leaving for graduate school. For reasons not yet clear, males tend to develop anorexia several years later in life than do females. Also unlike females, nearly one fourth of male anorexics are homosexual. This suggests that their disorder might be related to the stress involved in being gay in a society that is more homophobic toward gay males than toward lesbians. For other males, sports training can lead to an eating disorder. For example, male gymnasts, jockeys, and runners might initially try to lose weight in order to improve their athletic performance. In the process, though, they can become anorexic or bulimic (Hamlett & Curry, 1990).

Because no single factor is common to all anorexics or to all bulimics, the ways to prevent or to treat their disorders differ. In some cases, antidepressant drugs help, although most young people with eating disorders are not clinically depressed (Harrington, 1994). In other cases, therapists work with the family to change those dynamics that might be contributing to the eating disorder. Helping young people boost their self-esteem in ways other than focusing on their appearance and pleasing their parents can also be helpful. When the eating disorder appears to be related to traumas such as rape, incest, or physical abuse or to issues related to the person's sexual orientation, the therapist focuses as those issues, as well as on the eating disorder itself.

PERCEPTIONS, SELF-DECEPTIONS, AND WELL-BEING

It is striking that anorexics, delinquents, and psychologically disturbed teenagers so often have one problem in common: ways of perceiving life that are often inaccurate and self-destructive. Their negative, distorted, or pessimistic styles of thinking lead many of them to continue to engage in the very behaviors that are so self-destructive. As explained, the delinquent often has overly hostile ways of interpreting and reacting to the world; whereas the psychologically disturbed teenager has an overly pessimistic, grossly distorted, angry perception. These teenagers live out a self-destructive "life story" due to their maladaptive attributional styles. Many delinquent and psychologically disturbed youngsters, therefore, have extremely biased and distorted memories of the past, interpretations of the present, and expectations for the future. Listening to someone tell about their family or their past can reveal more about how well-adjusted or how emotionally disturbed they are today than about the truth of what actually happened to them in the past or in their families. Unfortunately, the things we trick ourselves into denying or believing about our "life stories" influence our behavior and our mental health (Bowlby, 1988; Gergen, 1992; Gilovich, 1991).

Many delinquent and psychologically disturbed teenagers can be seen as people whose "life story has gone mad." In this sense, when we say that these troubled teenagers "need more self-esteem," we are saying that they need help readjusting the lens through which they view themselves and others. For example, even when their parents were not overly critical and their childhoods were relatively happy, teenagers with schizophrenic disorders rarely remember the past favorably (Goldstein, 1990; Goleman, 1985). Likewise, what teenagers and young adults remember about their childhoods are colored by what each parent has told them and by how well their own lives are going in the present (Halverson, 1988; McCrae & Costa, 1988). We cannot change events that occurred in the past for delinquents or psychologically troubled teenagers. We can, however, help them "repair" their life stories and readjust the angry, hostile, or pessimistic lens through which they are misperceiving the world and themselves (Miller, 1990; Seligman, 1991; Weiner, 1992).

CONCLUSION

The vast majority of teenagers are psychologically and socially well-adjusted. Only a small percentage suffer from delinquent behavior, suicidal tendencies, clinical depression, or schizophrenic, borderline personality, or eating disorders. On the other hand, we could do more to reduce the numbers of young people affected by these externalizing and internalizing disorders. Whatever we can do as a society or within our individual families to prevent and reduce delinquency and children's mental disorders benefits us all—not only financially, but emotionally and spiritually as well.

Review/Test Questions

Support each of your answers with specific statistics and research results as applicable.

1. How prevalent are crime, murder, and delinquency among teenagers?
2. In what ways do environmental, genetic, and family factors contribute to delinquent and aggressive behavior?
3. What are the symptoms of each of the psychological disorders associated with aggressive, defiant, or violent behavior?
4. What are 10 problems that affect adolescents in our country? How prevalent is each? What are the links to race, income, and gender?
5. What distinguishes neurotic, socialized, and psychotic delinquents?
6. How might delinquency be prevented, and what are the best ways for rehabilitating delinquents?
7. How do delinquency and aggression differ by race, income, and gender? What accounts for these differences?
8. What are the symptoms of schizophrenic, schizoid, and borderline personality disorders?
9. Which biological, family, and environmental factors are most likely to contribute to

schizophrenic and borderline disorders?
10. In what ways are teenagers with schizophrenic and borderline disorders alike, and in what ways are they different?
11. How do therapists help teenagers with schizophrenic and borderline disorders?
12. How are each of the following related to adolescents' violent behavior or to schizophrenic and borderline disorders: anhedonia, attention deficit disorders, attribution bias, dysthymia, enmeshment, generational boundaries, locus of control, and splitting?
13. What are the common symptoms of depression and suicidal thinking?
14. Which adolescents are most likely to become depressed or to try to kill themselves? Why?
15. How do genetic and environmental factors contribute to depression and suicide?
16. What are the differences between dysthymia, bipolar depression, and a depressive episode?
17. In what ways are the treatments for depression different from those for schizophrenic and borderline disorders? Alike?
18. How do splitting, hostile attribution bias, and external locus of control attitudes affect an adolescent's mental health?

19. How do environmental, family, and biological factors contribute to eating disorders?
20. How do distorted styles of thinking contribute to low self-esteem, delinquency, eating disorders, depression, and schizophrenic or borderline disorders?

Questions for Discussion and Debate

1. Aside from the ideas mentioned in this chapter, how do you think we should go about reducing delinquency and violence among teenagers?
2. Which laws have you or your friends broken, and what were the outcomes? How did this affect your development or theirs?
3. Who was the most violent, most aggressive, or least law-abiding person you knew as an adolescent? What accounted for his or her behavior?
4. Considering the family factors and family dynamics that contribute to the problems discussed in this chapter, what is healthy and unhealthy about your own family?
5. If you know anyone who has or has had a psychological disorder: What do you believe contributed to his or her developing the problem?
6. What factors have contributed most to your being psychologically well-adjusted or psychologically troubled?
7. Thinking back to the times in your life when you have felt the saddest and most disheartened, what helped you most to recover? How could this be applied to helping depressed or psychologically disturbed teenagers?
8. Which problems discussed in this chapter struck closest to home for you?
9. If you or anyone you know has had an eating disorder: How did the problem affect you? How do you feel about your own body weight and about dieting?
10. How have you used schizophrenic thinking, splitting, or self-deception to deal with problems in your own life?

Glossary

affective disorders, p. 590
anhedonia, p. 590
anorexia nervosa, p. 600
antisocial disorder, p. 568
attention deficit disorder, p. 570
bipolar disorder, p. 592
borderline personality disorder, p. 575
borderline schizophrenia, p. 575
bulimia, p. 601

conduct disorder, p. 568
defiant personality disorder, p. 568
depressive episode, p. 591
displacement, p. 578
dysthymia, p. 592
enmeshment, p. 582
external locus of control, p. 594
generational boundaries, p. 583
hostile attribution bias, p. 570

manic, p. 592
neurotic, p. 593
Prozac, p. 594
psychopharmacology, p. 594
purging, p. 601
role reversal, p. 582
schizoid, p. 575
schizophrenia, p. 574
splitting, p. 578
status offense, p. 564

References

Ainsworth, M., & Eichberg, C. (1991). Effects of mother's unresolved loss of an attachment figure. In C. Parkes, J. Hinde, & P. Marris (Eds.), *Attachment across the life cycle* (pp. 160–183). New York: Routledge.

Allgood, M., Lewinsohn, P., & Hyman, H. (1990). Sex differences and adolescent depression. *Journal of Abnormal Psychology, 99*, 55–93.

American Psychiatric Association. (1994). *Diagnostic and statistical manual of mental disorders.* Washington, DC: Author.

American Psychological Association. (1993). *Violence and youth.* Washington, DC: Author.

Anderson, E. (1992). *Streetwise.* Chicago: University of Chicago Press.

Asher, S., & Coie, J. (1990). *Peer rejection in childhood.* New York: Cambridge University Press.

Bandura, A. (1991). Self-efficacy: impact of self-beliefs on adolescent life paths. In R. Lerner, A. Petersen, & J. Brooks-Gunn (Eds.), *Encyclopedia of adolescence.* New York: Garland.

Belsky, J., & Cassidy, J. (1994). Attachment: Theory and evidence. In M. Rutter, D. Hays, & S. Baron (Eds.), *Developmental principles and clinical issues in psychology and psychiatry.* Blackwell, England: Oxford Press.

Berman, A., & Jobes, D. (1991). *Adolescent suicide.* Washington, DC: American Psychological Association.

Biller, H. (1993). *Fathers and families: Paternal factors in child development.* Westport, CT: Auburn House.

Block, J., & Gjerde, P. (1991). Preadolescent antecedents of depressive symptomatology at age 18. *Journal of Youth and Adolescence, 20*, 217–231.

Bordo, S. (1993). *Unbearable weight: Feminism, Western culture and the body.* New York: Norton.

Bowen, M. (1978). *Family therapy in clinical practice.* New York: Aronson.

Bowlby, J. (1988). *A secure base.* New York: Basic Books.

Brown, J., & Siegel, J. (1988). Exercise as a buffer of life stress. *Health Psychology, 7,* 341–353.

Carlson, N. (1986). *Physiology of behavior.* Boston, MA: Allyn & Bacon.

Chess, S., & Thomas, A. (1993). Continuities and discontinuities in temperament. In R. Robins & M. Rutter (Eds.), *Straight and devious pathways from childhood to adulthood* (pp. 205–220). New York: Cambridge University Press.

Cicchetti, D. (1992). Peer relations in maltreated children. In R. Parke & G. Ladd (Eds.), *Family peer relationships: Modes of linkage* (pp. 345–383). Hillsdale, NJ: Erlbaum.

Clarizio, H. (1994). *Assessment and treatment of depression in children and adolescents.* Brandon, VT: Clinical Psychology Publishing Co.

Cohen, P. (1990). Common and uncommon pathways to adolescent psychopathology and problem behavior. In L. Robins & M. Rutter (Eds.), *Straight and devious pathways from childhood to adulthood* (pp. 242–259). New York: Cambridge University Press.

Colten, M., Gore, S., & Aseltine, R. (1991). Patterning of distress & disorder in a sample of high school aged youth. In M. Colten & S. Gore (Eds.), *Adolescent stress* (pp. 157–180). New York: Aldine De Gruyter.

Dabbs, J., & Morris, R. (1990). Testosterone, social class, and antisocial behavior. *Psychological Science, 1,* 209–211.

Diegmueller, K. (1994). Harnessing the power of positive peer pressure. *Education Week, June 8,* 28–32.

Dornbusch, S., Mont-Reynaud, R., Ritter, P., Zeng-yin, C., & Steinberg, L. (1991). Stressful events and their correlates among adolescents of diverse backgrounds. In M. Colten & S. Gore (Eds.), *Adolescent stress* (pp. 111–131). New

York: Aldine De Gruyter.

Ebata, A., Petersen, A., & Conger, J. (1990). The development of psychopathology in adolescence. In J. Rolf, A. Masten, D. Cicchetti, K. Nuechterlein, & S. Weintraub (Eds.), *Risk and protective factors in the development of psychopathology* (pp. 308–334). New York: Cambridge University Press.

Elicker, J., Englund, M., & Stroufe, L. (1992). Predicting peer competence and peer relationships from early parent-child relationships. In R. Parke & G. Ladd (Eds.), *Family peer relationships: Modes of linkages.* Hillsdale, NJ: Erlbaum.

Farrington, D., Loeber, R., & VanKammen, W. (1990). Long term criminal outcomes of hyperactivity-impulsivity-attention deficit and conduct problems in childhood. In L. Robins & M. Rutter (Eds.), *Straight and devious pathways from childhood to adulthood* (pp. 62–81). New York: Cambridge University.

Federal Bureau of Investigation. (1994). *Juvenile crime and delinquency prevention.* Washington, DC: U.S. Department of Justice.

Fisher, C., & Brone, R. (1991). Eating disorders in adolescence. In R. Lerner, A. Peterson, & J. Brooks-Gunn (Eds.), *Encyclopedia of adolescence* (pp. 156–172). New York: Garland.

Fisher, M. (1991). Eating attitudes and health risk behaviors. *Journal of Adolescent Health, 12,* 377–384.

Furstenberg, F., & Cherlin, A. (1991). *Divided families.* Cambridge, MA: Harvard University Press.

Gergen, M. (1992). Life stories: Pieces of a dream. In G. Rosenwald & R. Ochberg (Eds.), *Storied Lives.* New Haven, CT: Yale University Press.

Gilovich, T. (1991). *How we know what isn't so: The fallibility of human reason in everyday life.* New York: Macmillan.

Goldstein, M. (1990). Family relations as risk factors for schizophrenia. In J. Rolf (Ed.), *Risk and protective factors in the development of psy-chopathology* (pp. 408–424). New York: Cambridge University Press.

Goleman, D. (1985). *Vital lies, simple truths: The psychology of self-deception.* New York: Simon & Schuster.

Greenberg, M., Cicchetti, D., & Cummings, E. (1990). *Attachment in the preschool years.* Chicago: University of Chicago.

Guidubaldi, J. (1988). Differences in children's divorce adjustment across grade level and gender. In S. Wolchik & P. Karoly (Eds.), *Children of divorce* (pp. 185–231). Lexington, MA: Lexington Books.

Halverson, C. (1988). Remembering your parents. *Journal of Personality, 56,* 434–443.

Hamlett, K., & Curry, J. (1990). Anorexia nervosa in adolescent males. *Journal of Eating Disorders, 21,* 79–94.

Hanson, D., Gottesman, I., & Heston, L. (1990). Long range schizophrenia forecasting. In J. Rolf (Ed.), *Risk and protective factors in the development of psychopathology* (pp. 424–444). New York: Cambridge University Press.

Harrington, L. (1994). *Depressive disorder in childhood and adolescence.* New York: Wiley.

Hetherington, M. (1991). Families, lies and videotapes. *Journal of Research on Adolescence, 1,* 323–348.

Hinde, R., & Stevenson, J. (1995). *Relation between relationships within families.* Cambridge, England: Oxford University Press.

Jack, D. (1991). *Silencing the self: Women and depression.* New York: HarperCollins.

Kagan, J. (1989). *Unstable ideas: Temperament, cognition and self.* Cambridge, MA: Harvard University Press.

Kalter, N. (1990). *Growing up with divorce.* New York: Ballantine.

Karen, R. (1994). *Becoming attached.* New York: Time Warner.

Koestner, R., Zuroff, D., & Powers, T. (1991). Family origins of adolescent self-criticism and its continuity into adulthood. *Journal of Abnormal*

Psychology, 100, 191–197.

Kramer, P. (1993). *Listening to Prozac.* New York: Viking.

Kupersmidt, J., Coie, J., & Dodge, K. (1993). The role of poor peer relationships in the development of disorder. In S. Asher & J. Coie (Eds.), *Peer rejection in childhood* (pp. 274–309). New York: Cambridge University Press.

Lamb, M. (1994). *Adolescent problem behaviors.* New York: Erlbaum.

Larson, R., & Asmussen, L. (1991). Anger, worry, and hurt in early adolescence. In M. Colten & S. Gore (Eds.), *Adolescent stress* (pp. 21–42). New York: Aldine De Gruyter.

Lehnert, K., Overholser, J., & Spirito, A. (1994). Internalized and externalized anger in adolescent suicide attempts. *Journal of Adolescent Research, 9,* 105–119.

MacKinnon, C., Lamb, M., Arbuckle, B., Baradaran, L., & Volling, B. (1992). The relationship between biased maternal and filial attributions and the aggressiveness of their interactions. *Development and Psychopatholgy, 4,* 403–415.

Madrid, A., & Schwartz, M. (1991). Maternal infant bonding and pediatric asthma. *Pre and Perinatal Psychology, 5,* 347–358.

Magnusson, D. (1988). *Paths through life.* Hillsdale, NJ: Erlbaum.

Main, M. (1993). *A typology of human attachment organization.* New York: Cambridge University Press.

McCall, N. (1994). *Makes me wanna holler.* New York: Random House.

McCrae, R., & Costa, P. (1986). *Emerging lives, enduring dispositions.* Boston: Little Brown.

McCrae, R., & Costa, P. (1988). Recalled parent child relations and adult personality. *Journal of Personality, 56,* 417–434.

McGrath, E., Keita, G., Strickland, B., & Russo, N. (1990). *Women and depression.* Washington, DC: American Psychological Association.

Miedzian, M. (1991). *Boys will be boys:*

Breaking the link between masculinity and violence. New York: Doubleday.

Miller, A. (1990). *Banished knowledge: Facing childhood injuries.* New York: Doubleday.

Miller, B., & Wood, B. (1991). Childhood asthma. *Journal of Asthma, 28,* 405–414.

Minuchin, P. (1988). Relationships within the family. In R. Hinde & J. Stevenson-Hinde (Eds.), *Family interaction and psychopathology* (pp. 7–26). New York: Plenum.

Minuchin, S., & Fishman, H. (1981). *Family therapy techniques.* Cambridge, MA: Harvard University Press.

Murr, A. (1990, May 7). When gangs meet the handicapped. *Newsweek,* p. 70.

National Center for Health Statistics. (1991). *Vital statistics of the U.S.: Mortality.* Washington, DC: Author.

Newell, G. (1990). Self concept as a factor in the quality of diets of adolescent girls. *Adolescence, 25,* 117–130.

Nolen-Hoeksema, S. (1990). *Sex differences in depression.* Palo Alto, CA: Stanford University Press.

Olweus, D., Block, J., & Radke-Yarrow, M. (1985). *The development of antisocial and prosocial behavior.* New York: Academic Press.

Parke, R., & Ladd, G. (1992). *Family-peer relationships: Modes of linkage.* Hillsdale, NJ: Erlbaum.

Parker, G. (1983). *Parental overprotection: A risk factor in psychosocial development.* New York: Grune & Stratton.

Parkes, C., Stevenson-Hinde, J., & Marris, P. (1991). *Attachment across the life cycle.* New York: Tavistock/Routledge.

Patterson, G., Reid, J., & Dishion, T. (1992). *A social learning approach: Antisocial boys.* Eugene, OR: Castalia.

Peplar, D., & Rubin, K. (1994). *The development and treatment of childhood aggression.* Hillsdale, NJ: Erlbaum.

Perry, S., Frances, A., & Clarkin, J. (1990). *A DSM Casebook of Treatment Selection.* New York: Bruner-Mazel.

Petersen, A., Kennedy, R., & Sullivan, P. (1991). Coping with adolescence. In M. Colten & S. Gore (Eds.), *Adolescent stress* (pp. 93–110). New York: Aldine De Gruyter.

Peterson, A., Sarigiani, P., & Kennedy, R. (1991). Adolescent depression: Why more girls? *Journal of Youth & Adolescence, 20,* 247–271.

Phares, V., & Compas, B. (1992). The role of fathers in child and adolescent psychopathology. *Psychological Bulletin, 111,* 387–412.

Pianta, B., Egeland, B., & Stroufe, A. (1990). Maternal stress and children's development. In J. Rolf, A. Masten, K. Nuechterlain, & .W. Weintraub (Eds.), *Risk and protective factors in the development of psychopathology* (pp. 215–236). New York: Cambridge University Press.

Pleck, J., Sonnenstein, G., & Ku, I. (1993). Problem behaviors and masculine ideology in adolescent males. In R. Ketterlinus & M. Lamb (Eds.), *Adolescent problem behaviors.* Hillsdale, NJ: Erlbaum.

Radke-Yarrow, M. (1991). Attachment patterns in children of depressed mothers. In C. Parkes (Ed.), *Attachment across the life cycle.* New York: Routledge.

Reynolds, W. (1992). *Internalizing disorders in children and adolescents.* New York: Wiley.

Robins, L., & Rutter, M. (1990). *Straight and devious pathways from childhood to adulthood.* New York: Cambridge University Press.

Robinson, M. (1993). *Family transformation during divorce & remarriage.* New York: Routledge.

Rodin, J. (1990). Risk and protective factors for bulimia nervosa. In J. Rolf (Ed.), *Risk and protective factors in the development of psychopathology* (pp. 361–383). New York: Cambridge University Press.

Rolf, J., Masten, A., Cicchetti, D., Neuchterlain, K., & Weintraub, S. (1993). *Risk and protective factors in the development of psychopathology.* New York: Cambridge University Press.

Rubin, K., Lemare, L., & Lollis, S. (1990). Social withdrawal in childhood. In S. Asher & J. Coie (Eds.), *Peer rejection in childhood* (pp. 51–72). Hillsdale, NJ: Erlbaum.

Rutter, M., Hays, D., & Baron, S. (1994). *Developmental principles and clinical issues in psychology and psychiatry.* New York: Oxford University Press.

Safyer, A., & Hauser, S. (1994). Exploring adolescent emotional expression. *Journal of Adolescent Research, 9,* 50–66.

Seligman, M. (1991). *Learned optimism.* New York: Random House.

Sholevar, G., & Perkel, R. (1990). Family systems intervention and physical illness. *General Hospital Psychiatry, 12,* 363–372.

Sigel, I., McGillicuddy, A., & Goodnow, J. (1992). *Parental belief systems: The psychological consequences for children.* Hillsdale, NJ: Erlbaum.

Sigman, G., & Flanery, R. (1992). Eating disorders. In E. Greydanus & M. Wolraich (Eds.), *Behavioral pediatrics* (pp. 181–201). New York: Springer-Verlag.

Slaby, A., & Garfinkel, L. (1994). *Why teens kill themselves.* New York: Norton.

Snarey, J. (1993). *How fathers care for the next generation.* Cambridge, MA: Harvard University Press.

Strack, F., & Argyle, M. (1990). *The social psychology of subjective well-being.* Oxford, England: Pergamon Press.

Stroufe, A. (1989). Relationships and relationship disturbances. In A. Sameroff & R. Ende (Eds.), *Relationship disturbances in early childhood* (pp. 97–124). New York: Basic Books.

Thompson, B. (1995). *A hunger so wide and so deep: Women speaking out on eating problems.* Minneapolis: University of Minnesota.

Tucker, L. (1990). Physical fitness and

psychological distress. *International Journal of Sport Psychology, 21,* 185–201.

Tuckman, B., & Hinkle, J. (1988). An experimental study of the physical and psychological effects of aerobic exercise on schoolchildren. In B. Melamed (Ed.), *Child Health Psychology* (pp. 221–232). Hillsdale, NJ: Erlbaum.

VanBuskirk, A., & Duke, M. (1991). Coping style and loneliness in adolescents. *Genetic Psychology, 152,* 145–157.

Wallerstein, J. (1991). The long term effects of divorce on children: A review. *Journal of American Academy of Child Psychiatry, 30,* 349–360.

Waxler, C., Denham, S., Iannotti, R., &
Cummings, M. (1992). Peer relations in children with a depressed caregiver. In R. Parke & G. Ladd (Eds.), *Family peer relationships: Modes of linkage* (pp. 317–344). Hillsdale, NJ: Erlbaum.

Weiner, I. (1992). *Psychological disturbance in adolescence.* New York: Wiley.

Werner, E. (1987). Vulnerability and resiliency in children. In J. Burchard & S. Burchard (Eds.), *Prevention of delinquent behavior* (pp. 68–84). Beverly Hills, CA: Sage.

Wolf, N. (1992). *The beauty myth: How images of beauty are used against women.* New York: Doubleday.

Woodbury, R. (1991, September 2). Putting the brakes on crime. *Time,* p. 65.

Glossary

absolutist thinking—Reasoning in childlike extremes; "either-or" reasoning.

accelerated ego development—Developing a mature ego sooner than most people of the same age.

accommodation—As used by Piaget, the change in an existing schema that enables us to understand new concepts or new experience.

acculturation— Adopting the values and behavior of the majority race in a society.

acid—Lysergic acid diethylamide. *See* LSD.

acute anxiety disorders—Extreme nervousness or excessive fears.

adipose tissue—Fat tissue.

AFDC—Aid to Families with Dependent Children; national welfare program for poor mothers and their children.

agnostic—Someone who professes ignorance of a deity of afterlife, or the impossibility of knowing whether a deity or an afterlife exist.

Amish —A conservative Protestant sect of Mennonites that rejects most aspects of modernized American life.

amphetamines—Drugs that speed up or stimulate the central nervous system.

anal period—According to psychoanalytic theory, the stage from ages 2 to 4 when we need to develop some self-control and feel securely loved by our primary caretaker.

androcentric—Centered on males, or male issues and male values.

androgen—The steroid hormones that cause masculine secondary sex characteristics to develop.

androgyny—Possessing both masculine and feminine personality traits. For example, being both nurturing and assertive.

Angel Dust—Popular name for the drug Phencyclidine. *See* PCP.

anhedonia—Inability to derive pleasure from any relationship or activity.

anorexia nervosa—An eating disorder characterized by its victim's obsession with weight loss, to the point of self-starvation.

antisocial personality disorder— Psychological disorder marked by aggressive, defiant, or violent disregard for others. *See* Insert 5–2 for symptoms.

anxiety disorders—Psychological disorders marked by excessive worrying. *See* Insert 5–2 for specific symptoms.

areola—The dark colored skin around the nipple.

arrested ego development—Condition in which victim lags behind others of the same age in social and moral reasoning skills, individuation from parents, and identity formation. *See* Inserts 4–1 and 4–5.

assimilation—As used by Piaget, the process of fitting new concepts or new experience into existing beliefs and ways of thinking.

AT or AG—Academically talented or academically gifted. Terms for students who have exceptionally high IQ test scores.

atheist—Someone who does not believe in a deity or an afterlife.

attachment theory—An extension of psychoanalytic theory that explores the links between early childhood relationships with parents to later relationships with people outside the family as adolescents and adults.

attention deficit hyperactivity disorder—A neurological disorder that causes hyperactivity and inattentiveness. *See* Insert 10–3.

attribution bias—Attributing other people's behavior to hostile motives.

attribution theory—Theories that examine a person's explanatory styles.

attributional styles—*See* locus of control attitudes.

autonomous morality—According to Kohlberg, the ability to reason independently with less regard for obedience to authorities. *See* Inserts 12–1 and 12–2.

avoidant personality disorder—Psychological disorder marked by extreme shyness and social withdrawal. *See* Insert 5–2 for specific symptoms.

bar mitzvah—Jewish ceremony marking the acceptance of a teenage boy as an adult member of the Jewish community.

barbiturates—Drugs that slow down or depress the central nervous system.

basal metabolism rate—The rate at which the body converts calories into sugar for energy.

bat mitzvah—Jewish ceremony marking the acceptance of a teenage girl as an adult member of the Jewish community.

behaviorism—The theory that most human behavior is a consequence of reward and punishment. Synonym: Skinnerian psychology.

bicultural—Able to function equally well in two different cultures.

bilateralized—The brain's ability to process certain types of information in either hemisphere.

bilingual—Able to speak two languages.

binuclear family—A situation in which children spend roughly the same amount of time living with each divorced parent; dual residency.

biosocial theories—The theory that human behavior is a consequence of both biological and environmental factors.

bipolar disorder—Manic depression, characterized by the depressed victim's occasional periods of overly optimistic, energized, exuberant thinking. *See* Insert 5–7.

blended family—A family composed of two married adults, at least one of whom brings children from a former marriage.

borderline disorder—Psychological disorder in which a person's style of thinking and ways of relating to people are maladaptive and distorted. *See* Insert 15–6.

born again—Sudden conversion to Christianity involving very emotional commitment to Jesus.

boundaries—The unwritten rules and expectations separating children's roles from those of adults in a family.

brain lateralization—Refers to the brain's division into left and right hemispheres, with control of certain mental and physical functions located in one half or the other.

brittle ego—Unable to adapt easily to new situations, new people, or situations that are unpredictable and uncontrollable.

bulimia—An eating disorder in which the person induces vomiting or uses laxatives in order not to gain weight.

cervix—The tip of the uterus that extends into the vagina.

circumcision—Surgical removal of the skin covering the head of the penis.

class inclusion—The ability to reason simultaneously about parts of a whole and the whole itself.

clitoris—The organ of sexual arousal in females.

codependent—A person whose self-worth is determined almost wholly by putting his or her own needs second to the needs of others in ways that put the person into emotionally harmful relationships.

coercive parenting—Methods of trying to control and discipline children such as whining, begging, pleading, acquiescing, and bargaining—in contrast to more democratic, well-reasoned discipline.

cognitive dissonance—The unpleasant feeling that occurs upon encountering information or experiences that contradict or don't fit into existing beliefs or patterns of thinking.

cognitive stage theories—The theories that children and adolescents pass through a series of cognitive stages, each associated with characteristic ways of reasoning.

cohort group—A group of people possessing common characteristics, usually born in the same year.

concrete operations—According to Piaget, the cognitive stage that occurs from ages 7 to 11 during which we learn the rules of equivalence, reversibility, class inclusion and associativity.

conduct disorders—Psychological disorders characterized by defiant disregard for others. *See* Insert 5–2 for symptoms.

confluence theory—The belief that family size and birth order at least partially determine our personalities.

confounding variable—Any factor, such as race, gender, or income, that might confuse or interfere with whatever is being measured.

conservation—According to Piaget, the concept grasped at about the age of 7 that the amount of something stays the same regardless of changes in its shape or number of parts into which it is divided.

control group—A group of people as closely matched as possible to those in the experimental group.

conventional reasoning—According to Piaget, child-like reasoning that relies on obedience to authorities and simplistic ways of judging right and wrong.

convergent thinking—Thinking along conventional lines in order to find a single best answer or solution.

correlation coefficient—The number derived from a statistical formula that indicates the strength and the direction of the relationship between the variables being studied.

correlational research—Studies that compare the strength and the direction of the relationship among two or more variables.

Crack—Cocaine in crystallized form.

cross-sectional research—Studies that compare people from different age groups on the dependent variable.

culture-fair test—A test designed in ways that make it less likely to discriminate against people on the basis of race or class.

dependent personality disorder—Psychological disorder characterized by an excessive need to be taken care of. *See* Insert 5–2 for symptoms.

dependent variable—The variable being measured that can increase or decrease as a consequence of the other (independent) variables.

disequilibrium—In Piaget's theory, the unpleasant feelings that arise when we encounter new information that contradicts the information in our existing schema.

displacement—Directing your anger at someone other than the person who actually deserves it.

disposition—*See* temperament.

diuretics—Foods or medicines that cause weight loss by forcing water out of the body's tissues.

divergent thinking—Thinking that is creative and original.

Down's syndrome—A genetic abnormality that often results in mental retardation.

dual residency—A legal agreement in which children live about 50% of the time with each divorced parent.

dualistic thinking—A child-like way of reasoning in which the person perceives situations and people in only two totally opposite ways. For example: "always or never" rather than "sometimes." "Good or evil" rather than "flawed."

dysthymia—Depression that last for years.

dysthymic—Extremely melancholic, depressed disposition.

Ecstasy—Popular name for the drug MDMA.

ego—A person's basic ways of behaving and of interpreting the world around him or her.

ego development—Through the process of individuation, the development of an identity, or an "ego" of one's own.

egocentric thinking—Thinking from a self-focused viewpoint; lacking empathy for others' views or feelings.

egocentrism—A central characteristic of child-like reasoning and behavior in which the person can't consider or empathize with other people's feelings or perspectives; the inability to see things from another person's perspective or to consider different perspectives simultaneously.

Electra complex—According to Freudians, a daughter's being in love with her father in ways that make her jealous of her mother and that prevent her from forming healthy relationships with boys her own age.

endorphins—Chemicals released by the brain that act as natural painkillers and mood elevators.

enmeshment—A psychologically damaging relationship in which two people, usually within a family, are overly involved in one another's lives and feelings; failing to separate their identities from one another, they become entwined in each other's lives in damaging ways. *See* Inserts 4–4 and 4–5 for examples.

ESL—English as a second language; classes offered for students who are not native speakers of English.

estrogen—The hormone in both males and females that at proper levels produces female secondary sex characteristics.

ethnocentric—Perceiving one's own race, ethnic group, or culture as the standard for behavior, appearance, taste, and so forth; inclined to regard one's own social group as the center of culture.

evangelical—Fundamentalist Protestant denominations endorsing very literal, conservative interpretations of the Bible.

experimental research—Studies that, because of the way they must be designed, can be used to prove or disprove causality.

explanatory styles—*See* locus of control attitudes.

external locus of control—*See* locus of control.

extraneous variable—Confounding variable.

extrovert—Person who is usually outgoing and willing to try new experiences and approach challenging tasks.

Fair Labor Standards Act—Federal laws which legislate the hours & types of jobs which teenagers may and may not work

Fallopian tubes—The small tubes that connect the ovaries to the uterus.

false self—A personality one adopts in order to try to win the approval of others, even though it is not a real representation of one's own needs or interests.

family systems theories—Theories that explore how family interactions affect each member's individual behavior beyond the family.

field research—Studies in which the researcher records the subjects' behavior in their natural settings.

flashbulb memory—Remembering explicit details of an event as a result of the emotionally charged nature of the situation.

flexible ego—Characteristic of a resilient person who is adapts easily to change.

foreskin—The skin covering the head of the penis before circumcision.

formal operations—According to Piaget, the most advanced stage of cognitive development in which we are able to reason most logically and abstractly.

Foxfire project—Nationally famous vocational and teacher training program established in Georgia during the 1970s. *See* Insert 11–2.

Freudian theories—*See* Psychoanalytic theories.

gender roles—The behaviors and attitudes prescribed by each society as appropriate for males and for females. Synonym: sex roles.

gender schema theory—A cognitive theory stating that our behavior as males and females is influenced by how we fit our experiences into our existing systems of beliefs (schema).

generational boundary—The rules and expectations that grant adults more power and more responsibilities than children.

genital stage—According to Freudians, the adolescent stage during which we should separate enough from our parents to form intimate relationships with our peers.

glans—The head of the penis.

gonadotropins—Hormones released by the pituitary gland that cause the ovaries and the testes to increase the production of estrogen and testosterone.

gonads—The ovaries or testes.

GT—Gifted and talented; refers to students with exceptionally high IQ test scores.

hemisphericity—Brain lateralization.

hermaphrodite—A person born with both male and female organs or glands

HIV—Human immunodeficiency virus, the virus that causes acquired immune deficiency syndrome (AIDS).

homophobia—Hatred, fear of, or distorted perceptions of homosexuals.

hostile attribution bias—Chronically ascribing hostile, malevolent motives to other people when none exist.

HPV—Human pappilomavirus; the virus that causes genital warts.

hymen—The membrane that partially covers the external opening to the vagina. Slang/synonyms: cherry, maidenhead.

hypothalamus—The upper part of the brain stem that signals the pituitary gland to release the hormones that begin puberty.

Ice—Popular name for methamphetamine; an amphetamine.

identification—In early childhood, the process of bonding with your same-sex parent.

imaginary audience—Extreme self-consciousness most common during early adolescence that derives from the person's belief that "everyone is watching" and judging.

independent variable—Any factor, such as race or gender, that is constant and unaffected by changes in other variables.

individuation—In psychoanalytic theory, the process of creating an identity separate from our parents during our adolescence.

information processing theories—Research focused on the ways humans process stimuli, data, and experiences; memory, thinking, problem solving, and so on.

intentionality—The tendency to direct one's own goals rather than reacting to the wishes or demands of others.

internal locus of control—*See* locus of control.

introvert—Person who is uncomfortable around others and reluctant to try new experiences or approach challenging tasks.

inverse correlation—Negative correlation.

Jehovah's Witnesses—Conservative, evangelical Protestant sect that rejects many aspects of modern American life.

joint custody—A legal agreement in which each divorced parent retains the legal right to be consulted about decisions related to major issues affecting their children, such as education, religious training, and health care.

Judaism—Non-Christian religion based on a belief in one God.

kinesthetic intelligence—The mental ability to analyze the world spatially that consequently enhances the ability to move quickly and with great facility; for example, athletes display high kinesthetic intelligence.

Klinefelter's syndrome—Genetic abnormality that prevents secondary sex characteristics from developing at puberty in affected males.

labia—The folds of skin surrounding the vulva.

labile—*See* neurotic.

latchkey children—Children who take care of themselves after school or during vacations because their parents are away at work.

latency—According to psychoanalytic theory, the period occurring from ages 6 to 12 when we should develop a sense of industry and self-motivation.

learned helplessness—Extremely external locus of control attitudes.

learned pessimism—*See* learned helplessness.

learning disabilities—Physiological disorders which interfere with a child's progress in school such as dyslexia and attention deficit disorder.

LEP—Limited English proficiency; students whose English skills are limited because their native language is not English.

locus of control—A person's beliefs about whether they control most of what happens in their lives (internal locus of control) or whether factors beyond their control determine most of what happens (external locus of control). *See* Insert 5–3 for test.

longitudinal research—Studies that measure the same dependent variables of the same group of people across a period of time.

LSD—Lysergic acid diethylamide, a hallucinogen, that enhances perceptions and sensations and supposedly helps the user become more insightful.

mammary glands—The milk-producing glands in the female breast.

manic—*See* bipolar.

MDMA—A hallucinatory drug.

mean—The arithmetic average.

median—The number at midpoint of a distribution that has been ranked from highest to lowest or largest to smallest; half the distribution occurs on greater side of that midpoint, half on the lesser side.

moral realism—According to Piaget and Kohlberg, the stage of moral and social development in which young children think and behave in accord with simplistic rules such as obeying authorities without question. *See* Inserts 4–2 and 12–1 for characteristics of moral stages.

Mormon—A member of the Church of Latter Day Saints, 'LDS' or 'Saints' being the preferred term for most contemporary members. A religion based on the Bible plus the Book of Mormon.

Muslim—Non-Christian religion based on the principles of Mohammed, belief in Allah.

negative correlation—A relationship in which an increase in one variable is associated with a decrease in the other variable.

neurotic—A person with an extremely moody, irritable, withdrawn, volatile, overly sensitive, pessimistic personality. Synonym: labile.

nocturnal emissions—Wet dreams; male orgasm during sleep.

Norplant—Contraceptive capsules inserted beneath the woman's skin that release hormones for five years.

object permanence—According to Piaget, the awareness that objects or people still exist even when out of sight.

occupational types—A system of identifying the types of jobs for which a person would be best suited on the basis of his or her personality.

Oedipal complex—According to Freudians, a boy's being in love with his mother in ways that make him jealous of his father and unable to form relationships with girls his own age. *See* Insert 8–4 for a case study.

oppositional defiant disorders—A personality disorder contributing to aggressive, defiant, abusive behavior.

oral stage—According to Freudians, the stage between birth and age 2 when we should acquire a lifelong trust toward other people.

os—The opening in the cervix through which menstrual fluid flows and which expands during childbirth for the baby's passage.

ovulation—The release of the egg from the ovary each month; the fertile period.

PCP—The hallucinatory drug Phencyclidine.

personal fable—The "bulletproof" attitude that nothing bad can happen to you, regardless of your behavior; common among young adolescents.

phallic stage—According to Freudians, the stage around the age of 4 or 5 when we should identify with our same-sex parent and become increasingly self-reliant.

Piagetian theories—Cognitive stage theories. *See* Insert 3–4 for a description of stages.

PMS—Premenstrual syndrome; a condition causing extreme shifts in mood and behavior in some females before each menstrual period.

postconventional reasoning—According to Kohlberg, the most advanced stage of moral reasoning in which people think and behave from the least egocentric perspective.

poverty level—The income determined by the government below which a family is considered to be living in poverty; in 1994 about $14,000 for a family of four.

preconventional stage—According to Piaget and Kohlberg, the stage before adolescence in which we reason very egocentrically.

preoperational stage—According to Piaget, the egocentric stage between 2 and 7 when we develop such new skills as object permanence.

prepuce—The protective hood of skin covering the end of the clitoris or the end of the penis.

prostate gland—The male gland that produces semen.

psychoanalytic theories—Theories derived from Freud based on the premise that personality is established in the first few years of life, primarily by dynamics within the family.

psychometrics—The study of human intelligence through written and verbal tests.

psychopharmacology—The study of how certain drugs and body chemicals affect behavior and moods.

regression—According to Freudians, "going backward" in development; thinking or behaving as you did as a young child.

reliability—The ability of a test to yield basically the same score when the same person retakes the test.

relocation centers—Camps in which Japanese Americans were imprisoned in the United States during World War II.

reversibility—The ability to see a problem from several different angles or to be able to turn the problem backwards and forwards.

role diffusion—*See* role reversal.

role reversal—A situation in which a parent converts the hierarchical relationship with his or her children into a friendship in which the child assumes the role of adult by being

the parent's counselor, friend or confidante. *See* Inserts 4–4 and 4–5 for examples.

RU-486—The "morning after" contraceptive pill that causes the menstrual period to start.

rule of equivalence—The ability to understand the relationship between seemingly different objects or ideas. For example: if a=b, and b=c, then a=c.

schema—Piaget's term for the mental framework into which new information or new experiences are integrated as we mature.

schizoid personality disorder—Psychological disorder characterized by extreme shyness, social withdrawal, and distorted reasoning; less severe form of schizophrenia. *See* Inserts 5–4 and 5–5 for symptoms.

schizophrenia—Disorder in which extremely distorted styles of thinking put the person out of touch with reality; initial symptoms often include extreme shyness and social withdrawal. *See* Inserts 5–4 and 5–5 for symptoms.

scrotum—The pouch of skin that contains the testes.

sect—An extreme or heretical religious body, especially one that tries to preserve its doctrines by isolating members from the modern world; sometimes called a cult.

self-efficacy—Internal locus of control attitudes.

semen—The fluid released during male orgasm which contains sperm and other seminal fluids.

seminal fluid—*See* semen.

seminal vesicles—Tubes where the sperm is stored.

sensorimotor stage—According to Piaget, the cognitive stage from birth to age 2 in which we learn to use primitive symbols.

separation anxiety disorder—Psychological disorder characterized by fear of being separated from loved ones. *See* Insert 5–2 for symptoms.

serialization—The ability to arrange objects in proper order according to a criterion such as dimension, magnitude, or volume.

Seventh Day Adventist—Conservative, evangelical Protestant sect.

sexual orientation—Characteristic that determines one's preferred gender for sexual partner; can range from completely homosexual to completely heterosexual and might vary as one moves through different phases of life.

Skinnerian psychology—*See* behavioralism.

social cognition—Ways of thinking about and behaving in social situations; level of understanding of human behavior.

social learning theories—The view that most human behavior is determined by imitating other people and through reinforcement and punishment.

social phobia—Extreme shyness; fear of people.

SOMPA—System of multicultural pluralistic assessment; an intelligence test that takes into account the child's race, family income, and other environmental influences on IQ scores.

splitting—An immature, distorted denial of reality in which other people, events, and relationships are perceived in "all-or-nothing" terms; exaggerating events, distorting facts, caricaturizing people.

Stanford-Binet—An intelligence test. *See* Insert 3–1 for sample questions.

STD—Sexually transmitted disease. *See* Table 13–1 for specific diseases.

steroids—Synthetically made drugs that result in increased muscle mass and other male characteristics such as body hair.

temperament—Disposition; enduring traits of personality from infancy on.

temperamentally inhibited—Small percentage of extremely shy people with low, perhaps genetic, threshold to anything new or different.

testicles—Male sexual glands.

testosterone—Hormones that, at sufficient levels, produce male secondary sex characteristics in either sex.

Title IX—Federal law stating that no person shall be discriminated against in education or athletics on the basis of his or her gender.

tracking—Separating students into separate classes & separate curriculum on the basis of their academic abilities.

trait theorists—Those who believe that human behavior is primarily determined by enduring and inborn personality traits.

triangulation—A damaging situation in which parent and child are aligned as peers against the other parent. *See* Inserts 4–4 and 4–5 for examples.

tubal ligation—Female sterilization procedure in which the Fallopian tubes are either clamped or cauterized so the egg cannot come into contact with sperm.

Turner's syndrome—Genetic abnormality in females that prevents secondary sex characteristics from developing at puberty.

Unitarian—A religious denomination that stresses individual freedom of belief, the free use of reason in religion, a united world community, and liberal social action.

urethra—In males and females the tube that carries urine outside the body from the bladder.

uterus—Womb; the organ in which the fetus develops during pregnancy.

vagina—The passageway from the uterus to the outside of the body that holds the penis during intercourse.

validity—A test's ability to measure accurately what it claims to be measuring.

values clarification—Classroom activities designed to improve adolescents' social and moral reasoning. *See* Insert 5–5 for examples.

vas deferens—Tubes that carry sperm from the testicles to the seminal vesicles.

vasectomy—Male sterilization procedure in which the vas deferens are surgically cut so that sperm cannot mix with the seminal fluid, thus preventing sperm from reaching the egg.

vocational interest inventory—A test of a person's skills & interests designed to identify the types of jobs for which a person would be best suited. *See* Insert 11–3.

vulva—The external female genitals.

WAIS-R—Wechsler Adult Intelligence Scale, Revised; an intelligence test. *See* Insert 3–1 for sample questions.

WISC-III R—Wechsler Intelligence Scale for Children, Third Revision; an intelligence test.

Work to School Act—Federal laws enacted in 1994 which provide money for vocational education for adolescents and young adults.

working poor—Adults with jobs that generate income below the poverty level.

Photo Credits

p. 1, © 1993 Chuck Savage/The Stock Market; p. 8, © Ken Heyman Photography; p. 11, The Bettmann Archive; p. 12, The Bettmann Archive; p. 25, © 1993 Jose L. Pelaez/The Stock Market; p. 31, Courtesy of Wake Forest University; p. 37, Dr. Bob Jones; p. 52, © J.B. Akers/Steve Guerini; p. 56, © Courtesy of Wake Forest University; p. 65, © Mugshots/The Stock Market; p. 92, Photo by Bill Ray III, Wake Forest University Office of Public Affairs; p. 96, author; p. 101, © Joel Gordon 1992; p. 108, Dr. Bob Jones; p. 109, Dr. Bob Jones; p. 116, Dr. Bob Jones; p. 128, Dr. Bob Jones; p. 131, author; p. 144, © 1993 Tom & Dee McCarthy/The Stock Market; p. 147, Courtesy of Wake Forest University; p. 150, Dr. Bob Jones; p. 157, Dr. Bob Jones; p. 165, Courtesy of Wake Forest University; p. 179, Dr. Bob Jones; p. 192, © 1989 Hangarter/ Lightwave; p. 208, Photo by A. Libermon; p. 213, Courtesy of North Carolina School of the Arts, Winston–Salem; p. 215, Dr. Bob Jones; p. 217, author; p. 225, Courtesy of Wake Forest University; p. 240, © 1985 Ruth Anne Clarke-Mason; p. 248, Courtesy of Wake Forest University; p. 252, Dr. Bob Jones; p. 274, © 1987 Bob Shaw/The Stock Market; p. 276, author; p. 284, © Skjold/Lightwave; p. 287, author; p. 299, author; p. 304, author; p. 312, author; p. 348, Dr. Bob Jones; p. 399, © 1988 Charles Gupton/The Stock Market; p. 408, author; p. 420, Courtesy of Wake Forest University; p. 425, © 1987 Susan Mullally-Clark, Wake Forest University Office of Public Affairs; p. 429, author; p. 431, author; p. 437, © Joel Gordon 1988; p. 451, author; p. 455, Courtesy of Wake Forest University; p. 463, © Steve McCurry/Magnum Photos; p. 480, author; p. 487, © 1985 Ruth Anne Clarke-Mason; p. 494, author; p. 499, Reproduced with permission of The Children's Defense Fund; p. 507, © Richard Hutchings/ Photo Researchers, Inc.; p. 518, author; p. 524, author; p. 525, Dr. Bob Jones; p. 535, © Roy Morsch/The Stock Market; p. 561, © Bruce Davidson/Magnum Photos; p. 565, © 1985 Ruth Anne Clarke-Mason; p. 590, Dr. Bob Jones; p. 600, © George S. Zimbel/Monkmeyer Press.

Name Index

Subject Index